Welcome to Mexico

*The management of this hotel and the
publishers of this book welcome you.
We hope this publication will help to
make your stay with us more enjoyable.*

*We ask that you kindly leave this book in the
room for the next guest.*

You can buy this book:

1. At the newsstand or gift shop of most hotels.
2. By mail, using one of the coupons in the back of this book.
3. Through the Internet at: travelguidemexico.com

FONATUR - Loreto, Baja California

Brought to you by the editors of
Travelers Guide to Mexico

travelguidemexico.com

Bruce Herman · Copper Canyon

Mexico

Kayaking in Sumidero Canyon – Fondo Chiapas

• TOP RESORTS • LEADING HOTELS • DINING & SHOPPING
• SIGHTSEEING • LIVING IN MEXICO • NATURE & ADVENTURE
• COLONIAL MEXICO • ARCHAEOLOGY • BUSINESS & INVESTING

SECRETARÍA DE TURISMO | SECTUR

Friends and visitors:

Welcome to Mexico, an always-hospitable country!

It's an honor to have you visit Mexico, where the Federal Government, through the Ministry of Tourism, promotes programs designed to make tourism an industry that is at the vanguard; where the attention, the quality and hospitality offered tourists are a high priority.

Our wealth of tourism attractions is very varied. We have the world's fourth largest biodiversity and, in addition, we have historical and cultural resources that amaze millions of people.

Mexico has everything to please our visitors: sun and beach destinations, archaeological zones, music, art, gastronomy, traditional fiestas, and the best options for holding meetings, conventions, fairs and expositions.

In the north, as well as the central and southern parts of Mexico, there are hundreds of destinations from which to choose, each with its own particular attraction, where the tourism industry is being diversified to satisfy the most demanding tourist.

No one should miss the opportunity to visit Mexico's beaches, to see our colonial cities that have been declared World Heritage Sites by UNESCO, or visit the states that form part of the "Ruta de los Dioses" (Route of the Gods), "Mundo Maya" (Maya World) and "Pueblos Magicos" (Magical Towns).

Welcome, then, to this magical country, where the fun and the experiences will be unforgettable.

To help you plan your trip to our land starting now, it will assist you greatly to read the pages of *Travelers Guide to Mexico*, whose information, photographs and recommendations will guide you to make your stay an even more pleasant one.

LIC. RODOLFO ELIZONDO TORRES,
Secretario de Turismo del Gobierno de la República.

MÉXICO
PRESIDENCIA DE
LA REPÚBLICA

Dear Friends:

I most cordially welcome you to Mexico, a country that offers millions of visitors each year the widest range of possibilities: gorgeous beaches, colonial cities of surprising beauty, fascinating pre-Hispanic ruins, camp grounds and dive sites, a variety of eco-tourism activities and nature reserves that protect the country's biological diversity.

In these pages, TRAVELERS GUIDE TO MEXICO gives you an idea of the many things you can discover in a country where the customs and warmth of its people accompany you at all times.

For all types of travelers, Mexico has an infinite number of alternatives. Mexico is a country with immense business potential. Here is where the modern and the traditional meet; the forests, the sea, the mountains; the streets full of life in hundreds of friendly cities.

As well as being varied, Mexico is welcoming by tradition. That is why we offer our visitors the most extensive selection of dishes, which have made Mexican cuisine one of the world's most prestigious.

I most cordially invite you to enjoy Mexico, taking with you memories of a unique and unforgettable journey.

Fox

VICENTE FOX QUESADA

Residencia Oficial de los Pinos

TRAVELERS GUIDE TO MEXICO

Editor & Publisher
CHRIS A. LUHNOW

Executive Editor
SHOOKA SHEMIRANI

Advertising Director
REBECA SAUCEDO

Advertising & Production Manager
LAILY KO

Design & Production Director
RADDY MENDIETA

Administrative Manager
ANA LORENA
DE MONTALVO

Book Sales & Distribution
GUILLERMINA VAZQUEZ

Assistant to Publisher
LAURA ARIAS

Contributing Editors
SUE BEERE
STUART J. BARNES
JIM BUDD
TRACY EHRENBERG
SILVIA L. ELIAS
JOHN GLAAB
CHARLES KINDER
LETICIA KLEIN
RON LAVENDER
WENDY LUFT
LINDA NEIL
DEBORAH RINER
MIKE SCHAIBLE
CLARE SIMONS
TOODY WALTON
BARBARA WAUGH

Travelers Guide to Mexico (TGM) is published
annually and placed in more than 30,000 rooms
of first-class hotels in the major tourist areas of
Mexico, where more than 250,000 visitors read
it each month. Twenty-seventh edition, June,
2004. TGM es editada y distribuída por
Promociones de Mercados Turísticos, S.A. de
C.V., General Juan Cano No. 68, Col. San Miguel
Chapultepec, C.P. 11580, México, D.F. Tels.
(52-55) 5515-0925, 5271-4736. Fax: (52-55)
5272-5942 (tg2m@prodigy.net.mx.) Editor
responsable Christian A. Luhnow Lomax.
Certificado de Licitud de Título No. 8238,
Certificado de Licitud de Contenido No. 5806,
No. de Reserva de Derechos de Autor 04-2003-
090817502800-102. Código ISSN 1405-5724.
Preprensa digital e impresión: Litografía Magno
Graf, S.A. de C.V., Calle E #6, Parque Ind.
Puebla 2000, Puebla. Tel. en México, D.F. 5598-
1261 (ventas@magnograf.com.mx). All rights
reserved under International and Pan American
Copyright Conventions. No part of this book may
be reproduced, stored or transmitted in any
form. Derechos reservados conforme a la ley. El
contenido de este libro es propiedad de
Promociones de Mercados Turísticos, S.A. de
C.V., por lo tanto queda estrictamente prohibida
la reproducción total o parcial de los textos,
imágenes, mapas o fotografías que aparecen en
esta edición, aún citando su lugar de procedencia.

Table of

ivm®
Instituto Verificador de Medios
Circulación Certificada: Registro 280/01

Contents

MOCTEZUMA
& ASOCIADOS
INVESTIGACIÓN DE
LA COMUNICACIÓN

Perfil del Lector

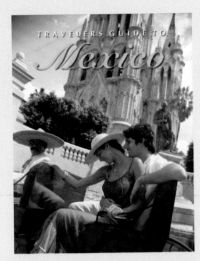

COVER: Colonial San Miguel de Allende's tree shaded plaza, dominated by an unusual neo-Gothic parish church, is a touch of the Left Bank. This cosmopolitan town is located about a four-hour drive northwest of Mexico City, in the heart of the colonial highlands, Mexico's Independence Country. Its many beautifully restored colonial mansions house delightful boutique hotels, patio restaurants, and fine shops. In addition, students of all ages come here to study art, painting, weaving, sculpting, photography and Spanish.

PHOTOGRAPHY

Bruce Herman, Director

Guillermo Aldana	Robert Campbell
John Elkins	RickGomez
Susan Kaye	Chris Luhnow
Carlos Sanchez Pereyra	John G. Youden

TGM would like to give special thanks to the Mexico Tourism Board for their support and participation, as well as to FONATUR and the Ministry of Tourism for providing several excellent photographs. Also thanks to the Acapulco Convention and Visitors Bureau, Los Cabos Convention and Visitors Bureau, Puerto Vallarta Convention and Visitors Bureau, Mexico City Tourism Authority, and the state tourism departments of Puebla, Chihuahua, Guanajuato, Monterrey and Nuevo Leon. And to John G. Youden, Vallarta Lifestyles and Mexico Boutique Hotels, as well as Barba Editores in Guadalajara. Hotels that generously provided photos include Las Brisas (Acapulco), Four Seasons (Punta Mita), Villa del Sol (Zihuatanejo), Maroma (Riviera Maya), Fiesta Americana (Guadalajara), Posada de la Mision (Taxco), Velas Vallarta (Puerto Vallarta), and Casa Careyes. Also thanks to restaurants Thai Gardens in Mexico City and Café Des Artistes in Puerto Vallarta, Tabachines Golf Course in Cuernavaca, and Ballesteros silver emporium and Centro Santa Fe shopping center in Mexico City.

Dear Visitor:

There's a good reason why Travelers Guide to Mexico is the largest selling guide book to Mexico in the world. In fact, there are several reasons:

IT'S COMPLETE: It covers the entire country, featuring the places most frequented by international and domestic tourists. It contains a wide variety of information—history, geography, climate, customs, business and investments, living and retiring, real estate, outdoor sports and activities, transportation, hotels, restaurants and shopping. (See pages 4 and 5 for the full range of contents).

IT'S AUTHORITATIVE: Travelers Guide staff and writers live in Mexico and know the country intimately. With few exceptions, the editors have personally visited the places recommended.

IT'S UP TO DATE: Each year, all the information contained in Travelers Guide is meticulously verified by checking directly with the establishments listed. We add what is new and remove what is no longer applicable.

IT'S OBJECTIVE: Readers have confidence in Travelers Guide because its recommendations are based on a completely objective evaluation. Advertising is accepted only from establishments that we regard as worthy of being recommended. To protect the tourist, we turn down considerable advertising from establishments of doubtful prestige, quality or service.

Occasionally, of course, a visitor is dissatisfied with a recommended establishment and lets us know about it. We try to learn whether it was just an isolated lapse or part of a pattern. If failings persist, we withdraw the recommendation. Consequently, if you have any complaints—or compliments—about specific establishments listed in Travelers Guide, please let us know. The results of our investigation may affect subsequent issues.

TRAVELERS GUIDE TO MEXICO is placed in more than 30,000 rooms of the best hotels throughout Mexico as a service to the traveler. It is given by us to the hotels for placement in their rooms and they do their best to keep it there in good condition and to see to it that the book is on sale at the newsstand in the lobby. Please do not take it from the room. For more information on how to obtain the book, please see the last page.

HAPPY TRAVELING—AND COME BACK SOON.

Chris A. Luhnow
EDITOR & PUBLISHER

REGIONAL SALES OFFICES

Acapulco: Francisco Medina. Tel. (744) 482-4601. **Cancun**: Patricia Fernández H. Tel. (998) 884-4869. **Chihuahua**: Katharine Renpenning. Tel. (614) 414-0118. **Cuernavaca**: Aurora Cervera Medina. Tel. (777) 322-5086. **Guadalajara**: Eduardo Plaza. Tel. (33) 3823-0100. **Ixtapa-Zihuatanejo**: Judith Whitehead. Tel. (755) 554-6226. **Los Cabos**: Gay Herrera. Tel. (624) 143-6351. **Mazatlan**: Elba Téllez. Tel. (669) 916-5402. **Mexico City**: Marisol Aguirre, Dolores Corona. Tel. (55) 5515-0925, 5271-4736. **Monterrey**: Martha Lozano. Tel. (81) 8352-6899. **Puebla**: Adriana Carrera de Pérez. Tel. (222) 240-5246. **Puerto Vallarta**: Toody Walton. Tel. (322) 224-0029. **San Miguel de Allende, Queretaro, Guanajuato, Morelia, Zacatecas**: Martha Beckhart. Tel. (415) 152-3401. **Taxco**: Leopoldo Sanchez Miranda. Tel. (762) 622-6351.

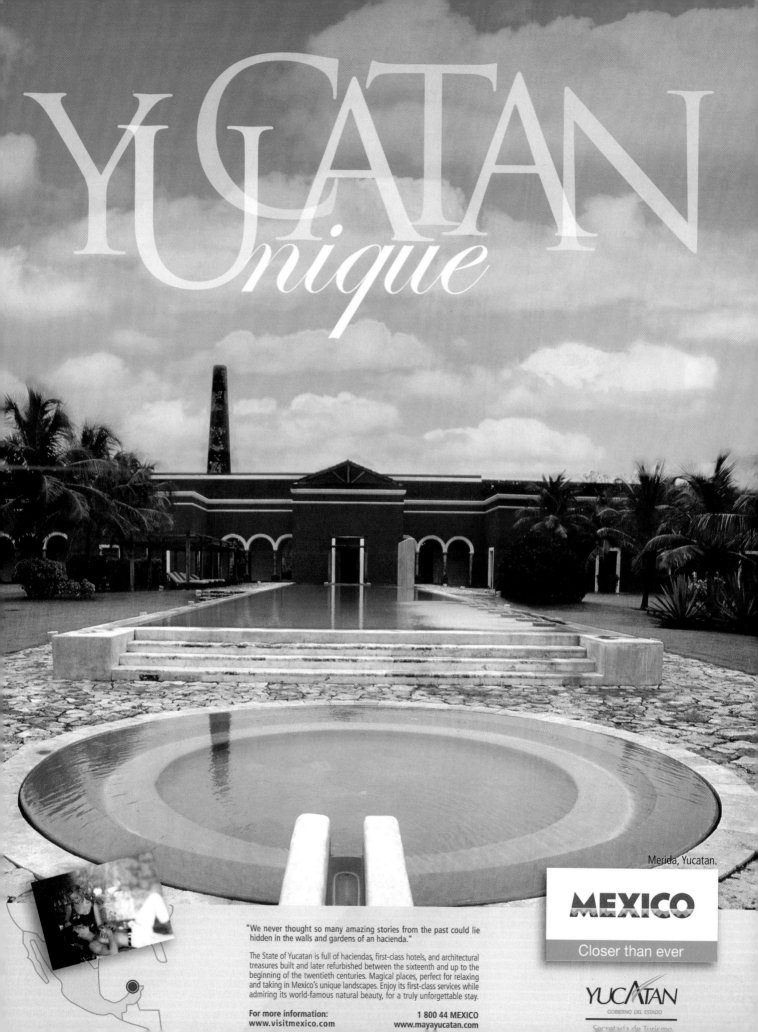

YUCATAN
Unique

Merida, Yucatan.

San Diego
Calexico
Tijuana
MEXICALI
Ensenada
Puerto Peñasco
Nogales
San Felipe
Nogales
El Paso
Ciudad Juarez
UN
Kino Bay
HERMOSILLO
CHIHUAHUA
Piedras Negra
Guerrero
Negro
Guaymas
Delicias
Ciudad Obregon
Santa Rosalia
Ferry
Alamos
Chihuahua-Pacific R.R.
Mulege
Monclova
Loreto
SEA OF CORTEZ
Los Mochis
Topolobampo
Torreon
SALTILLO
Ferry
CULIACAN
La Paz
Ferry
DURANGO
N
San Jose del Cabo
Fresnillo
W
E
Cabo San Lucas
Mazatlan
ZACATECAS
S
AGUASCALIENTES
TEPIC
Leon
© TRAVELERS GUIDE TO MEXICO 2004
GUANAJUAT
Total or partial reproduction of this map
is strictly prohibited. All rights reserved
Irapuato
under international and Pan-American
copyright conventions. Derechos
GUADALAJARA
reservados conforme a la ley.
Puerto
Impreso en México. Printed in Mexico.
Vallarta
Chapala
© Copyright by:
TRAVELERS GUIDE TO MEXICO
Barra de
Uruapan
Navidad
COLIMA
Patz
Manzanillo
Lazaro Ca
Ixta

Mexico

D STATES OF AMERICA

Eagle Pass

Laredo
Laredo

Mc Allen

MONTERREY   Reynosa
                Brownsville

                Matamoros

CIUDAD VICTORIA

GULF OF
MEXICO

Ciudad Valles   Tampico

Miguel de Allende

QUERETARO   Tuxpan

PACHUCA   Poza Rica
                    Tajin

MEXICO   JALAPA
CITY

TOLUCA   TLAXCALA

CUERNAVACA   PUEBLA   Cordoba   Veracruz

Taxco   Orizaba   Alvarado

                Tehuacan   Coatzacoalcos

CHILPANCINGO   VILLAHERMOSA

Acapulco   OAXACA
        Monte Alban   TUXTLA
                            GUTIERREZ   San Cristobal
                Mitla   de las Casas

        Tehuantepec

Puerto   Puerto
Escondido   Angel
        Huatulco   Tapachula

Isla Mujeres
                Cancun
        Progreso   Ria Lagartos
MERIDA   Valladolid   Playa del
                                Carmen   Ferry
Celestun   Chichen-Itza   Cozumel
        Uxmal   Tulum

                CAMPECHE

Cd. del Carmen   CHETUMAL   CARIBBEAN
                                        SEA

        Palenque   Belize City

                Tikal   Belmopan

                Flores

                            CENTRAL
                            AMERICA

Guatemala City

IXTAPA ZIHUATANEJO
Unbeatable

MEXICO
Closer than ever

TRAVELERS GUIDE TO
Mexico

*Mexico offers a wide variety of tourist destinations,
from colonial towns to beach resorts.*

Introduction

Mexico is a unique country, providing visitors with an endless variety of choices. It offers big-city sophistication or small-town intimacy, a chance to frolic on shimmering beaches or trek through lush tropical jungles, an opportunity to kick back and relax or pursue a growing number of business ventures.

Major changes in the past few years—including a democratic transition of power, and the promotion of ecotourism and free trade—have made it even more appealing to travelers with a wide range of interests.

If you're looking for sun, sand and surf, you can jet to some of the world's most famous beach resorts, such as Acapulco, Cancun or Puerto Vallarta, or newer resorts such as Ixtapa, Huatulco and Los Cabos. Here a few days' stay can be as relaxing or frenetic as you want it to be—sprawl on the beach or golf, snorkel, horseback ride, and dance till dawn.

If you like to fish or hunt, Mexico offers ideal spots. If you'd rather shoot wildlife with a camera, it is one of the world's five most biologically diverse nations.

As growing industrial and financial centers, Guadalajara, Monterrey and, of course, Mexico City are handling an ever-increasing number of business travelers each day.

Central Mexico's charming colonial towns, including Guanajuato, Morelia and Queretaro, invite you to explore the country's tumultuous history and struggle for independence, while cities in the southern states of Oaxaca and Chiapas offer a look at the nation's Indian roots.

A temazcal (pre-Hispanic sweat lodge) at Maroma, Riviera Maya

Chris Luhnow

World Heritage Sites

Mexico ranks first in the Americas and eighth worldwide in number of World Heritage Sites, with 23 in all. These sites, considered by the United Nations Educational, Scientific and Cultural Organization (UNESCO) to be "of outstanding universal value," include the historic downtown areas of the colonial cities mentioned above, as well as Zacatecas, Puebla, Campeche, Tlacotalpan, Oaxaca (and its nearby ruins of Monte Alban) and Mexico City (and its floating gardens of Xochimilco). In fact, Mexico has more cities with World Heritage Sites than any other country.

Other sites on UNESCO's list are Teotihuacan, Palenque, Chichen-Itza, El Tajin, Uxmal, Paquimé, Xochicalco, Calakmul, Sian Ka'an, the whale sanctuary of El Vizcaino and rock paintings of Sierra de San Francisco in Baja California, the 16th-century monasteries on the slopes of the Popocatepetl volcano, the Hospicio Cabañas in Guadalajara, and the Franciscan Missions in the Sierra Gorda region of Queretaro state.

Land of Contrasts

Mexico is a land of contrasts, geographically and socially. Indian communities nestled in mountain villages maintain centuries-old customs not far from where wealthy businessmen stride down the manicured streets of major cities. In Mexico you will discover beauty and squalor, wealth and poverty, efficiency and ineptitude coexisting in one of the world's most complex societies. These paradoxes make Mexico a truly foreign experience for the visitor, difficult to understand but always interesting. Add it up, and it could only be Mexico, so near, yet so different.

Mexicans refuse to enslave themselves to clocks, except where it is essential. Thus, airline, bus, and train schedules, as well as business appointments, are fairly adhered to, and the bullfights always begin precisely on time. But a more relaxed attitude applies for social gatherings.

Confronting the unexpected is always more of a hassle abroad than at home. If you run afoul of the law, things can get unpleasant because legal and judicial procedures bear little resemblance to those at home. Mexico's police are infamous for hitting up locals and foreigners alike for a *mordida* (literally "bite"), a bribe, often for phantom infractions. Big cities have big city crime. Don't push through crowds with pockets unprotected or purses open, and beware of pickpockets when riding a bus or subway, especially during rush hour.

One unsettling feature for tourists may be the occasional army inspection points on interstate highways. Don't be alarmed, they are there to watch for drugs, since Mexico is a convenient funnel for drugs destined for the United States from South America.

Mexico is still a developing country, even though it is one of the world's top oil producers, has one of the world's largest cities, dozens of world-class companies and its own satellite in space. Its economy has not yet fulfilled the promise of its rich resources, and the country still has a spotty human rights record. But major changes have been taking place in the past few years. With its recent and decisive integration into the world economy, Mexico hopes to spur its development and modernization. On the political front, the country has entered the 21st century with a more open and democratic government, having put an end to 70 years of one-party rule in 2000 by electing an opposition candidate to the presidency.

So, what can you expect in Mexico? Plenty! And that's what the rest of this book is about. It invites you to find out more about this fascinating country, its people, culture, and wealth of new experiences.

Welcome!

A Brief History

A Land Torn by Conquest, Independence and Revolution

As early as 40,000 years ago, prehistoric man roamed across the Bering Strait, leaving Asia and entering the territory that would come to be called America. In their pursuit of game, these early nomads crossed into the uninhabited lands of the Western Hemisphere.

By 10,000 B.C., clans of hunter-gatherers were scattered throughout the continent. As subsistence patterns changed and farming took precedence over hunting, many settled in the fertile regions of Mesoamerica. Others wandered farther south, their descendants eventually reaching the tip of Argentina.

The first highly developed civilization to emerge in the New World belonged to the Olmecs, who flourished between 1200 and 500 B.C. in the lowland jungles of Veracruz and Tabasco.

Today the Olmecs are most readily identified with the massive stone heads they sculpted. They are also credited, however, with originating much that would be adapted by later cultures, principally the Maya. The Olmecs developed a calendar and hieroglyphic writing. And aspects of their religion, architecture, art and an elementary numerical system were expanded on for centuries to come.

Olmec influence was carried via extensive trade routes to central Mexico, the states of Guerrero and Oaxaca, and throughout the Maya region. San Lorenzo, one of three main Olmec archaeological sites, is probably the oldest, having thrived between 1200 and 900 B.C.

Cathedral, Guanajuato

Mexico Tourism Board

Teotihuacan

Many of the wandering tribes started congregating in central Mexico. Some of these people built the sprawling city we call Teotihuacan, a name the Aztecs gave to it, meaning "Place Where Gods Are Made."

Teotihuacan was a true city that at its peak, around 500 A.D., may have reached a population of 200,000, and maintained extensive contacts throughout Mesoamerica. Teotihuacan was long in ruins by the time the Aztecs arrived.

Contemporary with Teotihuacan was Cholula, a city near Puebla that managed to survive as a religious center through many changes in cultural dominance. It was still a revered city at the time of the Spanish Conquest in 1521.

At this same time, the Maya were busy building great cities, which today are largely buried in the rain forests of Guatemala and Chiapas. Such leaders as Pacal of Palenque and Bird Jaguar of Yaxchilan left records of their times in hieroglyphic writing.

Many scholars have been attracted to the Maya, working to understand their ancient writings, and every year more is learned, transforming prehistory, that time before a written record existed, into history.

The Toltecs, whose capital, Tula, is a couple of hours north of Mexico City, became known to later generations as possessors of all that was fine in richly-decorated temples, elegant speech and intellectual pursuits. Many Aztec nobles were known to have altered their family trees in order to show a direct ancestral link with the exalted Toltecs.

Quetzalcoatl

Quetzalcoatl, the Feathered Serpent, is one of the most prominent gods of Mesoamerica. The earliest signs go back to the Olmecs, followed by an association with the rain god Tlaloc at Teotihuacan.

The Toltec city of Tula was his home, and here history and legend intertwine; several rulers took the name of the god, confusing history. Through deception by the god Tezcatlipoca, the fair Quetzalcoatl was forced to flee Tula and head east to the Yucatan Peninsula, where he became known as Kukulcan. When he left, he proclaimed his intention to return.

Among the many wandering Chichimeca tribes of the north were the Mexica, whose leader Xolotl gained legendary status as founder of the Aztec nation. In painted codices, Xolotl is depicted as a skin-clad hunter leading his people from their ancestral home, Aztlan, from which the name Aztec is derived.

These Mexica eventually would give their name to all of Mexico. The sign given by their god Huitzilopochtli for recognizing their destined homeland—an eagle sitting on a cactus—would become the national symbol. Later, a snake was added to the eagle's beak.

In 1492, when Columbus arrived in the New World, the Aztec empire was strong and growing. Emperor Ahuitzotl was engaged in a four-year campaign to add Pacific coast lands around present-day Acapulco to his realm.

In 1519 a 34-year-old Spaniard named Hernan Cortes led a band of 550 sailor-explorers on an unauthorized expedition from Cuba. Landing first at Cozumel and later on the gulf coast of Tabasco, he established a settlement just north of today's city of Veracruz.

The Aztec empire controlled vast lands stretching from the Yucatan Peninsula to the Pacific, with at least 370 individual nations subject to their capital city, Tenochtitlan.

The Aztecs' demand for heavy tribute was a significant factor in their downfall. Many natives were anxious to join the foreigners in their assault on the capital.

Post-conquest chroniclers tell us 1519 was the year Quetzalcoatl had promised his followers he would return from the east. When strange-looking men arrived aboard huge houses that moved on water, and appeared dressed in heavy armor, astride animals never seen before, speaking a strange tongue—then certainly their light-skinned leader must be Quetzalcoatl.

After two difficult years and the loss of many lives, especially among the Indians, who were decimated by the smallpox virus introduced into the New World by the conquistadors, the Spaniards defeated the Aztecs under their last ruler, Cuauhtemoc. Thus began 300 years of colonial rule.

An important figure in the conquest was Malinche, a multilingual Indian woman reputed to have been of noble birth, but reduced to slavery through family rivalries. She was a gift to Cortes from the chiefs of Tabasco and acted as interpreter and adviser on native customs. Eventually she bore Cortes a son, Martin.

Colonial Era

Religious fervor and greed were two driving forces of colonization. In every town, native Indians newly converted to Catholicism were forced to construct churches—many built from the rubble of demolished pre-Hispanic temples, such as at Tenochtitlan, today Mexico City.

The Inquisition proved most useful, since in rooting out so-called heretics it eliminated anyone opposed to the status quo. Critics of the church were accused of having questionable moral character, labeled a threat to society, and tortured into repudiating their beliefs, or killed.

The conquerors were awarded parcels of land for their labors to the crown and thus began the era of large land holdings. Silver lying below the ground in Taxco, Guanajuato and Zacatecas attracted many Spaniards, who forced the natives to work the mines.

Over the next 300 years Spain sent 61 viceroys to govern New Spain. Many beautiful buildings were constructed, which are still in use today. Spanish speech, dress and customs replaced indigenous cultures in the cities, but always with adaptations to the climate and the unique way of life in this vast new country.

Independence

A priest from the town of Dolores, near San Miguel de Allende, was instrumental in cutting ties with Spain. Father Miguel Hidalgo's impassioned plea to his countrymen on the morning of September 16, 1810, urged them to "recover the lands stolen 300 years ago from your forefathers by the hated Spaniards."

The impoverished Indian citizenry was quick to follow Hidalgo, and the image of the revered dark-skinned Virgin of Guadalupe, dear to all Mexicans, was wisely chosen as the emblem of the independence movement.

Every September 15 at 11 p.m., Hidalgo's "Grito de Dolores," or Cry of Dolores, is re-enacted in ceremonies in that town, in the capital, and in plazas throughout Mexico. It was the decisive first step toward Mexican independence, which would come 12 years later and bring to prominence men like Ignacio Allende and Vicente Guerrero, names honored today throughout Mexico.

General Agustin Iturbide was instrumental in drafting the peace plan that brought an end to fighting. Shortly after, he proclaimed himself emperor, but his monarchy lasted less than a year. Led by Antonio Lopez de Santa Anna, opposition forces quickly gathered support and in February of 1823 Iturbide abdicated and the rebel army entered Mexico City unopposed.

In 1824 a constitution was adopted and Mexico's first president, Guadalupe Victoria, was sworn into office. The following year both England and the United States officially recognized the Republic of Mexico.

But stability was short lived. Between 1833 and 1855 the presidency changed hands 33 times—including 11 terms held by Santa Anna. It was this same Santa Anna who led the bloody siege against the Alamo in 1836, when settlers in northern territories fought to cut ties with Mexico and form the independent Republic of Texas.

Eleven years later the Mexico-U.S. border and the ownership of the territories of California and New Mexico were still a subject of dispute. U.S. General Winfield Scott's army of occupation landed in Veracruz in March of 1847, and marched to the capital. References throughout Mexico to the "Niños Heroes" (Child Heroes) honor the young military cadets who defended Chapultepec Castle, the last position in the city to fall. It is said that one of the boys wrapped himself in the Mexican flag and plunged over the cliff to his death rather than surrender. They are remembered every September 13 in a ceremony at their monument in Chapultepec Park.

In 1861, with Santa Anna ousted for the last time, a Zapotec Indian from the state of Oaxaca was elected president. An orphan who left his uncle's home at age 12 speaking only a few words of Spanish, Benito Juarez studied hard, became a lawyer and was elected governor of his state. The story of his success against great odds and the struggles of his presidency make him one of Mexico's most beloved historical figures.

The French Intervention

Faced with overwhelming debts and an empty treasury, Juarez announced a two-year moratorium on payment of the foreign debt, primarily owed to France, Spain and England. French Emperor Napoleon III sent an army to Veracruz in late 1861, hoping to cash in on Mexico's indebtedness and buoyed by the support of the increasingly powerful Catholic church, which was in constant conflict with the Mexican government. French soldiers marched to Puebla, but were repelled by a ragtag Mexican army, adding a new national holiday to the calendar on May 5, Cinco de Mayo.

It was a short-lived celebration, however. A year later the French were able to take both Puebla and Mexico City. Austrian Archduke Ferdinand Maximilian of Hapsburg was sent to be the French emperor in Mexico, marking the beginning of a period of great elegance. Maximilian converted the Chapultepec fortress into his palace and ordered the construction of the European-style Paseo de la Reforma, which leads across town from the base of the castle.

Historians generally agree that Maximilian and his wife Charlotte, known here as Carlota, were well-meaning people who were misled into thinking they would be warmly welcomed in Mexico. It was a situation with no hope of success. Attempting to satisfy both liberals and conservatives, Maximilian only alienated everyone.

Mexican States and Capitals

Aguascalientes	Aguascalientes
Baja California	Mexicali
Baja Calif. Sur	La Paz
Campeche	Campeche
Coahuila	Saltillo
Colima	Colima
Chiapas	Tuxtla Gutierrez
Chihuahua	Chihuahua
Durango	Durango
Guanajuato	Guanajuato
Guerrero	Chilpancingo
Hidalgo	Pachuca
Jalisco	Guadalajara
Mexico	Toluca
Michoacan	Morelia
Morelos	Cuernavaca
Nayarit	Tepic
Nuevo Leon	Monterrey
Oaxaca	Oaxaca
Puebla	Puebla
Queretaro	Queretaro
Quintana Roo	Chetumal
San Luis Potosi	San Luis Potosi
Sinaloa	Culiacan
Sonora	Hermosillo
Tabasco	Villahermosa
Tamaulipas	Ciudad Victoria
Tlaxcala	Tlaxcala
Veracruz	Jalapa
Yucatan	Merida
Zacatecas	Zacatecas

On June 19, 1866, Maximilian was executed by firing squad on a hill outside the city of Queretaro. Carlota was in Europe, begging Napoleon to send additional troops in support of her husband. That tragic experience, compounded by her desire but inability to have children, reportedly drove her insane.

In 1867, Juarez was elected to a third term. Among his accomplishments were completion of a railroad connecting Mexico City and Veracruz, and the reorganization of the educational system, making primary school attendance free and obligatory.

For a third of a century, 1876-1910, Mexico was in the hands of dictator Porfirio Diaz. This was a period of rapidly developing industry, an expanded railway system and extensive foreign investment. Large land holdings also increased tremendously—one man alone owned an incredible 7 million acres in northern Mexico.

This level of wealth was supported through the exploitation of the indigenous Indians, who were subjected to forced labor and physical abuse. More than a quarter of their infants died through malnutrition and lack of medical care.

Revolution

The turn of the century was a colorful time of the dashing *charro,* or cowboy, entertaining friends at his numerous cattle ranching haciendas around the country. But Porfirio Diaz had emphasized industrial development at the expense of the masses. Modernization without social improvement only made their lives unendurable and set the stage for revolution.

Six years of fighting and the death of about one million Mexicans ended the Porfiriato regime and brought into prominence men like Emiliano Zapata, Francisco Madero and Pancho Villa. November 20, a national holiday, honors the beginning of the bloody 1910 Revolution.

At the end of the revolution, for the first time since Cortes captured Cuauhtemoc, Mexicans were in control of Mexico. Private ownership was a privilege, not a right, with lands subject to expropriation for the public interest. Lands seized during the Porfiriato were ordered restored to the local communities, and foreign ownership of land and mining rights was limited. A minimum wage was established and workers were allowed collective bargaining and the right to strike. The power of the church was considerably reduced, with construction of new church buildings requiring government approval.

The early 1920s saw an end to the violence that had plagued the country for so long. In the 1930s, Mexico's beloved President Lazaro Cardenas continued the redistribution of land promised after the revolution. Most of the land went to communities, to be worked by individuals given a right to use the land, but not own it. It was during Cardenas' term that the nation's oil companies, mostly foreign owned, were nationalized and the state petroleum company, Pemex, was established. The Confederation of Mexican Workers (CTM) was formed, playing a key role for years to come.

Today

The nation's past presidential election signalled the beginning of a new era as former businessman and political maverick Vicente Fox defeated the long-ruling Institutional Revolutionary Party (PRI) in a stunning election victory. Mexicans put an end to the PRI's 71 year-reign on July 2, 2000 by overwhelmingly voting for Fox, a member of the pro-business National Action Party (PAN).

Since its founding in 1929, the PRI had ruled uninterrupted, surrounded by all the trappings of a democracy, namely regularly held local and state elections that were, invariably, tainted by accusations of fraud. At the national level, outgoing presidents simply hand-picked their successors.

Peruvian novelist Mario Vargas Llosa called Mexico "the perfect dictatorship." Officials were horrified, but average Mexicans agreed it was an apt description of a multi-party system with one party enjoying a 70-year winning streak.

Rampant corruption, economic mismanagement, and a string of scandals, including the assassination of top-level *PRIistas* by fellow party members, weakened the PRI's grip on power. Compounding the party's self-inflicted wounds was the 1994 New Year's Day uprising by poor peasants in the southern state of Chiapas. Led by charismatic rebel leader *Subcomandante* Marcos, the ragtag Zapatista Army of National Liberation focused world attention on the desperate plight of Mexico's indigenous communities and deeply embarrassed the government.

Ex-President Ernesto Zedillo (1994-2000) has been both praised and pilloried for engineering the clean, competitive elections that allowed the opposition to win.

The PRI's old guard, known here as "dinosaurs," resents Zedillo for letting the reins slip through his hands, while others have hailed him as a champion of democracy. He will most likely be remembered in the history books as a key political reformer.

Fox, a former Coca-Cola executive and rancher known for his pragmatic business sense and signature cowboy boots, is leading a country with age-old problems of poverty and corruption but a new taste for democracy into the 21st century.

A little more than halfway through his six-year administration, which began December 1, 2000, potential successors are already jockeying to replace Fox, who is limited by the constitution to a single term.

Mexico's presidential hopefuls include his wife Martha Sahagun, who, despite her husband's assertions to the contrary, has repeatedly hinted she might run; popular Mexico City Mayor Andres Manuel Lopez Obrador; Fox's controversial former Foreign Minister Jorge Castañeda; and a host of PRI bosses eager to reinstate their party's leadership.

On a brief visit to Mexico recently, Vargas Llosa reappraised the nation, deeming it no longer to be a perfect dictatorship, but "an imperfect democracy."

Important Dates in Mexican History

B.C.

1200	Height of Olmec civilization.
31	Earliest recorded calendar date in New World.

A.D.

100-700	Teotihuacan influence spreads, declines.
600-900	Height of Mayan civilization
600-1200	El Tajin (Gulf Coast), Monte Alban, Mitla (Oaxaca) flourish.
987	Queztalcoatl departs from Tula.
1168	Fall of Tula, Toltec capital.
1325	Tenochtitlan founded.
1428	Defeat of Tepanecs of Atzcapotzalco.
1472	Death of Nezahualcoyotl of Texcoco.
1517	Cordoba's expedition to Yucatan.
1519	Cortes lands in Veracruz (April 21).
1521	Fall of Tenochtitlan (Aug. 13).
1535	First Spanish viceroy arrives in Mexico.
1810	Father Hidalgo's "Grito," start of War of Independence from Spain (Sept. 16).
1822	Gen. Agustin de Iturbide declares himself emperor (May 19).
1824	First president elected; constitution adopted.
1847	Gen. Winfield Scott victorious at Chapultepec Castle (Sept.13).
1855	Benito Juarez elected president.
1857	New constitution adopted with bill of rights, abolition of slavery.
1862	Battle of Puebla (May 5).
1864-67	French Intervention.
1876-1910	Porfirio Diaz dictatorship.
1910	Start of the Revolution (Nov. 20).
1917	New constitution adopted; revolution continues another three years.
1938	Nationalization of oil companies (March 18).
1952	University City completed.
1964	National Museum of Anthropology opens.
1974	Quintana Roo, Baja California Sur last states to join the Republic.
1978	Aztec Templo Mayor discovered in Mexico City.
1982	Private banks nationalized
1991	Reprivatization of banks
1994	North American Free Trade Agreement goes into effect; Zapatista army launches uprising (both Jan. 1).
1997	Mexico City makes democratic transition from president-appointed regent to popularly elected mayor.
2000	Vicente Fox wins presidency, ousting the world's longest-ruling party, the PRI (July 7).

Traveling Through Mexico

Making the Most of Your Trip

Mazunte, Puerto Escondido

Mexico Tourism Board

Traveling through Mexico has never been easier.

The two national airlines, *Mexicana* and *Aeromexico*, connect cities throughout the country with the capital and destinations abroad, upstart *Azteca* is making inroads with its budget fares, and small regional carriers, such as *Aerocaribe* and *Aeroliteral*, link more remote destinations.

But it is land transportation that has made the most headway in the past few years.

The nation's network of highways has been expanded, making driving between certain popular tourist destinations easier. Visitors to Morelia, the colonial capital of Michoacan state, for example, can now take a short, three and a half hour drive to Ixtapa-Zihuatanejo, on the Pacific coast. Highway access to Oaxaca and Guadalajara has also improved.

Motorists who decide to leave their car at home have more car rental options than ever before. All of the leading car rental companies—familiar names like Avis, Thrifty, Dollar, Hertz, National and Alamo—now have offices in Mexico's major cities and resorts.

Mexico's motor coach industry is today considered to be one of the world's best thanks to modern buses, economical fares and flexible routes. In fact, first-class service in most cases outshines that of the U.S. and rivals Europe's.

Standard first-class bus features include reserved seating, reclining seats, air-conditioning and heating, rest room, and TV monitors for video viewing.

Luxury bus service may include greater leg room or one-across seating, exclusive waiting rooms at terminals, snacks and refreshments, and even an on-board attendant. First-class and deluxe buses also stick to a certain speed limit on the highways, usually 95 kilometers per hour/59 mph.

For added convenience, some bus companies sell seven- to 21-day bus passes offering unlimited travel.

The nation's moribund state-owned railroad was sold not long ago, paving the way for much needed private investment. Now passenger trains are making a comeback.

Money has been invested in upgrading both the trains and stations of Mexico's most famous rail journey, the Chihuahua al Pacifico, which traverses the Copper Canyon in northern Mexico.

Passenger, dining and lounge cars on the Copper Canyon Express have been remodeled, with roomy, newly upholstered reclining seats and large windows that let you appreciate the passing scenery.

In the south, the recently launched Maya Express connects premier archaeological sites with colonial cities of the Yucatan Peninsula.

The rail journey begins in Merida, or Villahermosa, and takes in the Mayan ruins of Chichen-Itza, Uxmal and Palenque, as well as the colonial city of Campeche, as it winds its way through Mexico's Mundo Maya. The five-day train tour, aboard restored 1940's vintage cars, is offered by The Train Collection.

In central Mexico, the Independence Express aims to trace the country's struggle to break away from Spain as it winds its way through the colonial cities of Queretaro, Guanajuato, San Miguel de Allende, Zacatecas and San Luis Potosi.

Tourists take in the goings on at Oaxaca's main square

Chris Luhnow

Where to Stay

A few short years ago, Mexico offered visitors the usual menu of hotels: modern highrise or small inn, chain property or independent operation, standard or all inclusive.

Today, visitors have a greater variety of accommodations to choose from, including converted haciendas, increasingly popular bed-and-breakfasts, and historical colonial-era mansions.

This wider range of options is nowhere better reflected than in Mexico Boutique Hotels. This young association of hotels unites unique properties throughout Mexico that have in common an intimate size, idyllic setting, personalized service and individual style. Some play on a sense of grandeur, others offer a return to the basics of palm-thatched bungalows. All member hotels exemplify the charm and uniqueness that is part of Mexico's allure.

In preparing this book, the editors and correspondents of Travelers Guide to Mexico visit numerous hotels and study hundreds of detailed questionnaires sent in by them. Consequently, we collect a great amount of current data that we use to update our hotel recommendations.

Professional hotel directories seldom give more than the bare facts about a hotel. Here we try to be a bit more subjective and give you a feeling for the place.

Because hotel rates tend to fluctuate considerably, we use a code that indicates a general price range rather than a specific rate (see rates box). In general, prices are for standard double rooms, without meals. Only where specified are meals included in the rate, with AP standing for American Plan (three meals a day), and MAP for Modified American Plan (two meals a day). When the rate includes breakfast, it is mentioned next to the code. The codes applied to all-inclusive hotels, where daily rates cover all meals, beverages and most activities, reflect the per-person rate.

The principal factor in assigning a code to each hotel is its price range. Since we use the winter rate, usually the highest, to assign a code, the classification may not apply for all seasons. Remember that rates can vary greatly from low to high season, especially in coastal areas, where most hotels reduce their rates by as much as 50 percent during summer months, particularly as part of air-hotel packages. Inland hotels generally maintain the same year-round rate. In some instances, hotels apply the American Plan or Modified American Plan only during the winter season.

The code should also be evaluated with the hotel description and location in mind (inland hotels tend to charge lower rates than beach resorts, even for equivalent facilities). Whatever the rate given here, it is intended only as a guide, giving an approximate range of the cost of a double room. We welcome your comments on hotels you visit so we can take them into account in our subsequent editions.

In the following pages you'll find detailed information on transportation and other useful information designed to help you make the most of your trip to Mexico.

HOTEL RATES

LX: luxury hotel, with nightly rates above 375 USD

DX: deluxe hotel, with rates between 250-375 USD

FC: first-class hotel, with rates between 150-250 USD

MD: moderate hotel, with rates between 75-150 USD

ECON: economical (often excellent) hotel, with rates under 75 USD

Tips on Renting a Car in Mexico

1. Even if you're in a hurry, you can often save time and headaches by spending a few minutes checking out the vehicle:

a. Make sure its spare tire and tools are in place. You may need them—and you could be charged if the car is turned in and they are missing.

b. Give the car a visual check to see that it has no dents or broken glass. If you see anything, report it at once to the attendant so it gets noted on the contract.

c. Inside, check to see that the windows wind up and down, that the wipers, headlights, taillights, dimmer and parking lights work, and that there are no mysteries about dashboard controls, especially the air-conditioning, if the car has it.

d. Ask the attendant to show you what the registration card looks like and where it is kept. If you are stopped by the authorities they will ask to see it.

2. Sometimes the car will be delivered with just enough gas to get to the nearest filling station. Whatever the gas gauge registers, fill it up to that same point when you turn the car in. Otherwise, you may be charged extra for the difference.

3. If you receive a dirty car—one that has just been turned in, for example—and you don't want to wait to have it cleaned, most companies will be glad to have it washed the next day.

4. Check the oil level at the first gas fill-up (as well as levels in cars with power brakes and power steering) and make regular subsequent checks if the car is in use for several days.

5. Keep tire pressure at the recommended levels to assure better road control and mileage. Make sure the spare tire has air.

6. If you rent a car in Mexico City, or at any other point well above sea level, and drive to lower altitudes or to sea level, the motor may start to "ping" during acceleration or when it's pulling. A certain amount of this is normal because the car's carburetor is adjusted for rarefied air at the higher altitudes.

Conversely, if the car is rented at a lower altitude and goes up to the 7,000-foot level of Mexico City (or into surrounding mountains with altitudes of up to 10,000 feet), it will probably perform sluggishly on hills and during acceleration. This, again, is normal.

7. Even though it is expensive, you should buy insurance. Remember there is a deductible amount, so there is no reason to be less careful of the rental car than you would be of your own. And never leave the car open, or with the keys inside!

8. If you have a confirmed reservation, make sure you carry the confirmation slip when you claim your car. If you change your schedule, advise the rental company to insure that your car will be available.

The vision of turning beauty into opportunity.

Loreto · Los Cabos · Ixtapa · Huatulco · Cancun · Nayarit · Mar de Cortes · Huatulco · Costa Maya · Cancun · Los Cabos

Useful Information

When packing for a trip to Mexico, make sure your wardrobe coincides with the climate of the areas you plan to visit—cool in the central plateau and mountain zones, warm to hot in the coastal regions. Remember, it can get chilly enough at night for a thick sweater even in the tropics; and it can rain during the dry season.

The type of clothing depends also on the places you visit. You'll need comfortable footwear for getting around archaeological sites and climbing pyramids. For your own comfort, observe certain local customs—reserve outlandish or revealing attire for beach resorts and big cities, and dress more conservatively in the rest of the country.

The sun at Mexican resorts is strong and deceptive, so be careful. Suntan lotion and sunblock are available just about everywhere in Mexico, but if you need a special sunblock it's best to bring it with you. If you plan to visit areas near lush vegetation (archaeological sites in the tropical zones), insect repellent is an absolute must. Some beaches also attract gnats during certain seasons.

If you shoot slides, bring film for your camera, or stock up in Mexico's major cities before heading to the countryside.

Entry Requirements

U.S. and Canadian visitors to Mexico are not required to have valid passports. A tourist card, valid for up to 180 days (the length of time is specified on the permit), can be obtained at the border on presenting proof of nationality (passport or certified birth certificate). The permit costs about 20 dollars.

Those who travel by air can obtain the tourist permit from the airline at the time they purchase their tickets, or from their travel agents. Frequent visitors who enter by car or on foot are subject to the fee only once in a six-month period; they must carry their stamped visas, or tourist cards, to show they have already paid it.

Anyone remaining within 16 miles of the border or less than 72 hours in the country is exempt from the charge. U.S. citizens born of

A candle vigil forms part of the Day of the Dead ceremonies

Bruce Herman

Mexican parents are also exempt.

If your intention is to remain in Mexico for the maximum stay (180 days or six months), you should insist on this period being specified on the tourist card. Obtaining extensions once you are in the country can be time consuming.

U.S. citizens are not required to show proof of smallpox vaccination to enter or leave Mexico, unless they are arriving from a nation from which proof of vaccination is required. In the latter case, Mexican health authorities will administer the necessary vaccination without charge.

Mexican Customs

In addition to clothing, and photographic and sports equipment for their personal use, all flight or ship passengers entering Mexico are allowed up to 300 dollars in merchandise (50 dollars if traveling by land). Additionally, merchandise worth up to 3,000 dollars (1,000 dollars by land) per person may be introduced, but will be subject to a 38.8% global tax.

Each incoming traveler must complete a Customs Declaration Form and the belongings of all incoming travelers (except diplomatic personnel) are subject to spot check inspection by Mexican Customs authorities at entry points, land or air. For regulations concerning entering Mexico with a vehicle, please see the following chapter.

U.S. Customs and Others

Each U.S. citizen returning to the United States has a personal exemption of 400 dollars, and not more than 100 cigars or one quart of alcoholic beverages can be included in the exemption. There are restrictions on firearms, fruits and vegetables, as well as gold coins and jewelry containing them if minted after 1959. Naturally, narcotics and illegal drugs are prohibited, as are lottery tickets, products made from crocodile skins, ivory, sea turtles, wildcat fur, and animals (live or stuffed) such as birds or iguanas. The Generalized System of Preferences no longer includes most hand-crafted items, but duty charges are quite low, so this shouldn't keep you from making a purchase.

Canadians may bring back duty-free purchases of 100 dollars, or 300 dollars if they have been away for seven days or more. This

National Holidays 2004/2005

Jan. 1*	New Year's Day	Oct. 12	Day of the Race (Columbus Day)
Jan. 6	Three Kings Day		
Feb. 5	Constitution Day	Sept. 1*	President's State of the Union Address
March 21*	Benito Juarez' Birthday		
April 11	Easter Sunday 2004	Nov. 1-2	Day of the Dead
March 27	Easter Sunday 2005	Nov. 20*	Revolution Day
May 1*	Labor Day	Dec. 12	Virgin of Guadalupe Day
May 5	Battle of Puebla	Dec. 25*	Christmas Day
Sept. 16*	Independence Day		
			* Legal Holidays

MAKING A CALL TO THE U.S.

From any private or Telmex public phone, you can dial the following toll-free AT&T, MCI, SPRINT or TELMEX access numbers for multiple payment options, such as having calls charged to your telephone bill back home or major credit card, or making collect calls.

AT&T	(01) 800 288 2872
MCI	(001) 800 674 7000
SPRINT	(001) 800 877 8000
Telmex	(01) 800 SAVINGS
or	(01) 800 728 4647

Worldwide recognition from the Beach to the City

Mexico City

Ideal for business trips. Excellent facilities and sophisticated equipment. A gourmet center with international haute cuisine.

Guadalajara

Conveniently located. It offers the best convention and group facilities. Excellent service for your business or leisure trips.

Monterrey

Undoubtedly a great option for business trips. Infrastructure, flexibility and experience in one of the most important business and financial cities of Mexico.

Cancun

Enjoy the beauty of the Mexican Caribbean in a hotel that features first class facilities, excellent service and international food, plus the resort´s best beach.

Cozumel

An exclusive hotel on this paradisiacal island. White sands and more than a half mile of private beach. First class services and facilities.

Los Cabos

Remodeled and extended, this all-inclusive hotel offers 6 restaurants, 4 swimming-pools and 24-hour food and premium beverage service. Full activities program.

Ixtapa

An all-inclusive hotel with a wide range of recreational activities for the whole family, 24-hour food and premium beverage service.

Puerto Vallarta

Excellent facilities, recreational activities, 24-hour food and premium beverage service.

Paraiso de la Bonita

The first Boutique-Hotel with a Thalasso Center in the Americas operated by Presidente Inter-Continental Hotels & Resorts. Relax in one of our luxurious suites decorated in six different styles: Mediterranean, African, Indian, Balinese, Asian and Caribbean.

Dancers at Veracruz's main square

Rick Gomez

includes 200 cigarettes, 50 cigars, two pounds of tobacco, and 40 oz. of liquor. Packages marked "unsolicited gift—value under 25 U.S. dollars" may be mailed to Canada duty free.

British residents may return with 250 dollars of duty-free purchases plus 200 cigarettes (or 50 cigars, or 250 grams of tobacco), one liter of alcohol over 38.8% proof (or two liters of alcohol under 38.8% proof), two liters of table wine, and 50 grams of perfume.

Banking, Money Exchange

Currency can be exchanged at banks and money exchange houses (*casas de cambio*). Banking hours generally run from 9 a.m. to 5 p.m., Monday through Friday (certain banks open Saturdays also). Most exchange houses open 9 a.m. to 5 p.m. weekdays; a few also open half a day Saturdays. Some ATMs belong to the Cirrus and Plus systems, enabling travelers to access their accounts; withdrawals are made in pesos.

Peso coins come in denominations of five, 10, 20 and 50 centavos (cents) and one, two, five, 10 and 20 pesos. Peso bills come in denominations of 20, 50, 100, 200 and 500 (colors and sizes vary, but the 50, 100 and 500 peso bills are all reddish-purplish hues, so pay special attention).

The peso-dollar exchange rate stood at 11.4 pesos to the dollar in mid-June 2004. Whatever the current rate is, it will be posted prominently at all banks and places catering to tourists.

Major credit cards, such as American Express and Visa, are accepted at most establishments. Travelers checks can be used for purchases with normal identification procedures, but shops and restaurants do not usually offer the best exchange rate; it's best to cash travelers checks at banks.

Technically the peso is the only legal tender in Mexico, but establishments at some resorts accept dollars readily, especially in Los Cabos and, to a lesser degree, Cancun and Cozumel.

Medical Emergencies

There are excellent hospitals with modern facilities and English-speaking staff in Mexico City and increasingly at major beach resorts, such as Mazatlan, Puerto Vallarta and Los Cabos.

In Mexico City, the American British Cowdray Hospital (ABC)—tel. 5230-8000—is affiliated with Baylor University Medical Center in Dallas, Texas, and a member of the American Hospital Association. The ABC will recommend English-speaking specialists in other Mexican cities and tourist resorts, as will the U.S. Embassy.

Hospital Angeles del Pedregal, in the south of the city, is also excellent. Tel. 5652-2011.

Check the fine print on your insurance policies as to their applicability in Mexico. There are special policies for travelers, covering medical and life insurance, that can be purchased just for your trip. It is advisable to deal with these matters before leaving home.

If the worst should happen and you or a traveling companion needs to return home for medical care, Austin-based Air Ambulance America is on 24-hour standby to fly out sick or injured tourists from anywhere in Mexico. U.S. toll-free number 1 (800) 222-3564, or call collect (512) 479-8000.

Embassies

The U.S. Embassy is located at Paseo de la Reforma 305, Mexico 06500, D.F. Tel. 5080-2000.

The Canadian Embassy is at Schiller 529, Mexico 11550, D.F. Tel. 5724-7900.

The U.S. State Department operates a Citizens Emergency Center hotline, where callers receive up-to-date information on relevant matters, such as political unrest or health hazards at a prospective visiting site. The center will contact authorities abroad in an attempt to locate a traveler, deliver an urgent message and offer general assistance in emergencies. Phone: (202) 647-5255, weekdays from 8 a.m. to 5 p.m.; Saturdays, 9 a.m. to 3 p.m.

Other Useful Information

Telephones: Public phones in more than 150 cities throughout the country operate with pre-paid phone cards. The 20-, 30-, 50-, or 100-peso cards can be purchased at newsstands, convenience stores or any establishment displaying a sign that reads "LADATEL de venta aqui" (LADATEL sold here). Public phones marked "LADA" offer long-distance service, and those operated by Telmex, Mexico's national telephone company, appear to be applying the most competitive rates.

You can charge your long-distance calls to your telephone bill back home, a service offered by Mexico's national telephone company, Telmex, as well as major U.S. telephone companies AT&T, MCI and Sprint.

Cellular phones and pagers are available for daily rental.

Telephone numbers in Mexico's three largest cities—Mexico City, Monterrey, Guadalajara—are eight digits long, with a two-digit area code; in the rest of the country, numbers are seven digits with a three-digit area code.

Ministry of Tourism: This government ministry is located in

Useful Numbers

National

Toll-Free 24-Hour

Tourist Assistance:	(01 800) 903-9200
Emergency Assistance:	060
Information:	040
Operator-Assisted Nat'l Long Distance:	020
Operator-Assisted Int'l Long Distance:	090
Automatic Nat'l Long Distance:	01
Automatic Long Distance to U.S./Canada:	001
Automatic Long Distance Worldwide:	00

In Mexico City

Tourist Assistance:	5250-0123
Ambulance:	5523-1719
Fire Department:	5768-3700
Highway Police:	5684-2142
Int'l Telegrams:	5709-8625
Highway Assistance:	5250-8221
Missing Persons:	5658-1111

Mexico City at Presidente Masaryk 172 in Polanco. You can call their 24-hour English-speaking information service at 5250-0123 with any questions or problems. For information from anywhere within the country, the 24-hour toll-free number is 01 (800) 903-9200; from the United States 1 (800) 482-9832.

You can also address complaints, in English, to: Direccion General, Depto. de Quejas, Secretaria de Turismo, Presidente Masaryk 172, Mexico 11550, D.F. Regional offices are located in most major resorts, listed in the telephone directory under "Secretaria de Turismo."

Mail: Post offices in most all major cities are open 8 a.m. to 2 p.m. Monday through Friday; to noon Saturday. Mexico City's Palacio Postal (the main post office and a historic monument well worth visiting) is open 8 a.m. to 7:30 p.m. Monday to Friday, 9 a.m. to 4 p.m. Saturday. Standard airmail letters or postcards to the U.S. or Canada cost 8.50 pesos (or less than 80 U.S. cents). Surface mail is not recommended unless you don't care when the letter arrives. For especially urgent matters, you may want to use a courier service.

The U.S. embassy, in Mexico City

Sales Tax: A 15% value-added sales tax (called "IVA" in Spanish) is applied to most goods and services, although some items (medicine, for example) are exempt. It is not required to be itemized separately on your bill, and is usually included in the retail price of goods. The IVA is 10% in the states of Quintana Roo and Baja California. Hotels charge an additional 2% lodging tax.

Tipping: For baggage handlers and porters calculate about a dollar per person; chambermaids a dollar per day; and tour guides and drivers a dollar a day, minimum. It is customary to leave waiters anywhere from a 10% to a 20% tip, depending on the service. A parking lot or valet parking attendant should receive a small tip. Taxi drivers expect a tip only when they provide an extra service.

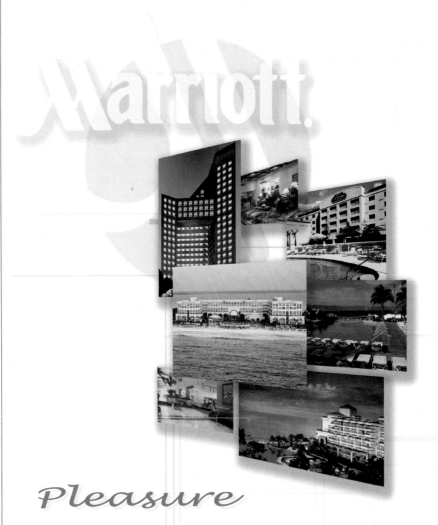

Transportation

AIRLINES

Mexicana and *Aeromexico*, Mexico's two national airlines, provide extensive service throughout the country, as well as to major U.S., Canadian and European cities. New budget carrier *Azteca* is gradually increasing its roster of destinations. And several regional carriers serve more remote areas.

More than 25 of the world's major international airlines serve Mexico and they include American Airlines, British Airways, Canadian, Continental, Delta, United, Air France, Japan Airlines, Iberia, KLM and Lufthansa.

The capital is the primary hub for incoming international flights, but several international carriers have direct flights from U.S. cities to such destinations as Cancun, Ixtapa-Zihuatanejo, Manzanillo, Puerto Vallarta, Mazatlan, Los Cabos and Monterrey.

European visitors can reach Mexico City on direct flights from Amsterdam (KLM), Frankfurt (Lufthansa), London (British Airways), Madrid (Iberia) and Paris (Air France).

AUTOMOBILES

Driving is one of the best ways to explore Mexico, but there is some paperwork involved in bringing a car into the country.

Entry Requirements: An import permit (Permiso Temporal de Importacion) is required for any vehicle (automobile, camper, etc.) entering the country. In order to obtain the permit, tourists are required to show proof of direct ownership of their vehicle and a driver's license, and pay a nominal fee (about 20 dollars) with an international credit card or post a bond of between 200 and 400 dollars, depending on the type of vehicle. The permit application form is available over the Internet.

While cumbersome, these restrictions are designed to ensure the vehicle (as well as its accessories, such as stereos, air-conditioners, etc.) leaves the country when the tourist does, minimizing cross-border trade in stolen cars. Should a tourist need to make an emergency air trip back home, special permission from the Secretaria de Gobernacion (Ministry of the Interior) may be obtained to leave the vehicle in the country. Airlines are not permitted to issue boarding passes to passengers with vehicular information noted on their tourist cards unless they have a special exit permit. Take care of this at least 24 hours prior to departure.

Since most U.S. and Canadian insurance policies do not cover the vehicle while it is out of the country, tourists entering Mexico with a vehicle should purchase Mexican insurance (full coverage or third party) for the duration of their stay (see below).

Who can drive the car while it is in Mexico? Any family member or other tourist who has a valid U.S. or foreign driver's license; Mexican citizens not related to the permit holder can drive the car only if accompanied by that person.

Insurance: Your vehicle's U.S. insurance policy will almost certainly not be valid in Mexico, but coverage can be obtained at virtually all border crossing points. *Sanborn's Mexico Insurance* (toll-free tel. 1 (800) 222-0158) is an experienced outfit with offices at major border cities and an agent in San Miguel de Allende.

Insurance rates are government controlled, but the minimum coverage usually provides no payment for medical expenses, car repairs or theft, so it is important to read your policy carefully. If you happen to be involved in an accident, you must provide on-the-spot proof of your financial ability to cover damage costs—even if the other party is responsible. Keep in mind that in Mexico insurance is not just a way to pay off damages, it is also a "stay out of jail" policy. The Napoleonic Code of Justice (you are guilty until proven innocent) prevails throughout Mexico; you'll have to tell it to the judge if you lack insurance or plenty of cash.

Gasoline: Pemex, the government-owned oil company, franchises all gas stations. Although you shouldn't have trouble finding unleaded gas, filling stations may run out, especially off the main tourist routes. Occasionally you will run into long stretches of road where filling stations are few and far between. It's always a good idea to fill up whenever possible. Unleaded *Premium* gasoline is the highest-octane fuel available. Unleaded *Magna Sin* has an octane level of 87 and is comparable to Regular Unleaded in the United States.

Driving Tips

Major highways in Mexico are generally very good. They range from miles of straight, flat highways in the north to very winding ones in spectacular mountainous terrain in other parts of the country.

When you cross the border into Mexico, your car will be inspected and your car trunk and individual valises will be sealed. Don't break the seals until you have passed through the second checkpoint—usually less than 50 miles from the border. Otherwise your belongings will undergo another time-consuming inspection.

It is still good advice for the visitor not to drive after dark. Emergency situations are always more difficult to cope with at night. Even if you have plenty of fuel to make it to the next town over a stretch of rural highway, be sure to fill up before starting out. Fuel deliveries at times are erratic and stations in remote towns may not have fuel.

Remember to always lock your car and take out valuables, or at least lock them in the trunk. Do not pick up any hitchhikers, even your fellow countrymen. You may be robbed or be the unwitting accomplice to narcotics transport, for which you can be implicated and your car confiscated.

City driving can be a little hectic for the foreigner. Street names often change from one block to another, signs may be in an unfamiliar language, and traffic circles (*glorietas*) seem to engage drivers in a game of Russian Roulette. In Mexico City, freeways tend to be anything but "free," especially during rush hour, at which time the main freeway, the Periferico, is referred to as the city's largest parking lot.

Watch out for *topes*—those three- to six-inch-high, concrete or metal speed bumps which are often unmarked. And always look both ways, even on a one-way street. Never take the right-of-way for granted!

Car Rental

Many major U.S. car rental firms operate in Mexico. It's best to stick to the well-known ones, as many of the lesser-known franchises are not properly supervised.

Rental fees are, in general, higher than in the United States, Canada and Europe. A compact here will cost between 75 and 85 dollars a day, depending on whether it's a standard or automatic. You must return your vehicle only to the office where you rented it or an additional pickup fee of about 45 dollars is added. Often during the high season demand exceeds supply at airport rental agencies. You can try to avoid this by reserving in advance through your travel agent or directly with a car rental company.

Alamo. Mexico City Tel. 5250-0055.
Toll-free nationwide: 01 (800) 849-8001.
Avis. Mexico City Tel. 5588-8888.
Toll-free nationwide: 01 (800) 288-8888.
Budget. Mexico City Tel. 5566-6800.
Toll-free nationwide: 01 (800) 700-1700.
Hertz. Mexico City Tel. 5592-8343.
Toll-free nationwide: 01 (800) 709-5000.
National. Mexico City Tel. 5661-5000.
Toll-free nationwide: 01 (800) 716-6625.
Thrifty. Mexico City Tel. 5280-5847.
Toll-free nationwide: 01 (800) 021-2277.

Mexican Highways

Listed below are the major highways leading into Mexico from towns along the U.S. border. All are accessed by the U.S. interstate highway system.

U.S. 89 ends in Arizona just across the border from Nogales, where it becomes Mexico Highway 15 and heads south to the Pacific coast and Mazatlan, 763 miles south.

Ciudad Juarez, across the border from El Paso, Texas, is the starting point for Mex 45, (known also as the Interamerican Highway), which travels through the states of Chihuahua, Torreon, Durango, and Zacatecas on its way to Mexico City, 1,130 miles southeast.

Mex 57 begins across the border from Eagle Pass, Texas, and continues to Mexico City via

Going on a trip ?
We´ll take you there !

To the beaches
Pto. Peñasco
Bahía Kino
Guaymas
Topolobampo
Mazatlán
San Blas
Pto. Vallarta
Manzanillo
Lázaro Cárdenas
Ixtapa Zihuatanejo
Acapulco
Pto. Escondido
Pto. Angel
Huatulco
Salina Cruz

To the border
Tijuana
Mexicali
Sonoyta
S.L. Río Colorado
Nogales
Naco
Agua Prieta
Cd. Juárez
Ojinaga
Cd. Acuña
Piedras Negras
Nvo. Laredo
Reynosa
Matamoros

GRUPO ESTRELLA BLANCA

www.estrellablanca.com.mx

Now buy your tickets in stores:

We take you to more than 1,200 destinations in 27 states throughout Mexico and, for your safety and convenience, sell tickets to the U.S. and Canada on Greyhound

For information, reservations, rentals and sales, call

Guadalajara
01 33 **3679 ★ 0404**

Mexico City
01 55 **5729 ★ 0707**

Monterrey
01 81 **8318 ★ 3737/38**

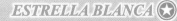

some of the country's most interesting northern and central cities—Monterrey, Saltillo, San Luis Potosi and Queretaro. After crossing a 250-mile northern stretch of bleak, arid desert plateau, the highway continues past the hills of Mexico's richest mining regions to the fertile farmlands of the central highlands, where beautiful trees, rivers, ranches and maguey fields dominate the landscape. It is the best access highway to Mexico City and you will find good, moderately priced accommodations all along the way.

Take Mex 85 in Nuevo Laredo, across the border from Laredo, Texas, and change 140 miles south, in Monterrey, to Mex 40 to Saltillo, and then change to Mex 57 to Mexico City, where it ends at Chapultepec Park on the Paseo de la Reforma, 758 miles from Laredo. This route is part of the Pan-American Highway, which becomes Mex 190 between Mexico City and the Guatemalan border.

Mex 180 runs along the coast of the Gulf of Mexico, from Matamoros, just south of Brownsville, Texas, to Veracruz, 609 miles southeast.

Highway Assistance

The Mexican Tourism Ministry operates a fleet of vehicles known as *Angeles Verdes* (Green Angels), which patrol the major highways and offer assistance to motorists in trouble. There is no charge for their services.

These radio-equipped vehicles, painted green and white, patrol the highways every day of the year from 7 a.m. to 6 p.m. They are manned by English-speaking expert mechanics who in addition to providing emergency service can administer first aid and provide information on highway conditions and tourist destinations. They carry a supply of minor spare parts as well as emergency gasoline and oil, which they can sell you at cost.

The Green Angels constitute one of Mexico's most appreciated tourism innovations. No matter what your highway trouble is, you can count on a Green Angel unit to come along sooner or later and help you out. You can also call their headquarters in Mexico City at 5250-8221.

BUSES

Buses offer a comfortable and economical way to travel. The level of service on first-class and deluxe buses is much higher than in the United States and comparable to European standards.

Almost all first-class buses are equipped with air conditioning, on-board bathrooms, and TV monitors for video viewing. Deluxe service may also feature three-across seating rather than four, a self-service bar stocked with coffee, tea and softdrinks, and private waiting lounges at bus terminals. On the Mexico City-Acapulco route, deluxe service often includes attendants serving drinks and snacks.

The terms used to identify these services—*ejecutivo, de lujo, diamante, crucero*—vary from company to company, so ask about the amenities you are getting. The

only drawback to bus travel is a lack of English-speaking personnel, so you may want to consult a travel agent.

First-class buses invariably travel on toll roads, which are safer, and take passengers only at designated terminals. For added security, travel by day.

Travelers can make reservations and purchase tickets for bus lines operating on the U.S. side of the border, as well as secure tickets on Mexican bus lines for the return trip north through Mexican territory. Contact *Estrella Blanca* (see below).

It is always best to purchase tickets in advance, especially if you plan to travel during the holidays or a long weekend. The leading bus lines accept credit card purchases by phone; passengers can then collect their tickets at the terminal before departure.

Most of the major bus lines in Mexico City depart from one of four terminals, depending

Estrella Blanca

on the region of the country served: Northern Terminal (*Terminal Central del Norte*), Av. de los Cien Metros 4907; Southern Terminal (*Terminal Central del Sur*), Taxqueña 1320; Eastern Terminal (*Terminal Central del Oriente*), Calzada Ignacio Zaragoza 200; Western Terminal (*Terminal Central del Poniente*), Av. Sur 122. A few of the bus lines recommended below depart from more convenient locations.

Autobuses de Oriente (ADO). Service to more than 20 cities throughout eastern Mexico, including the states of Quintana Roo, Yucatan, Campeche, Tabasco, Oaxaca, Veracruz and Puebla, and Mexico City. Deluxe "GL" service to such Mundo Maya destinations as Campeche, Cancun, Merida, Playa del Carmen and Villahermosa. ADO Buspass offers unlimited travel for a fixed price. The seven-, 14- and 21-day passes are available through authorized travel agents in Europe, Canada and the United States. Tel. 5133-2424.

Enlaces Terrestres Nacionales (ETN). Deluxe service to central Mexico's Bajio region, and a few coastal destinations. From Ter-

minal Central Poniente, service to Morelia, Toluca and Uruapan. From Terminal Central del Norte, service to Aguascalientes, Colima, Guadalajara, Leon, Manzanillo, Puerto Vallarta, Queretaro, San Luis Potosi, San Miguel de Allende and Zamora. Tel. 5277-6529.

Estrella Blanca. A leading transportation company operating luxury Turistar Ejecutivo, and first-class Futura and Elite bus lines, among others, to more than 1,200 destinations in 27 states, with connections to the U.S. and Canada on Greyhound. Also bus rentals, travel packages and tailored itineraries. Tel. 5729-0707.

Estrella de Oro. Terminal Central del Sur. Deluxe "Diamante" service to Acapulco, Ixtapa-Zihuatanejo and Taxco. Tickets can be reserved over the phone with a credit card. Tel. 5549-8520 to 29.

Estrella Roja/ADO GL: Deluxe service to Puebla from three convenient departure points in Mexico City: Rio Lerma 154 (Del Angel Hotel), Frontera 217 (Benidorm Hotel), and the international airport. Tel. 5133-2424.

Omnibus Cristobal Colon. Terminal Central del Oriente. Deluxe "Plus" service to the states of Chiapas, Morelos and Oaxaca. Connections to Guatemala and Central America. Tel. 5756-9926.

Primera AeroPlus: Deluxe service to Queretaro departing from Mexico City's international airport. Tel. (442) 229-0090.

Pullman de Morelos. Deluxe "Ejecutivo Dorado" service to destinations in Morelos state, including service to Cuernavaca from Mexico City's international airport, and service to Tepoztlan from Terminal Central del Sur. Tel. 5549-3505 to 08.

Transportes Chihuahuenses. Terminal Central del Norte. Pullman express cruisers to El Paso, Texas, connecting with Greyhound lines for the U.S. and Canada. Also service to Chihuahua, Ciudad Juarez, Durango, Queretaro and Zacatecas. Tel. 5729-0707.

Transportes del Norte. Terminal Central del Norte. Direct service to Laredo, Texas, connecting with Greyhound lines for the U.S. and Canada. Also serves Durango, Matamoros, Monterrey, Queretaro, Saltillo and San Luis Potosi. Tel. 5729-0707.

Uno. Terminal Central del Oriente. Deluxe service on buses with just 25 seats, serving Coatzacoalcos, Jalapa, Oaxaca, Tampico, Veracruz and Villahermosa. Tel. 5133-2424.

TRAINS

Neglected for years—with nearly 80 percent of its 16,000 miles of tracks dating from before the 1910 revolution—Mexico's national railroad system was sold to private enterprise in 2001.

Still, three special rail journeys offer a nostalgic and scenic way to travel—the Copper Canyon Express through Copper Canyon, and the new Independence Express through central Mexico and Maya Express through the Yucatan. You can find out more about these train tours in the North Mexico, Central Mexico and Mundo Maya sections.

The Great Outdoors

Sports, Ecotourism and Adventure Travel

Golfing in Mexico

By Charles Kinder

Today 6.5 billion dollars worth of golf-related resort and real estate development is taking place around Mexico, making golf one of the fastest growing and most important segments of Mexico's tourism industry.

Recent surveys show Mexico is the second most popular destination outside of the continental United States for U.S. golfers (Hawaii is No. 1). This popularity is due in no small part to the fact that many of the top names in the world of golf design, including Jack Nicklaus, Robert Trent Jones and the Dyes, are behind Mexico's best courses.

Without a doubt, Los Cabos is the leader in the development of world-class golf in Mexico. This burgeoning resort located at the tip of the Baja California Peninsula recently ranked 14th in a listing of the 50 most popular golf destinations in the world.

Los Cabos' climate and setting are perfect, like Palm Springs on the ocean. A 20-mile stretch of coast between the two towns of Los Cabos, Cabo San Lucas and San Jose del Cabo, is home to some of the world's best oceanside courses, carved out of a landscape where stark desert meets an azure sea.

Three Nicklaus signature courses are open along this corridor, including the top-rated *Cabo del Sol*, ranked 70th in Golf Magazine's top 100 courses in the world. The course boasts five oceanfront holes, including the "finest three finishing holes in golf," according to its designer.

Cabo del Sol hosted the 1995 and 1998 PGA Senior Slams as well as Shell's 1996 Wonderful World of Golf match featuring Lee Treviño and Nicklaus himself. These made-for-TV events brought Los Cabos into the homes of millions of viewers who then flocked to play golf south of the border.

Tom Weiskopf has added a desert course to Cabo del Sol's ocean course. His masterful inland layout, featuring 180-degree views of the sea from nearly every hole, takes advantage of natural river washes, subtle changes in elevation and dramatic bunkering as it weaves

> *No longer just a lazy one-course town, Puerto Vallarta may be destined to become the next major golf destination in North America.*

through lush desert landscape.

Up the road, at the legendary Palmilla resort, you'll find Nicklaus' first signature course in Latin America, with 27 holes featuring the ocean, arroyo and mountain nines.

In the middle of the Los Cabos corridor is Cabo Real, a master-planned golf resort featuring such deluxe hotels as the Westin Regina and Dreams Los Cabos, as well as the ultra-luxurious Las Ventanas al Paraiso. Tiger Woods escaped to Las Ventanas right after his runaway performance at the U.S. Open at Pebble Beach. Unable to resist the beauty of his golf

surroundings for even a few days, Woods was seen working on his game at Cabo Real's *El Dorado* golf course.

Cabo Real boasts two courses: the *Cabo Real* course by Robert Trent Jones II and the newer, spectacular, oceanfront El Dorado by Nicklaus, with six holes on the beach along the Sea of Cortez. El Dorado hosted the very successful 2000 U.S. Collegiate Championship featuring teams from 12 of the best golf schools in the country and broadcast by ESPN. The course record of 68, held by Nicklaus himself, was bettered each day of the event, ending with a final round of 61 played by Jess Daly of Northwestern University.

Los Cabos' newest course, *Querencia*, opened in November 2000 as part of the resort's first private country club. The world-class 18-hole course is Tom Fazio's first signature course in Mexico but certainly not his last.

Closer to Cabo San Lucas is the *Cabo San Lucas Country Club* designed by Roy and Matt Dye, featuring a more open layout with a view to Land's End, Los Cabos' most photographed landmark. This is the location of Los Cabos Golf Resorts for golf-focused guests who like the idea of owning a villa for a week or more on a golf course close to town. As part of American Golf's premier National Golf Club, members enjoy exchange privileges with more than 20 top-rated U.S. courses and resorts.

At the opposite end of the corridor, more affordable golf is found at the *Los Cabos Golf Club* in San Jose del Cabo, with nine very playable holes pleasantly priced at 60 dollars for a round of 18 holes.

Leading Golf Courses

Acapulco:	Acapulco Princess (18)
	Puerto Marques (18)
	Tres Vidas (18)
Cancun:	Hilton (18)
	Playacar (18)
	Pok-Ta-Pok (18)
	Puerto Aventuras (9)
Cozumel:	Cozumel (18)
Cuernavaca:	Lomas de Cocoyoc (18)
	San Gaspar (18)
	Santa Fe (18)
	Tabachines (18)
Guadalajara:	Atlas (18)
	Las Cañadas (18)
	Santa Anita (18)
Huatulco:	Huatulco Golf (18)
Ixtapa:	Marina (18)
	Palma Real (18)
Loreto:	Loreto (18)
Los Cabos:	Cabo del Sol (18)
	Cabo Real (18)
	Cabo San Lucas (18)
	El Dorado (18)
	Palmilla (27)
	Querencia (18)
Manzanillo:	El Tamarindo (18)
	Isla Navidad (27)
	La Mantarraya (18)
Mazatlan:	El Cid (27)
	Estrella del Mar (18)
Mexico City:	Bellavista (18)
	Campestre (18)
	Chapultepec (18)
	Chiluca (18)
	La Hacienda (18)
	Mexico (18)
	San Carlos (18)
	Vallescondido (18)
Merida:	Yucatan (18)
Monterrey:	Las Misiones (18)
	Club Campestre (18)
	Valle Alto (18)
Puebla:	Puebla (18)
Puerto Vallarta:	Flamingos (18)
	Four Seasons (19)
	Marina Vallarta (18)
	Mayan Palace
	Vista Vallarta (18+18)
Queretaro:	Jurica (18)
	San Gil (18)
	Tequisquiapan (18)
San Carlos:	San Carlos (18)
S.M. de Allende:	Malanquin (18)
Tijuana:	Bajamar (27)
	Real Del Mar (18)
	Tijuana (18)
Valle de Bravo:	Avandaro (18)
Veracruz:	La Villa Rica (18)
	Xalapa (18)

During the winter season in Los Cabos, an advance tee time reservation is a must, and available via the Internet at www.thegolfer.com. It's also a good idea to rent a car to make the most of your golf vacation; with the variety of golf courses and fine restaurants located along the corridor, you will want to drive up and down on your own schedule. Expect to pay premium prices in Los Cabos, often referred to as Newport Beach south, for accommodations and play.

For a free Best's Golf Guide to Los Cabos, contact Golf Publishing International at (949) 494-8561.

Mexican Riviera

Good golf travel advice wouldn't be complete without a few words about the Mexican Riviera on Mexico's Pacific coast. From Manzanillo to Puerto Vallarta, and Punta Mita beyond, this area has a legitimate claim to some of the best golf in the world.

More than 25 years ago, billionaire tin magnate Antenor Patiño gave us a golf course rated "10" at Las Hadas. Designed in 1969 by Pete and Roy Dye, *La Mantarraya* began the move to hire top-rated U.S. golf architects to design courses in Mexico. This is the Dye family, including Andy, at its best, with a wonderfully crafted course of greens surrounded by sand traps and sand traps in the middle of the green. An addition to the original plan is the famous million-dollar hole—a 144-yard par three 18th hole with the green positioned on a man-made island built in the ocean. The view from the tee is spectacular, with the all white Las Hadas resort in the background. The best advice is to take a couple of extra balls!

Next door, the all-inclusive Karmina Palace also has a spectacular view of the 18th hole and offers a super package that includes golf and many other activities for the entire family.

Heading north up the coast is the "kingdom" of *Isla Navidad* and its deluxe Grand Bay Hotel, one of only two properties in Mexico to receive Golf Magazine's 1998 Gold Award (the other is Los Cabos' Palmilla). Here Robert von Hagge has built a masterpiece with 27 holes of oceanfront and bay front fairways and greens.

Nearby is *El Tamarindo*, a spectacular, modern wonder in the world of golf with its own unique villagelike hideaway and an oceanside golf course in the jungle designed by David Fleming. This destination requires special consideration as it may not be for everyone. The right kind of adventurous golfer, however, will be able to brag to his friends about his experience with jungle golf.

Top-notch courses combined with reasonable prices are set to make the Mexican Riviera a fast-growth area for golf. In fact, Puerto Vallarta hosted the PGA-sponsored World Cup in December 2002.

Puerto Vallarta is no longer just a lazy one-course town. The opening of the *Vista Vallarta Golf Club* and its two dynamic championship courses is destined to make Vallarta the next major golf destination in North America. Occupying the property's highest elevations, the first course is designed by Nicklaus and offers

golfers a variety of terrain and challenges as they play across rolling hillsides, dense forests of palms and giant ficus trees, and at least a dozen natural arroyos. With dramatic views of the town and bay, golfers will want to play this course twice—once with a camera, and again with their clubs.

The second course, designed by Tom Weiskopf, takes players across deep natural ravines and swift creeks, all characteristic of the property's lowest elevations. Weiskopf has done a masterful job of working the terrain's natural features into an incredibly playable and memorable course, from the first tee to the green of the "driveable" 18th hole.

Diamond Golf Construction, the leading golf course builder in Mexico, transformed the property from wild jungle into landscaped fairways and greens. And preserving the natural beauty of this idyllic setting appears to have been a key directive throughout the project. The result is, in the words of ClubCorp's director of course development Bobby Heine, "the best golf complex in Mexico…difficult to duplicate anywhere in the world."

The *Marina Vallarta Golf Course* designed by Joe Finger was the resort's first course. Located between the marina and the ocean, the course is owned and managed by ClubCorp. Resident director of golf Greg Scott maintains U.S. standards, services and upkeep. Surrounding the course are several notable hotels, one is located right on the course. Along the 10th fairway are ClubCorp's timeshare villas, offering membership privileges and exchange abilities with some of their other premier properties, including Homestead and Barton Creek.

One of the most promising newer courses is 40 minutes north of Puerto Vallarta at Punta Mita. Developed by Dine and operated by the Four Seasons, it is a Nicklaus signature venue designed as a private club for hotel guests, and Punta Mita residents and their invited guests. The course has 19 holes; no typo here. When water or tide conditions prevent players from reaching the unique par three third hole, called The Tale of the Whale, with its green situated on a natural island 180 yards off the coast, then an optional par three is played.

The master-planned residential-resort community of Punta Mita is Four Seasons' first resort in Latin America, offering both award-winning luxury hotel services and vacation ownership with a lifetime of Four Seasons amenities. Plans call for two additional championship golf courses.

Farther north, Mazatlan offers two good options. At *El Cid*, a mega resort with more than a thousand rooms to meet your budget needs, Lee Treviño has built nine new holes and plans to redesign the existing 18. Down the road, *Estrella del Mar* boasts a Trent Jones masterpiece, and future vacation homes and hotel accommodations. Golf in Mazatlan is still relatively unknown, so those who discover it practically have the courses to themselves! Word, however, is spreading fast.

Acapulco is regaining its luster as a wonderful destination due in part to the *Tres Vidas Golf Club*, site of the Chrysler Cup Championship, and The Fairmont *Acapulco Princess* and *Pierre*

Marques hotels which, along with their respective courses, were recently bought by Canadian Pacific Hotels.

These courses have famous histories: renowned golfer-architect Ted Robinson designed the Acapulco Princess and Robert Trent Jones, Sr., redesigned the Pierre Marques, which served as the site of the 1960's World Cup. Plus, Acapulco offers great daytime golf followed by the best nightlife in Mexico.

Caribbean Courses

Cancun, and the Mundo Maya region in general, has its sights on gaining market share in the world of golf. Rumor has it that the Riviera Maya will see six courses open over the next five years. Cancun's Robert Trent Jones-designed *Pok-Ta-Pok* course is currently getting an overhaul via the good folks at ClubCorp, and near Playa del Carmen is the highly rated Robert von Hagge course at *Playacar*.

Off the coast of the Yucatan Peninsula, the island of Cozumel has unveiled its first golf course, designed by Nicklaus. Having been granted the first permit in almost 20 years for golf construction in the Yucatan, ClubCorp in conjunction with Diamond Golf Construction fashioned a championship course that is expected to serve as the ecological model for all future golf development in the Yucatan. From pulverizing rock into bunker sand to hewing trees into lumber for a bridge over a mangrove swamp, this project is an environmental masterpiece. For years, Cozumel has been known for its world-class reef diving, but this new course will encourage any diver to trade in his fins for a set of clubs.

Among inland resorts, Guadalajara is considered the golf capital of Mexico. Often overlooked in favor of beach locations, this city is home to five outstanding private country clubs with an open door policy for foreign golfers. Guadalajara offers golfers the opportunity to play the Riviera Country Clubs or Oak Hills of Mexico, and they jump at the chance. Add friendly veteran caddies and the intimate country club environment, and you have a golf vacation that can't be matched.

Guadalajara's *Atlas Country Club* has one of the longest courses in the country and is host to several annual tournaments. *El Palomar* is a newer, upscale course overlooking Mexico's second largest city. It has quickly become a hit among local golfers and will be a source of great satisfaction to visitors who play this course high above Guadalajara.

Golf Tours of Guadalajara ensures client satisfaction via several well-qualified tour guides who provide just the right amount of hand holding, from meeting golfers at the airport to course transfers, introductions to course staff, and lessons in English or Spanish. Tel. 3817-0540. For an interesting golfing adventure, combine three or four nights in Guadalajara with three or four nights on the Mexican Riviera, a short 45-minute flight away.

Visit www.golfinmexico.com for more information.

Charles Kinder publishes the Golf Guide to Mexico and Los Cabos.

Sport Fishing

Sport fishing in Mexico can be an experience you won't soon forget because of the great abundance of different fish and the generous limits and long seasons set by the Mexican government.

For saltwater fishing, practically all popular vacation spots, such as Acapulco, Puerto Vallarta, Manzanillo, Mazatlan, Guaymas, Loreto, La Paz, Cancun, Cozumel, Tampico, Veracruz and Los Cabos, have much improved their facilities in recent years. Good charter boats are available with expert crews who know where the fish are biting. The tackle is on the heavy side. If you're a light-tackle angler, bring your own. Tackle is allowed into the country duty-free as long as it is for personal use.

Your concierge can give you information on how to contact charter boats, as well as some idea of their rates. To avoid misunderstandings, reach an agreement in advance with the boat captain regarding rates, provisions and length of time you'll be out.

Most charter boat captains acquire fishing licenses for their customers for a small service fee. The Fisheries Department has offices in more than 125 cities throughout Mexico where licenses can be obtained for one day or up to a year.

Changes in the Fishing Law make it necessary to check with the charter boat captains or guides just how many fish and of what species may be caught per day per angler.

Every year several deep-sea fishing tournaments are held, and these are attended by Mexican as well as foreign anglers who come with their famous Rybovich, Hatteras and Bertram boats. The most famous tournaments are held in Acapulco, Los Cabos, Cozumel and Mazatlan. Bass tournaments are held in Tampico, Tamaulipas.

You can fish in Mexico almost year-round. Marine species are found in almost unlimited quantities along the more than 6,000 miles of coastline with which Mexico is blessed. Most fishing in Mexico, however, is seasonal. Many saltwater fish migrate either along the shoreline or to deeper water at certain times of the year. Experience has taught local boat captains when and where to fish for different species. A convenient group to contact is *Club Mex*. They publish a bimonthly newsletter and offer

insurance, renewals, boat permits, Mexican fishing licenses, tourist cards, books and general information on the area. Their mailing address is 3450 Bonita Road, Suite 103, Chula Vista, CA 91910; tel. (619) 585-3033 or (800) 423-2646.

In the Gulf of Mexico and the Caribbean, facilities for renting good charter boats are best in Cancun, Cozumel and Isla Mujeres. In Cozumel, you have *Caleta El Presidente*, next to the Presidente InterContinental Hotel, and *Club Nautico*, which has a modern marina with all conveniences for the visiting angler who comes in his own boat, and also operates fishing charters in nearby Playa del Carmen.

Triple centrifuged diesel fuel, Amber Plus, is available at a reasonable price.

For more information, refer to the Los Cabos chapter.

Freshwater Fishing

During the past few years Mexico has become famous for some of the best black bass fishing in the world. Many hot spots advertised in U.S. sports magazines can easily be reached from the Texas border.

One such place is Vicente Guerrero Dam, near Ciudad Victoria, Tamaulipas. Fishing li-

Posing with the day's catch

Bruce Herman

censes cost under 20 dollars per person for fishing from a boat. Other good fishing spots in Tamaulipas are the San Lorenzo Dam, near Xicotencatl, and El Mante.

The Comedero Dam in Sinaloa has caused a sensation in bass fishing circles, with scores of fishermen from Texas, Arkansas and Oklahoma going there to catch large mouth bass. Fishing trips to this dam are arranged by *Ron Speed Adventures*, 1013 Country Lane, Malakoff, Texas 75148. Tel. (903) 489-1656; fax 489-2856.

Trout fishing in wild rivers is no longer possible because the stock has been depleted by native fishermen who use mesh sacks to take out even the smallest fish. However, there are several large fish hatcheries near Mexico City where you pay for your catch by the kilo. One of the best is Club Arcoiris in the town of Rio Frio, on the way to Puebla, and San Bernardino Dam, near Tehuacan, Puebla, both well stocked with rainbow trout. Another good place to fish for rainbow trout is in Metepec, Puebla. You take the toll road to Puebla and continue about seven miles to the Atlixco exit. Follow the signs to Metepec and ask for the Social Security Camp. You pay for what you catch, but it is well worth it.

Fishing for rainbows is also great near the lovely Hacienda San Miguel Regla Hotel in Huasca, Hidalgo.

Fishing tackle can be obtained at sporting goods stores in Mexico City, Tampico and Veracruz, as well as in Mexico's popular beach resorts. Prices, however, will seem high to the average tourist because all the items are imported.

Bonefishing

For those who know what it is to catch a bonefish out on the flats of a secluded spot, some of the best bonefishing in the world is in Quintana Roo, not far from Cancun. The famous camp that caters to U.S. anglers and is well equipped with new boats, outboard motors, nice accommodations and good food, as well as experienced guides, is *Boca Paila*, in the Sian Ka'an reserve. The fishing is excellent.

Many U.S. sportsmen come once and return, lured by abundant bonefish and tarpon, as well as barracuda, snook and jack. Accommodations are set in a coconut grove plantation only a few steps from miles of white sand, colorful reefs and crystal-clear waters. Fresh seafood is prepared daily and in many different ways.

Besides fishing, there are many things to see and do, such as visiting the Mayan ruins at magnificent Tulum, just a half hour away, or touring the nearby villages and markets that have changed little over the centuries. There is also great bird-watching at Sian Ka'an.

Boca Paila can be reached by car from Cancun.

For more information, contact *Turismo Boca Paila*, Apartado Postal 59, Cozumel, Quintana Roo, Mexico 77600. Tel. (987) 872-1176 or 887-4353; fax 872-0053.

You can also book tours to Boca Paila through Pittsburgh-based *Frontiers* travel agency at (800) 245-1950.

Diving in Mexico

Few other sports have developed more swiftly in the past decade than scuba diving. To an ever increasing extent, Mexico offers opportunities to those who enjoy exploring the underwater world of rivers, lakes, oceans and now *cenotes*, beautiful natural pools, some underground, found throughout the Yucatan Peninsula.

Mexico is blessed with almost 6,000 miles of coastline and an incredible variety of underwater landscapes. With the exception of the relatively cold waters along the Pacific coast of Baja California, Mexican waters are temperate to tropical, creating warm and inviting surroundings for exploring marine flora and fauna and underwater coral structures.

The surprising thing is that there are diving areas not only along the coast, but in many inland waters as well, including at such freshwater sites as Las Estacas and Lake Tequesquitengo, and the aforementioned cenotes. All these provide unforgettable diving experiences.

All of Mexico's major resort areas have good diving services (scuba equipment, instructors and, increasingly, decompression chambers). To explore areas off the beaten track, come prepared with your own gear.

Inland Sites

Many lakes and rivers where diving is good

Huatulco

Bruce Herman

are within a short distance of Mexico City. This is true of the charming Las Estacas river in Morelos state, less than two hours from the capital. The river bursts out of the ground at El Borbollon (The Bubble) from underground springs common around Cuernavaca and Cuautla, near the volcanoes of Iztaccihuatl and Popocatepetl. The water emerges crystal clear, although somewhat cold. Once born at The Bubble, the river current winds through an area of exuberant vegetation, reaching depths of more than 20 feet.

Las Estacas was the location for the filming of many Tarzan movies, and divers can follow the current past "Tarzan's Pool" to the "Blue Pool," where transparent waters (visibility is about 60 feet) provide an exceptional view of the abundant underwater life.

Not far from Las Estacas, in the same state, is Lake Tequesquitengo, where a favorite pastime of divers is exploring the submerged colonial town that was covered by the lake many decades ago. Still visible are the remains of a 17th-century church, whose steeple lies about 10 feet below the surface. There are also underwater houses, aqueduct arches and even a cemetery. Lake depth is about 60 feet, and visibility is somewhat limited (three to 10 feet).

About 18 miles from the city of Toluca, in the State of Mexico, is the place for "high divers" in the literal sense. The extinct Nevado de Toluca volcano has two lakes in its craters; the Lake of the Sun and Lake of the Moon are more than 14,000 feet above sea level. Pre-Hispanic Indians regarded the lakes as sacred and deposited offerings in the clear waters, which are so cold that wet suits are required.

There are numerous volcanic craters in the state of Puebla, many of them offering opportunities for adventurous divers. A few of these are Aljojuca, Atexcax, Quechulac, La Preciosa, Tecuilapa and Alchichica. Alchichica's highly carbonated and bitter waters are more than 200 feet deep and, like other crater lakes, quite cold. Among the inhabitants of the depths are salamanders.

Somewhat more distant from Mexico City, in the state of San Luis Potosi, is the Manantial de la Media Luna (Spring of the Half Moon), where waters reach a depth of more than 100 feet, with temperatures varying between 68 and 75 degrees Fahrenheit. Night diving here is especially fascinating, and there are campsites along the banks of the spring.

Pacific Coast

Construction of the Baja California highway opened up myriad spots where diving can be a rewarding experience. On the Pacific side of the peninsula, experienced divers can maneuver through endless masses of undersea vegetation, with fronds reaching incredible lengths. The waters in the northern zone, like those off the coast of California, tend to be cold and drop off sharply to depths of more than 250 feet.

Water temperatures are a bit higher near the southern tip of the peninsula although wet suits are recommended, not only for protection against the cold, but against tiny organisms known as Hydrozoa, which are highly irritant and cause skin allergies.

Waters on the Sea of Cortez (Gulf of California) side of the peninsula are more invitingly warm than on the Pacific side, and divers can explore the rocky beds off Pichilingue, near La Paz, or watch tiny colored fish at Gaviotas Island.

A spot for experienced divers is just off Cabo San Lucas, where sand sliding down the slopes has formed fascinating "sand falls" with depths of up to 200 feet. Diving is more risky here, and it's best to go with guides who are familiar with the area and its dangers.

Farther north, in the gulf, is Espiritu Santo Island and its lovely Tecolote beach, where a sunken vessel has become the playground and refuge for a vast variety of marine life. Fish are also quite abundant among the corals at La Cueva del Leon, just off Cerralvo Island.

Across the Sea of Cortez, in Mazatlan, diving is still relatively unexploited, although there are some shops that provide equipment and guides for exploring the offshore islands, including Venado.

There's excellent diving service at Puerto Vallarta, nestled in Mexico's largest bay, Ba-

hia de Banderas. A favorite site is Los Arcos, which has been designated a marine refuge. Here the beauty of the undersea waters is breathtaking, with colorful fish, coral, giant clams and graceful sea plants. Just outside the bay itself are the Marieta Islands, with a rocky ocean bottom and larger fish such as barracuda and sharks. Other sites include Mismaloya Beach.

In Manzanillo, down the coast from Puerto Vallarta, arrangements can be made for rental equipment at most of the large hotels.

Moving south along Mexico's Pacific coast, other diving areas are at Ixtapa-Zihuatanejo and Acapulco in the state of Guerrero, and Huatulco and Puerto Escondido on the Oaxaca coast.

The sandy sea bottoms near Ixtapa contain an almost endless variety of marine life, including succulent lobsters and clams. More than 25 diving sites have been located, including Los Morros del Potosi, La Solitaria, El Bajo de Tintoral and La Caleta del Ensueño, where marine flora and fauna can be photographed in their natural settings. Guides are recommended when exploring undersea zones in this area as sharks are not uncommon.

Acapulco is well organized for diving, with several diving schools along the Costera Miguel Aleman, though it suffers from the effects of pollution. Underwater sites boast sunken vessels, such as the Rio de la Plata and the Santa Teresa, which have been adopted by schools of fish. Near Roqueta Island, just a few minutes' boat ride from Caleta Beach, is the underwater shrine of the Virgin of Guadalupe. Other popular spots include El Bajo del Matador,

Snorkeling at Xel-Ha

Palmitos, Punta Guano, El Jardin, La Quinta Sueños, Punta Diamante and La Ensenada del Peregrino.

Caribbean, Gulf of Mexico

Mexico's most fabulous diving area is off its Caribbean coast, with warm and remarkably transparent turquoise waters that are ideal for underwater exploring.

The island of Cozumel, in the state of

Nature and Adventure

Quintana Roo, for example, is a world-famous diving center, with its nearby coral reefs, such as Palancar, Santa Rosa, Chankanaab and San Francisco, regarded as some of the finest in the world.

Here divers can mingle with sea urchins, algae, starfish, fan corals, sponges and multi-colored fish. Since the Caribbean was the domain of pirates, there are numerous sunken ships, many of which struck the reefs in tropical storms and sank to the bottom. Wrecks are particularly common in the waters around Xel-Ha and Akumal. The latter is a renowned center for divers, who have uncovered hundreds of underwater objects from the early days of Mexican exploration and colonization.

Many of the best dive spots are accessible from Cancun, where diving services are well organized. The best sites include the area around nearby Isla Mujeres, such as Los Manchones, Bandera and Garrafon, as well as around Cancun itself, such as Punta Nizuc, where the sea bottom resembles huge underwater gardens. Experts say that only Australia's Great Barrier Reef surpasses the Mexican Caribbean for its variety and abundance of marine life and organisms.

The Yucatan Peninsula offers unique diving experiences in its numerous *cenotes*, or natural freshwater pools. Yucatan has no rivers and its water is found in deposits formed by underground currents over millions of years. The cenotes played an important role in Mayan settlements and religious ceremonies, including rites of human sacrifice.

The most-frequented cenotes are Noc-Ac, with its marine fossils, Tunel de Chelentum and Bolon-Xojol, whose transparent waters reflect the rays of the sun on the walls of the grotto, staging a fabulous dance of contrasting shades of gold and blue.

Merida and Cancun are good bases from which to explore the cenotes, about 40 of which are considered safe by diving associations for exploration. Refer to the Cancun section for more information.

Diving sites are abundant along the Gulf of Mexico, from Tampico down to Veracruz. But while there are interesting coral formations just outside the port of Tampico, the whole area is so busy with sea traffic and so contaminated from nearby petroleum and petrochemical plants that divers tend to avoid the area.

The port of Veracruz has coral reef systems just outside the port itself and to the south, at the village of Anton Lizardo. La Blanquilla reef has been designated a refuge, and there is a sunken vessel at Verde Island that serves as an abode for fish and other marine creatures. The reefs off Anton Lizardo offer fascinating opportunities for exploring shelves and grottoes at depths varying from a few yards to as deep as 150 feet, inhabited by fish, sea worms, sponges and coral.

Off the port of Progreso, on the northern tip of the Yucatan Peninsula, is a reef zone known as Alacranes. This requires a day's boat trip into the gulf from Progreso, which is about half an hour north of Merida.

These are only a sample of the many fascinating underwater worlds Mexico offers.

Ecotourism and adventure travel in Mexico runs the gamut from white-water rafting to bird-watching. It offers an opportunity to witness and experience such unforgettable sights as a forest carpeted by millions of monarch butterflies, a close encounter with curious and friendly gray whales, or a family of spider monkeys jeering at earthbound mortals while happily swinging from treetops overhead.

Why is Mexico so blessed? Because its land is a unique mosaic of ecosystems, ranging from desert in the north, to pine forests and snow-capped mountains in the middle, and tropical jungle in the south. Add to that 6,000 miles of coastline along the Caribbean, Pacific and Baja California coasts, and you could have the most varied natural landscape on earth.

Mexico is one of the world's five richest countries in terms of biological diversity. It has a greater variety of plants and animals than any country except Brazil, Colombia and Thailand. It is home to more reptiles than any other nation, and to the second largest number of mammals and amphibians. Some of its well-known treasures include the jaguar, quetzal bird, and Kemp's Ridley sea turtle, but Mexico also has more unique species than any place in the Americas.

Among Monarchs

Every autumn, millions of black-and-orange monarch butterflies fly some 3,600 kilometers (2,200 miles) from southern Canada and the northern United States to a tiny niche of mountains in the central Mexican states of Michoacan and Mexico. Once there, the butterflies roost in the high, cool trees of the fir forest to spend the winter months before heading north again in the spring. The millions of monarchs paint the otherwise green forest landscape a bright orange. It is one of the rare instances such natural phenomena can be so easily glimpsed and captured on film.

The best months to see the butterflies are February and early March, but any time from late November through March is fine. One of the most accessible butterfly sanctuaries is three hours away from Mexico City or two hours from Michoacan's capital city of Morelia, in Zitacuaro in central Michoacan. It makes for an unforgettable day trip.

Organized tours of from two to eight days are also available that combine the butterflies with visits to nearby sites of interest, such as the pyramids of Teotihuacan, the town of Patzcuaro and the capital city of Morelia.

Copper Canyon

A popular joke among Mexican naturalists is that the Copper Canyon in northwestern Mexico is what the Grand Canyon wants to be when it grows up.

One of Mexico's greatest natural wonders, the Copper Canyon, or Las Barrancas del Cobre in Spanish, is actually a series of interconnecting canyons, some of them deeper than their famous cousin in Arizona.

Part of the western Sierra Madre mountain range, the canyon's terrain ranges from below sea level to more than 10,000 feet at its peaks. Because of that, the canyon features three completely different ecosystems: cold evergreen forests grace the canyon tops, warmer-weather chaparral fills the plateaus on the way down, and tropical desert dominates the canyon floor. Mexico's tallest waterfall, the 984-foot (300-meter) Cascada de Basaseachi, is found here, as well as a variety of plant life. Unfortunately, most animal life was driven out by excessive hunting earlier this century.

The Tarahumara Indians who inhabit the region preserve their unique traditions and way of life, adding a rich cultural dimension to a canyon trip. Many of the hiking excursions follow ancient trading trails first blazed by the reclusive Tarahumara, who are famed for their ability to run long distances barefoot.

During the rainy season in late summer and early fall, canyon vistas are particularly lush and the cloud formations spectacular. In mid-December and at Easter, Tarahumara communities hold elaborate religious celebrations and festivals. During winter months, however, nighttime temperatures on canyon rims can dip below freezing.

One of the most colorful ways to see this natural marvel is to ride the Copper Canyon Express train that runs between the Pacific coast city of Topolobampo and Chihuahua city, traversing the canyon along the way. A new road is also facilitating car access.

For soft adventure, you can combine train travel with hiking. Setting off from Los Mochis, just 11 kilometers (about 7 miles) from the seashore, the train makes stops at El Fuerte, Bahuichivo, Divisadero, Creel, Cuauhtemoc and Chihuahua. From those stops, hikers can visit picturesque villages, waterfalls, hot springs, valleys, a lake and native Tarahumara Indian dwellings. There are options for experienced hikers and beginners.

Two U.S. tour operators specializing in the Copper Canyon are *Columbus Travel*, (800) 843-1060, and *Wilderness Research Expeditions*, (520) 882-5341, which offers excursions with an environmental, cultural or scientific bent. In Mexico, Los Mochis-based *Balderrama Tours* is an area expert. Tel. (668) 812-1613. For more information, consult the North Mexico section of this book.

Baja Wildlife

Named after the Spanish explorer who conquered Mexico, the Sea of Cortez (known south of the border as the Gulf of California) has been described as an upside-down rain forest—here a profusion of life exists below the water. Up to a third of the world's cetacean species (whales, dolphin, porpoise) are found in these waters, including the world's smallest porpoise—the vaquita—found nowhere else.

Nearly 100 pristine desert islands dot the azure waters off the east coast of the Baja peninsula. More than 3,500 species of plants, mostly cactus, thrive on this dry land, and hundreds of birds live here or migrate to feed on the sea life.

The best starting points to the area are Guaymas, Sonora, on the mainland, or La Paz, on the Baja peninsula. From there, boat trips can be arranged to the islands, many of which are federally protected.

A resident colony of sea lions live on the coast of San Pedro Nolasco island. Many tours include a scuba-diving session in the cold water with the sea lions. The island of San Pedro Martir houses ancient stone ruins of the Yaqui tribe, plus the world's most important colony of adorable blue-footed booby birds. Rasa Island provides an ideal nesting ground for 95 percent of the world's elegant terns and Hermann's gulls. Nearby, Angel de la Guarda Island offers beautiful desert beaches lapped by clear blue waters.

You can easily spot gray whales all along the stretch of water between the islands. Another good place to see the whales is Ojo de Liebre Lagoon, on the Pacific side of the Baja peninsula, near the Guerrero Negro desert. The best time to see the whales and birds is from late December to late March. Consult the Los Cabos section for more information.

A highly-regarded San Diego-based outfit offering tours to the Baja area is *Baja Expeditions*, run by Tim Means. Tel. (858) 581-3311, or (612) 125-3828 in La Paz; www.bajaex. com. For a luxurious and extensive excursion of the Baja area, try *Special Expeditions* run by the Swedish-born Sven-Olaf Lindblad. Tel. (212) 765-7740 or (800) 397-3348; www. expeditions.com.

Xcaret

Yucatan Peninsula

If it were a country unto itself, the southeastern Yucatan Peninsula would be considered an ecologically important nation. From its Caribbean waters to its natural sunken pools, or *cenotes*, from its jungles to its arid landscapes, Yucatan is blessed.

The *Sian Ka'an Biosphere Reserve*, 15 minutes south of Tulum or about two hours south of Cancun, is Mexico's third largest protected area and a UNESCO-designated World Heritage Site.

True to its name—in Mayan meaning "where the sky is born"—Sian Ka'an's soft, pale blue waters melt into the sky at the horizon. Spanning more than 2,000 square miles between Tulum and Akumal, just north of Belize, the reserve boasts tropical forest, mangrove wetland, freshwater canals, lagoons, savannah prairie and 70 miles of the second-longest barrier reef in the world, all rolled up into one dense "hot spot" of life.

Not surprisingly, the varied landscape is home to an abundance of birds and animals. More than 345 species of birds thrive here, including the rare Jabiru stork and more than a million wintering migratory song birds from the U.S. and Canada, which make wintertime tours ideal for bird-watching aficionados. All of the endangered cat species of southern Mexico are also found here, including the jaguar, puma and ocelot, though their nocturnal habits make sightings rare.

What's more, the remnants of some 27 Mayan sites, including one building which may have served as a customs check point for traders transporting goods via the canals, have been found on the reserve.

A local ecology group—*Amigos de Sian Ka'an*—offers day tours of the reserve with an expert biologist acting as host and guide. The tour includes a three-hour boat ride through the wetlands and the chance to swim in the

clear, winding canals. The water, originating in underground rivers flowing across the state and emerging at Sian Ka'an, is clean enough to drink.

Apart from the day tour, Amigos offers a seven-night package tour featuring the region's most ecologically important areas, including Sian Ka'an, Coba, a Mayan archaeological site in the midst of an extensive tropical forest, Contoy Island, a protected breeding colony for thousands of sea birds, and a boat tour around Nichupte Lagoon, to see what Cancun was like before it was developed into a major resort.

The tour price includes a tax-deductible contribution to The Nature Conservancy, which goes to fund conservation programs in the Sian Ka'an Biosphere Reserve. For more information, consult the Riviera Maya chapter in the Cancun section.

Ria Lagartos is a 200 square mile nature reserve of eight ecosystems dominated by salty lagoons and coastal waters. Lagartos lies in the northern part of the state of Yucatan, a four hour drive from Cancun.

Although named by Spanish explorers for the crocodiles that no doubt made exploring the area a miserable task, reptiles are not the reason Ria Lagartos is well known today. Lagartos still offers crocodiles for the adventuresome tourist, but its nature comes mostly in a flash of pink—as in flamingos.

Drawn to the lagoon's salty waters—where macrobiotic algae and life proliferate—the flamingos nest from summer to fall, then migrate a few hundred kilometers west to Rio Celestun, another biosphere reserve in Yucatan, about an hour and a half from Merida.

Although tourists are not allowed to barge in on nesting sites, boat trips in both areas invariably arrive upon flocks of feeding flamingos within an hour. Aside from the timid flamingos, there are 270 other species of birds here. More than a third of the area's birds are winter travelers from up north. The sandpiper, the scarlet tanager, the black and white warbler and the ovenbird are some of the migratory species found in the early hours of the day.

An hour's boat ride from Cancun sits *Contoy Island*, home to 70 species of resident or migratory birds. Contoy Island's four miles of interior lagoons, mangrove swamps and seashore provide an ideal home to species like the frigate, double-crested cormorant, roseate spoonbill, brown pelican and pink heron.

Punta Laguna is a small haven of semi-evergreen forest just south of Cancun. Of their own initiative, the mostly Mayan-speaking residents of this town decided to attract tourists to their natural spider monkey and bird sanctuary in a bid to protect the forest from loggers.

Located on the highway between Nuevo Xcan and Coba, Punta Laguna is a good place to visit in the morning hours before an afternoon trip to the ruins of Coba. Once there, ask for Don Serapio Canul, the man who began the reserve. The spider monkeys—and the local children eager to point them out to you—make the trip worthwhile. For more information, you can call Yucatan's *Pronatura* ecology group, tel. (999) 944-2290, in Merida, which advises the community on how to run the reserve.

Rafting in Veracruz

Ministry of Tourism

White-Water Rafting

Veracruz's rivers are ideal for combining sightseeing with a little—or a lot of—adventure. Visitors can enjoy the state's natural beauty and a few of its archaeological sites while navigating the *Filo-Bobos, Antigua, Pescados* and *Actopan*, the region's four main rafting rivers.

Rivers for white-water enthusiasts are rated from class one to six, and all categories are found here. Class one to three rivers are ideal for the beginning rafter. Class four and five are great for experienced rafters and kayakers, and class six is like plunging off Niagara Falls. Most rapids in Veracruz are easily navigated by the inexperienced rafter and offer a great opportunity to get started in this exciting sport.

Located between the city of Veracruz and Jalapa, the Actopan is a class one to three river that runs through a beautiful canyon lined with mango groves. The trip begins at a crystal-clear spring that pours out of a cliff, forming a 50-foot-high and 70-foot-wide waterfall.

Farther towards Jalapa, on the banks of the Antigua, sit the hot springs of Carrizal. The area has a few modest hotels, restaurant, and swimming pools. From here, travelers set off for the Antigua—which has pleasant, exciting descents that are perfect for the newcomer to the sport—and the Pescados, one of its tributaries and a class four to five river suited to those seeking high adventure. Boat trips can last from a few hours to a few days.

Veracruz's real showcase river is the Filo-Bobos, which can vary from class one to class five, depending on the time of year and water level. This trip begins at a beautiful ranch, continues through a 10,000 hectare natural reserve, and features three recently-discovered archaeological sites, as well as the beautiful El Encanto waterfall, which cascades 300 feet into a pool ideal for swimming. Rafting trips down the Filo-Bobos usually last two days, with an option to camp overnight along the river's banks. The river rafting season in Mexico coincides with the rainy season, running from June to October.

Well-known ecotourism outfits specializing in kayaking and river rafting tours in Veracruz, as well as the beautiful Huasteca region of San Luis Potosi, include Guadalajara-based *Expediciones Mexico Verde* (tel. 3641-1005, or 5255-4400 in Mexico City); and Mexico City-based *Rio y Montaña* (5520-2041). Both are members of Amtave, with certified guides and insurance, and have garnered high marks for their tours and camp sites.

Mountain Climbing

Two towering mountain ranges run down eastern and western Mexico. The central plateau between them is the highest populated region in the world after Bolivia and Tibet. Mexico City itself is perched at 7,350 feet.

A series of volcanoes along the central plateau makes up the trans-volcanic region. Five peaks stand taller than any in the continental United States. The tallest, *Pico de Orizaba* (18,850 ft.), is the third highest peak in North America and is located in Veracruz. The next tallest peaks are *Popocatepetl* (17,887), meaning "Smoking Mountain" in Nahuatl, and *Iztaccihuatl* (17,343), "Sleeping Lady," which stand side by side southeast of Mexico City.

The more popular of the pair is Popo, since the five- or six-hour climb to its summit rewards hikers with unparalleled views of Mexico City and neighboring Puebla, as well as the peaks of surrounding volcanoes poking through the clouds below, including Orizaba, Malinche and at times Nevado de Toluca (15,433). However, Popo has been off-limits since, true to its name, it began to billow smoke in early 1994 and finally had a minor eruption in late 2000.

The climb up Izta is much longer, even though the peak is not as high, taking on average about 12 hours. Done in two stages, the climb begins with a trek to the Tlamacas camp ground that serves as a starting point for hikers and rents gear. But the terrain is much more interesting here than on Popo, and the views as good.

Popo-Izta Park lies in the state of Mexico and is a two-hour drive from Mexico City on the road to Cuautla. Outside Mexico City, take the turnoff for Amecameca, a village resting at 8,000 feet on the northern slope of the volcanoes. From there, it is an easy drive to the volcanoes.

Although a gentler slope than Popo, Orizaba's height makes it a serious climbing challenge. The volcano sits 140 miles east of Mexico City on the eastern edge of the state of Puebla. Since the area has less infrastructure, climbers will need to take all the necessary gear. A 10-hour hike to the peak is about average.

A drive to the *Nevado de Toluca*, an hour and a half southwest of Mexico City, is an easy way to see a volcano up close. This inactive volcano, Mexico's fourth highest, is easily accessible by car via a road that leads directly into the crater, where two lakes reflect the occasionally snow-capped peaks. Surprisingly, snow is more abundant in the rainy summer months.

Club Alpino Mexicano (tel. 5574-9683) is a reputable outfit that organizes climbs to all of Mexico's major volcanoes, with expert guides leading the way. One stateside group offering high altitude mountaineering in Mexico is the *American Alpine Institute*. Tel. (360) 671-1505.

Tropical Forests

Mexico's southern states of Chiapas, Oaxaca, Tabasco, Veracruz, Quintana Roo and Campeche all have lush folds of tropical forests.

Of all of Mexico's forests, perhaps none is as blessed as the *Lacandona* rain forest in southern Chiapas. In just one hectare of forest, there are an estimated 30 species of trees, 50 of orchids, 40 of birds, 20 of mammals, 300 of butterflies and 5,000 or more of insects.

Lacandona's wildlife includes the jaguar,

harpy eagles, toucans, more than 50 varieties of bats, scarlet and green macaws, tapirs, and spider and howler monkeys. Together with the Peten rain forest in Guatemala, the Lacandona forms part of the largest tract of tropical rain forest north of the Brazilian Amazon.

For centuries, the river that traverses this forest, Rio Usumacinta, was the most important form of communication between the Maya Indians. And today navigating the river is one of the best ways to enjoy the area's natural beauty and Mayan heritage.

Expeditions on the Usumacinta include visits to the archaeological sites of Bonampak, Yaxchilan and Piedras Negras, a place not accessible by land and therefore visited by only a very few.

Two outfits offering expeditions to the Mundo Maya's Lacandon area via Rio Usumacinta are *Rio y Montaña* and *Expediciones Mexico Verde*.

Sitting 3,000 feet higher than the Lacandona's sea-level altitude, the *El Triunfo* cloud forest in Chiapas is a different version of tropical forest life. Near constant cloud cover and rainfall make this one of the Mexico's wettest and greenest areas. The cool climate provides an ideal habitat for one of Mexico's grandest prizes: the quetzal bird. With two-foot-long iridescent tail feathers, the quetzal is believed by many to be the world's most beautiful bird.

Trips to this area, usually in cooperation with the Chiapas Natural History Institute, generally include three days of camping in the heart of the reserve, plus a day in the Chiapas capital of Tuxtla Gutierrez to visit the world-famous zoo (inhabited only by animals native to Chiapas) and take a boat trip down the Grijalva river that runs through Sumidero Canyon.

Oaxacan Wonders

Seven of the world's eight sea turtle species nest on Mexican beaches in a ritual that dates back some 150 million years. The world's most endangered sea turtle, the Kemp's Ridley, nests

exclusively on the beaches of Rancho Nuevo, Tamaulipas, about 40 minutes from Tampico on the Gulf of Mexico.

But the best nesting beaches are found on the Pacific coast, where tens of thousands of sea turtles nest each year from June to December. Escobilla, a beach near Puerto Escondido on the Oaxacan coast, receives as many as 20,000 female sea turtles on some nights.

Most of turtle nesting beaches, including Escobilla, are federally protected and have no tourist facilities. There are some alternatives, however.

Tours are available from Puerto Escondido and Huatulco to *Mazunte*, the site of a former sea turtle slaughtering house that was turned into a sanctuary for the embattled species. Mazunte's Marine Turtle Museum is an aquarium and breeding center featuring the different varieties of the species that arrive at Mexico's shores.

Nearby, two lagoons offer great examples of Oaxaca's little known coastal wildlife, which includes more than 200 species of birds, crocodiles and dolphins, as well as sea turtles.

The first is *Manialtepec*, a mangrove encircled lagoon that is home to an unusual variety of tropical birds, including the roseate spoonbill, white-fronted parrot and tiger heron.

The second is the federally-protected *Chacagua Lagoon*, with mangroves that also host an array of birds. During late March and early April, you can spot nesting colonies of wood stork and roseate spoonbill.

The person to call for these trips is Canadian naturalist Michael Malone, who can be reached from December to April at *Viajes Escondidos/Hidden Voyages* in Oaxaca. Tel. (954) 582-0737. E-mail: pelewing@wincom.net.

For more information about ecotourism and adventure travel in Mexico, contact the Mexican Association of Ecological and Adventure Tourism (known by its Spanish acronym Amtave). E-mail: info@amtave.com. Web site: www.amtave.com.

Buying Real Estate in Coastal or Border Areas

By Linda Neil, A.B.R.

Laws regulating ownership of real estate in Mexico are different from those in other parts of the world largely due to Article 27 of the Mexican Constitution of 1917, which prohibits foreigners from owning residential real estate within 30 miles (50 km.) of any coastline or 60 miles (100 km.) of either border. These areas are known as the "restricted" zones.

To allow foreigners to purchase vacation or retirement homes in these zones, and bring in much needed dollars, the Mexican bank trust, or *fideicomiso*, was established in 1973. The trust places legal title in the name of a Mexican bank under a permit from the Secretary of Foreign Relations, so the bank may administrate the property on behalf of the buyer/beneficiary, who enjoys the same rights of ownership as does a Mexican national.

A permit to establish a trust can be obtained for a period of 50 years and then renewed. In other words, a trust established in 2003 will expire in 2053. In the sale of a property with an existing trust, the seller may assign the rights so that the buyer can enjoy the term established in the original trust.

The cost for the permit and record in the foreign investment registry is currently about 1,450 dollars and bank trust administration fees generally range from 200 dollars to 750 dollars annually. There are other expenses involved in the acquisition of a property, and it is wise to request a written estimate prior to beginning the transfer process.

The Mexican corporation as a vehicle for acquisition of "restricted" property: Under the 1993 Foreign Investment Law, a corporation established in Mexico is considered Mexican under the law, even if all shareholders are foreign. Thus a Mexican corporation with 100% foreign ownership can acquire property in the restricted zone. This applies *only* to non-residential property: a hotel, restaurant or other type of business. It is a violation of the foreign investment law to place a retirement or vacation home in the name of a Mexican corporation, and generally it is more costly due to taxes on corporate assets.

Title investigations and the Public Registry: Title, whether through direct ownership or a trust, must be registered in order to give notice to third parties as to the interest of the property. A certificate obtained from the local Public Registry will in addition provide information as to encumbrances on title. Title insurance is now available through both Mexican and U.S. companies and should be considered an absolute must.

There is no licensing law for real estate or escrow agents in Mexico and regulation of attorneys is virtually nonexistent. A foreigner considering the purchase of property in Mexico should consider the following guidelines:

• **Carefully select your real estate broker.** Confirm that the agent you are considering is an active member of the Mexican Association of Real Estate Professionals (AMPI). AMPI members operate under a code of ethics, and are affiliated with the U.S. National Association of Realtors (NAR) and the Canadian Association of Realtors (CREA). Check with others who have dealt with the broker.

• **Be wary of ejidal property.** More than 50% of all land in Mexico is ejidal (e-HEE-dal), or communal land, meaning it is government property at the service of a community, much like Indian lands in the United States and Canada. Certain provisions in the law now allow *ejidos* to be converted into private property, but until the conversion process is complete, it may be risky.

• **Confirm the value to be registered in your deed is the full amount you paid.** In many communities it is customary to use an appraised value, rather than full value, as the basis for cost. Since appraisal values can often be 40% to 60% of true commercial value, the buyer will save money at the onset in both acquisition taxes (2% of declared value) and property taxes. Nonetheless, using a value less than full purchase price is illegal and can be costly when selling since the capital gains tax paid on the sale will be based on the value declared in the deed at the time of original purchase. Thus a seller may end up paying a hefty capital gains tax on a fictitious book value. Better to declare it correctly at the beginning than be stuck with unwelcome taxes when it is later sold.

• **Insist that title, whether through direct ownership or a trust, be recorded in the local Public Registry.** Some attorneys in Mexico still insist this is not necessary. This is an error! Should a lien attach, correctly or incorrectly, to the trusted property, no beneficiary may transfer his rights to the property unless they have been registered in his name prior to the attachment of a lien.

• **Select a neutral third party to handle the transfer of your title.** Escrow companies operate under Articles 193 to 208 of the Mexican Commercial Code, and perform services as neutral third parties and/or consultants in the transfer of titles. Since there is no licensing for these companies either, it is prudent to insist on references and an examination of track records in much the same way you would in selecting the realtor representing you.

• **Spend the money necessary to research and obtain a valid transfer of title.** Closing costs can range from 3% to 20% of property value. A less expensive property will cost more, percentage-wise, to transfer with the percentage decreasing as the price increases. To protect your investment, it is of utmost importance to budget money for a correct transfer.

• **Insist upon a binding arbitration clause.** Lawsuits can be costly and time consuming. It is far less expensive for the parties to agree ahead of time to resolve any possible dispute through binding arbitration.

Linda Neil is founder and CEO of the settlement company®, consultants and land use professionals specializing in legal and tax matters affecting real properties in Mexico. The company provides escrow services and supervises the transfer of titles on Mexican properties located anywhere in the country. Ms. Neil, a California-licensed real estate broker with 30 years of experience in Mexican real estate, is a member of AMPI, NAR and FIABCI. For further information on these subjects, e-mail: info@settlement-co.com.

Bruce Herman

Living and Retiring

Enjoying Mexico's Warmth for Good

By Stuart J. Barnes

It is estimated that nearly half a million Americans, Canadians and British citizens call Mexico home on a full-time or part-time basis, including retirees living in benevolent climes, and businessmen and women working in Mexico City or Mexico's other industrial and financial centers.

When you ask retired Americans why they chose Mexico, you get a wide variety of responses. Some cite the temperate weather and their desire to escape blizzards, icy streets and mounting heating bills. Others came for economic reasons; dollar pensions generally go further here. Others looked for a change of scenery, enchanted by Mexico's coastal resorts or colonial towns, all within relatively easy reach by air or highway. Still others were drawn by the unique Mexican lifestyle and rich cultural heritage. Most came because of all of those reasons.

Prior to retiring in Mexico, most retirees check out alternative communities in the United States, and weigh the advantages and disadvantages. By whatever yardstick they employ, Mexico rates a high score.

If they are interested in a small cottage in a quiet setting, they find it in places like Chapala or Ajijic. If their tastes run to the fully bucolic, no Mexican city is very far from a rural village. If there is still something of the swinger in them, they find just the spots in resorts along Mexico's Pacific Riviera, like Acapulco, Manzanillo and Puerto Vallarta, or in large yet picturesque cities like Guadalajara and Cuernavaca. They find a wide choice of living accommodations, suited to just about every taste or income level. They can rent or purchase comfortable homes or apartments, or buy, rent or "share time" in elegant condos.

Some have managed to arrange for the best of both worlds, living in the United States part of the year and migrating annually to a home away from the numbing cold or the blazing heat. These "snow birds" make up a substantial, if transitory, part of the growing numbers of Americans who have put down new roots in Mexico's hospitable soil.

Playa Mazunte
Ministry of Tourism

Foreign But Near

Few places in Mexico are more than a three- or four-hour flight from most U.S. cities (slightly longer from the northern U.S. or Canada). This means little time or expense in getting back home to visit the kids, grandchildren, friends or relatives. Even driving back once or twice a year isn't much of a chore.

Whatever sense of isolation a newcomer feels at the beginning is rapidly dissipated by the presence of other Americans doing their thing in Mexico and forming their own social circles. There is usually a special camaraderie among members of retirement communities who share similar interests and more or less equal golfing handicaps.

It is important to remember, however, that retiring in Mexico requires just as much planning and preparation as any other major life decision. It means taking a close look at the land and the people, and analyzing yourself and your ability to adapt to a new lifestyle and a different environment.

Above all, avoid hasty and shallow-based judgments. You must know what the country, and the specific area you choose, have to offer and what they lack. Your decision should be based on your personal tastes, interests, temperament, cultural requisites, income, eating habits and schedules, and general tolerance of things new and often unpredictable.

What You May Miss

Don't sell the family homestead and head for Mexico until you are absolutely sure what you are getting into, and certain that it is compatible with who you are and what you expect out of retirement living.

The different pace at which things tend to get done in Mexico (auto and plumbing repairs, restaurant service, deliveries, etc.) can be irritating for some, amusing for others.

If you like the theater you will have to cope with productions in Spanish. In places like Mexico City, Cuernavaca and Chapala, there are occasional English-language theater productions.

Americans accustomed to TV dinners and a gamut of instant foods may have to make a transition to fresh vegetables and fruits—a very pleasant change in most cases. Selections in the supermarkets are likely to be somewhat limited: you may not find your favorite cereal on the shelves, and meat is generally cut differently. In larger cities, supermarkets do carry a wide variety of imported goods.

Driving in congested Mexico City and on some of the highways can be an ordeal for people long accustomed to freeway mobility and discipline.

If your pension is a bit tight, you will find that Mexican law governing retirees does not permit you any gainful employment, either regular or moonlighting, until after you acquire full resident status, which takes five years. Generally speaking, however, a U.S. dollar pension converts into a better living standard than it would back home.

Mexico preserves the Spanish propensity for bureaucratic processes. Paperwork abounds and slows down most dealings with local, state and federal authorities. Mexico is governed under the Napoleonic system of law, which requires every detail to be spelled out (usually in multiple copies), in contrast with the English legal system, which leaves a great deal to judicial interpretation and precedents.

Another factor to consider is the restrictions on real estate ownership. Land ownership in Mexico does not include subsoil rights, and foreigners must comply with special regulations and procedures. For them, direct title is permitted in the interior of the country, but ownership in coastal or border areas has to be through a trust arrangement. In compensation, however, property values are usually well under U.S. rates, as are property taxes for equivalent residences.

For some retirees, an impediment to living in Mexico may be the absence of Medicare and Medicaid benefits. Although the U.S. Congress has been considering legislation to extend this type of coverage to Americans living abroad, it is not available in Mexico.

Time, Newsweek and other major magazines have home delivery here, but the mail is slow. Major U.S. newspapers, such as the *Miami Herald, New York Times, Los Angeles Times* and *USA Today*, can be picked up at newsstands in major cities.

The good news is you no longer have to forgo U.S. television programming; satellite dishes are widely available. And there are other options, like Cablevision, which carries the Fox and Sony networks in addition to other channels, and is available in a wide area of Mexico City. Multivision, a national microwave system that you can easily rent, also has U.S. programming, ranging from CNN to ESPN.

Internet access is widespread not just in major cities, but in resort towns as well, especially Puerto Vallarta and Los Cabos, where cybercafes have sprung up near major tourist centers. Even smaller resort communities are connected, including Puerto Peñasco (Rocky Point) and San Carlos, both south of Arizona, in Sonora.

What Kind of Investment?

Before scouting for your ideal retirement location, consider the type of investment you want to make—to rent on a long-term basis, rent for a given number of months out of the year, purchase or build a home, buy a condo apartment, or get into timesharing. Only you can decide which is best for your tastes and needs. Here are a few tips:

• Subscribe to a few English-language newspapers and magazines to get a sense of the community. They are fairly inexpensive and the subscriptions pay off with good information.

• Decide what you want: a beachfront condo, a colonial retreat or a cosmopolitan setting.

• Travel to the most popular communities that fit your basic desire: San Miguel de Allende, Cuernavaca, Puerto Vallarta, Guadalajara or Chapala.

• Attend some English-language functions, such as VFW, American Legion, AA or American Society meetings or church services, and talk to participants about their experiences. These activities are commonly listed in such newspapers as *The Herald*, Guadalajara's *The Colony Reporter* and *Vallarta Today*.

• Consider your size of investment: Do you want to purchase a home or just rent? The advantage of renting—at least at the beginning—is that you can always pull up and go somewhere else (or back home) with minimal economic loss. Think about purchasing only when you are convinced that living in Mexico is what you want, and you are fully satisfied with the city you have selected.

How you finally settle the housing issue will depend on your special circumstances and budget, and how much flexibility you want in the arrangement. You may be renting a house you have grown fond of to find the owner no longer wants to renew the lease. Or a purchase might lock you into a place that no longer appeals to you, and selling may become more of a task than you anticipated. The same may apply to condo rental or purchase.

You will find it generally less expensive to buy or build in Mexico than in the United States. Building your own home, of course, presents hazards anywhere and should be undertaken in Mexico only if you have full confidence in the builder or contractor and can communicate with him frequently and fluently.

The experience of tens of thousands of delighted Americans has proved that retirement in Mexico can be rewarding and enjoyable. The point is to come in with your eyes open. While there are conditions and situations in Mexico you would not find in a U.S. retirement community, most of the problems are the same ones you encounter anywhere you may decide to live.

You will find more information on the most popular places to visit and live further in this book. Some sections, such as Puerto Vallarta and Los Cabos, have real estate articles to help guide you. But whatever you do, don't fail to consult with one or more real estate professionals. Laws, customs and practices are different here, so don't go it alone.

In most places you will find a good selection of English-speaking real estate agents. Check their credentials, see how long they've been in business, talk with one or two of their recent clients, and ask if they are a member of AMPI, the Mexican Association of Professional Realtors.

Making a Start

Once you have made a general decision about the characteristics you are looking for in a retirement area, many of the places that fail to meet your requisites are automatically eliminated. The best method is to take a "toe test" by coming down as a tourist and doing some exploring. You may discover a spot that no one else ever thought about. Or you may go the way of other U.S. retirees before you.

Once you've made a tentative decision, take another six months or so (tourist visas are issued for up to 180 days) to live in the area and learn firsthand and from other retirees all there is to know about its advantages and disadvantages. Only after you are fully convinced that Mexico is for you, should you make financial commitments for a place of residence.

If you do decide in favor of Mexico, you will be echoing decisions made by thousands of American retirees and semi-retirees who have found fun, friendship and adventure to enrich their sunset years.

Stuart J. Barnes arrived in Mexico in 1952 and was for 22 years editor of the monthly business magazine Mexican-American Review, published by the American Chamber of Commerce of Mexico. He was editor-in-chief of Travelers Guide to Mexico from 1981 to 1988. He also served as editorialist for Mexico's former English-language daily, The News. He is now retired.

Doing Business and Investing

Understanding Mexico's Business and Investment Climate

By Deborah Riner

The year 2000 marked the beginning of a new chapter in Mexico's history, as well as a new millennium. Vicente Fox's victory in the July 2000 presidential race ousted the Institutional Revolutionary Party (Partido Revolucionario Institucional, PRI) from the presidency for the first time since that party's formation seven decades earlier.

The PRI had lost its control of Mexico's bicameral Congress three years earlier, in the July 1997 elections, converting the Congress from a rubber-stamp institution to a body that could make or break the administration's agenda.

The Supreme Court, too, has become an institution that is assuming its rightful role as an independent power of government.

Fox's administration took over with an economic agenda that had three critical objectives, as stated by his Economy Minister Luis Ernesto Derbez. Halfway through his term, let's assess the progress his administration has made in fulfilling them.

1. "Achieving high and sustainable rates of economic growth."

The first year of the Fox administration, the economy was essentially flat. That was, in fact, a triumph. This was the first administration in a quarter of a century not to start its six-year term with a major economic debacle. That the economy contracted –0.3% was a striking contrast to the –6% contraction that occurred in 1995. Unfortunately, macroeconomic stability was accompanied by minimal growth in the next two years: the economy grew just 0.9% in 2002, picking up slightly to 1.3% in 2003.

Achieving the 7% growth target Fox had set for his government in any one of the three years that comprise the second half of his term (2004-2006) will not happen unless further structural reforms are enacted. However, if, as seems likely, the economy grows at a steady average annual rate of 3% to 4% with low inflation and interest rates and without abrupt changes in the exchange rate, Mexico will be doing quite well.

2. "Providing economically stable conditions, so that the recurrent cycles of inflation and devaluation are forever eradicated from Mexico's economy."

Fox and his team, building on work done in previous administra-

tions, are well on the road to achieving this goal. The peso has ever been the bellwether of the economy. Between 1998 and 2001, the inconceivable actually happened: the peso appreciated 7.5%. The peso was so strong that there were widespread demands that the government do something to weaken the currency!

When the peso depreciated a cumulative 22.6% in 2002 and 2003, it was greeted with relief, not panic. The depreciation simply was not a major event, something unimaginable only a few years earlier. In fact, Mexico's international reserves were so high in early 2003 (over 50 billion dollars, record levels then, and about 10 billion dollars higher a year later) that the Exchange Commission introduced a mechanism to limit the accumulation of reserves! Over the last nine years, Mexicans have learned that the peso can appreciate as well as depreciate.

Inflation has been brought down below 5%. For three consecutive years, inflation came in below target, an accomplishment that seemed nothing short of miraculous. In 2002, inflation exceeded the government and central bank's 4.5% objective but, at 5.7%, was certainly not out of control. In 2003, inflation met the 3%, plus or minus 1%, target range. This year, inflation will be slightly higher. Inflation should remain under 5% this year and in the coming two.

3. "Improving the lot of Mexico's most economically vulnerable population by ensuring that they are provided opportunities to benefit from the economic reforms that Mexico has implemented since the 1980s."

This is the most difficult of the three objectives. Certainly, the poor benefit from macroeconomic stability and growth. Low inflation rates help the poor, whose incomes never keep up in times of high inflation. When inflation is low, real (discounting inflation) wage gains are higher, helping workers.

But macroeconomic stability, growth and low inflation, while necessary, aren't enough. The Fox administration, with Congress's approval, has been channeling more government expenditures into health, education and social areas, but the need far outstrips the resources available. Greater efficiency in administering the available resources is equally critical.

As in the United States, job creation and increasing productivity are and will be ongoing challenges.

Investing in Mexico

The North American Free Trade Agreement (NAFTA) has made the geographical fact an economic reality: Mexico is a part of North America.

The more time that has elapsed since the treaty took effect on January 1, 1994, the more integrated the three North American economies have become.

Trade flows between the United States and Mexico have more than tripled. Bilateral trade in the last year before NAFTA took effect, 1993, totaled 81 billion dollars. By 2001, bilateral trade had soared to 262 billion dollars. Two years later, recession notwithstanding, it remained over 235 billion dollars.

Direct foreign investment, roughly three-fifths to two-thirds of which comes from the United States in any given year, has more than quadrupled, from an average annual level of 3.2 billion dollars in the eight years preceding NAFTA to an average level of 13.1 billion dollars in the 10 years since its implementation.

A good barometer of how the financial markets perceive Mexico is what happens to the exchange rate following a crisis outside of Mexico.

In 1998 and early 1999, the de-facto Russian default and the devaluation of the Brazilian real sent the peso reeling. The cost of a dollar jumped from 9 pesos to more than 10 pesos in the fall of 1998. The "samba effect" pushed the cost of a dollar, briefly, to 11 pesos. Three years later, Mexico remained remarkably immune to the "tango effect" unleashed by the meltdown of Argentina's economy. In fact, the peso strengthened and the rating agency Standard and Poor's awarded the coveted "investment grade" rating to Mexican public sector foreign debt early in 2002!

Investment in Mexico can be either direct or portfolio. Direct investment can take the form of building a production facility or buying a company. Portfolio investment can take the form of buying Mexican stocks or investing in fixed income, debt obligations issued by the public or private sector. Both forms of investing are flourishing. It is noteworthy that in October 2003 the Mexican government successfully placed a 20-year, peso-denominated debt obligation at a fixed rate of less than 9%.

Direct Foreign Investment

Mexico is the logical "first stop" for U.S. companies who are opening their first international facility. An increasing number of foreign companies are locating in Mexico. The consumer market is growing rapidly. Skilled labor is available and relatively cheap, compared to the United States. Communications and transportation are improving rapidly. The United States and Mexico have signed a workable tax treaty. There is ready and preferential access to U.S. markets: NAFTA is working as projected and providing attractive trade benefits.

Mexico's consumer market offers attractive possibilities for all kinds of foreign businesses. Most of the Fortune 500 companies have been in Mexico for decades: a number have celebrated their 75th anniversary in Mexico in the last 10 years. But since NAFTA was initiated, a host of smaller companies have made direct investments in the economy, not only to profit from local market possibilities, but also to follow their customers and/or initiate export operations.

The numbers speak for themselves. In the 1970s, when Mexico was a closed economy, direct foreign investment flows averaged barely half a billion dollars a year. As the economy opened, under President De la Madrid, direct foreign investment was encouraged and average annual flows jumped to about 2.5 billion dollars.

In the Salinas administration, when NAFTA was negotiated and implemented, direct foreign investment flows doubled, averaging 5 billion dollars a year.

During Zedillo's presidency, with the flourishing of NAFTA, direct foreign investment climbed to an annual average of 11.8 billion dollars.

In the first year of the Fox administration, direct foreign investment soared to 24.7 billion dollars. Citi Group's purchase of Banamex (a leading Mexican bank) accounted for half that total, but even without Citi's purchase, direct foreign investment in 2001 was at historically high levels. In the next two years, direct foreign investment averaged 12.2 billion dollars a year.

Foreigners think Mexico is a smart place to invest. That doesn't mean there aren't concerns. There are three areas of current concern, all of which should be resolved as the economy evolves and as the democratic process is refined.

The first concern is a high crime rate, particularly in urban areas and along the nation's highways. An increasing number of trucks are being hijacked and robbed, and there is growing concern for personal safety among tourists and residents in cities such as Mexico City and Guadalajara. The government is working hard to solve this problem, but it is one that does not have a short-term solution. In the interim, tourists and foreign businessmen are advised to stay alert to possible dangers, exercise caution and refrain from dressing or acting ostentatiously.

A second concern, especially over the short term, is the future direction of the peso-dollar exchange rate. Businessmen and investors must pay careful attention to exchange rate tendencies, since good business and good investments in peso terms could look very different when translated into dollars, especially if the peso abruptly and unexpectedly depreciates.

Shortly after the 1994 peso devaluation, the government revised its policy concerning the currency, allowing the peso to float in accordance with supply and demand.

The government has, under certain circumstances, intervened in exchange markets, but it has not attempted to freeze or peg the peso's value to the dollar in any way.

Due to these conditions, the peso can no longer "be devalued" as in the past and the exchange rate should reflect justifiable and perceived value.

With the exchange rate allowed to reflect the forces of supply and demand, and reserves at historically high levels, the peso may experience volatility, but it should not suffer a massive devaluation.

The downside of this policy, of course, is the inability to predict either the short- or long-term value of the currency, making it difficult for business to quote prices for future delivery, or make any long-term commitments for imports. If asked, however, most businessmen would prefer this uncertainty to an overvalued peso that inevitably leads to devaluations. Peso slippage can be planned for, but devaluation cannot.

All current political and economic concerns eventually end up affecting the exchange rate. However, there is a political consensus that the floating exchange regime has served the country well since 1995 when it was adopted. While the government may attempt to influence currency flows through interest rates and non-discretional direct interventions in exchange markets, the peso will continue to float in the foreseeable future.

The third concern has to do with improving Mexico's competitiveness. In today's global economy, no country or company can afford to rest on its laurels. More reforms are needed to cement the foundations for a higher

Dial

01 800
Savings

01 800 728 4647

US Local Calling Cards

Collect calls to Mexico and USA
Llamadas por cobrar a México y USA

THE SMART WAY TO CALL HOME

- Bilingual operators are available 24 hours a day.
- Available from any private or Telmex public telephone by simply dialing 01 800 Savings.

- Gives you multiple payment options:
  - Charge to any major credit card.
  - Your local company card.
  - Collect Calls.

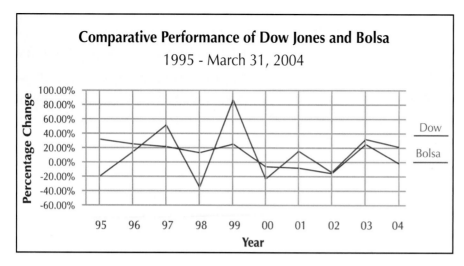

Comparative Performance of Dow Jones and Bolsa
1995 - March 31, 2004

average sustainable growth rate in the context of macroeconomic stability.

Stocks, Bonds, Deposits

Just as the amount of direct foreign investment has mushroomed in recent years, so has the amount of foreign investment in Mexican stocks, bonds and deposits.

Portfolio investment only really became important in Mexico in the 1990s. Between 1990 and 1994, Mexico attracted 44.6 billion dollars of portfolio investment.

The bursting of the bubble in 1995 saw 13.3 billion dollars flow out that year. However, the very painful but necessary economic measures taken by the Zedillo administration restored confidence: between 1996 and 2000, portfolio investment in Mexico totaled 10.1 billion dollars.

The first three years of the Fox administration saw another 1.9 billion dollars of portfolio investment flow into Mexican equities and fixed income instruments, hardly an amount to cause a balance of payments crisis.

As of February 29, 2004, foreign investment in equities totaled 63.8 billion dollars in a stock market with a capitalization of 139.4 billion dollars. Foreign investment in government money market obligations, as of February 29 stood at 4.4 billion dollars.

A large number of Mexican stocks are traded as American Depositary Receipts (ADRs) on the New York Stock Exchange and many of the larger U.S. brokers and funds now have direct Mexican representation. Most of Mexico's large companies are registered for trading on the Bolsa and trading volumes have increased dramatically during recent years. According to Bolsa figures, the value of Mexican equities traded in February 2004 reached 8.2 million dollars; half of that trading occurred outside Mexico.

A few foreign mutual funds operate almost exclusively in Mexican securities and there are hundreds of local mutual funds catering to the desires of both speculative and conservative investors.

Money market accounts, time deposits and income-oriented mutual funds offered by Mexican banks and brokerage houses are perhaps the country's most trusted and widely used form of investment.

Until May of 2001, interest rates were normally in double-digits. As Mexican inflation dropped to under 5%, local interest rates also fell. Since May of 2001, interest rates on the benchmark one-month government debt obligation have been normally between 5% and 9%. That is still a considerable premium over those offered in the United States and Europe, but the difference between U.S. and Mexican interest rates has declined. All deposits are, of course, denominated in Mexican pesos, so investors must carefully consider exchange risks before making a commitment to local markets.

A cardinal precept of investing is that investors willing to take higher risk reap higher returns. Since investing in Mexico entails assuming more risk than investing in the United States, returns should be higher. An interesting comparison on the relative returns from investing in Mexican equities and U.S. stocks is what's happened in the two markets since their peaks in March 2000.

In March 2004, the Dow Jones index was still about 8% off its historical high. The Bolsa index, measured in dollars, was up over 6%. It is striking that the dollar value of an investment in Mexican equities, as measured by the Bolsa index, is significantly higher than that of the much less risky Dow Jones index.

Because Mexico is a riskier investment, returns should be higher and that certainly has been the case in the last five years and the first quarter of 2004. The Dow Jones index rose 13.9% while the Bolsa index climbed 95.9% in dollar terms, more than doubling in peso terms. In the first quarter of this year, the Dow dipped 1.0% while the Bolsa index rose 21.1% in dollar terms. Riskier markets are more volatile and that opens up the prospect of handsome returns for investors who get their timing right.

Tax Considerations

Interest payments made by Mexican banks and mutual funds are made after a tax has been withheld and paid to the Mexican government. Yields (locally advertised) are net or after tax. Any tax withheld may be applied as a tax credit in many other countries, including the United States.

A 15% tax is withheld from dividend payments and dividends are paid net to stockholders. When stocks are purchased and sold on the Bolsa, there are no Mexican capital gains taxes for non-Mexican residents. Unearned income from different sources is not accumulated for purposes of Mexican taxation for non-Mexican residents. Taxes on earned income are roughly equivalent to U.S. income tax rates. There are no Mexican estate taxes for non-Mexican residents.

Beginning in 2003, the tax treatment for Mexicans changed. As of July 2, 2002, banks have had to report all interest paid and Mexicans have been required to report all income exceeding one million pesos from any source. No taxes were levied on that income in 2002. In 2003, Mexicans were required to report income from any source in excess of 500,000 pesos and income from all sources, totaled and taxed at a global rate, irrespective of source.

Of course, it is important to consult a tax specialist to confirm the tax treatment your investment will be subject to.

Doing business and investing in Mexico is much the same as in many other countries. However, it would be unwise to make assumptions concerning local risks and rewards without proper analysis and expert local advice. There are large numbers of excellent accounting and law firms, headhunters, banks, brokers and chambers of commerce that can provide the potential investor with important and necessary help.

The longer-term outlook for Mexican business and the economy is positive and, if reforms to promote competitiveness are made, excellent. Its location and economic potential make Mexico a country no thoughtful businessman or investor can afford to ignore.

Timing is critical. The floating exchange rate will continue to be the key to successful investment for years.

Politics and its effect on the economy must be watched carefully, but competitive elections, the developing independence of the press, and a congress not beholden to the president have all worked to eliminate any president's power to alter the country's course by fiat.

There is always more that needs to be done in terms of growth and macroeconomic stability as well as the development of a working democracy. But, what has been accomplished without violence over the last decade is indeed impressive. Political stability is not an issue in Mexico. Neither is macroeconomic stability. Mexico's future looks clearer than it ever has and it looks good.

Deborah Riner, editor of Mexletter, has been Chief Economist of the American Chamber of Commerce of Mexico since 1993. Dr. Riner, who holds a Ph.D. in political economy from Princeton University, was a guest fellow at the Overseas Development Council, the Brookings Institution, the Royal Institute of International Studies (London), Universidad Catolica in Santiago, Chile, and CEDES in Buenos Aires. She has held fellowships from the Social Science Research Council and Organization of American States, among others.

Wining and Dining

Enjoying Mexican Cuisine

Ixtapa Tourism Board

"Fiesta," the Spanish word for party, literally means feast. And that's what Mexico is all about—a feast of colors, textures, aromas and flavors.

Numerous foods enjoyed worldwide originated in Mexico, including the avocado, chocolate (xocolatl in Nahuatl), tomatoes, peanuts, squash, vanilla, turkey and corn. Today many of these ingredients are enjoyed in Mexico in restaurants and dishes representing every corner of the globe.

You can dine out any way you like, and on any budget. The purpose of this article is only to whet your appetite. The rest is up to you. As a visitor, of course, you'll be eating mostly in restaurants and hotels. Take a little time to choose well, and you'll add a whole new dimension to your trip.

Few cities anywhere offer the variety of excellent restaurants Mexico City does—the very best rank among the world's leading spots. And while they're not inexpensive, your bill is almost certain to be considerably less than if you were dining in San Francisco, London, New York or Montreal. A curbstone estimate of the price of dinner for two at a good restaurant is about 60 dollars (including a drink and the tip). The same is true of most resorts in Mexico.

Italian, Mediterranean and Oriental restaurants are making new inroads. Much of this activity is due to the North American Free Trade Agreement, which went into effect January 1, 1994. NAFTA opened up the food service industry to new challenges and opportunities. Foreign foodstuffs and exotic ingredients have become readily available, allowing the diligent restaurateur much greater scope in preparing menus and recipes. U.S. beef, veal and lamb are on the wholesale markets, so you can get a truly fine steak or prime rib.

An Affair to Remember

Dining out is no small affair in Mexico. Mexicans like to take their time and enjoy the ambiance. As a result, you'll often find music, even in the middle of the day, and service that may not be prompt but almost always gracious. Remember that the check won't arrive until you ask for it.

Mexicans eat their main meal in the early afternoon, which is why restaurants are usually bustling at lunch time and quiet at night. The big rush begins after 2 p.m., so if you can get to the restaurant of your choice by 1:30 p.m., you'll have no trouble finding a table. Mexicans take advantage of these luncheons to meet business associates and clients, which means it's often 5 p.m. before the major restaurants begin to empty.

Many Mexico City restaurants usually remain open right through the afternoon into their evening shift, so you can dine as early as you like. However, many of the finer restaurants don't begin dinner seating until 7 p.m. Mexicans work late and, therefore, eat late. They rarely have dinner before 9 p.m.

Power breakfasts have taken off in Mexico—they're fast and cheap (involving no alcohol). They're also a good way to visit some of the finer restaurants economically. Weekend brunches are extremely popular, and usually lively, extended-family affairs.

At resorts, most people prefer a light lunch. Around sundown it's customary to enjoy a prolonged cocktail hour, followed by a late dinner.

Key Ingredients

Once known only for its contribution to lowly Tex-Mex food—the often greasy, always carbohydrate-driven hybrid born at the U.S.-Mexico border—Mexico's culinary tradition has been elevated in recent years to a cuisine in its own right.

It seems that a couple of noteworthy new restaurants open each month in Mexico City and popular resorts. And many of the smartest establishments feature what some call Mexican nouvelle cuisine or new Mexican cuisine, a happy marriage of regional ingredients with European cooking techniques and presentation.

Not all Mexican dishes are spicy, though hot peppers, or *chiles*, do play a prominent part in Mexican cuisine, particularly in sauces. Indeed,

Mexicans cook with more than 200 different varieties of chiles, ranging from mild to scorching. The latter is usually served on the side and is only for experienced aficionados. Restaurants catering to tourists understand their low boiling point.

For centuries before Hernan Cortes landed in Mexico, corn was the staple of the native diet and was even deified. The most important use of corn was and still is to make tortillas, the foundation of dozens of dishes, including *enchiladas*. You're probably already familiar with the standard, thin, flat, pancakelike tortilla—after all, annual tortilla sales in the United States surpass 2 billion dollars.

The method of preparing cornmeal dough is basically the same today as when the con-quistadors arrived in the New World. Dried corn kernels are cooked with water and limestone until soft. After standing for a day, kernels are skinned and ground to form a dough. In remote parts of Mexico, the stone mortars and pestles used in ancient times are still used to do the job, but in more populated areas the process has been mechanized. Depending on the region, however, tortillas can be made of yellow, blue or red corn and vary in size from about two inches in diameter to as large as the foot-wide varieties found in the markets of Oaxaca. In northern Mexico, wheat tortillas are more common.

Cornmeal dough is also used to make *tamales*, corn husk or banana leaf filled with dough, meat or chicken and a chile sauce, rolled and steamed. Sweet tamales are made with fruit pulp and often filled with jam. Cornmeal is even used to make a sweet, piping hot drink called *atole*.

A taco, the staple of Mexican fast food, can simply be a hot tortilla topped with beef, pork or chicken. More elaborate versions call for a crisp-fried tortilla piled high with shredded chicken, guacamole, cream, shredded lettuce and grated cheese.

Don't miss an opportunity to try *mole poblano*. A specialty from the state of Puebla, this rich, dark, spicy sauce made of more than 20 ingredients, including several kinds of chiles, peanuts, chocolate and tomatoes, is usually served over chicken and sprinkled with sesame seeds. Oaxaca has its own variety, *mole negro*. More recently, the tangy flesh of the tamarind pod has been used to make a delicious sweet-and-sour sauce called *mole tamarindo*. Also try *chiles rellenos* (chile poblano stuffed with ground beef or cheese) and *quesadillas* (tortillas stuffed with cheese, mushrooms or other fillings).

Seafood lovers should try *ceviche*, the popular Pacific coast fish or seafood cocktail marinated in lime juice and mixed with chopped tomatoes, onions and chile serrano, and *huachinango*, red snapper, prepared countless ways. Mexicans love seafood and export large amounts of it, from shrimp to lobster. One favorite dish is *langostino*, a large river crawfish usually cooked *al mojo de ajo*. If you're not a garlic fan, skip the ajo.

Mexican cooking is also noted for its wonderful soups, a favorite being *sopa Azteca* (also called *caldo Xochitl*), chicken broth with chunks of chicken, rice, vegetables, a slice or two of avocado and a *chile chipotle*. Other popular soups are *sopa de tortilla*, chicken-tomato broth served over strips of fried tortilla, and *sopa de frijol*, black bean soup usually served with a garnish of fried tortilla strips and a dollop of cream. Be warned that shrimp soup (*sopa de camaron*) is one of Mexico's spiciest dishes.

You will almost always find a plate of lime slices, along with salt and the ubiquitous salsa, on the tables of a typical Mexican restaurant. Mexicans use limes, almost as much as they do chiles, to add zing to fruits, potato chips, broths, beer, tequila, fish and even meat.

If you are in Mexico during the two-month period beginning in August, try *chiles en nogada,* a popular dish that sports the colors of the national flag. This is the time of year fresh walnuts are harvested. It is also the height of the season for chile poblano and pomegranate, all key ingredients in this sweet-and-spicy dish that is usually served cold. The chiles (green) are filled with ground beef stewed with several seasonal fruits, raisins, almonds and spices. Then they are dipped in batter, fried, and served in a sauce (white) made of cream pureed with ground fresh walnuts. A sprinkling of pomegranate seeds (red) is the final garnish. Chiles en nogada season peaks during mid-September's independence festivities, when all things patriotic are celebrated.

In addition to the Mexican foods the world is already familiar with, there are many others for you to discover. Try *crema de flor de calabaza,*

Mexican Foods
Items You're Likely to Find on the Menu

Ate: A jellied paste made from the pulp of fruits, most commonly quince or guava. Often served after a meal with slices of *manchego*, a mild yellow cheese.

Barbacoa: Goat wrapped in a maguey leaf and pit roasted.

Cabrito: Roast kid, popular in northern Mexico.

Cajeta: Caramelized milk (usually goat milk) often used to make crepes.

Ceviche: A cocktail of marinated fish or seafood with chopped onion, tomato, chili, olive oil and lemon juice.

Chia: A lemonadelike beverage with tiny native seeds.

Chicharron: Deep-fried pork rind.

Chiles en nogada: A seasonal dish (August-September) of poblano pepper stuffed with ground beef and raisins, bathed in a walnut cream sauce, garnished with pomegranate seeds. Usually served cold.

Chiles rellenos: Poblano peppers stuffed with cheese or ground beef, fried in egg batter, bathed in a spicy tomato sauce.

Chongos: Sweet curdled milk mixed with egg; syrup and cinnamon added.

Cochinita pibil: A Yucatecan specialty of marinated suckling pig slow cooked in banana leaves.

Cuitlacoche: Sometimes called *huitlacoche*, this purplish-black corn fungus has an earthy, mushroomlike flavor.

Enchilada: A rolled tortilla filled with chicken or cheese and cooked in *salsa verde* (green) or *rojo* (red). Swiss enchiladas are red with cream.

Escamoles: Ant eggs, usually served with tortillas and guacamole.

Guacamole: Mashed avocado mixed with onions, tomatoes and serrano chili, served as a side dish or dip with tortilla chips.

Gusanos de maguey: Maguey worms, usually served crisp-fried.

Horchata: A sweet, milky-white beverage made from rice.

Jumiles: Grasshopper-like insects, usually served roasted.

Machaca: Dried shredded beef, similar to beef jerky, popular in northern Mexico. Also called *carne seca*.

Mixiote: A piquant orange-colored sauce used to marinate mutton, chicken or fish which are then slow cooked in maguey skin, corn husks or banana leaves.

Mole: A dark, rich sauce made of dozens of ingredients, principally chocolate, tomato, chili and spices, and served with chicken or enchiladas. Also *mole verde* and *mole rojo*.

Picadillo: Minced meat mixed with tomato and onion, and seasoned. Used in chiles rellenos and quesadillas.

Pozole: A hearty, highly seasoned soup made with hominy kernels and pork; garnished with five different ingredients. Popular in Guerrero.

Quesadilla: A tortilla folded in half and stuffed with just about anything—cheese, mushrooms, squash flower, mashed potato—and fried.

Sangrita: Tangy, chili-spiced, orange and tomato juice concoction served as a tequila chaser.

Tamales: Corn meal stuffed with pork or chicken, chili sauce, then steam-cooked in corn husks or banana leaves (the Oaxacan variety).

Tamarindo: A brown pod whose tangy flesh is used to make a dark sweet-and-sour sauce.

Torta: A sandwich made with a bread roll (*bolillo*) cut in half.

Tortilla: A staple of the Mexican diet, this thin pancake of corn meal (wheat in the northern states) is used in countless ways.

a delicately flavored, creamy broth made from the bright yellow flowers of the squash plant.

Don't miss *cuitlacoche*—the purplish-black corn mushroom is used to make quesadillas or, at many deluxe restaurants, soup, crepe filling or sauce.

The truly adventurous will want to try *gusanos de maguey* (maguey worms) and *escamoles* (ant eggs), pre-Hispanic dishes generally served with tortillas and guacamole.

Breakfasts in Mexico are elaborate affairs. You'll find juice, usually fresh-squeezed, toast and cold cereals on nearly every menu, but try Mexico's regional specialties if you can. A plate of fresh tropical fruits often begins a morning meal. And the three most popular egg dishes are *huevos rancheros* (fried eggs served on a tortilla and bathed in a spicy tomato sauce), *huevos a la mexicana* (scrambled eggs with chopped tomato, chile and onion), and *huevos con chorizo* (scrambled eggs with a Spanish-style sausage), all accompanied by refried beans.

In the Yucatan, delicious multilayered *huevos motuleños* are the breakfast staple, while in northern cities such as Monterrey it's *huevos machacados*, scrambled eggs mixed with dry shredded beef.

Other typical breakfast dishes are *chilaquiles* (tortilla chips cooked in a spicy sauce and served with grated cheese and cream) and *puntas de filete* (beef stew).

Breakfasts and *meriendas* (light suppers) are usually accompanied by *cafe con leche* (coffee with hot milk) or *chocolate caliente* (hot chocolate). Most restaurants serve cappuccino and espresso. Mexican restaurants occasionally, but unfortunately not always, offer *cafe de olla*, a delicious combination of coffee simmered with cinnamon, sugar and other spices.

Desserts, long the least interesting items in Mexican cuisine, have gotten a boost in recent years with the application of European cooking know-how to native ingredients. Today light mousses made of exotic fruits like mamey, guanabana and mango are featured at the better Mexican restaurants. *Flan* (creme caramel) and *crepas de cajeta* (crepes served with a syrup made from caramelized goat milk) continue to be traditional favorites, as are *ates* (jellied fruit) served with soft cheese, *arroz con leche* (rice pudding), *natilla* (vanilla pudding) and *chongos* (a curdled egg, milk and sugar mixture served in a cinnamon-flavored syrup).

Spirits

The popularity of tequila, Mexico's national drink, has been at an all time high. Not only are better-quality brands being produced, but at a time when Americans have been generally cutting back on distilled liquor, tequila sales in the United States have continued to grow dramatically.

The same is true of mezcal, a spirit made of agave grown in

A seaside buffet, Puerto Vallarta

Oaxaca. (To find out more about these two uniquely Mexican beverages, see "Tequila, Mexico's Gift to the World.")

While Cuba, Puerto Rico and Jamaica are famed for their rum, all tropical countries in the Western Hemisphere are sugar producers. Mexico has a great variety of rum from both cane and molasses. You'll find many familiar brands here, but you should also experiment with the great local varieties ranging from white and dry to the heavier, dark ambrosias.

A great deal of brandy is produced as well that rivals both rum and tequila as the most popular spirit in Mexico. In fact, party-goers will notice that the drink of choice for many Mexicans is Cuba Libre, traditionally a blend of rum and cola that's made here with brandy.

All of the finest after-dinner drinks, including top-of-the-line cognacs, are readily avail-

able in Mexico. Visitors can also try Mexico's unique regional specialties:

Coffee Liqueurs. Mexican coffee liqueurs, of which Kahlua is the most popular, are much exported and famous the world over. Smooth and sweet with your coffee, straight, on ice, or poured over vanilla ice cream.

Crema de Lima. Tastes like a distillation of Scottish orange marmalade, and that's pretty close to how it's made.

Damiana. An infusion of the herb of the same name from Baja California and Sinaloa. Distillers claim it is an aphrodisiac.

Tequila Almendrada. Sweetened and flavored with almonds.

Xtabentun. (Shta-ben-TOON) An anise-flavored, honey-based liqueur from the Yucatan. *Liqueurs from native fruit.* Ask for *crema de guanabana, nanche* or *platano.*

Harvesting time at a Baja vineyard

Tequila: Mexico's Gift to the World

Mexico's national drink, tequila, has a long history. Its source, the agave—which despite its fleshy, pointy, cactuslike appearance is not a cactus—served Mexico's pre-Hispanic cultures much like the buffalo did the American Indians. All parts were put to good use: the fibers were used to weave mats and baskets, the "skin" to make parchmentlike paper, sandals and rope, and the juice to make *pulque*, a mildly alcoholic beverage that regardless of its slimy consistency and bland taste was considered special enough to be used in religious ceremonies.

The naturally fermented sap of an agave plant, pulque is slightly foamy and viscous, with an alcoholic content similar to beer. Though it has experienced considerable fall from grace, in comparison with its ancient place in society and role in ritual, it is still drunk, usually to excess, at *pulquerias*, cantinas that exclusively dispense pulque.

At the Baskin Robbins of pulquerias, *Pulqueria Familiar La Hortencia,* in Mexico City's Plaza Garibaldi, the drink is offered plain or in a variety of fruit and nut flavors.

It wasn't until the Spanish arrived, bringing with them knowledge of distillation, that tequila was obtained from the juice of the agave (pulque is the result of fermentation only). Another important difference is that only blue agave can be used to make tequila (*Agave tequilana Weber azul*), while any of 200 varieties of the plant can be used to make pulque.

Mexicans customarily savor tequila straight and at room temperature; served in a clear, tall shot glass called a *caballito* or, at more pretentious establishments, in a miniature cognac snifter.

A chili-spiced, tomato-and-orange juice concoction called *sangrita* is usually served as a chaser, offsetting tequila's herbaceous, peppery taste with its sweet-and-sour tanginess.

White tequila, as opposed to aged, doesn't get the same treatment, being primarily used as a cocktail mix in such drinks as a margarita, tequila sunrise, or *palomita* (tequila with lime soda, usually Fresca, and a pinch of salt).

The way Mexicans drink finer tequila, however, is by far the best way to enjoy its unique qualities.

A growing appreciation of tequila's singular flavor has spurred producers to make more top-of-the-line brands that often come in the kind of elegant packaging more commonly associated with cognac—a stately bottle, perhaps with the words "limited production" printed across the label.

Just as cognac gets its name from its place of origin, tequila gets its name from the Tequila region of Jalisco state, where the blue agave flourishes. When the plant matures, at 6 to 12 years of age, the leaves are removed, revealing a pineapple-shaped heart (called a *piña*) which can weigh anywhere up to 300 pounds. The heart is harvested by hand, but from here on the process is largely industrialized, with the piñas roasted to turn the starches into sugars, then mashed, fermented, and distilled twice to obtain the silvery spirit. Some tequila is then aged in oak barrels and takes on a golden hue. Tequila labeled "*reposado*" has been aged a minimum of two months, "*añejo,*" a minimum of 12 months.

Beer

Mexico's leading export beer, Corona Extra, overtook the competition in the late 1990s to become the No. 1 selling foreign brand in the United States. Corona's sales have placed it ahead of Heineken, which had held the top spot since it was first imported in 1933, the year Prohibition was repealed. The rise in popularity of Corona is all the more impressive when you consider that its brewer, Grupo Modelo, did not begin exporting until 1977.

In pre-Columbian Mexico, there were certain drinks that resembled beer. When Spanish conquistador Alfonso de Herrera was sent by Cortes to Spain, he asked King Carlos V for permission to begin producing beer in Mexico. In 1542 he brought brew masters from the coast of Flanders and other areas to the New World, and by 1554 he could report that the first brewery in the Americas was prospering. Today, Mexico has 17 breweries throughout the country.

Mexico produces many kinds of beer, or *cerveza*, and they are basically divided into three categories: light (*clara*), dark (*oscura*) and campechana (in-between).

Here are some of the brand names you will encounter: Negra Modelo (dark), Corona (light), Dos Equis-XX (lager and dark), Indio (dark), Bohemia (light, aromatic), Leon (dark, from Yucatan state), Montejo (campechana, from Yucatan state), Sol (light), Victoria (campechana), Pacifico (Mazatlan's light local brew) and Casta, a new microbrewed brand. Nochebuena is a dark seasonal beer available only around Christmas time.

One popular way to drink a "*chela*" (the slang term for beer), especially in hotter coastal climates, is poured over lime juice and ice in a salt-rimmed glass. This combination is usually called "*chelada.*" The addition of a pinch of red chili powder, and a dash of Tabasco and Worcestershire sauce (or something like it) is often called "*michelada.*" The names may vary depending on where you are, so ask about what you're getting first. In Mexico City, a michelada comes with just the lime juice and a "*michelada Cubana*" has the added spices. In Oaxaca, beer with lime juice is called "*suero*" (or serum), and the spicy version is a michelada.

If it all sounds too confusing, just point, there's bound to be someone at the next table enjoying one. Salud!

Leading Mexican Wines

RED

Casa de Piedra: Tempranillo-Cabernet
Casa Mogor Badan: Cabernet Franc, Cabernet Sauvignon
Chateau Camou: Flor de Guadalupe, Gran Vino Tinto
Domecq: Chateau Domecq Cava Reservada, Cabernet Sauvignon X-A, Chateau Domecq Vino Tinto
L.A. Cetto: Cabernet Sauvignon Reserva Privada, Nebiolo Reserva Limitada, Petite Sirah
Madero: Cabernet Sauvignon Casa Grande, Merlot, San Lorenzo Vino Tinto
Monte Xanic: Cabernet Franc, Cabernet Sauvignon, Cabernet Sauvignon-Merlot, Merlot
Santo Tomas: Duetto (coproduced with Wente), Merlot, Tempranillo-Cabernet
Viñas de Liceaga: Merlot Gran Reserva

WHITE

Chateau Camou: Chardonnay, Fume Blanc
Domecq: Chateau Domecq Vino Blanco
L.A. Cetto: Chardonnay Reserva Privada
Madero: Chardonnay Casa Grande, Chenin Blanc, San Lorenzo Vino Blanco

Robert Campbell

*Latin America's tallest building, the 55-story Torre Mayor,
overlooks Paseo de la Reforma Boulevard.*

Introduction

Indisputably one of the world's largest metropolises, Mexico City is also the Western Hemisphere's oldest urban center—taking into account the Aztec capital Tenochtitlan.

Even in those days, the city had a way of impressing newcomers. Reporting back to King Carlos V about the wonders of the Aztec seat of power, Spanish conqueror Hernan Cortes wrote he had seen things "… which cannot be adequately described in words."

The sight of the Aztecs' imposing temples left Cortes and his men awestruck. Struggling to convey the majesty of what he saw, Cortes compared this new world with the old. Imagine the king's surprise at learning that "one of the plazas is twice the size of that of Salamanca," and "the principal pyramid is taller than the tower of the cathedral at Seville," or that the stone and wood craftsmanship that adorned these monuments "could nowhere be bettered."

The conquistadors were amazed at what they found, though just a short time later they would destroy it to make way for the Spanish reign that followed.

Nowhere is Mexico's explosive past better depicted than at its central plaza, the Zocalo. Surrounded by some of the finest buildings of the colonial era, lie the remnants of one of the Aztecs' principal monuments, the Templo Mayor. Its mysterious shapes stand as a haunting tribute to the pre-Hispanic civilization that flourished here long ago.

Officially known as the Federal District (Distrito Federal), the country's capital ranks as the world's second-largest city, after Tokyo, with some 23 million inhabitants in the metropolitan area.

For decades, the federal government was concentrated in the old quarter, here called the Historic Center (Centro Historico). The official headquarters of the president, the Palacio Nacional, is still there, but the various ministries are now scattered all over the city.

The poshest residential areas lie to the west, in an area called Las Lomas (The Heights), and to the south, in San Angel and Coyoacan, once independent towns and still delightfully colonial in style. Other interesting neighborhoods, or *colonias*, are Condesa, Mexico City's answer to SoHo, and Roma.

Most major cities grapple with urban problems—a city this size, all the more so. Notorious levels of air pollution (especially during

Xochimilco Ecological Park

Robert Campbell

the winter months), crime, traffic congestion, slums, beggars, overpopulation, and lack of sanitation plague the city. To curb pollution levels, a one-day-without-a-car program is in place.

The weather is usually mild. Cold snaps are short lived, so few homes have central heating. Summer is the rainy season, but showers rarely last more than an hour and usually occur in the late afternoons or evenings. Spring and fall are warm, but not hot. Air-conditioning is rare.

Elevation is important. At 7,350 feet the air is much thinner and takes getting used to. One drink packs the wallop of two. It's also best to eat light when first arriving.

Driving aside, life here generally moves at a slower pace. People seldom hurry and when punctuality is expected you'll be told to function on "English time."

Keeping in touch with things back home is easy. All major newspapers are available and *The Herald*, Mexico's English-language newspaper, carries national and international news, as well as notices of community events.

Taxis: Avoid flagging a regular taxi—as-

saults have been known to occur, and tourists, often toting cameras and recent purchases, are especially vulnerable. *Sitios*, or radio cabs, offer a convenient, reasonably-priced and safe way to get around town. Radio cabs usually add a surcharge to the amount registered on the taximeter. Hotels and restaurants are accustomed to calling radio cabs for their guests and clients.

Regular cabs are mostly old, green VW Beetles or newer red-and-white four-doors. The word "*Libre*" ("Free") in the front windshield means it is available. Ensure the taximeter is working before getting in. If it's not, wait for another cab—such an irregularity could be a sign of a rogue taxi.

Upon arrival in Mexico City, take only taxis belonging to the special airport concession. Prices are fixed according to destination and tickets can be purchased at clearly marked booths found both in the baggage claim area and next to major airport exits.

Metro: The Metro, or subway, is user-friendly and a bargain to boot. A ticket, sold at booths inside the station (which also offer free subway maps), costs two pesos. Trains run from 5 a.m. (6 a.m. Saturdays, 7 a.m. Sundays and holidays) to half past midnight (1:30 a.m. Saturdays, 1 a.m. Sundays and holidays) and each station displays a map of the network. At peak morning and afternoon hours, separate cars are reserved for women. Avoid the subway during rush hour and watch your wallet or purse when taking any public transit.

Peseros: These minibuses—originally called *peseros* because a ride cost one peso, but now also known as *colectivos* or *combis*—shuttle along fixed routes. The minimum fare is 2.50 to 3.50 pesos. The farther you go, the higher the fare, though it's rarely more than five or six pesos.

Buses: Buses run regularly and during non-rush hour are an easy way to get to museums in the Chapultepec Park area. The two-peso fare must be in exact change.

Tours: See "What to See and Do" for touring information.

Safety: Don't carry a lot of money with you or wear anything too flashy; leave valuables in your hotel safe or deposit them at the front desk. Only withdraw money from ATMs during the day and preferably from machines located inside shopping malls and supermarkets.

A Brief History

Sensing the Ghosts of the Past

Teotihuacan, home of the Sun and Moon pyramids

In the year 1300 much of the area covered today by Mexico City was an enormous lake in the Valley of Anahuac, or Valley of Mexico. On the shores of this lake, Lake Texcoco, three powerful groups, dominated by the Tepanecs of Azcapotzalco, controlled the smaller subject communities.

At this time a semi-nomadic tribe called the Mexica arrived, directed by their god Huitzilopochtli on a lengthy journey from their place of origin, Aztlan. The Aztec empire they were to establish was named for this mythical homeland. The newcomers were not welcome, and their aggressive behavior did little to endear them to their neighbors. Good land around the lake was already scarce and the Mexica were soon expelled from their first settlements and forced onto the most inhospitable area around—a region of volcanic rock teeming with snakes. The Mexica ate the snakes, cultivated what fertile ground existed, and thrived until their quarrelsome ways made new enemies and they were forced to flee to a small island near the western edge of Lake Texcoco.

Tenochtitlan

Huitzilopochtli chose this moment to speak with the Mexica priest-ruler, Tenoch, telling him that the sight of an eagle perched on a cactus would mark the spot where his people would build a permanent home. The following day the Mexica saw the sign and set about building a temple to Huitzilopochtli. The year was 1345 and under the leadership of Tenoch the Mexica established the city they would name Tenochtitlan.

As subjects of the Tepanecs, on the western side of the lake, the Mexica took part in military expeditions and were rewarded with land for their role in subjugating outlying regions. The Mexica paid tribute, contracted advantageous marriages, and finally came to be considered good neighbors.

An aristocracy evolved and in 1372 a man named Acamapichtli became the first Aztec emperor. At this point they were still Tepanec subjects under the thumb of the ruthless Tezozomoc, and often forced to pay excessive tributes.

By the early 1400s the town of Texcoco, on the eastern bank of the lake, had risen to a position of importance. Much of this was due to a remarkable leader named Nezahualcoyotl, and his father, Ixtlilxochitl.

In 1428, two years after Tezozomoc's death, the Mexica and their allies defeated the Tepanecs, with considerable credit to Nezahualcoyotl and his uncle, the emperor Izcoatl.

Nezahualcoyotl

Nezahualcoyotl established Texcoco as his capital, and the center of Aztec art and learning. The "purest" form of Nahuatl was reportedly spoken here. The ruler held poetry competitions at his mountain-top retreat, Texcotzinco, where his baths carved out of rock can still be seen. His gardens, palaces and libraries were legendary.

The poet-king was a lawmaker, establishing much of the groundwork for the legal system used by the Aztec Triple Alliance of Tenochtitlan, Texcoco and Azcapotzalco. And he was also an engineer. In 1459 Emperor Moctezuma I asked Nezahualcoyotl to design a massive causeway to connect Tenochtitlan to the mainland and bring freshwater from the surrounding hillsides.

Another influential man of the time was Tlacaelel, son, nephew and half brother of four Aztec emperors. For more than 40 years, as chief consul to three emperors, he ranked second only to the man on the throne.

With increased power, it was natural for Aztec rulers to want to expand their territories. The entire course of Aztec history was one of conquest, extending their realm, collecting tribute from distant lands, and making Tenochtitlan ever more magnificent. Traders were a special class who traveled on expeditions lasting years and returned loaded with riches. Because these merchants often served a double purpose, as spies on distant rulers, theirs was at times a dangerous profession.

Hernan Cortes

Since 1517, the year Spaniards first approached the Yucatan Peninsula in their ships, messengers had been bringing Emperor Moctezuma II drawings of the mysterious *acalli*, or waterhouses, sighted off the coast. In 1519 the situation turned critical when Hernan Cortes and his men landed on the Gulf coast and built a settlement named La Villa Rica de la Vera Cruz (today, Veracruz).

Initially the emperor believed the light skinned, bearded warrior to be the fair god Quetzalcoatl who, according to Aztec legend, had been forced to flee east, but promised to return. Thus inclined toward appeasement, Moctezuma sent gifts of gold, silver and finely woven garments, which merely fueled the Spaniards' lust for riches.

As he made his way across the mountains, Cortes gathered the support of Indians eager to sever their allegiance to the distant capital.

Arriving at Tenochtitlan, Spanish chroniclers recorded their amazement at finding a city "grander than any in Spain."

Dominated by the towering Great Temple—Templo Mayor—with twin altars dedicated to Huitzilopochtli and the rain god, Tlaloc, Tenochtitlan was a city of canals connecting residential areas to the main plaza. It spanned from today's Zocalo to the Latin American Tower, and north past Tlatelolco.

The Spaniards were welcomed and treated royally, a situation they exploited to the point of taking over Moctezuma's palace and imprisoning their host. The citizens of Tenochtitlan, disillusioned by their leader's weakness, removed him from office. He was later stoned to death by an angry mob he had been trying to calm.

Moctezuma's brother, Cuitlahuac, succeeded him, but reigned for only 80 days, succumbing to smallpox, a disease brought over by the Spaniards. Their 26-year-old cousin, Cuauhtemoc, who was outspoken in his resistance against the Spanish, became the last Aztec emperor. It was Cuauhtemoc who led the Aztecs in the final battles, and who is most revered today.

Conquest

The Aztecs actually won the first battle, driving the Spaniards out of Tenochtitlan on a night known to history as "La Noche Triste" (The Sad Night). Many Spaniards drowned in Lake Texcoco, weighed down by stolen gold. Cortes is said to have rested under a large tree

in the town of Tacuba during the retreat and wept over his losses. What's left of a tree said to be the very same one, is still preserved. The Spaniards subsequently spent nine months building brigantines to cross Lake Texcoco.

Many factors contributed to the Spanish victory. Lured by reports of gold, reinforcements arrived from Cuba; an important alliance was formed with nearby Tlaxcala, a never-conquered enemy of the Aztec empire; Spanish weapons were considerably better; the Spaniards killed their enemies instead of saving them for sacrifice; and an indecisive, obsessively religious ruler was on the throne when the Spaniards arrived.

Equally important were the diseases, including smallpox, that the conquistadors introduced into the New World with devastating effects for the indigenous population.

Tenochtitlan was blockaded for nearly four months while its citizens slowly died of hunger, thirst and foreign diseases.

Cuauhtemoc was taken prisoner on August 13, 1521, at the site of what today is the Church of the Conception, near Tlatelolco. The Tlaxcalan allies are blamed for burning the famed palaces and libraries of Texcoco.

Before the Spaniards arrived, Tenochtitlan-Tlatelolco was larger than any European city, with possibly 300,000 inhabitants. Forty years later, the indigenous population was recorded at 75,000.

Colonial Era

Following the conquest, the Spaniards filled in Lake Texcoco and used the stones of the Aztec capital's great palaces and temples to construct their own churches and buildings.

Cortes returned to Spain and remained in his country's service, though always intending to spend his retirement in Mexico. He died in Spain, however, in 1547 at the age of 63. His remains were sent, at his request, to the Hospital de Jesus, which he established near the Zocalo in Mexico City. They are still today.

During the colonial era, the capital grew, acquiring a distinctively Spanish look with both European and Moorish architectural styles, not to mention a citizenry clad in European fashions.

The Spanish also instituted their own class system, dominated by the aristocracy and followed, in descending order of social status, by Mexican-born Spaniards (*criollos*), those of mixed Indian and Spanish blood (*mestizos*), and slaves.

Mexico City Today

The capital is not just the country's political, financial and artistic center, but also its historical vortex, where modern-day Mexico began and evolved.

Walking around the Centro Historico, it is impossible not to sense the ghosts and picture the people who constructed the buildings—those still standing and those lying buried below—to imagine their struggles and admire their achievements.

Colonial Coyoacan

Bruce Herman

What to See and Do

From Squares to Pyramids

A double-decker Turibus tours the city

Robert Campbell

Declared a World Heritage Site by UNESCO in 1988, the four-square-mile (10-square-kilometer) Centro Historico, or historic downtown area, radiates out from the city's main square. It is home to important constructions from pre-Hispanic times to the present: ruins of the Aztec capital of Tenochtitlan dating from the 14th century, colonial-era churches and mansions built over 300 years, between the time of the Spanish Conquest (1521) and Mexico's Independence from Spain (1821), and lavish European-style homes and monuments built during Mexico's industrial boom. A major Historic Center restoration project is currently underway.

The main square, officially named Plaza de la Constitucion but known to everybody simply as the "Zocalo," is an ideal place to begin a city tour. The Spanish word "*zocalo*" means "pedestal," and the square derived its name from the base of a statue that was never erected.

You'll find a smaller version of the Zocalo in virtually every city and town in Mexico, usu-

ally flanked by the cathedral and City Hall, sometimes with a gazebo at its center.

Mexico City's is the second largest plaza in the world, surpassed only by Moscow's Red Square. It has gone through many transformations, having at different times featured lovely gardens, fountains, statues, a rotunda and a bandstand.

The Zocalo subway station displays models of the plaza as it was in Aztec days, the colonial era, and at the turn of the century. The square was completely cleared and paved with concrete in the 1950s. Its only adornment today is a large Mexican flag.

To the northeast of the Zocalo is a brass model of the Aztec capital of Tenochtitlan as it was when the Spanish came upon it. The Aztecs enjoyed a view of the entire valley fringed by mountains, with two volcanoes, Popocatepetl (Smoking Mountain) and Iztaccihuatl (Sleeping Lady), towering on the eastern horizon. On a rare clear day you can still see the impressive snow-capped volcanoes.

One of the most thought-provoking descriptions of the plaza as it was in Aztec times is found in Hernan Cortes' dispatches to Spain's King Carlos V: "This city has many open squares where markets and trade are continuous. One of the plazas is twice the size of that of Salamanca; it has a portico all the way around, where daily more than 60,000 people meet to buy and sell all kinds of goods.... In this great plaza there is a large building like a courthouse where always are seated perhaps 10 or 12 judges who try all the marketplace cases and questions which arise there and have the guilty punished..."

The Zocalo, where the Halls of Moctezuma once stood, served as the center of Tenochtitlan, then an island about a mile square containing palaces and pyramids, including the *Templo Mayor* (Great Temple). Completed in 1487, the Templo Mayor had two altars dedicated to the Aztec war god, Huitzilopochtli, and the rain god, Tlaloc. The dedication ceremony lasted four days and several thousand victims were sacrificed. Today, only the lower layers remain since the conquistadors destroyed the temple, using the volcanic rock to build a cathedral nearby.

The beautifully designed *Templo Mayor Museum* depicts the lives of the Aztecs and how they came to settle here, with dramatically displayed artifacts from the ruins of Tenochtitlan, including life-size figures of eagle warriors alongside the skulls of sacrificial victims. A large model shows the grandeur of the city. From tiny jade beads to huge warrior figures, the artifacts draw you into an ancient culture cut short in its prime.

Buried beneath the colonial buildings facing what remains of the temple are the remnants of other great Aztec architectural feats that have not been, and may never be, unearthed.

The Zocalo is also home to twin City Hall buildings to the south, the National Pawnshop (Monte de Piedad) to the west, the National Palace (Palacio Nacional) to the east, and the Metropolitan Cathedral to the north.

Construction of the *Metropolitan Cathedral* began in 1567, but having taken some 250 years to complete, it combines three major architectural styles from the 16th through the 19th centuries, including Gothic, baroque and neoclassical. While the cathedral is a melange of styles, the adjoining parish church, El Sagrario, is a fine example of pure churrigueresque architecture. Modeled after its counterpart in Seville, this cathedral is the largest in Latin America and home to prized works of colonial art.

An elaborate light-and-sound show called "Voices of the Cathedral" brings the early history of Mexico to life, and highlights the building's more impressive features. Dramatized by actors and musicians in period costume, performances are held Wednesday evenings. The cathedral also offers guided visits of usually off-limits areas, such as the sacristy and bell tower, and nighttime tours. For more information, call 5510-0440.

The *Palacio Nacional*, built from the ruins of the Aztec temple, was erected on the site of the

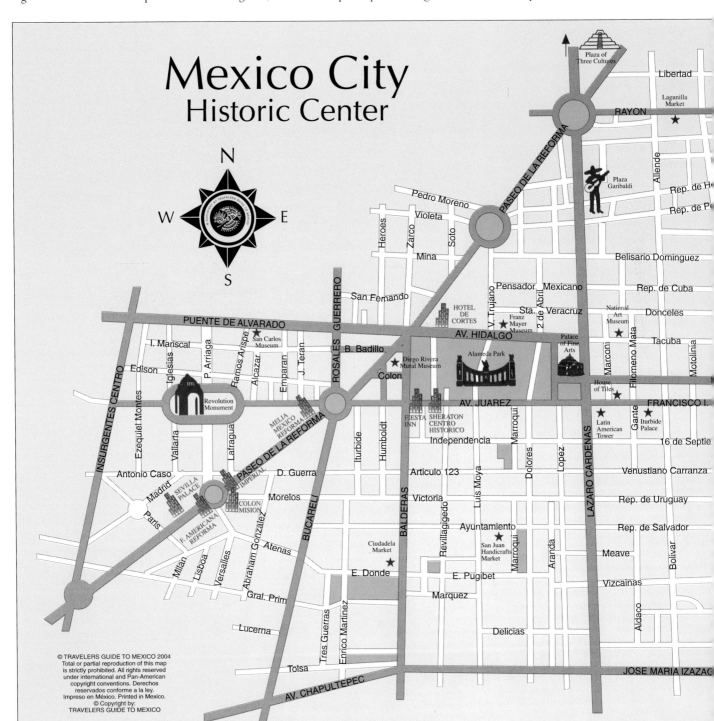

former palace of Moctezuma, and Cortes maintained his headquarters here. Today the National Palace houses offices of the president and the Finance Ministry. The central staircase and mezzanine are decorated with some of Diego Rivera's most stirring murals, giving a vivid pictorial history of Mexico. The bell over the central portal is said to be the one Father Miguel Hidalgo rang in Dolores, Guanajuato, to signal the start of the War of Independence.

In the Recinto Juarez, or Juarez Chamber, visitors can see the office and living quarters of Mexico's most revered president, Benito Juarez. Juarez was the author of the 1858 Reform Laws which curbed the considerable power of the church by, among other things,

nationalizing church property. Try to visit the National Palace in the late afternoon to witness the flag-lowering ceremony in the Zocalo.

A block east of the Templo Mayor, on Academia Street, is the *Jose Luis Cuevas Museum* in what was originally the Santa Ines convent. It houses the Mexican painter's private collection of contemporary Latin American art, which he donated to the city.

City Hall consists of the two buildings across the plaza from the cathedral. One building dates to just after the Spanish Conquest, the other is less than four decades old. The original City Hall building was erected in 1532 and enlarged in 1564. A fire started by rioters destroyed it in 1692, and its reconstruction was completed in 1724. Remodeling under Porfirio Diaz added another floor and a new facade. The building was divided to make way

for Avenida 20 de Noviembre (named for the day the 1910 Revolution began) and another floor was added in 1948.

The *Monte de Piedad* (National Pawnshop) was under construction while Jefferson was writing the U.S. Declaration of Independence. This hock shop is one of the world's most unique. Items range from electronic equipment to antique jewelry. It was begun by Pedro Romero de Terreros in 1777 as a charitable organization and it continues to help finance the construction of schools and retirement homes with revenue from its pawning operation. Each year before Easter and other holidays, families low on cash flock to the Monte de Piedad to hock their valuables to finance their vacations.

Near City Hall, on Avenida 20 de Noviembre, are the city's leading department stores, Palacio de Hierro and Liverpool. The city's

House of Tiles

growth and the consequent difficulty of getting downtown have induced these companies to open branches in newer parts of town.

Three blocks behind the cathedral is *Plaza de Santo Domingo*. Seated at antique typewriters under the shade of the arcades that line the west side of the square, scribes known in Mexico as "evangelists" pound out love letters or missives to folks back home for a modest sum. Such requests are becoming rarer as literacy increases, but the scribes do not appear to be in danger of extinction; their main job these days is filling out legal forms—bureaucracy thrives in Mexico.

Within the Zocalo area is the Supreme Court, a huge stone building erected on the site where the Aztec empire's legal matters were handled. The original building was razed by Cortes to make room for games and bullfights. Later it became a market, which was demolished in 1929 to make way for the Supreme Court building, completed in 1941.

To the northeast of the cathedral, across from Plaza Santo Domingo, is the *Ministry of Public Education*, housing impressive Rivera murals. About two blocks east, on Justo Sierra Street, sits the *Museo de San Ildefonso*, site of major art exhibits, a wonderful gift shop, and a showcase of early Mexican mural art, especially by Jose Clemente Orozco.

The Americas' first printing press sits at the corner of Licenciado Verdad and Moneda streets, next to the Temple of Santa Teresa la Antigua. The 16th-century *Antiguo Palacio del Arzobispado*, at Moneda 4, houses the modern art collection of the Finance Ministry, comprised of the tax contributions of some of Mexico's leading contemporary artists. The *Mayorazgo de Guerrero*, once the estate of a Cortes lieutenant, is on Correo Mayor Street, near the Temple of Santa Ines, with its huge doors of elaborately carved wood. The *San Carlos Academy*, opened in 1785 to teach painting, sculpture and architecture, is on the corner of Academia and Moneda streets.

The *Mexico City Museum*, which documents the history of the city since pre-Columbian times, is housed in a colonial masterpiece on Pino Suarez Street.

Touring

Turibus, a recently launched sightseeing service aboard bright red, open-topped double-decker buses, offers visitors a comprehensive look at the world's second largest city. The three-hour tour shows passengers both the seedy and the sublime sides of Mexico City as it makes its way through overcrowded downtown neighborhoods, where thousands of street vendors hawk their wares, and the wide solitary boulevards of upscale residential zones.

Tickets cost about 10 dollars (half price for kids) and are valid for 24 hours, letting passengers get on and off at their convenience at more than 25 sites of interest. Buses leave from the Auditorio Nacional at 9 a.m., 12, 3, 6 and 9 p.m. (nighttime tours are offered Thursdays and cost slightly more.)

Old-fashioned trolley cars offer half-hour mini-tours of the Historic Center, 10 a.m. to 5 p.m., to 8 p.m. weekends. Tours depart from in front of the Palacio de Bellas Artes. Trolley tours of the Coyoacan district leave from Calle Paris 190, in Colonia Del Carmen, every day from 10 a.m.

A fun way of getting around the Centro Historico is riding one of the green-and-yellow bicycle-pulled rickshaw-type "taxis" that are parked on the north side of the Zocalo in front of the cathedral.

The fanciest street in the old part of town is Francisco I. Madero, named after Mexico's first president following the revolution. It used to be known as the Avenue of the Silversmiths and is still flanked by shops selling silver and gold jewelry.

Madero, which runs westward from the Zocalo, is really the start of the city's main street since it leads into Juarez Avenue which, in turn, joins Paseo de la Reforma, the capital's fashionable central thoroughfare.

Just off Madero, at Isabel la Catolica 30, is *El Bazar del Centro*, a pearl and jewelry center housed in a beautifully-remodelled 17th-century house.

Among the landmark buildings lining Madero is the 18th-century *Iturbide Palace*, where Agustin Iturbide lived during his brief reign as emperor (1821-1823) following Mexico's independence from Spain. The building, at No. 7, houses the Palacio de Cultura Banamex and features the art collection of one of Mexico's largest banks.

Toward the end of Madero is the *Church of San Francisco*, begun in 1524 shortly after the conquest. And across the way is the famous *House of Tiles*, dating to 1596. According to legend, it was built by the son of a count in response to his father's assertion that he would "never have a house of tiles," an expression which finds its modern-day equivalent in "you'll never amount to anything." To prove his father wrong, the son built a grand mansion and covered every inch of it with beautiful blue-and-white Talavera tiles. Today the building houses Sanborns, a first-class general store with a beautiful restaurant and soda fountain.

Turning right on Lazaro Cardenas, at the end of Madero, you'll pass two extraordinarily beautiful turn-of-the-century buildings, the *Bank of Mexico* followed by the *Central Post Office*. Continuing on to Tacuba Street, you can return toward the Zocalo, passing the *National Museum of Art*, at Tacuba 8. A fine collection of Mexican art, largely of the classical European school, from the conquest and colonial periods, is displayed in this restored palace.

In front of the museum is a massive and impressive equestrian statue built by Manuel Tolsa in honor of Spain's King Carlos IV. "El Caballito," or "The Little Horse," as it is called, has not been preserved out of appreciation for the lackluster monarch, but because it is the work of one of the greatest architects of the colonial era and one of the finest statues of its kind in the world. Across the street is the old School of Mining.

The street named in honor of former President Lazaro Cardenas marks the western boundary of the Centro Historico, but there are encroachments. On the corner of Madero and Lazaro Cardenas is the *Latin American Tower*, a pillar of glass 44 stories high, with an observation deck at the top. It's a fun place to visit on a clear day; you can see several major landmarks and monuments, including Alameda Park, the Revolution Monument, the cathedral and National Palace—all fringed by the city's surrounding mountains. This landmark was for years Mexico's tallest building. Today it ranks 4th after the World Trade Center, Pemex Tower and Torre Mayor, a new skyscraper at Reforma 505 that is Latin America's tallest structure at 225 meters (about 740 feet).

Diagonally across the street is the *Palacio de Bellas Artes* (Palace of Fine Arts), Mexico's principal opera house, and home of the National Folkloric Ballet, important murals, and several exhibit halls. An architectural masterpiece inside and out, its interiors are a beautiful blend of art deco and art nouveau styles. In the main theater is a magnificent Tiffany stained-glass curtain depicting the Valley of Mexico with its two imposing volcanoes, Popocatepetl and Iztaccihuatl. This marble palace, completed in 1934, has sunk more than 15 feet into the spongy subsoil but, like the newer Latin American Tower, is built on a "floating" foundation which allows for more or less even sinking. An art deco-style cafe and bar to the left of the lobby offers a small but varied snack menu, and tables on a sunny terrace overlooking Alameda Park.

Alameda Park

At Lazaro Cardenas, Madero becomes Juarez Avenue. Newly renovated, it now boasts a wide promenade on each side. Diego Rivera's famous mural "Dream of a Sunday Afternoon in Alameda Park" is housed just steps away inside the *Diego Rivera Mural Museum*. Much of the area from the Zocalo west along Juarez and Reforma was badly damaged by a severe earthquake in 1985, including the building that originally housed the prized mural, the Del Prado Hotel. The museum's only treasure is this mural, an engaging depiction of famous political, entertainment and society figures of the time.

Alameda Park begins here. In colonial times the park was the exclusive realm of the rich and fenced off to the masses. Later it was where victims of the Spanish Inquisition were burned at the stake. Today it throbs with pedestrian traffic and plays host to lunch-time idlers and enamored couples. The park is dominated by a marble monument honoring 19th-century President Benito Juarez, "Mexico's Abe Lincoln." It also boasts several handsome fountains and statues brought from Paris by President Porfirio Diaz at the turn of the century (the originals are housed at the National Museum of Art).

Dressed in Mexican cowboy, or *charro*, gear, a new mounted police corps patrols Alameda Park. Wearing mariachi-style uniforms with tapered pants decked with silver buckles, bolero jackets and wide-brimmed sombreros, and armed with machetes and a basic knowledge of English, these picturesque police officers are mostly there to assist tourists.

Behind Alameda Park, at Hidalgo 45, on Plaza de la Santa Veracruz, is the *Franz Mayer Museum*. Situated between two colonial-era churches, the building dates to the 16th century, when it was a hospital. It was later used as an orphanage. Today it houses a vast collection of exquisite colonial-era art and rare items accumulated by Mayer and donated to the people of Mexico. Called a "museum of applied arts," it features mostly functional pieces, such as furniture, watches, trunks, utensils and altarpieces.

Nearby, also on Hidalgo, is the historical *Hotel de Cortes*, with a pleasant, plant-filled courtyard restaurant that offers a perfect respite from sightseeing.

At Juarez 89 is a *Fonart* handicraft store, carrying an excellent selection of beautifully made crafts from around the country.

Juarez Avenue leads to the *Revolution Monument*. Its giant dome was originally built to be placed atop a new capitol, but the Mexican Revolution put an end to those plans. Under the monument there is the *Museum of the Revolution*, containing interesting items (including satirical cartoons) from those turbulent years. The remains of revolutionary heroes are entombed within the monument's massive columns.

Three blocks away, at Puente de Alvarado and Ramos Arizpe streets, is the *San Carlos Museum*. Housed in a graceful mansion that was designed by Manuel Tolsa, the museum contains a fine selection of European art, part of which was donated by the King of Spain to the San Carlos Academy in the 18th century. This is one of the few museums in Mexico City that is open on Mondays (it closes Tuesdays).

Reforma

Juarez leads into elegant Paseo de la Reforma, a boulevard which continues west through Chapultepec Park and north toward the Plaza of the Three Cultures, the Ministry of Foreign Relations, and the Basilica of Our Lady of Guadalupe.

Reforma is a paradox. Ordered built by Emperor Maximilian, it was the most ambitious project carried out during the Austrian's three-year reign (1864-1867), yet it bears the name of the Reform program backed by the man who eventually defeated him, Benito Juarez. The broad boulevard is believed to have been modeled after Brussels' main avenue, Louise, in deference to his Belgian-born wife, Carlota.

At the Juarez-Reforma intersection are the *National Lottery* buildings. Drawings are held three nights a week in the older building, and the lucky winners are paid in the newer one. A century ago, the Juarez-Reforma intersection was on the edge of town, and was once the site of Mexico City's first bullfighting ring.

The handsomest street in the city, Reforma is lined by towering bank buildings, luxury hotels, fine restaurants, airline offices, and cinemas along its central segment, and by palatial residences and embassies at its western end.

At various junctions, Reforma is intercepted by traffic circles, called *"glorietas"* in Spanish. Heading west from the Zocalo, the first glorieta honors Columbus, who stands, arm extended, as if hailing a cab. Cuauhtemoc, the last of the Aztec emperors, is commemorated at the next glorieta. This is where Insurgentes Avenue, named in honor of the insurgents who rose against Spain in the War of Independence, crosses Reforma.

Zona Rosa

Roughly covering a four-by-10 block area beginning at the palm tree glorieta, where Niza meets Reforma, is the Zona Rosa, or Pink Zone. How the area got its name is a minor mystery. One version holds that a reporter at a local newspaper once referred to it as the "Pink Light District." Though no one knows why he called it that, the name stuck anyway.

Once an upscale shopping and dining enclave, the Zona Rosa lost its exclusivity with the advent of the Metro. The neighborhood

Major Museums

Chapultepec Park Area

Chapultepec Castle (National Museum of History). Open 9 a.m. to 5 p.m. Closed Mon. Fee for cameras; no flash permitted. Tel. 5286-0700.
National Museum of Anthropology. Reforma and Ghandi. Open 9 a.m. to 7 p.m.; Sun. and holidays, 10 a.m. to 6 p.m. Closed Mon. Fee for cameras; no flash or tripod permitted. Tel. 5553-6381.
Rufino Tamayo Museum. Reforma and Ghandi. Open 10 a.m. to 6 p.m. Closed Mon. Tel. 5286-6519.
Museum of Modern Art. Reforma and Ghandi Open 10 a.m. to 6 p.m. Closed Mon. Tel. 5211-8729.
Papalote Children's Museum. Chapultepec Park. Open Mon. to Sun., 9 a.m. to 1 p.m. and 2 to 6 p.m.; Thu., 7 to 11 p.m. also. Tel. 5237-1774.

Historic Center

Templo Mayor Museum (Great Temple). Northeast corner of the Zocalo. Open 9 a.m. to 5 p.m. Closed Mon. Tel. 5542-4943.
National Palace. Zocalo. Houses Diego Rivera murals. Open daily, 9 a.m. to 5 p.m. Free. Tel. 5512-0614.
Diego Rivera Mural Museum. Balderas and Colon. Open 10 a.m. to 2 p.m. and 3 to 6 p.m. Closed Mon. Free. Tel. 5510-2329.
Palacio de Bellas Artes. Alameda Park. Open 10 a.m. to 6 p.m. Closed Mon. Tel. 5550-3983.
Franz Mayer Museum. Hidalgo 45. Open 10 a.m. to 5 p.m. Closed Mon. Tel. 5518-2265.
Jose Luis Cuevas Museum. Academia 13. Open Mon., Tue., Thu. and Fri. from noon to 8 p.m.; Sat. and Sun. from 10 a.m. to 6 p.m. Free. Tel. 5542-6198.
National Museum of Art. Tacuba 8. Open 10 a.m. to 6 p.m. Closed Mon. Tel. 5130-3400.
Mexico City Museum. Pino Suarez 30. Open 10 a.m. to 5 p.m. Closed Mon. Tel. 5542-0083.
San Ildefonso Museum. Justo Sierra 16. Open 10 a.m. to 5:30 p.m. Closed Mon. Tel. 5702-6378.
San Carlos Museum. Puente del Alvarado and Ramos Arizpe. Open 10 a.m. to 6 p.m. Closed Tue. Tel. 5566-8522.

South

Frida Kahlo Museum. Londres 247, Coyoacan. Open 10 a.m. to 6 p.m. Closed Mon. Tel. 5554-5999.
Diego Rivera & Frida Kahlo Studio Museum. Diego Rivera 2, San Angel. Open 10 a.m. to 6 p.m. Closed Mon. Tel. 5548-3032.
Dolores Olmedo Museum. Av. Mexico 5843, Xochimilco. Open 10 a.m. to 6 p.m. Closed Mon. Tel. 5676-1055.

North and Environs

Pyramids of Teotihuacan. Open 7 a.m. to 6 p.m. Tel. (594) 956-0276.
Basilica of Guadalupe. Plaza of the Americas. Museum open 9 a.m. to 6 p.m. Closed Mon. Basilica open 6 a.m. to 8:45 p.m. Tel. 5577-6022.
Viceregency Museum. Tepotzotlan Convent, 45 min. northwest. Open 10 a.m. to 5 p.m. Closed Mon. Tel. 5876-0245.

The "Angel" monument overlooks Reforma Boulevard

reflects its past and present status in the way fast-food franchises and tacky nightclubs share the streets with swank jewelry stores, smart boutiques, antique shops, and genteel teahouses.

There are sidewalk cafes and restaurants for people-watching, such as those on Copenhague and Genova streets, both of which are closed to traffic. One of the city's better markets, *Mercado Insurgentes*, is located between Londres and Liverpool streets.

While pleasant for window shopping during the day, Zona Rosa's streets at night become jammed with cars, revelers and nightclub hawkers, appearing more like a red-light district than a pink zone.

Across Reforma, which marks the Zona Rosa's northern boundary, is the U.S. Embassy. An imposing marble-covered structure built in 1964, it houses one of the largest U.S. diplomatic missions in the world. Next door is the Sheraton Maria Isabel, one of the city's leading hotels.

The Pink Zone more or less ends at the *Monument to Independence*, a tall marble column supporting a gilded statue of the winged Goddess of Liberty. "The Angel," as she is com-

monly known, toppled off her column in a 1957 earthquake and was carefully restored. Best known of the capital's monuments, it is a common gathering place during demonstrations as well as mass celebrations, as it is every time Mexico's national soccer team wins a World Cup match.

The fountain at the next circle was built in 1992 for the specific purpose of showing off Mexico's famous statue of *Diana the Huntress*.

Chapultepec Park

A few blocks west, past the luxurious *Marquis Reforma* and *Four Seasons* hotels, begins Chapultepec Park, 2,100 acres of greenery with woods, marble statues, playgrounds, jogging paths, restaurants, man-made lakes with small boats, botanical gardens, a fine zoo and a children's petting zoo.

Few cities anywhere in the world boast such a spacious park and as many as half a million residents head for the grounds on Sundays.

Royal Aztec hunting grounds and imperial home of Emperor Maximilian, Chapultepec remains even today the seat of the country's ruler. Los Pinos (The Pines), the official resi-

dence of Mexican presidents, is in the park.

Crowning it all is the hilltop *Chapultepec Castle*, former home of Maximilian and current home of the *National Museum of History*. The castle was begun late in the 18th century by one of the last viceroys. He chose the highest site in the city, a hill known as "Chapultepec," a Nahuatl name meaning "Grasshopper Hill," to be the home of the Spanish crown's representatives in New Spain. Building was slow in those days and the castle was never really completed, the War of Independence having much to do with slowing things down. The republic took over the project and turned it into the National Military Academy.

When Maximilian of Hapsburg became emperor of Mexico, he converted the castle into his palace. The beautiful building and surrounding gardens are largely a remnant of Mexico's brief fling with monarchy. After Maximilian was executed, the castle served for years as the official home of presidents.

Visitors to the castle can see the various salons and their opulent furnishings, the splendid imperial carriage, and parts of a stunning second-story stained-glass window. Impressive murals by Orozco, Siqueiros and O'Gorman

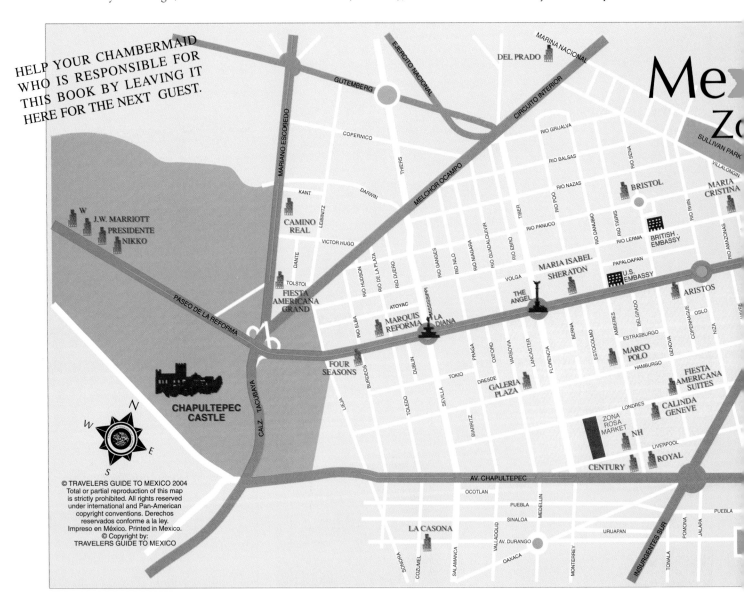

are also housed here. But the panoramic view and magnificent grounds alone make the trip to the castle worthwhile.

One of the most picturesque ways to arrive at the castle is via the entrance on Avenida Constituyentes, where there is a small flower market. The path winds past several beautiful marble statues and monuments. A staircase leading up to the castle is open on weekends and holidays.

Just off the path leading uphill to the castle is the *Museo del Caracol*, a spiral-shaped showplace ("*caracol*" means "snail") depicting Mexico's struggle for freedom.

Chapultepec Park is also home of the National Auditorium, the Papalote Children's Museum (see "Special Attractions"), the Rufino Tamayo Museum, and the museums of Natural History, Modern Art, and Anthropology.

The *Museum of Modern Art* is set in a sculpture garden. The interior walls display an excellent permanent collection of Mexican art, including works by Diego Rivera, Frida Kahlo, Orozco, Velasco, Siqueiros and Tamayo. There are also temporary exhibits by contemporary artists.

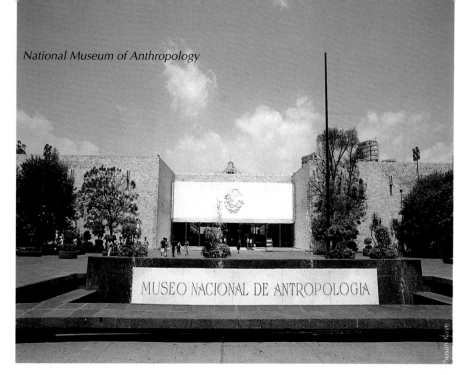

National Museum of Anthropology

MUSEO NACIONAL DE ANTROPOLOGIA

Another major attraction is the *Rufino Tamayo Museum*, which, in addition to some of Tamayo's own creations, contains his collection of about 300 works by world-famous artists. The museum hosts temporary exhibits and has an art library, coffee shop and gift shop.

Chapultepec also has a popular amusement park (La Feria), a new attraction that features the country's famous monuments in miniature (Mexico Magico), and a zoo with more than 300 types of animals, including pandas; Mexico is the only country that has been able to successfully breed these rare animals in captivity.

The park has a few excellent restaurants, including El Lago and Del Bosque, both overlooking a beautifully landscaped lake.

Anthropology Museum

The world-renowned National Museum of Anthropology, designed by famed Mexican architect Pedro Ramirez Vazquez and considered one of the finest of its kind in the world, has been a major city attraction since it opened in 1964.

It contains sections devoted to all regions of the country, from the earliest humans to arrive on the continent to the arrival of the Spaniards in 1519. Here you'll find the famous Aztec Calendar Stone, unofficial symbol of the Mexican nation, along with models of Tenochtitlan and a fascinating marketplace diorama.

Some of the most popular exhibits include giant stone Olmec heads from the jungles of Tabasco and Veracruz; the terrifyingly impressive statue of the snake-headed Aztec goddess Coatlicue, wearing a necklace of human hands and hearts, and a skirt of writhing snakes; treasures recovered from sacred Mayan wells; striking gold creations excavated from Zapotec tombs in Oaxaca; and a reproduction of the famous Bonampak murals near Mexico's border with Guatemala. Among the relics on display are even some found while excavating for the Mexico City subway, including a figure of Ehecatl, the wind god.

Days can be spent here without ever reaching the second floor with its fascinating ethnological displays of rural Mexican life. English-speaking guides are available.

Polanco

Once exclusively residential, the fashionable Polanco district north of the Nikko, Presidente InterContinental, JW Marriott and W hotels, has become a major commercial district with many of the city's most upscale boutiques, shopping centers, and restaurants lining its main thoroughfare, Avenida Presidente Masaryk.

Beyond the park, Reforma becomes a tree-lined avenue that passes through one of Mexico City's most exclusive residential areas, Las Lomas (The Heights). Here the homes are built in what is known as California style (or what Californians call Spanish colonial). Home to movie stars, business tycoons and diplomats, the imaginative mansions are surrounded by gardens and very often high walls.

Although the geographical boundaries of the Federal District extend halfway to Toluca, it wasn't so long ago that Lomas was thought of as the western edge of the city. Over the past 20 years, however, settlements have sprung up alongside the highway that winds through the hills to Toluca.

Insurgentes

Insurgentes is the longest street in Mexico City, running the entire length of the capital from north to south. It actually begins at the Texas border, in Laredo, and continues on to Acapulco. Its southern tract is flanked by shops and restaurants, while the northern section heads to the pyramids of Teotihuacan.

Insurgentes Sur, the southern half, begins at Reforma and the Cuauhtemoc monument. A few blocks from Reforma, Insurgentes runs into a large, circular plaza which serves as the Insurgentes Metro station. From there, a short stroll down Oaxaca Street leads you to a traffic circle featuring a bronze reproduction of Madrid's famous Cibeles fountain, a gift from grateful Spanish Republican residents of Mexico City.

Nearby is *Colonia Condesa*, Mexico City's own SoHo. Its art deco buildings and European-style townhouses dating from the Porfirian era (1876-1910) have attracted the artistic and bohemian community. The area is worth exploring on foot. Many of its notable buildings surround Parque Mexico (officially called Parque San Martin, but popularly known by the name of the avenue that encircles it, Avenida Mexico). Small offbeat boutiques, and sidewalk cafes and restaurants line its major avenues, especially Michoacan, from Mazatlan to Tamaulipas.

Back on Insurgentes, past the Miguel Aleman highway, is the 51-story *World Trade Center* and convention facility. The WTC is the country's third tallest structure, after the Torre Mayor, a new skyscraper at Reforma 505, and the Pemex Tower, which is the headquarters of the national oil company.

Few men have the opportunity to build their own monuments, which is just what renowned muralist David Alfaro Siqueiros did with his *Poliforum* on Insurgentes, adjoining the WTC. The Poliforum's upper level houses the largest mural ever painted, "The March of Humanity," covering an area of 27,000 square feet. The three-dimensional mural, or "sculpto-painting," is a combination of metals and acrylics on asbestos-concrete panels over iron. A 25-minute light and sound show, narrated in Siqueiros' own voice, is offered Saturdays and Sundays at 11:30 a.m. and 12:45 and 5 p.m.

Just off Insurgentes is *Plaza Mexico*, the world's largest bullfighting ring. It is, literally, a bowl dug into the ground. Spectators enter at street level and find themselves nearly at the top of the monumental stadium, built to seat 50,000. City officials, however, believe that to be too big a crowd in case of an emergency and limit attendance to 42,000.

Farther south on Insurgentes is *Parque Hundido* (Sunken Park), with fiberglass reproductions by Daniel Rios Zertuche of relics found in Mexico's archaeological zones, and the *Insurgentes Theater* (not to be confused with the Insurgentes Cinema). Its facade is a vast mosaic mural, the type Mexico is famed for, depicting the history of Mexican theater. Executed by Diego Rivera, it covers some 60 square meters with Mexico's famous comedian, Cantinflas, at center stage.

San Angel and Coyoacan

Farther south, Insurgentes leads to San Angel, once an independent village, and now a charming colonial-style district. A landmark here is the monument to Alvaro Obregon, who was assassinated at an Insurgentes restaurant in 1928 after being elected to a second term as president. The law has since been changed so that no president can run for a second term.

San Angel retains the feel of a picturesque village seemingly miles from the capital, with cobblestone streets and quaint homes. It is a residential area favored by prominent artists and writers.

San Angel's most publicized attraction is *Bazaar Sabado*, an upscale Saturday market for artisans producing clothing, jewelry, glassware, ceramics and other items. The bazaar is located on Plaza San Jacinto. On the same block is the *Isidro Fabela Museum*, also known as the Casa del Risco, most noteworthy for its unusual fountain made entirely of pieces of porcelain.

Worth a visit is beautiful *San Angel Inn*, once a coach stop and hacienda, today a grand Mexican restaurant, and the *Museo Casa Estudio Diego Rivera y Frida Kahlo*, just across the street. The neighborhood's *Ex-Convento del Carmen* is a handsome monument from the days of the viceroys, containing colonial art and a bizarre exhibition of mummies once buried nearby.

Sundays are especially pleasant in the neighboring district of Coyoacan, where Cortes had one of his many homes. Cobblestone streets surround the main church, *San Juan Bautista,* and plaza. Behind the church is the old Cortes residence, and just a few blocks away are the *Frida Kahlo Museum* (the artist's former home and studio) and the *Churubusco Convent*, housing the *Museum of Interventions*, which records the number of times Mexico has been invaded.

The *Anahuacalli Museum*, which was built by Diego Rivera to showcase his collection of 60,000 pre-Hispanic artifacts, is also in Coyoacan. Russian history buffs will want to visit the *Leon Trotsky Museum*.

Trolleys offering tours of the Coyoacan area leave from Calle Paris 190, in Colonia Del Carmen, every day from 10 a.m.

San Angel blends into an area known as *Pedregal*. Once a bleak terrain of volcanic rock, scorpions and cacti, it has developed into a posh bedroom community famed for its ultramodern homes.

University City

University City, the campus of the Autonomous National University of Mexico (UNAM), is in Pedregal, straddling both sides of Insurgentes. The university, the oldest in the Western hemisphere, was for centuries located downtown in buildings near the Zocalo. Work began on the present 800-acre campus about 40 years ago. Four years later, architecturally and artistically, it became one of the world's most beautiful learning centers. Many of Mexico's greatest muralists and designers took part in its construction. A campus landmark is the library, its walls covered with mosaic murals by Juan O'Gorman, who was also its architect.

Opposite the library is the Olympic Stadium. Featuring mosaic murals by Diego Rivera, the stadium was originally designed in Brazil when that country hoped to host the Olympics. Brazil lost out, but the planned stadium, built here in the 50s, became the site of the opening and closing ceremonies, and the track and field events of the 1968 Olympic Games. It is designed to resemble the crater of a volcano.

UNAM is not the only institution of higher

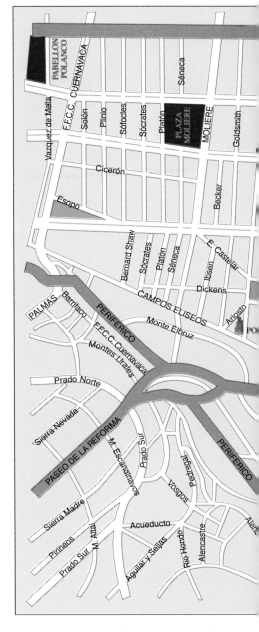

learning in the capital. Others include the Ibero-Americana, Anahuac, Metropolitan, and the National Polytechnic Institute. There are a number of excellent universities in the provinces as well, such as Monterrey Tech and the Autonomous University of Guadalajara, which receives hundreds of medical students each year from the United States.

Nezahualcoyotl Hall

The 3.3 million-dollar Nezahualcoyotl Hall is an outstanding auditorium named in honor of the venerated ruler of Texcoco, which was part of the Aztec Triple Alliance. It is North America's first wraparound concert hall, with 2,500 seats on various levels surrounding the stage. Ever since the Cleveland Orchestra performed Beethoven's Ninth Symphony in the fall of 1977, this has ranked as one of the world's great concert halls.

South of the auditorium and beyond the Periferico (Beltway) is *Cuicuilco*, a pyramid built around 600 B.C. Around 300 A.D., the site

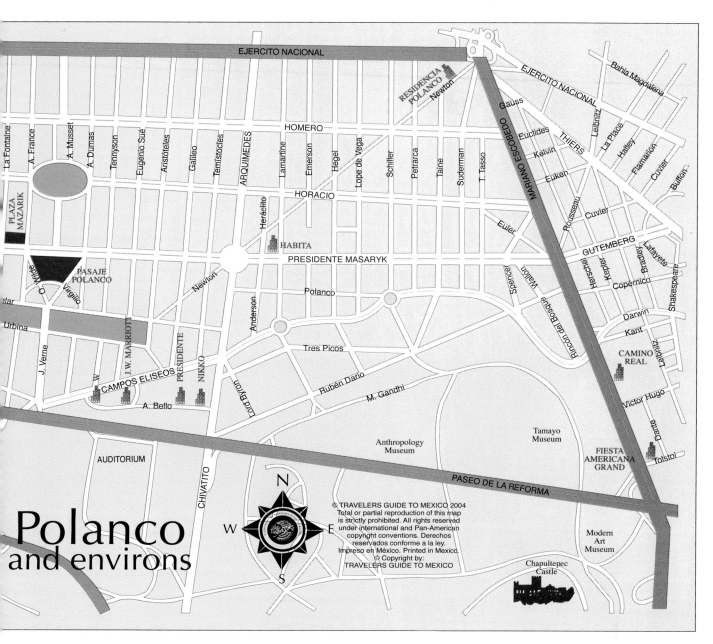

Polanco
and environs

was buried under 20 feet of lava, but is now partially unearthed.

Insurgentes goes on to *Tlalpan*, another "village" within the city. Tlalpan's charming plaza, dating from its days as an independent municipality, serves as a site for Sunday concerts. From here, Insurgentes continues on to Cuernavaca, Taxco and Acapulco.

Xochimilco

Also in the south are Mexico City's famed floating gardens of Xochimilco.

In Aztec times the Valley of Mexico was filled by a lake and Tenochtitlan, the capital, was built on an island. Since farmland was scarce, the Aztecs created additional land for cultivation by placing heaps of mud in wooden frames to create rich soil. Willow trees were then planted along the edges of the "plots" to develop a strong root system. The newly formed "floating gardens," or *"chinampas,"* were used to grow fruits, vegetables and flowers for the capital. The system died out, but ef-

forts are being made to revive it.

Trajineras (flat-bottomed boats that serve as a kind of Mexican gondola), bedecked with artificial flowers, are pole-propelled along the canals, and make for a delightful ride. Mariachi and marimba bands are boat-borne, too, as are taco and beer vendors, and sellers of all kinds of flowers and wares.

Xochimilco can be very crowded on weekends, when Mexican families gather for a day outdoors. To avoid the bumper to bumper traffic on the canals, you can go on a weekday, but you may miss a lot of the flavor and carnival atmosphere. Nighttime trajinera rides can also be arranged.

Nearby, the *Dolores Olmedo Museum* contains the most representative collection of works by muralist Diego Rivera and painter Frida Kahlo. Their works, as well as a great collection of pre-Hispanic ceramic art, are displayed in a beautiful, rambling estate belonging to Olmedo, a former socialite who modelled for Rivera, and an avid collector. The museum is located at Avenida México 5843; you can take the Metro

to Tasqueña and from there the Tren Ligero to La Noria station.

During Day of the Dead celebrations, All Saints and All Souls days on November 1 and 2, Mexican and foreign tourists flock to the town of *Mixquic* to witness the fascinating rituals. Again, be prepared for crowds.

In *Ixtapalapa* is the Cerro de la Estrella (Hill of the Star), where fires were rekindled at the beginning of each 52-year cycle of the Aztec calendar. This is also the site of an elaborate Passion Play each year on Good Friday.

Insurgentes Norte

Heading north on Insurgentes, crossing Reforma, you are on the old road to Laredo, Texas (the new road, to the west, passes through Queretaro and San Luis Potosi). This end of the avenue is quite different from Insurgentes Sur. The north side of town is filled with factories and sprawling working-class neighborhoods.

Next door to the now defunct train station

Tile murals deck campus buildings at UNAM

Mexico Tourism Board

is *Buenavista Market*, which started out large and expanded to enormous. Their prices are fixed, and you often find better bargains by shopping around town—but they do have a vast selection of Mexican crafts under one roof.

The *Monument to the Race*, on Insurgentes, is a pyramid (of recent construction) dedicated to the blending of Spanish and indigenous blood that gave rise to Mexico's *mestizo* culture.

A few streets over from Insurgentes is the *Plaza of the Three Cultures*, so called because an Aztec ruin and a colonial-era church are found juxtaposed with the modern offices of the Ministry of Foreign Relations, symbolizing the Indian, European and mestizo peoples.

Shrine of Guadalupe

The hilltop Basilica of Our Lady of Guadalupe, considered by Catholics to be the holiest site in the Western Hemisphere, has been visited by such dignitaries as John F. Kennedy, Charles de Gaulle and Pope John Paul II.

According to legend, it was on this hill in December, 1531, that an Aztec Indian recently converted to Catholicism and baptized Juan Diego saw a vision of the Virgin Mary. He was on his way to mass when the Virgin appeared, requesting that a church be built at the site. Juan Diego reported the encounter and request to the bishop, who asked for proof of the apparition.

On December 12 the Virgin reappeared and told Juan Diego to gather in his cloak roses she had miraculously made appear on the barren hilltop and carry them back to the bishop as proof. When Juan Diego later unfolded his cloak, the flowers were gone, but an image of a dark-skinned Virgin was imprinted on the fabric.

Skeptics, some of the earliest arriving from Rome itself, came to examine the cloak and went away baffled. Eventually the church was

built and consecrated as a shrine. The Virgin of Guadalupe was declared Patroness of Mexico and Empress of the Americas. To this day no one has been able to provide a scientific explanation of the image on Juan Diego's cloak. The portrait hangs encased in glass above the central altar of a modern basilica built at the site.

In July 2002, on his fifth visit to Mexico, Pope John Paul canonized Juan Diego, making him the first indigenous saint of the Americas.

Some believe the legend of Juan Diego was fabricated by the Spanish to win Indian converts to Christianity. Tepeyac Hill was already sacred to the Aztecs for its association with the mother-goddess Tonantzin.

Visitors to Mexico will find Guadalupe's image almost everywhere. Indeed, it was Mexico's first flag, the banner Father Miguel Hidalgo raised to urge his parishioners to oust the Spaniards and fight for an independent Mexico.

December 12 is a national though unofficial holiday and sees hundreds of thousands of the faithful make a pilgrimage to the shrine, the most repentant or grateful on their knees.

The basilica can be reached by driving up Insurgentes Norte and turning right at the Lindavista Cinema. An on-site museum displays colonial-era relics and a fine collection of ex-votos.

Teotihuacan

Beyond the basilica is the turnoff to the pyramids of Teotihuacan, 31 miles northeast of Mexico City. The site is one of Mexico's most popular tourist attractions and its first true city, at its peak extending several miles in each direction, with a population of possibly 200,000.

Teotihuacan's religious, cultural and eco-

nomic influence peaked between 500 and 700 A.D. Craftsmen from distant regions brought their specialties here. Obsidian was prevalent, and today local men still make figurines from the iridescent black stone to sell to tourists.

Much of the city was later destroyed by fire and became a ghost town. It was in ruins when the Aztecs discovered it centuries later, and it remains a place of great mystery and reverence. Experts believe the city's builders came from the east about 2,000 years ago, their culture based on worship of the rain god.

Today the language and history of this ancient city—even its original name—are lost. Its present name—meaning "Place Where Gods Are Made"—was given to it by the Aztecs, who could only surmise from the monumental ruins of the abandoned city that they had stumbled onto divine territory. It was here, they believed, that the gods created the universe and the world as we know it, called the "Fifth Sun," the previous four creations having been destroyed by nature.

Quetzalcoatl is here closely associated with the goggle-eyed rain god Tlaloc and other water symbols, such as seashells, which decorate his temple and appear in murals in the Atetelco, Tetitla and Tepanitla areas. Aside from the major buildings, these are probably the most beautiful.

The pyramids of the Sun and Moon, the Ciudadela, or Citadel, with its Temple of Quetzalcoatl (the Plumed Serpent) and the Palace of Quetzalpapalotl (Plumed Butterfly) are the major constructions along the site's nearly mile-long main thoroughfare, the Avenue of the Dead. The Pyramid of the Sun is the largest, standing 210 feet high. Teotihuacan monuments were built as flat-topped bases for ceremonial temples reaching high into the sky, to be near the gods.

Even though explorations have continued nonstop since the late 1920s, only a small portion of the site has been excavated and more discoveries are expected.

It's a good idea to begin your visit at the museum next to the Sun Pyramid (one of three in-situ museums) to get an overview of the site. If you plan to climb, wear comfortable shoes and don't be surprised to find souvenir vendors at the top. The site is open 7 a.m. to 6 p.m. daily. Tel. (594) 956-0276.

Buses leave from Central del Norte terminal for the one hour and 15 minute ride to the site. Just steps from the ruins, Club Med's *Villa Arqueologica* (tel. (594) 956-0909) offers a pleasant place to lunch or spend the night. Also nearby, *La Gruta* features traditional Mexican cooking and folkloric entertainment in a colorful setting inside a mammoth cavern (tel. (594) 956-0127).

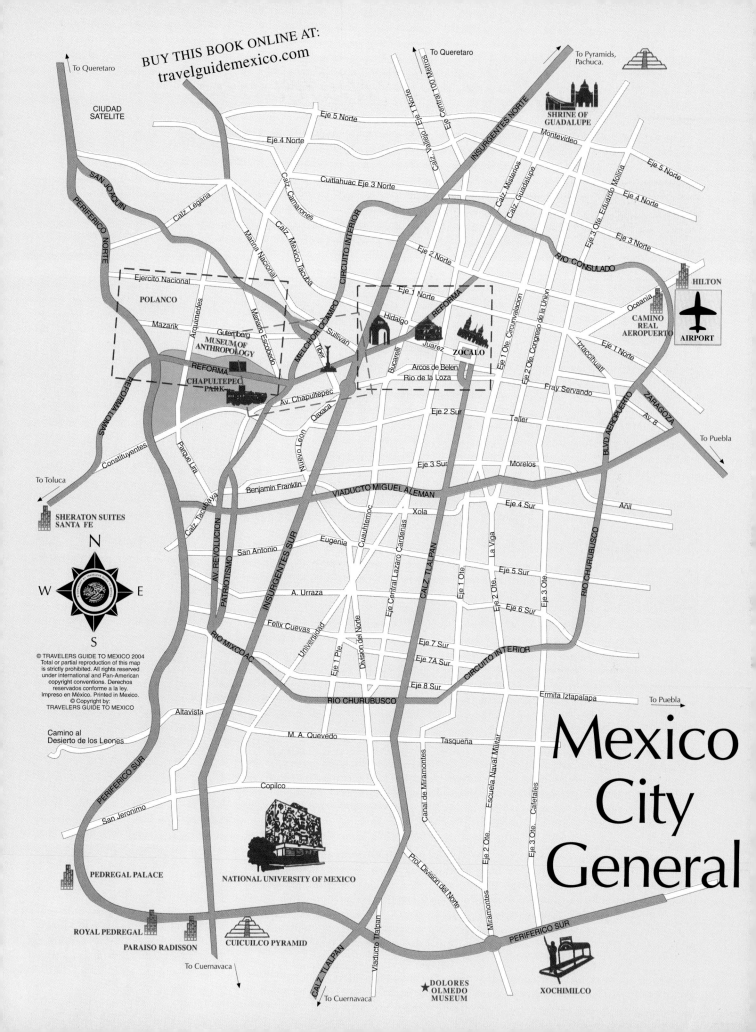

To Queretaro

CIUDAD
SATELITE

SAN JOAQUIN

PERIFERICO NORTE

Eje 5 Norte

Eje 4 Norte

Calz. Legaria

Calz. Camarones

Cuitlahuac Eje 3 Norte

Marina Nacional

Calz. Mexico Tacuba

CIRCUITO INTERIOR

To Queretaro

Eje 5 Norte
Eje 1 Norte
Eje Central 100 Metros

INSURGENTES NORTE

Calz. Vallejo

Calz. Misterios

Calz. Guadalupe

To Pyramids,
Pachuca.

SHRINE OF
GUADALUPE

Montevideo

Eje 5 Norte

Eje 4 Norte

Eje 3 Ote-Eduardo Molina

Eje 3 Norte

Eje 2 Norte

RIO CONSULADO

HILTON

Ejercito Nacional

POLANCO

Mazarik

Arquimedes

Mariano Escobedo

MELCHOR OCAMPO

Gutemberg
MUSEUM OF
ANTHROPOLOGY

REFORMA

REFORMA LOMAS

CHAPULTEPEC
PARK

Sullivan

Tiber

Hidalgo

REFORMA

Juarez

Bucareli

ZOCALO

Eje 1 Ote. Circunvalacion

Eje 2 Ote. Congreso de la Union

CAMINO
REAL
AEROPUERTO

AIRPORT

Oceania

Iztaccihuatl

Eje 1 Norte

Av. Chapultepec

Oaxaca

Nuevo Leon

Arcos de Belen
Rio de la Loza

Eje 2 Sur

Taller

Fray Servando

BLVD AEROPUERTO

ZARAGOZA

Av. 8

To Puebla

Constituyentes

REFORMA LOMAS

Parque Lira

Eje 3 Sur

Morelos

To Toluca

SHERATON SUITES
SANTA FE

Calz. Tacubaya

Benjamin Franklin

VIADUCTO MIGUEL ALEMAN

Xola

Eje 4 Sur

Añil

N

W   E

S

AV. REVOLUCION

PATRIOTISMO

San Antonio

INSURGENTES SUR

Eugenia

Cuauhtemoc

Eje Central Lazaro Cardenas

CALZ. TLALPAN

Eje 1 Ote

Eje 5 Sur

RIO CHURUBUSCO

© TRAVELERS GUIDE TO MEXICO 2004
Total or partial reproduction of this map
is strictly prohibited. All rights reserved
under international and Pan-American
copyright conventions. Derechos
reservados conforme a la ley.
Impreso en México. Printed in Mexico.
© Copyright by:
TRAVELERS GUIDE TO MEXICO

A. Urraza

Felix Cuevas

Universidad

Eje 1 Pte.

Division del Norte

Eje 2 Ote.

Eje 6 Sur

Eje 7 Sur

Eje 7A Sur

CIRCUITO INTERIOR

Eje 3 Ote.

RIO MIXCOAC

Altavista

Eje 8 Sur

Ermita Iztapalapa

To Puebla

Camino al
Desierto de los Leones

M. A. Quevedo

Tasqueña

PERIFERICO SUR

San Jeronimo

Copilco

Canal de Miramontes

Escuela Naval Militar

Cafetales

Eje 2 Ote.

Eje 3 Ote.

Mexico
City
General

PEDREGAL PALACE

NATIONAL UNIVERSITY OF MEXICO

Prol. Division del Norte

Miramontes

ROYAL PEDREGAL

PARAISO RADISSON

CUICUILCO PYRAMID

CALZ. TLALPAN

Viaducto Tlalpan

PERIFERICO SUR

DOLORES
OLMEDO
MUSEUM

XOCHIMILCO

To Cuernavaca

To Cuernavaca

Special Attractions

Visitors admire the gardens at Chapultepec Castle

Folkloric Ballet

No one should miss the spectacular presentation of Mexico's Folkloric Ballet at the Palacio de Bellas Artes. What began in 1952 as a small dance company founded by the late dancer and choreographer Amalia Hernandez, is now one of Mexico's largest and most important artistic enterprises, performing at major venues throughout the world.

It is a tour de force of traditional music and dance from the days of the Aztecs to the fiestas that are still celebrated throughout Mexico today. You'll see some of the most popular regional dances performed with skill in a colorful and exciting show staged at a gorgeous venue.

Performances are held Wednesdays at 8:30 p.m., and Sundays at 9:30 a.m. and 8:30 p.m. Taking photos, without flash, is permitted. Tel. 5529-9320.

Bus & Trolley Tours

A new fleet of red double-decker open-topped buses, called Turibus, shuttle along the city's main boulevard, Paseo de la Reforma, taking in some 25 sites of interest (headsets offer information in several languages). A ticket, costing about 10 dollars, lets passengers board throughout the day; evening tours are also available.

Old-fashioned trolley cars offer half-hour mini-tours of the Centro Historico, highlighting well-known and a few obscure but interesting historic landmarks, including the Mexico City Museum, where Hernan Cortes first met with Aztec Emperor Moctezuma in 1519. Tours leave daily from 10 a.m. to 6 p.m. from the corner of Bellas Artes. Large groups can book English-language tours in advance by calling 5512-1012, ext. 0202 or 0230.

Trolleys offering tours of the city's colonial Coyoacan district leave from Calle Paris 190, in Colonia Del Carmen, every day from 10 a.m.

Chapultepec Castle

Hilltop Chapultepec Castle, famed as the former home of Emperor Maximilian, today houses the *National Museum of History*. A tour of the grounds and building, which features various salons and their opulent furnishings, a splendid imperial carriage, stunning stained-glass windows, and impressive murals by Orozco, Siqueiros and O'Gorman, helps bring Mexico's history to life. Though the panoramic view alone can make a trip to the castle worthwhile.

The beautiful building and surrounding gardens are largely a remnant of Mexico's brief fling with monarchy. After Maximilian was executed, the castle served for years as the official home of presidents.

Markets

One of the most colorful spots for Mexican handicrafts and some Guatemalan textiles is *La Ciudadela,* an attractive open-air market located on Balderas, about four blocks south of Avenida Juarez. The displays, offering everything from leather goods to silver jewelry, are built around a small courtyard. Facing the courtyard, a *comida corrida,* or Mexican-style fast-food spot, offers tasty typical fare.

In the heart of Zona Rosa is *Mercado Insur-*

gentes, which is crammed to the rafters with goods, especially a wide variety of sterling silver jewelry and tableware. *Lagunilla*, at Reforma and Rayon, offers a bustling Sunday flea market featuring everything from antique furniture to vinyl records. You'll even find shoes and pets for sale among the aisles. *Centro Artesanal San Juan*, downtown on Ayuntamiento and Dolores, is a newly renovated handicraft and curios market. You won't find any handicrafts at *Mercado de Sonora*, about three blocks from the Merced Metro station, but it is famed for its medicinal herbs and magic potions.

Bazaar Sabado, at Plaza San Jacinto in San Angel, is an upscale market for sophisticated artisans selling creative jewelry, glassware, ceramics and home decorations. An open-air patio offers a Mexican buffet and marimba music. As its name implies, it's open only Saturdays, 10 a.m. to 7 p.m.

Kid Stuff

The *Papalote Children's Museum*, described by The New York Times as one of the largest and most technologically sophisticated "touch and do" museums in the world, is located in Chapultepec Park. The complex contains 250 interactive exhibits grouped into five different themes related to art, science and technology. Adults seem to enjoy the museum as much as their younger companions do, especially the computerized games, so Thursday evenings have been set aside especially for them. An IMAX auditorium screens breathtaking films on Mexican culture and archaeology, as well as other topics. Tel. 5224-1260.

Kid's City, known in Spanish as La Ciudad de los Niños, is a recreational center where children get to play at being adults surrounded by miniature versions of banks, stores, airplanes, etc. A recent recipient of the THEA Award, considered the Oscar of the theme park industry, Kid's City is located at Centro Santa Fe.

In the south, Mexico City's *Six Flags* amusement park offers the latest heart-thumping rides, games and attractions, including mega-rollercoasters Batman The Ride and Medusa, and the Kilauea rocket launcher. Open Tuesday to Sunday from 10 a.m. to 7 p.m. Tel. 5728-7292.

Art in the Park

Open-air art exhibits are a weekend staple: On Saturday, artists display their work at *Plaza San Jacinto* in San Angel, just outside Bazaar Sabado. On Sunday, paintings and sculptures are on show at *Sullivan Park*, two blocks from the Reforma-Insurgentes intersection. The works represent a wide variety of styles and come in all price ranges.

Hearing Voices

"Voices of the Cathedral," an elaborate light-and-sound show, brings the Metropolitan Cathedral's history to life with actors and musicians in period costume. Performances are Wednesdays at 8:30 p.m.; English-language shows can be arranged in advance.

The cathedral also offers guided tours, with access to otherwise off-limits areas such as the bell tower and sacristy, Monday to Saturday at 8, 10:30, noon, 3 and 5:30, as well as nighttime tours. For information, call 5521-7737.

Floating Gardens

At the famed "floating gardens" of Xochimilco, dating from Aztec times, colorful *trajineras* (Mexican-style gondolas) propel passengers along canals flanked by plant nurseries.

The one- or two-hour excursions are like floating picnics, with couples, families or groups of friends (sometimes in two or three boats tied together) enjoying an on-board meal. Passing boats—carrying taco and beer vendors, marimba bands or mariachi musicians—supply both food and music. Expect bumper-to-bumper traffic on weekends, especially on Sunday.

Teotihuacan

Located 31 miles northeast of the capital, this fascinating archaeological site derived its name—meaning "Place Where Gods Are Made"—from the Aztecs, who surmised from the monumental ruins of the abandoned city that they had stumbled onto divine territory. It was here, they believed, that the gods created the universe.

The Sun and Moon pyramids, the Ciudadela, or Citadel, with its Temple of Quetzalcoatl (the Plumed Serpent), and the Palace of Quetzalpapalotl (Plumed Butterfly) are the major constructions along the site's nearly mile-long Avenue of the Dead.

Three museums, including one by the Sun Pyramid, display regional artifacts. The site is open 7 a.m. to 6 p.m. daily. We recommend taking a morning tour, so there is plenty of

Palacio de Bellas Artes

Mexico City Tourism Authority

time to look around. Tel. (594) 956-0276.

Bullfights

Winter is the big season for bullfights in Mexico, when the full-fledged matadors perform. During spring, summer and autumn, the plaza features novices—the best the country has, but novices nevertheless—who hope some day to win the coveted title of matador. To the aficionado the difference is considerable, but the visitor about to witness his first fight has no reason to thumb his nose at the *novillero* (a *novillo* is a young bull under the official weight limit, and the novice who fights it is known as a *novillero*).

Bullfights are staged most Sundays of the year at 4 p.m. The most hassle-free way to attend is with a tour.

Arroyo, a restaurant complex located in the south of the city, offers a good alternative for those interested in taking in a bullfight. It hosts a *novillada* each Saturday at noon from May through August at its miniature bullfighting ring. Families who come to attend the bullfight usually stay to enjoy a traditional Mexican meal afterwards, complete with folkloric dancing and music. See "Where to Dine" for details.

Fans of the bullfight stress the danger presented by the bull, which they say bears about as much resemblance to its barnyard cousin as a tabby does to a jaguar. Indeed in a contest between a bull and a lion, the smart money would be on the bull—but don't cheer for the bull, it's not considered good form.

A Day at the Races

El Hipodromo de Las Americas, the city's newly revamped horse racing track, draws nearly 4,000 spectators on an average racing day. Races are held Fridays from 4:30 p.m., and Saturdays and Sundays from 2:30 p.m. You can reserve your table at the Club House at 2122-1515.

Athletic and sporting events from around the globe are featured at the site's Sportsbook every day from 10 to 2 a.m., as well as at Zipango, a sophisticated restaurant-bar overlooking the track. A work in progress, the complex will include an equestrian museum, hotels and boutiques when completed.

Urban Cowboys

A *charreada* is a Mexican-style rodeo featuring feats of horsemanship. Its origins are traced to Mexico's old haciendas, where ranchers skilled in the art of riding and lassoing honed their art by competing against each other. The most original and daring moves, and fanciest attire, have been enshrined in today's Fiesta Charra.

The best time to see a charreada is when the Feria del Charro (usually held at the end of May, first week of June) brings riders from around the nation to compete against one another. Year-round, chareadas are held Sundays at at Rancho del Charro (Constituyentes 500, tel. 5277-8706) or at Lienzo del Charro, in the south.

45 AMFAR

Expo Decoración y Regalo

The Gift & Accessories Mexican Show

Del 26 al 30 de Julio de 2004
July 26-30 2004

La Exposición más grande
de Latinoamérica
20 Años de experiencia
600 Expositores en 850 Stands
Experiencia Profesional en
Organización de Exposiciones

The largest Gift show in Latin America
20 Years of experience
600 Exhibitors in 850 Booths

20º ANIVERSARIO
20º ANNIVERSARY

46 amfar | **Del 17 al 21 de Enero 2005**
Expo Decoración y Regalo | January 17-21 2005

Solo es cuestión
de tiempo...
It's just a matter of time...

¡Regístrese en
www.amfar.com
Imprima su gafete e
Ingrese sin demoras!*

Register online, print your badge and
Access without delays!*

*Consulte Restricciones
Check Restrictions

World Trade Center
Ciudad de México

AMFAR A.C.
Guanajuato 214 Col. Roma 06700 México D.F.
Tel. 5564 4564 Fax 5574 9709
www.amfar.com amfar@amfar.com

Business Information

The Visiting Executive's Guide for Getting Around Town

The American Chamber of Commerce of Mexico can be of great help to business travelers, offering information and orientation. AmCham operates a high-tech *InfoCenter* with CD-ROM databases and a library of trade directories, and has a staff of trade specialists.

The InfoCenter can provide up-to-date information on matters relating to U.S.-Mexico trade, including NAFTA, laws regulating trade, statistics, forecasts and business opportunities.

AmCham also publishes numerous studies on economics and business in Mexico that are usually available for sale.

AmCham members have free access to the center; non-members pay a nominal but varied research fee. The InfoCenter is open Monday to Friday, 9 a.m. to 1 p.m. and 3 to 5 p.m., at Lucerna 78, Colonia Juarez, just steps from Reforma. Tel. 5141-3800. E-mail: amchammx@amcham.com.mx.

The American Chamber also has branches in Monterrey and Guadalajara.

U.S. Embassy Offices

The Foreign Commercial Service of the U.S. Commerce Department staffs the Commercial Section of the U.S. Embassy in Mexico City.

Commercial officers and specialists brief U.S. visitors on local business conditions and assist in locating potential agents, distributors, licensees or joint venture partners.

Other embassy officers are available for consultation on banking and finance, labor relations, fisheries, petroleum and mining.

The U.S. Commerce Department operates a U.S. Trade Center in Mexico City to promote U.S. goods in Mexico. It provides businessmen looking to do business here with office space for lease and other services, including help in arranging business appointments for visiting executives. The center can also supply background information on firms with which the visitor has meetings.

The U.S. Embassy-run Benjamin Franklin Library, at Liverpool 31, just a few blocks from the American Chamber of Commerce, is a good source of information in English. It has a good selection of reference material, as well

Mexico's stock exchange towers over Reforma.

Robert Campbell

as microfilm and photocopying services. It is open Monday and Friday from 11 to 7 p.m. Tel. 5080-2733.

Investment Board

The Mexican Investment Board, a government agency, acts as a clearinghouse of information for foreigners who want to do business in Mexico. It is also designed to help cut through red tape, so foreigners who are interested in establishing an office here should work with the investment board.

Mexican Investment Board (Consejo Mexicano de Inversion), Reforma 915, Lomas de Chapultepec, Mexico, D.F. 11000. Tel. 5202-7804.

Conventions

Mexico City convention and exposition sites include the Banamex Convention Center at the Hipodromo de Las Americas (overlooking the city's horse racing track) and a new exposition venue at Santa Fe, as well as the World Trade Center (WTCMx), Palacio de los Deportes, and National Auditorium. In addition, meeting and convention planners have several unique historical venues to choose from for hosting social events, such as Chapultepec Castle.

To help promote Mexico as a meetings and conventions destination, the government recently created Mexico's Meetings and Conventions Bureau. Headed by tourism sector veteran Eduardo Chaillo, the bureau aims to lure some of the world's 102.3 billion-dollar meetings and conventions business to Mexico. In 2003, Mexico hosted about 1,500 conventions, representing about 1% of the total world market. By comparison, the United States hosts upwards of 700,000 conventions a year.

The Mexico City Convention & Visitors Bureau can help you coordinate and organize your next meeting or convention. Call 5211-2136 or e-mail: info@cvbmexicocity.gob.mx.

World Trade Center

Mexico City's World Trade Center (WTCMx) features a modern International Exposition and Convention Center (CIEC). This attractive, modern low-rise, built exclusively to host expos, is the first center of its kind in Mexico with loading and unloading installations, services that facilitate the mounting and dismantling of exhibits.

The center hosts as many as 75 expos a year, including a semiannual gifts fair and expo organized by the Mexico City-based Compañia Integradora de Articulos Para Regalos (CIAR), which has 15 years of experience in its field.

WTCMx: Tel. 5488-2566. Fax 5628-8395. E-mail: dirciec@wtcmexico.com.mx.

CIAR: Tel. 5564-4564. Fax 5574-9709. E-mail: amfar@amfar.com.

International Business Club

Located at the city's international airport, this business center is available 24 hours a day, 365 days a year.

Air Travel Information

To facilitate air travel, the Mexico City International Airport recommends travelers keep the following information in mind:

• Passengers should arrive two hours before a national flight and three hours before an international flight.
• Each passenger is allowed up to 25 km/55 lb of baggage for national flights and up to 30 km/66 lb for international flight (excess baggage carries a charge).
• Carry on luggage must measure no more than: 45 cm/18 in in length, 35 cm/14 in in width, and 20 cm/8 in in depth.
• Passengers should arrive at their boarding gate 45 minutes before departure.
• Among the articles prohibited in boarding areas and onboard are: umbrellas, any opened food or beverage, matches, adhesive and measuring tapes, and some powders (such as detergents). These items should be packed in checked luggage.
• For 24-hour storage of luggage, contact: Lockers, Sala E3, international wing, tel: 5726-0467; or Mexicana de Lockers, outside Sala A1, national wing, tel: 5786-9048.

For more information, visit www.aicm.com.mx or call 5571-3600, ext. 2259 and 2303.

Aero California. Tel. 5207-1392.	**British Airways.** Tel. 5387-0300.
Aeromar. Tel. 5133-1111.	**Canadian.** Tel. 5207-8683.
Aeromexico. Tel. 5133-4010.	**Continental.** Tel. 5283-5500.
American Airlines. Tel. 5209-1400.	**Delta Airlines.** Tel. 5279-0909.
Aviacsa. Tel. 5716-9004.	**Mexicana.** Tel. 5448-0990.
Azteca. Tel. 5716-8989.	**United Airlines.** Tel. 5627-0222.

Services include fully-equipped offices and meeting rooms, computers, Internet access, bilingual staff, and more.

International Terminal, second floor. Tel. 5764-6900. Fax 5764-6901. www.ibcmexico.com.

Important Telephone Numbers

Emergency
All-purpose — 060
Mobile Intensive Care — 5598-6222
ABC Hospital — 5230-8000

Airlines
Aeromexico — 5133-4010
American — 5209-1400
British Airways — 5387-0300
Canadian — 5207-8683
Continental — 5283-5500
Delta — 5279-0909
Mexicana — 5448-0990
United — 5627-0222

Long Distance Calls
National — 01
US & Canada — 001
Worldwide — 00
AT&T — 01(800)288-2872
MCI — 001(800)674-7000
Sprint — 001(800)877-8000
Telmex — 01(800) SAVINGS

To report loss of credit cards
American Express — 5326-2666
Diners Club — 5258-3220
Visa — 001(800)847-2911
Mastercard — 001(800)307-7309

Radio Taxis
Servitaxis — 5516-6020
Taxi Radio — 5566-0077

U.S. State Offices

A visit with representatives of one of the nearly dozen U.S. state offices in Mexico (most located in the capital) can provide a visiting businessman with a wealth of information.

Each state office has a trade representative who can answer questions about trade in general, plus larger offices with staff dedicated to particular areas of trade, such as agriculture.

State offices will also arrange some business meetings and organize trade missions. While it is a good idea to contact these offices before coming to Mexico, they do not discourage drop-in visitors.

Chambers of Commerce

American Chamber of Commerce of Mexico
Lucerna 78, Col. Juarez
Tel. 5141-3800.
British Chamber of Commerce
Rio de la Plata 30, Col. Cuauhtemoc
Tel. 5256-0901.
Canadian Chamber of Commerce
Cantu 11, Col. Anzures
Tel. 5545-4090.
German Chamber of Commerce
Bosques de Ciruelos 130,
Col. Bosques de las Lomas
Tel. 5251-4022.
Mexico City Chamber of Commerce
Reforma 42, 3rd Floor,
Col. Juarez
Tel. 5705-0424.

Commercial Affairs Offices

British Embassy
Commercial Affairs Office
Rio Lerma 71, Col. Cuauhtemoc
Tel. 5207-2089.

Canadian Embassy
Commercial Affairs Section
Schiller 529, Col. Polanco
Tel. 5724-7900.
Japanese Embassy
Commercial Affairs
Reforma 395, Col. Cuauhtemoc
Tel. 5211-0028.
U.S. Embassy
Commercial Section
Reforma 305, Col. Cuauhtemoc
Tel. 5080-2000.

Publications

Business Mexico: Published 10 times a year by the American Chamber of Commerce of Mexico.

Doing Business in Mexico: One of a series of books on business conditions in the countries in which Price Waterhouse firms have offices. Published by Price Waterhouse World Firm Limited.

Intercambio: Published quarterly by the British Chamber of Commerce.

Lloyd Mexican Economic Report: A monthly newsletter published by Guadalajara-based Allen W. Lloyd y Asociados. Tel.: (33) 3880-2000. E-mail: lloyd@lloyd.com.mx

Mexletter: A monthly analysis of Mexico's investment panorama. Tel.: 5533-3600. E-mail: mexletter@webtelmex.net.mx

The Challenge of Working and Living in Mexico: Written by psychologist Dr. Marc I. Ehrlich, a comprehensive guide to success-

Clubs & Associations

Alcoholics Anonymous
Union Church.
Reforma 1870, Lomas.
Wednesday at 7:30 p.m.
Information: 5585-1569.

American Legion
Celaya 25, Condesa.
Tel. 5564-3386.

American Society of Mexico
Montes Escandinavos 405, Lomas.
Tel. 5202-4600.

Anezeh Temple (Shrine)
Hegel 416.

Junior League
Platon 211, Polanco.
Tel. 5395-4067.

Lions Club
Ures 13.
Tel. 5564-1260.

Newcomers Club
Union Church, Rm. 205.
Reforma 1870, Lomas.
Tel. 5520-6912.

Rotary Club
Dinamarca 67.

Salvation Army
San Borja 1456, Narvarte.
Tel. 5575-1042.

fully making the cultural transition. Tel.: 5251-0824. E-mail: marc@mehrlich.com

The Guide to Mexico for Business: A comprehensive, introductory guide to doing business with Mexico, published by the American Chamber of Commerce of Mexico. (Relocating to Mexico: The Insider's Guide to Living in Mexico City, Guadalajara, Monterrey is a supplement to the above mentioned publication.)

The Herald, Mexico's new English-language newspaper is a joint venture between The Miami Herald and El Universal. National and world coverage of politics, business and finance, arts and leisure, sports. www.herald.com. Subscriptions: Tel.: 5237-0807.

Services

Languages: Those interested in learning Spanish have several long-established language schools to choose from.

The *Centro de Enseñanza Para Extranjeros* (CEPE) at *Mexico's National Autonomous University* (UNAM) offers six-week group courses, with either morning or afternoon schedules, as well as Mexican studies (history, literature, art), at its campus in the south of the city. Tel. 5622-2470.

Lanser de Mexico, located in the city's posh Lomas de Chapultepec residential and commercial zone, offers language instruction, as well as translation and simultaneous interpretation services. Tel. 5540-0575.

The *Instituto Anglo-Mexicano de Cultura,* located not far from the Zona Rosa district, offers both group sessions and individually-tailored programs. Tel. 5566-7771.

Car Rental: Many major U.S. car rental firms operate throughout Mexico. Some rental companies offer chauffeur-driven cars with hourly or daily rates, such as the Avis Driven program, which can also be contracted for out of town travel.

Alamo. Tel. 5250-0055.
Avis. Tel. 5588-8888.
Budget. Tel. 5566-6800.
Hertz. Tel. 5592-8343.
National. Tel. 5661-5000.
Thrifty. Tel. 5280-5847.

Medical Facilities: For visitors who may require emergency medical care, there are excellent hospitals with modern facilities and English-speaking personnel. The *American British Cowdray Hospital* (ABC, tel. 5230-8000) is affiliated with Baylor University Hospital in Dallas, Texas, and is a member of the American Hospital Association. *Hospital Angeles del Pedregal* (tel. 5652-2011) is also excellent.

Housing. Trying to find a house or apartment can be very time consuming. If you can't dedicate much time to the task of finding the perfect place to live or work, the following relocation companies can help: *Crown Relocations* (tel. 5596-9562), *KIBRIT* (5596-2310), *Brokers Inmobiliarios* (1998-7221), *Rojkind* (5393-6088) and *International Relocation Services* (5291-5344).

Cellular Phones. If you need the convenience of a cellular phone, you can rent one easily from either of Mexico's leading cellular phone companies, *Iusacell* and *Telcel*. These companies require their foreign clients to show valid identification and leave a credit card voucher. Both charge a flat daily rental rate, plus varying rates per minute for local and long-distance calls.

Iusacell has offices in Polanco (tel. 5502-1051) and Zona Rosa (5500-0383). Telcel distributors are located around the city, including in Zona Rosa (5514-6775). The companies deliver the phone to clients wherever they may be. *Skytel* rents pagers at the airport. Tel. 5229-7000.

Couriers. For speedy or overnight deliveries, there are several established courier companies operating in Mexico, most with branches throughout the city.

Airborne Express: Tel. 5203-6811.
Estafeta: Tel. 5270-8301.
Federal Express: Tel. 5228-9904.
DHL: Tel. 5345-7000.
UPS: Tel. 5228-7900.

MONEY EXCHANGE TABLE

First determine the daily exchange rate of the peso; the local newspaper, bank or hotel cashier can tell you. Then choose the closest rate (10.50, 11, 11.50, 12) on the horizontal scale at the top of the chart. Go down this column until you reach the peso amount you wish to convert, as seen in the vertical column on the left. The answer is the approximate dollar value of your pesos. Use the same procedure for converting dollars into pesos.

PESOS TO DOLLARS					DOLLARS TO PESOS				
	10.50	11.00	11.50	12.00		10.50	11.00	11.50	12
PESOS					DOLLARS				
1	0.10	0.09	0.09	0.08	1	10.50	11.00	11.50	12
2	0.19	0.18	0.17	0.17	2	21.00	22.00	23.00	24
3	0.29	0.27	0.26	0.25	3	31.50	33.00	34.50	36
4	0.38	0.36	0.35	0.33	4	42.00	44.00	46.00	48
5	0.48	0.45	0.43	0.42	5	52.50	55.00	57.50	60
6	0.57	0.55	0.52	0.50	6	63.00	66.00	69.00	72
7	0.67	0.64	0.61	0.58	7	73.50	77.00	80.50	84
8	0.76	0.73	0.70	0.67	8	84.00	88.00	92.00	96
9	0.86	0.82	0.78	0.75	9	94.50	99.00	103.50	108
10	0.95	0.91	0.87	0.83	10	105	110	115.00	120
20	1.90	1.82	1.74	1.67	20	210	220	230.00	240
50	4.76	4.55	4.35	4.17	50	525	550	575.00	600
100	9.52	9.09	8.70	8.33	100	1,050	1,100	1,150	1,200
500	48	45	43	42	500	5,250	5,500	5,750	6,000
1,000	95	91	87	83	1,000	10,500	11,000	11,500	12,000
5,000	476	455	435	417	5,000	52,500	55,000	57,500	60,000
10,000	952	909	870	833	10,000	105,000	110,000	115,000	120,000

50 Centavos	1 Peso	2 Pesos
About 5 US cents	About 10 US cents	About 20 US Cents

5 Pesos	10 Pesos	20 Pesos
About 50 US Cents	About 1 US Dollar	About 2 US Dollars

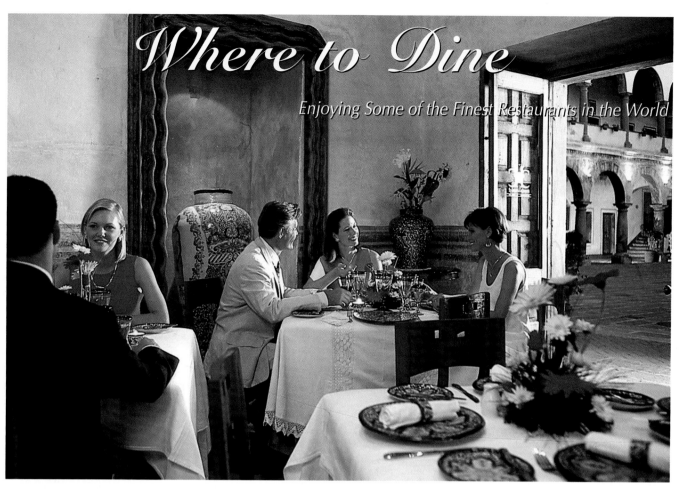

Where to Dine

Enjoying Some of the Finest Restaurants in the World

In a city this size, it's not surprising to find hundreds of restaurants serving cuisine from around the globe. Mexico's affection for classic continental fare and increasing appetite for Italian and Mediterranean cuisine is apparent in the number of restaurants specializing in these types of dishes.

Don't miss the opportunity to try Mexico's own cuisine, especially out of fear that it may be too spicy. Many fine restaurants have opened in recent years that combine home-grown ingredients with sophisticated European cooking techniques and presentation. The happy outcome has been an increase in subtler, more refined, innovative dishes that retain their unique Mexican flavor.

What's more, Mexico's varied regional cuisines can all be sampled in Mexico City, including culinary fare from Puebla, Oaxaca, Yucatan and Veracruz.

Mexicans place a great deal of importance on dining, and meals are more often than not social events that celebrate ties between family, friends and associates. Lunch is the main meal of the day. While restaurants usually open around 1:30 p.m., you won't find many customers until 2. A languid two- to three-hour lunch is typical and tends to push the dinner hour back to about 9:30 or 10 p.m.

Keep in mind, too, that Mexicans dress for dinner; ultra-casual attire is not appreciated at better restaurants. It's always wise to make reservations. Many restaurants close on Sundays, or open for lunch only.

International

Barraca
Insurgentes Sur 905, near World Trade Center
Tel. 5523-9169
Part of an award-winning Mexican chain of restaurants. Its lively, casual ambiance and good food have made it a popular place among locals. International and Mexican menu. Excellent service. Open 1 p.m. to midnight; to 6:30 p.m. Sunday.

Barraca Orraca Oyster Bar & Grill
Palmas 275, Lomas de Chapultepec
Tel. 5520-9084
An elegant New England-style venue for enjoying fish and seafood specialties, including Boston clam chowder and oysters Rockefeller, as well as prime rib. Open 1 p.m. to midnight; to 6:30 p.m. Sunday.

Bondy
Galileo 38, corner of Newton, Polanco
Tel. 5281-1818
This quaint restaurant and pastry shop, housed in a two-story converted residence, is famed for its delicious European-style pastries, brought to you on a platter so you can select your favorite (it won't be easy). Also offers tasty beef, chicken and fish dishes, including grilled tenderloin with mushrooms and paté, Hungarian beef goulash, and roasted veal. Dine indoors or on a covered terrace. Open 9 a.m. to 10 p.m. Closed Monday.

Casa Blanca
Moliere 48, Polanco
Tel. 5281-8151
Shades of terra cotta mark this north African-style setting for Mediterranean cuisine with a Moroccan touch. Begin with Spanish tapas and Greek mezzes, including dates stuffed with paté, or smoked salmon and potato pie, and follow up with such specialties as hearty couscous tomato soup and the "vegetarian dream," featuring eight varieties of eggplant. The *café marroquí*, made with coffee mousse, Kahlua and a double shot of espresso, is a wonderful way to end the meal.

Ciboulette
Plaza Zentro, Polanco
Tel. 5282-0722
An attractive minimalist setting and gourmet Mediterranean cuisine created by French chef Olivier Lombard. Try fresh clams sautéed with butter and parsley, quails cooked in Port, variety of pastas, salads, and soufflés, the house specialty.

Como
Horacio 253, Polanco
Tel. 5250-1596
This popular neighborhood eatery offers a cozy setting for enjoying international cuisine and Italian specialties. Try any of their homemade pastas with a choice of 15 different sauces, four types of ravioli, grilled marinated chicken breast, or Argentinian-style grilled rib-eye. Live

blues Friday and Saturday nights. Extremely popular.

Don Amador
Presidente Masaryk 275, Polanco
Tel. 5282-3478
Named in honor of late restaurateur Amador Prendes, owner of Mexico City's once-famed Prendes restaurant, this place aims to carry on the tradition of fine dining and attentive, personalized service that was the hallmark of his establishment. The menu features charcoal-broiled marinated tuna, *chistorra* (Argentinean sausage) cooked in white wine, rib eye in foie gras, shrimp brochettes, and glazed duck with red wine and honey.

El Campanario
Holiday Inn Zocalo Hotel, Historic Center
Tel. 5521-2121
Breakfast, lunch or dinner with a sweeping view of the Zocalo from its open-air top-floor terrace. Breakfast and lunch buffets, a la carte dinners. Weekend brunch 9 to noon, and *parrillada* (barbecue) 1 to 5 p.m. Open 7 a.m. to 11 p.m.

El Lago
Chapultepec Park, 2nd Section
Tel. 5515-9586
This fine restaurant features floor-to-ceiling glass walls that overlook a lovely lake and spectacular fountain—rainbow spotting is a lunchtime sport. Gourmet international fare, some of it with a Mexican touch. Try the hot and cold foie gras with green salad, red snapper fillet with sesame seed sauce, award-winning pork dish and cappuccino cup with coffee mousse. Extensive wine list, attentive service. Soft violin and piano music from 9:30 p.m. Coat and tie required. Open 1:30 to 11 p.m.; Sunday brunch 11 a.m. to 4 p.m. Reservations recommended.

Fonda Garufa
Michoacan 91-1, Condesa
Tel. 5286-8295
An informal and popular sidewalk eatery specializing in Argentinian-style grilled meats and pastas. Bar serves beer and wine only. Reservations not accepted.

Ici
Tennyson 102, Polanco
Tel. 5281-0736
Mediterranean cuisine in a chic setting with potted palms and a long, sleek bar. Basque chefs Pablo San Roman and Santiago Ortega's creative menu features tabule salad, fettuccini with lobster sauce, tiramisu with cinnamon syrup. Live jazz, bossa nova Thursday to Saturday nights. Open 1 p.m. to 1 a.m.; to 8 p.m. Sunday.

Konditori
Genova 61, Zona Rosa. Tel. 5208-1846
Euler and Masaryk, Polanco. Tel. 5250-1032
Insurgentes Sur 1261. Tel. 5611-1792
Coyoacan 2000. Tel. 5605-4704
Centro Santa Fe mall. Tel. 5258-0820
European-style restaurant-cafes popular for their good food, deli-style sandwiches, pastries and coffees. Zona Rosa branch's covered sidewalk seating is great for people-watching. Popular pancake brunch weekends accompanied by live music. Open 7 a.m. to midnight.

La Galvia
Campos Eliseos 247, Polanco
Tel. 5281-2310
An elegant setting for nouvelle cuisine with a Mexican touch and a new light menu, designed by a nutritionist, that features delicious low-calorie specialties, Try the Portobello mushrooms in balsamic vinaigrette, artichoke hearts with slivers of parmesan, seared yellowfin tuna, or charcoal-grilled venison. Coat and tie required weekdays. Open 1:30 to 6 p.m.; 2 to 11 p.m. Saturday; 2 to 5 p.m. Sunday. Reservations recommended.

La Hacienda
Fiesta Americana Hotel
Tel. 5140-4100
This attractive restaurant features a front-row view of the city's main thoroughfare, Paseo de la Reforma, at Columbus Circle, and well prepared Mexican specialties and fine cuts of beef. Menu highlights include grilled seafood platter with lobster and shrimp, and mesquite-grilled Angus beef with baked potato and cream of spinach. Open 7 a.m. to midnight; from 6 p.m. Saturday. Closed Sunday.

La Hacienda de los Morales
Vazquez de Mella 525, Polanco
Tel. 5096-3055
Set in a former hacienda that flourished on the outskirts of the capital in the 16th century, this restaurant today offers the quintessential Mexican fine dining experience right in the heart of Mexico City. Colonial splendor greets guests at the entrance, where graceful arches give way to a carved stone fountain and cobblestone drive that is lit at night by flaming torches. The hacienda's interior dining rooms, bar area, courtyard, gardens and private rooms are unique settings for any occasion. Have a drink in the charming and relaxing cocktail lounge, with live piano and violin music. The excellent Mexican cuisine and international dishes, as well as the gracious service, reflect the more than 36 years this restaurant has been in business. The extensive menu features red snapper

meuniere with coriander, and squash flower crepes, two of the house specialties, and beef tenderloin tips grilled with sliced onions and mushrooms. Trio music at lunch Sundays in the covered patio. Formal attire/jacket suggested after 6 p.m. Open 1 p.m. to midnight. Reservations recommended.

La Jolla
Marquis Reforma Hotel, near Zona Rosa
Tel. 5229-1200
Gourmet continental cuisine served in an intimate award-winning restaurant decorated with beautiful art deco accents. Menu highlights include fettuccini with smoked salmon, lobster fricassee and luscious desserts. Fixed-price executive menu offered weekdays. Extensive wine list. Private and semiprivate dining rooms available, all overlooking Reforma. Piano music afternoons and evenings. Open 7:30 a.m. to 11 p.m. Closed weekends.

Lamm
Alvaro Obregon 99, corner of Orizaba, Roma
Tel. 5514-8501
Housed in a beautifully renovated European-style mansion, this dynamic venue is not just a restaurant and bar, but a place to pass the time, indoors or out, surrounded by books, art and live music. Traditional Mexican cuisine with a contemporary flair, extensive selection of wines, including by the glass, and ample cocktail menu. Try the cuitlacoche (corn truffle) quiche, chilled avocado soup, tuna in tamarind sauce.

Landó Grill
Emilio Castelar 121, Polanco
Tel. 5282-3052
This exclusive bistro-style restaurant popular with captains of industry, celebrities and political figures offers excellent cuisine and a distinguished yet relaxed setting decked with wood panelling; jazz background music. The varied menu features such signature dishes as Portobello mushroom and artichoke carpaccio, an exquisite rack of lamb, a luscious chocolate bomb. A wide selection of seafood and grilled steaks also available. Extensive wine cellar. Reservations recommended.

Le Cirque
Camino Real Hotel, Polanco
Tel. 5263-8881
The Mexico branch of the famed New York City eatery features the same whimsical setting and gourmet cuisine. Try the foie gras terrine with prunes marinated in port, duck magret in honey and hazelnuts, and Paris-Mexico, a delicious combination of light orange-flavored pastry and bitter chocolate mousse. Lavish buffet brunch served Sundays. Catering service. Open 1 p.m. to 1 a.m.; from 7 p.m. Saturday; from noon to 5 p.m. Sunday.

Ostrica
Parque Duraznos mall, Bosques de Duraznos 39, Bosques de las Lomas
Tel. 5596-2214
An attractive, airy setting for contemporary Mediterranean cuisine. Menu features sea bass

with white wine and mushroom risotto, duck with raspberry sauce and wild rice, apple tart with warm foie gras and honey. Also pizzas and sandwiches. Open 1 p.m. to midnight; 1:30 to 7 p.m. Sunday.

Palm
Presidente InterContinental Hotel, Polanco
Tel. 5327-7700
This branch of the celebrated New York eatery features the same inviting setting, with caricatures of famous celebrities and captains of industry adorning the walls, and winning dishes, including thick cuts of U.S. prime beef and jumbo lobsters from Nova Scotia. Also extensive wine selection and outstanding service. Open 1 to 11 p.m.; 1:30 p.m. to midnight Saturday; to 10 p.m. Sunday.

Pujol
Petrarca 254, Polanco
Tel. 5545-4111
The contemporary international fare often surprises with its innovative combination of ingredients. Try the heart of palm ceviche flavored with oranges, avocados and cilantro, three-fish "fish n' chips" (tuna, salmon and sea bass), lobster spring roll with mango dip, tuna fillet in black sesame seed crust, or rib eye with cabernet sauvignon sauce. Desserts are equally creative, including the pineapple strudel with coconut ice cream. A tasting menu makes the decision making easier. Wine aficionados will love their wide variety by the glass and a selection that's been awarded by Wine Spectator

magazine. Closed Sunday.

Reforma 500
Four Seasons Hotel, near Zona Rosa
Tel. 5230-1818
This AAA Five Diamond award-winning restaurant features contemporary Mediterranean
cuisine served in a sunny plant-filled courtyard
or simple yet elegant dining room. Characteristically light and balanced, dishes are an exquisite blend of flavors and aromas derived
from fine herbs, olive oils, dried fruits, fresh
pastas, and quality meats, fish and seafood.
Open 6:30 a.m. to 11:30 p.m.

Rincon Argentino
Presidente Masaryk 177, Polanco
Tel. 5254-8744
Argentinian home cooking and imported cuts
of beef cooked to your exact order. The bron-
tosaur-sized grilled steaks, ribs, sausages and
other meat specialties are ideal for sharing.
Also wide choice of salads, pastas, grilled fish
or chicken, and for dessert, light mousses made
of seasonal fruits. The impressive ranch-house
setting, complete with blue skies above, looks
just like a Hollywood movie set. Open 12:30
p.m. to midnight; to 10:30 p.m. Sunday.

Salammbo
Fiesta Americana Grand Hotel, Polanco
Tel. 2581-1553
Oversized arm chairs and tabletop statues give
this sleek ultra-urban restaurant a cozy, playful air. The innovative menu matches the creative decor. Try the mussels and morels in a
cream sauce (generous enough for two), fresh
tuna carpaccio with fried parsley, award-winning salmon in black bean crust with cilantro
vinaigrette, and almond terrine with seasonal
fruits.

Salute!
Prado Norte 125, Lomas de Chapultepec
Tel. 5540-3302
A bright, airy setting with an open kitchen,
colorful wall-sized mural, terrace tables shaded
by umbrellas, and Mediterranean-style dishes.

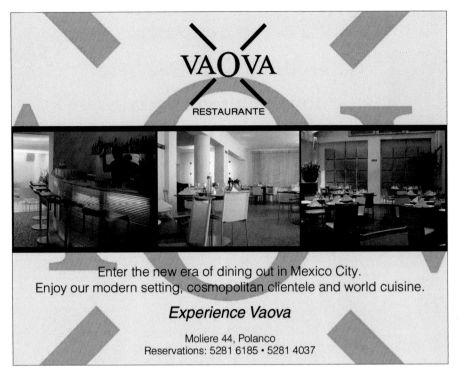
huitlacoche, crepes filled with corn truffle, *chiles rellenos,* poblano peppers stuffed with cheese and ground beef, and *robalo a la Veracruzana,* fillet of sea bass with green olives, tomatoes and other vegetables, as well as shrimp Rockefeller, steak tartare, and roast duck. Top off dinner with a fiery *cafe diablo* and strawberries with Bavarian cream. Wandering trios. Excellent service. Winner of the Dirona Award (2002). Coat and tie suggested. Open 1 p.m. to 1 a.m.; to 10 p.m. Sunday. Reservations recommended.

SeDe Vino
Campos Eliseos 199, Polanco. Tel. 5280-4825
Sheraton Centro Historico Hotel. Tel. 5518-2494
For lovers of wine and those who want to learn more about Mexico's leading wineries, this sleek and stylish wine bar offers 50 varieties from around the world by the glass and about 130 varieties by the bottle. Prices range from 30 to 145 pesos a glass; up to 250 pesos for the sparkling wines. There's a range of tasty tapas to accompany your selections. Polanco branch open noon to midnight, except Sunday; Sheraton branch open noon to 10 p.m. daily.

Sir Winston Churchill's
Avila Camacho 67, Polanco
Tel. 5280-6070
With a name like that, how could it not be authentic? Owners Jane and Raymundo Fernandez remodeled a Tudor-style mansion with meticulous authenticity. The wood panelling, beamed ceilings and billiard room are all traditionally British, as is the food. Specialties include trout and salmon paté, oxtail soup, sword of seafood in a Romesco sauce, prime rib of roast beef with Yorkshire pudding, Cambridge sausages and, for dessert, sherry trifle and Irish coffee. Piano music from 3 to 11 p.m. Private dining rooms available for six or as many as 50 people. Excellent wine cellar. Jackets required, except on Saturday afternoon. Open 1 p.m. to 1 a.m. Closed Sunday. Reservations recommended.

Solea
W Hotel, Polanco
Tel. 9138-1800
A striking contemporary setting, with seating areas separated by red glass partitions and an eye-catching sunken 12-seat dining room. The innovative coastal cuisine features fresh seafood from both the Caribbean and Pacific. A blend of local ingredients and Asian flair, the menu offers cod-filled squash flower tempura, crab soup with coriander and corn cake, whole roasted fish, sea bass with wild mushrooms, and red snapper with chorizo. Breakfast and lunch are served on the terrace, a popular spot for nighttime drinks and a light meal.

Vaova
Moliere 44, Polanco
Tel. 5281-4037
Located in Mexico City's fast-growing restaurant row, this new addition to the local dining scene is already a hit with trend setters. A striking modern setting sets the stage for an eclectic offering of global cuisine. Architect Daniel Estebaranz's use of light gives the place a re-

Try the Caesar salad with deep-fried calamari and anchovies, homemade pastas, and grilled rib eye or salmon. Very popular. Branch at Escenaria San Jeronimo 263 (tel. 5616-2333).

San Angel Inn
Diego Rivera 50, San Angel

Tel. 5616-1402
A magnificently restored 18th-century hacienda houses this award-winning restaurant. Have a margarita around the elegant flower-filled patio, then sample selections from the hors d'oeuvre table. Highlights from the Mexican and international menu include *crepas de*

laxed, fun and lively atmosphere. Executive chef Juan Pablo Rullan's innovative menu brings together haute cuisine from different parts of the world, including Mexican-style lobster pozole, Japanese shabu-shabu, fine Mediterranean carpaccios, and exquisite coastal ceviches. There's a good list of wines to accompany your selections. Open 1:30 to 6 p.m. Sunday and Monday; to 11:30 p.m. Tuesday and Wednesday; to 12:30 a.m. Thursday and Saturday. Tel. 5281-6185.

Mexican

Aguila y Sol
Moliere 42, Polanco
Tel. 5281-8354
Reinventing the concept of Mexican cooking, this restaurant features New Mexican Cuisine that combines traditional ingredients in a whole new way. Try the guacamole with *requeson* cheese and pomegranate seeds, squash blossom soup with almonds, red snapper a la marimba Veracruzana, chicken breast in pistachio *pipian,* or grilled rib eye with Don Porfirio-style salsa *borracha* and beans. Open 1:30 p.m. to 1 a.m.; Sunday to 5:30 p.m.

Arroyo
Insurgentes Sur 4003, Tlalpan
Tel. 5573-4322
Like a small Mexican town unto itself (including a bullfighting ring that can seat a thousand). Traditional Mexican dishes, tequila, homemade tortillas, plus folkloric singing and dancing every afternoon starting at 4. On Saturdays, Mexican families come to see a *novillada* (bullfight) and lunch afterwards. Bullfights May through August. Open 8 a.m. to 7 p.m.

Cafe Tacuba
Tacuba 28, Historic Center
Tel. 5521-2048
A picturesque restaurant serving traditional Mexican food since 1913, including enchiladas, *chiles rellenos,* and beef in *mole.* The tile work on the walls is wonderful. Entertainment Friday and Saturday nights. Very popular for lunch on weekends. Open 8 a.m. to 11:30 p.m.

Casa Merlos
Victoriano Zepeda 80, behind Observatorio
Tel. 5277-4360
Off the beaten track, but well worth it for its incomparable Pueblan cuisine. Open 1 to 6 p.m. Thursday to Sunday.

Cualli
Camino Real Aeropuerto Hotel
Tel. 3003-0033
The ideal oasis before, after and between flights, this restaurant offers a tranquil, elegant setting for enjoying refined Mexican cuisine as well as international dishes. Try the chicken breast stuffed with squash flowers, and mango mousse for dessert. Open 7 a.m. to 11 p.m. Closed Sunday.

El Bajio
Cuitlahuac 2709, Azcapotzalco
Tel. 5341-9889

Off the beaten track, but famed nevertheless for its delicious homestyle Mexican cooking and friendly ambiance. Dishes from all parts of the country, tasty *carnitas,* handmade tortillas, terrific typical breakfasts. Open 8 a.m. to 7 p.m.; 9 a.m. to 6:30 p.m. weekends.

Fonda El Refugio
Liverpool 166, Zona Rosa
Tel. 5525-8128
In business for 50 years, this leading Mexican restaurant features truly authentic cuisine in a charming, tranquil setting—a converted home decorated with folk art and handicrafts. An English-language menu and the English-speaking staff can help you select the perfect dish. Everything from the fresh guacamole to the *crema quemada* dessert is excellent. Winner of the Holiday Magazine and Dirona (Distinguished Restaurants of North America) awards. Open 1 p.m. to 2 a.m.; to 10 p.m. Sunday.

Gallo Centenario
Republica de Cuba 79, Historic Center
Tel. 5521-7866
Turn-of-the-century opulence is reflected in the hand-painted walls, antique-filled armoires and elaborate table settings, a sense of whimsy is evident in the collection of roosters that peer out from unexpected corners. Refined Mexican cuisine. Open 1:30 p.m. to 1 a.m.; to 2 a.m. Saturday; to 6 p.m. Sunday.

Hacienda El Mortero
NH Hotel, Zona Rosa

Tel. 5228-9928

Dinner a la carte, breakfast and lunch buffets. Try the *ceviche*, chunks of tangy fish marinated in lemon with chopped onion, parsley and serrano chili; *queso fundido*, Mexican-style cheese fondue with Argentinian lean sausage and flour tortillas; and *mixiote de pollo*, chicken marinated in a piquant guajillo chili sauce and slow cooked in a maguey leaf. Live music in the afternoons. Open 7 to 1 a.m.

Hosteria de Santo Domingo

Belisario Dominguez 72, Historic Center
Tel. 5526-5276

In business since 1860, it claims to be the oldest restaurant in town. The traditional Mexican fare features *pechuga ranchera a la nata*, ten-der chicken breast in a delicious cream sauce you'll want to scoop up with the fresh baked tortillas, and *chiles en nogada*, poblano peppers stuffed with ground beef and raisins, and covered in walnut sauce, a seasonal dish that's served here year-round. Very picturesque and popular. Piano and violin duet. Open 9 a.m. to 10 p.m.

Izote

Presidente Masaryk 513, Polanco
Tel. 5280-1671

Contemporary Mexican cuisine by well-known Mexican chef Patricia Quintana. Try the assorted tamales, including squash blossom, Acapulco-style ceviche, lobster enchiladas in *pipian verde*, shrimp in tamarind *mole*, or fish in pulque essence. Open 1 p.m. to midnight; to 6 p.m. Sunday.

La Calle

Centro Santa Fe mall
Tel. 5257-0885

Part of an award-winning Mexican chain of restaurants, this spot features delicious regional Mexican dishes in a setting resembling a typical folkloric Mexico City street circa 1940, complete with sidewalk fruit stands, overhead balconies and a road leading to a mural of a cityscape twinkling with lights. Don't miss the *queso frito en salsa verde*, a spicy crunchy treat. Excellent service. Open 1 p.m. to midnight; to 6:30 p.m. Sunday.

La Casa de las Sirenas

Guatemala 32, Historic Center
Tel. 5704-3225

A turn-of-the-century home converted into a multilevel restaurant with a ground-floor cantina. Tables indoors or on a top-floor terrace with a view of the cathedral. Try the guacamole accompanied by crispy pork rind, *cetas al chipotle con queso fundido* (sizzling mushrooms in a cheesy chili broth), and *gallina al mango* (tender chicken in a sweet-and-sour sauce). Open for breakfast, lunch and dinner.

La Destileria

Pabellon Polanco mall
Tel. 5557-8336

Dine in a setting that pays tribute to tequila with colorful murals and antique souvenirs of its early production days. You can even devise your own taste test; they have more than 100 varieties of Mexico's national drink. Tasty Mexican cuisine, especially dishes from Jalisco—tequila country—and grilled meats. Indoor and outdoor seating under umbrellas. Open 1 p.m. to midnight; to 6:30 p.m. Sunday.

La Valentina

Plaza Mazarik mall, Polanco. Tel. 5282-2297
La Piazza, near Interlomas mall. Tel. 5290-3848

A treat for the senses, these establishments offer attractive hacienda-style surroundings, great Mexican cuisine, and romantic trio music in the evenings from 9 p.m. to midnight. Favorite menu items include the seasoned fish tacos Don Elias, *pollo a la fogata* (blackened marinated chicken), or *filete mextli* (tender beef fillet in a creamy huitlacoche sauce). The warm chocolate cake with vanilla ice cream is a favorite dessert. Open 1 p.m. to midnight; to 10 p.m. Sunday.

Los Almendros

Campos Eliseos 164, Polanco. Tel. 5531-6646
Insurgentes Sur 1759. Tel. 5661-2658

Great Yucatecan restaurants that bring the look, feel and famed cuisine of that region to the big city. Begin with the excellent *tacos de venado* (venison tacos) or *taquitos de cochinita pibil* (shredded pork marinated in a spicy sauce and wrapped in flour tortillas). Follow with the sizzling grilled venison or crisp-fried shrimp in a coconut shell. Try an ice cold Montejo beer, Yucatan's local brew. At the Polanco branch a

LA VALENTINA POLANCO, PRESIDENTE MASARYK 393 TEL 52822297
INTERLOMAS LA PIAZZA, BLVD INTERLOMAS 401 TEL 52903848 EXT 226

trova Yucateca or marimba band plays at lunch and dinner. Open 7:30 a.m. to midnight; 8 a.m. to midnight Saturday; 8 a.m. to 10 p.m. Sunday.

French

Au Pied de Cochon
Presidente InterContinental Hotel, Polanco
Tel. 5327-7766
A favorite of captains of industry, politicians and celebrities, this faithful replica of the popular French bistro offers a relaxed yet elegant setting, and an extensive menu featuring a variety of seafood, classic onion soup, and the dish it was named after, pig's knuckles. Excellent breakfast specials. Open 24 hours a day.

Le Bouchon
Julio Verne 102, at Virgilio, Polanco
Tel. 5281-7902
Styled after a "bouchon Lyonnais," or family restaurant in Lyon, this attractive brasserie features country-style specialties served indoors or in a sunny open-air patio. Menu highlights include poached egg salad with croutons and bacon, mussels in white wine, and other French classics.

Les Moustaches
Rio Sena 88, near Zona Rosa
Tel. 5533-3390
Ideally located two blocks from "The Angel" monument and the U.S. embassy, this outstanding restaurant has over 30 years consistently ranked among the city's top 10 dining establishments, thanks to its fine cuisine and impeccable service in an elegant atmosphere. Housed in a charming, European-style mansion, it offers diners a choice of settings: a sleek, modern ground-floor dining room, an elegant "fin de siecle" upstairs salon, private rooms, and a cozy bar. Enjoy the classics of French cuisine and exquisite desserts, as well as three types of champagne by the glass. Private dining rooms for groups of 4 to 60 or more people at no extra charge. Open 1 p.m. to midnight. Closed Sunday.

Italian

Alfredo di Roma
Presidente InterContinental Hotel, Polanco
Tel. 5327-7766
The Mexico City branch of the Italian restaurant famed for its fettuccini Alfredo, prepared table-side with rich cream, light semolina noodles, and fresh parmesan cheese. The dishes are complemented by fine wines and attentive service. Open 1 to 11:30 p.m.; to 5 p.m. Sunday.

Bice Bistro
Camino Real Hotel, Polanco
Tel. 5263-8888
Sophisticated Italian cuisine from Tuscany in an elegant, contemporary art deco setting. Highlights from the extensive menu include the grilled vegetable tower with goat cheese and tomato sauce, veal osso bucco with saffron rice, prime beef in cognac and Madagascar

pepper, and ricotta cheesecake topped with raspberries. Open 7 a.m. to 11 p.m.; 1 p.m. to 12:30 a.m. Saturday; to 5:30 p.m. Sunday.

Casa Rolandi
Presidente Masaryk 110, Polanco
Tel. 9126-0256

An extravagantly designed two-story restaurant promising a memorable dining experience. Glass cases displaying designer luxury items add to the lavish setting. Chef-owner Fabio Peiti's Swiss-Italian cooking features the enhanced flavors of a wood-burning oven, fresh baked bread, and a changing weekly menu that highlights seasonal ingredients. Try the lobster-filled black raviolis topped with lobster sauce, roasted veal in white wine and rosemary, grilled whole fish, and gourmet pizzas. Second-floor piano bar with live music from 9 p.m. Open 1:30 p.m. to 2 a.m.; to 6 p.m. Sunday.

Il Punto
Emilio Castelar 213, Polanco
Tel. 5280-3623
This attractive restaurant, with covered sidewalk seating, offers a culinary tour of Italy with hearty dishes from the country's different provinces. Favorite menu items include imported Italian prosciutto di Parma; farfalle al tequila, short pasta with shrimp in a tequila cream sauce; juicy veal scallopine with grilled vegetables and mixed mushrooms in lemon; and such sumptuous desserts as Pavlova, merengue topped with fresh seasonal fruits, or cheese mousse with raspberries. Open 1 p.m. to 1 a.m. Reservations recommended.

La Bottiglia
Edgar Allan Poe 8, Polanco
Tel. 5280-0609
Traditional Italian fare served in a cozy setting. Open 8 a.m. to 11:30 p.m.; to 6:30 p.m. Sunday.

La Griglia
JW Marriott Hotel, Polanco
Tel. 5999-0000
Intimate and sophisticated with a well-crafted Italian/Mediterranean menu designed by Italian head chef Enzo Fornito. Extensive anti-

pasto bar, homemade pasta, beef, chicken and seafood specialties, luscious desserts. Open 7 a.m. to 11 p.m. Closed Saturday

Maremma
Bosques de Duraznos 39, Bosques de las Lomas
Tel. 5596-2214
A casual, modern setting for regional specialties from Tuscany, including more than 20 different antipasto plates prepared daily and a variety of beef, fish, poultry, pasta and pizza specialties made with fine herbs, olive oil, basil and other classic Italian ingredients. Open 1 p.m. to midnight; to 1 a.m. Thursday to Saturday. A wine bar-lounge offers more than 80 varieties to choose from.

Melée
Pabellon Polanco mall
Tel. 5395-5500
Casual wood-panelled setting with overhead ceiling fans and a menu that offers many traditional favorites. The generous portions of select cuts of beef, pastas, pizzas and salads are ideal for sharing. Wine served in soda glasses adds to the casual atmosphere. Open 1 p.m. to midnight; to 1 a.m. Friday and Saturday; to 9 p.m. Sunday.

Stuffa
Centro Santa Fe mall
Tel. 5570-8223
A rustic setting for traditional Italian favorites, from pizzas and pastas to charcoal-broiled specialties. Menu features oven-baked veal osso bucco in red wine and rosemary sauce, Mediterranean-style sea bass, and charcoal-broiled salmon or shrimp brochettes, tuna steak, rib eye or chicken. Open for lunch and dinner.

Tuscan Grill
Presidente Masaryk 275, second floor, Polanco
Tel. 5282-3291
Sleek and contemporary, with a great selection of wines in all price ranges. Begin with the *charcuteria Toscana,* a platter of prosciutto, panceta, salami, warm bread and cheese, and follow with the Tuscan Grill chicken or artichoke tortellini with fresh ricotta bathed in a buttery, tomato-based herb sauce.

Portuguese

Casa Portuguesa
Emilio Castelar 121-K, Polanco
Tel. 5281-0075
A slice of Portugal in Mexico, this intimate restaurant with sidewalk tables overlooking a park offers traditional cuisine, music and ambiance. Try the national staple, *bacalhau* (codfish), prepared a number of creative ways, from charcoal grilled with a touch of olive oil to au gratin, breaded and deep fried as croquettes, marinated and tossed with a fresh salad. Other favorite dishes include *sardinas* and *feijoada.* The live music (a talented singer accompanied by string instruments) is a treat. Very popular. Open 1 to 10:30 p.m.; to 11:30 p.m. Thursday to Saturday; 10 a.m. to 6 p.m. Sunday. Closed Monday.

THE BEST RESTAURANTS ARE IN OUR GOURMET CENTER

French cuisine

The authentic King of Fettuccine

Serving jumbo lobsters and prime aged beef

Mexican cuisine

You'll always find good taste at the Presidente Inter-Continental's specialty restaurants. Reservations: 55 5327 7700

PRESIDENTE
INTERCONTINENTAL.
MEXICO

Campos Eliseos 218, Polanco Mexico City

Thai Gardens Restaurant

Seafood

Acqua
Presidente Masaryk 275, Polanco
Tel. 5282-3292
An informal, light-filled setting for seafood and casual fare. Menu offers green curried shrimp, tropical ceviche, and banana leaf wrapped red snapper in red curry, as well as California-style pizza and Black Angus burgers.

Bistrot Central
Presidente Masaryk 214
Tel. 5280-7800
From the enormous fish tanks and open kitchen to the seafood market-style displays of fresh fish and seafood, this innovative spot promises a memorable experience. Design your own dish or choose from an extensive menu that features charcoal-grilled specialties. Beef, lamb, poultry also available. Extensive selection of wines.

El Danubio
Republica de Uruguay 3, Historic Center
Tel. 5521-0912
Steeped in nostalgia, with old-fashioned photographs covering the walls, and praised for its fine fish and seafood dishes, this place has been a favorite with area bankers and businessmen for more than 50 years. Try the grilled crayfish, red or green fish soup, and Gulf of Mexico stone crabs. Open 1 to 10 p.m.

La Pigua
Alejandro Dumas 16, Polanco
Tel. 5281-1302
The Mexico City branch of Campeche's popular fish and seafood restaurant features the same delectable specialties of the Gulf Coast and Yucatan Peninsula in a charming mansion

dating from the early 1900s. Don't miss the crisp coconut jumbo shrimp served in a coconut shell with apple chutney, Sir Francis calamari with almonds and *guajillo* chili, excellent seafood salads, and coconut desserts. Piano player Thursday to Saturday nights. Open 1:30 to 11 p.m.

Spanish

Centro Castellano
Camino Real Hotel, Polanco
Tel. 5263-8888
A new branch of a Mexico City favorite since 1952, this spot serves classic Spanish cuisine. Popular menu items include suckling pig roasted in a wood-burning oven, jumbo shrimp, baby lamb, and *bacalao a la Vizcaina* (codfish simmered in a spicy sauce). The *tartaletas de arroz con leche*, or rice pudding tarts, are a perfect way to end a meal. Open for lunch and dinner. Closed Sunday.

Tezka
Royal Zona Rosa Hotel
Tel. 5228-9918
The acclaimed gourmet cuisine features the traditional dishes (especially seafood) of Spain's coastal Basque region. Try the asparagus soup with shrimp and fried leeks, *huachinango* (red snapper) with crisp vegetable strips in a light walnut vinaigrette, and, for dessert, coconut soup with mango cubes and lemon butter ice cream. Open 1 to 5 p.m. for lunch Monday to Saturday and 8 to 11 p.m. for dinner Thursday and Friday. Closed Sunday. Branch at Royal Pedregal hotel offers the same menu, but operates with different hours. Reservations recommended.

Torre de Castilla
Esopo 31, Polanco
Tel. 5281-0906
A medieval castle decked with swords, shields and armor sets the stage for Spanish cuisine. This newest addition to the Centro Castellano restaurant group features specialties from Spain's different regions, including dishes from the Basque provinces and Andalusia. Try the jumbo shrimp, smoked marlin with special *habanero* sauce, wood-burning oven-baked lamb, and Segovia-style roasted suckling pig. Patio and terrace dining, private wine cellar-dining rooms. Open 1 to 11 p.m.; to 7 p.m. Sunday.

Chinese

Hunan
Reforma 2210, Lomas. Tel. 5596-5011
G. Ogazon 102, San Angel. Tel. 5661-6414
A sleek, elegant and exclusive Chinese restaurant specializing in the Hunan-style cuisine of chef James Wang. Menu highlights include a warm appetizer for two with sweet-and-sour pork ribs, spring rolls, and fried dumplings; Peking duck; and crispy shrimp in a honey dip. Open 1:30 p.m. to midnight; to 6 p.m. Sunday.

Luau
Niza 38-B, Zona Rosa
Tel. 5525-7474
In business for over 40 years, this restaurant features authentic Chinese cuisine and decor in a romantic setting with a fountain. Specialties include roast duck, sweet-and-sour pork, orange-flavored chicken. Take out and delivery service. Open noon to 11 p.m.; to midnight Friday and Saturday; to 10 p.m. Sunday.

Oriental

China Grill
Camino Real Hotel, Polanco
Tel. 5263-8888
The newly opened Mexico branch of the famed Miami restaurant features the same gourmet international fare with an Oriental touch. Menu highlights include crunchy calamari salad, plum-glazed pork ribs with sesame seeds, and Szechuan-style broiled beef. Also extensive sushi bar.

Noodles

Moliere 50, Polanco
Tel. 5281-8111

A pair of lions welcome diners to this Oriental oasis featuring pan-Asian cuisine, a blend of Thai, Vietnamese, Chinese, Malaysian, Filipino, Balinese and Fijian culinary traditions. Try their assortment of noodle dishes (which, they recommend, should be slurped like fine wine "to bring out their subtle flavors") and other specialties, including dancing shrimp dim sum with ginger-peach dip, crispy catfish salad with spicy mango sauce, Atlantic noodle soup with vermicelli and salmon in coconut milk. Accompany with sake served in a bamboo shoot.

O'mei

Nikko Hotel, Polanco
Tel. 5281-6828

The best of Oriental cuisine—a combination of Chinese, Thai and Vietnamese culinary traditions—in a light-filled, contemporary setting. The menu features Peking duck elegantly served in two courses—a first course of crispy duck skin wrapped in mandarin pancakes and a second course of minced, stir-fried duck and vegetables in a lettuce pouch. Other specialties include basil chicken and red curry coconut beef. Watch the talented chefs (from China, Vietnam and Hong Kong) prepare your dishes in their open kitchen. Private rooms available. Open 1:30 to 5 p.m. and 7:30 to 11 p.m., 1:30 to 6 p.m. Sunday.

Japanese

Benkay

Nikko Hotel, Polanco
Tel. 5283-8700

Enjoy authentic, exotic Japanese cuisine in a simple setting with tables facing a glass-enclosed bubbling brook, sushi bar and private tatami rooms. Chef's suggestions include asparagus rolled with smoked salmon, marinated jelly fish, and grilled duck or eel with Teriyaki sauce. Try the lovely green tea ice cream. Prices are steep, dishes are spare but elaborate. Open 7 to 10:30 a.m., 1:30 to 5:30 p.m. and 7:30 to 11 p.m.; Sunday buffet 1:30 to 5:30 p.m. Reservations recommended.

Teppan Grill & Tong Fong Sake Bar

Nikko Hotel, Polanco
Tel. 5283-8700

The specialty is fine cuts of national and imported beef, fish and seafood prepared at your table teppanyaki-style by expert cooks. Also sushi, kushiage and tempura. The service is excellent and the food authentic. The bar stocks an extensive variety of sake and Japanese-style snacks. Pleasant atmosphere, especially in the evenings. Open 1:30 to 11 p.m. Bar open 7:30 to 11 p.m., except Sunday.

Thai

Thai Gardens

Calderon de la Barca 72, Polanco
Tel. 5281-3850

Beautiful tropical palms by a cooling fountain set the tone for exotic Thai cuisine and warm, attentive Oriental-style service. Try the house specialty, "floating market," a hot and spicy seafood soup of shrimp, squid and mussels steeped in the Oriental aromas of lemongrass and ginger. Also notable are the tasting menu, for those who want to get a taste of everything, and *pla ma nao,* steamed sea bass flavored with chili and lemon. Desserts include tropical fruits with creamy *flan* and chocolate mousse with coconut. Open 2 p.m. to midnight; to 1 a.m. Thursday to Saturday; to 6 p.m. Sunday.

Tacos

El Tizoncito

Tamaulipas 122, Condesa

Tel. 5286-7819

People from all walks of life come here for Mexico's staple food in its many variations. Try the gyro-style *tacos al pastor* topped with shredded pork, and delicious *quesadillas* with cheese and vegetable fillings. Bustling, especially late at night. Branches throughout the city.

Tako's Takos

Edgar Allan Poe 14-A, Polanco
Tel. 5280-8948

Unlike your more traditional *taqueria,* this upscale venue lets you accompany your tacos and *quesadillas* with a tequila or glass of wine and top off your meal with a cappuccino or espresso. Indoor or sidewalk seating. Open 1 p.m. to midnight.

THAÏ GARDENS

Royal Thaï Cuisine

Jorge Juan, 5
28001 Madrid
Tel. 91 577 88 84

Diputación, 273
08007 Barcelona
Tel. 93 487 98 98

Calderón de la Barca, 72
Col. Polanco, México, D.F.
Tel. (52 55) 5281 3850

Avenue de la Cote d'Emeraude s/n
Anfa (Casablanca)
Tel. (212) 2279 7579

Paris – Opening in June 2004

Nightlife

Mexico City nightspots, ranging from mariachi music venues to techno lounges, are generally concentrated in a few key neighborhoods such as Condesa, Roma, Polanco and the Centro Historico.

Legendary *Plaza Garibaldi,* a gritty square located northwest of the Zocalo, is where the city's mariachi bands hang out, taking requests (the going rate is about 50 pesos a song) while waiting to be hired to play at a wedding, birthday or sidewalk serenade. If you want to enjoy the revelry indoors, one of the more reputable cantinas on the plaza is *Tenampa.* Leave your valuables at home; this is a heavily trafficked area, attracting people from all walks of life.

Folkloric shows are staged at the *Arroyo* restaurant. Mariachi, marimba, *estudiantina* and other types of Mexican music can be heard at *La Hacienda de los Morales* and *Cafe Tacuba* restaurants, and at the *Jorongo* nightclub. See their individual listings for more details.

Palacio de Bellas Artes (Palace of Fine Arts) hosts concerts, operas and, most important, performances of the National Folkloric Ballet. The *National Auditorium* hosts frequent concerts by popular Mexican entertainers as well as renowned international artists.

The major hotels have popular lobby bars, some with entertainment, including the W, which attracts a young crowd, the Presidente InterContinental, JW Marriott, Camino Real and Nikko.

Movie houses are abundant but some films arrive about three months after their U.S. releases. Most are screened in the original language with Spanish subtitles, unless they are animations or children's films. Admission is about half of the price back home.

For listings of movies, concerts, and other cultural and entertainment events, consult *Donde Ir* and *Tiempo Libre* magazines, both available at newsstands.

Finally, keep the following tips in mind:
• Nightlife starts later here. Many bars and discos don't open till at least 9:30 p.m., with peak hours being from midnight to 2 a.m. At most nightclubs, shows don't begin before 11 p.m.
• Remember the altitude—one drink packs the punch of two, at least.
• Always have the number of a *sitio,* or radio cab company, with you, or ask your waiter to call one for you. Never flag a taxi in the evenings.

Cantinas

Centenario
Vicente Suarez 42, Condesa
One of the neighborhood's most popular spots for soaking up Mexican atmosphere.

El Nivel
Moneda 2, Historic Center
Tel. 5522-9755
Located on the main square, this cantina is reputedly the city's first. Open from noon, except Sunday.

Karisma
Campos Eliseos 219, Polanco
Tel. 5280-1872
People watch from sidewlk tables or play dominos or *cubilete* (similar to poker, but louder and played with dice) and listen to Mexican music. Good variety of tequilas and Mexican snacks. Noisy but fun.

La Casa de las Sirenas
Guatemala 32, Historic Center
Tel. 5704-3465
This charming colonial-era building behind the cathedral houses a cozy ground-floor cantina and tequila bar. Open Thursday to Saturday, 9 p.m. to 2 a.m.

La Guadalupana
Higuera 14, Coyoacan
Tel. 5554-6253
Founded in 1932, this colorful cantina is situated in one of the city's most picturesque colonial-era neighborhoods. Open 1 to 11 p.m., except Sunday.

La Opera
Cinco de Mayo 10, Historic Center
Tel. 5512-8959
An authentic 19th-century cantina with a lot of tradition. Adding to the charm of its stately period decor and architecture is a bullet hole in the ceiling courtesy of Pancho Villa. Great margaritas and Mexican snacks. Guitar playing trio or quartet from 5 p.m. Thursday to Saturday. Open 1 p.m. to midnight. Closed Sunday.

Tenampa
Plaza Garibaldi 12, Historic Center
Tel. 5526-6176
One of the best spots at "mariachi square," this cantina was founded in 1925 and is still going strong. Colorful and boisterous, with paintings paying homage to Mexican movie idols and roving mariachi bands playing all at once. Open 1 p.m. to 3 a.m.

Bars

Blue Lounge
Camino Real Hotel, Polanco
Tel. 5263-8888
A very liquid environment—tables are "suspended" over a pool—for martinis and other cocktails. Live music. Very popular.

Celtics
Tamaulipas 36, Condesa
Tel. 5211-9081
A trendy pub popular for its roomy bar and cozy "living room," as well as Guinness, beer-battered shrimp, and Irish Orgasm (a blend of amaretto, hazelnut liqueur and Irish Cream).

Colmillo
Versailles 52, Roma
Tel. 5553-0262
A spacious lounge bar with a separate, sunken dance area and top floor jazz club. The eclectic music gives way to techno as the night wears on. Guinness beer. Cover charge: 65 pesos. Open Wednesday to Saturday from 10 p.m.

El Bar
Four Seasons Hotel, near Zona Rosa
Tel. 5230-1818
Wood panelling, book-laden shelves, plush sofas and armchairs evoke the refined yet cozy atmosphere of a private English library; also terrace seating. An extensive selection of wine, national and imported beer, champagne by the glass, more than 110 brands of tequila, and mezcal from Oaxaca. If you'd like a fine imported cigar to go with any of that, they have them too. Hors d'oeuvres served throughout the day. String music in the evening. Open 1 p.m. to 1 a.m.; to midnight Sunday.

El Estribo
Vazquez de Mella 525, Polanco
Tel. 5096-3055
Part of La Hacienda de los Morales restaurant, a beautifully restored 16th-century hacienda, this cozy bar has live music and a large selection of tequilas.

El Hijo del Cuervo
Plaza Jardin Centenario 17, Coyoacan
Tel. 5659-8959
Nice location, overlooking the main square. The decor is simple and sleek, and the bar attracts a young crowd. Drinks and a snack menu. Adjoining rooms feature poetry readings, bands, variety shows. Open 1 p.m. to 1 a.m.

Gallo Centenario
Republica de Cuba 79, Historic Center
Tel. 5521-7866
Occupying the ground floor of a restored 17-century mansion, this picturesque bar recalls an opulent turn-of-the-century bordello. Talented wandering trios and lively rumba bands entertain nightly. Best nights are Thursday, Friday and Saturday. Open 1 p.m. to 2 a.m.; to 8 p.m. Sunday.

Hard Rock Cafe

Campos Eliseos 290, Polanco
Tel. 5327-7100
The Mexico City branch of the world-famous rock 'n' roll haven has live music, mostly by cover bands, Tuesday to Saturday nights. Next-door concert venue features international artists. One of the few bars open late on a Sunday night. Open 1 p.m. to 2 a.m.

La Martinera

Plaza Mazarik mall, Polanco
Tel. 5281-7235
Trendy martini bar with lounge music, acid jazz. Open from 1 p.m.

Moon Bar

Camino Real Hotel, Polanco
Tel. 5263-8888
Drinks under the stars, in a candle-lit garden setting decked with plush sofas, water beds, canopies. Try the dragon sushi roll and lychee martini. Open Friday and Saturday from 8 p.m. to 2 a.m.

Shelty

Nikko Hotel, Polanco
Tel. 5283-8700
An attractive, wood-panelled piano bar resembling a swank British pub. A nice place to meet, have a drink and savor their exquisite hors d'oeuvres. Live piano music in the evenings. Open 4 p.m. to 1 a.m.; to midnight Sunday.

The Dubliner

Mariano Escobedo 434, Polanco
Tel. 5250-8105
This Irish-style pub features an authentic atmosphere, Guinness and other imported beers. Open noon to 2 a.m.

Windows

Av. de las Naciones 1, Napoles
Tel. 5628-8304
Part of a revolving restaurant on the 45th floor of the World Trade Center, offering a 360-degree panoramic view of the city every 45 minutes. Snack and dinner menu available. Open from 1 p.m.

Whiskey Bar

W Hotel, Polanco
Tel. 9138-1800
The hotel's popular lobby bar, decked with inviting sofas, attracts a young crowd.

Yuppie's Sports Cafe

Genova 34, Zona Rosa
Tel. 5208-2267
Wall-to-wall sports memorabilia and casual pub setting. Great for watching sporting events. Also covered sidewalk seating. Open 1 p.m. to 1 a.m.

Zipango

At the Hipodromo (race track)
Tel. 2122-3000
A trendy, multilevel restaurant-bar and sportsbook with a view of the race track. TV monitors broadcast races and sporting events from around the world. Open till 3 a.m.

Tropical Music

Bar Leon

Republica de Brasil 5, Historic Center
Tel. 5510-3093
A tropical music haven featuring live music and small but often packed dance floor. Fun but grungy. Free salsa classes Saturdays, 5 to 7 p.m. Open Wednesday to Saturday from 9 p.m. to 3 a.m. Reservations suggested weekends.

Barfly

Plaza Mazarik mall, Polanco
Tel. 5282-2906
An intimate two-level bar featuring good Cuban dance bands from 11 p.m. Small dance floor. Dinner and snack menu. Cover charge. Open Tuesday to Saturday from 8 p.m.

La Bodeguita del Medio

Cozumel 37, Roma. Tel. 5553-0246
Insurgentes Sur 1798. Tel. 5661-4400
Replica of the celebrated 1940s Havana nightclub famed for its autograph-covered walls. Cuban food, music and ambiance. Try a *mojito*, the island's favorite drink. Open from 2 p.m.

Mama Rumba

Queretaro 230, Roma. Tel. 5564-6920
Plaza San Jacinto 23, San Angel
Tel. 5550-8099
Lively restaurant-bar featuring Caribbean music. Bands play Tuesday to Saturday from 9 p.m. Cover charge.

Nightclubs

El Habito

Madrid 13, Coyoacan
Tel. 5659-6305
Inspired social and political satire based on current events, as well as musical shows offering everything from burlesque to tango. All in Spanish, but worthwhile if you've mastered it. Shows Friday and Saturday from 10:30 p.m. Reservations a must.

Jorongo Bar

Sheraton Maria Isabel Hotel, near Zona Rosa
Tel. 5242-5555
For a night out *a la Mexicana*. In business for 40 years, this nightclub features excellent mariachi bands and romantic trios. Cover charge. Open 7 p.m. to 3 a.m.

La Bodega/El Bataclan

Amsterdam and Popocatepetl, Condesa
Tel. 5525-2473
A favorite with the over-25 crowd for its relaxed atmosphere and bohemian-chic decor. Rumba bands, bolero singers, rumba/flamenco troupe, depending on the night. Political and social satire Friday and Saturday nights, often featuring Mexican comedienne Astrid Hadad. Also sidewalk seating. Reservations recommended for shows; cover charge for bands and shows only. Open from 1 p.m. Closed Sunday.

La Casa de Paquita la del Barrio

Zarco 202, Guerrero
Tel. 5583-8131

This venue is where Mexico's celebrated torch singer, Paquita, performs her ballads of spurned love, including "Give My Regards to Your Lover" and "Are You Listening to Me, Stupid?" Paquita performs only about four times a month (when not touring through Europe and other parts of the world), otherwise there are guest performers. Call ahead for dates. Shows are at 7, 9 and 11 p.m. Thursday to Saturday.

Upstairs

Versailles 52, Roma
Tel. 5553-0262
Top floor of Colmillo bar. Live jazz Thursday to Saturday from 10 p.m. The cover charge also gets you access to the downstairs bar.

Elegance is

a virtue only few

can attain ...

Where to Shop

The Best Boutiques and Most Colorful Markets

You will find most everything that is made in Mexico in Mexico City. Handicrafts, silver, leather, carved wood furniture and folk art from around the country are sold here for not much more than you would pay in the regions where they are made.

Polanco, an upscale residential and commercial district located behind the Nikko, Presidente InterContinental and JW Marriott hotels, is where you'll find Mexico's answer to Rodeo Drive, Avenida Presidente Masaryk, the neighborhood's main boulevard and address to many designer boutiques, from Armani to Zegna.

Plaza Moliere dos 22 is Polanco's newest mall, with a branch of Palacio de Hierro, one of the city's leading department stores. *Pabellon Polanco*, on the corner of Homero and Vazquez de Mella, is the neighborhood's largest mall. *Plaza Zentro*, at the corner of Presidente Masaryk and La Fontaine, has a small concentration of exclusive shops. Next door to Plaza Zentro is *Plaza Mazarik*, another exclusive mini mall.

Zona Rosa, or the Pink Zone, is home to scattered souvenir shops and a few smart boutiques (almost all of which are on Calle Amberes), but the neighborhood is best known as the city's antiques center. Antique lovers will find much to browse through at the *Bazar de Antiguedades*, a passageway located between Hamburgo and Londres streets. The shops here are almost exclusively dedicated to

the sale of antiques, from Mexican colonial furniture to ceramic dolls. On Saturdays, shopkeepers and other vendors of antiques, vintage

Talleres de los Ballesteros

clothing or simply souvenirs of bygone eras, display their goods in the bazaar's passageways and around its courtyard.

Searching for fine handicrafts and folk art is made easy thanks to *Fonart,* a government agency that promotes artisans around the country and displays their work at retail stores throughout Mexico, including two branches in the capital.

Mexico's colorful markets are another good source for handicrafts (see their individual listings under "Handicrafts"). Bargain hunters may want to check out the city's main flea market Sundays at *Lagunilla.* Stretching the length of about three city blocks starting from the corner of Reforma and Rayon, stands sell everything from tie-dyed T-shirts to pets. Dress for comfort, and don't wear or carry anything too flashy. Consult the chapter titled "Special Attractions" for more information on markets.

Don't miss *Bazaar Sabado*, an upscale Saturday bazaar in the city's southern San Angel neighborhood. Built around a courtyard, the bazaar features the work of some of Mexico's finest artisans in silver, enamel, pottery, glass and textiles.

Stores in Mexico City usually open at 10 or 11 a.m., and remain open until 7 or 8 p.m. Many specialized stores open only half a day Saturday, and most stores close on Sunday, except those in shopping centers.

Department Stores

Liverpool
20 de Noviembre, Historic Center; Horacio and Mariano Escobedo, Polanco; and five other locations
Tel. 5522-8520
Founded in 1847, this leading department store chain has everything from plants to pets.

Of special interest to the visitor are the Mexican and international designers, Mexican handicrafts and sweets.

Palacio de Hierro

20 de Noviembre, Historic Center; Plaza Moliere, Polanco; Centro Santa Fe mall, and four other locations
Tel. 5229-1999
One of Mexico's leading department store chains, Palacio de Hierro has come to be associated with quality and a wide range of selections. You'll find top designers, both international and national, brand name goods, and a gourmet section carrying top-of-the-line tequilas, Mexican wines and foodstuffs. Also Mexican handicrafts, travel agency.

Sanborns

Madero 4; Reforma, at "The Angel" monument; and other locations
Less than a department store, but still a great convenience for travelers, carrying everything from shaving cream to jewelry, handicrafts, records and tapes. Cafe, restaurant, bar and browser-friendly magazine section with English-language publications.

Sears

Tel. 5557-0055
Eight branches throughout the city, including Pabellon Polanco and Centro Santa Fe malls. A familiar name to most North Americans, this department store chain has grown rapidly in Mexico

Handicrafts

Adobe Diseño

Centro Santa Fe mall
Tel. 5257-1454
Creative Mexican-made furniture and decorative items for the home from Mexico's handicraft mecca of Tlaquepaque (in Guadalajara). Everything from leather backgammon boards to forged-iron tables in the shape of cactus. Items made to order. Packing and shipping.

Artesania Magica

Edgar Allan Poe 308, Polanco
Tel. 5531-3984
A breathtaking selection of prized handicrafts

Plaza Moliere shopping center

you won't easily find anywhere else, such as brightly-painted wooden trays inlaid with mother of pearl.

Bazaar Sabado

Plaza San Jacinto 11, San Angel
An upscale bazaar featuring unique handicrafts by selected expert artisans, including ornate costume jewelry, contemporary silver jewelry, embroidered cotton apparel and accents for the home, enamel work, blown glass, and more. A wonderful place to browse and admire the handiwork. You can also enjoy a traditional buffet lunch and regional music in the central courtyard. Open 10 a.m. to 7 p.m. Saturday only.

Buenavista

Aldama 187, Guerrero
Tel. 5526-0315
Rather charmless, but big as a warehouse, with aisles and aisles of handicrafts at fixed prices. Open 9 a.m. to 6 p.m.

Carretones

Carretones 5, Historic Center
Tel. 5522-5311
Founded in 1889, this factory makes colorful Mexican-style blown-glass. They do a large export business, make glassware to order and speak English. The small factory store brims over with vases, glasses, bowls and myriad items at bargain prices. Weekdays you can see the glass being blown and shaped. Clients get personalized attention from sisters Lydia and Maria Luisa Vazquez Castrellon. Tucked away in one of the city's grittier neighborhoods, so take a taxi. Open 10 a.m. to 2 p.m. and 3 to 5 p.m.; to 2 p.m. Saturday. Closed Sunday.

Fonart

Juarez 89, Historic Center. Tel. 5521-0171
Patriotismo 691, Mixcoac. Tel. 5563-4060
Wonderful stores for picking up fine Mexican folk art or just stocking up on gifts and souvenirs. Fonart retail shops, part of a national fund for the promotion of Mexican handicrafts, offer the best from every region of the country, including carved-wood furniture from central Mexico, black pottery from Oaxaca, Talavera ceramics from Puebla, hand-painted Olinala boxes from Guerrero, ethnic and antique silver jewelry, woven baskets, wool blankets, and even Paquimé-style pottery from Chihuahua. Experts at packing and shipping. Fixed prices. Open 9 a.m. to 8 p.m.; 10 a.m. to 7 p.m. Sunday.

Insurgentes Market

On Londres, near Florencia, Zona Rosa
This handicraft market is worthwhile for its large silver selections.

La Ciudadela Market

Balderas and Ayuntamiento, downtown
One of the city's most colorful and inviting handicraft markets.

Las Artesanias

Oscar Wilde 29, Pasaje Polanco
Tel. 5280-9515
Hidden inside a small shopping plaza, this three-story shop carries a large selection of ceramics from Puebla and Guanajuato, and some select handicrafts from other parts of the country, including silk shawls, lacquered trays and chests. Also attractive all-cotton clothing by Mexican designer Alejandro Julian Nuñez, some of it featuring distinctive Huichol hand embroidery. Open 10 a.m. to 8 p.m.; noon to 6 p.m. Sunday.

Mil Manos

Montes de Oca 13, Condesa
Tel. 5286-3731
A longtime manufacturer and distributor of fine handicrafts that has opened its doors to the public with this attractive factory showroom. A tasteful selection of handmade decorative items for the home, some designed exclusively for Mil Manos, fills various rooms: tile mirrors, pewter bathroom accessories, painted pottery, lamps and more. Open 11 a.m. to 7 p.m.; noon to 5 p.m. Saturday; closed Sunday.

San Juan Handicrafts Market
Ayuntamiento and Aranda, Historic Center
Tel. 5512-2790
One of the city's oldest and most tradtional markets carries handicrafts from throughout the country. You'll find everything from Olinala lacquerware to Talavera from Puebla, and even regional costumes. Open 10 a.m. to 7 p.m.; to 5 p.m. Sunday.

Uriarte
Alejandro Dumas 77, Polanco. Tel. 5282-2849
Four Seasons Hotel. Tel. 5231-4828
The Mexico City showrooms of one of Puebla's most prestigious makers of Talavera pottery display wonderful pieces in all sizes, from giant urns to tiny cookie jars. Also reproductions of museum pieces. Expert shipping. Branch in San Antonio. You can visit their factory in Puebla and watch the artisans at work.

Jewelry & Sterling Silver

Aplijsa
Isabel la Catolica 30, Historic Center
Tel. 5521-1923
Presidente Masaryk 281, Polanco
Tel. 5280-0870
The downtown branch, housed in a beautifully preserved 17th-century mansion that has been declared a historical monument, serves as a unique backdrop for precious and semiprecious gems, both loose and worked into beautiful jewelry. Aplijsa specializes in loose, high-quality stones, from De Belder diamonds to pearls of every variety, but also carries finished pieces. Even if you're not in a buying mood, this is a great place to browse and learn about pearls and gems. Look around and admire the colonial setting with a mural by artist Manuel R. Lozano. Open 10 a.m. to 7 p.m.; to 3 p.m. Saturday; closed Sunday.

Daniel Espinosa Jewelry
Tamaulipas 72, Condesa
Tel. 5211-3994

Bold, contemporary designs in silver by the talented Taxco-based jeweler, including many pieces with semiprecious stones. Espinosa's creativity and sense of fun is evident in his tie-style chokers made of silver cubes and red beads, hypnotic silver rings with black enamel swirls, and other unique jewelry.

Emilia Castillo
Camino Real Hotel, Polanco
Tel. 5531-8873
Daughter Emilia, of Taxco's famed family of silversmiths, displays her own sterling silver creations here, many of them incorporating a wildlife motif or animal prints.

Entenaya
Montes de Oca 47, Condesa
Tel. 5286-1535
Unique sterling silver creations by 15 talented Mexican designers. Together they offer an eclectic collection of jewelry and accessories, ranging from bold pieces with wildlife motifs to intricate necklaces, rings, earrings set with semiprecious stones. Open noon to 8 p.m.

Gigi Mizrahi
Julio Verne 112, Pasaje Polanco
Tel. 5280-9195
A wonderful selection of sterling silver jewelry, many pieces inspired by pre-Hispanic, Mayan themes.

Izta
Alejandro Dumas 7-A, Polanco
Tel. 5282-0024
Tucked away in a corner near the JW Marriott hotel, this small shop carries finely-crafted silver creations that are uniquely Mexican. Many items are sterling silver versions of handicrafts traditionally fashioned out of pottery, wood, straw or other materials.

Sergio Bustamante
Nikko Hotel, Polanco
Tel. 5282-2638

Stunning 22 karat gold, gold-plated silver, and silver jewelry by the celebrated Guadalajara-born artist; also his sculpture. The jewelry features his signature blazing suns and moons.

Sub Chrono
Presidente Masaryk 360, Pasaje Polanco
Tel. 5281-1219
Sexy, sporty timepieces from St. Tropez with interchangeable bands and faces. Prices range from 250 to 5,000 dollars for a diamond-encrusted model.

Talleres de los Ballesteros
Presidente Masaryk 126, Polanco
Tel. 5545-1666
Amberes 24, Zona Rosa. Tel. 5511-8281
Insurgentes Sur 1971. Tel. 5663-5080
Exquisite sterling silver jewelry, silverware, table settings and decorative accents for the home, all crafted by the famed Taxco-based Ballesteros family of silversmiths. Ballesteros creations reflect the creativity and fine workmanship that comes from years of experience. The Presidente Masaryk branch is a multilevel emporium of silver items.

Tane
Presidente Masaryk 430, Polanco
Tel. 5281-4775
A veritable museum of silver treasures, featuring expertly crafted jewelry and decorations, limited edition silver sculptures by renowned artists, and a permanent collection of silver objets d'art. Branches around the city.

Tanya Moss Designer Jewelry
Presidente Masaryk 360, Pasaje Polanco
Tel. 5281-0697
Original gold and sterling silver jewelry, and wearable art by designer Tanya Moss, whose innovative and sophisticated designs reflect their Mexican heritage. Individually handcrafted by skilled artisans, many of her creations incorporate freshwater pearls, amber, precious or semiprecious stones.

Centro Santa Fe shopping center

Clothing

Antonio Solito
Presidente Masaryk 320, Polanco
Tel. 5282-1600
This exclusive men's shop offers classic custom-made suits using only the finest imported fabrics, such as Loro Piana and Drapers, as well as finely-tailored clothing by Brioni, Longhi, Borrelli and others.

Ermenegildo Zegna
Presidente Masaryk 454, Polanco
Tel. 5282-0810
Offering three distinct collections of men's wear and accessories, from formal suits (Sartorial Collection) to leisure and active wear (Sportswear Collection).

Girasol
Londres 161, Zona Rosa
Tel. 5525-4901

Attractive all-cotton Spanish-style clothing for women, including gypsy-style skirts, romantic tops, embroidered jackets.

Hermés
Presidente Masaryk 422, Polanco
Tel. 5282-2118
This beautiful two-story emporium of signature clothing and accessories from the famed French design house is a wonderful place for browsing and picking up gift items.

Roberto Cavalli
Plaza Zentro, locales 7 and 8, Polanco
Tel. 5282-3463
Clothing and accessories by the famed Italian designer known for his fabulous prints, sensual fabrics. His celebrity clients include Jennifer Lopez, Cindy Crawford, Cristina Aguilera, Shakira, Thalia etc. On this continent, Cavalli boutiques can be found in New York, Miami (Bal Harbor) and Mexico City only.

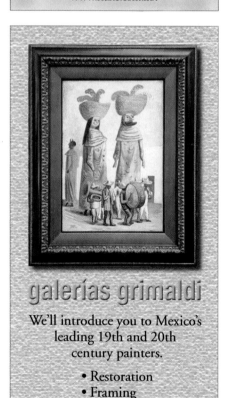

Versace
Presidente Masaryk 422-B, Polanco
Tel. 5282-2454
A chic two-story boutique featuring Versace clothing and accessories for men and women, including Versace Jeans Couture designer denim.

Leather

Aries
Presidente InterContinental and Camino Real Hotels, Polanco; Florencia 14, Zona Rosa; Sheraton Maria Isabel Hotel; Centro Santa Fe and Perisur malls.
Selections of the country's finest leather work. Fashionable bags, coats, jackets, suits, and luggage, plus gift items.

Antiques

Bazar de Antiguedades
Between Hamburgo and Londres streets, opposite the Insurgentes Market, Zona Rosa
An antiques center with more than 30 stores lining the passageways on two levels. On Saturdays, shopkeepers and other vendors of antiques, vintage clothing or souvenirs of bygone eras, display their goods in and around the bazaar's courtyard. An interesting place to browse. Prices are negotiable. Open daily 10 a.m. to 8 p.m.; Saturday flea market 10 a.m. to 4 p.m.

Rodrigo Rivero Lake
Campos Eliseos 199-1001, Polanco
Tel. 5281-5505
A passion for art and antiques has led Rivero to travel the world in search of unique collector's items, from museum quality pieces to decorative art from around the globe. His collection contains many one-of-a-kind items you might find in a museum display, such as a 16th-century gate to a city or a complete colonial altar. Don't miss a chance to talk to him and get his book. By appointment only.

Special

Celaya
Cinco de Mayo 39, Historic Center
Tel. 5521-1787
Founded in 1874, this landmark art nouveau-style shop exclusively sells Mexican sweets, from candied coconut-filled limes to powdery *polvorones*. Also has branches at Colima 143 and Orizaba 37, both in Colonia Roma.

El Secreto
Altavista 13, San Angel. Tel. 5550-3622
Cda. Monte Libano 13, Lomas de Chapultepec
Tel. 5520-1953
Traditional Mexican sweets, handmade from the finest ingredients and beautifully packaged. Try the sesame or pumpkin seed brittle, creamy coconut drops, and Mexican-style animal crackers made of molasses.

La Casa del Habano
Amberes 1, Zona Rosa

Tel. 5514-7464
A good source for fine Cuban cigars, with each box bearing its seal of authenticity, plus a wide selection of stylish accessories for the cigar aficionado. Branches at Plaza Mazarik and Plaza Loreto malls.

SeDe Vino
Campos Eliseos 199, Polanco
Tel. 5280-4825
Sheraton Centro Historico Hotel
Tel. 5518-2492
For lovers of wine and those who want to learn more about Mexico's leading wineries, this attractive wine bar and store carries about 130 wines from Mexico and around the world, plus original Riedel glassware. Polanco branch open noon to midnight, except Sunday; Sheraton branch open noon to 10 p.m. daily.

Shopping Centers

Centro Santa Fe
Vasco de Quiroga 3800
Tel. 5259-4500
Mexico City's premier shopping center is a dining and entertainment complex with dozens of restaurants, movie houses, a groundbreaking recreational center for kids, and even a golf practice range. Shops offer everything from designer clothing and accessories to handmade Mexican furniture and decorative items. Anchored at each end by Mexico's two leading department stores, *Palacio de Hierro* and *Liverpool*. Also has an American Express office and money exchange houses. Located in the western part of the city; we recommend you take a taxi.

Centro Coyoacan
Universidad and Rio Churubusco, Coyoacan
A large, modern, two-story shopping center convenient to visitors staying in the south.

Pabellon Polanco
Homero and Vazquez de Mella, Polanco
The area's largest mall features several fine boutiques, a cineplex, and good restaurant options, including *La Destileria* for Mexican cuisine and atmosphere, and *Melée* for steaks, pastas and pizzas.

Plaza Moliere dos 22
On Moliere, Polanco
Within easy walking distance of the major hotels. This shopping center features an upscale *Palacio de Hierro* department store, boutiques and restaurants.

Plaza Zentro
Presidente Masaryk and La Fontaine, Polanco
An exclusive and upscale mini mall featuring designer boutiques, popular restaurants and nightspots.

Plaza Mazarik
Presidente Masaryk and La Fontaine, Polanco
Like its sister mall, Plaza Mazarik houses just a handful of fine shops. One of the city's most popular Mexican restaurants, *La Valentina*, is on the second level.

Where to Stay

Calinda Geneve
Londres 130, Zona Rosa
Tel. (55) 5080-0800
www.hotelescalinda.com.mx
Following major renovation, this traditional hotel in the heart of the Pink Zone offers 270 rooms with satellite TV, minibar, a/c, safe, iron/ironing board, hair dryer; rooms are well appointed, but on the small side. Business center with two small meeting rooms, six computer stations; gym with sauna, steam room, spa treatments; casual restaurant, lobby bar with live music. Rates FC.

Camino Real
Mariano Escobedo 700, Polanco
Tel. (55) 5263-8888
www.caminoreal.com
A unique city landmark, this modern Mexican resort on seven acres has 678 rooms and 36 suites with all first-class amenities. Excellent restaurants, bars, swimming pools surrounded by gardens, tennis courts, gym. Extensive banquet and convention facilities for up to 1,500 people, executive club floors. One of The Leading Hotels of the World. Rates FC.

Camino Real Aeropuerto
Puerto Mexico 80
Tel. (55) 3003-0000
www.caminoreal.com
Connected via a pedestrian skywalk to the international airport, this attractive property offers 600 refurbished rooms and suites equipped with irons and ironing boards, hair dryers and other first-class amenities; 24-hour room service. There's a fully-equipped fitness cen-

ter with indoor pool. Business center with three computer stations, executive floor and lounge, extensive meeting and banquet facilities, first-class convention services. Good restaurants and lobby bar with live music. Rates FC.

Century Zona Rosa
Liverpool 152, Zona Rosa
Tel. (55) 5726-9911

www.century.com.mx
Ideally located in the city's popular Zona Rosa district, this modern building has 142 rooms and suites, all with private balconies, marble bathtubs, a/c, satellite TV, minibar, phone with modem and fax hookups, safe. Heated outdoor pool, small meeting rooms, business center. Rates MD.

City Suites
Kant 25, near Polanco
Tel. (55) 1101-1370
www.cityexpress.com.mx
Ideal for extended stays, with one- and two-bedroom apartmentlike units with well equipped kitchenettes, living room, high-speed Internet access, satellite TV, DVD player, concierge service (they'll rent your movies for you). There's also a penthouse suite with spacious terrace. Business center, room service. Hotel rates adjusted according to length of stay. Rates MD (includes continental breakfast).

De Cortes Best Western
Hidalgo 85, Historic Center

Galería Plaza méxico, d.f.
BRISAS HOTELS & RESORTS

Because of its location, service and facilities, Galería Plaza is ideal for your next convention or business trip. Ideally located in the Zona Rosa, next to Paseo de la Reforma Avenue and near the Independence Monument.

Comfortable rooms, professional group services and outstanding restaurants are but a few of the advantages that Galería Plaza offers for today's demanding business and leisure traveler.

When Mexico City is on your agenda, think of Galería Plaza, your best choice.

Please ask about our Special offers.

Mexico 01 800 227 4727
U.S./Canada 1 888 559 43 29
www.brisas.com.mx
galeria.plaza@brisas.com.mx
Tel. 52 (55) 5230 1717
Fax 52 (55) 5207 5867
01 800 717 9223
Hamburgo 195, Col. Juárez
Mexico City

Tel. (55) 5518-2181
www.hoteldecortes.com.mx
Facing Alameda Park, this colonial-era monument is the oldest and most authentically Mexican hotel in the capital. The 19 rooms and 10 well-decorated suites overlook the park or a charming patio restaurant with plants and a fountain, and have been recently remodeled to offer such modern conveniences as data ports. Mexican Fiesta Friday evenings. Rates MD.

Excalibur
Hamburgo 49, near Zona Rosa
Tel. (55) 5535-0007
www.hotel-excalibur.com
This conveniently located hotel just steps from the main boulevard, Reforma, offers 40 clean, comfortable, air-conditioned rooms with color TV. Rates ECON (continental breakfast included).

Fiesta Americana Grand
Mariano Escobedo 756, Polanco
Tel. (55) 5326-6900
www.fiestamericana.com
This attractive, new Art Deco-style high-rise features spectacular views of Chapultepec Park and Castle from its 203 spacious guest rooms and meeting facilities. Rooms, including 6 apartmentlike suites, have all deluxe amenities and services, including 24-hour room service and concierge. Executive floors and lounge, rooftop health club, rooftop ballroom for 250, meeting rooms. Fine restaurant, lobby bar. One of The Leading Hotels of the World. Rates FC.

Fiesta Americana Reforma
Reforma 80, close to Zona Rosa
Tel. (55) 5140-4100
www.fiestamericana.com
A 25-story hotel with 610 rooms and suites with a/c, cable TV, minibar, phone. Restaurant, coffee shop, lobby bar. Gym. Business center and extensive convention and banquet facilities for up to 1,000 people. Rates MD.

Fiesta Americana Suites
Londres 115, Zona Rosa
Tel. (55) 5080-0700
www.fiestamericana.com
Ideal for extended stays, with 60 well-appointed suites designed for the business traveler: four phones, two lines, high-speed Internet connection, microwave, work station, and more. Coffee shop, lobby bar. Business center, small meeting rooms. Gym, terrace with jacuzzi. Rates MD.

Fiesta Inn
Periferico Sur 5230

Tel. (55) 5096-9300
www.fiestamericana.com
This 14-story hotel in the south offers an attractive setting and comfortable accommodations for the business traveler, with 220 rooms with work station, coffee maker, hair dryer. Coffee shop, room service, lobby bar. Business center, swimming pool with jacuzzi, gym. Rates MD.

Four Seasons

Reforma 500
Tel. (55) 5230-1818
www.fourseasons.com
Located on the city's central and fashionable Paseo de la Reforma, this luxury hotel offers superior service and amenities. Colonial-style architecture and interiors that recall a comfortably and tastefully furnished residence. The 240 spacious rooms and suites, some of the largest in the city, overlook a flower-filled courtyard with a fountain, as do the fine restaurant and bar. Well equipped health club, spa services, heated pool, whirlpool and sun deck. Extensive meeting and banquet facilities, fully equipped and staffed business center. Special amenities and services available for families traveling with infants or children, 24-hour room service. Rates DX.

Galeria Plaza

Hamburgo 195 and Varsovia, Zona Rosa
Tel. (55) 5230-1717
www.brisas.com.mx
Ideally located, this modern high-rise offers

439 spacious rooms and suites with all deluxe in-room amenities. The penthouse-level gym and pool with sun deck offer a panoramic view. Pleasant a la carte and buffet restaurants, popular lobby bar. Business center, well-equipped meeting rooms for up to 250 people, executive club floors and lounge. Rates FC.

Gran Melia

Reforma 1, corner of Juarez
Tel. (55) 5128-5000
www.solmelia.com
Upgraded to "Gran Melia" category following a 12 million-dollar renovation, this hotel and convention center with an airy 22-story atrium lobby and business bent now features a state-of-the-art spa. There are 489 attractive rooms with executive amenities, including Royal Service floors with personalized service. Convention facilities for 2,500 guests, business center. Health club with covered swimming pool, terrace with a view. Specialties restaurant, steak house, cafeteria, espresso bar, lobby bar, non-smoking and rooms for handicapped. One of The Leading Hotels of the World. Rates FC.

Habita

Presidente Masaryk 201, Polanco
Tel. (55) 5282-3100
www.hotelhabita.com
A strong fashion statement, this sleek hotel features minimalist interiors and a trendy rooftop lounge-bar. Ground-floor restaurant, spa

with sauna and whirlpool, open-air heated pool and solarium, 24-hour room service, complimentary valet parking and garage. The 32 rooms and four junior suites have 27" flat-screen TV, minibar, safe, Internet access, in-house music channels. Business center, meeting room. Rates DX.

Hilton

Mexico City International Airport
Tel. (55) 5133-0505
www.hilton.com
Located in the international terminal, third floor, this newly refurbished 129-room hotel designed for the business traveler offers first-class accommodations and amenities, including multilingual concierge service, restaurant, lobby bar overlooking the landing strips, small well-equipped gym, meeting rooms and business center. The soundproofed rooms have work stations, three phones, safe, minibar, satellite TV with flight information. Rates FC.

Holiday Inn Zocalo

Cinco de Mayo 61, Historic Center
Tel. (55) 5521-2121
www.holidayinnzocalo.com.mx
Incorporating the facade of a colonial-era building, this hotel overlooking the Zocalo offers comfortable, modern lodgings in the heart of the Historic Center. Rustic wood furnishings and hand-painted pottery give the property a Mexican feel. The 100 standard double rooms are on the small side, but attractively furnished with first-class amenities, including

big-screen satellite TV, coffee maker, safe, clock radio, hair dryer; 10 spacious suites overlook the plaza, five with jacuzzi. Terrace dining, excellent buffet breakfast, lobby bar. Lovely banquet hall with terrace overlooking the plaza. Business center and fitness room. Parking. Rates MD.

JW Marriott
Andres Bello 29, Polanco
Tel. (55) 5999-0000
www.marriott.com.mx
This modern, 20-story high-rise offers luxurious accommodations and amenities. All 311 guest rooms, including 12 suites or duplex apartments, are beautifully appointed and overlook Chapultepec Park or Polanco; extended stay apartments have kitchenettes. There's a 24-hour business center with state-of-the-art computers, two fully-equipped offices for rent, executive floors, and extensive meeting facilities. Excellent fitness center and spa services, heated outdoor swimming pool with sun deck. Fine formal and informal restaurants. Rates DX.

La Casona
Durango 280, Colonia Roma
Tel. (55) 5286-3001
www.hotellacasona.com.mx
Housed in a renovated turn-of-the-century mansion near the Zona Rosa, this charming European-style hotel offers a wonderful alternative to the city's larger hotels. The 29 individually decorated guest rooms are well-equipped with cable TV, phone, robes, safe, hair dryer. Continental breakfasts placed in "butler box" for guests' convenience. Cozy lounge, restaurant, gym, sun deck, small meeting room, business center. Member of Mexico Boutique Hotels. Rates FC (highest rate 160 USD; includes continental breakfast).

Majestic Best Western
Madero 73, Historic Center
Tel. (55) 5521-8601
www.majestic.com.mx
A charming hotel housed in a seven-story colonial-era building overlooking the Zocalo, with 85 attractive rooms with remote-control TV, radio, alarm clock, phone, minibar. Rooftop restaurant with terrace overlooking the main square, bar. Rates MD.

Marquis Reforma
Paseo de la Reforma 465, near Zona Rosa
Tel. (55) 5229-1200
www.marquisreforma.com
Despite its size, this charming hotel has an intimate ambiance with cozy interiors and inviting corners decorated with a mix of Mexican art and Art Deco. There are 125 rooms and 83 suites well equipped for the business traveler, three executive floors, business center with three computer stations, meeting and banquet facilities for up to 2,000. Fully-equipped gym and spa with outdoor jacuzzis and sun deck. Excellent gourmet restaurant and cafes. Outstanding service. One of The Leading Hotels of the World and member of Small Luxury Hotels of the World. Rates DX.

NH Mexico City
Liverpool 155, Zona Rosa
Tel. (55) 5228-9928
www.nh-hoteles.com
This recently remodelled first-class high-rise in the heart of the Pink Zone has 302 rooms and suites. Restaurant, heated outdoor pool, gym. Executive floors and services, meeting rooms for up to 300 people, business center. Rates MD.

Nikko Mexico
Campos Eliseos 204, Polanco
Tel. (55) 5283-8700
www.hotelnikkomexico.com

Part of an international Japanese chain of luxury hotels, this modern high-rise offers 720 attractive rooms and 24 elegant suites with all deluxe amenities. Oriental and Japanese restaurants, bars, 24-hour room service. State-of-the-art Athletic Club with indoor pool, sun deck, gym, golf driving range, lighted tennis courts. Extensive convention facilities with simultaneous translation channels, 24-hour business center, executive floors with separate check-in. Rates DX.

Pedregal Palace
Periferico Sur 3487, in the south
Tel. (55) 5681-1290

www.pedregalpalace.com.mx
Formerly Continental Plaza Pedregal, this small exclusive hotel has 57 rooms and six suites with cable TV, a/c, minibar, phone. International restaurant, bar, small meeting rooms and business center, gym, jacuzzi, solarium. Rates MD.

Polanco
Edgar Allan Poe 8, Polanco
Tel. (55) 5280-8082
www.hotelpolanco.com
Located in one of the city's poshest neighborhoods, this moderately priced hotel offers 71 comfortable rooms with safe, color cable TV, direct-dial phone with data-port; gym, Internet parlor, meeting room for 20. Rooms are on the small side, but comfortable and clean, and the location and price can't be beat. Rates MD.

Presidente InterContinental
Campos Eliseos 218, Polanco
Tel. (55) 5327-7777
www.intercontinental.com
Continually refurbished, this modern 42-story high-rise offers an ideal location, numerous fine restaurants, and 659 elegant rooms and suites with spectacular views of Chapultepec Park or Polanco. Nonsmoking rooms. Business center, convention and banquet facilities for up to 1,800 people. Its famed international restaurants let you embark on a culinary world tour: visit London (Balmoral), New York (Palm), Rome (Alfredo di Roma) Paris (Au Pied de Cochon); also popular lobby bar with live jazz. Winner of AAA's Four Diamond Award and the Distintivo H (hygiene) award from Mexico's ministries of health and tourism. Rates DX.

Radisson Paraiso
Cuspide 53, Parques del Pedregal
Tel. (55) 5927-5959
www.radisson.com
In the south, opposite Perisur shopping center, with 236 modern, spacious rooms and suites with all first-class amenities, including satellite TV, minibar. Executive floor, business center with computer station, and six meeting rooms for up to 350 people. Well-equipped gym with sauna. Lobby bar, restaurants. Rates MD.

Residencia Polanco
Newton 272, Polanco
Tel. (55) 5203-9144
www.mexicoboutiquehotels.com
Ideal for longer stays, this modern-colonial-style hotel offers 23 attractively furnished one-bedroom suites with a living room and kitchenette, cable TV and safe. Plants, original paintings and rustic furnishings make for a cozy ambiance. Roof-garden restaurant and bar, solarium, jacuzzi, spa. Meeting rooms and secretarial services. Member of Mexico Boutique Hotels. Rates MD.

Royal Zona Rosa
Amberes 78, Zona Rosa
Tel. (55) 5228-9918
www.hotelroyalzr.com
A renovated modern high-rise with 161 rooms

and a master suite, all with remote-control satellite TV, phone with dataport, minibar and safe. Specialties restaurant, cafe, top-floor terrace bar with panoramic view. Heated swimming pool, solarium, gym with steam room, access to Club de Golf Mexico. Meeting facilities for 120, business center. Rates MD.

Royal Pedregal
Periferico Sur 4363
Tel. (55) 5449-4000
www.hotelesroyal.com.mx
One of the best options in the south of the city, with 314 deluxe rooms and suites with remote-control satellite TV, safe, 24-hour room service, other amenities. Indoor and outdoor pools, well-equipped health club. Basque specialties restaurant (Tezka), lobby bar, meeting, banquet and exhibition facilities for up to 1,200 people. Rates FC.

Sevilla Palace
Reforma 105
Tel. (55) 5705-2800
www.sevillapalace.com.mx
This well-located high-rise has 413 rooms with cable TV, minibar, a/c, safe, data port, hair dryer. Restaurant, cafeteria, piano bar. Gym, steam room, massage services, covered rooftop pool and jacuzzi. Business center with computer stations, meeting rooms for up to 400 people. Rates MD.

Sheraton Centro Historico
Juarez 70, Historic Center
Tel. (55) 5202-1837
www.sheratonmexico.com
This newly inaugurated, modern 20-story tower is poised to become the city's leading convention hotel, with a state-of-the-art venue that can accommodate up to 3,000 people. Guests at the 457-room hotel enjoy privileged views of Alameda Park and other historic landmarks, as well as a rooftop garden, fitness center and spa, business center, restaurant, wine bar, and other amenities. Ample parking facilities. Rates FC.

Sheraton Maria Isabel
Reforma 325, opposite Zona Rosa
Tel. (55) 5242-5555
www.starwood.com
Facing "The Angel" monument, this city landmark is centrally located. Sporting an attractive face-lift, plus refurbished rooms and a renovated lobby/shopping arcade, this traditional favorite offers 755 spacious rooms and suites, excellent service, good restaurants, popular mariachi nightclub, lobby bar, health club, pool and tennis. Business center, high-tech banquet and convention facilities for 2,000. Exclusive Towers section. Rates FC.

Sheraton Suites Santa Fe
G.G. Camarena 200, Ciudad Santa Fe
Tel. (55) 5258-8500
www.sheraton/santafe.com
A modern low-rise designed for the business traveler. The 194 suites have kitchenette with microwave, three phones with dataports, ironing board; master suites also have whirlpool bath. Executive club floors. Gym and spa services. Business center, meeting facilities for up to 700. Restaurant, bar. Rates DX.

Villa Arqueologica
San Juan Teotihuacan, State of Mexico
Tel. (55) 5836-9020
www.teotihuacaninfo.com
Located a short walk from the archaeological site. A Club Med cultural hotel with 40 Moroccan-style rooms with cable TV, phone, air-conditioning and heating; indoor/outdoor dining, cozy bar with fireplace, heated pool, playground, lounge, pool table and library. Rates ECON.

W
Campos Eliseos and Andres Bello, Polanco
Tel. 9138-1800
www.starwood.com
This architecturally striking 25-story 237-room hotel features a popular bar and restaurant, spa, banquet/meeting facilities. Guest rooms stand out for their large work areas, oversized desks and ample seating for small meetings, as well as open bathrooms with floor-to-ceiling window views. In-room amenities include high-speed Internet access, 27" TV with advanced in-room entertainment system. Business center, 24-hour room service, concierge. A signature W program designed to liven up meetings, "Sensory Setup," is available to ease guests into a creative frame of mind, with lively music, smells, tastes and visuals.

A privileged location, unbeatable rates.

Conveniently located a few steps from Mexico City's main boulevard, Paseo de la Reforma, and near major museums, shopping centers, sites of interest, such as Chapultepec Castle and Zoo, and the National Auditorium, this first-class hotel offers 71 comfortable rooms with cable TV, safe, direct-dial telephone with Internet access, and other amenities such as a gymnasium, Internet parlor and a meeting facility for 20.

Edgar Alan Poe No. 8, Col. Polanco, México, D.F. 11560
Tel. 5280-8082 Fax 5280-8082, ext. 101 Toll-free in México 01 800 221-9044
E-mail: hotelpolanco@prodigy.net.mx   www.hotelpolanco.com

Mexico City Side Trips

Numerous day trips or longer jaunts are possible from Mexico City. You can read about the major ones in the pages ahead. Below are a few other options:

Tepotzotlan and Tula

Tepotzotlan, 40 km./25 mi. to the northwest, is famous for its ornate 16th-century Jesuit seminary and church, which today houses a museum of viceregal art and hosts Nativity plays, called *pastorelas*, at Christmas time.

In the neighboring state of Hidalgo, about 49 km./31 mi. north of Tepotzotlan, and 96 km./60 mi. north of Mexico City, is Tula, the ruins of a Toltec city known for the giant 15-foot stone warriors, called "atlantes," that stand atop the main Pyramid of the Morning Star. Tula was founded around 1000 A.D.

Toluca

Industrial Toluca, capital of the State of Mexico, lies 46 miles west of Mexico City and less than 25 miles from the world's only drive-in volcano, *Nevado de Toluca*. You can actually drive into the crater, home of the lakes of the *Sun* and *Moon*.

Around Toluca's main square shops sell everything from an orange-flavored liqueur called *moscos* to locally made red or green *chorizo* (sausage). On the east side of the plaza is *Cosmo Vitral*, a lovely botanical garden under stained glass. Across the street, a restaurant specializes in *chapulines*, a pre-Hispanic dish of seasoned grasshoppers. Paseo Tollocan is home to the leading restaurants, including *La Destileria* (Tollocan 1202), which serves Mexican dishes and grilled meats in a setting that pays tribute to tequila with colorful murals. Tel. 211-5404.

Centro Cultural Mexiquense houses various interesting museums, including the *Museum of Folk Art*, displaying a fine collection of regional arts and crafts, including impressive trees of life.

Malinalco

Once a ceremonial center for Aztec warriors, *Malinalco* is located in a picturesque town of the same name (40 mi./64 km south of Toluca, via Hwy. Mex. 55). Easy to reach via 400 steps and well worth the effort, the circular temple is renowned for its magnificent jaguar and eagle figures carved out of the mountain. The temple's interior chamber is off limits, but the new and impressive *Museo Universitario* features a beautiful replica. On the main square, *Los Placeres* restaurant is an excellent spot for a meal.

Valle de Bravo

A popular weekend retreat for well-heeled Mexico City residents, "Valle" is set on a mountain slope beside a beautiful lake. Cobblestone streets, red-tile rooftops, attractive shops, and traditionally-dressed Mazahua Indians from surrounding villages who come to sell their handicrafts are all part of its charm. (Though only 87 miles away, the drive takes about three hours because of the winding road.)

Lush hills around the lake are considered excellent for hang-gliding—in fact, you can usually spot gliders floating in the sky above town. For lessons, contact Erick Salgado (tel. 262-0048). For the less action oriented, there are boat rides around the lake. For the ultimate in tranquility, visit *Maranatha*, a beautiful retreat, likened to an Italian palazzo, run by Carmelite nuns.

Leading restaurants around town include *Mozzarella*, at the Batucada Hotel, *Mostazas*, Santa Maria 118, and *Los Veleros*, Salitre 104. Overlooking the lake are *Indigo*, at Marina Club, and *Lagartos*, near the city dock. Overlooking the square are *El Portal* and *La Cueva del Leon*. In the evenings, boats offer a moonlight cruise called a "Lunada." On land, revelers like to gather at the beautiful and cozy *Bar des Artistes*, Bocanegra 103, and at *La Pila Seca*, Cinco de Mayo 100.

Recommended hotels include the *Batucada* and *Meson del Viento*, both located downtown, and *Avandaro Golf & Spa Resort*, about 15 minutes from town.

Real del Monte

Hidalgo state's own little Taxco is located just 9 km./6 mi. from its capital, Pachuca, which is 90 km./56 mi. northeast of Mexico City. The narrow cobblestone streets of this fairy talelike colonial-era mining town are lined with pastel-colored shops selling silver jewelry (products of the town's two active silver mines) or *pastes*, meat-filled turnovers (Cornish pasties) introduced to the region in the 1800s by miners from Cornwall, England.

Dolores Hidalgo

On September 16, 1810, Father Miguel Hidalgo, the priest of the village of Dolores, urged his parishioners to join the movement to overthrow the Spanish viceregal government. Officially known as the "Grito de Dolores" (Cry of Dolores), his call to arms is considered the high point of Mexican history. Each year on the eve of Independence Day, Mexico's president reenacts the *grito* at Mexico City's main square with cries of "Viva Mexico!" Reenactments on a smaller scale take place in every city and village throughout the country.

Ceramics, pottery and Talavera tile have been the special handicrafts of Dolores Hidalgo ever since Father Hidalgo founded the town's first ceramics workshop in the early 19th century.

Few people know that Dolores Hidalgo is also famous for its ice cream, which comes in a variety of unusual flavors, including avocado, corn, cheese and honey.

San Luis Potosi

The state of San Luis Potosi, home to the scenic *Huasteca Potosina*, has been actively promoting its outdoor life in the past few years. Whitewater rafting along the Huasteca region's clear blue Santa Maria River is especially popular.

The region's best known towns are Valles, which serves as a gateway to the Huasteca, and Xilitla (pronounced hee-LEET-lah), where some 50 years ago an eccentric Englishman called Edward James built surreal works of art in the jungle. El Castillo, James' former jungle hideaway, serves as a small inn and base from which to see area attractions. The inn is operated by American couple Avery and Leonore Danziger. Tel. 365-0038.

During the 16th century San Luis Potosi was the third largest province in New Spain, its boundaries extending from Louisiana to New Mexico. Many of its towns preserve their colonial character, and the most unique of these is *Real de Catorce*, a former mining center that was abandoned when the mines dried up. One arrives through a nearly two-mile-long tunnel built in 1901, adding to the air of mystery surrounding this ghost town.

Not to be missed when visiting the capital, also called San Luis Potosi, are the churches of *San Francisco* and *Carmen*, the *Regional Museum*, and especially the *Museum of the Mask*, where more than 700 ceremonial masks are on display. Recommended hotels include the Westin, Holiday Inn and Real de Minas.

Aguascalientes

This former mining city is today best known for hosting one of the oldest and most famous festivals in all of Mexico, the *San Marcos Fair*. Spanning the last two weeks of April and first week of May, what began in 1828 as an agricultural and livestock show has grown into a 22-day extravaganza attended by about a million people.

A good way to begin a visit to the city is to take a stroll through lovely *San Marcos Park*. Don't miss the beautifully proportioned *Government Palace*, with its striking central courtyard and murals depicting state history and scenes of the San Marcos Fair. Also worth visiting are the *Aguascalientes* and *Guadalupe Posada* museums, and *Discover: Interactive Museum of Science and Technology*, where visitors can experience virtual reality. Recommended hotels include the Quinta Real, Fiesta Americana, De Andrea Alameda and Fiesta Inn.

Just 13 kilometers/8 miles outside of town, on the road to Zacatecas, is one of the country's leading wineries, *Bodegas de Santo Tomas*.

Mexico City and Vicinity

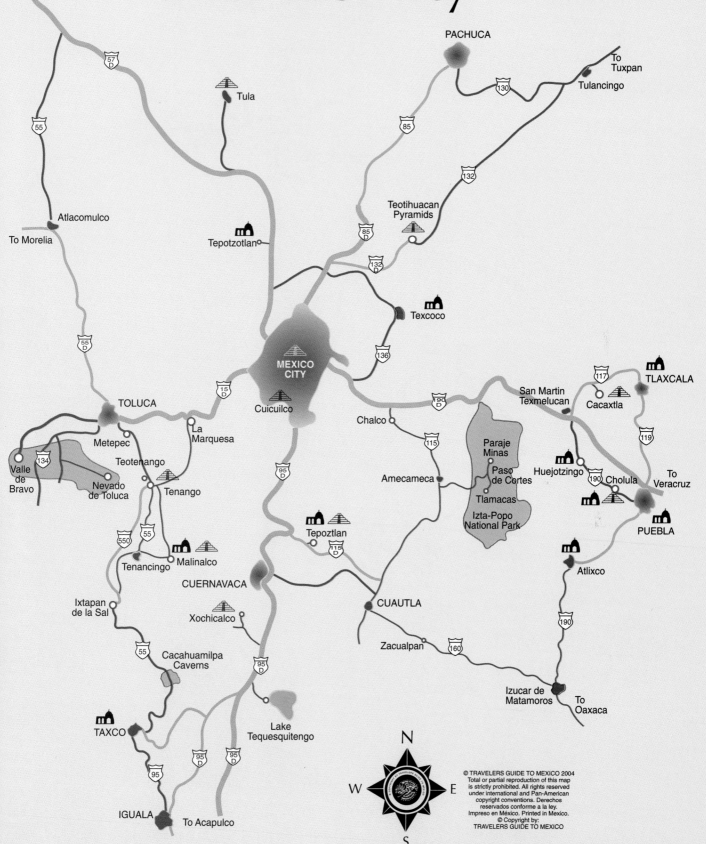

To Queretaro
Tequisquiapan
57 D
55
55 D
Atlacomulco
To Morelia
Tula
Tepotzotlan
PACHUCA
To Tuxpan
Tulancingo
130
85
132
Teotihuacan Pyramids
85 D
132 D
Texcoco
136
MEXICO CITY
15 D
Cuicuilco
TOLUCA
La Marquesa
Metepec
Teotenango
Valle de Bravo
134
Nevado de Toluca
Tenango
550
55
Tenancingo
Malinalco
CUERNAVACA
Tepoztlan
115 D
Chalco
115
Amecameca
Paraje Minas
Paso de Cortes
Tlamacas
Izta-Popo National Park
San Martin Texmelucan
190
117
TLAXCALA
Cacaxtla
119
Huejotzingo
190
Cholula
To Veracruz
PUEBLA
Atlixco
190
Ixtapan de la Sal
Xochicalco
CUAUTLA
Zacualpan
160
Cacahuamilpa Caverns
95 D
Lake Tequesquitengo
Izucar de Matamoros
To Oaxaca
TAXCO
95 D
95 D
95
IGUALA
To Acapulco

N
W E
S

TRAVELERS GUIDE TO
Central Mexico

Bruce Herman

An intricately carved pyramid at Xochicalco, near Cuernavaca, pays tribute to the Plumed Serpent deity

Cuernavaca

The Aztec City of Eternal Spring

Tabachines

Resort towns are nothing new to Mexico. When Hernán Cortés and his troops arrived in the central highlands, they learned from the Aztecs how to escape Mexico City's winter chill by spending the colder months in a town about 40 miles south, beyond the mountains. Its name, *Cuauhnahuac,* meant "place of great trees" in native Nahuatl. To the Spanish it sounded like *cuerno de vaca,* which in their native tongue means "horn of a cow," and that's how we got Cuernavaca, or so the story goes. Despite its less-than-flattering name, people have been going there to get away from the hectic pace of the capital ever since.

When his adventuring days were over, Cortés chose to retire in Cuernavaca. The silver barons of the colonial era also built homes here. Even Emperor Maximilian and his wife, Carlota, had their weekend retreat.

Things are not so different today. Thanks to its perennial springlike weather, Cuernavaca continues to be a weekend getaway for Mexico City residents and home to a growing colony of retired Americans. The town is filled with country club-style hotels and homes with swimming pools. In fact, Cuernavaca has more pools per capita than any city in the world exceeding a million inhabitants. When not swimming, everyone seems to gather at the plaza to have a drink at a sidewalk cafe or lounge on a bench and watch other people watch them.

The center of town surrounds not one, but two big plazas. Overlooking the larger one is the *Palacio de Cortés,* built by the conqueror in 1526 and said to be the only monument to him in Mexico. The building was once the home of the Morelos State Legislature and now houses one of the city's major cultural attractions, the *Cuauhnahuac Museum,* with a collection of pre-Columbian and conquest-era exhibits, plus several superb Diego Rivera murals. The murals were commissioned by Dwight Morrow, U.S. ambassador to Mexico from 1927 to 1930. The museum is open Tuesday to Sunday, 9 a.m. to 6 p.m.

Morrow was an outstanding envoy who did much to restore good relations between the two countries after the torment of the revolution. Among his many accomplishments, he awakened Mexican interest in regional handicrafts and probably did more than any other person to keep the industry from dying. The street where he lived in Cuernavaca is fondly named after him and one of Cuernavaca's leading restaurants, La India Bonita, is in his former residence, Casa Mañana (which reputedly got its name from the architect, who would respond to Mrs. Morrow's incessant queries about when the house would be finished with these words: *"Mañana acabamos, Señora. Mañana!"*).

It was Morrow's daughter, however, who put Cuernavaca on the map. She often spent weekends in town with her parents. And when she did, a shy young man with a world-famous name came to call. Miss Morrow eventually became Mrs. Charles Lindbergh.

A focal point of a visit to Cuernavaca is the *cathedral,* at the corner of Hidalgo and Morelos. Started in 1525 (nearly 100 years before the Pilgrims set foot on Plymouth Rock), it is among the oldest churches in the country. Due to a renovation in 1959, it is also among the most modern. Adorning some of the walls are a series of murals depicting the crucifixion in

Japan of a 16th-century Mexican saint, Felipe de Jesus. The cathedral is especially renowned for the Mariachi Mass held Sundays at 11 a.m. and 8 p.m.

Just across the street from the cathedral is *Jardin Borda.* Joseph de la Borde, a wandering Frenchman who struck it rich in Mexican silver back in the 18th century, altered his name to the Spanish-sounding Jose de la Borda, but kept many of his French ways. Among them was a penchant for gardens, the sort Louis XIV liked. Borda spent a fortune on his own private park. A century later, Carlota and Maximilian discovered the park and turned the grounds into a summer residence. According to royal household gossips, the imperial couple favored the gardens for romantic after-dark rendezvous—with their lovers. Today, the Borda Gardens have been restored to reflect some of their former glory. Open Tuesday to Sunday, 10 a.m. to 5:30 p.m.

Behind the cathedral is *Museo Casa de la Torre* (formerly known as the Robert Brady Museum), housed in the former Convent of San Francisco. The collection of 1,300 artworks and antiques belonged to the late Robert Brady, an American expatriate who lived in the building until his death in 1986. Dating from pre-Hispanic times to the 20th century, the displays include Frida Kahlo's most renowned painting, "Self Portrait With Monkey," and African tribal masks. A cantina, old-fashioned tiled Mexican kitchen and walled gardens make this an enjoyable place to visit. Open 10 a.m. to 6 p.m., except Monday. Guided tours in several languages are available by appointment. Tel. 318-8554 or 314-3529.

MUROS, a cultural center opened by Costco, partly in atonement for having razed a traditional landmark to make way for one of its mega-sized super stores, presents visitors with a new sightseeing option. In addition to housing murals that were rescued from the dismantled Casino de la Selva Hotel, the center features the art collection of Jacques and Natasha Gelman, more than 300 pieces that include works by Kahlo, Rivera, Toledo, and Alvarez Bravo. Tel. 364-5588.

A small photographic museum, *El Castillito,* on Agustin Guemes, opposite Las Mañanitas restaurant, offers a glimpse into the area's fascinating history. Near the railroad station, about a mile from the center of town, is *Teopanzolco,* whose one standing building is the only remnant in town of the Aztecs.

Cuernavaca is close enough to Mexico City for you to drive over for lunch and be back before dusk, traffic permitting, via a six-lane toll highway. But the town, with its hills, ravines and one-way streets, is a complicated place to maneuver around; it's best to park and take cabs, or take a tour.

Aerolineas Internacionales flies to Cuernavaca from Mexico City and also connects Cuernavaca with other destinations in Mexico, such as Acapulco, Monterrey, Tijuana, Guadalajara and Cancun. Call 311-5115 in Cuernavaca, or 5543-1223 in Mexico City.

For excellent guided tours of Cuernavaca and its surroundings, including the Zapata Route, which traces the footsteps of revolutionary hero Emiliano Zapata, contact *Ludel Tours,* run by the multilingual and well-informed Eleonora Isunza. Tel. 318-1015.

Where to Dine

A sumptuous, relaxed meal in a semitropical garden setting can be the sole objective of a trip to Cuernavaca, as guests at the famed *Las Mañanitas* can tell you.

At the market or in small towns and villages around Cuernavaca, you are more likely to find typical regional fare, including tacos filled with *colorin* flowers, tamales stuffed with beans, blue

Cuernavaca's cathedral

Mexico Tourism Board (CPTM)

tortillas wrapped around *jumiles* (an insect), *cecina* (Mexican-style beef jerky) with cream and fresh cheese, rabbit in *chileajo,* and Tlayacapan-style *mole.*

Bugambilias
Jacarandas Hotel, Cuauhtemoc 133
Tel. 315-7777
In Colonia Chapultepec. In business for 40 years, and recently completely refurbished, this hotel and restaurant is set amid beautifully kept tropical gardens. The Mexican and international menu features Greek salad and beef medallions in a three-pepper sauce. Open 7 a.m. to 11 p.m.

Carlos 'n Charlie's
Domingo Diez 711
Tel. 313-0626
Housed in a former mansion-turned-fun house, this restaurant is one of the liveliest and most popular places in town. Great food, terrace

dining and a very popular bar. Don't miss it!

Casa Hidalgo
Jardin de los Heroes 6, on the main square
Tel. 312-2749
This beautifully renovated colonial-era building offers international and Mexican specialties in an attractive contemporary setting, and romantic balcony tables overlooking the plaza. Try the cream of Brie soup and *Fileton Hidalgo,* breaded fillet of beef stuffed with manchego cheese and prosciutto. Open 1:30 to 11 p.m.; to midnight Saturday; to 10:30 p.m. Sunday.

El Amate
Hacienda San Gabriel de las Palmas Hotel
Tel. 348-0636
In Amacuzac, 20 minutes from Cuernavaca. This lavish hacienda built in 1529 offers gourmet international fare in an elegant indoor or garden setting. Menu highlights include green salad with avocados, pears, strawberries and goat cheese in a honey-mustard dressing, beef specialties *arrachera del hacendado* and *cecina San Gabriel,* and Mandarin duck. Open 8:30 a.m. to 10:30 p.m.

El Faisan
Zapata 1233
Tel. 317-5281
Four blocks south of the Zapata monument. This popular Yucatecan restaurant, founded in Mexico City some 40 years ago, is a real treat for those who love to explore new flavors. Open for breakfast, lunch and dinner.

El Gallinero
Leyva 94, downtown
Tel. 312-7444
International fare in an elegant Bohemian-style restaurant-bar-bookstore-bakery and nightclub. Try the *tacos sudados de cochinita pibil* and *robalo al ajillo.* Open 2 to 10:30 p.m.; to 7 p.m. Sunday. Closed Monday.

El Laurel
Plaza El Pueblito
Tel. 318-9559
Excellent Mexican and international cuisine served in a charming, relaxed, European-style setting. Specialties include chicken breast stuffed with squash blossoms, brains in black butter and Norwegian salmon. Open for breakfast, lunch and dinner.

El Madrigal
Sonora 115, Colonia Vista Hermosa
Tel. 316-7878
Ruben Cerda, who managed Las Mañanitas for years, has opened this contemporary hacienda hotel offering excellent dining overlooking an attractive garden with waterfall.

El Nido
Galeana 119, downtown
Tel. 314-2993
"The Nest," as it's called, offers fine dining in a chic art-filled setting with a great view of the city, plus live jazz on Friday and Saturday evenings.

Cuernavaca

HOSTERIA LAS QUINTAS
RESORT · SPA
HOTEL · SPA · BOTANIC GARDEN

Our home is Your home

To be well taken care of
and enjoy the tranquility of a beautiful space is the longing of every man.

the pleasure of rest

Delight in our regional and international cuisine

Hosteria Las Quintas, located an hour and a half from Mexico City, offers the perfect atmosphere so that your mind and body can be in harmony with nature.

We offer 90 beautiful terrace and Jacuzzi suites with 80,000 square feet of magnificent gardens, trees, sculptures, fountains and waterfalls, all framed within a setting of our singular Mexican architecture.

Beauty a la carte in our Spa

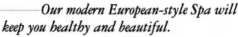

Our modern European-style Spa will keep you healthy and beautiful.

Let yourself be pampered with facial and body treatments, massages, sauna, steam bath and gym. Return to daily life completely revitalized.

90 individually decorated terrace Jacuzzi suites

Our restaurant-bar with international and Mexican cuisine has been recognized for its quality and service.

Enjoy your favorite drink under the canopy of a giant laurel tree surrounded by beautiful floral landscaping.

More than 180 friendly and happy people offer our guests personalized service so you feel at home.

2 heated pools, outdoor Jacuzzi

Blvd. Díaz Ordaz 9, C.P. 62440
tel: 01 (777) 362 3949
fax: 318 3895

toll free fax in U.S.A. & Canada
1-888-SPAS-MEX
1-888-772-7639
spa@blasquintas.com

lasquintas@blasquintas.com
www.blasquintas.com

Cuernavaca · Morelos · Mexico

El Patio

Cuernavaca Racquet Club
Francisco Villa 100, in Rancho Cortes
Tel. 311-2400

At midday it's fun to dine on the terrace overlooking the action on the nine hard-surface tennis courts set in a lovely garden among a grove of royal palms. Evenings are for candlelight dinners next to an attractive courtyard in this exclusive club.

Gaia

Benito Juarez 102, just off the main square
Tel. 312-3656

One of Cuernavaca's leading restaurants, it offers an attractive setting for contemporary Mediterranean cuisine with a Mexican touch. This used to be the home of the late Mario Moreno "Cantinflas". Try the *taquitos de jaiba*, mini crab tacos with tamarind sauce and guacamole; and salmon Gaia, a fresh fillet in a sweet-and-spicy *chabacano* (apricot) and chipotle chili sauce. Open 1 p.m. to midnight; to 8 p.m. Sunday. Closed Monday.

Hacienda de Cortes

Plaza Kennedy 90, Colonia Atlacomulco
Tel. 315-8844

This historic monument, which has served as the setting for several films, was built by Hernan Cortes. Destroyed during Mexico's revolution, it was later restored and converted into a hotel with a romantic restaurant with an international menu and lovely gardens with enough flowers, fountains and history to overwhelm you.

Hosteria Las Quintas

Diaz Ordaz 9
Tel. 318-3949

This popular and newly-expanded retreat, which recently celebrated its 30th anniversary, features more than 10,000 square meters of lush semitropical gardens ideal for banquets and special events. A new specialty restaurant serves fine international and Mexican cuisine, and a "light" spa menu. Las Quintas was founded by the late Salvador Castañeda y Mendoza and is managed by his son, Salvador,

with the same attention to quality and service.

La Calandria

Posada Maria Cristina Hotel
Juarez 300, corner of Abasolo
Tel. 318-2981

Built in the mid-16th century by one of Hernan Cortes' men on the site of the orchards and stables of Cortes' palace, this former hacienda features a fine restaurant-bar overlooking a garden with fountain. Try the *camarones angeles a caballo,* jumbo shrimp stuffed with cheese and wrapped in bacon, served on a bed of croutons in white wine sauce. Open for breakfast, lunch and dinner.

La India Bonita

Dwight Morrow 15, in Casa Mañana
Tel. 312-5021

A longtime Cuernavaca favorite offering authentic Mexican fare in a charming colonial-style setting with garden seating. Try the *India Bonita* soup, made with squash blossoms and corn; *filete Maximiliano,* fillet of beef stuffed with

Cuernavaca Real Estate

By Barbara Waugh

Cuernavaca's perfect climate and proximity to Mexico City have made it a favorite weekend retreat and the destination of choice for a large expatriate community.

If you've ever dreamed of owning (foreigners *can* own property in their own name) or renting your own Mexican villa, this is the place, whether you're looking for a winter retreat, summer vacation home, or year-round residence. A strong buyers market exists for properties in all styles, sizes and prices, usually with a pool and garden. But as prices rise, many of the real bargains are being snapped up, from the tree-shaded heights of Rancho Cortes and Vista Hermosa to the tropical gardens of Palmira and Acapantzingo.

Mexico City is an easy hour's drive via a modern six-lane highway, and its international airport is a half-hour farther. Mexicana regional carrier Aerocaribe recently inaugurated Cuernavaca to Guadalajara and Monterrey flights, while Aeromexico connects the city with Tijuana. The airport, located on the outskirts of the city, serves private jets as well. Travelers who want to see the beauty and variety of Mexico can make the drive down from the U.S. border on divided highways with spectacular scenery and plenty of service stations, some with snack shops. There are fascinating towns and villages along the way.

Both Travel and Leisure and The Robb Report, two popular U.S. luxury lifestyle publications, have chosen Cuernavaca as one of the best communities in the world in which to live. Forbes magazine has on several occasions featured a luxury Cuernavaca property on its website as its "Property of the Week."

At a lower cost than other world-class resorts, residents and visitors can enjoy golf, tennis and horseback riding, as well as European-style and holistic spas, U.S. and international television programming, fine restaurants, cultural events, recreational parks, thermal springs and much more.

Many foreigners choose Cuernavaca over life in the suburbs, citing privacy, security, convenience and cultural diversity. Other resort destinations in the area, such as Tepoztlan, a charming village with a lively crafts market, and Cocoyoc, home to a popular golf course, have their admirers, but no suburban destination offers those four important qualities to the extent that Cuernavaca does.

Some prospective buyers decide to rent while they are looking to buy. Rent prices are higher during the high season, roughly Thanksgiving to Easter, when it's freezing in the north. A house with all services, garden, pool and staff, rents from 250 dollars a day, or about 7,500 dollars a month, depending on size. Yearly rentals cost less proportionally, but offer fewer services.

Good neighborhoods in all areas offer a wide choice of property locations. Unlike other Mexican towns popular with expatriates, Cuernavaca's foreign community is not concentrated in one area. You can choose to be in the Historic Center, near the impressive 16th-century cathedral and the Cortes Palace, or in a quiet gated community, on a golf course, near equestrian facilities, around the racquet club, on a broad avenue or a cobblestone street — the choices are numerous. Many residents live on a *privada*, a private street a block or two long with controlled access, security and no through traffic. A home built by a known architect on a privada with a lovely terrace, pool and garden is priced from about 450,000 dollars.

One key factor in deciding where to buy or rent is temperature: south Cuernavaca is 1,000 feet lower than its northern counterpart, and can be as much as 10 degrees Fahrenheit warmer.

Building in a foreign country and therefore in a foreign language shouldn't be an obstacle: English-speaking architects can help. However, it's cheaper and easier to buy a property than build, and prices are negotiable. Besides, most of the best sites are already built on.

As an owner, you may be able to rent your property during the seasonal months for enough to cover the yearly maintenance. Absentee ownership will require a good administrator, which is easy to find. Timeshares are almost nonexistent, except among groups of friends or relatives who make their own arrangements, and there are few condominiums.

Title insurance for Mexican real estate (TIMR) protects against risks involved in the transfer of property rights. The price of the policy may vary between 0.5 percent and 1 percent of the property value, according to an attorney familiar with the insurance.

Following are several recommended English-speaking real estate agents in the area:

Lourdes Borbolla: 313-3030
Alejandra Reza: 318-4049
Suzanna Rodriguez: 313-8460
Barbara Waugh: 312-5730

A real estate agent for 30 years, Barbara Waugh is Christie's Great Estates affiliate for Cuernavaca (and most of Mexico) and a member of Who's Who in Luxury Real Estate. For more information, visit www.barbarawaugh.com and www.cuernavaca properties.com, or e-mail bw@barbarawaugh.com.

Turn off the noise,
light up *your* **spirit**

MISIÓN DEL SOL
RESORT & SPA
UN ESPACIO DE LUZ

An exceptional ecological Resort in Cuernavaca, specially designed to offer a renewal experience.
In Mision del Sol you will find relaxing and revitalizing Spa therapy treatments, an exquisite menu from
our exclusive International Cuisine and Spa á la Carte

*Come to Mision del Sol and live a unique experience of balancing relaxation
for your mind, body and soul.*

Cuernavaca's main square

huitlacoche (corn truffle) and bathed in avocado sauce; *cecina de Yecapixtla* accompanied with refried beans, corn tortillas and other Mexican staples. Closed Monday.

La Pancha
Rufino Tamayo 26, Colonia Acapantzingo
Tel. 312-8186
Housed in a charming Italian villa-style hotel, this restaurant-bar offers a popular open-air setting for Mexican fare with a Mediterranean touch. Try the fish with fried parsley and the duck tacos.

La Strada
Salazar 38, next to the Palace of Cortes
Tel. 318-6085
A beautiful spot featuring Italian specialties served in a romantic, candlelit colonial patio. The delicious dishes, ample portions and reasonable prices have made this one of Cuernavaca's favorite spots. And you can savor a variety of wines from around the world (they have more than 120) at their European-style bar on the second floor, Caffé Central. Open from 1:30 p.m.; from 2 p.m. Sunday. Closed Monday. Reservations suggested.

Las Mañanitas
Ricardo Linares 107, downtown
Tel. 314-1466
One of Mexico's most famous restaurants features alfresco dining in a colonial setting overlooking a lush garden, where cranes, peacocks and flamingos wander amid elegant Zuñiga sculptures. The lovely surroundings, fine cuisine and gracious service (on chilly nights portable "fireplaces" are arranged around tables so diners can enjoy the beautiful outdoors in comfort) make for a memorable meal. Specialties include tortilla soup, *escamoles* (ant eggs), fettuccini Alfredo, grilled red snapper, and chocolate pie. Las Mañanitas was selected by the Franklin Mint for its "Demitasse Collection" of the 25 most famous restaurants in the world, and is a member of the prestigious Relais & Chateaux.

Marco Polo
Hidalgo 30, across from the Cathedral
Tel. 312-3484
A fine Italian-Mediterranean restaurant serving authentic regional specialties prepared with fresh homemade pastas and delicious sauces. Charming Mediterranean setting.

Rancho Cuernavaca
Callejon del Arrastradero 10
Tel. 313-3962
In the Chamilpa neighborhood, off the road to Tepoztlan. This upscale hideaway on a seven-acre former ranch with expansive gardens, fountains and charming colonial-style architecture offers outdoor dining under the arcades or in an elegantly appointed dining room.

Reposado
Netzahualcoyotl 33, downtown
Tel. 312-9575
This beautifully converted mansion features nouvelle Mexican cuisine. Try the huitlacoche (corn truffle) fondue in crusty campesino bread, tortilla soup (the house specialty), and salmon in sweet adobo sauce. The Azotea, their open-air terrace lounge, offers drinks with a view of the cathedral, as well as king-size beds for lounging.

Sumiya
Camino Real Sumiya Hotel
Tel. 329-9888
About 15 minutes south of town via the Civac exit on the Acapulco highway. The converted home of late heiress Barbara Hutton is set amid Japanese gardens and contemplation pools whose imported stones were ceremoniously placed by a Japanese priest from Kyoto. Dining is on a terrace overlooking the valley. A variety of fish and seafood specialties include

squid sashimi, shrimp in peanut sauce. Open 1 to 11 p.m., except Monday and Tuesday.

Villa del Conquistador
Paseo del Conquistador 134
Tel. 313-1188
In Colonia Lomas de Cortes, this first-class hotel and restaurant features expansive gardens and a wonderful panoramic view of the city.

Nightlife

Although Cuernavaca is more famous for its sunny days, nighttime activities are on the increase. Enjoying a drink in the garden at Las Mañanitas is always pleasant. Casa Tamayo Hotel's *La Pancha* bar is another popular alfresco alternative.

For dinner theater, try *La Comedia*, at Casa de Las Campanas shopping center, Comonfort 2. For reservations, call 314-3445.

Barbazul, a popular disco at Prado 10, features laser light shows and music for the young set; an adjoining bar has lovely gardens and jazz from 8 p.m. Other good discos include *Ta'izz* and *Alebrije,* both popular with the Mexico City crowd. For dancing to tropical music, there's *Zumbale,* at Bajada Chapultepec 13-A, with live bands and an over-25 crowd (open from 9:30 p.m. Thursday to Saturday, tel. 322-5344).

Shopping

Rustic furniture and glazed pottery are some of Cuernavaca's best buys. The market has a good selection of Mexican handicrafts at fair prices, but for unique finds try the specialty shops.

Small shopping centers around town, including *Plaza Cuernavaca, Plaza Esmeralda* and *La Cascada Galerias,* house some nice stores and galleries. *Art Collection Gallery* (Plaza Cuernavaca) displays fine abstract paintings. *Centro de Expresion Cultural,* on Gutemberg, below Harry's Grill, has a permanent exhibit of erotic paintings and sculpture by local artists. *Arte Para Todos,* opposite Bio Art, handles a wide variety of paintings and styles. *Galeria de Arte Contemporaneo,* at Cuauhtemoc 518, displays works by some of Mexico's top contemporary artists.

Azahares
Zapata 810, near the Zapata monument
Tel. 317-0132
This large and colorful Mexican crafts store features a wide variety of traditional hand-painted Talavera and Majolica ceramics, from pots to plates, as well as rustic, wood Mexican colonial furniture and blown glass. Mario Solis and his wife Rufina are the cordial and informative hosts.

Bio Art
Diaz Ordaz and Alta Tension
Tel. 314-1458
One block from Hosteria Las Quintas. A treasure trove of Mexican handicrafts, from accent pieces for the home to furniture sets—one of the best in the country. Here you will find an exceptional selection of truly unique creations in wood, clay, ceramics, glass and textile, as well as some authentic antiques.

Carlos de Villa
Actores 111, Colonia La Jolla, Area No. 20
Tel. 313-0067
The works of this Cuernavaca artist, whose painting "Iconoclasta" hangs in the Jose Luis Cuevas museum in Mexico City, can be seen at his home/studio/workshop. Carlos de Villa has participated in several individual and collective exhibits in Mexico and the United States. He works in a style he calls "buffo hyperrealism," a mixture of surrealism and hyperrealism.

Casillas Artesanias
San Diego 805, Colonia Vista Hermosa
Tel. 316-3598
Two blocks from the Lumiere Cinema. Handmade furnishings, home decorations and handicrafts from the states of Michoacan and Guanajuato, as well as handicrafts from Oaxaca, Puebla and Jalisco. Open 10 a.m. to 7 p.m.; 11 a.m. to 4 p.m. Sunday.

Ceramica Santa Maria
Zapata 900
Tel. 313-0670
Well-known for their fine hand-painted pottery, expert craftsman Jose Sanchez and family have been creating new techniques and designs for more than 42 years. Workshop open to visitors.

Devi
Plaza Crystal
Designer Manola Ruiz's original and attractive silver jewelry. Well worth a visit.

Emilia Castillo
Sonora 115, Colonia Vista Hermosa
Tel. 316-7878
Emilia Castillo, member of the famed Taxco-based family of silversmiths, displays her fine silver jewelry and decorative items at a small shop inside El Madrigal Hotel.

Escaré
Plaza El Pueblito
Tel. 318-7753
A wide selection of unique jewelry and gifts for all occasions, as well as interesting and creative household decorations. English spoken.

Gabriel Contreras Gallery
Abasolo 513, downtown
Tel. 318-9502
A delightful gallery specializing in watercolors, Mexican landscapes, folk paintings, and portraits in oils.

La Casa de Las Campanas
Opposite the Cathedral
One of the city's oldest and most exclusive shops offers original Mexican handicrafts and traditional Mexican apparel for women. Movie actress Manola Saavedra is the owner.

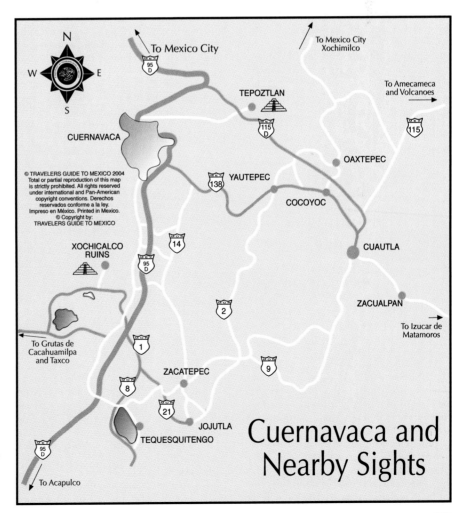

Cuernavaca and Nearby Sights

Tepoztlan

La Puerta del Sol
Reforma 401, corner of Teopanzolco
Tel. 313-9095
An emporium of finely hand-carved, antique-style furnishings, as well as decorative items for the home, including woven rugs, wrought iron, *equipales* and blown glass.

Takana
Alvaro Obregon 154, downtown
An attractive shop carrying fine hand-crafted gifts and decorative items for the home. Open Wednesday to Saturday 11 a.m. to 2 p.m. and 4 to 7 p.m.; 11 a.m. to 3 p.m. Sunday.

Side Trips

South of Cuernavaca is *Xochicalco,* where an intricately carved pyramid pays tribute to the god Quetzalcoatl, or Plumed Serpent. Declared a World Heritage Site by UNESCO in 1999, Xochicalco's artistic styles tie in cultures from central Mexico, the Gulf Coast, the Mayan region and the Mixtec-Zapotec area of Oaxaca state. An impressive, ultramodern, on-site museum tells Xochicalco's fascinating history.

Eight miles from Xochicalco and 11 miles from Cuernavaca is the town of *Xochitepec,* one of the few truly picturesque colonial towns in the state of Morelos. This sleepy town has a colorful Sunday market and 16th-century Franciscan church.

Just 23 miles from Cuernavaca is *Las Estacas,* an oasis that has served as the jungle backdrop for several Tarzan films. The crowning jewel of this nature resort is a crystal clear mile-long river fed by an underwater spring. You can walk the length of the river to its source and enjoy the surrounding exuberant vegetation, or swim, snorkel, scuba dive or just float along its calm surface in an inner tube. Crowded on weekends, but wonderfully tranquil midweek, the park has swimming pools, playgrounds, mini-golf, horseback riding, a restaurant-bar, cabins, campgrounds and meeting facilities. Tel. 345-0350.

East of Cuernavaca, near the town of Cuautla, is the very early site of *Chalcatzingo.* Enigmatic Olmec-style bas-reliefs associated with the water deity, agricultural rites and possibly fertility symbols were carved into the mountainside as long ago as 1100 B.C.

Located some 30 miles east of Cuernavaca, *Cuautla* is famous as the stomping grounds of revolutionary hero Emiliano Zapata; Zapata was born in Anenecuilco, today a suburb of Cuautla. *La Ruta de Zapata,* a tour inspired by the rebel's life and times, is a good way to get to know this region and its people, with visits to the mud shack where he was born, a former sugar plantation now in ruins that remains a powerful symbol of the oppressive colonial system he fought to eradicate, and his empty mausoleum, among other sites. Cuautla is also known for its sulphurous springs, including *Balneario Agua Hedionda,* located on Calle Progreso.

Half an hour past Cuautla (two hours from Mexico City) is *La Casa de Los Arboles,* a country house-turned-holistic retreat set in a landscape of exuberant rose orchards and a smoldering volcano. This haven for the mind and body is located in Zacualpan, a quintessentially Mexican village where men on horseback canter along cobblestone streets, a majestic 17th-century church and former convent dominates the town square, and the overgrown ruins of a once sprawling hacienda hark back to the colonial era. In this timeless setting, the family-run Los Arboles offers sanctuary from the stress and pace of urban life, in addition to spa treatments to rejuvenate and replenish.

Golf aficionados can play nine holes at the attractive *Hacienda Cocoyoc* resort, or 18 holes at *Club Campestre* country club, both in the Cuernavaca area.

About 23 miles south of Cuernavaca is *Hacienda Vista Hermosa.* It once served as a retreat for Hernan Cortes and became the first sugar cane mill in Mexico. Zapata and his rebels burned much of it and most other haciendas in Morelos during the revolution. The sturdy stone structures survived, however, and were restored to house a hotel and restaurant that opened in 1945.

Popular with water-skiers is *Lake Tequesquitengo,* a four-mile-long and nearly two-mile-wide body of water just 20 minutes from downtown Cuernavaca. Weekend residences and a few hotel-restaurant-ski clubs surround the lake, including *Molacho's* and *Villa Bejar.*

Between Tequesquitengo and Taxco, just off the free road, are the largest caverns in central Mexico, the *Grutas de Cacahuamilpa,* which compare in size to those at Carlsbad, New Mexico. The wide variety of stalactites and stalagmites are often interpreted by local guides as resembling religious figures or well-known personalities.

Tepoztlan

The town of Tepoztlan, just 25 minutes from Cuernavaca or one hour from Mexico City, is a delightful place in one of the most beautiful settings imaginable, beneath towering vertical mountains.

Tepoztlan is so typical a Mexican village that it has long been studied by sociologists and economists, from Stuart Chase to Oscar Lewis. Lewis, of "The Children of Sanchez" fame, wrote about it in his book "Five Families." Carlos Coccioli started his novel "Manuel the Mexican" in Tepoztlan.

The town made headlines not long ago when residents prevented the building of a golf course and country club by overthrowing the local government and running the mayor out of town (he had unilaterally approved the project). Their successful small-scale rebellion received ample coverage in *The New York Times.*

Ruins of a temple dating from the late 1400s are located north of town, atop a majestic mountain, 1,200 feet above the valley. It is a difficult climb, but the view is rewarding. The temple was dedicated to Tepoztecatl, the god of *pulque,* a still popular fermented drink made from the spiky maguey plant. The site also was associated with Tlaloc, the rain god, whose presence can be felt when dark storm clouds cling to the mountain top. Give yourself at least an hour and a half to reach the top, and stop along the way to rest and take in the scenery. The site opens no earlier than 10 a.m. and closes at 4:30 p.m. sharp.

The Sunday crafts market is one of the best in central Mexico. Also, the town's main street, Avenida Revolucion, is home to several wonderful shops, most of them selling attractive, rustic home furnishings and decorative items.

For a memorable meal, try the hilltop *Posada del Tepozteco Hotel,* with its castlelike aura, charming dining room and garden tables with a panoramic view. Tel. 395-0010. *Luna Mextli,* Revolucion 16 (395-1114), is a favorite restaurant for its pleasant setting around a garden patio and bohemian ambiance. *El Ciruelo,* Zaragoza 17 (395-1037), serves gourmet fare in an attractive covered courtyard and draws a trendy crowd. Prior to Christmas, the restaurant stages *pastorelas,* irreverent renditions of a Nativity play, followed by dinner, and piñata games for kids. *Casa Piñon,* Revolucion 42 (395-2052), features French cooking on a sunny terrace.

The valley of Tepoztlan is attracting a growing number of spas and holistic retreats, such as the *Posada del Valle* and *Villas Valle Mistico,* and *Hostal de la Luz* in nearby Amatlan.

Where to Stay

Argento

Rio Mayo 1001, Colonia Vista Hermosa
Tel. (777) 316-3286
www.hotelargento.com
Newly-opened in a residential zone and near the Acapulco-Mexico City Highway, this hotel offers 51 spacious, air-conditioned rooms with cable TV, safe. Restaurant, wine cellar-style bar, elegant wood-paneled meeting room for 15, conference room for 50, heated outdoor pool. Colonial decorative touches and royal palms add charm. Rates MD.

Camino Real Sumiya

In Jiutepec, 10 minutes from the city center
Tel. (777) 329-9888
www.caminoreal.com
The former Oriental-style estate of the late heiress Barbara Hutton serves as a deluxe hotel with rambling gardens and pagoda-inspired architecture. There are 163 rooms and suites with deluxe amenities, two lovely pools, eight tennis courts, gym, meeting facilities for up to 600 people. Rates FC.

Casa Colonial

Netzahualcoyotl 37, downtown
Tel. (777) 312-7033
Housed in a beautifully converted 18th-century building near the cathedral, with 16 individually-decorated rooms, each with a fireplace, antique decor. Lovely gardens, swimming pool, cable TV, small meeting room. Rates MD.

Casa Tamayo

Rufino Tamayo 26, Colonia Acapantzingo
Tel. (777) 312-8186
A charming Italian villa-style hotel with just nine guest rooms with terrace and cable TV, a popular open-air restaurant-bar, swimming pool. Rates MD.

Cuernavaca Racquet Club

Francisco Villa 100, in Rancho Cortes
Tel. (777) 311-2400
www.mexicoboutiquehotels.com
A charming modern-colonial-style hotel and tennis club featuring nine Laykold courts (four illuminated), 52 guest rooms with cable TV, restaurant, bar, pool, fitness center. Meeting rooms for up to 200 people. Member of Mexico Boutique Hotels. Rates FC.

El Nido

Galeana 119, in Las Palmas, downtown
Tel. (777) 314-2993
www.elnido.com.mx
"The Nest" offers 14 guest rooms with terrace, marble bath and cable TV; fine dining in a setting with a great view of the city. Heated swimming pool. Rates MD.

Las Mañanitas

Hacienda Cocoyoc

About 30 minutes from Cuernavaca
Tel. (777) 356-2211
www.cocoyoc.com.mx
This converted sugar plantation and onetime summer home of Hernan Cortes resembles a colonial-style country club. There are 289 spacious colonial-style rooms and suites (23 with private wading pools), restaurant, nine-hole golf course, tennis, pools, jacuzzi, horseback riding. Fitness center. Convention facilities for up to 2,000. Rates MD.

Hacienda de Cortes

Plaza Kennedy 90, Colonia Atlacomulco
Tel. (777) 315-8844
A beautifully restored 16th-century hacienda built by Hernan Cortes has been converted into a picturesque hotel with 23 colorfully decorated suites. Lovely gardens, pool, meet-

ing facilities, and indoor or terrace dining on fine international cuisine. Rates MD.

Hacienda San Gabriel de las Palmas
Cuernavaca-Chilpancingo Hwy., Km. 41.8
Tel. (777) 348-0636
www.hacienda-sangabriel.com.mx
In Amacuzac, 20 minutes from Cuernavaca. This lavishly decorated hacienda built in 1529 has served as a Franciscan monastery, sugar plantation and headquarters of Emiliano Zapata. Today it houses 15 guest rooms decorated with period furnishings and original artwork, some with balconies, indoor and outdoor restaurants, swimming pool, tennis court, *temazcal* steam room, game room, meeting and banquet rooms. Horseback riding, massage services. Member of Mexico Boutique Hotels. Rates FC.

Hacienda Vista Hermosa
Alpuyeca-Tequesquitengo Hwy., Km. 7
Tel. (777) 345-5361
Off the Jojutla exit of the Acapulco toll road. South of Cuernavaca in San Jose de Vista Hermosa, close to Lake Tequesquitengo, this beautiful 17th-century hacienda has 105 spacious colonial-style rooms and suites, fine Mexican restaurant, bars, huge pool, myriad outdoor activities, including horseback riding and tennis, game room, and six well-equipped meeting rooms. Rates MD.

Hosteria Las Quintas Resort & Spa
Diaz Ordaz 9, in Cantarranas

Tel. (777) 362-3949
www.hlasquintas.com
More than 10,000 square meters of gardens for banquets and special events, a first-class spa, and five-star service have made this charming owner-managed hostelry one of Cuernavaca's favorite retreats. Newly expanded, it offers 90 spacious terrace and jacuzzi suites with cable TV, fine dining and gourmet "light" cuisine. The spa offers a wide range of services, including a *temazcal*, or pre-Hispanic sweat lodge; the latest in relaxation therapy, called "floating"; and massages, scrubs, wraps and facials. Also three swimming pools, gym, access to golf and tennis clubs. Meeting rooms for 10 to 300 people. Rates MD.

Jacarandas
Cuauhtemoc 133
Tel. (777) 315-7777
www.jacarandas.com.mx
Completely refurbished, with seven charming, individually-decorated suites and 80 balconied guest rooms overlooking beautifully-kept tropical gardens. Three swimming pools, two tennis courts, squash, Ping-Pong, and other recreational facilities. Good open-air restaurant. Meeting rooms. Rates MD.

Las Mañanitas
Ricardo Linares 107, downtown
Tel. (777) 314-1401
www.lasmananitas.com.mx
Everyone's favorite small hotel is famous for its outstanding gourmet restaurant. If you can get

a room (there are only 21 suites), you'll enjoy extensive gardens and a private pool area. A wonderful setting for special events; also small meeting rooms. Impeccable service, outstanding staff. Member of Relais & Chateaux and Mexico Boutique Hotels. Rates DX.

Las Villas de Bellavista
Tabachin 133, in Bellavista
Tel./Fax (777) 317-1893
This colonial-style property, run by an expatriate from New York, is ideal for longer stays, with eight one- to three-bedroom villas with cable TV, phone, fully-equipped kitchen, living-dining area, terrace and private garden, some also with fireplace. Heated swimming pool, bar area. Maid service. Rates MD.

Mision del Sol
Gral. Diego Diaz Gonzalez 31
Tel. (777) 321-0999
www.misiondelsol.com
About 15 minutes from downtown. An upscale health retreat with 40 rooms and 12 villas surrounded by gardens with fountains; guest quarters have no phones or TVs to distract. Full-service spa, lovely swimming pool, tennis court, gym. Restaurant with a vegetarian bent (no red meat). Water recycling and solar power. No children under 13. Rates FC.

Posada Maria Cristina
Juarez 300, corner of Abasolo
www.maria-cristina.com
Tel. (777) 318-2981
Built in the mid-16th century by one of Hernan Cortes' men on the site of the orchards and stables of Cortes' palace, this former hacienda features 20 well-appointed suites around 7,000 square meters of gardens. Swimming pool, fine restaurant-bar, small meeting rooms. Meetings, banquets and events coordinator. Rates MD (includes breakfast).

Rancho Cuernavaca
Callejon del Arrastradero 10
Tel. (777) 313-3962
www.ranchocuernavaca.com
In the Chamilpa neighborhood, off the road to Tepoztlan. This upscale hideaway on a seven-acre former ranch with expansive gardens, fountains and charming colonial-style architecture is ideal for romantic getaways, executive retreats, weddings and other gala events. Each of the 12 guest rooms has marble floors and a fireplace, and is decorated with fine European antiques. Accommodations range from standard doubles to private two-bedroom cottages with a kitchen. Outdoor dining under the arcades or in an elegantly appointed dining room. On-site stables for horseback riding, rodeo ring, bar with billiards, and large swimming pool. Rates FC (includes breakfast).

Reposado
Netzahualcoyotl 33, downtown
Tel. (777) 312-9575
www.reposado.com.mx
This lovely converted mansion ideally located behind the cathedral offers just three guest rooms, pool, fine dining.

Villa Bejar

Domingo Diez 2350
Tel. (777) 311-3300
www.villabejar.com
A Moorish-style property with 69 suites, restaurant, bar, two pools, tennis courts, spa, kids club, extensive meeting and banquet facilities. Rates MD.

Villa Bejar Beach Club & Spa

Blvd. Tequesquitengo and Lomas Tropicales
Tel. (734) 347-0179
www.villabejar.com
On a private beach on Lake Tequesquitengo, with 45 suites, spa, restaurant, pool, jacuzzi, marina. Rates MD.

Villa del Conquistador

Paseo del Conquistador 134, in Lomas de Cortes
Tel. (777) 313-1166
www.conquistador.com.mx
Expansive gardens and a panoramic view of the city are among its best features. The 40 spacious rooms and suites are equipped with color cable TV and phone. Large pool, restaurant, bar, squash, tennis, children's playground, and ample meeting facilities. Rates MD.

Vista Hermosa

Rio Panuco 600
Tel. (777) 315-2374
www.hotelvistahermosa.com.mx
In the Vista Hermosa neighborhood, this attractive hacienda-style hotel offers 35 suites and five master suites, each with terrace, ceiling fan, cable TV, phone. Outdoor swimming pool, open-air restaurant-bar overlooking the gardens, meeting room for up to 50 people. Rates MD.

Tepoztlan

Posada del Tepozteco

Paraiso 3, on a hilltop overlooking town
Tel. (739) 395-0010
www.tepozteco.com
This charming hotel with a castle motif has lovely grounds, panoramic view and an excellent restaurant. There are 20 colonial-style guest rooms and suites, most with terrace and jacuzzi. Gardens, two swimming pools (one heated), tennis, Ping-Pong. Small meeting room. Rates MD (includes continental breakfast).

Zacualpan

La Casa de Los Arboles

Abasolo 9
Tel. (731) 357-4106
www.lacasadelosarboles.com
Half an hour past Cuautla, two hours from Mexico City. For utter tranquility in a splendid setting, this family-run retreat features 35 rooms and suites amid exuberant gardens, health and beauty treatments, including a pre-Hispanic-style steam bath, yoga, meditation, floating tank and *janzu* pool. Outdoor and covered swimming pools. Fine dining, open-air bar and game room. Guided walking tours of nearby sites of interest. Rates FC (AP).

www.puebla.gob.mx

Come to Puebla for the Arts and Crafts

"I was finally able to come back to Puebla. I was very excited about buying a new set of ceramic dishes and I found them at El Parián, even though it was a hard decision, I wanted to take it all, lamps, pots, well everything they have is gorgeous. Later on I found a small antique cedar table at the Plazuela de los Sapos and I could not resist the temptation. From all that walking around I was famished... so I met up with my husband at a restaurant we both love. The dishes prepared with mole were exquisite. Since we needed some time to rest, we decided to stay ONE MORE DAY."

The home of Mole!

Puebla

Mexico's Spanish City of Tiles

Colonial cupolas mark Puebla's skyline

Puebla Convention & Visitors Bureau

Mexico's fourth largest city is perhaps its most characteristically Spanish, with lovely, typically colonial architecture giving it great dignity and charm. Set in the foothills of the Sierra Madre, Puebla is flanked by four of Mexico's best known volcanoes—Popocatepetl, Iztaccihuatl, Malinche and Citlaltepetl, also called Pico de Orizaba.

Puebla was settled after the conquest as a Spanish stronghold between the coast and Mexico City. Three centuries later a ragtag Mexican army of 2,000 men defeated 6,000 invading French troops in the famous Battle of Puebla on May 5, 1862. This is the origin of the Cinco de Mayo holiday and the reason streets throughout Mexico bear that name.

Famous for hand-painted Talavera tile, Puebla was the first city in New Spain to master the art of decorating and glazing fire-baked clay, an art introduced by the Spanish, who had in turn learned it from the Arabs. Spanish tile makers took up residence in Puebla and set a standard of excellence that prevails to this day. You'll see tiles adorning many churches and other buildings around town.

The city's long history as a pottery center actually began before the Spaniards arrived. In his "True History of the Conquest of Mexico," historian and conquistador Bernal Diaz de Castillo noted the "excellent manufacture of earthenware of three colors—red, black and white," adding that when the conquerors dined with Emperor Moctezuma, service was on earthenware from Cholula.

The "City of Tiles" is about 80 miles from Mexico City via an excellent toll road. You can take the toll highway one way and the longer free route the other; the scenery on both is lovely. First-class buses make the trip departing from the airport, or the Del Angel and Benidorm hotels (call 5133-2424, ext. 350 for information). There are also 15-minute flights from Mexico City; and air links between Puebla and San Antonio on *Aeromexico*, and Monterrey, Nuevo Leon, on *Mexicana*.

What to See and Do

The main plaza, or *zocalo*, is a good place to begin sightseeing. Surrounded by arcades on three sides and dominated by the cathedral on the fourth, it is a pleasant spot for people-watching or having coffee at a sidewalk restaurant.

The *Cathedral of the Immaculate Conception*, a combination of medieval, Renaissance and neoclassical architecture, is one of Mexico's most impressive churches, with two massive bell towers, a somber dark-grey carved facade and enormous doors that open onto an opulent interior with 14 gilded and painted chapels.

Beautifully housed in a lovely colonial building at Calle 2 Sur 708, almost three blocks from the main square, is Puebla's most spectacular museum (streets running north to south are *calles*, those running east to west, *avenidas*). Not to be missed, the *Amparo Museum* showcases an extraordinary collection of pre-Hispanic and colonial-era art, as well as some contemporary works. The museum is equipped with ultramodern audio-visual systems, and is probably one of the first, if not the first, museums in Mexico to post explanations in both Spanish and English. Open 10 a.m. to 6 p.m., except Tuesday.

Two blocks from the zocalo, on 5 de Mayo between 4 Poniente and 6 Poniente, is the rosary chapel of the *Church of Santo Domingo,* with a jeweled Virgin and walls covered with tile, gold leaf, sculptured figures and carvings.

On the corner of 6 Norte and 4 Poniente is the *Regional Museum of Puebla* in the *Casa del Alfeñique,* or Sugarcake House. This mansion, dating from the 17th century, houses an archaeological and historical display on the first floor, with the second floor furnished as a typical colonial home.

The *Secret Convent of Santa Monica,* at 18 Poniente 103, off 5 de Mayo, has a fascinating history. After 1857 church reform laws abolished convents, it was operated clandestinely until its discovery in 1935. Now a religious museum, it has 39 rooms full of paintings and relics from this and other secret convents. You enter through a house with a secret passageway. Guide service is available.

Other sightseeing attractions include the *Museum of Popular Arts*, with its authentic Puebla-tile kitchen, located in the former *Santa Rosa Convent; Bello Museum; Church of San Francisco; Guadalupe Fort; Palafox Library* (one of the oldest in the hemisphere); the ultra-modern *Convention Center,* located in the heart of the historic downtown area; *Plaza of the Americas; Puebla State University;* and the baroque *Iglesia de la Compañia,* the final resting place of "La China Poblana."

Bright red, open-topped double-decker buses offer sightseeing tours of the city. The service, called *Turibus*, operates from the convention center from 9 a.m. to 9 p.m. daily, including weekends and holidays. The 90-peso fare (half price for chidren) lets you get on and off as many times as you want at any of the 13 sites of interest.

Africam Safari, an impressive drive-through wild animal park, is located 15 minutes from Puebla. It's especially fun for kids, with pony and llama rides. Nighttime safaris can be arranged for groups. The park operates its own private transportation from Calle 4 Norte 1004. Tel. 235-8700.

Puebla hosts its annual fair at the end of April, with festivities culminating on Cinco de Mayo, or May 5, commemoration day of the Battle of Puebla.

City maps are available at the Tourism Office on the main plaza, which has an efficient and friendly staff, and displays a good selection of folk art. For more information, call 230-2631.

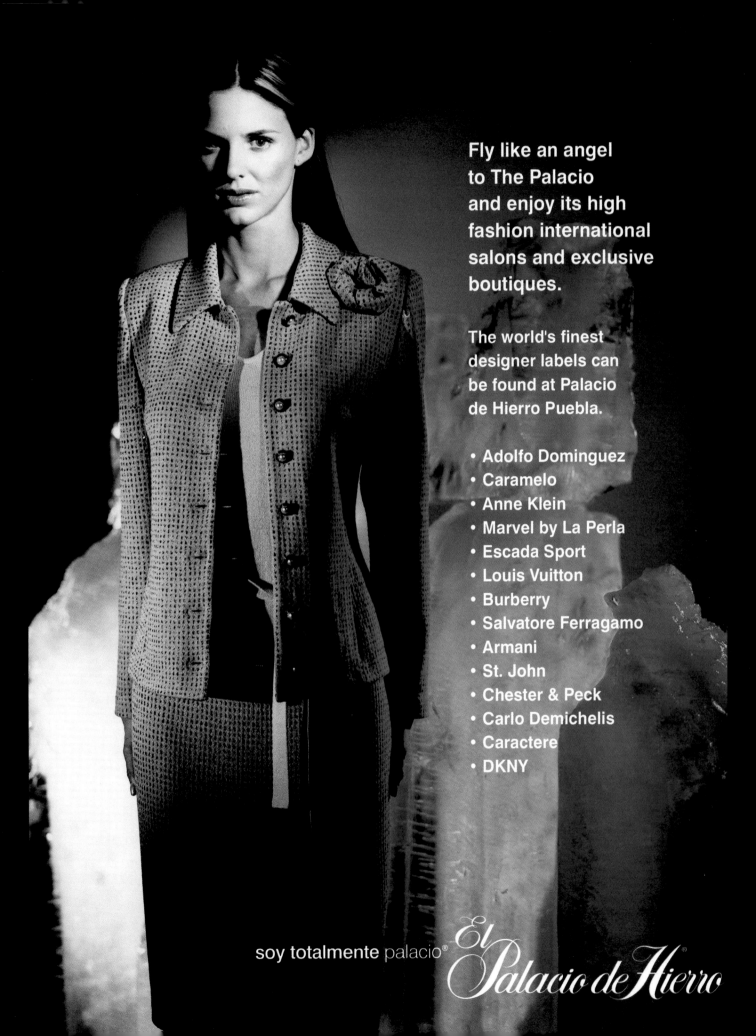

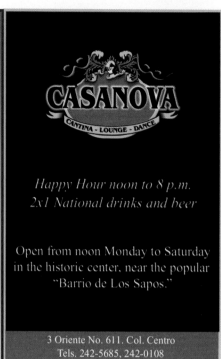
of a nun," "almond dolls" and "little drunk ones."

You'll find piles of Talavera and sweets, as well as onyx, marble, textiles, amate paper from the village of Pahuatlán, terra-cotta from the village of Izucar de Matamoros fashioned into "trees of life," and other regional crafts at the *Parian Market,* about three blocks from the main plaza, on 6 Norte, between 2 Oriente and 4 Oriente.

Other good places to browse are the *Barrio de los Artistas,* a small plaza and promenade located at 6 Oriente and 6 Norte that is flanked by artist's studios, and the *Plazuela de los Sapos,* a small plaza at 5 Oriente and 6 Sur that is ringed by antiques shops. On Saturday and Sunday the Plazuela turns into a bustling outdoor flea market.

On Sunday, natives from surrounding towns come to sell their crafts at the Mercado Municipal (Calle 11 Norte, between Av. 2 and Av. 6 Poniente). It's also fun to attend market day in at least one of the surrounding villages: Texmeluca, Tuesday and Friday; Huejotzingo, Saturday; Tepeaca, Friday.

Shopping

Throughout Puebla, vivid Talavera tile decorates church domes and facades, and other buildings. Introduced to Mexico by artisans from Talavera de la Reina, near Toledo, Spain, this art form is still practiced today, using much the same techniques used in colonial times.

Uriarte, a well-known manufacturer of fine Talavera, has been producing top-quality handmade, hand-painted ceramics since 1827. A brief tour of their factory and showroom at Av. 4 Poniente 911 lets you see the Talavera-making process from start to finish, including the time-tested method of mixing and refining the colors used. All items can be expertly packaged and shipped anywhere. Tours of the installations are offered Monday through Friday at 11,

noon and 1 p.m. Tel. 232-1598. Uriarte has a smaller store at Ex-Hacienda La Noria, 41 Poniente 2120-2, and shops in Mexico City.

At *Casa Poblana,* Calle 6 Sur 306, you'll find Taladura, Talavera-style earthenware specially designed to be microwave safe. Tel. 232-6043.

Daniel Espinosa Jewelry, at the Angelopolis shopping center and the Crowne Plaza Hotel, features bold, contemporary designs in silver, including many pieces with semiprecious stones. Espinosa's creativity and sense of fun is evident in his tie-style chokers made of silver, hypnotic silver rings with black enamel swirls, and other unique items.

Don't miss a stroll along Calle 6 Oriente, "La Calle de los Dulces," which is flanked on both sides by shops selling a mind-boggling array of regional candies with names like "sighs

Dining

No dish is more Mexican than *mole* (pronounced mo-LAY), a rich, dark sauce created centuries ago by nuns of the local Santa Rosa Convent. Traditionally served over chicken and sprinkled with sesame seeds, the spicy-bittersweet concoction is said to be made of more than 20 ingredients, including ground chilies and chocolate.

Another Pueblan original is *chiles en nogada.* Made of stuffed green chilies bathed in a white walnut sauce and sprinkled with red pomegranate seeds, it is the culinary counterpart of the Mexican flag. Appropriately, the dish is featured during independence celebrations in September. A few restaurants serve it year-round, but mid-August to mid-October is the season for chiles en nogada.

Chalupas, another culinary specialty, are

made of mini corn tortillas topped with shredded pork, sizzling lard, chopped onion, and red or green chili sauce. At *Paseo de San Francisco,* billed as the birthplace of chalupas, family-run restaurants feature this and other local favorites.

Recommended restaurants in the downtown area include *Meson Sacristia de la Compañia,* featuring delicious traditional Mexican cooking in an antique-bedecked dining room and intimate sunny patio, and *Meson Sacristia de las Capuchinas. Fonda de Santa Clara* specializes in regional Poblano cuisine (with three branches: 3 Poniente 920, closed Tuesday; 3 Poniente 307, opposite the Bello Museum, closed Monday; and at Angelopolis).

Mi Ciudad, Juarez 507, near the Fuente de la Paz monument, is a colorful restaurant and cantina that pays tribute to the city with murals and replicas of its colonial landmarks. The menu offers traditional Poblano cuisine and attention to detail is evident in the handmade tortillas.

Las Bodegas del Molino, a longtime favorite for its international and nouvelle Mexican cuisine in an authentic colonial-era setting, is located 15 minutes from the main plaza at Calzada del Bosque 12. Open for lunch and dinner, the hacienda has banquet rooms and a fine wine cellar.

For fine international cooking in a refined setting, there's *Armadía* at Circuito Juan Pablo II, in Las Animas. *El Sindicato,* located in a converted theater at Fuentes de San Miguel 75, offers good food in a spectacular setting, as do *Los Amorosos, La Tecla, La Noria, La Garita, La Conjura* and *1800.*

Many of the better restaurants close early Sundays. For good food round the clock, there's *Sanborns,* a cafeteria-restaurant that stays open late.

The Camino Real has an attractive bar that's ideal for an aperitif or after-dinner drink. *Charlie's China Poblana,* at Av. Juarez 1908, is a lively restaurant and night spot located in an upscale neighborhood. Mexican-style sports bar *No Que No,* at Juarez 2302, offers a friendly setting for drinks, with televised broadcasts and table games.

Near Plazuela de los Sapos, a colorful cantina called *La Pasita* serves a delicious regional liqueur made of raisins (*pasitas* in Spanish). You can try a shot of pasita, traditionally served with a raisin and cube of cheese, or buy a bottle to take home.

Cholula

About five miles west of Puebla lies Cholula. Once known only as a city of churches—a popular but apocryphal story claims it has 365 churches, one for each day of the year—it is now famed as having been a significant religious site through more than 2,000 years of occupation. Predating Teotihuacan by perhaps 400 years, it was still an active spiritual center at the time of the conquest in 1521.

Cholula is home to the world's largest pyramid, covering 46 acres, built in several stages during the first 800 years A.D. Its size is one of two unusual features: atop the 200-foot-high structure the Spanish built a church, *Santuario de los Remedios,* in 1666. The fascinating pre-Hispanic temples, plazas and tunnels that have been excavated so far have yielded significant finds. Much more remains to be uncovered, but excavations are hampered in part by the church.

Less than five miles from Cholula two spectacular churches—*Tonantzintla* and *Acatepec*—are prime examples of the zeal with which inspired Indian artists interpreted Biblical teachings.

Outside Tonantzintla's church, you can find an excellent selection of handicrafts at *Tonantzin Artesanias.*

Tlaxcala

Surrounded by Puebla on three sides, little-known Tlaxcala literally lives in the shadow of its more famous neighbor. Yet Mexico's smallest state offers visitors numerous attractions, certainly more than its size would warrant. It has colonial masterpieces, stunning pre-Hispanic murals, colorful religious festivals, and even an annual Pamplona-style running of the bulls, all in an area slightly larger than Rhode Island, in other words, all within minutes of each other. Plus it is located just an hour and a half (120 kilometers/75 miles) from Mexico City via an excellent toll road.

Tlaxcala's capital, also called Tlaxcala, is a colonial gem in miniature, retaining its distinctive small-town charm. On weekends, residents gather at the main square to hear the lo-

cal band play *danzon,* and a school dance atmosphere descends on the plaza.

On the north side of the main square, the 16th-century *Palacio de Gobierno* features brilliantly colored and intricate 20th-century murals depicting Tlaxcala's intriguing history. The Tlaxcalan Indians, fiercely independent and quite capable of ruling themselves under a democratic-style system, for years resisted Aztec domination. But by the time Hernan Cortes and his army arrived in 1521, they had been overpowered and were paying heavy taxes and tributes to Tenochtitlan, the Aztec capital. Not surprisingly, the disgruntled Tlaxcalans became eager allies in Cortes' campaign to subjugate the Aztecs, and with their help he was able to conquer the New World.

Nearby, the *Museo de la Memoria* (Museum of Memory) relates Tlaxcalan history through intriguing codices and other displays. The fusion of ultramodern and colonial architecture alone makes this museum worth seeing. Open 10 a.m. to 5 p.m., except Mondays.

The former *San Francisco Convent,* up the hill from Plaza Xicohtencatl, boasts a beautiful Moorish-style open-air chapel built in 1537 and houses the *Regional Museum of Tlaxcaala.*

Just east of town is the *Sanctuary of Ocotlan.* Its *Camerin de la Virgen,* the Virgin's dressing room, where not an inch of wall or ceiling is devoid of stucco decorations, paintings and wood carvings, took Tlaxcalan artist Francisco Miguel Tlayotlehuamaintzin 25 years to complete. To see the Camerin, it's best to visit between 10 a.m. and 1 p.m.

The *Museum of Popular Arts and Traditions,* which displays masks and costumes worn during festivities, is worth visiting. Weavers can sometimes be seen carding wool and working at handlooms. There is also a small gift shop.

Under the main plaza's arcades, or *portales,* traditional restaurants serve delicious Mexican fare with regional twists, including *crema de frijol,* or cream of bean soup, served with cubes of avocado and cheese, chopped toasted *guajillo* chili, and fried pork rind croutons; *mixiote* (pronounced mee-sho-te), a favorite dish made of mutton marinated in a piquant sauce, wrapped in the skin of a maguey leaf, and steam-cooked until the meat falls from the bone; and for dessert, *buñuelo,* similar to a deep-fried crepe sprinkled with sugar and topped with a ball of vanilla ice cream. *Fonda del Convento,* up the hill from Plaza Xicohtencatl, serves regional dishes in a charming traditional setting. For a fancier meal, try the restaurants at the Posada San Francisco, which faces the main square.

The tourism office, located a block from the main square at Juarez and Lardizabal, offers excellent tours of the city and its surroundings every Saturday starting at 10:30 a.m., including transportation. They also provide maps highlighting all of the attractions, and they speak English.

Just 19 kilometers/12 miles away from downtown Tlaxcala, ancient pre-Columbian murals at the archaeological site of *Cacaxtla* relate more distant history.

Discovered by looters in 1974, these precious remnants from the Olmec-Xicalanca civilization that flourished here between 650 and 900 A.D. are distinctly and mysteriously Mayan in style, recalling the murals of Bonampak in Chiapas. The paintings portray armed warriors, high-ranking figures in elaborate attire and, in

Popocatepetl volcano

Raúl Gil

one of the earliest examples of surrealism, corn stalks sprouting human heads instead of ears of corn, a brilliant and bizarre depiction perhaps of the pre-Hispanic conception of corn as the source of life. The most gripping mural, depicting a fierce battle scene pitting warriors clad in bird feathers against warriors in jaguar skins, is graphic enough to warrant viewer discretion.

The incredibly well-preserved murals survived for more than a thousand years under layers of dirt. Today they are protected from the sun and rain by an enormous corrugated steel ceiling, so unsightly in fact that Cacaxtla has been snubbed by UNESCO for inclusion on its list of World Heritage Sites. Because of the protective shell, lighting at the site is often dim, so take super fast film if you want to take pictures (no flash permitted). A pair of opera glasses could also come in handy to appreciate the murals' finer details; some of them are a bit removed from the viewing platforms.

Just up the hill from the entrance to the site there is a pleasant restaurant, called Cacaxtla, offering good food and a panoramic vista.

Near Cacaxtla (about a 20 minute walk through beautiful country fields) is the more recent discovery of *Xochitecatl.* Opened to the public in 1994, this hilltop site has a unique spiral-shaped pyramid. It's an easy climb and one you wouldn't want to miss since the site's most unforgettable feature is at the top: a spectacular 360° view of the surrounding highland plateau, taking in the Popocatepetl and Iztaccihuatl volcanoes to the west, the Pico de Orizaba volcano to the east, and La Malinche to the south. Since Xochitecatl is uphill from Cacaxtla, it's easier to go there first, then hike down the hillside to Cacaxtla, where you can lunch later.

In August, the town of *Huamantla,* located 45 kilometers (28 miles) from the city of Tlaxcala, hosts a 10-day fair revolving around the feast day of the Virgen de la Caridad. In her honor, huge tracts in front of the town basilica are carpeted with flowers assembled in her image. Scattered around the atrium, clusters of costumed pilgrims march, twirl and stomp, each to a different religious beat. In one corner, the battle between the Moors and Christians is vividly re-enacted by a group of machete-swinging, Ray Ban-wearing faithful.

This being fighting bull-breeding country, the *Huamantlada,* or running of the bulls, is another featured event of the fair, with 12 to 14 800-pound bulls released into the streets.

Huamantla is also home to the *National Puppet Museum,* an earnest and first-rate tribute to the universal art of puppeteering and to native son Don Julian Aranda, who established a family puppeteering enterprise in 1850 that became famous throughout Mexico. There are puppets from around the world, including dreamlike shadow puppets from India, Pakistan and Indonesia. The museum is open Tuesday to Sunday, 10 a.m. to 2 p.m. and 5 to 8 p.m.

About five minutes outside of town, the picturesque restaurant-inn *La Escondida* is where locals and visitors head for a leisurely weekend meal.

The rainy season in this temperate climate runs from April to October, with usually warm sunny mornings followed by late-afternoon showers and cool temperatures. The *Feria de Tlaxcala* takes place from mid-October to about mid-November. On the third Monday of May, there are celebrations in honor of the Virgen de Ocotlan.

For more information, contact the Tlaxcala Tourism Office at 462-0027.

Where to Stay

Camino Real

7 Poniente 105, downtown
Tel. (222) 229-0909
www.caminoreal.com
Two blocks from the main plaza. Dating from 1594, this converted convent houses 75 deluxe rooms and 9 suites, all decorated with priceless colonial art—walls even feature original 16th-century frescoes. Restaurant with outdoor tables facing an expansive courtyard, bar built into a 13th-century Hindu balcony. Business center and meeting facilities for 300. Rates FC.

Crowne Plaza

Hermanos Serdan 141
Tel. (222) 213-7070
www.crowneplazapuebla.com.mx
At the main entrance to the city, this attractive, colonial-style property offers Mexican hospitality and modern comfort, with facilities for the business traveler and executive club floor. 216 rooms, business center, meeting facilities for up to 550 people, indoor pool, fine restaurant, lobby bar. Rates MD.

El Sueño

9 Oriente 12, downtown
Tel. (222) 232-6489
www.elsueno-hotel.com
Housed in a converted 18th-century mansion that beautifully blends colonial and contemporary design, this attractive hotel and spa offers 12 suites with cable TV, Internet access and room service, among other amenities; spa with outdoor solarium and jacuzzi, sauna, massage area and gym; covered open-air coffee bar, lounge bar featuring martinis and light gourmet fare. Rates FC.

Fiesta Americana

La Vista Country Club
Tel. (222) 225-9300
www.fiestamericana.com
This 200-room hotel, overlooking a Robert von Hagge-designed 18-hole golf course, offers guests many club amenities, including access to the course and tennis courts. Indoor-outdoor meeting facilities, business center, exclusive Fiesta Club section, restaurant, lobby bar, heated pool. Rates MD.

Holiday Inn

2 Oriente 211
Tel. (222) 223-6600
A block and a half from the main square. This newly-refurbished hotel geared to the business traveler offers a colonial-style setting with modern amenities: 80 rooms with work stations, meeting facilities, rooftop pool and sun deck, dining room, parking. Rates MD.

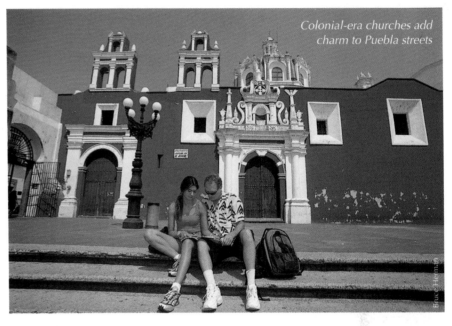

Colonial-era churches add charm to Puebla streets

Hostal De Velasco

8 Oriente 813
Tel. (222) 232-2981
On Antigua Calle de Mesones, downtown. This beautifully preserved 17th-century mansion offers guests the unique opportunity to stay in an authentic historical monument, surrounded by original antiques and works of art. A private home-turned-luxury B&B, the building has been in the De Velasco family for 13 generations. It features 15 guest rooms, a lavish 18th-century French baroque music parlor, an English-style library, open-air patio and terrace. An ideal setting for exclusive gatherings and events. Rates FC.

Hostal Santa Maria

3 Oriente 603

Tel. (222) 141-2000
www.marriott.com
This attractive hotel at the main entrance to the city (formerly Real Meson del Angel) offers nicely-kept grounds with gardens, and 192 rooms and suites with balconies and all first-class amenities; 70 rooms housed in a separate executive section with added services, including daily continental breakfast, secretarial assistance. Mexican-international restaurant, bar, swimming pool, tennis, gym, business center and meeting facilities for 800 people. Rates FC.

Meson Sacristia de la Compañia
6 Sur 304 (on "Callejon de los Sapos")
Tel. (222) 242-3554
www.mesones-sacristia.com
A stunning downtown colonial hostelry with just seven guest rooms and two suites, all exquisitely decorated with fine antiques and antique-style furnishings, many of them for sale. Fine gourmet Mexican restaurant, and bar with live music. Guests enjoy access to nearby private clubs with golf, tennis and swimming pool. Member of Mexico Boutique Hotels. Rates FC.

Meson Sacristia de las Capuchinas
9 Oriente 16, downtown
Tel. (222) 232-8088
www.mesones-sacristia.com
This seven-room sister hotel to Meson Sacristia de la Compañia is housed in a luxuriously renovated 16th-century home just steps from the Amparo Museum. Gourmet restaurant. Guests enjoy access to nearby private clubs with golf, tennis and swimming pool. Member of Mexico Boutique Hotels. Rates FC.

Radisson
Circuito Juan Pablo II 1936
Tel. (222) 211-9000
www.radisson.com
A 150-room hotel designed for the business traveler, with extensive meeting facilities, restaurant-coffee shop, lobby bar, swimming

Tel. (222) 298-8240
Around the corner from "Callejon de los Sapos." This colorfully refurbished colonial hostelry (facade is bright yellow, foyer hot pink) offers six well appointed guest rooms with cable TV, coffee maker, phone and friendly family-run management. Rates ECON.

Las Calandrias
In Atlixco

Tel. (222) 266-5393
www.lascalandrias.com.mx
This charming hotel-spa offers personalized service and pampering in a country setting just minutes from Puebla, with five exclusive suites, heated pool, pre-Hispanic-style sweat lodge and other body treatments.

Marriott Real Puebla
Hermanos Serdan 807

pool, game room, gym, cable TV. Rates MD.

Cholula

La Quinta Luna
Calle 3 Sur 702, downtown
www.mexicoboutiquehotels.com
This 17th-century mansion, a bonafide historical monument, features just six guest rooms and a wonderful restaurant housed in the former chapel; guests may also dine on the patio or in their own room.

Villa Arqueologica
2 Poniente 601, in Cholula
Tel. (222) 273-7900
At the foot of the great pyramid. A member of Club Med's chain of rustic cultural hotels, it offers 54 rooms and suites, good restaurant, heated pool, tennis court, library-video room. Rates ECON.

Tlaxcala

Calinda
Tlaxcala-Apizaco Hwy., Km. 10
Tel. (246) 461-0000
www.hotelescalinda.com.mx
Located on the outskirts of town, this property is surrounded by gardens and faces a waterfall. The 102 rooms and suites are distributed in a *"cascada"* section or more secluded *"hacienda"* section. Freestanding business center, banquet room. Indoor swimming pool and jacuzzi, well-equipped gym, tennis, restaurant,

bar, parking and playground. Rates MD.

Posada San Francisco
Plaza de la Constiucion 17
Tel. (246) 462-6022
Ideally located on the main square, this renovated colonial-era mansion features 62 rooms and six suites built around a large swimming pool or around a quieter courtyard with fountain; all rooms have cable TV, phone, heaters. Ground-level rooms are attractively rustic, upper-level rooms more modern but less charming. Tennis courts, billiard table, good restaurants, cozy bar, meeting facilities. Rates MD.

Taxco

An Old World Town Paved With Silver

As recently as 70 years ago, most traveling to and from Taxco was on horseback, taking the better part of a week. Today, via modern toll roads that eliminate the tortuous 300 curves of the former approach, the enchanting colonial town can be reached from Mexico City in approximately two hours. The trip takes you through spectacular mountains and fields before a sea of whitewashed homes with red-tile roofs, and the filigree spires of Santa Prisca church suddenly appear over the last crest of the journey.

While a steady trickle of foreign visitors tackle the town's steep cobblestone streets, Taxco's mainstay is the manufacture of silver. Silver shops line the main plaza and all the streets leading to it, and the clerks' relaxed, hands-off approach towards the casual browser bespeaks a brisk export business.

A Rich History

Shortly after the Spanish Conquest of Mexico in 1521, conquistador Hernan Cortes learned that the Indians living in the mountains south of what is now Mexico City paid an earlier conqueror, Moctezuma I, in blocks of silver and gold.

Engineers were promptly dispatched to the area called "Tlachco," an ancient Aztec word meaning "a place to play ball." Eventually, the Spanish corruption of the name turned it into "Taxco" (Tahs-co).

The Indians were set to work extracting tons of silver and gold ore from what became known as the King's Shaft. The mine, considered to be one of the oldest in North America, cannot be entered today, though the original entrance is still partially visible.

When the royal shaft petered out, the search for minerals was continued by local prospectors. One of these suggested to his brother, Jose de la Borda, a Frenchman living in Spain, that he also try his luck at surface

Taxco's famed Santa Prisca church, on the main plaza

mining. Swinging a pick axe, Borda rushed over to the New World. He was about to return home after several months of fruitless toil, however, when he finally struck it rich. As the story goes, one day his horse slipped on a steep hillside, dislodging a stone and revealing a rich lode of silver. Taxco's famed *Santa Prisca Parish Church*, some say, is built on the spot where Borda's stumbling beast exposed the vein of silver.

Borda made and lost a fortune several times over, but ultimately fared so well that he is said to have declared, rather pithily, "God gives to Borda, so Borda gives to God," and set about erecting a magnificent church in the manner of a cathedral.

Single-handedly financing the entire project, inside and out, Borda commissioned the finest artisans from Spain and France to build what is considered to be one of the most beautiful examples of 18th-century Mexican baroque architecture. A somewhat histrionic-sounding plaque bearing the words "It's Over" announces the church was completed in eight years and dedicated in May, 1759.

The church houses 12 ornately carved and gilded altars arranged according to size, intricacy and hierarchical religious content, from the most modest to the most ambitious. An adjoining portrait gallery serves as a pictorial Who's Who of prominent *Taxqueños*, including oil paintings of Borda, his son and Santa Prisca's first priest, Manuel, and Juan Ruiz de Alarcon, the famous playwright and native son (born 1581), who is to Taxco what Miguel de Cervantes is to Guanajuato.

A law enacted in the early 1930s declared Taxco a national colonial monument and ensured the preservation of the mansions built by the city's early silver barons, who flocked to Taxco after Borda's discovery. *Casa Borda*, a spacious townhouse the silver magnate built for himself on the main plaza, is one of these. The handsome building is now a cultural center.

As a mining center, Taxco languished until the early 20th century, when newly-developed equipment resurrected the industry which today employs almost half of the town's inhabitants.

William Spratling

In the mid-1920s, William Spratling, a young professor of architecture at New Orleans' Tulane University, was invited to Mexico City to give a series of lectures. Fascinated by the countryside, he journeyed south on horse-back to see life in the small villages. He later published his travel experiences under the title "Little Mexico." In 1929, then U.S. Ambassador to Mexico Dwight W. Morrow, aware of Spratling's love for the country, persuaded his friend to settle in Taxco and to put his vast knowledge of design to use.

Spratling set up a workshop and took on apprentices. At the same time a young man named Antonio Castillo was sent to live with relatives in Taxco, where his aunt got Spratling to agree to giving Antonio and his cousin English classes. The two young men became apprentices as well as English students. And when the whole family moved to Taxco, three more Castillo boys joined as apprentices. Thus began the flourishing industry that has given Taxco its nickname, "The Silver Capital of the World," and made the name Castillo synonymous with quality silver craftsmanship.

Weavers and carpenters were brought to the Spratling factory located a few steps south of Santa Prisca (the space is today occupied by the Bora-Bora pizza parlor), and there they made rugs, shawls and exquisite Spratling-designed furniture, silverware and jewelry. There were few tourists in those days, but as word spread of Spratling's products, more arrived. Hotels were built to accommodate them and soon Taxco became Mexico's most popular tourist destination after Mexico City.

During World War II, when the supply of jewelry from Europe and the Orient was cut off, merchants from New York and other U.S. cities clamored for Spratling's entire output.

At the height of his success, Spratling formed a partnership with a rich American. He was unaware, he said later, that his "partner" needed to show a tax loss and that he purposely sank the company to get it. Spratling and a few of his craftsmen retired to a chicken ranch south of Taxco, where he rebuilt the business and, to his credit, personally paid back every *centavo* his friends had lost when the company went bankrupt.

After Spratling's death in 1967, a good friend named Alberto Ulrich bought the workshop and store, where he continues manufacturing Spratling Silver from the original molds.

You can visit the *Spratling Ranch,* located in Taxco Viejo, and watch craftsmen creating Spratling-designed silverware and jewelry. The pieces range in price from about 100 to about 3,000 dollars. Both the workshop and store are open Monday to Saturday, 8 a.m. to 1 p.m. and 2 to 5 p.m. Tel. 622-6108.

One of the first of Spratling's apprentices to strike out on his own was Antonio Castillo. With his three brothers, he established a family business and the name Castillo came to stand for quality silver products, especially items inlaid with mother of pearl. Shops carrying Castillo creations are found in various cities, including Mexico City, Cancun, Acapulco and Puerto Vallarta, as well as Dallas and Paris. You can visit the family-run workshop and store at the beautiful *Rancho la Cascada*, also located in Taxco Viejo. The workshop is open weekdays, the store Monday to Saturday. Tel. 622-1016.

Taxco Viejo, located about 15 minutes outside of town, can be easily reached by taxi or, more economically, by *peseros*, collective taxis that regularly cover the route.

What to See and Do

Taxco's tiny main plaza, *Plaza Borda*, is the hub of activity day and night. The beautiful Santa Prisca Parish Church regularly hosts weddings. And almost all the buildings perched on the square house ground-floor silver shops and top-floor restaurants with flower-decked balconies overlooking the scene. At meal time, in fact, you'll be hard pressed to find any vacant balconies, which provide an ideal vantage point for admiring Santa Prisca's elaborately carved pink-hued facade.

Next to whiling away the time at a front-row balcony seat, the best way to enjoy Taxco is on foot, weaving in and out of the myriad silver shops, discovering little plazas, and taking in the colonial atmosphere. Be sure to wear your most comfortable, flat shoes; pedestrians share the narrow streets and alleyways with traffic, and cars are often revving their engines in an attempt to make it up the steep roads.

While a small museum located directly behind Santa Prisca bears Spratling's name, it displays not silver, but an interesting collection of pre-Hispanic archaeological relics found in the region.

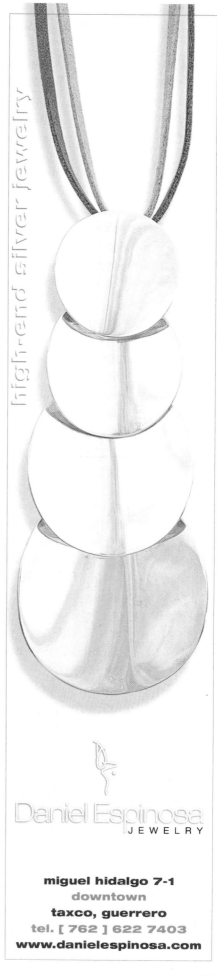

Nearby, at Juan Ruiz de Alarcon 6, is *Casa Humboldt*, named in honor of German naturalist Baron Alexander von Humboldt, who stayed here during his travels. The 17th-century building served as a hospital during the revolution, as Taxco's first movie theater, as a fine hotel, and is now home to the *Museo de Arte Virreinal*, which displays liturgical objects from Santa Prisca.

The *Hacienda del Chorillo*, originally built around 1542 to house Spanish engineers sent to supervise the mines, today serves as the Taxco campus of Mexico's National Autonomous University (UNAM), which offers courses by professors and artisans in literature, Spanish, art history, painting, sculpture, woodworking and jewelry making. For information, call 622-3690.

A nearby smelter, originally ordered built by Cortes himself, has been redesigned and rebuilt to house the Taxco Convention Center, a tourism office and a large outdoor theater for special events.

Taxco hosts world famous and awe-inspiring religious festivals during *Holy Week*, the week between Palm Sunday and Easter. Visitors come to see thousands of pilgrims and penitents participate in the reenactments of the crucifixion of Christ. Once observed, the rituals are not easily forgotten.

In May the town hosts *Las Jornadas Alarconianas* in honor of its favorite son, playwright Juan Ruiz de Alarcon, featuring a variety of cultural events, such as plays, concerts, exhibits, and festivities.

On the first Monday following Day of the Dead celebrations on November 1 and 2, the *Festival del Jumil,* a type of beetle found in abundance this time of year, has the town combing the hills for these edible insects.

The last Saturday of November marks the beginning of the week-long *National Silver Fair*, during which popular concerts are staged nightly at the main plaza, and entries in a nationwide silver contest, from sleek hair ornaments to garish stone-encrusted fountains made of silver, are displayed at Casa Borda.

About 30 minutes outside of town, *Zoofari* features free-roaming wild animals and an opportunity to enjoy close encounters with elephants, zebras, elks, llamas, ostriches and other creatures from all corners of the world. Visitors drive through this zoo and breeding center, viewing and feeding (special feed is provided) the animals at the park, located at Km. 55 of the old, free road leading north to Cuernavaca. The park, including a restaurant, is open 9 a.m. to 5 p.m. daily. Tel. 320-9723.

The *Grutas de Cacahuamilpa*, a string of more than 20 caverns featuring dramatic stalactite and stalagmite formations, is located a 30-minute drive north of Taxco, on the Toluca highway. Some of the "rooms" in these caves are larger than Radio City Music Hall and one, in fact, has seats and a stage for concerts. Emperor Maximilian and his wife Carlota often visited this natural wonder, and former president/dictator Porfirio Diaz (1876-1910) used to host state receptions inside. The site is open 10 a.m. to 5 p.m. daily; set aside two hours for

the guided tour of the well-illuminated caves.

An easy scenic drive from Taxco is to the village of *Ixcateopan*, the birthplace of Mexico's Emperor Cuauhtemoc, and the resting place of his remains. The stone outcroppings en route to the site are not granite, but pure white marble. The village is home to the *Museum of Indigenous Resistance*, which depicts the struggle of Mexico's Indians against the Spanish conquistadors.

Dining and Nightlife

Overlooking the main square is *Paco,* a wonderful place to eat good food, have a drink and people-watch. Diners get a bowl of freshly-popped popcorn to munch on while waiting for their orders, and curried dishes are one of their specialties. Open from 1 p.m. Reservations are recommended, especially during the holidays: 622-0064. Next door, *La Parroquia* offers a good option for breakfast, lunch and dinner, with deliciously-prepared meat specialties.

La Hacienda restaurant and *La Terraza* cafe and bar, both at the Agua Escondida Hotel on the square, offer good food in simple settings with a good view of the plaza.

At *Pozoleria Tia Calla*, also on main square, at Plaza Borda 1, you can try Guerrero-style *pozole*, a hearty pork or chicken and hominy stew that is traditionally found on menus on Thursdays. Tel. 622-5602; closed Tuesday.

Farther from the square, the Posada de la Mision Hotel's *El Mural* restaurant offers excellent international cuisine, including the best fish and steaks in town. There's an indoor dining room and an open-air, plant-filled terrace featuring a spectacular view of the downtown area. It's open for breakfast, lunch and dinner. Tel. 622-0063.

Next to the Palacio Municipal, at Benito Juarez 12, is *Sotavento*, a popular restaurant-bar-gallery serving creative international dishes in a colonial setting with an attractive patio. Open noon to 11 p.m.

At the tiny Plazuela de San Juan, behind the square, there are two good restaurants: the pretty *El Adobe*, featuring Mexican cuisine, and *La Concha Nostra*, a friendly bohemian place serving Italian fare and pizzas.

For coffee and dessert, try *Neveria Vicky* at Plaza Borda 5, upper level. Here you can enjoy your cappuccino or espresso, along with homemade cakes or cookies and ice-cream, from any of three balconies facing the main plaza. Open 9 a.m. to 9 p.m.

For nighttime entertainment, there is the Posada de la Mision Hotel's popular disco and piano bar; the MonteTaxco Hotel's *Windows* disco, featuring the Voladores de Papantla (a group of dancers that twirl suspended by ropes from a pole), and *PlaneTaxco*, a disco near the square, at Cuauhtemoc 8, that has futuristic interior decor and an upstairs bar-cafe (disco open Friday to Sunday; cafe open Monday to Thursday.

Shopping

There are literally hundreds of silver shops in Taxco's two major shopping areas—along

the main highway and around Plaza Borda. Many of the shops sell both retail and wholesale, and also produce custom-made pieces.

The most eye-catching shops on the main plaza are *Pineda's Taxco* and *Sebastian*. One of the most opulent shops downtown, *Elena de los Ballesteros,* is located near Pineda's.

Daniel Espinosa Jewelry, at Miguel Hidalgo 7-1, features bold, contemporary designs in silver, including many pieces with semiprecious stones. Espinosa's creativity and sense of fun is evident in his tie-style chokers made of silver, hypnotic silver rings with black enamel swirls, and other unique items. *Talleres de los Ballesteros,* a family-run business since 1937, is located at Avenida de los Plateros 68. Silver manufacturer *Uriland*, whose showroom is at Veracruz 5, is a leading wholesaler and exporter.

Emilia Castillo, daughter of the renowned Taxco family of silversmiths, has a shop displaying her own creations at Juan Ruiz de Alarcon 7. Her work features silver-inlaid ceramics, many incorporating wild animal motifs.

The town market offers heaps of silver items, as well as belts, *huaraches* (good footwear for Taxco's hilly cobblestone streets) and other leather goods.

Where to Stay

Agua Escondida. Plaza Borda 4, on the main plaza. Plain to look at, but excellent location in the heart of town and outstanding views. A rambling old building with 50 rooms, large rooftop pool, terrace restaurant, game room. Rates ECON. Tel. (762) 622-0726. www.aguaescondida.com.

Hacienda el Solar. Paraje del Solar, south of town, off Hwy. 95. This charming hilltop hotel offers a spectacular view and 23 colonial-style rooms and suites, some with balconies. Swimming pool, tennis. Restaurant-bar. No children under 12 allowed. Rates MD. Tel./Fax (762) 622-0323. www.haciendadelsolar.com.mx.

MonteTaxco. Lomas de Taxco. This 170-room neo-colonial-style hotel is located high on a mountain top above town; guests can ride a cable car down to a road leading into the city. Popular with Mexican families for its many outdoor activities, including tennis, golf, poolside games. Restaurants, disco, nightclub, gym. Rates MD. Tel. (762) 622-1300. www.montetaxco.com.mx.

Posada de la Mision. Cerro de la Mision 32, just off the highway leading into town. Located on a hilltop, yet within walking distance of the main plaza, this wonderful colonial-style property features a panoramic view of Taxco and excellent dining. The 150 individually decorated, spacious guest rooms range from standard doubles with cable TV, a/c and phone to two-bedroom suites with a kitchenette, fireplace and terrace with a sweeping vista. Amenities include swimming pool, gardens, fine restaurant, bar, handicrafts shops, travel agency, and meeting facilities for up to 500 people. Excellent service, tranquil setting. Rates ECON. Tel. (762) 622-0063.

Queretaro

Baroque Splendor

Queretaro abounds with parks and plazas

Mexico Tourism Board

Just two and a half hours north of Mexico City by car lies one of Mexico's most cherished colonial jewels—the city of Queretaro.

The picturesque town is studded with charming and amazingly well-preserved baroque churches, temples and mansions boasting graceful balconies and ornate facades. Nestled among these architectural masterpieces are well-tended plazas featuring fountains or statues paying homage to famous local sons and, at least in one case, daughters. The city of 850,000 residents is also capital of the state of Queretaro, which encompasses numerous other attractions for the visitor, from archaeological sites to spa resorts.

Queretaro's central location made it an important crossroads in Mexican history. The area was first inhabited by the Otomies and later the Purepechas and Mexicas.

The name "Queretaro" is believed to be Purepecha for "site of the ballgame" or "place where there are rocks." If the second translation is true, perhaps the rocks the Indians were referring to were the opals, amethysts and other semiprecious stones found in rich supply throughout the mountainous region. Even

today Queretaro and the nearby towns of San Juan del Rio and Tequisquiapan are Mexico's gem-cutting centers, where opals and other semiprecious stones are cut and polished. Many stores carry the stones loose or worked

Well-tended plazas featuring fountains or statues pay homage to famous local sons and, at least in one case, daughters.

into jewelry; buying them from street vendors is not recommended.

In 1531, the city was overtaken by the Spanish. It became a point of transit for anyone traveling between the nation's capital and the interior provinces, and its prominence was

acknowledged with the designation "Third City of New Spain." It later played a leading role in both the struggle for independence and the revolution. It was here that Mexico's constitution was written and signed.

The city's most prominent landmark is an eight-kilometer-long, 74-arch aqueduct built in the early 1700s to supply the city with water. It runs through one of the city's main thoroughfares, with intersections laced through its high arches. Appropriately, a fountain built in the city's main square, the diminutive *Plaza de Armas* or *Plaza de la Independencia*, pays tribute to the man who financed the 12-year project (1726-38), Don Juan Antonio Urrutia, the Marquis de la Villa del Villar del Aguila.

The main square is the ideal starting point of any walking tour, with its attractive buildings and intriguing legends. A tale of two buildings, standing side by side, tells of fiercely competitive neighbors who tried so hard to outdo one another in residential splendor that city officials were forced to intervene before yet another architectural enhancement threatened to take another bite out of the already minute plaza. The case went to court and the verdict is

See for yourself
we offer more than you ever imagined
History - Culture - Tradition - Fun - Entertainment - Rest & Relaxation

 FIPROTUR MEXICO

Querétaro is *Better*

> Santa Rosa de Viterbo Church > Aqueduct > Peña de Bernal

Sites of interest in the State of Querétaro

SECRETARÍA DE TURISMO DE GOBIERNO DEL ESTADO DE QUERÉTARO

Pasteur 4 Nte. Centro Histórico, Santiago de Querétaro. Tel. (442) 238•50•00 ext. 5067 y 5212

del interior del país llame sin costo al 01•800•715•1742 From U.S. toll free 1•888•811•6130

www.queretaro.gob.mx/turismo Correo-e: turismo@queretaro.gob.mx plainly written on the loser's facade.

The state tourism office, at Pasteur 4 on the main square, conducts a variety of walking tours in Spanish and English, relating the city's history and highlighting monuments. Tours are every day starting at 10 or 10:30 a.m., depending on their duration. Tel. 238-5000.

Trolley Tours

An old-fashioned *trolley* offers tours of the downtown area, with a bilingual guide to explain the 21 historic buildings and monuments passed along the way. The trolley sets out from the state tourism office at 9, 10 and 11 a.m., and 4, 5 and 6 p.m., except Mondays. Passengers can also board at the Mirador al Acueducto and Cerro de las Campanas.

For a schedule of trolley tours to nearby sights of interest, including Tequisquiapan, San Juan del Rio and Cadereyta, call 238-5067.

It is in downtown Queretaro where many of the baroque buildings for which the city is famous are concentrated. Most are in use today, housing government agencies, museums or luxury hotels.

The former San Agustin Monastery, with its exquisitely proportioned patio, now houses the *Museum of Art,* and the equally lovely former Convent of San Francisco is home to the *Regional Museum of Queretaro.*

The 18th-century *Templo de Santa Rosa de Viterbo,* at Arteago and Ezequiel Montes, is one of the most exotic examples of ecclesiastical architecture in Mexico. It has two enormous flying buttresses flanked by dragon heads, an intricate bell tower fashioned after an Oriental pagoda, an octagonal cupola, and the first multiple-face clock built in the Americas. The interior is a mass of gilt, carved wood with inlaid marble, and filigree work.

Points of historical interest include the *Cerro de las Campanas,* where Emperor Maximilian was executed in 1867, and the *Casa de la Corregidora,* home of independence heroine Doña Josefa Ortiz de Dominguez. It was from

this house, now seat of the state government, that Doña Josefa was able to relay instructions—by whispering them through a keyhole—that ultimately led to the ouster of the Spanish viceroys. A monument to Doña Josefa graces the city's Plaza Corregidora.

Radiating from the main plaza is *Andador Libertad,* where most of the city's street vendors have been relocated to permanent stands, creating a kind of outdoor flea market. Stores line both sides of this pedestrian-only promenade, including *Casa Queretana de las Artesanias* (Andador Libertad 52, tel. 224-3326). A showcase of handicrafts from around the state, this government-backed shop occupies three adjacent locales, each dedicated to different hand-made items, such as embroidered fabrics and Talavera-style pottery.

Another shop worth visiting is *Casa Canela,* housed inside a historic building at Andador Cinco de Mayo 39, *La Casona de los Cinco Patios.* Here you'll find excellent handicrafts in both traditional and contemporary designs.

The *Independence Express* (Expreso de la Independencia), a train that tours major cities in Central Mexico such as Guanajuato, San Miguel, Zacatecas and San Luis Potosi, begins and ends its rail journey in Queretaro. Departing from a quaint, antique station that's considered one of the prettiest in the country, the train offers five-day midweek or three-day weekend tours aboard vintage Pullman-style sleeping and dining cars. Packages include guided visits, meals and train accommodations. For more information, call (444) 812-5411 in San Luis Potosi.

Colorful fiestas attract visitors to Queretaro from many parts of the country, especially in mid-September and at Christmas. This area is also notable for its vineyards; wines such as *Hidalgo* are important regional products.

Dining and Nightlife

There's good dining at the leading hotels, especially La Casa de la Marquesa, Meson de

Santa Rosa and Doña Urraca, all of which feature nouvelle Mexican cuisine.

Popular outdoor cafes and restaurants line two sides of the main square, as well as nearby Plaza Corregidora. *1810,* facing the main plaza at Andador Libertad 64, is a great place to try the regional specialty, *enchiladas Queretanas.* This twist on the traditional enchilada dish includes a topping of potato, sausage and carrots in an adobe sauce. The restaurant offers international as well as Mexican cuisine and has both sidewalk seating and indoor dining rooms. Open 8 a.m. to midnight.

Around the corner from the main plaza, at Andador Cinco de Mayo 39, is *La Casona de los Cinco Patios,* a historical colonial-era mansion that today houses a gorgeous restaurant, *San Miguelito,* and two bars, *La Viejoteca* (open Tuesday to Saturday) and the bullfighting-themed *Rincon de Juli* (open Friday and Saturday). The restaurant, a feast for the eyes with each table and setting inspired by a different Mexican icon, is open daily from 1 p.m. to midnight. Tel. 224-2760.

Don't miss an opportunity to have a traditional Mexican meal, accompanied by trio and mariachi music, at *Hacienda Los Laureles.* This beautiful converted hacienda features canopied tables in a sunny, flower-filled patio, and delicious regional specialties like *carnitas,* or fried pork. Km. 8 on the Queretaro-S.L.P. Hwy. Tel. 218-1118.

Side Trips

The state of Queretaro comprises numerous towns and sites of historical interest and natural beauty. Most of these sites are within easy driving distance of its capital. Many of them, including the Sierra Gorda region's old Spanish missions in the northern part of the state, are just beginning to attract travelers.

Tequisquiapan

About a 45-minute drive, or 68 kilometers, from the city of Queretaro and a nearly two-hour drive from Mexico City, is the picturesque town of Tequisquiapan.

Situated over volcanic springs, that have now largely dried up, the town gained the nickname "The Fountain of Eternal Youth" because of its once abundant thermal waters touted as being mildly radioactive and therapeutic, believed to relieve arthritis, insomnia and gout.

Because of its relative proximity to Mexico City, "Tequis" has long been popular with capital residents for its unhurried pace and ideal climate—invariably warm and sunny by day, cool and, in winter months, brisk at night. Each year in late May to early June, the town hosts a national wine and cheese fair featuring the products of regional vineyards.

A thriving arts and crafts center, the town square is ringed with shops selling pottery, glassware, rustic wooden furniture and decorative items. A

Mexico Tourism Board

nearby out door market specializes in rattan goods and hand-woven baskets, and select shops carry Mexican antiques and unique handicrafts. *Casa Queretana de las Artesanias,* a government-run handicrafts shop, is at Andador Morelos 12 (tel. 273-1551).

There is little to do except lounge around outdoor pools, go hiking in the countryside along the river banks or up the hill to the *potrero* (a place where bulls are pastured), or go horseback riding through the surrounding fields. You can also golf at two nearby courses.

Gourmet French-Mexican cuisine is served at *Capricho's,* 20 de Noviembre No. 2 (tel. 273-0108), and Mexican dishes at *La Valentina,* a restaurant and cantina on the main square, at Juarez 10 (tel. 273-0005).

Cadereyta

Located just 36 kilometers north of Tequisquiapan, en route to the Sierra Gorda missions, is the small town of Cadereyta, home to Latin America's largest greenhouse.

The *Fernando Schmoll Greenhouse* contains more than 4,000 varieties of cactus and 2.5 million plants covering an area of eight hectares. Founded in 1920, the botanical center is unique in its concentration of cactus plants cultivated through seed planting. The greenhouse is open to the public and if you see something you like, you can buy the seed or fledgling version. They ship all over the world.

San Juan del Rio

As the gateway to the state of Queretaro for visitors arriving from Mexico City, San Juan del Rio is considered the state's second most important town.

Located 51 kilometers southwest of the city of Queretaro and 170 kilometers (about 90 minutes) from the country's capital, San Juan del Rio offers the visitor small-town charm and interesting constructions dating from the 16th, 17th and 18th centuries.

The town, with its nearly 127,000 inhabitants, generates most of its revenue from agriculture, especially the cultivation of grapes for wine making. Other regional products include hand-embroidered tablecloths and other textiles, woven baskets, and opals. Each year an agricultural, industrial and handicrafts fair takes place in June.

Bernal

This small town, situated at the entrance to Queretaro's Sierra Gorda region, has just one main attraction, but it's a singular feature that you're not likely to ever forget—*Peña Bernal,* a huge monolith believed to be one of the world's three largest (the biggest is Australia's Ayer's Rock).

Locals have endowed the monolith with all manner of magical powers, but it appears to cast a spell mostly on rock climbing aficionados, who converge on the town on weekends.

Bernal is also known for its woolen serapes, blankets and rugs that are woven on homemade looms, and locally-made candies. The

best time to visit Bernal, an easy two-hour drive from Mexico City, is during Feast of the Holy Cross celebrations on May 3 and 4, which feature a procession to the rock, where mass is held.

Ruins

Queretaro's archaeological sites of *Toluquilla* and *Las Ranas* are situated north of Cadereyta, around the town of San Joaquin.

Las Ranas is believed to have been a fortress settlement and ceremonial center, and shows influences of the Gulf Coast cultures. It was abandoned between 900 and 1000 A.D., and occupied by the Chichimecas—the name given to Indians from the northern territories who migrated to Central Mexico—up to the arrival of the Spanish. Situated on a hilltop, Toluquilla is also considered to have been a fortress city. The ruins here show a Huasteca influence.

Missions of the Sierra Gorda

During the mid-1700s, Queretaro served as headquarters of the Spanish missionary undertakings and the Sierra Gorda region to the north proved to be one of the most resistant.

In 1750, Franciscan friar Junipero Serra, widely credited with the spiritual conquest of the Indians, traveled into the Sierra Gorda, where he helped found the five renowned missions of the

region in *Jalpan, Tancoyol, Landa, Tilaco* and *Conca*. Built before Serra headed north to establish his now famous California missions, these are larger and considered finer than those found in the United States.

All five missions, declared by UNESCO as World Heritage Sites, share the same well-planned architectural layout, and display amazingly intricate facades that combine Spanish and Indian cultural influences, such as Christian saints and other religious figures with plants, animals and other pre-Hispanic icons.

Expect a two-and-a-half to three-hour drive over a very winding road to reach the missions and their spectacular setting in the Sierra Gorda, where the landscape varies from desert to forest.

Where to Stay

Doña Urraca
Cinco de Mayo 117, downtown
Tel. (442) 238-5400
www.donaurraca.com
This beautiful Mediterranean-style hotel just four blocks from the main square incorporates remnants of a colonial mansion renovated with contemporary flair. There are 24 spacious suites, each named after a bird, as is the hotel itself, fine restaurant, swimming pool, spa with outdoor jacuzzi and sun deck, and wide range of treatments. Rates FC.

Fiesta Americana Hacienda Galindo
Amealco Hwy., Km. 5, in San Juan del Rio
Tel. (427) 271-8200
www.fiestamericana.com
This lovely 16th-century hacienda is replete with legend and history. One of the country's most charming resorts, with 143 rooms and 25 suites (with jacuzzi), three restaurants, nightclub, tennis, swimming pool, jacuzzi, billiards, horseback riding, conference and banquet facilities for 900 people. Rates MD.

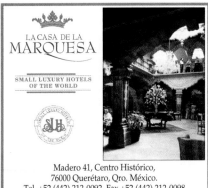

Hacienda Jurica
Mexico-S.L.P. Hwy., Km. 229
Tel. (442) 218-0022
www.brisas.com.mx
About six miles north of town, just off Hwy. 57. This beautiful 16th-century hacienda has been converted into a beautiful resort on 35 acres of gardens. It features 182 rooms and suites, excellent restaurant, two bars, two swimming pools, tennis, horseback riding, convention facilities. Rates MD.

Holiday Inn
Cinco de Febrero 110, road to San Luis Potosi
Tel. (442) 216-0202
A modern-colonial-style inn surrounded by gardens, with 171 rooms and suites. Restaurant, cafeteria, lobby bar. Swimming pool, two tennis courts, gym, putting green, playground. Business center, meeting facilities for 700, resident convention coordinator. Rates MD.

La Casa de la Marquesa
Madero 41, downtown
Tel. (442) 212-0092
www.lacasadelamarquesa.com

A baroque, 18th-century mansion rich in detail converted into a unique, luxury hotel with just 25 guest rooms (11 of them in an adjoining building), each individually decorated with antiques and antique-style furnishings, and equipped with all modern conveniences, including air-conditioning, cable TV and phone. Restaurant, bar, handicrafts and antiques shop. Member of Small Luxury Hotels of the World. Rates FC (includes continental breakfast).

Meson de Santa Rosa
Luis Pasteur 17, downtown
Tel. (442) 224-2623
Dating to the late 1700s, this wonderfully-renovated colonial building houses 21 over-sized suites with cable TV, phone, some with balconies, all beautifully designed and decorated. Good patio restaurant, central courtyard with fountain, heated pool. Rates MD.

Mision Juriquilla
Villas del Meson 56, in Juriquilla
Tel. (442) 234-0000
www.misionjuriquilla.com
This countryside resort features first-class hospitality and Mision service, plus 200 comfortable rooms, extensive convention facilities, and beautiful landscapes, all just 15 minutes from Queretaro and 35 minutes from San Miguel de Allende, among many other nearby sites. The numerous recreational facilities, including golf course, tennis courts, heated pool, make for a fun-filled vacation. Rates MD.

Mision La Mansion
Mexico-Queretaro Hwy., Km. 172
Tel./Fax (427) 271-0096
www.hotelesmision.com.mx
In San Juan del Rio, next to the San Gil Golf Club. A converted hacienda with 22 suites and 126 standard rooms distributed in a building of recent construction. Pool, tennis, garden, restaurant, tequila bar. Rates MD.

Plaza Camelinas
Cinco de Febrero 201
Tel. (442) 216-5494
This modern hacienda-style hotel near the industrial sector boasts a spacious lobby with a grand central staircase, gardens and heated pool. There are 158 well-appointed rooms and suites with satellite TV, and a sumptuous master suite with dome ceiling, jacuzzi and terrace overlooking the gardens. Mexican restaurant, video bar, piano bar, banquet and meeting facilities for 500 people. Rates MD.

Villa Antigua
Km. 11.5, between Tequisquiapan and San Juan del Rio
Tel. (414) 273-3322
A lovely hacienda-style hotel offering gourmet dining, 20 attractive guest rooms, garden and outdoor pool, facilities for small meetings, and gracious service.

Mexico Tourism Board

Zacatecas

Zacatecas, the capital of the state of the same name, is called "the city with the pink stone face and silver heart." Elegant, almost regal, and a true colonial gem, it is one of Mexico's most photogenic cities and was declared a World Heritage Site by UNESCO in 1993. Beautifully preserved pink stone buildings adorned with delicate wrought iron balconies line a labyrinth of spotless narrow streets that twist and turn through the city.

One of Mexico's highest cities (8,000 feet), Zacatecas is squeezed into a narrow gully between two bare hills. Spanish conquistadors discovered rich lodes of silver in the Cerro de La Bufa, and just two years later, in 1546, the initial settlement was proclaimed a city. In more modern times, a decline in silver production caused Zacatecas to fall on bad times and into virtual oblivion. For years the state's main source of revenue has been remittances from Zacatecans who have gone north seeking work in the United States. But within the last 15 years or so, Zacatecas has been "rediscovered." It has even become one of Mexico's top producers of silver again.

Recommended hotels include the *Quinta Real,* built around the remnants of a colonial-era bullfighting ring, and *Meson de Jobito.*

Jerez, a beautifully preserved colonial city founded in 1536, makes for an interesting side trip. Its horseshoe-shaped *Hinojosa Theater,* which was built seven years after the assassination of Abraham Lincoln, is a replica of Washington, D.C.'s Ford's Theater.

It's a long (seven hour) but easy drive from Mexico City, and service is available aboard deluxe buses. *Mexicana* offers direct flights between Zacatecas and several U.S. cities such as Los Angeles, the U.S. city with the largest Zacatecan community, Chicago and Denver, as well as destinations throughout Mexico.

What to See and Do

The downtown area is best explored on foot, beginning at the Plaza de Armas, or main square. Facing the plaza is the Palace of Justice, more commonly known as the *Palace of the Bad Night.* According to local legend, Manuel Retegui, a mine owner, went broke building it.

One night, in a state of deep depression he contemplated suicide, but was saved from this fate when news arrived that a rich vein had been discovered in his mine.

Just southwest of the plaza is the art nouveau *Gonzalez Ortega Market.* Once the city's central produce market, it has been totally remodeled and transformed into a charming mall. Here you'll find shops selling silver jewelry, regional wine, riding gear and local sweets.

Further southwest (it's best to take a cab), off Enrique Estrada Park, is the *Francisco Goitia Museum.* Zacatecas' most famous painter, Goitia is considered to be the precursor of

Zacatecas' ancient aqueduct frames the cathedral

Carlos Sanchez Pereyra

modern Mexican art and the most Mexican of the country's painters. Exhibited are his works and that of other renowned Zacatecan artists, including Julio Ruelas, Manuel Felguerez, brothers Pedro and Rafael Coronel, and Jose Kuri Breña.

In the opposite direction is the *Rafael Coronel Museum,* one of the most exciting in the country, not only because of the unusual nature of its contents, but also for the originality of the displays. The former San Francisco church and monastery provides an exquisite setting for Coronel's collection of 5,000 Mexican masks and pre-Hispanic pottery. There's a special hall for a creatively displayed collection of marionettes from the famous Rosette Aranda Theater. (Before radio and television, this theater traveled throughout the country

and was its most important source of entertainment). Also on the premises is a delightful cafe and gift shop.

The *Pedro Coronel Museum* exhibits one of the finest art collections in the country. Coronel, a renowned Zacatecan artist, left his large collection of pre-Hispanic artifacts (mostly from the state of Guerrero), as well as an important collection of colonial, European, African, Greek and Oriental art, to his home state. Displayed are marvelous African masks, Chinese and Japanese urns and screens, a complete set of Goya's "Disparates," as well as works by Miro, Dali, Picasso, Motherwell, Hogarth and Piranesi.

A visit to this city should include a tour of *Eden Mine,* which functioned from 1586 until the beginning of this century. The entrance to the mine is located on the outskirts of town, but its tunnels honeycomb throughout the city. A small train takes you to the beginning of the shafts. From there you continue through winding paths and over rickety (but safe) wooden bridges that cross terrifying chasms that drop some 1,500 meters. The tour, conducted in Spanish, is fascinating, explaining how the miners' only access was via shaky wooden ladders or ropes. They worked seven-day weeks and never saw the light of day. Yearly fatalities numbered in the thousands. Given the severity of the working conditions, the name—Eden—more fittingly describes the lives of the owners.

For a view of the entire city, take the cable car just a few feet from the exit of El Eden. The ride takes you straight up over the old part of town to *Cerro de La Bufa,* where you'll have a commanding view of the entire city and the bare hills beyond. Atop La Bufa is the *Chapel of Our Lady of Zacatecas,* a religious shrine, a dramatic equestrian monument to the famous Battle of Zacatecas, and a museum which pays homage to the heroes of the Mexican revolution.

The city's traditional flavor makes it an ideal place to study Spanish. Founded in 1973, the *Fenix Language Institute* combines class instruction with field trips and other activities to promote language proficiency. They also help place students with host families. Tel. 922-1643.

Fenix Language Institute
Spanish & Cultural Studies in Mexico

Ledezma 210 Centro. Zacatecas, Zac.
Tel./Fax (492) 922-1643/922-3732.
E-mail: fenixmex@terra.com.mx
http://fenixmex.tripod.com.mx

RESTAURANT-BAR
AZADORES
DE ZACATECAS

Callejón de la Palma 104, Col. Centro
Tel. 922-0382
Tel/Fax. 924-2653

Guanajuato STATE

is history, culture, architectural jewels, friendly people; a state that shines through in the heart of Mexico. Its admirable monuments are valuable reminders of Mexico's rich history; authentic colonial jewels. The capable hands of its people breathe life into Mexico's beautiful handicrafts and genuine works of art. Its excellent geographic location is enhanced by modern four-lane toll roads and highways, clear signs of its penchant for progress. Such routes have made Guanajuato State readily accessible from Mexico City, Guadalajara and Monterrey. For those traveling by plane, Guanajuato International Airport (BJX) offers direct flights to Houston, Dallas, Los Angeles and Chicago, as well as to all major Mexican cities and seaside resorts, and it is serviced by top international carriers. Because of all these qualities, plus its magnificent temperate climate and the variety of its natural beauty, the State of Guanajuato is known today as...

The door to Mexico

San Miguel de Allende

A Colonial Center for the Arts

Hilltop view of San Miguel de Allende

Susan Kaye

San Miguel de Allende's tree shaded plaza, dominated by an unusual neo-Gothic parish church, is a touch of the Left Bank. The plaza is the heart of a cosmopolitan town with a colonial setting, so strikingly lovely in its architecture that it has been designated a national monument. Its many beautifully restored colonial mansions house delightful boutique hotels, patio restaurants, and fine shops. In addition to the visitors who come to enjoy the town's beauty, climate and colorful fiestas, students of all ages come to study art, painting, weaving, sculpting, photography and Spanish. All this makes the city a fascinating place to spend a few hours, a few days or a few weeks.

About a four-hour drive northwest of Mexico City, San Miguel is nestled in the heart of the colonial highlands, Mexico's Independence Country. Its name honors Ignacio Allende, a leader in the war to gain independence from Spain.

The parish church, *La Parroquia,* has long set the town apart from its neighbors. Legend has it that the builder, Ceferino Gutierrez, was inspired by a European postcard and, sketching outlines in the sand, set his workers to build-

ing a Mexican-Indian version of a Gothic cathedral. The result is a mass of pink spires poking into the blue sky.

It was the *Instituto Allende,* however, that really put San Miguel on the map. Founded in 1951 on the grounds of an abandoned hacienda, the institute grew over the years into one of Latin America's largest schools of fine arts for English-speaking students. Year-round classes offer degrees in fine arts, crafts, photography and, of course, Spanish. Language studies are given an added dimension with field trips to historic and cultural sites. E-mail: allende@instituto-allende.edu.mx

Centro Cultural Ignacio Ramirez "El Nigroman-te" is a thriving cultural center that presents a variety of events throughout the year, such as art exhibits, theater productions, dance performances, and concerts. It is also a school of music and art, offering classes in painting, ceramics, stained glass, sculpture, weaving, theater and dance. An autonomous institution under the umbrella of Mexico's National Institute of Fine Arts, the center is housed in a glorious former convent built in the mid-18th century with the dowry of a nun, Sor Maria

Josefa Lina de la Canal y Hervas. Tel. 152-0289.

The *Academia Hispano Americana,* founded in 1959 and housed in an 18th-century mansion declared a national monument, offers intensive four- to six-hour a day Spanish courses, among others. Tel. 152-0349.

San Miguel's unspoiled provincial character—no neon, no billboards, no swarms of guides or vendors, no mobs of tourists (except on the biggest fiesta weekends)—combined with its level of cultural activity make it one of Mexico's truly stimulating travel destinations.

What to See and Do

San Miguel has its share of historical sites, including the recently restored *Allende* home, birthplace of patriot and town namesake Ignacio Allende. It is worth a visit, largely because of the building itself. Stately and graceful, with sunlit patios, it is the perfect example of a typical San Miguel colonial-era mansion. Another beautiful example of the architecture of the period is the *House of the Counts of Canal,* now occupied by a bank branch. It hosts temporary exhibits that are open to the public.

The best way to appreciate San Miguel is on foot. For a customized walking tour of the town you can call *Helene Kahn* (152-0849), who runs a personalized guide service of San Miguel and the surrounding Bajio area. Kahn also offers a shopping tour of San Miguel.

PMC (Promotion of Mexican Culture) *Tours*, at Hidalgo 16 (152-0121), offers an interesting selection of tours in and around San Miguel. *Servitur*, at Recreo 11, arranges tours as well as international home exchanges. Mountain bike excursions through the countryside are offered by *Bici-Burro*, Hospicio 152, and *Aventuras San Miguel,* Recreo 10 (153-5489). For horseback tours of San Miguel and hot-air balloon rides, contact *Coyote Canyon* (154-4193).

El Charco del Ingenio, a botanical garden located east of the city, features walking trails that take visitors past a variety of cacti and an orchid house. Established for the study and preservation of regional flora, this ecological reserve also sells a variety of fledgling cactus.

San Miguel celebrates Mexico's numerous national holidays with verve, and also has many of its own local fiestas.

In mid-June, around the Feast Day of St. Anthony of Padua (St. Anthony is seen in Mexico as a kind of Catholic cupid), young men and women dress up in crazy costumes for the *Fiesta de Los Locos* (Lunatics' Fiesta). Men dress as women and women as men; some dress to lampoon politicians. The festivities usually begin a few days earlier and end on the 13th with a parade through the main streets of town.

In late September, usually the third Saturday of the month, the town hosts a *Sanmiguelada*, a Pamplona-style running of the bulls accompanied by fireworks, concerts, religious processions and folk dances.

On September 29, the town celebrates the feast day of St. Michael the Archangel, its patron saint. The eve of St. Michael's Day is celebrated with night-long festivities. At 5 a.m. there is a parade with *mojigangas* (huge papier-mâché dolls), followed by fireworks in front of the parish church.

In August, the town hosts a *Chamber Music Festival*, which has been running for more than 20 years. Music lovers from around the world come to hear internationally-acclaimed ensembles perform in historic and architectur-

ally unique venues. Tel. 154-5141.

The bilingual *Public Library*, at Insurgentes 25, can provide information on local events. The library publishes the town's English-language weekly, *Atención San Miguel,* and is home to a small cafe. It also offers a Sunday house and garden tour that lets you peek behind the high walls of private mansions. Tel. 152-0293.

Golf and tennis aficionados can indulge in their favorite sports at the *Malanquin Club.* Some of the larger hotels in and around San Miguel have tennis courts.

Visitors who come to stay a while will want to prowl about the countryside. About nine miles north of San Miguel, on the way to the town of Dolores Hidalgo, is the mystic 18th-century shrine of *Atotonilco,* with its unique, rustic frescoes. If you want to overnight here, *El Viejo Rancho Hotel* is an excellent option, with hot springs, outdoor jacuzzi and a *palapa* restaurant-bar. The long road to Guanajuato, a spectacular mountain drive, goes through the little town of *Dolores Hidalgo,* a Talavera tile and pottery center, and birthplace of Mexican independence.

Real Estate

By Peggy Zavala

Leading publications, from Forbes to Money Magazine, Travel & Leisure, Conde Nast, the New York Times, Washington Post and USA Today, have listed San Miguel as a top community to retire in or visit, based on its amenities, climate, cost of living, safety, restaurants and the arts. That is why real estate in San Miguel has been and continues to be an excellent investment.

Properties for sale can be found advertised in the local English-language weekly newspaper, Atencion. The vast majority of properties for sale are listed with English speaking realtors, many from the United States, and prices are advertised in U.S. dollars. While there is no multiple listing service in San Miguel, realtors work cooperatively.

Many firms offer websites featuring properties for sale. Those buying real estate can choose from an average of 250 properties on the market at any one time and work with over 13 qualified real estate firms, all of which conform to national real estate standards set by AMPI (Mexican Association of Professional

Realtors), and collaborate with the leading notaries for legal real estate transactions.

The most desirable properties are located in "El Centro," a five-block radius around the town's main square. Homes in this historical district can be more than 300 years old, usually are colonial in style, and can be priced upwards of 350,000 dollars for a spectacular 2,000 square-foot property with a patio and fountain, arches, balconies, a profusion of flowers, and rooftop views of the Parroquia.

Neighborhoods within a 15-minute walk of the Centro frequently offer a real value, including San Antonio, Guadiana, Guadalupe and Mexiquito. The Los Balcones neighborhood located on a hill with views of town and westward offers homes built within the last few decades in a variety of styles and price ranges. Country club/golf course living is available at Club Malanquin. The planned community of Los Frailes, a 10 minute-drive south of town, offers space for gardening and views of lake *Presa*. A taxi ride to the Centro costs about 1.50 to 3 dollars and local buses charge about 30 cents per trip, making living in these neighborhoods quite convenient.

Cost for new construction (not including the price of land) can run from 70 to 90 dollars per square foot for quality construction incorporating handmade tiles, stone, and creative touches by experienced masons. Building sites in the Centro are virtually a thing of the past. However, many people buy homes and reconstruct them in keeping with municipal and federal government style regulations. Some

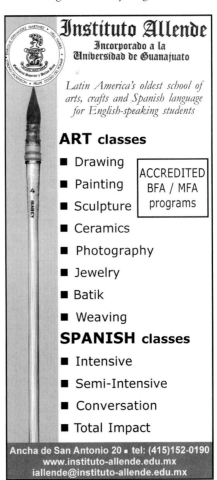

building lots can still be found in the Centro's surrounding neighborhoods.

Property taxes are very low compared to most U.S. communities. Domestic help is available for an average of 10 to 20 dollars a day (six hours). The cost of local produce is considerably lower than in the United States. Phone, cable, high-speed Internet access, and other services may be comparable to U.S. prices.

Modern hospitals and health care services are located in San Miguel and within an hour's drive. International health care insurance can be purchased for a reasonable price.

Tennis and golf facilities are minutes from the center of town, and there are nearby hot springs and day spas.

Lovely homes for rent by the week and month and be found on websites about San Miguel de Allende. Visit and check out the local real estate scene for yourself.

Originally from San Antonio, Texas, Peggy Zavala arrived in San Miguel 45 years ago and has been involved in local real estate for more than 20 years. For more information, visit www.sanmiguelhouses. com, or contact La Margarita Real Estate at 152-2893.

Shopping

A field day awaits shoppers in San Miguel. The beauty of the town appears to inspire regional artisans and the narrow cobblestone streets are flanked with stores displaying their handiwork.

Interesting little shops surround the main plaza, selling everything from embroidered *charro* (Mexican cowboy) outfits to glass-and-tin boxes. Zacateros, a street two blocks below the main plaza, is lined with shops displaying crafts for the home made of copper, brass, pewter and tin. Wrought-iron hinges, drawer-pulls and candelabra are prized items. There's a crafts market at Loreto and Andador Lucas Balderas, and steps away is the municipal market, which bustles with fruit and vegetable vendors.

Many shops pack and ship anywhere, but you can also contact *Border Crossings,* near the square at Correo 19 (tel. 152-2497). In business nearly 10 years, they also offer clients a stateside postal address and free Internet service. Most stores open from 9 or 10 a.m. to 2 p.m. and again from 4 to 8 or 9 p.m.

Art, Antiques, Decorations

Artesana Evos
Hernandez Macias 55
Tel. 152-0813
Spanish colonial classics in wood and iron, Oriental rugs, imported upholstered furniture and decorative items. Open 10 a.m. to 5:30 p.m. Closed Sunday.

Casa Canal
Canal 3
Tel. 152-0479
For nearly 30 years, this quality boutique has been known for its original hand-carved furniture created in a variety of designs and woods, including pine, mahogany and cedar. The shop also carries hand-embroidered clothing for men and women, and paintings and sculptures by well-known artists.

Casa Virreyes
Canal 21
Tel. 152-7389
A large selection of colonial-style home furnishings. Items made to order. Closed Thursday.

Casas Coloniales
Canal 36 and Canal 42
Tel. 152-0286
These stores feature Mexico-inspired furniture and accessories for the home, from a variety of colorful, hand-woven textiles to tiled decorative items. No. 36 is the main showroom, while No. 42 will help create tailor-made designs.

Casavieja
Mesones 83
Tel. 152-1284
A fine collection of art and antiques that will add a unique decorative touch to your home, includ-

ing Mexican ex-votos, carved wooden chests, and hand-painted furniture. Very select pieces.

Coleccion Cuatro Vientos
Road to Dolores Hidalgo, Km. 8
Tel. 154-7846
Located 10 minutes from San Miguel (call for an appointment; transportation provided), proprietor Milou de Montferrier's home-gallery features an extensive collection of country furniture and decorative items from around the world, many one-of-a-kind works of art and crafts, as well as unique jewelry. Open 10 a.m. to 2 p.m. Closed Sunday.

Galeria Atenea
Jesus 2
Tel. 152-0785
Housed in a beautifully restored 100-year-old home, this is one of the leading art galleries in town. In business since 1985, it features the work of Mexican contemporary artists, including sculptor Sergio Bustamante, who creates surreal sculptures in papier-mâché, bronze and copper, as well as a line of stunning gold and silver jewelry with his trademark faces, moons and blazing suns. Frequently hosts exhibits. Open 10 a.m. to 2 p.m. and 4 to 8 p.m.; Sunday, noon to 2 p.m.; closed Thursday.

Herco
Reloj 12
Tel. 152-0666 and 152-1434
This manufacturer and retailer of furniture and accessories for your home or business in solid brass, cast aluminum and wrought iron, or a combination of the three, has been in business since 1930. Specialists in bathroom and kitchen fixtures in unique, custom designs, including a very large selection of antique-style sinks and faucets. Special designs made to order. Closed Sunday.

Icpalli
Correo 43
Tel. 152-1236
Here you can find *equipales*, chairs of pre-Hispanic design which were considered by Huichol Indians to be fit for kings, in a variety of colors, sizes and shapes. Also a wonderful selection of Mexican folk art and handicrafts attractively displayed indoors and in an outdoor patio.

Josh Kligerman Gallery
San Francisco 11, just off the plaza
Tel. 152-0951
Known as San Miguel's "little museum," this gallery displays works by major Mexican and international contemporary artists, as well as African tribal art.

La Antigua Casa Canela
Umaran 20
Tel. 152-3428
Great for browsing, this extensive store features a large selection of fine quality antiques, colonial art, and home furnishings displayed around a courtyard. Also a wing with attractive cotton clothing. Run by a long-established family of designers.

La Vie de Chateau

Original creations in fabric-covered furniture, trimmings, curtains and decorative items.

La Zandunga

Hernandez Macias 129
Tel. 152-4608

A small shop featuring high-quality 100% wool rugs hand woven by Zapotec Indians from Oaxaca. Owner Rebecca Kamelhar imports colorfast Swiss dyes and oversees the designs. Most of the rugs are exported to New Mexico. Custom designs made to order. Expensive but beautiful.

Terra

Cuadrante 6
Tel. 152-2116

Attractive patio and garden furniture, and decorative items. Everything from seeds to pots and baskets. Great gifts for gardening buffs.

Handicrafts

Casa Maxwell

Canal 14 and Umaran 3
Tel. 152-0247

In business for 40 years, these well-stocked stores carry a great variety of well-chosen folk art, as well as furniture and decorations from all parts of the country.

Veryka

Zacateros 6

A gallery of folk art, featuring an interesting assortment of masks, ceramics and beaded Huichol work.

Jewelry and Accessories

Beckmann

Hernandez Macias 105
Tel. 152-0112

For more than 30 years, one of San Miguel's most prestigious jewelry shops. It specializes in beautifully crafted silver and silver plate—from decanters to Christmas ornaments—and gold and silver jewelry. Also custom designs and fine crsytal.

Cerroblanco

Plaza Colonial (Canal 21). Tel. 154-4888
Canal 17. Tel. 152-0502

The Cerroblanco family designs and manufactures its own collection of sterling silver and gold jewelry; the branch at Canal 17 specializes in accessories for men. Closed Sunday.

Talisman

San Francisco 7
Tel. 152-0438

Half a block from the main square. This interesting boutique carries a large selection of handmade rebozos, plus jewelry and accessories.

Dining

Locals say no other town this size in Mexico has such an ample selection of good restaurants. The more refined inns boast award-winning cuisine or simply first-rate restaurants, including *Casa de Sierra Nevada*, *Villa Jacaranda* and *La Puertecita*. There are also wonderful restaurants around town, each with its own particular flavor.

Azafran

Hernandez Macias 97
Tel. 152-7507

This new addition to the local dining scene offers memorable gourmet Mediterranean fare, including grilled vegetable salad with polenta, camembert with sauteéd apples, and salmon in anchovy butter. Menu changes weekly; indoor or patio dining. Reservations recommended. Closed Wednesday.

Bugambilia

Hidalgo 42
Tel. 152-0127

About two and a half blocks from the main plaza. In business for more than 50 years, this charming patio restaurant, housed in a beautiful colonial home, serves exquisite traditional Mexican food accompanied by pleasant guitar music. Open noon to 10:30 p.m.

Cafe de la Parroquia

Jesus 11
Tel. 152-3161

The ideal place for a delicious breakfast or lunch in a small, sun-filled patio. Good coffees, Mexican and international dishes, soft classical music. Very popular. Open 7:30 a.m. to 4 p.m.; to 2 p.m. Sunday. Closed Monday.

Capilla

Cuna de Allende 10
Tel. 154-4944

Housed in a beautifully restored 17th-century building, this restaurant features a fine collection of antiques from around the world, and regional and international dishes. Nestled next to the church, with a great view of the comings and goings at the main plaza from its garden patio and upstairs terrace, plus live music. An interior café called El Atrio de la Capilla offers an elegant setting for breakfast or a sweet snack, with homemade chocolates and cookies. Open for breakfast, lunch and dinner. Closed Tuesday.

Chamonix

Sollano 17-A
Tel. 154-8363

Intimate and popular, this romantic spot near the main square offers an innovative international menu. Try the *filete Suizo*, Vietnamese egg rolls, Sri Lanka-style curry. Live music Saturdays. Open 1 to 10 p.m. Closed Sunday and Monday.

El Asador Catalan
Carr. San Miguel-Queretaro, Km. 9.5
Tel. 152-7900
Locals head to this spot on the road to Queretaro for traditional Spanish fare and Catalan regional specialties, including paella and Segovia-style suckling pig baked in a wood-burning oven.

El Campanario
Canal 34
Tel. 152-0775
Celebrating 10 years in business, this elegant and very popular restaurant is housed in a colonial-era building decorated with stained-glass art. An extensive international menu features select cuts of beef in a variety of sauces, as well as fish and seafood specialties. Open-air terrace seating with a lovely view of the church towers. Trios, mariachis or soloists perform from 8 p.m. Open 1 to 11 p.m., except Thursday.

El Catrín
Canal 154, downtown
Tel. 152-1597
Dine in an elegant garden setting surrounded by more than 6,000 lights or in a converted antique Pullman dining car. This leading restaurant's international menu is as creative as its ambiance. The luncheon menu features "Chinese chicken wraps" or "drug store burgers." At dinner, try the char-grilled steaks, "double cut" lamb chops with serrano chili-mint jelly or New Orleans barbecue shrimp. Open 1 p.m. to 10 p.m.; to 6 p.m. Sunday.

El Correo
Correo 23
Tel. 152-4951
Authentic Mexican cuisine served in a cozy and colorful setting just off the main plaza. A fun place for lunch.

El Market Bistro
Hernandez Macias 95
Tel. 152-3229
Classic French specialties, from foie gras to escargot and chauteaubriand, served in a beautiful courtyard setting or cozy dining room with fireplace. Open 1 to 11 p.m.; to midnight Friday and Saturday. The Petite wine bar open from 6 p.m.

El Pegaso
Corregidora 6
Tel. 152-1351
A restaurant-bar serving everything from excellent sandwiches and soups to T-bone steaks. Folk art, including masks from throughout Mexico, deck the walls and are for sale. Popular gathering place for foreign residents. Open 8:30 a.m. to 10 p.m. Closed Sunday.

Harry's New Orleans Cafe & Oyster Bar
Hidalgo 2
Tel. 152-2645
A New Orleans-style restaurant offering a blend of Creole, Cajun and Mexican cooking. Menu features seafood gumbo, shrimp remoulade, Angus beef. Patio bar and oyster bar. Open noon to 1 a.m.

La Finestra
Canal 21
Tel. 152-8093
A cozy European-style restaurant-cafe that's great for people-watching. Their fresh-baked pastries and variety of coffees get the day off to a good start. Menu features nouveau Mexican cuisine. Live music weekend evenings. Open 9 a.m. to 11 p.m. Closed Tuesday.

La Grotta
Cuadrante 5
Tel. 152-4119
Located a block and a half from the main square, this popular spot has garnered a loyal clientele for its Italian favorites, including pastas made fresh daily, delicious pizzas and calzone. Closed Tuesday.

Nirvana
Hernandez Macias 56-A
Tel. 150-0067
A contemporary setting for creative fusion cuisine from owner-chef Juan Carlos Escalante, who studied in New York and has worked in Acapulco, Cancun and Spain. Open 1 to 10 p.m. Closed Tuesday.

Pueblo Viejo
Umaran 6, near the main plaza
Tel. 152-4977
Reminiscent of a typical Mexican village, this restaurant offers good Mexican and international food, including fine cuts of beef and delicious desserts. Their breakfast special is blueberry pancakes. Live folk music at lunch and dinner Monday to Wednesday; live jazz Thursday to Saturday. Open 8 to 1 a.m.

Tio Lucas
Mesones 103
Tel. 152-4996
In front of the Angela Peralta Theater. A popular watering hole for both locals and tourists, with a lively bar area, charming open-air patio, and a lot of decor dangling from the ceiling. Specialties are Mexican cuisine and fine cuts of beef with a variety of sauces, including chateaubriand. There's a good jazz/blues band in the evenings from 9. Owner Max Altamirano personally supervises everything. Open noon to midnight.

Nightlife

After dark painters abandon their easels, writers lay aside their pens, students close their books and together they form an eclectic crowd at several nightspots.

You're bound to run into everybody at *Mama Mia,* Umaran 8. There's a small dance floor at Mama's bar, since the bands invariably get people up and dancing to rock, blues and funk from Monday to Wednesday, and tropical music from Thursday to Sunday. You may even get a salsa dancing lesson if you show up early.

A newer and visually spectacular bar is *El Grito,* where larger-than-life sculptures and ornate columns evoke the interior of a lavish Italian opera house. Open Friday and Saturday nights at Umaran 15. Tel. 152-0048.

As in the rest of Mexico, nightlife starts late in San Miguel; few people dine before 9 p.m.

Spas

Donatella
Aldama 43, downtown
Tel. 152-0564
Soothing music and relaxing aromas mark this haven for the mind and body. Skin care products imported from Paris form part of their arsenal of anti-aging tools. Also slimming and relaxation massages.

The Spa
Hospicio 46
Tel. 152-3427
Written up in Vogue, this first-class colonial-style spa offers traditional facial and body treatments, as well as Oriental health and fitness regimens.

Hotels

Antigua Villa Santa Monica
Baeza 22, downtown
Tel. (415) 152-0427
www.antiguavillasantamonica.com
A charming hotel with just 14 well-appointed suites (including a bridal suite with jacuzzi), all with fireplace and private patio. Pool, lovely gardens with fountain, restaurant-bar. Rates MD (includes continental breakfast).

Casa de Liza...Villas en el Parque
Bajada del Chorro 7, corner of Recreo
Tel. (415) 152-0352
www.casaliza.com
Owner Liza Kisber's converted 17th-century estate houses a six-room B&B and orchid-filled greenhouse. Accommodations include a lavish two-story villa, penthouse with terrace, Moroccan suite overlooking the jacuzzi/pool, library suite, and Villa Carlotta with a wonderful terrace. Cable TV, laundry service, heated jacuzzi-pool. Rates MD (includes breakfast).

Casa de Sierra Nevada Quinta Real
Hospicio 35, downtown
Tel. (415) 152-7040
www.quintareal.com
Old World charm characterizes this sumptuous hotel comprised of adjoining colonial mansions which house 33 exquisitely furnished rooms and suites, some with private balconies or fireplace. Lounge bar, gourmet dining, heated pool, small meeting room. No children under 16. Sister hotel by Juarez Park. Member of Mexico Boutique Hotels. Rates DX.

Casa Rosada
Cuna de Allende 12
Tel. (415) 152-0382
www.casarosadahotel.com
Ideally located behind one of the town's main attractions, La Parroquia, this authentic colonial monument features 16 modern, comfortable and individually decorated rooms and suites, and spectacular views of the parish church from the patio, balconies and terraces. Among the architectural highlights is a chapel-turned-reception area with a magnificently decorated vault ceiling. Lounge bar, restaurant, meeting room. Idea for special events, including weddings and retreats. Rates FC (includes continental breakfast).

Casa Quetzal
Hospicio 34, downtown
Tel. (415) 152-0501
Originally built by a film company to accommodate visiting stars and producers, this hotel offers just three luxurious apartment suites, each sumptuously decorated to reflect a theme: zen, karma, voodoo. Suites have kitchenette,

living and dining room, minibar, satellite TV, phone, gas-log fireplace. Services include daily in-room breakfast, newspaper, hotel-airport transfers. Packing/unpacking and gourmet catering available. Rates DX (includes breakfast).

Dos Casas
Quebrada 101, downtown
Tel. (415) 154-4073
This contemporary Mexican home-turned-B&B features minimalist decor with Mexican touches. Five guest rooms furnished to offer all the comforts of home and then some, including DVD and CD players, fireplace or library. Also jacuzzi, solarium, patios, terraces, massages. Rates DX (includes breakfast).

El Atascadero
Prolongacion Santo Domingo
Tel. (415) 152-0206
www.redmex.com/atascadero
On a hilltop, five minutes from the city center. Surrounded by lovely gardens, this restored hacienda offers lots of tranquility, with 51 rooms and suites with fireplace and tasteful rustic decor. Tennis court, swimming pool, jacuzzi, sauna and sun deck. Good dining room. Courtesy transportation into town from 8 a.m. to 3 p.m.; after that cabs are available and inexpensive. Rates MD.

Hacienda Taboada
Km. 8 on the road to Dolores Hidalgo
Tel. (415) 152-0850

www.hoteltaboada.com
A 10-minute drive from San Miguel. This attractive Mediterranean-style hotel, with 70 guest rooms with first-class amenities, is set in a marvelous country setting with lush plant-filled grounds. Crystal-clear and odorless thermal waters, four pools, gym. Wide range of outdoor activities, including Ping-Pong, tennis, horseback riding, activities for kids. Superb food, nightlife. Friendly management. Meeting facilities for up to 300 people. Rates MD (MAP).

La Mansion del Bosque
Aldama 65, three blocks from downtown
Tel./Fax (415) 152-0277
Owned and managed by Ruth Hyba, this intimate guest house offers 22 rooms with fireplace, tiled baths, gas heating, Mexican decor. Dining room with meals served family style, bar, lounge-library. Rates MD (MAP).

La Puertecita
Santo Domingo 75
Tel. (415) 152-5011
www.lapuertecita.com
In an exclusive hilltop residential area five blocks from the town center. Highly rated by the Times of London as one of the top 100 hotels in the world, and a AAA Four Diamond Award winner, this friendly boutique hotel offers 36 charming rooms and suites distributed on a hillside and in villas across the road. Domed brick ceilings, rustic Mexican furniture and sculpted stone-framed windows give the accommodations their distinctive appeal; some have private patios, garden baths and fireplaces. Fine Mexican and international food served poolside, in the dining room, or on guest patios. Two heated pools, jacuzzi and fitness area. Arrangements made for biking, golf, tennis and tours to historic sites and hot springs. Rates FC (includes continental breakfast).

Mision de los Angeles
Km. 2 on road to Celaya
Tel. (415) 152-2099
www.realminas.com.mx
Known for its numerous domed brick ceilings (300), this colonial-style hotel overlooks Allende Dam, with 58 rooms with phone and TV, pool, restaurant, bar. Rates MD.

Posada de la Aldea
Calle Ancha de San Antonio 15
Tel. (415) 152-1022
www.naftaconnect.com/hotellaaldea
Located just five blocks from the main square, this pleasant Spanish-style hotel offers 66 spacious, comfortable rooms with phone and satellite TV. Swimming pool, tennis courts, expansive grounds, restaurant. Rates ECON.

Posada de San Francisco
Plaza Principal 2, on the main square
Tel. (415) 152-7213
www.naftaconnect.com/hsanfrancisco
Resembling an old Spanish-colonial monastery, this centrally located hostelry is simply furnished in good taste. There are 46 rooms with cable TV and phone, courtyard and patio, restaurant, coffee shop. Rates ECON.

Quinta Loreto
Lorcto 15
Tel. (415) 152-0042
www.travelbymexico.com/guan/quintaloreto
A modest colonial-style hotel three blocks from the main square with 40 rooms with TV and phone, gardens, tennis court, pool and good restaurant. Rates ECON.

Villa Jacaranda
Aldama 53, downtown
Tel. (415) 152-1015
www.villajacaranda.com
This beautifully converted mansion features attractive accommodations and gourmet dining in a charming, sunny plant-filled setting. The 15 suites and guest rooms, decorated in a warm colonial style, open onto private or shared patios and terraces, and have cable TV, phone, electric blankets, tubs and showers. Award-winning cuisine in a light-filled dining room, outdoors under majestic trees, or on a rooftop terrace with a view. A cozy bar with fireplace is where guests gather for a relaxing

drink. Giant jacuzzi, sun deck, gym. Guests enjoy access to country club golf course, tennis courts and swimming pool. Banquet facilities for 150. Parking on premises. Rates FC.

Villa Rivera
Cuadrante 3, downtown
Tel. (415) 152-2289
www.mexicoboutiquehotels.com
Art, good food and tastefully decorated surroundings await guests at this attractive colonial-style hotel located just steps from the main plaza. There are 12 suites with wood beam ceilings and wrought iron decorative touches, some with terraces; swimming pool, fine restaurant, bar, and valet parking. Member of Mexico Boutique Hotels. Rates FC.

Villas Mirasol
Pila Seca 35
Tel. (415) 152-6685
www.villamirasol.com
Located just four blocks from the main plaza, this hotel is housed in a converted hacienda with 10 rooms and suites, each with hand-painted tile bath, cable TV, phone, maid service; some with private patios or balconies. Lounge with TV, books, contemporary art. Guests enjoy the personalized service of host Carmen Avery. Rates MD (includes breakfast).

Guanajuato

Crowning Jewel of Colonial Cities

Colonial-era buildings flank Guanajuato's winding streets

Guanajuato State

Nestled in a narrow canyon between huge mountains, Guanajuato is a singular and perfectly preserved colonial city, and capital of the like-named state. Declared a World Heritage Site by UNESCO in 1988, the town is a photographer's delight with its quaint plazas, winding cobblestone streets and unique underground passageways.

The name "Guanajuato" is derived from the Tarascan Indian "quanashuato," meaning "mountainous place for frogs." When the Spanish arrived, they discovered the mountains were rich in silver and a mining town flourished that soon became the richest city in Mexico, producing more than a third of the world's silver by the turn of the 18th century.

The town is a maze of cobblestone streets that wind their way up steep, hilly inclines. Colonial buildings crowded together, and perched one atop the other, line the alleyways, or *callejones*, their balconies almost touching. That last architectural feature has even been immortalized in the legend of the *Callejon del Beso*, or Alley of the Kiss, so named because the top-floor balconies of two facing homes are close enough for their respective occupants to kiss. For a small contribution, local kids will eagerly retell the tale of the ill-fated lovers who liaised from the upper balconies.

There's more to Guanajuato's unique colonial landscape. An ancient subterranean tunnel, originally built to prevent flooding and currently used as a kind of medieval-style bypass, zigzags under the city. Part of the tunnel follows the original course of a dried up river, other parts were added later to alleviate traffic jams on the city's narrow streets.

Guanajuato played an important role in Mexico's War of Independence. In 1810 it was invaded by Father Miguel Hidalgo—a rebel priest and leader of Mexico's independence movement—and his ragtag army of farmers and mine workers. The wealthy mine owners fled to the town's granary, barricading themselves and their treasures behind its thick walls, until a brave young miner nicknamed El Pipila immortalized himself by breaking down the door and allowing the revolutionaries to kill their enemies and seize the city. A hilltop monument honoring Pipila is also the site of a lookout that offers a magnificent view of the town and its mazelike layout.

Though Guanajuato doesn't have a main square in the manner of other Mexican towns, the wedge-shaped *Jardin de la Union*—known locally as the "Pedazo de Queso" (slice of cheese)—is the favored gathering spot. Shaded by ancient trees, it features a charming old-fashioned bandstand where concerts are frequently held, and a few bustling sidewalk cafes. In the evenings *estudiantinas* (student troubadours) often perform in the streets.

Other pretty plazas include *Jardin de la Reforma*, *Plazuela San Roque*, which is the stage for outdoor theater productions during the Cervantino Festival, and *Plazuela San Fernando*. *Plaza de la Paz*, in front of the basilica, is surrounded by former mansions of local mining magnates.

Near the Jardin de la Union is the handsome and ornate *Teatro Juarez*, a magnificent theater that combines many architectural styles and is a testament to Guanajuato's mining boom. Eight carved muses crown the edifice, gilt carvings and velvet fabric adorn the interior, and graceful art nouveau railings line the tiers throughout. It has been called by one writer a "1900s version of classical Greece."

On the plaza is *San Diego Church*, noted especially for its beautiful and highly ornate doorway. Built in 1663 and almost destroyed by floods in the late 18th century, it is an outstanding example of churrigueresque art.

La Parroquia, also known as the Basilica of Our Lady of Guanajuato, on Plaza de la Paz, dates from the 17th century. Behind its coral and gold facade is a carved wood image of the Virgin Mary covered in jewels. It arrived in Guanajuato in 1557 as a gift from Felipe II of Spain. The statue, worshiped in Spain since 714, had supposedly been hidden from the Moors in a cave, and is presumed to be the oldest representation of Christian art in Mexico.

Another interesting church, with a particularly beautiful pink stone baroque facade and cupola reminiscent of St. Peter's in Rome, is the *Templo de la Compañia de Jesus*, behind the university. Completed in 1747, it was part of a Jesuit seminary.

The *Alhondiga de Granaditas*, the old granary and site of the first major rebel victory in Mexico's War of Independence, is now a regional museum filled with interesting artifacts that relate the history of the city, ranging from its pre-Hispanic past to the great flood of 1905 which inundated the town, and up to modern times. Not to be missed are the dramatic murals of Guanajuato's history painted by artist Jose Chavez Morado on the walls of the stairwell.

The *Museo Casa Diego Rivera*, the birthplace of Mexico's famed muralist, contains period furniture, including the brass bed in which Rivera was born in 1886, and a wonderful collection of his works, including sketches for the mural at New York City's Rockefeller Center.

Also worth visiting is the 17th century *Museo del Pueblo de Guanajuato*. Housed in the former mansion of a mining magnate, the museum features an art collection that ranges from colonial to modern times, and a powerful mural by Chavez Morado.

The *Museo de las Momias* is very popular if a bit gruesome with its assembly of mummified corpses encased in glass caskets. There are about a hundred cadavers on display, all remarkably well preserved thanks to mineral salts in the soil, and some are identified according to their particular mishap: hanged, drowned, mistakenly buried alive. Located at the entrance to the cemetery, the museum recently decided to play up its ghoulish side by incorporating some haunted house-style displays.

The suburb of *Valenciana*, about five kilometers north of town on a hill overlooking Guanajuato, is well worth the short bus trip or taxi ride to visit its famous mine, church and former mansion-turned-restaurant and handicraft emporium.

The *Valenciana Mine*, shut down after the Mexican Revolution, was reopened in 1968 and the grounds are open to the public. The first Count of Valenciana and owner of the mine commissioned the building of the incredibly beautiful *Church of San Cayetano*, popularly known as the Church of La Valenciana, in the 18th century. He spared no expense—the facade is spectacular and its interior dazzles with ornate altars heavily trimmed in gold leaf, stained glass, filigree carvings, grand paintings, and a pulpit imported from China. The *Casa del Conde de la Valenciana* houses a large, multilevel gallery of sophisticated Mexican arts and crafts, as well as one of the city's leading restaurants. The fine food is served in a lovely colonial setting with a great panoramic view. Hours are 10:30 a.m. to 6 p.m. Monday to Saturday; daily during the Cervantino Festival. Tel. 732-2550.

To see what life was like for the wealthy mine owners, visit the *Ex-Hacienda de San Gabriel de la Barrera*. The former hacienda of Captain Gabriel de la Barrera, a descendent of the first Count of Valenciana, was restored and opened as a museum in 1979. Set amidst magnificent gardens, the mansion is furnished in colonial antiques and period European furniture and art, and has a private chapel featuring an ornate gold-covered altar. There's a lovely outdoor cafe and wine bar, as well as a wonderful handicrafts shop on the grounds.

The city's poshest residential area surrounds a scenic reservoir, *Presa de la Olla*, built in 1742 by the Marquis de Rayas. The reservoir and park is a favorite spot for family picnics and boat rides on Sundays, but the rest of the week is quiet and peaceful. Stately turn-of-the-century homes line the neighborhood's main boulevard, Paseo de la Olla. Most now house government buildings, and one has been

Guanajuato State

converted into a small luxury hotel. On the first Monday in July, everyone comes up here for a big party celebrating the opening of the floodgates. The Feast Day of St. John is celebrated here from June 15 to 24 with dances, music, food and fireworks.

A huge monument of Christ, *Cristo Rey*, crowns a 9,442-foot mountain peak located 10 miles west of the city. Visible to travelers miles before they reach Guanajuato, the statue is 82 feet high and marks what is said to be the geographical center of Mexico.

Cervantino Festival

Each fall (usually in October) Guanajuato hosts the *Festival Internacional Cervantino*, a nearly month-long celebration of the performing arts. Named in honor of Spanish writer Miguel de Cervantes Saavedra, author of "Don Quixote," the cultural extravaganza features well-known soloists and ensembles, opera singers, jazz musicians, modern dance companies and folk dance troupes, as well as traditional and experimental theater groups from around the world. The entire city becomes a stage as many events take place at outdoor venues. The festival draws people from all over and is usually a sellout, so make plans in advance if you want to attend.

A magnificent collection of art inspired by Cervantes' tragic character, Don Quixote, is on display at the *Museo Iconografico del Quixote*. This eclectic collection of representations of the knight of La Mancha was donated to the city of Guanajuato by Mexican advertising mogul Eulalio Ferrer. The collection ranges from postage stamps to murals of the hapless hero and his sidekick Sancho Panza, and includes works by Pablo Picasso, Salvador Dali, Carlos Merida and Rafael Coronel.

Shopping and Dining

As already mentioned above, two of the best places for fine Mexican folk art, furniture and decorative items are the *Casa del Conde de la Valenciana* and *Ex-Hacienda de San Gabriel de la Barrera*.

The turn-of-the-century *Mercado Hidalgo* on Avenida Juarez is a huge vaulted iron and glass structure with elaborate grillwork. On the ground floor most of the vendors sell fruit, vegetables, meat and poultry, but upstairs you'll find dozens of stalls offering baskets, embroidered dresses, pottery, shawls and other local handicrafts.

Alfareria Tradicional produces hand-painted Majolica pottery using the same traditional techniques and original designs employed during the colonial era (1521-1810). The workshop was founded by master artisan *Gorky Gonzalez*, whose ceramic pieces have been displayed around the world. The store/workshop is located on Pastita, in Ex-Huerta de Montenegro. Tel. 731-0389.

Though not noted for its cuisine,

Trees and a lacy kiosk
deck a typical square

Guanajuato

Guanajuato has a few good restaurants in town and the better hotels usually offer excellent dining options. *La Casona del Cielo,* at Pastita 76, belongs to the Gorky Gonzalez family, so fine ceramics as well as paintings by local artists deck the walls of this colonial home-turned-restaurant. The menu offers international fare with a Mexican touch, and the popular bar features live jazz in the evenings. Open 1 to 10 p.m.; to 7 p.m. Sunday and Monday. Tel. 731-2000.

Casa del Conde de la Valenciana houses one of the city's leading restaurants. Here fine food is served in a lovely colonial setting and outdoor patio with a great panoramic view. Hours are 10:30 a.m. to 6 p.m. Monday to Saturday; daily during the Cervantino Festival. Tel. 732-2550.

One excellent alternative is *La Hacienda de Marfil,* an elegant yet rustic restaurant-bar housed in a former hacienda just outside Guanajuato, at Arcos de Guadalupe 3 in Marfil (tel. 733-1148). The creative menu, which features Mexican nouvelle cuisine and traditional French dishes, makes the short drive worthwhile. It's open 1:30 to 7 p.m., except Mondays.

Marfil was an important mining center in the 17th and 18th centuries, but a catastrophic flood in the early 1900s reduced it to a ghost town. Its charm and proximity to Guanajuato led to the growth of a small residential suburb, while the former haciendas have begun to attract tourism.

Located just steps from the main square is *Guanajuato Grill*, a popular bar and disco at Alonso 4, behind San Diego Church. There are cocktail lounges at the Castillo de Santa Cecilia, Parador de San Javier, Real de Minas and San Diego hotels.

On weekend evenings, *estudiantinas* entertain at the bar of the Castillo de Santa Cecilia Hotel, and occasionally at the Posada Santa Fe Hotel. Also on weekends, university students in period costume stage comic skits called *entremeses*; most of the performances take place outdoors at Plazuela San Roque.

Hotels in Guanajuato

Castillo de Santa Cecilia. Km. 1 on the road to La Valenciana. A romantic medieval castle motif incorporating some original colonial-era walls. 88 guest rooms, some with fireplace and excellent city views. Gardens, heated pool, restaurant, nightclub, meeting rooms. Rates ECON. Tel. (473) 732-0485.

Holiday Inn Express. Euquerio Guerrero 120, near the city's hilltop convention center. Designed for the business traveler, with 165 rooms, some with high-speed Internet access, business center, gym, covered, heated pool. Rates MD (includes breakfast). Tel. (473) 735-2000. www.hotelesmilenium.com.

La Casa de Espiritus Alegres. Ex-Hacienda La Trinidad 1, in Marfil, about 10 minutes from the city center. "The House of Good Spirits" dates back to the 17th century. Today it is a charming nonsmoking bed-and-breakfast with just five guest rooms and three suites, all decorated with Mexican and Indian crafts and folk art. All rooms have a fireplace, private bath, terrace or patio, or open onto a garden. Lots of color and ambiance. Rates MD (breakfast included). Tel./Fax (473) 733-1013.

Meson de los Poetas. Positos 35, corner of Juan Valle. Ideally located for sightseeing, this charming converted home offers 30 attractive guest rooms with terrace, kitchenette, cable TV, phone. Parking, meeting or banquet room. Rates MD. Tel./Fax (473) 732-0705.

Mision Guanajuato. Marfil-Guanajuato Hwy., Km. 2.5. This friendly, modern-colonial-style hotel is located 10 minutes from the downtown area, opposite Ex-Hacienda San Gabriel de la Barrera, a major tourist attraction with beautiful gardens, excellent crafts shop and museum. There are 139 spacious rooms, restaurant, lobby bar, covered pool, tennis. Courtesy transportation into town. Rates MD. Tel. (473) 732-3980. www.hotelesmision.com.mx.

Posada Santa Fe. Jardin de la Union 12, on the main plaza. Ideally located in the heart of the colonial city, this picturesque colonial-era hotel has been declared a national monument. Colonial decor and art representing the area's history and culture deck the walls and hallways. There are 49 rooms with satellite TV, one of the city's most popular sidewalk restaurants, rooftop jacuzzi. Rates MD. Tel. (473) 732-0084.

Quinta Las Acacias. Paseo de la Presa 168. A small romantic hotel housed in a renovated turn-of-the-century French-style mansion facing a park. Just nine guest rooms, each individually decorated with antiques; open-air jacuzzi, garden, library, satellite TV. No children under 12 allowed. Member of Mexico Boutique Hotels. Rates FC (AP). Tel. (473) 731-1517. www.mexicoboutiquehotels.com.

Hotels in Leon

Comanjilla Termas Spa. Carr. Panamericana, Km. 385. A delightful hacienda-style spa resort with 116 rooms and suites, restaurants, bars, enormous pool, tennis, steam baths, massages, 48 thermal water springs (water piped directly into each private bath), horseback riding, game room, Sunday mass. Rates MD. Tel. (477) 714-6522.

Fiesta Americana. Blvd. Lopez Mateos 1102. Located on the main boulevard, this attractive modern-colonial-style hotel has 211 rooms and suites, pool, tennis, gym, spa, restaurants, extensive meeting facilities and business center. Rates MD. Tel. (477) 713-6040. www.fiestamericana.com.

La Estancia. Blvd. Lopez Mateos 1311 Ote. Located on the main boulevard, this first-class, modern-colonial-style hotel (formerly the Camino Real) has 74 rooms and suites with cable TV; pool, restaurants, bar, business center. Conveniently located near the convention center and the downtown area. Rates MD. Tel. (477) 716-3939.

Studying Spanish

Being a university town, Guanajuato provides a perfect atmosphere for studying Spanish. The *University of Guanajuato* is a descendant of a school begun by the Jesuits in 1732 for the wealthy sons of mining families, and has been functioning continuously ever since. For information about their Spanish courses, you can write: Departamento de Servicios al Estudiante, Lascurain de Retana 5, 36000 Guanajuato, Gto. Tel. 732-2770. Fax 732-0278.

Michoacan

From the Majesty of Morelia to Monarch Butterflies

Tzintzuntzan, once the center of power of the Tarascan Indians.

The aristocrat of colonial cities and capital of Michoacan state, Morelia is characterized by wide, polished-stone streets and stately buildings. By and large, the architecture has been kept in the traditions of Old Spain.

Mexico's first viceroy, Antonio de Mendoza, founded the city in 1541 and named it Valladolid after his home in Spain. After Mexico's War of Independence, the city was named Morelia in honor of local hero Jose Maria Morelos.

In the center of the city, the lovely *Plaza de los Martires* is the focal point of town life and a good place to start sightseeing. It is flanked on one side by the pink-stone *cathedral*, one of the most beautiful in the country, with twin towers 200 feet high.

The most prominent architectural landmark in Morelia is its massive colonial aqueduct. Built in 1790 to carry water into the city from nearby springs, it has more than 250 arches, some of them 30 feet high.

The aqueduct ends at *Plaza Villalongin*, unmistakable for the large fountain adorned by statues of handsome Tarascan women holding aloft baskets of fruits and vegetables. While here, stop in at the *Sanctuary of Guadalupe*,

where every inch of the temple's interior is adorned with gold leaf and brightly-colored flowers. East of the Plaza walk down *Calzada Fray Antonio de San Miguel*, a beautiful shaded street flanked by elegant homes.

Worth a visit is the small and very old church of *Santa Rosa*, facing a beautiful plaza.

On the opposite side of the park, in the former Santa Rosa convent, is the *Conservatorio de las Rosas*, the first in the Americas, and today home of the Morelia Boys' Choir. The *Colegio de San Nicolas* is the second oldest educational institution in the Americas. It was founded by Bishop Vasco de Quiroga in Patzcuaro in 1540 and moved to its present site in 1580.

The *Regional Museum of Michoacan* is dedicated to regional customs and traditions, and includes a complete Morelian pharmacy dating from 1868. The *Michoacan Museum* houses a collection of archaeological artifacts and art, including Federico Cantu's impressive mural of the Four Horsemen of the Apocalypse.

History buffs will want to visit the *Jose Maria Morelos Museum*, once the home of the Mexican patriot. The *Museum of Colonial Art* displays an interesting collection of Christ figures made

from sugar and corn pulp, as well as some outstanding colonial paintings.

At Morelos Norte 485 is the *Casa de la Cultura*, one of the oldest and most impressive structures in the city. It contains an interesting *Mask Museum* with examples from many regions of Mexico.

For a real change of pace visit the *Benito Juarez Zoo*. It's a pleasant place with a variety of animals, a lake with rowboats for hire, a small train, picnic areas and a children's playground. The *Orchid Garden*, at the convention center, boasts a collection of 4,000 plants and is open 365 days a year.

The annual State Fair is held in Morelia from April 29 to May 20. One of the highlights of the fair is the organ festival that is held during the first two weeks of May featuring international artists.

If you're in central Mexico between late November and early March, be sure to visit the monarch butterfly refuge near Angangueo, Michoacan.

The drive from Morelia to Mexico City takes about four hours. A new highway connects Morelia with the seaside resort of Ixtapa in about three and a half hours

Hong Kong has hundreds of buildings...

Morelia,
Mexico
1,400 colonial gems

Morelia, the city of pink quarry, reflects in its magnificent
civil and religious monuments a grand historical past.
And today, it proudly stands as a Cultural World Heritage Site.
Morelia is lovelier than ever.

Come, fall in love with Michoacán

Morelia
more lovely than ever

Michoacán
the soul of México

MEXICO
Closer than ever

Copper goods dazzle the eye in Santa Clara del Cobre

Shopping

The state-run *Casa de las Artesanias* has a great selection of the lacquerware, wood carvings, pottery, and copper for which this region is noted. It is located downtown at Plaza Valladolid, between Humboldt and Bartolome de las Casas. There is also a museum of regional handicrafts on the premises. You'll find top quality here and they ship anywhere in the world.

Exquisite hand-carved, hand-painted wood furniture can be found at *Muebles Alanis*, Francisco Gonzalez Leon 96, in Santa Maria de Guido. High-quality pine and other woods are carved in Victor Alanis' workshop into colonial-style headboards, desks, wardrobes, chairs and other items that are then skillfully painted with exotic jungle scenes or other motifs. Tel. 323-5141.

Other shops specializing in colonial and rustic furniture are *Exportaciones Guare*, at Heroes de Nocupitaro 421, and *Fabrica Señal*, in Santa Maria de Guido, which also carries an excellent selection of folk art from all over Mexico.

At Guillermo Prieto 30, on the main plaza,

you will find *La Casa del Portal*, a fine restaurant and gallery selling colonial-style furniture and antiques.

Santa Sirenita Gallery, at Rey Tanganxoan 575, on the road to Santa Maria, carries fine colonial and contemporary art, plus handicrafts.

La Soterraña, at Plazuela Rayon 410, downtown, is another recommended gallery for folk art.

Candy lovers should head for the *Museo de Dulces*, located opposite the main post office, where regional sweets are displayed in a turn-of-the-century setting complete with sales clerks in period costume, or *Mercado de Dulces*, where dozens of stalls are piled high with locally-made candy.

Dining

Villa Montaña, a member of Small Luxury Hotels of the World, is a lovely showcase of fine colonial art and architecture with a gourmet restaurant offering seclusion and wonderful views just minutes from the downtown area.

Hotel de la Soledad, a charmingly reconstructed monastery, and *Virrey de Mendoza*, a colonial residence built in 1744, are popular with those who like to be near the central plaza, and both have good restaurants.

Los Juaninos, a restored colonial-era building on the main plaza, offers a rooftop restaurant and bar with a magnificent view of the cathedral. Also overlooking the plaza is *Casa del Portal*, an excellent restaurant in a wonderfully decorated mansion.

Housed in a beautifully restored turn-of-the-century home with garden seating, on Calzada Fray Antonio de San Miguel 344, *Casa de la Calzada* features excellent contemporary cuisine, including barbecued shrimp brochettes with mango salsa, a wide variety of grilled specialties, and luscious desserts. Tel. 313-5319.

San Miguelito restaurant-bar and bazaar, at Chopin 45, offers a great setting for dining and drinks, with a lively ambiance, unique decor and a very special shrine. If you take a liking to your table or tableware, you can take it with you—many of the antiques and antique-style furnishings are for sale. Tel. 324-2300.

Other good restaurants around town include *Fonda Las Mercedes* and *Los Mirasoles*.

Hotels

Hotel de la Soledad. Zaragoza 90, just off the main plaza. A beautiful converted monastery featuring a flower-filled central courtyard with a fountain framed by stone arches. The 49 rooms and nine suites are clean and simple with color TVs. Pleasant indoor/outdoor restaurant, bar with live music, heating. Rates MD. Tel. (443) 312-1888.

Los Juaninos. Morelos Sur 39, downtown, next to the cathedral. Wood-beam ceilings and stone arches recall the colonial past of this restored 18th-century building, while a polished-steel elevator and modern decorative touches point to the present day. There are 33 guest rooms with satellite TV, a/c, minibar, phone; small meeting room, lovely rooftop restaurant-bar with terrace tables and a great view of the cathedral. Member of Mexico Boutique Hotels. Rates FC. Tel. (443) 312-0036. www.hoteljuaninos.com.mx.

Villa Montaña. Patzimba 201, in the Santa Maria hills overlooking the city, five minutes from the downtown area. Recent million-dollar remodelling enhanced this already stunning property featuring multilevel colonial-style villas nestled in landscaped gardens. All 36 guest rooms, ranging from cozy studios to outsize one-bedroom suites with living rooms, are superbly decorated with fine antiques and local handicrafts. Rooms have a fireplace, satellite TV, phone, and deluxe bathroom amenities; some have private balconies. Heated pool, tennis court, gym; spa opening soon. Gourmet restaurant and bar with a panoramic view of the city. Small meeting and convention facilities. Nearby country club with golf course, horseback riding. Excellent guided tours to artisans' workshops, monarch butterfly sanctuary and other sites. No children under eight allowed December-February. Member of Small Luxury Hotels of the World and Mexico Boutique Hotels, winner of AAA's Four Diamond Award. Rates FC. Tel. (443) 314-0231. www.villamontana.com.mx.

Villa San Jose. Patzimba 77, in the Santa Maria hills overlooking the city. Very popular with families, these colonial-style villas house 43 rooms with fireplace, rustic wood furniture and hand-painted walls. Glass-enclosed restaurant with a view, bar with live music, heated outdoor pool, jacuzzi. Meeting room. Member of Mexico Boutique Hotels. Rates FC. Tel./Fax (443) 324-4545. www.villasanjose.com.mx.

Virrey de Mendoza. Madero Pte. 310, on the main plaza. Full of atmosphere, this colonial residence featuring a covered central patio with stone arches was built in 1565, a second floor was added in 1744, a meticulous restoration completed in 1991. There are 55 rooms and suites with cable TV, some with balconies overlooking the main plaza. Restaurant, bar. Rates MD. Tel. (443) 312-0633.

Patzcuaro

Once the capital of Purepecha Indians,

Patzcuaro is located on the southeast shore of Lake Patzcuaro, and is known for its famous butterfly-net fishing. Fishermen today employ more modern methods to catch the local whitefish, but still use the beautiful nets for visiting tourists near the *Island of Janitzio*, a short boat ride away.

Spanish soldiers, led by Nuño de Guzman, conquered the area in 1522. Their inhumanity to the Indians was such that the colonial government sent a bishop named Vasco de Quiroga to alleviate the situation. He arrived here in 1536 and encouraged each village around the lake to establish its own craft specialty, a tradition that continues to this day.

Patzcuaro is a beautiful town with a handsome central plaza. Friday mornings an Indian market moves into the main square to sell ceramics, wood carvings, lacquerware, copper, woven goods and even furniture.

The *Basilica de Nuestra Señora de la Salud* was originally planned by Vasco de Quiroga to be three times bigger than the Cathedral of Notre Dame in Paris. The present church is only one nave of the original plan. Its most interesting feature is the figure of the Virgin of Health that was created by Tarascans out of corn paste and wild orchids in the 16th century.

The attractive *Museo de Artes Populares* displays a large selection of Mexican folk art in charming rooms and gracious patios. Open 9 to 7 p.m.; to 3 p.m. Sunday; closed Monday.

Island of Janitzio

There are excellent arts and crafts shops near the plaza. The *Casa de los Once Patios*, a sprawling colonial-era home with interconnecting rooms built around numerous patios, houses the state-run arts and crafts store. It's a wonderful place to browse, and has a colorful restaurant-cafe.

Galeria del Arcangel, at Arciga 30, is one of the town's leading shops. Its different rooms contain a colorful selection of furniture and decorative items for the home, masks and other types of folk art, and creative sterling silver jewelry.

Posada de la Basilica, a modest hotel located in front of the church, offers a wonderfully picturesque place for a meal. The restaurant features excellent Mexican fare beautifully presented in striking black earthenware and the bar mixes a zesty margarita cocktail made with blackberry juice.

Patzcuaro and Janitzio are most famous for their Day of the Dead celebrations on the 1st

Carpet weaving, the old-fashioned way

Bruce Herman

and 2nd of November. This is not a time of grieving, but a time when families remember their lost ones, whose spirits are said to return to the realm of the living on those days. Small boats carry people across the lake to the Island of Janitzio to visit the cemeteries and decorate the graves with flowers and candles for an all-night vigil.

Tzintzuntzan, a Tarascan name meaning "place of the hummingbirds," was once the center of power of the Tarascan Indians. It is located 15 kilometers from Patzcuaro on the northeast edge of the lake. Here you can visit an archaeological site that contains the remains of five round structures, called *yacatas*, that were believed to have been burial centers for their leaders.

Not far from Patzcuaro is Villa Escalante, popularly known as *Santa Clara del Cobre* (a Clarist convent was established there in colonial times) and famous for its copperware. At the time of the conquest, the area's Purepecha Indians were experts at working the malleable metal found in the nearby Inguaran copper mines, and Vasco de Quiroga brought a group of Spanish craftsmen to the area to help the Indians refine their craft.

The Purepechas would start with a heavy chunk of metal fired with bellows until it was red hot, and with sheer imagination hammered it into a wonderful pitcher, urn, plate or pot, which was often a unique interpretation of a natural form. This technique is still used today and the sound of hammers pounding copper echoes everywhere. In mid-August, Santa Clara celebrates the National Copper Fair. The prize-winning pieces are on display in Santa Clara's *National Copper Museum*.

In the 1960s American artist James Metcalf and his wife, Ana Pellicer, settled in Santa Clara, introducing innovations to copper-making, such as outsize pieces, and luring women into the trade through jewelry making.

In the 1970s they helped establish an outstanding government-run school of arts and crafts. At *Galeria Tiamuri*, Pino Suarez 110, you can find the finest designs of Pellicer and students of the Adolfo Best Maugard Center for Creative Technical and Industrial Training.

Attractive copperware is also available at *Casa Felicitas, Taller El Porton,* and *Galeria Arte y Diseño en Cobre y Plata,* which displays outstanding designs by Ignacio Punzo Angel, a copper fair prize winner. The first two establishments are also workshops where you can see pieces being made.

About an hour's drive from Patzcuaro is pristine *Lake Zirahuen*. One dining option here is *La Troje de Ala*, an alpine-style restaurant set on the lake shore (open Friday to Sunday only.)

Recommended hotels in Patzcuaro include *Hacienda Mariposas*, a bed-and-breakfast owned and operated by Californian Shelley Ocana and her Mexican husband Rene; *La Casa de los Sueños,* a converted 17th-century mansion run by longtime resident Priscilla Madsen, originally from San Diego, Calif.; *Mansion Iturbe,* a converted 17th-century muleteer's home; and *Posada de la Basilica,* a modest yet charming hotel with an excellent top-floor restaurant.

Uruapan

Uruapan is a pleasant town west of Morelia and Patzcuaro. It was founded early in the colonial era, after the Aztec Empire collapsed and the Spanish sent expeditions to every area of Mexico. One of these expeditions, headed by Franciscan friar Juan de San Miguel, went into the mountainous region inhabited by the Tarascans and selected a spot believed to be the most beautiful in New Spain.

Here they founded the settlement of San Francisco Uruapan in 1532. Uruapan means "place where the flowers bloom," and it must have led the newcomers to suspect a tendency

towards understatement among Tarascans. The verdant beauty of Uruapan has fascinated visitors for years. It has cobblestone streets, a peaceful atmosphere, attractive homes and buildings, and flower-filled plazas.

In the area adjoining the plazas is *Guatapera*, a former chapel and hospital-turned-museum of folk art with stunning displays of the lacquerware for which the city has so long been famous. These unusual and highly prized objects include trays, small chests and wooden plates, all the result of a complex and intricate process of carving into the wood, setting color in the niches and applying the lacquer. There is no entrance fee, but a voluntary donation to the caretaker is much appreciated.

The *Mercado de Antojitos Tipicos*, a block north of the main plaza, is a good place to sample the regional dishes of Michoacan in a typical setting. Small restaurants flank the length of the entry, but an open-air courtyard in the back offers the nicest spot to sit and have a meal. The restaurants at the Plaza Uruapan and Victoria hotels are excellent.

On the outskirts of the city, but just a five-minute drive from the main square, is the *Eduardo Ruiz National Park* with its lovely fountains, river and spring, the source of the Cupatitzio River (said to be one of the most beautiful in the world). The 130-foot *Tzararacua Falls* are located downstream, surrounded by thick green shrubbery and trees, with an almost perpetual rainbow visible in the mist formed by the cascading water. Stairs lead down to the bottom of the waterfall, but you can also descend on horseback. Here vendors sell fresh coconuts, first making a hole for a straw so you can drink the juice and then cleaving the shell in half so you can scoop out the flesh.

Recommended hotels include *Mansion del Cupatitzio*, a charming Mexican-colonial hostelry at the edge of the park, and *Plaza Uruapan,* on the main plaza.

About 22 miles northwest is the town of *Angahuan*, from which one can visit the unique lava field originating from the 8,400-foot *Paricutin Volcano*, which sprang up out of the earth in 1943 and for eight years continued to spew lava before suddenly dying. It caused more than 4,000 people to flee their homes and buried the village of San Juan Parangaricutirimicuaro, called Parangaricutiro for short. Still visible is the village's church spire protruding from the lava bed.

Thirty miles north of Uruapan is *Paracho*, a town that produces violins and high quality guitars coveted by Mexican musicians. Returning to Mexico City from Uruapan by way of Morelia takes you through majestic scenery.

TRAVELERS GUIDE TO
Acapulco

*The Pacific coast resort features
a spectacular natural harbor.*

Introduction

A Resort With Celebrity Status

In Acapulco's heyday, the world's jet set flocked to its Pacific shores as often as to the French Riviera. Initially, Hollywood stars came to vacation away from the cameras. Leading man Errol Flynn threw lavish parties aboard his private yacht. Johnny "Tarzan" Weismuller, who is buried at a local cemetery, hosted beach bashes. And members of Hollywood's Rat Pack were regulars, as was Elizabeth Taylor, who married Mike Todd here.

Due to the sheer scope of its early fame, Acapulco still retains its celebrity status, though it has lost its former ranking as a leading international tourist destination to younger, more upstart resorts.

While Acapulco no longer evokes the star-studded image of its earlier days, celebrities continue to drop in on a fairly regular basis, especially at its legendary Las Brisas Hotel. Las Brisas has hosted so many luminaries over the years that it has its own version of the Hollywood Walk of Fame—the Wall of Fame, adorned with the cement handprints and signatures of eminent guests.

Acapulco continues to be a favorite resort for Mexicans, rich or poor, near or far. It is the closest beach to Mexico City, so it has the world's most populous urban center as its captive market. In fact, the ultimate way to end a wild party or night out in the big city has traditionally been the *"acapulcazo,"* or the impulsive, last-minute decision to veer onto the Acapulco highway and spend the following day recovering at the beach. Fortunately, a four-lane highway built in the early 1990s cut driving time between the two destinations from six to three and a half hours.

At night, Acapulco is breathtaking, with thousands of shimmering lights blanketing the mountainsides that surround this spectacular natural harbor. Away from the hotel zone, the city has a warm small-town feel to it, despite being home to 1.5 million inhabitants. As you walk along the beach near the downtown area you may see locals playing beach volleyball, or fishermen reeling in their nets, and selling a fish or two from the day's catch to passersby.

A major long-term program is underway to improve the resort and reposition it as a leading international and national destination. To be implemented in stages from now till the year 2025, it calls for additional wastewater treatment plants, the renovation of the seafront, and the construction of a bridge leading from the cruise ship pier to the historic fort and museum, among other things.

Acapulco has shown remarkable resilience and is often described as experiencing a renaissance. 1997's Hurricane Pauline, for example, battered the resort, but after the clean-up—a major priority since tourism is the port's main money earner—Acapulco looked better than ever.

Trade With the Orient

Evidence of human presence in and around Acapulco has been dated to as early as 3,000 B.C., making it one of Mesoamerica's earliest settlement sites. In 1530 Spanish conqueror Hernan Cortes and his men reached Acapulco, then a sleepy fishing village.

Having stumbled on to another sea, Cortes had ships built and, some

Acapulco Convention & Visitor Bureau

say, dreamt of adding China to his conquests. If so, he was disappointed. But ships from Acapulco did reach another jewel in the Spanish crown, Peru. They also headed northward, exploring the Sea of Cortez, and even far up the Colorado River.

After seizing Mexico and most of the Americas, the Spaniards set out to conquer the Philippines. In 1565 the first Spanish vessel sailed east from Manila and eventually arrived in Acapulco, marking the opening of one of the world's most important trade routes. For more than 200 years Acapulco played a major role in world trade as goods from China and Japan regularly arrived at the port, where they were traded for merchandise from Spain and the Americas.

Cargo aboard the famed Manila Galleon was valued at what today would amount to tens of millions of dollars, and before long pirates infested the waters not far from shore. Among the more notorious buccaneers was England's Sir Francis Drake.

To protect the thriving port, work began in 1616 on the San Diego Fort, now a historical museum and one of the oldest constructions in Acapulco. In 1818, the fort was besieged by Mexican troops during the War for Independence. The Spaniards held on for awhile, then retreated to their ships, sailing away forever. With them went the trade with the Orient and Acapulco went into decline.

A century later, Acapulco had all but ceased to exist. The trip from the capital took more than a week. A rail line ran only as far as Iguala, and from there the journey had to be made on horseback.

The first road from the capital was inaugurated on November 12, 1927. A few hearty souls made the long drive from Mexico City, which still took a week, and one or two boarding houses opened.

Acapulco Rediscovered

Acapulco's true potential was recognized only after World War II. Affluent Americans, yearning to travel abroad and all but barred from Europe and its Riviera, turned to Mexico, "so near, and yet so foreign."

John Wayne, Fred McMurray and Red Skelton were among the partners who acquired one of the resort's earliest hotels, Los Flamingos, which is still operating and well worth a visit. Soon, the name "Acapulco" began to appear regularly in the society columns of major U.S. newspapers.

But it was the jet age that really put Acapulco on the map. In 1964 direct international flights arrived for the first time. A construction boom followed as new vacation palaces, shops and restaurants were built.

These days a boom of sorts is taking place east of town, in an area known as *Acapulco Diamante*. Though it lies just 15 minutes from Acapulco's main strip, at the eastern tip of the bay, it is a different world, with lush, jungle-covered hills towering over wide beaches pounded by the surf of the open Pacific. Slated for major development, this area is now home to the luxury Quinta Real Hotel.

Today the resort city is an oasis along a primitive coast, a mirage amid barren mountains. She falls in and out of favor with international tourists, but continues to be a favorite holiday retreat among Mexicans, and the rich and famous who maintain opulent villas overlooking the Pacific.

What to See and Do

Beaches, Cliff Divers, Water Sports and More

Boats in dock at Acapulco's marina

Acapulco Convention & Visitors Bureau

Acapulco stretches around the bay and beyond, and is too spread out to see on foot. A new fleet of old-fashioned trolley cars offer a colorful way to cruise the main boulevard, Costera Miguel Aleman, named after the man who was president when it was built, Miguel Aleman Velasco (1946-1952). The *Tranvia Turistico* visits 25 sites of interest on its two-hour tour of the port.

The center of town is jammed together around an overly-adorned main plaza with a brick gazebo, potted palms, benches and fountains. An architecturally unconventional cathedral with Moorish-style spires that resemble mosque minarets is hidden behind the square's many ornamental features.

Here the resort changes into a bustling tropical port town. The main square more or less faces the dock crowded with small fishing boats and seafaring freighters. Occasionally, a brightly-lit luxury cruise liner dominates this scene. Fisherman's Walk, the area's seaside promenade, is a lovely place to stroll along the beach or sit on a bench under the shade of a palm tree.

Beaches

This is a town of many beaches, each with a character all its own, so try more than one during your stay.

Playa Caleta used to be the place to spend the morning. It's still popular, but almost exclusively among locals as it is removed from the hotel zone. Situated at the westernmost tip of the bay, or on the opposite end from the airport, Caleta's placid waters attract families with kids, and on weekends and holidays it teems with activity.

Two traditional hotels in Caleta, each with its own special charm, are good options for day visitors. The intimate *Boca Chica* lets non-guests use its facilities, including a private cove (no beach) and small swimming pool, for a nominal consumption charge at its excellent restaurant and bar. The sprawling *Caleta* features a private beach, two large swimming pools, restaurants, bars and expansive grounds.

Glass-bottom boats take passengers from Caleta to *Roqueta Island*, just a few hundred yards and some 10 minutes away, where you

High-rise hotels line Acapulco Bay

Robert Campbell

Pie de la Cuesta

If you want to see the sun go down in style, head for Pie de la Cuesta. Located just a few miles north of Acapulco (where the sun sets behind the mountains), this strip of beach is beyond the bay and offers an unobstructed view of the brilliant tropical sunset.

You can laze in a chair or stretch out in a hammock, sip a *coco loco*, a rum-laced coconut drink (order a *conga* for whoever is driving—no alcohol), perhaps call over a trio to sing a few songs, and watch what is beyond question one of the most beautiful shows in Acapulco. *Hacienda Vayma,* one of the better small beachfront hotels, offers a pleasant beach club and grill. Tel. 460-2882.

Pie de la Cuesta divides the Pacific Ocean from a large lagoon called *Coyuca,* which has its own attractions. Its calm surface is ideal for water-skiing and at the *Tres Marias* ski club you'll find experienced instructors ready to teach you how to ski—with or without skis. Tel. 460-0013.

A Jungle Tour of the lagoon lets you see the many species of birds that inhabit its palm-lined shores, as well as visit its two islands, the film locations of "Rambo 2" and the "Tarzan" television series, and try a mud mask. Tel. 481-2103.

At the northern end of the beach, the all-inclusive *Parador del Sol Hotel* offers spacious bungalows on both the Pacific and lagoon. Tel. 444-4050.

will find a less crowded but still well-attended beach. The boat ride offers a close look at area marine life, especially when one of the boat hands dives in, grabs a sea urchin and feeds it to the fish under the boat, causing quite a stir both above and below water. Boats making the return trip to Caleta leave every few minutes. On a tiny island joined to Caleta by a footbridge is *Magico Mundo Marino*, an aquarium popular with local children.

Playa Condesa has traditionally been Acapulco's most active beach. This beautiful strip of sand between the Continental Plaza and El Presidente hotels is where Mexico's spring-breakers converge. If there is a happening beach in town, this is it. There are several restaurant-beach clubs here where you can dine and dance to live music, and bungee jump.

Playa Los Hornos, the traditional afternoon beach, is where local fishermen set out in their boats in search of the day's catch. The preferred method is net fishing, and nets are cast just 50 to 100 meters from shore, then slowly reeled in. Invariably, a passerby buys a fish or two on the spot before the catch is taken to market.

Remember to check the beach flags and stay out of the water when the red flag is up. At times the undertow is powerful, so it is not a good idea to swim alone or at night.

Vendors of beach apparel, souvenirs, silver jewelry, snacks and other items ply the beaches despite government efforts to relocate them to permanent stands along the boulevard.

After lunch, a siesta is a time-honored tradition in Acapulco. Residents close up shop from 2 to 4 or 5 p.m. Visitors catch on quickly.

Puerto Marques

For years a tranquil little bay flanked by mountains and trees, with a little beach in the middle, Puerto Marques is today burdened with too many small businesses vying for too few clients.

The entire stretch of beach is crammed with about 40 identical concrete restaurants which fiercely compete with one another for business. This nearly uninterrupted wall of cement doesn't appear to discourage locals from flocking here on weekends and holidays, especially wind-surfing aficionados, who find the conditions ideal.

At the far end of the bay, the Puerto Marques branch of Acapulco's popular Pipo's seafood restaurant offers a nice place to have a drink or meal with a view of the comings and goings on the beach.

Acapulco Diamante

For a fun trip, drive east over the mountain toward the airport to Playa Revolcadero. In many ways this is the most beautiful beach of all. It faces the open sea and pounding surf, its soft sand stretching southward to Playa Diamante

Parachute gliding offers a bird's-eye-view of the resort

Acapulco Convention & Visitors Bureau

and Barra Vieja, and then off into the horizon. Though ideal for surfers, swimmers should practice caution.

A public beach with swaying palms offers *palapas*, or palm-thatched sunshades, a large swimming pool, open-air restaurant, and ample parking. To get there, pass the traffic circle at the bottom of the mountain as you leave Acapulco toward the airport, then turn right where you see the big sign at the gasoline station.

Farther south on the same beach is the deluxe all-inclusive Fairmont Pierre Marques Hotel with an 18-hole golf course; Fairmont Acapulco Princess, dominating the area with its pyramid-shaped main building surrounded by another 18-hole golf course; the impressive Mayan Palace, and the Tres Vidas golf club.

Revolcadero is sandwiched between Punta Diamante on the west and Playa Diamante on the east, all forming part of what is known as *Acapulco Diamante*, an area of almost 3,000 acres that stretches eastward from the end of the hotel zone. The Quinta Real Hotel and spa is one of Acapulco Diamante's most important developments. This beautiful setting with incomparable views will eventually be home to several five-star hotels, condominiums, villas, shopping centers, recreational facilities and beach clubs.

Continuing south about 15 miles is *Barra Vieja*. Don't expect to get away from the crowds here. Though this beach with pounding surf is unknown to most tourists, it is extremely popular among Mexicans. Here the *Tres Palos Lagoon* meets the Pacific Ocean. The lagoon, pretty well hidden from the road by trees and bushes, is a haven for birds in winter. Local fishermen offer sightseeing tours and fishing excursions in the lagoon. Several typical beachfront restaurants serve *pescado a la talla* (an Acapulco specialty made of whole fish rubbed with spices and roasted on a spit).

Cliff Divers

A trip to Acapulco isn't complete until you've seen the world-famous divers at La Quebrada make their spectacular 130-foot leaps off the cliffs into just 11 feet of water. Divers plunge into a narrow cove, which is safe only when a wave has come in. Needless to say, they must dive at exactly the right moment.

You can see the dives, for a nominal entrance fee, from balconies built into the cliffs opposite the diving sites. Dives are scheduled at 1 p.m., and nightly at 7:30, 8:30, 9:30 and 10:30 p.m. At night, the last divers carry lighted torches as they plunge into the water—an unforgettable sight.

You can also watch the dives from La Perla restaurant-bar at the El Mirador Hotel, which is built into the cliffs above. There's a minimum consumption charge.

La Quebrada can be reached on foot by following the street that bears its name from its base behind the cathedral.

Bay Cruises

A variety of boats offer day and nighttime cruises of the bay. *Bonanza*, which has a swimming pool and stern platform that lowers to sea level for swimming in the bay when the boat makes a brief stop, has day cruises departing at 11 a.m., sunset cruises at 4:30 p.m., and moonlight cruises at 10:30 p.m. Friday to Sunday and holidays. Tel. 482-2055.

Palao takes passengers on a four-hour tour to Roqueta Island, with a buffet lunch and open bar. Tel. 482-4313. *Divers de Mexico* offers a sunset Champagne cruise to see the cliff divers. Tel. 482-1398. Call ahead for current departure times, which may vary from summer to winter.

Water Sports

A sport you can master in Acapulco is water-skiing. You will have no trouble finding a teacher. Sit on the beach five minutes and you'll see. But beginners will have a better time in the tranquil waters of Coyuca Lagoon or Puerto Marques.

If you want to try scuba diving, the waters are calm and the instructors top-notch. The favorite diving spots include Piedra del Elefante and Piedra de la Hierbabuena reefs, and the Virgen Sumergida (an underwater shrine) off the shores of Roqueta Island where the currents are gentle. American-owned Divers de Mexico offers diving excursions that

Acapulco's famed divers jump off the rocky cliffs of La Quebrada

include an introductory in-pool lesson for beginners and an English-speaking captain. Tel. 482-1398.

Equipment rental and instruction are also available from *Aqua Mundo* (482-1041) and *Hermanos Arnold* (482-1877).

Snorkeling is fun most anywhere, especially around Roqueta. Extra caution should be used here, because many tourist boats visit the area.

You will also find a good assortment of paddle and surf boards, and catamarans, as well as windsurfing equipment.

One of the newest activities in Acapulco is a high-speed boat ride aboard the *Shotover Jet*. This New Zealand import takes passengers aboard a jet boat specially designed with an "impeller," an internal propeller that sucks in water and forces it out through a moveable nozzle, for extra maneuverability and speed in shallow water. Set aside about four hours for the trip. Consult your hotel travel desk or call 484-1154 for a reservation.

Chances of hooking a 100-pound game fish in Acapulco are excellent. Sailfish, tuna and red snapper are just a few of the varieties that make this a great fishing port. Full-day or half-day tours can be arranged for groups of four to eight. Divers de Mexico offers deep-sea fishing excursions and private yacht charters. Tel. 482-1398. Some pleasant freshwater fishing (mainly bass and catfish) is available at Coyuca Lagoon.

CICI Water Park is fun for the kids, with swimming pools with artificial waves and toboggans, an aquarium, dolphin and seal show, swimming with dolphins, and beach club. The park is open 10 a.m. to 6 p.m. Tel. 484-4035.

For a different kind of thrill, you might try parachute gliding. If you accept the risk and go up, you'll have an exhilarating view and no doubt be the only person on your block back home who's flown over Acapulco barefoot!

Golf and Tennis

Acapulco has four 18-hole golf courses and a nine-hole municipal course. *Tres Vidas Golf Club* features an 18-hole, par-72, Robert von

San Diego Fort

Acapulco Convention & Visitors Bureau

Hagge-designed course built right on the edge of the ocean. It is landscaped with nine lakes, dotted with palms, and home to a flock of ducks and other birds. Tel. 444-5135. *Mayan Palace Golf Club* also boasts an 18-hole course by the ocean's edge. Tel. 469-6000.

The *Acapulco Princess* and *Pierre Marques* hotels share two championship golf courses side by side, with driving ranges and practice areas. Tel. 469-1000. And Acapulco's *Club de Golf* offers a nine-hole municipal course just west of the convention center. Tel. 484-0781.

The Villa Vera Racquet Club has long been the favorite place to play tennis, but you'll find excellent courts at the Acapulco Princess, Pierre Marques, Las Brisas, Hyatt Regency, and Mayan Palace hotels, as well as at the Club Britania at Joyas de Brisamar Vista de Altamar (tel. 484-5292).

Spas

After a day spent in the sun, a deep-tissue or shiatsu massage or a hydrating body or facial treatment can help allay fatigue and prepare you for a night out.

The Quinta Real spa offers luxurious pampering and gourmet spa cuisine, while Villa Vera features romantic treatments for two at its *spa á deux.* The Hyatt's Alory Spa and the Willow Stream Spa at the Acapulco Princess are two of the resort's newest.

More to See

Acapulco's historic *San Diego Fort,* overlooking the bay from the north, was built in 1617 to defend the port from pirates looking to profit from Mexico's lucrative trade with the Orient. Virtually abandoned at the end of the 18th century, the fort today houses the *Acapulco Historical Museum,* which contains an interesting collection of art and artifacts relating the port's long history of trade with the Far East. It also displays relics from Acapulco's pre-Hispanic past and colonial era. Among the rare objects are an

ivory infant Jesus from Goa, an 18th-century one-piece cannon from Spain, and a pirate flag reputed to have belonged to Cromwell.

Newly renovated, the fort hosts a light-and-sound show Saturday evenings that brings the port's history to life (performances in English can be arranged for groups). Visiting hours are from 10 a.m. to 6:30 p.m., Tuesday through Sunday.

Down the hill from the fort's entrance is the *House of Masks*, which houses an interesting collection of hand-carved wooden masks from the state's seven regions. A resident artisan can be seen making masks out of different materials.

Recently opened to the public, the hilltop *Palma Sola* archaeological site features perhaps

A fisherman shows off his catch

Ministry of Tourism

some of the world's earliest drawings, stick figures carved in stone more than 1,200 years ago. Approximately 18 petroglyphs are scattered about a hillside. Stairs lead up to the site, but the climb can be arduous.

Fans of Mexican muralist Diego Rivera may want to see the home of Dolores Olmedo, a socialite and art collector who modeled for Rivera in her youth. In 1956 Rivera covered the facade of the house, on Calle Inalambrica 6 in downtown Acapulco, with a mural made of seashells and tiles. In tribute to Aztec lore, the mural depicts the feathered serpent deity Quetzalcoatl. He also painted interior walls, but the house is not open to the public.

The Acapulco bullfighting ring is a smaller version of the one in Mexico City, but it boasts the same pageantry and color. Unfortunately, you won't see the same caliber of fights, unless it is a special benefit event. Bullfights are held every Sunday at 5:30 p.m. from January to March. You can buy tickets to sit in the sun or shade.

The modern *Jai Alai* center on the Costera, near the Hyatt Regency, seems to attract bigger crowds to its giant bingo hall and sportsbook.

Centro Internacional Acapulco, on the Costera, just a two-minute drive past the Hyatt Regency Hotel toward town, is a 50 million-dollar, 35-acre convention and exposition center built in 1976. Each year it hosts Mexico's largest travel trade fair, the Tianguis Turistico, as well as other events. Tel. 484-3218.

Daily sightseeing tours take visitors to the main beaches and hotels as well as the downtown area. The cliff divers at La Quebrada are usually included. There are also nightclub tours in the evenings. The American Express office, located at the Gran Plaza mall, offers sightseeing tours as part of its travel services.

Depending on your length of stay, you can arrange one-, two- or three-day tours to the silver mining town of Taxco, the colonial town of Oaxaca, or the capital, Mexico City.

Getting Around

Taxis are abundant, but can be expensive. Posted in most hotel lobbies are the authorized fares. Taxis that pick you up directly at the hotel stick to this higher price list. Taxis hailed on the street charge a slightly lower rate, but it's best to negotiate a price before getting in.

A more economical option is to take the white-and-yellow collective cabs that cruise up and down the Costera, picking up and leaving passengers along the way; there are no designated stops.

Rickety buses that should have been retired years ago from active duty pass frequently and charge a minimal fare. A fleet of modern, air-conditioned, yellow buses called Acabus shuttle along the same route, from Playa Caleta to the Hyatt Regency Hotel, for slightly more, but they are less frequent. Rented jeeps are ideal for exploring on your own.

Real Estate

Living in a Resort Area That's Hard to Beat

By Ron Lavender

Acapulco is and probably always will be an important tourist destination. It has had its ups and downs, but with a natural setting so genuinely breathtaking—James Michner called it "one of the most beautiful bays in the world"—the warm waters of its protected bay, and a near-perfect climate (almost constant sunshine and year-round temperatures in the 80s), it's a resort area that's hard to beat.

Acapulco is a place for relaxing and playing. Here, when we discuss—and resolve—the problems of the world, we do it stretched out on an air mattress under the hot sun, while gliding over the surface of a pool, drink in hand. This feeling of relaxation, and Acapulco's easy accessibility by plane and by land (from Mexico City via the toll highway it is about a three and a half hour drive), are what make this port's real estate market so attractive.

Shortly after the first highway connected Mexico City to Acapulco in 1927, it became socially *de rigueur* for Mexico City's well-to-do families to own a seaside retreat. Many of those early mansions still exist in what is known as "traditional Acapulco."

During the administration of former President Miguel Aleman (1946-1952) the city progressed enormously with the construction of the Costera, the main boulevard; the airport; and the Carretera Escenica, the highway leading from the Naval Base, past Las Brisas, to Puerto Marques. The government's infrastructure improvements opened the way for private developers, and from the mid-40s to the mid-50s there were tremendous strides. The famous Las Brisas Hotel and residential subdivision was opened in 1957.

Acapulco's different real estate options—from the varied locations, to rentals or purchases, and beachfront condos versus hilltop villas—are discussed below.

Where to Buy

Las Playas: This area is home to the Acapulco Yacht Club and Marina Acapulco, and is also convenient to the *zocalo*, or main plaza, and the downtown area. Some good bargains are scattered around this neighborhood, and view conscious buyers will appreciate some of the lovely views available. As one of the city's older neighborhoods, streets and infrastructure may not be tip-top, but that is why prices here are attractive.

Los Cocos condominium units have their own dock, a good pool, great view, and appealing prices. Some of the older homes have good refurbishing potential. In brief, if you are a seafarer or somewhat economy minded, Las Pla-

A luxury villa overlooks the bay

YOU CAN BUY YOUR OWN COPY OF THIS BOOK. SEE THE LAST PAGE.

yas is a good bet.

Hornos Insurgentes: This district, located above and behind Papagayo Park, with some panoramic views, is central and reasonably priced. There are several single-family homes and a good variety of condominiums to choose from.

Magallanes: Also located above Papagayo Park, but below Hornos Insurgentes, this basically commercial area has several fine beachfront condominiums.

El Farallon/La Condesa: Located on the hillside above Playa Condesa, these two adjoining areas offer a number of quite spectacular homes and condominiums with good views, and are home to a solid upper middle-class residential population.

Club Deportivo: Surrounding the Acapulco Golf Club, this area offers above average homes and condos in the residential zone, and a great number of beachfront condos, ranging from moderate to opulent.

Costa Azul: This solid upper middle-class neighborhood, site of Oceanic 2000, is where many local business and professional people live. Flat and easy to build on, the land makes this a good real estate option in spite of the fact that most of the lots are without a view. The beach area is high quality condominium row.

Brisas Guitarron/Marina Brisa: Half a dozen of Acapulco's residential showplaces (with an average value above 5 million dollars) are situated along the waterfront in this area, clearly the high rent district. The hillside residential area is also prime real estate. Great views, good maintenance, and tight security characterize this gated community.

Las Brisas/Club Residencial Las Brisas: The market leaders, these areas offer panoramic views, well-kept grounds, tight security and excellent administration, plus a strong home owners association. The average price of a residence is one million dollars, with several villas running in high multiples of that. An added amenity for owners and guests is a private club with a semi-Olympic pool, gymnasium, tennis courts, meeting rooms and a theater, as well as 24-hour medical service.

Brisas Marques: This extensive area, known for being environmentally friendly, boasts good infrastructure, with wide streets. Depending on the section, the magnificent views are of Puerto Marques and the open Pacific, or of Acapulco Bay. Many very good lots are still available.

La Cima: Located along the mountain ridge above Las Brisas, this relatively new area has state-of-the-art infrastructure and fabulous views of Acapulco Bay, Puerto Marques and Revolcadero. There are many excellent lots to choose from; prices are very high.

Acapulco Diamante: This area has enjoyed tremendous growth during the past 10 years, and continues to do so. Running from the east side of Punta Diamante up to and including Tres Vidas, with broad Revolcadero Beach to the south and the airport highway to the north, it includes the Princess and Pierre Marques hotels (both Fairmont properties),

Mayan Palace, condos and villas, Playamar and Club Playamar condos, and the new Maralago complex, already half sold and still in construction.

Beachfront units at these upscale properties run from 350,000 to 650,000 dollars, while fairway villas at both the Princess and Mayan Palace run between 200,000 and 350,000 dollars.

A spectacular oceanfront golf club with five beachfront holes, Tres Vidas tops the list of four area golf courses.

The vast majority of owners in Acapulco Diamante, which is burgeoning and will continue to do so in the foreseeable future, are affluent Mexico City residents who weekend by the seaside.

Private hilltop homes feature panoramic views

What to Buy

Villa or condo? This one almost answers itself. Some people are gregarious, enjoy having neighbors to chat with, and want a place where they can turn the key and walk away. Others want quiet and privacy, with more space and more service. It's almost that simple. Of course, prices factor in also. Generally a villa will cost twice as much as an apartment. Keep in mind that no property should be left unattended, even an apartment. A maid should come once or twice a week to dust, water plants, ventilate the place for an hour or two. Villas, depending on size, usually come with a cook and housekeeper, maid and pool man-gardener.

Should you rent or buy? Villa rentals start at around 400 dollars a day (though there are not very many of these). The average cost is closer to 1,000 dollars a day for a four- or five-bedroom with a pool, panoramic view and good staff. For those who enjoy living like a Turkish pasha, there's an 11-bedroom, 14-bath villa that rents for 5,000 dollars a day, with two pools and a tennis court. Condominium apartments generally rent from 200 to 450 dollars a day, and range from very com-

fortable to quite lavish.

Many people prefer owning, knowing that their place will be available to them regardless of the season. In the long run this has worked well, many old-timers now have properties worth several times what they paid for them.

There are an abundance of homes on the market and it seems most people prefer to buy an existing property that suits their tastes than build. Good lots are almost exhausted in Las Brisas and residences with refurbishing potential have been pretty well used up. But there are other areas—Brisas Marques, La Cima and Tres Vidas—where attractive sites still exist. If building, consider hiring one of the excellent local architects or builders; they understand the lifestyle, predominant breezes, storm winds, etc.

Property Management

If you are an absentee owner, especially of a villa, it's a good idea to use an administrative service, and one that is well established. There are many sad tales of owners who relied on a maid, taxi driver or tradesman to pay the bills, supervise rentals and keep accounts. In the long run there is no responsible party to fall back on and what appears to be the cheaper route turns out to be more expensive.

Of critical importance, a strong and active owners association is a powerful guarantee for the buyer, ensuring good maintenance and security.

If you are buying a condominium, review the owners' covenant carefully, and determine with the manager how accounts stand with the current owners.

The Las Brisas residential subdivision has a strong association with an active board, as does Club Residencial Las Brisas. The same is true of the villas at the Acapulco Princess, Mayan Palace and Pichilingue Diamante.

Only recently have U.S. buyers been able to get financing from U.S. mortgage companies for the purchase of property in Mexico. Such companies typically offer loan terms of up to 25 years at an average annual interest rate of 10 percent.

Timesharing

There are several well established timeshares, some offered by such leading hotels as Mayan Palace, on Playa Revolcadero, and Hyatt Regency, in the hotel zone.

In general, a timeshare week can be purchased for a period of five, 10 or 25 years. The average price per year for a unit for two to four people runs from about 1,600 dollars for a low-season week to 2,800 dollars during the high season. A separate maintenance fee is charged annually; monthly payment programs are available.

Originally from the U.S. midwest, Ron Lavender has resided in Acapulco since 1954. He is on the board of the home owners associations for Las Brisas and Brisas Guitarron, and serves as president of Amigos de Acapulco, Acapulco's principal charitable organization.

MAYAN ⬙ PALACE
A C A P U L C O

The most spectacular resort in Latin America.

More than 200 acres of tropical paradise surrounded by lakes, waterfalls and the most beautiful gardens.

Conveniently located only 5 minutes away from Acapulco International Airport. The only one with over one half mile of beach front, 18-hole golf course, 12 covered tennis courts; also, over 20 acres of lakes and a private system of boats and canals as well as a railroad for access and enjoyment. We have the longest pool in the world!... and much more.

All these features and spectacular architecture make the

MAYAN ⬙ PALACE
A C A P U L C O

a breathtaking and exciting experience.

RESERVATIONS: U.S.A. AND CANADA 1-800-99 MAYAN. MEXICO 01 800 36 45600.

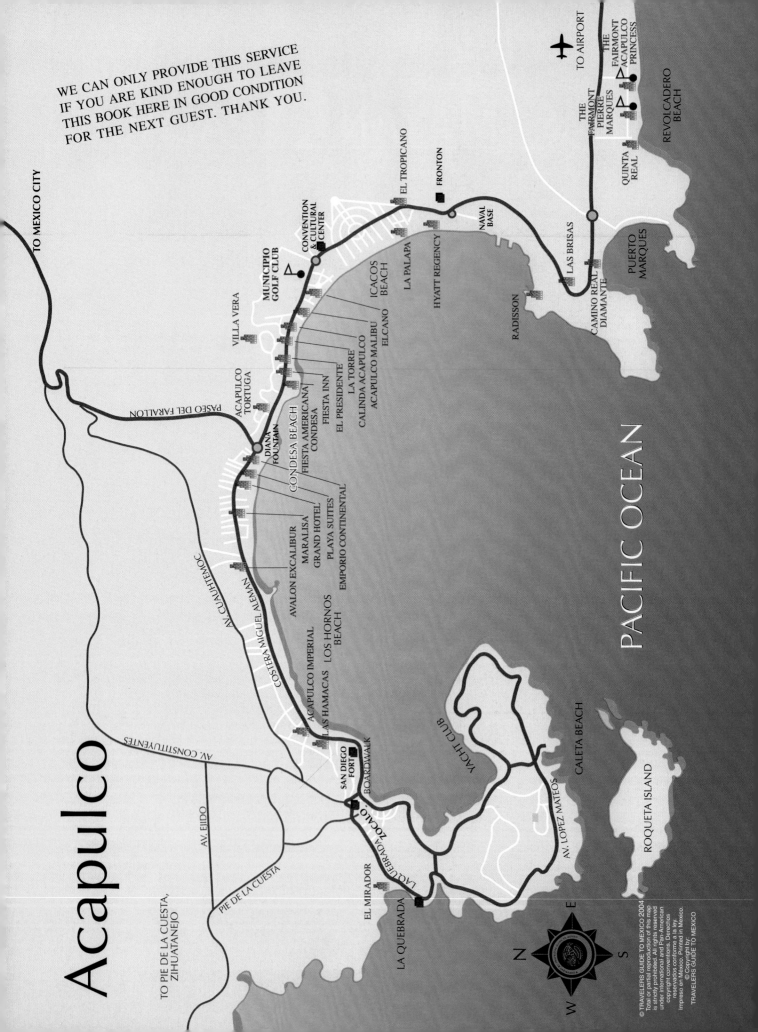

Acapulco

PACIFIC OCEAN

TO MEXICO CITY

TO AIRPORT

THE FAIRMONT ACAPULCO PRINCESS

THE FAIRMONT PIERRE MARQUES

REVOLCADERO BEACH

QUINTA REAL

PUERTO MARQUES

CAMINO REAL DIAMANTE

LAS BRISAS

NAVAL BASE

FRONTON

EL TROPICANO

CONVENTION & CULTURAL CENTER

MUNICIPIO GOLF CLUB

VILLA VERA

HYATT REGENCY

LA PALAPA

ICACOS BEACH

RADISSON

ELCANO

ACAPULCO MALIBU

CALINDA ACAPULCO

EL PRESIDENTE

LA TORRE

FIESTA INN

ACAPULCO TORTUGA

CONDESA

FIESTA AMERICANA

CONDESA BEACH

DIANA FOUNTAIN

PASEO DEL FARALLON

AVALON EXCALIBUR

MARALISA

GRAND HOTEL

PLAYA SUITES

EMPORIO CONTINENTAL

AV. CUAUHTEMOC

COSTERA MIGUEL ALEMAN

ACAPULCO IMPERIAL

LAS HAMACAS

LOS HORNOS BEACH

AV. CONSTITUYENTES

AV. EJIDO

PIE DE LA CUESTA

TO PIE DE LA CUESTA, ZIHUATANEJO

SAN DIEGO FORT

BOARDWALK

ZOCALO

LA QUEBRADA

EL MIRADOR

YACHT CLUB

CALETA BEACH

AV. LOPEZ MATEOS

ROQUETA ISLAND

N
E
S
W

Dining & Nightlife

From Fish-on-a-Stick to Chateaubriand

Mexico Tourism Board

Dining out in Acapulco can be memorable, whether it's at one of the resort's leading hotels, a romantic hilltop restaurant, or under a palm-thatched *palapa* overlooking the beach. Even the most modest restaurant can offer the freshest fish and seafood grilled to perfection and accompanied by an ice cold *chelada*—beer and lemon juice on ice served in a salt-rimmed glass. And you can begin with a favorite appetizer, *ceviche*, a marinated seafood cocktail imported from Peru during the 16th-century sea trade.

The main boulevard, Costera Miguel Aleman, follows Acapulco's shoreline from one end to the other and is home to most of the port's colorful eateries, many open-air restaurants overlooking the golden sand.

The hills that ring the bay are home to several top restaurants featuring fine cuisine and panoramic views that are especially breathtaking at night when the bay lights up with thousands of shimmering lights. Many of the best restaurants open only for dinner.

One of Guerrero state's most famous dishes is *pozole*, a hearty, highly seasoned stew made with hominy kernels and pork. Traditionally Thursday is pozole day, when you'll find almost every restaurant in town serving the dish accompanied by its usual bevy of garnish: toasted oregano, red chili powder, shredded lettuce, and chopped onion, parsley and radish.

Although many tourists are accustomed to having their meals at noon and 6 p.m., dining in Acapulco begins to take shape at about 2 p.m. for lunch and 9 p.m. for dinner.

Baikal
Carretera Escenica 22
Tel. 446-6867
Acapulco's newest hilltop restaurant is a feast for the senses, combining a stunning setting, spectacular view, gourmet cuisine, soft jazz and

even elegant short films that are projected onto retractable screens. The dishes successfully blend elements of classic French, Mediterranean and Asian cuisines. Menu highlights include salmon steak in a honey balsamic vinaigrette, Paris-Peking glazed duck, and goat cheese-stuffed chicken breast in a tomato-and-tarragon sauce. Separate upper level bar area. Reservations recommended.

Bambuco
Elcano Hotel
Tel. 484-1950
A breezy terrace restaurant-bar specializing in fine Spanish and seafood dishes. The menu favorite is paella Valenciana, made with saffron rice, succulent jumbo shrimp, clams, mussels and chunks of chicken and beef. Very popular at lunch with strolling guitar-strumming crooners singing Mexican tunes. Open 7 a.m. to 11:30 p.m.

Acapulco Convention & Visitors Bureau

Bellavista
Las Brisas Hotel
Tel. 469-6900
This attractive world-renowned restaurant offers breathtaking views from its terrace and features award-winning international gourmet cuisine accompanied by soft music and a spectacular bay view. The setting calls for elegant resort attire. Reservations a must. Open 7 to 11 p.m.

Cabo Diamante
Camino Real Hotel
Tel. 435-1010
Light, airy and thoroughly delightful with terraced seating that gives all diners a front-row view of Puerto Marques Bay. The international fare includes fish and seafood, meats and some Mexican specialties, all well prepared and beautifully presented. The striking paintings on the walls are by Salcido. Open 7 a.m. to 11 p.m.

Carlos'n Charlie's
Costera M. Aleman 112
Tel. 484-0039
You'll find good food and friendly service at this second-story, open-air terrace restaurant overlooking the main boulevard. Try the grilled shrimp bathed in their homemade barbecue sauce. Animated at night, with loud music and sassy waiters. Open 1 p.m. to 1 a.m.; bar to 3 a.m.

Casanova
Carretera Escenica 5256
Tel. 446-6237
This refined, multilevel Italian restaurant features a spectacular view; indoor and outdoor dining. The excellent menu offers international specialties as well. Arturo and Patricia Cordova, also owners of Coyuca 22, have added their personal touch to every aspect of the decor, design, menu and service. Consistent winner of the Dirona (Distinguished Restaurants of North America) award and the AAA's Four Diamond. Expensive. Reservations suggested. Open 7 p.m. to midnight.

Coyuca 22
Tel. 483-5030
The name is the address, high in the hills overlooking the bay. *The New York Times* has called it "one of the most beautiful restaurants in the world." Unique and elegant, it is the perfect choice for a special evening. Menu favorites include pepper steak and lobster tail. Winner of the AAA's Four Diamond award. Reservations recommended. Open for dinner only, November through April.

El Faro
Costera M. Aleman 75
Tel. 484-3100
The Lighthouse, as it's called, offers fish and seafood specialties with a Mediterranean touch, in a setting resembling a luxury cruise liner. Try the grilled catch of the day; broiled lobster with truffle, tarragon and parsley butter; or barbecued rib-eye for two. Separate bar area. Open 12:30 to 11:30 p.m. Closed Monday.

El Olvido
Plaza Marbella
Tel. 481-0203
Favored for its stunning alfresco setting facing the bay and bold architectural design. The gourmet dishes combine the flavors of Mexico and cuisines from around the world. Menu highlights include black bean soup with sour cream, salmon in mango vinaigrette, and sea bass in avocado sauce with fried *epazote* herb. Leave room for their delicious *crema quemada* dessert (a Mexican-style creme brulée). Open 6 p.m. to 1:30 a.m.

El Pescador
Hyatt Regency Hotel
Tel. 469-1234
Great fresh fish and seafood, wood-burning oven pizzas, and sizzling steaks served in an attractive, relaxed, open-air restaurant suspended over the beach, with a wonderful view. Try the *pescado a la talla* for two, broiled fish rubbed with spices, an Acapulco specialty, and fried bananas with a scoop of coconut ice cream, a great way to end any meal. Excellent service. Open 12:30 to 11:30 p.m.

Gourmet
Quinta Real Hotel
Tel. 469-1500
Gourmet Mexican and international cuisine in an elegant setting with views of Punta Diamante. Specialties include red snapper in citrus sauce and shrimp-stuffed cactus leaves. Open 7 a.m. to noon and 6 p.m. to midnight.

Kookaburra
Carretera Escenica Las Brisas
Tel. 446-6039
Breathtaking view of the bay and delicious, innovative seafood dishes created by talented chef Roberto Thomas, who blends the flavors of Mexico and other countries with his French-style cooking. Try the crab cakes in sweet-and-sour sauce, his original recipe for shrimp in tamarind sauce, shrimp carpaccio with cream of caviar, and mahi-mahi ceviche with salmon caviar and fried wontons. Equally creative duck, lamb and beef specialties. Indoor and outdoor terrace dining, and separate bar. Open noon to midnight.

La Perla
El Mirador Hotel
Tel. 483-1155
Offering front-row seats to the famous cliff divers, and international fare. The 130-foot dives are held nightly at 7:30, 8:30, 9:30 and 10:30.

La Trattoria
Fiesta Americana Hotel
Tel. 484-2828
An informal open-air Mediterranean restaurant serving a variety of pasta dishes. Live music. Open 6 p.m. to 1 a.m.

La Vela
Camino Real Hotel
Tel. 435-1010
Excellent setting and seafood. Umbrella-

shaded tables on a breezy wharf offer wonderful views of the comings and goings at Puerto Marques Bay. Begin with any of a wide variety of refreshing *ceviches,* marinated fish or seafood cocktails. Everything is expertly prepared and presented. Open 1 to 11 p.m.

Le Jardin des Artistes
Vicente Yañez Pinzon 11
Tel. 484-8344
Located just off the Costera, this pleasant alfresco restaurant offers gourmet French cuisine in an outdoor patio decked with art; very romantic at night when tables are candle lit. Specialties include fresh goose foie gras, tender beef fillet with black pepper, sumptuous desserts, and a good selection of French wines. Open from 7 p.m.

Madeiras
Carretera Escenica 33
Tel. 446-5636
Two-tiered dining, with a terrace that provides a lovely view of the bay. Delicious international dishes from a fixed-price four-course menu. Reservations suggested. Open for dinner only.

Mezzanotte
Carretera Escenica, La Vista Shopping Center
Tel. 446-5728
This popular restaurant-cum-nightclub features innovative Italian cuisine and seafood, nightly entertainment, and a panoramic view of the bay. Favorite menu items include any of their charcoal-grilled specialties, including whole red snapper or duck marinated in fine herbs, and gourmet wood-oven pizzas made with smoked salmon, prosciutto di Parma, smoked Provolone or other imported ingredients. Music and dancing from 10 p.m. Open 2 to 11:30 p.m.; to 1:30 a.m. Thursday to Sunday.

Palma Real
Villa Vera Hotel
Tel. 484-0333
Once a celebrity haunt and still infused with a bygone glamour, this hotel offers relaxed elegance in a glass-enclosed restaurant overlooking the town and bay. Menu highlights include Pacific coast crepes filled with seafood in a white wine sauce, whole grilled fish, and regional specialty pozole served Thursdays. Pleasant at lunch, romantic at dinner. Reservations recommended since hotel guests often don't stray far. Open 7:30 a.m. to 10:30 p.m.

Paradise
Costera M. Aleman 107, on Playa Condesa
Tel. 484-5988
One of the oldest establishments in town, and still going strong. Good food at reasonable prices served in a casual hutlike setting overlooking the beach. Try the grilled whole red snapper. Music and dancing (the waiters put on a show) from noon; not the place for a quiet meal. Open for lunch and dinner.

Pipo's
Costera M. Aleman, opposite convention center
Tel. 484-0165

Started by a mother-and-son team, this popular restaurant serves fresh fish and seafood dishes. Try the whole red snapper, grilled crispy outside and flaky inside. Open 1:30 to 9:30 p.m. Also has a branch downtown.

Salamandras
Club del Mar Beach Club
Tel. 466-2683
Adjacent to the Quinta Real Hotel, this new dining option offers innovative Thai-Mexican cuisine in a lavish seaside setting. Tables are set under a giant palapa or around the landscaped gardens and three circular pools. Specialties of the fusion cuisine include crisp summer rolls, tropical chicken satai, fish wrapped in banana leaves, tuna-stuffed *chile ancho*, lobster tail, sea bass, shrimp and more. Open Fridays only, 8 p.m. to 2 a.m. (the beach club is open daily, 10 a.m. to 6 p.m.). Reservations a must.

Señor Frog's
Carretera Escenica, La Vista Shopping Center
Tel. 446-5734

A great view, cooling breeze and utter tranquillity by day; frat party atmosphere at night with the resident DJ playing the latest pop tunes and diners dancing on the table tops. Entertainment provided by the wacky maxims that deck every inch of wall and ceiling space, and the riotous waiters. The food is good, too. The regional specialty, pozole, is served Thursdays. Open noon to 12:30 a.m.; bar 1 p.m. to 3 a.m.

Suntory
Costera M. Aleman 36
Tel. 484-8088
This attractive restaurant brings a slice of Japan to the Pacific coast resort. Dine indoors or, in the cooler evening hours, on a balcony overlooking a lovely Japanese garden with a refreshing pond and waterfall. Good traditional favorites. Open 2 p.m. to midnight.

Tabachin
The Fairmont Pierre Marques
Tel. 469-1000
Acapulco's first renowned restaurant is mak-

ing a comeback thanks to chef Gino Guercio and his innovative cuisine, a blend of French and Asian culinary traditions.

Zapata, Villa & Cia
Hyatt Regency Hotel
Tel. 469-1234
Take a trip back in time to the days of the Mexican Revolution. The Mexican and seafood specialties include oversized Tampiqueña steak, sizzling chicken and beef fajitas, marinated choice cuts of U.S. beef, chicken and shrimp. Nearly 100 varieties of tequila. The food and service are both outstanding, with that wonderful Hyatt flare and attention to detail. Open 7 to 11:30 p.m. Closed Sunday.

Nightlife

Acapulco is famed for its nightlife, especially its hilltop glass-walled discotheques, which command a sweeping view of the bay.

The resort is also home to one particularly famous disco, *Baby'O*, whose success has over the years inspired discos around the country to adopt similar names, like Dady'O, Lady'O and Mamy'O. Even a notorious Tijuana cartel drug kingpin, by the name of Francisco Arellano Felix, briefly operated a disco in Mazatlan called Frankie'O.

There are nightclubs to suit every taste, age and pocketbook. Some of the best may be right in your own hotel, or on the main boulevard, or perched on the hills above the bay.

Nighttime activity gets started late in Acapulco and often lasts till dawn (knowing you can lie on the beach recharging the next day can help keep you going). Combine that with fun-loving weekenders (mostly from Mexico City) and you have the Pacific coast's most popular after-dark resort.

It's not easy getting into the top discos during the high season. You might ask your hotel concierge to make a reservation, but your best bet is to get there by 10, before the crowds.

Baby'O
Costera M. Aleman 22, near the Hyatt
Tel. 484-7474
In business nearly 25 years and still going strong, this legendary disco is one of Acapulco's favorites. Built to resemble a large cavern, the interior features a sunken dance floor/stage with seating arranged in tiers above. Good dance music and a laser light show keep the pace moving. There's a breakfast room downstairs. Very popular with all age groups. Dress code: sophisticated resort wear. Open from 10:30 until sunrise.

Disco Beach
Costera M. Aleman 111, at Playa Condesa
Tel. 484-8230

This beachside bar and disco, featuring foam parties and bikini contests, is hugely popular with the young set. Street-level open-air bar area, beach-level bar with pool tables, video games, dance floor. Open Thursday to Sunday. Dress code: very casual. Open 8:30 p.m. to 6 a.m.

El Alebrije
Costera M. Aleman
Tel. 484-5904
Situated across from the Hyatt, this cavernous disco bills itself as the world's largest, with a capacity for 5,000 people. Rock and pop music. Open 11 p.m. to 5 a.m.

Susan Kaye

Hard Rock Cafe
Costera M. Aleman 37
Tel. 484-0047
The Acapulco branch of the world-famous restaurant-bar features rock bands every evening from 11 p.m. The bartenders entertain with nifty beer bottle tricks. A small dance floor, huge bar, and wall-to-wall rock memorabilia. Bar open noon to 2 a.m.

Mandara/Siboney
Carretera Escenica Las Brisas
Tel. 446-5711
Elegant and popular, with a dramatic bay view, this glass-walled disco houses two different venues. The larger one offers disco music and the occasional Latin dance tune. The smaller one, called Siboney, is an intimate piano bar romantically lit by a cut crystal chandelier.

O Bleu
Costera M. Aleman
Tel. 484-2252
An innovative setting that combines open-air spaces with creatively lit interiors. Gymnasts, trapeze artists, swimmers and professional dancers add to the fun.

Palladium
Carretera Escenica Las Brisas
Tel. 446-5490
This expansive glass-walled, hilltop disco features a spectacular view and a magnificent waterfall. House music and hip-hop. Very popular with the young crowd.

Pepe's Piano Bar
Carretera Escenica, La Vista Shopping Center
Tel. 446-5736
The place in Acapulco where Mexicans indulge their passion for singing, with piano accompaniment. Open 9 p.m. to 4 a.m.

Planet Hollywood
Costera M. Aleman 2917
Tel. 484-4284
Acapulco's branch of the well-known restaurant-bar chain offers a lively place for drinks. Open noon to 2 a.m.

Salon Q
Costera M. Aleman
Tel. 481-0114
Billing itself as "the cathedral of salsa," this huge dance hall is for tropical music lovers. Live bands play salsa, cumbia and other Latin rhythms.

Yuca
The Fairmont Acapulco Princess
Tel. 469-1015
Hot Latin rhythms by Cuban bands; a new group arrives from Havana every three months.

Zucca
Carretera Escenica, La Vista Shopping Center
Tel. 446-5690
Smaller and more intimate than other hilltop discos, but with an equally wonderful view of the bay. Great laser show, good drinks, ultra-modern sound system, and a more adult clientele. Hits from the 70s, 80s and 90s. Dress code: dressy.

Mexican Fiestas

Fiestas Mexicanas, featuring Mexican folk music and dancing, are usually staged during the high season (November through April), with a Mexican buffet and national drinks like tequila, margaritas, and beer.

The hilltop Las Brisas Hotel hosts an excellent one Friday evenings (in high season), complete with fireworks, mariachis and a handicrafts fair. Reservations are a must. Tel. 469-6900.

Shopping

Where the Buys Are

If you travel light, you'll find everything you need in Acapulco.

Attire here is usually casual by day and dressy at night. You'll see no men in jackets and neckties, unless they are stepping off the plane.

The *guayabera*—the tailored shirt of the tropics—is popular among Mexican men. You can find simple, short-sleeved cotton ones to wear to the beach and more elaborate, long-sleeved embroidered ones for an evening out.

The best silver and gold jewelry, clothing and handicraft shops are located at or near the better hotels. The silver shops feature some of the country's best works, and there are beautiful, original designs in gold. Most silver shops along the Costera anticipate bargaining, so don't settle for the first price.

The two-story *Plaza Bahia*, located next to the Grand Hotel Acapulco on Costera Miguel Aleman, Acapulco's main boulevard and shopping strip, is one of the resort's two leading malls. There's a fast food patio, shops offering everything from jeans and resort wear to arts and crafts, and a bowling alley. For movie buffs, a cinema on the second floor screens relatively recent releases. The mall is open 10 a.m. to 10 p.m.

Acapulco's largest shopping center is *Gran Plaza*, located on the Costera. *Fabricas de Francia*, a Mexican department store chain, has a branch here, as does *American Express*, *Foot Locker* and *Radio Shack*. Most of the stores carry attractive, casual clothing for a young crowd. Open 9 a.m. to 9 p.m.

A small *Sears* department store is located at Cuauhtemoc 30, two blocks inland from the Costera.

In an effort to clear Acapulco's beaches of vendors, the local government has set up several markets, most located at major intersections along the Costera. One is located at the Diana circle at the entrance to the highway from Mexico City. Downtown, next to the main square, you'll also find a handicrafts market selling kitschy souvenirs, leather goods, silver and other items.

The markets are colorful and fun, but keep in mind that you usually get what you pay for: that bargain-priced turquoise necklace may be nothing more than cleverly painted plaster of Paris.

With few exceptions, store hours in Acapulco are from 10 a.m. to 2 p.m. and 5 to 9 p.m.

Clothing

Aca Joe
Plaza Marbella, and other locations
The brand that single-handedly popularized T-shirts in Mexico. Active wear for men: shorts, pants, jackets, sweaters and more, in quality cotton.

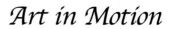

Chris Luhnow

Armando's
Costera M. Aleman 1252. Tel. 484-5111
Hyatt Regency Hotel. Tel. 484-0827
Finely embroidered light cotton jackets, dresses and other garments for women in tropical colors and styles. A unique addition to any wardrobe.

Esteban
Costera M. Aleman 2010
Tel. 484-3084
Renowned Acapulco designer Esteban's exclusive and finely-tailored evening wear for men and women, plus ready-to-wear apparel and accessories. Also carries a select range of handicrafts, including beaded art work by Huichol Indians. Esteban's complex has grown to include a small cafe, so you can take a coffee break while browsing. Next door, but accessed through the boutique, a small gallery is crammed with some interesting paintings and sculptures.

Guess?
Costera M. Aleman, opposite Disco Beach, and other locations.
Large and well stocked with stylish denim and all-cotton clothing for men, women and children.

KOS
Costera M. Aleman, near Playa Suites Hotel
A large selection of Gottex brand swim wear.

Macarena Gutierrez
Costera M. Aleman, opposite El Presidente Hotel
Attractive swim wear and beach accessories.

Martha Riestra
Grand Hotel Acapulco shopping arcade; Emporio Continental Hotel; and Plaza Bahia mall.
An interesting selection of casual and dressy resort wear for women, some in all cotton, some in clingy modern fabrics.

Tommy Hilfiger
Costera M. Aleman 117-2
Tel. 484-1146
Jeans, golf apparel, sportswear by the internationally-acclaimed American designer known for his rugged, stylish clothing and accessories, and trademark bold designs.

Handicrafts

AFA
Horacio Nelson, corner of James Cook, behind the Baby'O disco.
A supermarket of Mexican handicrafts.

Jewelry

Tane
Las Brisas and Hyatt Regency hotels
Tel. 469-1234
A long-established silversmith offering handmade reproductions of antique pieces and fine jewelry. Also exclusive contemporary sculptures by outstanding Mexican and foreign artists. The attractive silver items include trays, bowls, tea and coffee services, candle holders, picture frames, vases, tableware and place settings. Their attractive line of jewelry features gold and sterling silver combinations, including many limited pieces with lifetime warranties. Branches throughout the country, including in Mexico City.

Art

Galeria Espacio Pal Kepenyes
Costera Guitarron 140, on road to Radisson Hotel
Tel. 484-3738
Enigmatic works of art by Hungarian-born artist Pal Kepenyes, author of the radiant "Pueblo del Sol" ("People of the Sun") sculpture on the road leading to Playa Revolcadero. Kepenyes' most recent work features unique "interactive" sculptures—mobile pieces that can be displayed in different ways. Kepenyes also applies his talent to jewelry, creating bold, original pieces in brass, copper and silver, many with pre-Hispanic motifs. Call for an appointment.

Galeria Rudic
Yañez Pinzon, just off the Costera
Paintings, sculptures for collectors by leading Mexican artists, including Leonardo Nierman, Trinidad Osorio, Armando Amaya.

La Coleccion de Sergio Bustamante
Costera M. Aleman 120-9, Galerias Picuda
Tel. 484-4992
A fine assortment of Bustamante's wonderful and whimsical anthropomorphic suns, moons and animals in metal, papier-mâché and other materials. Also a small selection of his beautiful line of jewelry.

Special

Marti
Plaza Bahia. Tel. 485-1735
Plaza Marbella. Tel. 484-5733
Mexico's leading supplier of sporting goods carries extensive selections of sneakers, swimsuits and sweat suits, as well as gear for camping, snorkeling, etc.

Sanborns
Costera M. Aleman, downtown; Oceanic 2000; and other locations
An all-purpose store with an excellent pharmacy, good selection of handicrafts, and the largest selection in town of English-language magazines, newspapers and paperbacks.

Where to Stay

Camino Real Acapulco Diamante

Baja Catita S/N, Pichilingue Diamante
Tel. (744) 435-1010
www.caminoreal.com
Terraced on a hillside, this stunning property has 157 luxury rooms and suites with terraces overlooking a private little beach and the lush green peninsula beyond. Three swimming pools on different levels with a waterfall, jacuzzi, gym, spa services, beach club, kids club, tennis court, access to golf. Excellent restaurants. Ideal for small meetings and incentive groups. Rates DX.

Elcano

Costera M. Aleman 75
Tel. (744) 435-1500
www.hotel-elcano.com
An Acapulco favorite that received a complete make-over not long ago with stunning results. All 180 rooms and suites, decorated in crisp blue and white, have private balconies with ocean views, cable TV. Excellent restaurants, bar, pool with underwater music, kids' pool, three jacuzzis, gym with steam room. Meeting facilities for up to 300 people. Rates FC.

El Mirador

Quebrada 74, the famous cliff divers' site
Tel. (744) 483-1155
www.hotelelmiradoracapulco.com.mx
Built some 60 years ago, this well-maintained landmark features spectacular ocean views. There are 133 pleasant rooms and suites, two swimming pools, private beach club with salt-water pool, restaurant-bar with a view of the cliff divers. Rates MD.

Emporio Continental

Costera M. Aleman 121, Magallanes
Tel. (744) 469-5050
www.continentalemporio.com
Mexico's Emporio hotel chain has completely revamped the former Continental Plaza and brought it into the modern age. With a blue-lit bar and spacious minimalist lobby, this beachfront property features 419 remodeled air-conditioned rooms with bay views and cable TV, one of the largest freeform swimming pools, seafood and international restaurants, water sports, meeting and banquet facilities. Rates FC.

Fiesta Americana Condesa

Costera M. Aleman 97, Condesa Beach
Tel. (744) 484-2828
www.fiestamericana.com
Overlooking one of the most popular beaches in town, this tower houses 500 rooms with oceanview balconies, cable TV. Two swimming pools, open-air restaurants, lobby bar. Banquet and convention facilities. Popular with people who like to be where the action is. Rates FC.

Fiesta Inn

Costera M. Aleman 87
Tel. (744) 435-0500
www.fiestainn.com
This beachfront low-rise offers 220 rooms with ocean views and amenities for the business traveler, including Internet access, secretarial services. Swimming pool, cafeteria, parking. Rates MD.

Grand Hotel Acapulco

Costera M. Aleman 123, Magallanes
Tel. (744) 485-9050
www.grandhotelacapulco.com.mx
Formerly the Costa Club, this beachfront high-rise began hotel-wide remodeling in late 2003. Ample meeting and banquet facilities, pools, lighted tennis courts. Rates MD.

Hyatt Regency

Costera M. Aleman 1
Tel. (744) 469-1234
www.acapulco.regency.hyatt.com
This magnificent 23-story deluxe hotel features 640 spacious rooms and suites with balconies overlooking the bay. Excellent restaurants (with a kosher menu during the high season), bars, pool, gym (small entrance fee), Alory Spa, three lighted tennis courts next to the municipal golf course, shops, and extensive convention and banquet facilities. Camp Hyatt kids club during the season. Synagogue for group prayer or individual meditation. Superbly managed, and a center of activity year-round. Rates FC.

Las Brisas Acapulco

Carretera Escenica 5255
Tel. (744) 469-6900
www.brisas.com.mx
This hilltop hideaway, one of the most exclusive and romantic destinations in the world, is a favorite of celebrities, honeymooners and those who seek privacy. Set on 40 acres of lush hibiscus gardens overlooking famous Acapulco Bay, the pink-and-white resort has 263 bungalow-style guest rooms dotting the hillside, each simply yet attractively furnished, with pools. At La Concha, Acapulco's only private beach club, guests enjoy two saltwater pools and a freshwater pool with swim-up bar, snorkeling, and a relaxing ambience, as well as the finest seafood and live music. You'll feel miles away from it all, yet this fabulous seaside resort teems with activities: join a jeep safari for

colorful sunsets, tee up on a nearby championship 18-hole golf course, or treat yourself to a massage at the spa. Your stay is bound to be a memorable one. One of The Leading Hotels of the World. Rates DX.

La Marina
Costera M. Aleman 222, facing the marina
Tel. (744) 482-8556
www.lamarinahotel.com.mx
This modest yet attractive property features 45 airy bungalows with a/c and ceiling fans (some with kitchenette) amid nicely landscaped grounds with brick-lined walkways and lots of plants. Gym, small pool, restaurant-bar; spa and aroma-therapy garden under construction. Bridge access to nearby beach area. Rates MD (includes continental breakfast).

Mayan Palace
Costera de las Palmas 121
Tel. (744) 469-6000
www.mayanpalace.com
An expansive 200-acre hotel and time-share resort on the beach, 10 minutes from the airport, featuring beautiful Mayan-style architecture and an impressive palm-thatched lobby. The 366 deluxe units, with ocean and garden views, range in size from a studio with jacuzzi (Ocean-front Crown Suite; no children allowed) to a two-bedroom with kitchenette (Oceanview Luxury Suite; up to four adults/four kids). There are 12 covered tennis courts, an 18-hole golf course, kilometer-long pool with artificial cascades, boating along a network of canals, train transportation through the grounds, restaurants, bars, casino-style restaurant-bar. Rates FC.

Las Brisas

Quinta Real
Paseo de la Quinta 6, in Real Diamante
Tel. (744) 469-1500
www.quintareal.com
Nestled on a hilltop, this luxury hotel and spa overlooks its own secluded beach club on the open Pacific. There are 74 impeccably appointed suites with balconies, ocean views, color cable TV and minibar; some with private

plunge pools. Lovely gourmet restaurant and terrace bar. Luxurious spa and gourmet spa cuisine. Meeting and banquet facility for up to 250 people. Concierge, car rental, parking, 24-hour medical service. Arrangements made for golf, tennis, fishing and water sports. Member of Mexico Boutique Hotels. Rates LX.

Radisson Resort
Costera Guitarron 110
Tel. (744) 446-6565
www.radisson.com
Nestled on a tiny beach on the east end of Acapulco Bay, this multilevel, mazelike property has 212 rooms and suites (about 30 percent with bay views) distributed in villas built along the side of a hill. Tram shuttles guests between lobby and beach area. Two large pools, health club, sauna, restaurants, bar, meeting rooms. Rates FC.

The Fairmont Acapulco Princess
Playa Revolcadero
Tel. (744) 469-1000
www.fairmont.com
On a wide stretch of beach 20 minutes from town. Newly renovated, this massive luxury resort is comprised of three buildings, one shaped like an Aztec pyramid, with 1,017 rooms and suites. Spectacular lobby overflowing with plants, 18-hole golf course, indoor and outdoor tennis courts, fitness center, 14,000-square-foot spa, fine restaurants, saltwater and freshwater pools, shopping arcade, private disco. Extensive convention and banquet facilities for up to 2,000. Popular with groups. Rates DX (MAP).

The Fairmont Pierre Marques
Playa Revolcadero, next to the Princess
Tel. (744) 466-1000
www.fairmont.com
Originally the summer home of multimillionaire J. Paul Getty, this 480-acre all-inclusive property offers relaxed elegance in a tropical seaside setting. There are 343 deluxe rooms, suites and villas, most with ocean views, 18-hole, par 72, championship golf course, five lit tennis courts, three lovely pool areas, two kids pools, gym, fine dining, piano bar, meeting facilities. Specializes in hosting small and medium-sized groups. Rates FC (all inclusive).

Villa Vera Spa & Racquet Club
Lomas del Mar 35
Tel. (744) 484-0333
www.clubregina.com
This hilltop hotel, spa and racquet club exudes wonderful 50s-style glamour. The 67 guest rooms, nestled in 15 acres of subtropical gardens, include suites with shared or private pools, and two villas. There's a main pool with a panoramic view, jacuzzi, fine restaurant with a view, clay tennis courts, paddle courts, spa with gym, sauna, treatments for two, conference facilities for 110 people. No children under 16. Member of Mexico Boutique Hotels. Rates FC.

TRAVELERS GUIDE TO
Ixtapa-Zihuatanejo

YOU CAN BUY YOUR OWN COPY
OF THIS BOOK. THE LAST PAGE.

Palmar Bay is home to the resort's leading large hotels.

A Small, Beautiful, Secluded Resort

Looking to while away your time at a friendly, picturesque fishing village? Or in the mood to unwind at an ultramodern resort? Ixtapa-Zihuatanejo has both. Few destinations offer visitors these two strikingly different options—each within minutes of the other, both with unique attractions.

This slice of Pacific coastline remained "undiscovered" until recently, even though it lies just 150 miles northwest of Acapulco. Long overshadowed by that famed resort, Zihuatanejo, a lovely seaside village on Zihuatanejo Bay, was known only to locals and a few hardy travelers until a paved highway connected the two ports. Increasing numbers of tourists, foreign as well as Mexican, were drawn to the tranquility and seclusion of the charming village, its natural beauty, superb beaches and excellent fishing.

In the early 1970s the Mexican government selected an area around Palmar Bay, just four miles up the coast from Zihuatanejo, to build a major tourism complex. The virgin area, dominated by coconut palms, mangrove swamps, rocky cliffs pounded by surf and lovely, but almost inaccessible, beaches, came to be known as Ixtapa.

The highway between Acapulco and Zihuatanejo was extended to Ixtapa in 1972. A beautiful 18-hole professional golf course designed by Robert Trent Jones II was built. Beachfront lots were laid out and sold to hotels. And the small airstrip at Zihuatanejo was replaced by a modern international airport only 10 miles from town. The transformation was complete and Ixtapa opened to tourism in 1975.

Ixtapa's coastline is home to several world-class hotels, condominium developments, a marina and two golf courses. An impeccable, tree-lined boulevard divides the hotels on one side from a string of small-scale shopping centers on the other.

Ixtapa has become so popular that during the high season it is hard to get hotel accommodations and airplane seats. U.S. and Canadian tourists who visit Ixtapa are delighted by the warm surf, breathtaking sunsets and fine climate: the mean average temperature is 82ºF, and it's almost always sunny, because even during the summer rainy season showers are brief and usually in the late afternoon or evening.

Ixtapa-Zihuatanejo is a three hour drive from Acapulco, a three and a half to four hour drive from Morelia, via a new highway, and about a seven hour drive from Mexico City. By air it is a scant 45-minute flight from the capital. There are also direct flights from the United States.

Beaches

Ixtapa—a Nahuatl Indian word meaning "the white place," alluding to the beach—borders a wide bay dotted with small rocky islands that are inhabited solely by sea birds. The beach, *Playa del Palmar*, is a two-mile-long stretch of beautiful white sand covering the entire base of the bay. At times there can be a strong surf and undertow, so pay attention to the warning flags.

Paseo de Ixtapa takes you to the northern end of the beach, where you'll find *Marina Ixtapa*. Here a canal was opened from the sea and the swampy mainland converted into a modern, full-service marina with slips for more than 600 vessels. This is the sister project to Marina Vallarta in Puerto Vallarta, and it is the site of a large 500 million-dollar residential and commercial development covering some 400 acres. It has a yacht club, an 18-hole golf course, villas, condominiums, private homes,

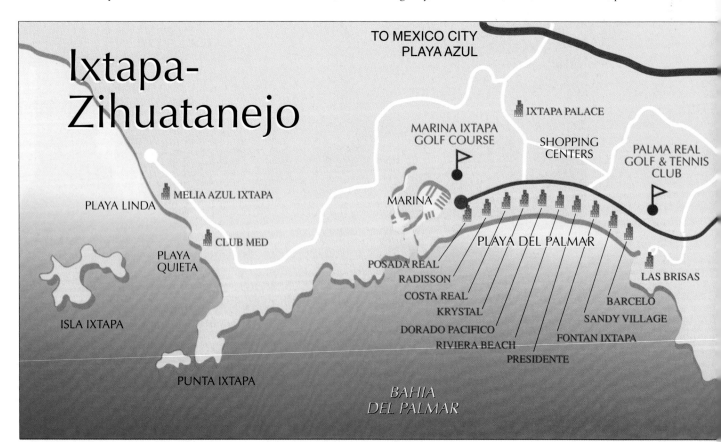

Ixtapa Marina

Ministry of Tourism

and several restaurants.

Past Marina Ixtapa, on the inland side of the waterways, following the road to Playa Linda, is the new residential development of *Punta Ixtapa*. Set on the hillside are private million-dollar homes designed by talented Mexican ar-

chitect Diego Villaseñor that have Playa las Cuatas as their private beach.

Playa Quieta, about a 20-minute drive north of Ixtapa's hotel zone on a road with bicycle paths, is a wide expanse of beach bordering on the 37-acre Club Med.

A few minutes north of Club Med is a lovely expanse of beach called *Playa Linda*, which on its southern end is home to the all-inclusive *Qualton Club*. Playa Linda is now dominated by the large-scale *Melia Azul Ixtapa Hotel*. Horses can be rented at the north end of the beach,

ZIHUATANEJO DOWNTOWN

IRMA
CASA CUITLATECA
QUINTA TROPPO
LA CASA QUE CANTA

PLAYA LA MADERA

PIER

SOTAVENTO
CATALINA

PLAYA LA ROPA

VILLA DEL SOL

VILLA VERA PUERTO MIO

PLAYA MAJAHUA

PLAYA LAS GATAS

AMULETO

TO AIRPORT, PLAYA LARGA ACAPULCO

N E W S

PACIFIC OCEAN

BAHIA ZIHUATANEJO

Golfers have two courses to choose from

John Elkins

where the Barrio Viejo River and its quiet lagoon meet the sea. Here also, a new pier serves as a departure point for *pangas*, or boat taxis, to Isla Ixtapa.

Just 15 minutes south of Zihuatanejo, past a narrow road lined with coconut groves, is *Playa Larga*, a beautiful stretch of beach recently chosen to be the site of a presidential vacation home.

A few small palm-thatched *enramadas* dot the beach and a short stroll brings you to the north end, where a sleepy lagoon teems with birds and marine life.

Another 20 minutes south of the airport is an extension of Playa Larga called *Playa Blanca*. At its southernmost tip is an old fishing village, Barra de Potosi, where numerous small restaurants serve up the local fishermen's latest catch.

You can kayak through the inlets and spy on the many species of wildlife that thrive in the wilderness of the area's large lagoon. Call *Zoe Tours* at 553-0496.

On the beach closer to the airport, the luxurious six-room *Las Palmas Hotel* features a delightful restaurant, serving lunch daily and dinner by reservations only (557-0634), and a pool.

Isla Ixtapa

One popular outing is by boat to charming Isla Ixtapa for swimming, snorkeling and relaxing on a sheltered beach facing the mainland, just north of Ixtapa's main beach. The island's beaches are excellent and practically free of surf.

Declared a national park, Isla Ixtapa is home to many bird and animal species, including deer, armadillos and raccoons. You can take tours and spend the better part of a day there. Or you can take a taxi to Playa Linda, on the mainland directly in front of the island; from there launches go back and forth until 5 p.m.

The island has several open-air *palapa*, or palm-thatched, restaurants serving fresh fish and cold beer. Playa Linda is a popular sailing and windsurfing beach because it has calm waters, thanks to Isla Ixtapa in front.

Water Sports

The waters around Zihuatanejo have long been famed for the abundance and variety of game fish, large and small, from sailfish and marlin to rooster fish, mackerel, wahoo, yellowtail and bonito. The best time to catch the big ones is from December through March, though you will seldom return empty-handed; remember this was a fishing village long before the advent of tourism. At the end of April the Billfish Tournament attracts lots of diehard fishermen hoping to catch "the big one." Fishermen can make their own rental arrangements at the pier in Zihuatanejo. Most of the boats available are modest pangas, but remember, it's always best to hire a boat with a radio.

Other popular activities include water-skiing, snorkeling, scuba diving, sailing and kayaking. Zihuatanejo Bay, especially Playa la Ropa, is ideal for water-skiing, as well as windsurfing, while Las Gatas and Isla Ixtapa are popular for snorkeling. Many fine dive sites are located off the coast of Ixtapa-Zihuatanejo, and excursions leave from Las Gatas and Isla Ixtapa.

Surfers find good surfing in Troncones' *Manzanillo Beach* area; up the coast at *Playa Petacalcos*, where the wave action is just right and delicious seafood is served at beachfront huts; and at *Playa la Saladita*.

You can enjoy the attractions of the Pacific coast aboard the *VLTAVA,* a fully-equipped classic '85 windjammer schooner with a capacity for 50 passengers, operated by the experienced team of Tony and Claire Piazza. Their Sunshine Cruise sails past the Ixtapa hotel zone to Isla Ixtapa, where passengers lunch, snorkel and swim. Other cruises feature the white beach and coral reef of Playa Manzanillo, and Pacific sunsets. Boat charters also available. Tel. 554-2694.

There is also parachute gliding, which involves being harnessed into a parachute that is pulled high over the bay by a speedboat. It's fun and usually safe, but accidents do happen, so be aware that it can be dangerous and there's no one to sue in case of an accident. Even more thrilling is a parachute jump over Palmar Bay, in tandem or solo (offered in high season only).

Golf and Tennis

Golfers find the 18-hole, par 72, Robert Trent Jones II-designed course at the *Palma Real Golf Course* a real challenge. Rolling expanses of fairways and greens are rimmed by tall coconut palms and dotted with small ponds and three lakes. It's also a game preserve, with many varieties of gorgeous birds and several lake-dwelling alligators. The course is surrounded by a residential development with scores of attractive homes. The final greens are right on the edge of the ocean, Pebble Beach style.

The newer *Marina Ixtapa Club de Golf* is an 18-hole, par 72, Robert von Hagge-designed championship course on 6,781 yards of rolling dunes with undulating greens. Rated one of Mexico's top courses by Golf Digest, it is a challenging course for the experienced golfer, but its four sets of tees make it enjoyable to all levels of players. The beautiful Mediterranean-style clubhouse houses a full-service restaurant, called The 19th Hole, and overlooks both the course and marina.

Both courses have pro shops fully stocked with name-brand, quality merchandise and well-maintained equipment and golf carts. The clubhouses serve snacks and drinks, and offer a mobile bar for the thirsty golfer. The Palma Real also has five adjoining lighted tennis courts.

Most of the hotels have tennis courts, lit during the evening, which is often the best time to play to avoid the heat of the day. In Zihuatanejo, the only place you will find tennis courts is at the *Villa del Sol Hotel*, where you can reserve time on one of two courts.

Other Activities

A countryside tour takes visitors to the base of the Sierra Madre mountains, through quaint fishing villages, coconut groves and mango orchards, and to *La Barra de Potosi* lagoon, with its colorful birds and vegetation, 14 miles south of Zihuatanejo. The final destination is a pristine beach favored by local residents, *Playa Blanca*.

A 25-minute drive north towards Lazaro Cardenas will bring you to the tiny fishing village of *Troncones*, a "gringo" beach community. You can surf and enjoy the beach, and arrange a horseback riding trip into the nearby mountains to see caves featuring stalagmites, stalactites and ancient cave paintings.

A few small hotels and B&Bs line the beachfront here: recommended are *The Inn at Manzanillo Bay, Casa Ki, Hacienda Eden* and *Casa de la Tortuga*, which was featured in Travel & Leisure as a pleasant alternative to the larger resorts. Manzanillo Bay owner Michael Bensal, a chef trained at the San Francisco Culinary Academy, creates simple yet exquisite dishes combining local ingredients with international cooking techniques. At Hacienda Eden's *Cocina del Sol* restaurant, chef Christian Schirmer serves a popular Sunday "lunch on the grill" topped by his signature peach or mango cobbler dessert. You can take a guided tour of the Troncones area or take a taxi (approximately 60 dollars round trip).

For nature and adventure tours, call *Adventours* at 553-1069. Their excursions range from soft adventure (bird watching, leisurely bike rides, nature trails) to mountain biking, uphill hiking and rappeling. Newly hatched sea turtles are released into the ocean from June to December and visitors can take part in this rare experience. Zip over the jungle canopy to the Majahua Caves with *Jaguar Tours*; reservations should be made 24 hours in advance (553-2862).

There is miniature golf at two locations, one in Ixtapa and one in Zihuatanejo. In Ixtapa, *Golfito,* run by a nice couple from Oregon, Ken and Merlinda, is behind the Las Fuentes mall. In Zihuatanejo, *Discovery Kids*, with its video arcade, is located on Nicolas Bravo.

A fun way to get around Ixtapa is by moped, scooter, or the new gasoline-powered golf carts, all of which are for rent at the malls. But be cautious, as accidents do happen. All the major car rental companies have offices here. Bicycles can be rented at the malls, and new bicycle paths run along Ixtapa Boulevard, to

Playa las Gatas

the marina and out to Playa Linda. During the high season, a leisurely way to go from one end of the boulevard to the other is aboard a horse-drawn carriage.

Zihuatanejo

The once sleepy fishing village of Zihuatanejo has picked up its pace quite a bit, but it remains a charming little town on a beautiful bay. Fishermen still bring their daily catch to the town dock in the mornings, the produce market still bustles with activity, and the local boys still play soccer on the beach at sunset.

It's fun just to walk around this town of 35,000 inhabitants, most involved in tourism, and enjoy the local scene. Take a stroll along *Paseo del Pescador* (Fisherman's Walk) by the waterfront and browse along Cuauhtemoc, Juan N. Alvarez and Pedro Ascencio streets, where you will see a few attractive and interesting stores.

A five-minute walk north takes you to the town pier, where the fishing and tour boats are moored, and the BIG catches are weighed. The fishing and excursion boats make Playa Principal (the town beach) not good for swimming. The waterfront walkway leads to a number

of seafood restaurants and several clean budget hotels. At night you can join the townsfolk at the plaza cheer on their favorite team in a local basketball game. Sunday evenings the plaza takes on a festive air with local bands, sidewalk art exhibits and occasional folk dancers.

The walkway south, which is romantically lit at night by gas lanterns, takes you past the archaeology museum, where for a nominal admission fee you can see the small but interesting collection of pre-Hispanic artifacts found in the region. The walkway winds southward along the rocky coast to *Playa la Madera,* a lovely hidden beach popular with families who frequent the more economical bungalows and hostelries.

Meanwhile, for excellent beaches and super panoramic views, take a 10-minute drive over the hill to *Playa la Ropa.* It's the same bay but another world. From the mountainside you have majestic views of the bay and town. Then you descend to the beach with its gentle waves and fine white sand. The hotels here are the best in the area.

Hotels in the Zihuatanejo Bay area are generally older and smaller than those in Ixtapa, and are often preferred for that very reason.

But the bay is also home to the resort's most exceptional hotels: *La Casa Que Canta,* an exclusive hilltop tropical retreat, and *Villa del Sol,* a chic hideaway right on the area's best beach.

Bed-and-breakfasts have caught on in Zihuatanejo in the past couple of years. The most charming is the eight-room *La Quinta Troppo,* run by gracious Australian David Ferguson.

During the day, buses shuttle between Ixtapa and Zihuatanejo. Going to Zihuatanejo, there's just one bus, but heading back, there are several, so be sure to ask the driver "Ixtapa?" before boarding.

Playa las Gatas

Further south along the bay is Playa las Gatas. This beautiful, semi-isolated beach lies at the far end of Zihuatanejo Bay and is really only accessible by the pangas that run between the town pier and a mini-dock on the beach. The last boats return at 5 p.m. Hardcore hikers can follow a rocky path around the water's edge from Playa la Ropa.

The beach is nestled at the foot of the mountains and protected by an underwater reef. It is popular for its informal open-air seafood restaurants specializing in delicious grilled lobster, a favorite being *Arnoldo's.*

A walk to the end of the coral and shell studded beach will bring you to Owen Lee's "ecological center," a place where you can sit under a big, shady tree and watch the sunset in perfect isolation. You can even rent a bungalow and stay for a few days.

The waters are ideal for snorkeling and diving, but it's a good idea to use tennis shoes or some kind of foot protection for walking on the rocky, shell-strewn bottom. Scuba or snorkel gear is for rent from *Carlos Scuba,* owned by former Jacques Cousteau diving companion Jean Claude; instructors are available.

Flies can be somewhat bothersome during the summer, so be sure to take along some insect repellent.

Real Estate

Don't overlook Ixtapa-Zihuatanejo as an investment possibility, whether you are looking for a hideaway beach home, vacation condo or retirement villa.

Ixtapa offers luxury homes and condominiums around the older Palma Real golf course or the newer, larger course at Marina Ixtapa. Zihuatanejo Bay is a growing area with new homes and condominiums on the surrounding hillsides offering great views—some overlook the area's best beach, Playa la Ropa. It can also offer a more traditional ambiance with smaller homes in Mexican neighborhoods.

In general, prices for homes and condos, and construction costs, are similar to those in the United States. In Ixtapa, two-bedroom condos cost from 90,000 to 500,000 dollars, depending on location and amenities. Homes in the area will run from 125,000 to 900,000 dollars. Zihuatanejo properties with ocean views can be a bit pricey, but lower-priced homes without views can be purchased in town.

Many small new developments, mostly condominiums but also homes with private docks, are being developed around Marina Ixtapa. Located across the channel leading into the marina is *Porto Ixtapa,* which opened its first condo units in the fall of 1994.

On the road north to Playa Linda several ultra-luxurious projects are under construction, including *Punta Ixtapa,* a gated residential community with homes and condominiums with ocean views and private beaches.

Pacifica and *Ixtapa Palace* are long-standing and successful timeshares. Many hotels in Ixtapa offer timeshare units.

La Casa Que Ve al Mar, the only new development overlooking La Ropa Beach and Zihuatanejo Bay, offers one- to three-bedroom condos, each with a spectacular view. Designed and constructed by foremost Mexican architect Enrique Zozaya (of Casa Que Canta, Villa del Sol, Quinta Troppo fame), the first 19 condominiums are selling between 130,000 and 250,000 dollars.

In Troncones, *Las MaraVillas* offers just four deluxe condominium units with inviting breezes and water views, also designed by Zozaya. Just finished, the units are selling at a starting price of 130,000 dollars.

The North American Free Trade Agreement has had an effect on the availability of mortgages in Mexico. Limited bank financing is becoming available to non-Mexicans for the purchase of homes and condos. And direct ownership (no trust required) by foreigners of tourism-related properties, such as hotels, has been legalized.

Following are several recommended real estate firms:

Century 21: Located at Ixtapa's La Puerta mall, the office is part of the worldwide realty chain. Tel. 553-0017. Fax 553-2358.

Marin Center Real Estate: Offering marina area properties. Marina Plaza, Locale 24. Tel. 553-1429. E-mail: marincenter@prodigy.net.mx.

Paradise Properties: Longtime Zihuatanejo resident and Travelers Guide to Mexico contributing editor Judith Whitehead puts her considerable real estate experience and knowledge of the area to work in sales, rentals and property management. Tel. 554-6226. Fax 553-1212. E-mail: jude@prodigy.net.mx.

Ticar: Owned and operated by Tim Sullivan, who will help you with rentals as well as sales. Tel. 553-1418. Fax 553-1199. E-mail: ticarsa@prodigy.net.mx.

Dining in Ixtapa

Al Cilantro
Colina de las Palomas 325
Tel. 553-0610
Hidden away in a private villa complex called "Tres Puertas," this elegant and intimate spot offers terrace dining beside an inviting pool in a perfumed garden. Owners Gabriela and Guillermo Braña offer an exquisite fusion of Mexican and Asian cuisine. She cooks while husband Guillermo serves as host, bartender and waiter. Reservations required. Open Thursday through Saturday, 7 to 11 p.m. (in high season only).

Arrecife
Riviera Beach Resort
Tel. 553-1066
Mediterranean cuisine with a Mexican touch in an outdoor setting overlooking the beach. Specialties include seafood and fine cuts of beef prepared on an open-air grill. Friendly, attentive service. Open during the high season from 6 to 11 p.m.

Beccofino
Veleros 7 and 8 at Marina Ixtapa
Tel. 553-1770
Consistently rated one of the resort's finest restaurants, this charming spot serves wonderful northern Italian cuisine in a casually elegant setting on the marina—tables are set on a teak wood deck right on the water. Host, owner and master chef Angelo "Rolly" Pavia, who hails from San Remo on the Italian Riviera, expertly prepares fish and seafood dishes, including a delicious fish fillet in black butter and rosemary. He makes an exquisite fine herbs sauce, and puts a surprising twist on the traditional tiramisu, here served in a bowl! Open for breakfast, lunch and dinner.

Bogart's
NH Krystal Hotel
Tel. 553-1770
Exotic Moroccan decor inspired by the film "Casablanca" and sophisticated international cuisine served by attentive waiters. Piano music. Open 6 to 11 p.m. Reservations necessary.

Bucanero's
Marina Ixtapa
Tel. 553-0916
Provençal cuisine beautifully prepared and served in a picturesque marina setting. Reservations suggested during the winter season. Open 8 a.m. to midnight.

Carlos'n Charlie's
On the beach, next to Posada Real Hotel
Tel. 553-0085
The usual fun atmosphere the Anderson chain is famous for, with a beach disco. Specializes in BBQ ribs. Restaurant open noon to midnight; dance club till 3 a.m.

Deborah's Mamma Norma
La Puerta mall
Tel. 553-0274
Deborah, the popular former manager of J.J.'s Lobster House, welcomes guests at this favorite sidewalk cafe. Excellent pastas, lobster specialties and various seafood dishes you won't find anywhere else. Try the grilled jumbo shrimp with a light orange-chipotle sauce and the spinach salad with honey vinaigrette—as close to perfect as you can get. Open 8 a.m. to 11 p.m. in high season.

Don Quijote
Barcelo Beach Resort
Tel. 555-2000
Enjoy excellent classic Spanish cuisine in a lovely setting decked with traditional Spanish decorative touches. Open 6 to 11:30 p.m. Closed Wednesday.

El Ancla
Riviera Beach Resort
Tel. 553-1066
A beautiful open-air setting facing the ocean that's ideal for breakfast, with one of the best cups of coffee poured anywhere, an ample breakfast buffet, and a la carte specialties like eggs Benedict. Also good for a casual lunch or dinner.

El Galeon
Marina Ixtapa
Tel. 553-2150
A small restaurant-bar with tables set on a "barge" overlooking the marina. Enjoy their Caesar salad, delicious homemade pastries and seafood prepared with a Mexican flair. Open 9 a.m. to midnight.

El Infierno y La Gloria
Galerias Ixtapa mall
Tel. 553-0272
A fun cantina-style restaurant serving good Mexican cuisine. Member of the popular Anderson chain of restaurants.

El Mexicano
Las Brisas Hotel
Tel. 553-2121
Authentic Mexican cuisine served in a refined setting reminiscent of a large Mexican hacienda, with tables around a colorful, plant-filled courtyard. For a memorable Mexican evening. Open 6 to 11 p.m. Reservations recommended.

Frank's Restaurant & Sports Bar
Plaza Ixpamar
Frank and his wife Miriam have made this a very popular place. Have one of their delicious hamburgers or steaks, and support your favorite team from home with vocal fellow fans who add to the excitement of the game. Open from 10 a.m. to 11 p.m.

J.J.'s Lobster & Shrimp
Paseo de Ixtapa, opposite Riviera Beach Resort
More of J.J.'s jazzy style. Sizzling grilled lobster (three sizes to choose from) and jumbo shrimp are part of the great menu. A seafood lover's dining destination. Now with dining tables in a back garden. Open 5 p.m. to midnight.

La Brisa II
Las Brisas Hotel
Tel. 553-2121
Exquisite international gourmet cuisine served on an open terrace facing the Pacific. Intimate and cozy, casual yet elegant. Open mid-December to mid-April, 6 to 11 p.m. Reservations recommended.

La Terraza
Radisson Hotel
Tel. 553-0003
This restaurant offers traditional Mexican dishes in a friendly atmosphere. Try their popular margaritas. Open 6 to 11 p.m. during the high season.

La Pasta Nostra
NH Krystal Hotel
Tel. 553-0333
Tasty pastas and other Italian specialties served in a relaxed atmosphere. Open 6 to 11 p.m.

Portofino
Las Brisas Hotel
Tel. 553-2121
An intimate *ristorante* with lovely decor and excellent gourmet Mediterranean-Italian cuisine. Freshly-made pastas, imported ingredients and a good selection of wines make for a memorable meal. Open 6 to 11 p.m. Reservations recommended.

Ruben's
Ixsol mall, next to Los Mandiles
Tel. 553-0055
Chela and family work their magic on delicious mesquite-grilled hamburgers and baked potatoes. Take-out available. Open noon to 10:30 p.m.

Ruben's Original Hamburgers
Next to Café Salsa, facing the Barcelo
English-speaking Ruben and son Ruben, Jr. serve up the mesquite-grilled hamburgers that the family is famous for, as well as baked potatoes and pitchers of Mexican fruit-flavored "waters." Open noon to 11 p.m.

Señor Frog's
La Puerta mall
Tel. 553-0672
The other local link in the famed Anderson

chain serves up a party atmosphere and typically delicious fare, such as BBQ ribs and Mexican favorites. Rock and pop hits. Open from 3 p.m.

Soleiado
Plaza Ambiente, facing Radisson Hotel
Tel. 553-2101
Canadian Chef Francesco and his wife Caroline personally welcome guests at their sidewalk cafe-style restaurant with open kitchen. Watch the cooks prepare your tuna Louisiana or shrimp and grapefruit salad. Their eggs Benedict for breakfast or brunch are the best in town. The key to their success (they have a loyal following) is freshness, from the home-grown herbs to the just caught fish. Open 7 a.m. to midnight. Reservations recommended in high season.

Veranda
Barcelo Beach Resort
Tel. 555-2000
A lavish breakfast buffet is served in their sun-filled atrium lobby. Open from 7 a.m. to 11:30 p.m.

Villa de la Selva
Paseo de la Roca, just past Las Brisas Hotel
Tel. 553-0362
This attractive hilltop home designed for a former Mexican president was converted in 1982 into a restaurant and sunset lover's delight. Enjoy a memorable evening in a spec-

tacular setting—dine on terraces overlooking the Pacific as the sun slowly descends into the ocean and the stars begin to appear in the night sky. The menu features tantalizing contemporary cuisine complemented by excellent service. Open 6 p.m. to 1 a.m. Reservations required.

Dining in Zihuatanejo

Amuleto
On Las Gatas Scenic Road
Tel. 544-6222
An exquisite view, romantic ambience and inspired menu created by Kau Kan chef and owner Ricardo Rodriguez make for an unfor-

gettable evening. Dine at the highest point overlooking the town and bay. The Brazilian owners of this boutique hotel and restaurant, Ricardo and Neglia Teitelroit (along with architect Zozaya), have created a true oasis. Open for dinner only, 6 p.m. to midnight. Reservations required.

Bay Club
On the road to Playa la Ropa
Under the management of restaurateur Jorge Elvira, this spot serves fine beef and fresh seafood in a beautiful setting high on a cliff overlooking Zihuatanejo Bay. Open for dinner till midnight in high season only. Live jazz some evenings.

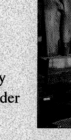

Casa Bahia Restaurant & Yacht Club
On road to Villa Vera Puerto Mio Hotel
Tel. 554-8666
Join owners Will and Walt for their tropical seafood and steaks with a panoramic view.

Casa Elvira
Paseo del Pescador 8, facing the beach
Tel. 554-2061
One of the oldest restaurants in town, it serves seafood and Mexican specialties. Open for lunch and dinner.

Coconuts
Pasaje Agustin Ramirez 1
Tel. 554-2518
A well-known garden restaurant located in one of the town's oldest historical buildings. The menu features fresh seafood, pastas and choice cuts of beef. Open for lunch and dinner. Closed during the summer. Reservations recommended.

El Chuleto
Paseo del Pescador, near La Sirena Gorda
The staff and fine recipes from the former Paul's (which closed with the passing away of its Swiss owner) have moved to this beachfront restaurant run by Luis Muñoz, well-known owner of La Sirena Gorda. Here you'll find all your favorite dishes, including the fresh artichokes, escargot in garlic, and shrimp in dill sauce. A full bar and good service keeps you coming back for more.

El Manglar
South end of La Ropa Beach
Tel. 554-3752
A wonderful surprise awaits you across the lagoon from the former Paraiso Hotel; walk the plank from the beach (and watch out for the crocodiles below!) or arrive via the arched driveway. You'll find some of the best food on the beach courtesy of owner Memo Armenta, who has garnered a loyal clientele for his unusual and exquisite recipes, like the mahi-mahi with spinach and goat cheese. Open noon to 9 p.m. Closed Wednesday.

Kau Kan
On road to Playa la Ropa
Tel. 554-8446
Former Casa Que Canta chef Ricardo Rodriguez offers a menu of inspired dishes, including stingray in black butter, salmon roll stuffed with sea bass, grilled mango and shrimp salad with a ginger vinaigrette, and their famous lobster patata (baked potato stuffed with whole lobster, ringed by jumbo shrimp in a basil sauce). Two romantic lantern-lit terraces, fine dining and impeccable service. You'll want to return again and again. Open from 6 to 11:30 p.m. Reservations recommended.

La Cala
Villa Vera Puerto Mio Hotel
Tel. 553-8166
This fine tropical restaurant and bar is built into a small cove where you can admire the view of the ocean and dine to the natural "music" of the surf rippling through the pebbles. Especially romantic at night, when the tables and surrounding rocks are candle lit. Beautifully prepared seafood specialties and attentive service. Open 7:30 a.m. to 11 p.m.

La Cantina Bar & Grill
Villa del Sol Hotel
Tel. 555-5500
This leading hotel's casual beachfront restaurant offers an exciting cantinalike setting and the delicious culinary creations of its accomplished European chef. Don't miss their festive Friday night Mexican buffet. Open 2 to 11 p.m. Reservations required during the high season.

La Casa Que Canta
La Casa Que Canta Hotel
Tel. 555-7030
This luxurious hotel, dramatically built into the cliffs between La Ropa and La Madera beaches, offers a memorable dining experience—exquisite dishes accompanied by a sweeping view of Zihuatanejo Bay. The menu features gourmet Mexican cuisine as well as fish and seafood specialties; heed their recommendations. The setting calls for elegant resort wear. Open 7 p.m. to midnight. Reservations required.

La Gaviota
Playa la Ropa, south end of the beach
Tel. 554-3816
One of the first family-owned restaurants on the beach offers excellent fresh fish and seafood in a pleasant beachside setting.

La Perla
Playa la Ropa
Tel. 554-2700
This typically Mexican, open-air restaurant on the beach offers a diverse seafood menu, full beverage service, and a pleasant place to spend the day—they have lounge chairs, palapas and service on the beach, as well as water sports facilities. A favorite beachside sports bar with satellite TV. Open 9:30 a.m. to 10 p.m.

La Sirena Gorda
Paseo del Pescador 90, next to the pier
Tel. 554-2687
Written up in Bon Appetit and deservedly so, with tasty fish and seafood dishes simply served in a rustic, alfresco setting resembling a beachside bungalow. Smoked fish and seafood tacos, and superburgers are their specialties. Great breakfasts too, including apple, raisin and walnut pancakes. Open 9 a.m. to 11 p.m. Closed Wednesday.

Orient Express
Vicente Guerrero and Calle Ejido
Cell phone: 044-755-79672
Asian and Filipino dishes prepared by owner and longtime resident Estela Buenaventura, who holds court and entertains as she whips up her wok specialties, including Imperial shrimp, chicken or pork, fried rice and her latest creation, spring rolls with plum sauce. Open 1 to 10 p.m. Take out available.

Villa del Sol
Villa del Sol Hotel
Tel. 555-5500
This chic hotel on Playa la Ropa offers wonderful dining options for every meal. You can enjoy lavish breakfast buffets with a view of the bay, and perfectly prepared gourmet dishes right on the beach or under a charmingly rustic palapa that's romantically lit at night with lanterns. Everything is excellent, from the tasty smoked tuna to the luscious frozen cappuccino dessert. Worth the trip into Zihuatanejo for a well spent afternoon or evening. Owner Helmut Leins personally supervises the smallest details—even the bread is made on the premises. The setting calls for elegant resort wear. Open 8:30 a.m. to 10:30 p.m. Reservations recommended.

Zihu@Rob's Internet Service Café
Vicente Guerrero 3-A
Tel. 554-3591
Personable English-speaking owner Rob Whitehead offers a pleasant air-conditioned setting where you can catch up on your e-mail and surf the net. Meet, mingle and share information in real time as well. Tech support, scanning service, good tourist information.

Nightlife

Carlos'n Charlie's
On the beach, next to Posada Real Hotel
Tel. 553-0085
This popular spot hosts a lively dance party in the evenings on a raised platform over the beach.

Christine
NH Krystal Hotel
Tel. 553-0333
A must for disco lovers. Great decor and sound system. Reservations necessary in season. Open from 10 p.m.

Galeria
Dorado Pacifico Hotel
Tel. 553-2025
A pleasant piano bar featuring "bohemian" singers.

Liquid
Between Mandiles restaurant and Bancomer bank branch
This glitzy after-hours bar features a cocktail menu of flavored martinis. Open 10 p.m. to 4 a.m.

Los Mandiles
Behind Galerias Ixtapa mall
Tel. 553-0379
This popular restaurant has an open-air disco on the upper level for dancing under the stars.

Sanca
Barcelo Beach Resort
Tel. 555-2000
A bar and nightclub with live music for dancing during the high season; check with the hotel for a schedule of shows. Happy Hour 9 to 10 p.m. Open till 1 a.m. Closed Tuesday.

Señor Frog's
La Puerta mall
Tel. 553-0272
Large and lively dance floor. Open from 3 p.m.

The Lighthouse
Marina Ixtapa
A perfect sunset bar with a panoramic view of the marina and all Ixtapa. Open from 5 p.m.

Zen Bar
Opposite the Radisson Hotel
Lounge bar with live music. Open 10 p.m. to 4 a.m.

Shopping in Ixtapa

Across the street from the beachfront hotels is a maze of shopping areas with dozens of boutiques—some of international renown—art galleries, pharmacies, banks, money exchange houses, travel agencies, restaurants. And, of course, there are artisan shops featuring handicrafts from all over Mexico.

Below are descriptions of several of the best shops in town; those in Ixtapa are grouped by shopping center.

Las Fuentes

La Casa de la Playa
Tel. 553-2415
Sophisticated Mexican-made home furnishings and decorative items, from frames made of cactus wood to creatively woven straw curtains. Owned and operated by architect Enrique Zozaya and his wife Veronica.

La Puerta

Alberto's
Tel. 554-2161
Outstanding for exclusive designs in silver and gold, with precious and semiprecious stones, cultured and freshwater pearls. Rings, necklaces and bracelets made to order. One of the most reputable shops here.

Mic-Mac
Tel. 553-1733
An unusual collection of art, handicrafts and clothing. Fine hand-loomed place mats and painted *alebrijes* from Oaxaca, along with Guatemalan textiles and leather goods. You're sure to find more than one item to remember your trip by. Branches in Huatulco and San Carlos.

Los Patios

Deshilados y Artesanias
Tel. 553-0221
Beautiful hand-embroidered textiles from Aguascalientes, including tablecloths, bed covers, pillow cases and more.

Galeria San Angel
One of the most interesting collections in the city. Brass boxes and mirrors, enamel work, sculpture and hand-painted scenes on copper. Many items inspired by pre-Columbian or colonial-era designs. There is also a Sergio Bustamante gallery displaying the highly original sculptures and home furnishings of the celebrated Guadalajara-born artist.

La Fuente
Tel. 553-0812
More of an art gallery than a store, it contains beautiful hand-painted wooden chests, unusual decorative items, Talavera pottery and fine clothing for women. Owned by Joel Lidouren, who also owns Mic-Mac at La Puerta mall.

Plaza Ixpamar

El Amanecer
A showcase of Mexican artistry at its best. There's a large selection of folk art along with contemporary regional handicrafts such as trees of life, clay pottery, painted fish and original, brightly-painted papier-mâché figures, called *alebrijes*, by the well-known Linares family of craftsmen. Also exquisite hand-embroidered cotton dresses and blouses.

Originales
A very interesting store specializing in one-of-a-kind hand-crafted designs, including candles and candelabras. Decorative art created by individual artists.

Shopping in Zihuatanejo

Alberto's
Cuauhtemoc 15
Tel. 554-2161
Featuring the silver and gold creations of master craftsman Alberto. Lovely gift items and jewelry repair. Branch in Ixtapa.

Arte Mexicano Nopal
Cinco de Mayo 56, facing indigenous market
Tel. 554-7530
One of the most charming stores in town thanks to owners Vicki and Rafael, who have collected a great selection of wicker furniture, baskets, large and small, and lots of unusual crafts, including colorful hand-painted canes, miniature masks, Oaxacan black clay pottery and trees of life.

Casa Marina
Paseo del Pescador 9, next to the square
Tel. 554-2373
Three stores in one: El Embarcadero has hand-woven, embroidered cotton clothing from Oaxaca and Guatemala, as well as colorful woven bags and wraps; La Zapoteca has a selection of wool rugs, wall hangings and serapes; and El Jumil displays masks from Guerrero and other handicrafts. All proceeds from the sale of its ASPCA-logo T-shirts go to helping animals.

Coco Cabaña
Vicente Guerrero, behind Coconuts restaurant
Tel. 554-2518
An interesting store full of collectible handicrafts for the home from all over Mexico. Many one-of-a-kind and signed pieces. Owned by Patsy Cummings, who also owns Coconuts, one of Zihuatanejo's most popular restaurants.

GalArt
Villa del Sol Hotel
Tel. 555-5500
A wonderful shop and gallery run by Rocio Madrazo, who handles such artists as metal sculptor D'Argenta, jewelry designers Judy Brown and Jette, and others. Open 10 a.m. to 2 p.m. and 5 to 8 p.m.

Galeria Maya
On Calle Cuauhtemoc
Tel. 554-4606
Ferocious carved masks, Indian dolls, embroidered clothing, Guatemalan textiles, leather goods and Mayan art. Also houses the Ixchel Gallery, featuring the collection of women and goddess sculptures of award-winning Michoacan sculptor Arturo Macias. Owner Tania Scales is as unique as the items displayed.

La Galeria
La Casa Que Canta Hotel
Tel. 555-7030
Lenore Lavalle, former owner of El Amancer in Ixtapa, features prize-winning handicrafts and one-of-a-kind jewelry from around the country handpicked for its unique artistry. Open 10 a.m. to 2 p.m. and 5 to 8 p.m.

Lupita's
Juan N. Alvarez 5
Tel. 554-2238
Exquisite hand-embroidered cotton clothing from Guatemala, Chiapas and Oaxaca, including Oaxacan "wedding skirts" and matching off-the-shoulder blouses, and woven shawls. Owned and managed by the charming Lupita Bravo, who will take special orders and mail items home.

Where to Stay

Villa del Sol overlooks Playa la Ropa

Ixtapa

Barcelo Beach Resort
On Ixtapa Blvd.
Tel. (755) 555-2000
www.barcelo.com
This all-inclusive high-rise hotel designed for recreation comprises two towers with panoramic elevators built around a central atrium. There are 333 rooms and suites, most with private balconies and ocean views. Extensive gardens surround a lovely large swimming pool and pool area, kids programs, wide beach, informal and specialties restaurants, great international shows, bars, three tennis courts, gym, daily activities program. Rates FC.

Club Med
On Playa Quieta
Tel. (755) 552-0044
www.clubmed.com
About 10 minutes from the Ixtapa hotel zone, this complex has 375 air-conditioned rooms. Two swimming pools, 12 tennis courts, a complete range of water sports and entertainment. Restaurants. Rates FC (all inclusive).

Costa Real
Ixtapa Blvd. 5
Tel. (755) 553-1175
www.realresorts.com.mx
A modern hacienda-style property (formerly Continental Plaza) with a large freeform pool, kids' pool, and 124 guest rooms with a/c, satellite TV, minibar. Informal restaurant overlooking the pool area, bars, game room. Meeting facilities, Internet access. Rates FC (all inclusive with room-only option).

Dorado Pacifico
On Ixtapa Blvd.
Tel. (755) 553-2025
www.doradopacifico.com
This 11-story high-rise has 285 spacious rooms, including 21 suites, with satellite TV and great views of the beach. Two lighted tennis courts (and a resident tennis instructor), large swimming pool with slides, kids pool and recreation area, massage services, lovely gardens, panoramic elevators. Numerous restaurants, bar, weekly Fiesta Mexicana dinnershow. Extensive convention and banquet facilities. Rates FC.

Las Brisas
On Playa Vista Hermosa
Tel. (755) 553-2121
www.brisas.com.mx
This award-winning property features 416 spacious oceanview lanai rooms and suites cascading down a hillside to a private secluded beach. Each unit opens onto a large semiprivate terrace with hammocks. Tropical gardens, 4 pools connected by waterfalls, 4 tennis courts, 3 restaurants, Sunset lobby bar, 24-hour room service, kids club, health and fitness center. Extensive convention facilities. Ideal for people who like to stroll, although there's a beach elevator and shuttle service to the pool. Winner of AAA's Four Diamond Award. Rates DX.

Melia Azul Ixtapa
Paseo Punta Ixtapa
Tel. (755) 555-0000
www.meliaazulixtapa.solmelia.com
A resort and convention center with 410 modern units facing the ocean, two large swimming pools with waterfalls, and the ultimate kids pool. Tennis courts, kids clubs, jacuzzis, fitness center. Nightly shows. Rates DX (all inclusive).

NH Krystal Ixtapa

On Ixtapa Blvd.
Tel. (755) 553-0333
www.nh-hotels.com
A deluxe beachfront hotel with 255 attractive rooms and suites with private terraces with ocean views, and color cable TV. Large free-form swimming pool, tennis, gym, kids club. Poolside palapa bar, popular disco and restaurant, meeting facilities. Rates FC.

Posada Real Ixtapa

On Ixtapa Blvd.
Tel. (755) 553-1685
www.posadareal.com.mx
Freshly-renovated, this intimate beachfront hotel offers 110 clean and comfortable air-conditioned rooms with a Mexican flavor. Lovely beachfront pool, bar, restaurant. A Best Western hotel. Rates MD.

Presidente InterContinental

On Ixtapa Blvd.
Tel. (755) 533-0018
www.intercontinental.com
Relaxed and informal, this upscale family-friendly all-inclusive resort features a garden setting with winding paths that lead to the swimming pools and beach. There are 420 contemporary Mexican-style rooms, many with balconies overlooking the Pacific ocean, all with air-conditioning, color cable TV and cozy sitting area. Meeting and banquet facilities for up to 450 people. Wide range of recreational activities, from tennis and golf to lessons in sand sculpture and dancing; there's also a kids club. Two restaurants, bars, wet bar. Rates DX (all inclusive).

Radisson Ixtapa

On Ixtapa Blvd.
Tel. (755) 553-0003
www.radisson.com/ixtapamx
Formerly the DoubleTree, this 14-story hotel has 275 rooms and suites, each with a private balcony overlooking the ocean. Good restaurant and palm-thatched snack bars, huge pool, meeting and banquet facilities for 450. Rates FC.

Riviera Beach Resort

On Ixtapa Blvd.
Tel. (755) 553-1066
www.riviera.com.mx
This 11-story tower on a superb beach offers excellent service in an attractive setting; sunny yellows, sun-bleached whites and tropical blues decorate the rooms as well as the bright open-air lobby facing the lovely pool area. There are 150 guest rooms with ocean or mountain views, and 23 spacious ocean-view suites, including two penthouse suites. In-room amenities include remote-control satellite TV, individually-controlled a/c, minibar, automatic safe, hair dryer. Informal and specialties restaurants overlooking the beach and ocean, sunset bar. Meeting rooms for up to 400 people. Large swimming pool, two lighted tennis courts, gym, spa with sauna and steam bath, beauty salon with wide range of services. Parking. Rates FC.

Zihuatanejo

Amuleto

Camino Escenico a Playa las Gatas
Tel. (755) 544-6222
www.amuleto.net
A new five-room boutique B&B designed by well known architect Enrique Zozaya. The uniquely handcrafted and tropically designed suites have individual infinity pools overlooking the bay and beaches from Cerro del Vigia hill, between La Ropa and Las Gatas beaches. Rates DX.

La Casa Que Canta

Camino Escenico a Playa la Ropa
Tel. (755) 555-7030
www.lacasaquecanta.com
This unique hotel is dramatically built into the cliffs, offering spectacular views of the bay. Rustic palm-thatched roofs, adobe walls, and folk art blend with modern amenities and fine service to offer a luxurious tropical retreat with just 28 suites. No in-room phones or TVs; but there's a lounge with satellite TV. (For the ultimate in luxury, the new El Murmullo Private Residence, located just below the main complex, features 4 suites with private plunge pool and direct access to La Ropa Beach.) Freshwater infinity pool, saltwater pool, jacuzzi, fitness center. Beach easily accessible via a private gate. Gourmet dining. No children under 16 allowed. Member of Small Luxury Hotels of the World. Rates DX.

Villa del Sol

Playa la Ropa
Tel. (755) 555-5500
www.hotelvilladelsol.net
This beach lover's paradise offers relaxed elegance in the tropics with 70 attractive guest rooms and suites overlooking the beach, a man-made lagoon, or gardens. None of the suites are more than a few steps from Zihuatanejo's favorite *playa*, and 12 incredibly sumptuous, super deluxe suites are right on the beach, with a private plunge pool and high-tech conveniences; second-story units offer great views. The superb service begins with a pre-breakfast eye-opener of aromatic coffee and crispy croissants. Excellent dining options, including a palapa restaurant and bar, and an exciting cantina with game tables. Tennis, Ping-Pong, a full service beauty salon offering massages on the beach, gym, swimming pools, including an infinity pool right on the beach and a 60-foot lap pool. Small meeting room. No children under 14 during the winter season. Member of Small Luxury Hotels of the World and Mexico Boutique Hotels. Rates DX (MAP).

HOTEL RATES

LX: luxury, rates above 375 USD
DX: deluxe, rates from 250-375 USD
FC: first-class, rates from 150-250 USD
MD: moderate, rates from 75-150 USD
ECON: economical, rates under 75 USD

Villa Vera Puerto Mio

Paseo del Morro 5
Tel. (755) 553-8165
A beautiful and secluded hotel located just inside the mouth of Zihuatanejo Bay, yet within walking distance of the downtown area. What this hotel lacks in beachfront it makes up for with wonderful views. A hilltop mansion with a lounge and pool area houses 16 elegantly simple balconied rooms and suites with spectacular vistas of the bay, some also with a lovely private pool with a view, lounge, luxurious tub. A short golf-cart ride down the hill brings you to a picturesque rocky cove that's home to a romantic restaurant, cozy bar and a freeform pool with a view. Private marina, spa services. Rates DX.

If you only live once, what better place to do it than here?

VERACRUZ
The State that has it all

Xalapa.

Adrenalin in Veracruz!
Come shoot our rapids, conquer our mountains on a bike or rappel, and experience over a thousand adventures. Are you ready?

Veracruz

Catemaco Lagoon.

Beaches at Chachalacas.

Veracruz

A Favorite Vacation Destination

Veracruz is without a doubt a favorite vacation destination for Mexicans from all walks of life. A year-round festive atmosphere, fresh seafood prepared myriad ways, and a wide variety of activities, from archaeological exploration to white-water rafting, are all part of its appeal.

Veracruzanos are also a big part of the allure. The people of Veracruz like to enjoy and celebrate life. There's always a party going on—Carnival in the port of Veracruz, the Festival de la Candelaria in Tlacotalpan, with its running of the bulls, and Easter celebrations. Then there's the nightly festivities in the central plaza of the port city of Veracruz. And that's the short list.

The state of Veracruz comprises a large part of Mexico's eastern coast. The state begins just across the river from Tampico, in northern Mexico, and stretches, much like California, 600 miles south along the Gulf of Mexico to Coatzacoalcos. The port city of Veracruz is at almost the same latitude as Mexico City, 261 miles due west.

Few places offer so much to discover as does the state of Veracruz. Within a relatively short distance, the adventurous traveler can go from sea level to 19,000 feet, and cover historic ground from before 3000 B.C. to the present. The culture reflects indigenous, Spanish, Afro-Caribbean and other influences, while major archaeological sites, ecological reserves, jungle rivers, beaches, and coral reefs provide unlimited experiences.

Veracruz is easily accessible by land or air. Both *Aeromexico* and *Mexicana* make the 45-minute flight from Mexico City several times a day. By car or bus, the drive passes through the state of Puebla and across the formidable Cumbres de Maltrata mountains down into the lush vegetation that characterizes just about the entire state of Veracruz. The drive between Mexico City and the port city of Veracruz takes under five hours on a toll road that has garnered a good rating from the American Automobile Association (AAA). Drivers should be aware that just outside Veracruz the return highway is at an 8,000-foot elevation and often enveloped in fog, making driving this stretch a bit of a challenge.

Travelers driving to the city of Veracruz from Mexico City pass through the colonial towns of Orizaba, Fortin de las Flores, and Cordoba.

Orizaba is nestled under the monumental mountain that gives the city its name. The snow-capped Pico de Orizaba is the second-highest volcano in North America; at 19,000 feet, it is Mexico's highest. A favorite training ground for mountain climbers, it is not to be treated lightly by inexperienced climbers. Guides are available and recommended. Orizaba is also home to one of Mexico's largest breweries and is a sugar processing center. The town, with its colonial buildings, is well worth exploring.

Fortin de las Flores is the next stop on the journey. "Flores," or "flowers," form part of its name and much of its landscape. Azaleas, bougainvillea, gardenias, orchids and many other varieties of flowering plants grow in abundance. There are several charming hotels and restaurants.

The small, industrial city of *Cordoba* is located about 10 minutes from Fortin. The town's central plaza—where Mexico's declaration of independence was signed—offers a nice place to enjoy a sip of coffee, beer or rum, all products of local industry in this coffee and sugar growing region. From here travelers descend through sugar cane fields on their way to Veracruz and its fast-growing neighbor-turned-suburb Boca del Rio.

Port of Veracruz

Colorful and lively, the city of Veracruz is the oldest post-Columbian city on the continent, and the state's central attraction. Few other Mexican cities have had a history as stormy. It is where conquistador Hernan Cortes landed in 1519, and is the first city established by the Spanish in Mexico. To frustrate the fainthearted among his crew, Cortes burned his boats prior to undertaking his march on the Aztec capital, which marked the beginning of one of the most remarkable sagas of conquest in all human history.

The Spanish named their settlement La Villa Rica de la Vera Cruz (The Rich Village of the True Cross). The original town was actually situated about 50 miles north of its present location and moved several times before Cortes built the fort that still guards the entrance to Mexico's largest and busiest port, Fuerte San Juan de Ulua.

The city has twice been the nation's capital at critical times: during The Reform (1858-1860) and from 1914 to 1915, during the Mexican Revolution. In the War of Independence, Spanish troops bombarded and almost leveled the city from San Juan de Ulua. The French did the same 17 years later. U.S. troops occupied Veracruz during the Mexican-Ame-

Veracruz's civil registry, a vestige of traditional port architecture

Mexico Board

Veracruz is a popular river rafting destination

Rick Gomez

rican War in 1847 and advanced on Mexico City. The French were back again in 1860, prior to the establishment of Maximilian's short-lived empire. And U.S. forces once more bombarded the port in 1914.

Veracruz has a well-deserved reputation as the liveliest of Mexican cities. Its atmosphere is reminiscent of pre-Castro Havana. Not only was it the starting point for the conquistadors, it has long been a port of entry for immigrants from Europe, the last wave consisting of refugees from the Spanish Civil War. The European influence may explain the presence of its sidewalk cafes. The Caribbean also has influenced Veracruz, especially in music and dance, and carnival time brings with it an uninhibited display of color and gaiety. But Veracruz's principal activity is that of a port, receiving the major share of Mexico's overseas imports and exporting goods to foreign destinations.

Boca del Rio, a former fishing village-turned suburb of Veracruz, attests to the port's growth. The area is home to a World Trade Center (with continual expositions of everything from cattle ranching and agriculture to construction and oil exploration), the Expover Convention Center, and five-star hotels and restaurants. Meaning "mouth of the river," Boca del Rio has its festive side as well. During the annual La Señora Santa Anna Festival, locals set a new record by making, and eating, the world's longest stuffed fish fillet. 1994's fillet made it into the Guinness Book of World Records by weighing in at a little more than 2 tons and measuring 136 meters in length. Veracruz actually holds eight Guinness records, including "world's largest shrimp cocktail" (also 2 tons), and "most cups of coffee served at one time." Naturally, it is seeking official recognition as the world's most record-breaking state.

What to See and Do

Plaza de Armas, as the city's main square is called, with its sidewalk cafes and restaurants, and the *malecon*, or waterfront promenade, with its souvenir shops, are both ideal for strolling, people-watching and taking in the port's unique ambiance.

Designed by the Spanish in the 16th century, the square is attractively landscaped with tall palms and tropical flowers, and lit with colored lights in the evening. Wandering musicians, string trios consisting of *jarana*, guitar and harp, and marimba bands serenade diners sitting at tables under the arcades. Often all the bands play at once, creating a memorable cacophony. Tuesday, Friday and Saturday evenings are reserved for *danzon*, a kind of tropical waltz, and people of all ages gather at the square to dance or watch.

Sightseeing in town should include *San Juan de Ulua*, a large island fortress that is Veracruz's prime historical landmark. The Spanish built the fort in the late 16th century to protect their New World interests from pirates; it was later used as a prison for criminals and political "undesirables," some of whom were thrust into dungeon holes that were half-flooded at high tide. Today it is a beautifully preserved maze of moats, ramparts, bridges, battlements and turrets, and houses a small museum with some colonial-era artifacts related to the fort's role in fighting off invaders. You can get there by bus or taxi. Open 10 a.m. to 4:30 p.m., except Monday.

Also worth visiting are the *Museo de Arte e Historia Veracruzana* (Museum of the City of Veracruz), which houses a collection of costumes used over the years in local carnival celebrations; and the *Baluarte de Santiago*. Built in 1625 to guard the city against frequent pirate attacks, this sentinel is the last of nine once linked by a protective wall that stretched around the city. A small museum displays some extraordinary pieces of gold found in the harbor, as well as ancient blueprints, maps and documents relating to the port.

Boats docked along the malecon offer half-hour tours of the harbor. The ride lets you appreciate the cityscape from a different angle, and brings you close to the huge cargo ships that arrive from around the world. There's no set schedule for the tours; a boat will leave whenever a sufficient number of passengers (about 15) make it worthwhile for the tour operators.

If you're in Veracruz between December and February, look for a replica of Christopher Columbus' flagship, the Santa Maria, docked in the harbor. The 15th-century-style ship was built using the original blueprints, which have been conserved in Spain's Marine Museum. Built to celebrate the 500th anniversary of Columbus' Atlantic crossing, the ship retraced that voyage, leaving Veracruz and arriving in Spain. Called *Marigalante*, the initial name of Columbus' ship, it contains a nautical museum and is usually in port during the months leading up to *carnaval*.

The *Veracruz Aquarium*, located at Playa de Hornos, is one of the city's major attractions, and rightly so. Its freshwater and salt-water tanks display some of the world's most exotic creatures. Plus, you can stand in the middle of an enormous doughnut-shaped Japanese-made tank with 13-foot-high acrylic windows and watch some of the deep's most awe-inspiring

San Juan de Ulua Fort

Susan Kaye

inhabitants, including sharks, barracudas and giant sea turtles, swim by.

Mexico's most famous composer Agustín Lara was a native of Veracruz (some say he was born in nearby Tlacotalpan), and one of his best-known songs is a tribute to his home state. An appreciative governor once presented Lara with a house in the port city, and now *La Casita Blanca,* or The Little White House, has been turned into a museum containing photographs and other memorabilia of Lara's song writing and acting careers. The museum is on Ruiz Cortines, corner of Avila Camacho.

City tours highlight the port's rich history with visits to monuments from the 15th to the 19th centuries, including the fort, churches, museums and government buildings. *VIP Tours,* which maintains a travel desk at the Crowne Plaza Torremar hotel, specializes in groups and conventions. Tel. 922-2077.

Beaches in the port city are usually shallow and safe, but often comprised of narrow strips of dark sand that aren't very inviting. The best beaches are south of town, especially at Mocambo. Four large reefs just off the coast offer little-known but worthwhile dive sites. One of them, La Blanquilla, was Mexico's first national underwater park.

Anglers go to Mandinga, where clusters of fishing shacks surround two lagoons, one fished for shrimp, the other for oysters. Perch and bass are also good here. You can do some river fishing at Boca del Rio, or fish at Catemaco Lake.

Restaurants

Jarochos, as natives of Veracruz are called, enjoy long midday meals that typically begin with *sopa de camaron* (shrimp soup) or *sopa de mariscos* (seafood chowder) followed by *arroz tumbada,* rice with seafood, or *picadas,* tortillas smothered with a spicy red sauce and garnished with chopped onion, beans and cheese. Then comes a platter overflowing with *mariscos* (seafood) or *salpicon de jaiba* (shredded crab), *huachinango a la veracruzana* (red snapper in a tomato sauce) or *camaron para pelar* (literally, shrimp for peeling), followed by a cup of coffee and *natilla,* a delicious pudding prepared with locally grown vanilla.

Jarochos are passionate about their coffee as well as cuisine. The countless sidewalk cafes around the port city's bustling downtown area are invariably so full you may wonder whether anyone ever goes to work, until you realize that much of the local wheeling and dealing takes place there. These spots are always crowded with regulars who meet to share the news of the day while enjoying a steaming glass of *lechero* (strong coffee with hot milk).

There's an art to ordering lechero and it's worth mastering if you're a coffee maven. A waiter will bring you a tall glass with a serving of coffee in it, and then leave, rather prematurely you'll think, to attend to some other table. Don't worry—it's not a matter of neglect, but division of labor. Clinking your glass with a spoon will summon another waiter with a kettle of hot milk in one hand and coffee in the other. He'll adjust the amount of coffee you want and then swing the milk kettle high in the air to fill your glass to the rim, amazingly, without spilling a drop.

One of the most traditional cafes, *La Parroquia,* was founded in 1810 and throughout the years gained near legendary status. A true democracy, members of Mexico's working class as well as the rich and famous rubbed shoulders at this no-frills landmark.

Its original location just off the main plaza, at Independencia and Zamora, is today home of the *Gran Cafe del Portal,* a coffeehouse and restaurant so popular that clients vie for the scarce outdoor tables under the arcades. The building preserves its high ceilings and period decor, and mural-sized photographs of its exterior circa 1900 cover the walls at one end. Open 6 a.m. to midnight.

La Parroquia relocated to other, less picturesque, locations, but still remains quite popular.

Restaurants at the leading hotels are usually good bets for dining out. The Fiesta Americana's *Rosato* serves good Italian fare for lunch and dinner, while Veracruz-style fish and shellfish is the specialty at *La Palapa* (open Tuesday to Sunday, 1 to 7 p.m.).

Veracruz's landmark Mocambo Hotel serves delicious seafood at *La Fragata* (closed Mondays), and lavish breakfast buffets weekends, accompanied by live marimba music, at its open-air terrace restaurant, *El Mirador.*

Try *Villa Rica,* at Calzada Mocambo 527, near the Mocambo Hotel, for some of the best seafood found anywhere. This attractive palm-thatched restaurant also has live music in the late afternoon from a talented group of strolling musicians.

Around the plaza and on the malecon there are many eateries, but few that stand out. The best places are *Bar Regis,* a popular restaurant-bar on the plaza known for its tasty *tortas,* or sandwiches; *Pardiños,* serving good seafood right across from the souvenir stalls; and *Papaloapan,* offering a great view of the harbor from the Emporio Hotel.

For a leisurely meal of fresh fish and seafood accompanied by a memorable sunset, go to nearby *Mandinga Lagoon.* Here *El Paisa* offers an exceptional selection of dishes, as well as live regional music and folk dancing.

Nightlife

Evenings, too, people congregate in the sidewalk cafes around the main plaza to have a drink or charge up on coffee for the night ahead, and listen to the sounds of marimba bands or strolling mariachis.

Residents and tourists alike turn out Tuesday, Friday and Saturday nights to watch *danzon* aficionados dance in the main plaza, accompanied by a live band. Simultaneously reserved and passionate, the regional dance and music is so popular that rain fails to cancel these events—everyone simply moves under the *portales,* or arcades, lining the square.

The picturesque bar at the Mocambo Hotel, *El Ancla,* features live music Thursday to Saturday from 9 p.m. For tropical rhythms, try Lois Hotel's *Carioca* nightclub. *Carlos 'n Charlie's,* a wild and crazy place at Avila Camacho and Heroles, in Boca del Rio, serves delicious "nude" crabs and offers a lively setting for drinks.

As in most of Mexico, nightlife here really begins around 10 p.m. and peaks after midnight, with revelers often timing their departures to coincide with the beautiful view of the sun rising over Sacrifice Island and the Gulf of Mexico.

Veracruz's main plaza hosts dancers and musicians

Bruce Herman

Shopping

In the downtown area, shops sell Panama-style hats and handmade cigars, two local specialties. Part of the malecon is also lined with stalls selling wonderfully kitschy souvenirs made of shells, and lots of imported knick-knacks from China and Taiwan. *El Mayab*, at Zaragoza 78, is a good place to pick up handicrafts.

In Boca del Rio's hotel zone two shopping centers stand out, *Plaza Mocambo* and *Plaza las Americas*. Las Americas, the newest of the two, is a two-story mall featuring a "river" that runs from one end to the other, culminating in a large waterfall that spills into a lovely pool. The mall contains four department stores—*Liverpool*, *Sears, Sanborns* and *Chedraui*—and lots of smaller shops.

Side Trips

To really complete a trip into this region's past, visitors should travel just north of the port to the ruins of *Cempoala* and the small village of *Antigua*.

The archaeological site of Cempoala, where Cortes and his men first made contact with the natives, features six major structures amid lush tropical vegetation, including *La Gran Piramide* (The Great Pyramid), constructed of riverbed stones, and *Las Caritas* (The Little Faces), adorned with niches containing small carved faces.

To garner support for his march against the Aztecs, Cortes convinced the local Totonac ruler, known to us as the Fat Chief, that the Spaniards had come to help outlying cities break free from the oppressive rule of imperial Tenochtitlan (today Mexico City). Often tribute would force a small city into a continual state of impoverishment, so the Totonacs were happy to cooperate. It was here that the two camps hatched plans for the long march over the mountains to Tenochtitlan.

Site of the first European settlement on the American continent, the quiet, friendly village of Antigua features the crumbling former home of Hernan Cortes and a small chapel reputed to be the oldest in the Western Hemisphere (built in 1529).

One of the best beaches in the state, *Chachalacas*, is located just north of Antigua, and is known for its enormous sand dunes.

Two hours south of Veracruz by bus is charming *Tlacotalpan*, a riveside village on Rio Papaloapan.

Named a World Heritage Site by UNESCO in 1999, the village boasts a lovely plaza with winding promenades and a Moorish-style kiosk, and streets lined with pastel-colored homes, some dating from the 1800s.

Tlacotalpan is known for its Candlemas Day celebrations in February featuring a Pamplona-style running of the bulls and a riverside candlelight procession.

Xalapa (also spelled Jalapa, and pronounced ha-LA-pa) is the capital of Veracruz and an attractive hillside college town. Located 66 miles (106 km) north of the port or a two-hour bus

ride away, Xalapa and the nearby colonial town of *Coatepec* offer some interesting sights.

Xalapa's main attraction is the spectacular *Museum of Anthropology,* which displays some 3,000 artifacts, including seven of the 10 colossal Olmec stone heads known to exist (two are at Mexico City's National Museum of Anthropology, and one remains where the giant relics were originally found, in San Lorenzo, in the southern part of the state). It was the Olmecs who established the first civilization in the New World, starting around 1000 B.C. Much of what you see at the museum influenced future cultures throughout Mesoamerica, and even North America. For fine regional fare, try *La Casa de Mama* (817-3144).

A 15 minute drive from Xalapa is Coatepec, Mexico's coffee-growing capital. Among the

A giant Olmec head at Xalapa's Museum of Anthropology

Susan Kaye

town's well-preserved colonial buildings is *Posada Coatepec,* offering a charming place to stay the night or have a meal.

In addition to coffee, and candy and liqueurs derived from the bean, this region is known for a marzapanlike sweet called *jamoncillo*. Produced exclusively by several different orders of cloistered nuns in both Xalapa and Coatepec, jamoncillo is made by first grinding pumpkin seeds into a fine paste that is then dyed and molded into fruit, flower or animal shapes.

Coatepec's *Museo Ex-Hacienda El Lencero,* a former sugar plantation and home of General Santa Ana, provides a good picture of what life was like on a colonial-era hacienda.

You can enjoy the state's natural beauty and a few of its archaeological sites while navigating its four main rafting rivers. For more information, consult the chapter titled "The Great Outdoors."

El Tajin

The crown jewel of Gulf Coast archaeology, *El Tajin* is located about 135 miles/216 kilometers northwest of Veracruz, near the vanilla-producing town of *Papantla.* Nestled among hills covered with tropical vegetation, it remained undiscovered until 1785. Its main feature is the awe-inspiring Pyramid of the Niches, so named because it is carved into 365 niches symbolizing the days of the year. There are also 11 ball courts decorated with bas-relief stone carvings of great craftsmanship and beauty.

Papantla, located seven miles/12 kilometers east of El Tajin, was once an important center of the Totonac culture, and is today famous for its vanilla and *voladores*, or "flying Indians." The ancient ceremony of the *Voladores de Papantla* involves four colorfully-dressed men led by a musician playing the flute who ascend a 60- to 90-foot pole fitted with a small platform on top. After the flutist plays a special tune paying homage to the East, West, North and South, the dancers, tied by long ropes to the pole, fall backward, spiraling down and around the pole as their ropes slowly unwind. They stop just inches from the ground. This performance can be seen today throughout Mexico, but it originated here.

While you're in the area, check local shops for unique flower and animal figures made of vanilla beans. You can also buy a vanilla liqueur called *Xanath,* and some of the most flavorful vanilla extract in the world. All these items are nearly impossible to find outside the area. The town has a few hotels, but better accommodations can be found in *Tuxpan,* a seaside resort 80 kilometers to the northeast.

Lake Catemaco

Southeast of Veracruz city, the highway follows the coast to the state's second port city, Coatzacoalcos. On the way are many interesting stopping points, among them *San Andres Tuxtla,* a pretty mountain village likened to Switzerland without the snow.

Just a few miles beyond San Andres and 75 miles/120 kilometers southeast of Veracruz is *Catemaco,* a small fishing village that's home to a beautiful 10-mile-wide (16-kilometer-wide) lake. A boat tour takes in two islands; Isla de los Changos and Isla de Agaltepec. The first is populated by a colony of red-cheeked mandrill monkeys brought from Africa by the University of Veracruz, which is involved in simian research. Other sights include El Tegal grotto, where the Virgin of Catemaco is said to have appeared to a fisherman in 1710, and beautiful *Teoteapan* waterfalls, accessible via hiking trails. Motorboats and water-ski rentals are also available.

Catemaco is famed as Mexico's witchcraft center and hosts an annual convention of witches. Here you can have a spell cast or a curse removed, or buy do-it-yourself potions.

Hotels in town are third-class at best, but on the shores of the lake are several pleasant inns and an ample supply of good restaurants. Two very acceptable stopping places are *La Finca,* a U.S.-style motel, and *Playa Azul,* a motel with bungalow-style rooms in a lush lakeside grove.

Located 11 miles/7 kilometers from Catemaco, *Nanciyaga Ecological Park* lets visitors admire regional wildlife, bathe in clay and aromatic herbs, take a dip in a pool of mineral water, consult with a *curandero* (witch doctor), or enjoy a pre-Hispanic-style steam bath in a *temazcal.* The park is accessible by car or motor boat. Tel. 943-0808.

Coatzacoalcos, a bustling industrial port at the mouth of the Coatzacoalcos River, derives its name from one of the most important events in pre-Hispanic mythology. According to legend, it was here that the Aztec god Quetzalcoatl, or Plumed Serpent, boarded a boat and set sail, promising to return. The name means "where the snake goes into hiding." When Spanish conquistador Hernan Cortes landed in the New World, the Indians believed him to be the returning god.

Home to the largest petrochemical plant in Latin America, Coatzacoalcos has little of interest to the tourist. Hotel accommodations are good, but the better hotels are liable to be all booked by engineers working in the area. Best to plan your overnight stop in Veracruz or Villahermosa.

Pyramid of the Niches, Tajin
Mexico Tourist Board

Hotels

Camino Real
Blvd. Manuel Avila Camacho 3650
Tel. (229) 923-5500
www.caminoreal.com
Leading Mexican hotel chain Camino Real has opened this first-rate 156-room hotel right on the beach, and just minutes from the WTC. Two restaurants, two bars, pool, business cen-

ter. Rates FC (includes breakfast).

Crowne Plaza Torremar
Blvd. Adolfo Ruiz Cortines 4300
Tel. (229) 989-2100
Facing Expover convention center. Newly-renovated thanks to its recent affiliation with the international hotel chain, this first-class hotel has 230 rooms and suites with cable TV and ocean view. Skimpy beach but nice pool area, lobby bar with live music, good restaurant, kids playroom, gym, business center, meeting rooms. Rates FC.

Emporio
Paseo del Malecon
Tel. (229) 932-0020
www.hotelesemporio.com

On the harbor, near the downtown area. This popular, modern hotel has 203 rooms and suites with satellite TV and a/c; each of the 50 suites have a jacuzzi. Three pools with slides (heated and indoor), gym with sauna, game room and kids activities, seafood restaurant with a great view of the harbor, bar, coffee shop, parking, car rental, and banquet/convention facilities for 1000. Rates MD.

Fiesta Americana
Blvd. M. Avila Camacho
Tel. (229) 989-8989
Corner of Bacalao, in Boca del Rio. One of the city's finest hotels is located on one of the safest and widest beaches. This attractive property offers 320 deluxe suites with all corresponding services and amenities. Nice pool

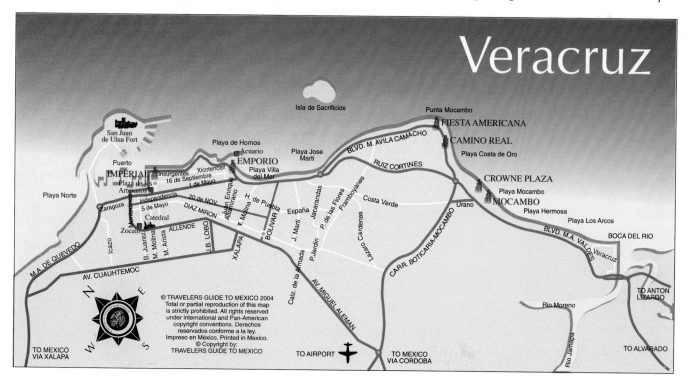

Veracruz

© TRAVELERS GUIDE TO MEXICO 2004
Total or partial reproduction of this map is strictly prohibited. All rights reserved under international and Pan-American copyright conventions. Derechos reservados conforme a la ley. Impreso en México. Printed in Mexico.
© Copyright by:
TRAVELERS GUIDE TO MEXICO

area. Extensive banquet and convention facilities. Rates MD.

Fiesta Inn
Blvd. M. Avila Camacho
Corner of Tortuga, in Boca del Rio
Tel. (229) 923-1000
An attractive new 200-room beachfront hotel with amenities for the business traveler, as well as a wonderful pool and sunning area. Facilities for small to medium-sized groups, business center, cafe-restaurant. Gym. Parking. Rates MD.

Holiday Inn Centro Historico
Morelos 225, downtown
Tel. (229) 932-4550
Housed in the former Convent of San Francisco, with its graceful colonial arches, garden patio and fountain, it has 45 comfortable air-conditioned rooms with cable TV, phone, safe, minibar. Restaurant-bar, room service, pool, meeting rooms, parking. Rates MD.

Mocambo
Blvd. Adolfo Ruiz Cortines 4000
Tel. (229) 922-0202
www.hotelmocambo.com.mx
In Boca del Rio. This stately, sprawling property reflects the glamor of a bygone era, when it served as *the* grand hotel on Mexico's Gulf coast. Built in the 1930s on the city's best

Catemaco

beach, it is larger than life, with high ceilings, spacious interiors, outdoor and indoor swimming pools, and tennis courts. Meandering paths and interconnecting bridges lend the property a delicious air of mystery. There are 123 rooms with a/c and TV, and four matrimonial suites; good restaurant and a piano bar.

Rates MD.

NH Krystal Express
Blvd. M. Avila Camacho
Tel. (229) 923-0201
www.nh-hotels.com
In Boca del Rio. Designed with the business traveler in mind: 115 well-equipped rooms with work stations, gym, sauna, pool, restaurant, bar, meeting rooms. Rates MD.

Hotels in Xalapa (Jalapa)

Meson del Alferez
Sebastian Camacho and Zaragoza
Tel. (228) 818-6351
Two blocks from Parque Juarez. This converted colonial mansion offers clean, comfortable and colorful accommodations, as well as a good restaurant, in the heart of the downtown area. Rates ECON.

Posada Coatepec
Hidalgo and Aldama
Tel. (228) 816-0544
In Coatepec, about a 15 minute drive from Xalapa. An exquisite provincial mansion converted into an exclusive hotel. The 23 spacious rooms and suites with cable TV are built around a delightful patio; also a two-floor villa with jacuzzi. The hotel houses an excellent restaurant, bar. Pool, tennis. Rates MD.

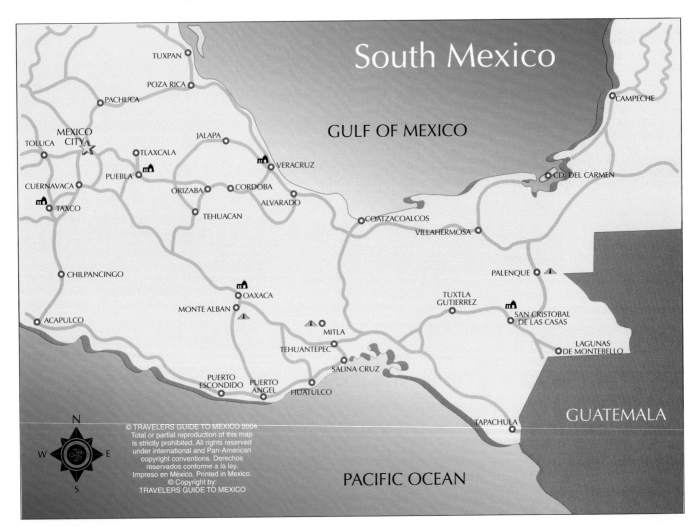

South Mexico

Oaxaca

A Glimpse Into Mexico's Roots

Monte Alban

Bruce Herman

Southern Mexico appeals to travelers who like to immerse themselves in the countries they visit. Geographically, this is where Mexico displays its affinity with tropical Central America and its lush green mountains, indigenous groups and incredible variety of wildlife. The area, easily the country's poorest economic region, is home to Mexico's largest Indian populations.

For the traveler's purpose, southern Mexico could be defined as the three states of Oaxaca, Chiapas and Tabasco, plus part of the state of Veracruz. Two of these southern states, Tabasco and Chiapas, border Guatemala; in fact, Chiapas used to be a part of Guatemala and still has more in common with it than with the rest of Mexico. Both Tabasco and Chiapas were part of the Mayan empire and as such are described in the Mundo Maya, or Maya World, section.

This region is of special interest to archaeologists. If there is still an "undiscovered" Mexico, it is here. It offers few of the sophisticated frills of glittering resorts, but reveals a face of Mexico the tourist will see nowhere else. For those with time and spirit, a visit to this beautiful and largely unspoiled area is richly rewarding and unforgettable.

Oaxaca City

Oaxaca, the capital of the state of the same name, lies 340 miles southeast of Mexico City and can be reached by plane or car. The toll road from Mexico City is fairly new and has cut driving time in half, from about 10 to just under five hours.

Located in a valley surrounded by the Sierra Madre del Sur, the city has a superb climate, making it a year-round favorite of visitors. Once the center of Mixtec and Zapotec civilizations, Oaxaca is a combination of pre-Hispanic, colonial and modern influences.

The early Zapotecs developed a great civilization at nearby Monte Alban centuries before the birth of Christ. Two of Mexico's most famous presidents, Benito Juarez and Porfirio Diaz, were of Zapotec origin.

After the Spanish conquered Oaxaca in 1533, the city quickly took on a Spanish flavor, with ornate buildings, churches, elegant archways, balconies, decorative grill work and charming plazas. Yet despite its colonial heritage, the city remains basically Indian at heart—wherein lies its charm.

Oaxaca is easily explored on foot. Almost everything there is to see is concentrated around the main square, or *Zocalo*, or situated along the principal pedestrian promenade, Macedonio Alcala.

Shaded by giant Indian laurels and framed by graceful arcades, the central square is one of the most active and colorful in Mexico. Sidewalk cafes, three to four tables deep, do a brisk business, hosting resi-

Santo Domingo Church

Mexico Tourist Board

Dominicans in 1608, is considered one of the finest baroque churches in the Western world. Thanks to restoration work carried out in the 1950s, its ceiling and 30-foot-thick walls are ablaze with gold and polychrome bas-relief, some of it depicting the family tree of the founder of the order, Santo Domingo de Guzman.

The adjoining *Santo Domingo Cultural Center,* resplendent following recent restoration work, houses the *Museum of the Cultures of Oaxaca.* The museum's stellar attraction is a roomful of gold artifacts excavated at Monte Alban. More than three and a half metric tons of gold, silver, jade, turquoise, crystal and pearl jewelry and relics were found there in a single tomb, known as Tomb 7. Archaeologists believe the tomb was filled long after Monte Alban had been abandoned.

The museum has a cactus garden and cafe, and has plans to open a national school of fine arts, as well as arts and crafts workshops. The museum is open until 8 p.m., and closes Mondays.

Opposite Santo Domingo, renowned Oaxacan painter Francisco Toledo established the *Oaxacan Institute of Graphic Arts,* which features photography and graphic arts exhibits. It is also open till 8 p.m., but closes Tuesdays.

Just a few doors down, the *Oaxacan Museum of Contemporary Art (MACO)* features a collection of Tamayos, Toledos and Nietos. MACO also functions as a cultural center, screening films and hosting concerts. MACO is open 10:30 a.m. to 8 p.m., except Tuesdays.

Not to be missed is the *Rufino Tamayo Museum of Mexican Pre-Hispanic Art,* located at Morelos 503, about four blocks from the main plaza. Housed in a charming colonial building is one of the country's finest collections of pre-Columbian statues and relics, all donated by the late Oaxacan artist. There are five halls, all color coordinated by him. The museum is open 10 a.m. to 2 p.m. and 4 to 7 p.m. (open half a day Sundays, till 3 p.m., and closed Tuesdays).

A couple of blocks away, at Garcia Vigil 609, is the house where Benito Juarez lived when he first came to Oaxaca. It was declared a national monument and opened to the public (closed Mondays).

For a panoramic view of the city and valley, take a cab to *Cerro del Fortin,* site of the hilltop amphitheater that hosts Oaxaca's famous yearly festival. Above it stands a statue of Juarez cast in Rome in 1891.

dents and visitors alike. This casual interaction between Oaxacans and the mostly American, Canadian, German, English, French and Spanish travelers that come here gives the city an authentic cosmopolitan air. Balloon vendors and Indian women selling baskets, serapes and other handmade goods crisscross the square, adding to the hustle and bustle.

Every night, music of one kind or another fills the square. Especially popular are the marimba bands, which play several nights a week.

Just north of the Zocalo, facing Alameda Park and the post office, is the *Catedral de Oaxaca,* built in 1555. Its intricately carved facade stands in contrast to its plain interior.

A far more remarkable church is located a few blocks north of the plaza on Macedonio Alcala. The *Iglesia de Santo Domingo,* built by the

Festivals

Oaxaca's largest annual celebration, *La Guelaguetza,* is a dance festival featuring spectacularly costumed delegations from the state's seven regions, each showcasing its own distinctive songs, dances and regional dress.

The seven regions represented are: the Central Valleys, the Sierra Juarez, Cañada, Tuxtepec, Mixteca, the coast, and the Isthmus of Tehuantepec. Performances end with each group offering a *"guelaguetza,"* or gift (usually products typical of their region), to the public.

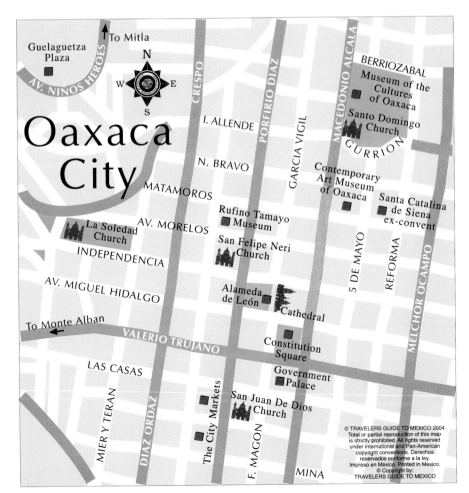

Oaxaca City

To Mitla

Guelaguetza Plaza

AV. NIÑOS HEROES

CRESPO

I. ALLENDE

N. BRAVO

MATAMOROS

PORFIRIO DIAZ

GARCIA VIGIL

MACEDONIO ALCALA

BERRIOZABAL

Museum of the Cultures of Oaxaca

Santo Domingo Church

GURRION

Contemporary Art Museum of Oaxaca

Rufino Tamayo Museum

San Felipe Neri Church

La Soledad Church

AV. MORELOS

INDEPENDENCIA

AV. MIGUEL HIDALGO

To Monte Alban

VALERIO TRUJANO

LAS CASAS

MIER Y TERAN

DIAZ ORDAZ

The City Markets

F. MAGON

Alameda de León

Cathedral

Constitution Square

Government Palace

San Juan De Dios Church

MINA

Santa Catalina de Siena ex-convent

5 DE MAYO

REFORMA

MELCHOR OCAMPO

For those not fortunate enough to be in Oaxaca in July, a mini version of the Guelaguetza is presented Wednesday and Friday nights at the Camino Real hotel, along with a delicious buffet. Similar shows are staged nightly at the *Monte Alban Hotel*, located in front of the cathedral at Alameda de Leon 1, and at *Casa de Cantera*, two blocks from the Zocalo on Murguia, between Cinco de Mayo and Macedonio Alcala.

In December, a festival ambiance prevails, peaking before Christmas with the celebration of the *Noche de los Rabanos*, or Night of the Radishes. This time-honored tradition, origin unknown, features sculptures, some about a foot long, carved out of the prized root.

Markets

The *Oaxaca Market*, located in the southwestern part of the city, is the second largest native crafts market in Mexico, after Toluca. Saturday is usually market day, when Indians from the surrounding villages bring their wares to the city, but it is worth a visit on any day. You will see marvelous wool rugs, green earthenware, famed Oaxacan black pottery, wonderfully imaginative hand-carved animals and masks, hand-loomed fabrics for dresses or tablecloths, hammocks, leather, gold jewelry and embroidered belts.

The most authentic market is held every Sunday in *Tlacolula*, a town 40 minutes east of Oaxaca. There you will be surrounded by Oaxacans speaking their native Indian dialects and wearing their traditional garb. This trip can also include a visit to the nearby ruins of Mitla.

You can attend a different market each day of the week since surrounding towns take turns hosting these events: on Mondays, there's a market in Miahuatlan, Tuesdays in Zimatlan, Wednesdays in Etla, Thursdays in Zaachila and Fridays in Ocotlan.

Craft Centers

The town of *Coyotepec*, a few miles south of the airport, is where artisans specialize in black pottery and give demonstrations of their craft. The town of *Atzompa*, a little northeast of the city, is where you can see the region's distinctive green-glazed pottery being made.

Teotitlan del Valle, a nearby town which was virtually unknown 10 years ago, is growing rapidly as the world learns of its expert rug weavers. The selections are seemingly limitless, from woven designs of pre-Hispanic figures to reproductions of cubist paintings. One of Teotitlan del Valle's master weavers, Emiliano Mendoza, has two shops, at Juarez 39 and at Venustiano Carranza 2. At the former, Abigail Mendoza runs a restaurant called *Tlamanalli* that serves tasty regional dishes. Here you can hear the staff speaking to one another in their native Zapotec.

Mezcal

Oaxaca is mezcal country. A close cousin of tequila, mezcal can be made from three different kinds of agave that thrive in Oaxacan soil. You can see the spirit being made at small family-owned distilleries in the countryside, most located on the road to Mitla. One popular mezcal production house is *Casa Chagoya*, but there are others in the small village of Matatlan.

Ruins

Monte Alban, meaning White Hill, is situated just six miles west of town on a mountain plateau 1,200 feet above the city. The site features a great central plaza flanked by various temples, more than 150 tombs, and mysterious stone slab figures called *danzantes* that were carved around 700 B.C. Though named "dancers," the significance of the figures is still unclear.

Archaeologists have discovered six distinct periods of occupation dating from 900 B.C., and strong trade relations with the Gulf Coast

Folk dancers take part in the Guelaguetza festival

Mexico Tourism Board

Olmecs, followed by ties with Teotihuacan. Most of the buildings date to this later period, when the Zapotec population numbered about 60,000.

Mixtec invaders took over the largely abandoned site around 1300 A.D. They were great craftsmen, judging by the jewelry and other art objects left behind, but they were not architects. Little new construction followed their arrival and old Zapotec tombs were re-used to bury members of the Mixtec elite.

Mitla, located 24 miles east of town, close to a village of the same name, was inhabited from the same early date as Monte Alban, but the Zapotecs did not begin constructing here until around 200 A.D. Its outstanding architectural features are elaborate carvings and mosaic works that experts believe represent the Sky Serpent, a variation of the omnipresent god Quetzalcoatl.

Mitla's recently renovated *Frisell Museum* has an extensive exhibit of Mixtec and Zapotec art, and a pleasant restaurant, *La Sorpresa*.

En route to the ruins, stop in the towns of *Tlacochahuaya* and *Tlacolula* to see some wonderful examples of the creativity of Oaxaca's native artists. The 16th-century former convent in Tlacochahuaya is renowned for its beautiful plateresque altars and especially for the painting of San Jeronimo by native artist Juan de Arrue. In the church of Nuestro Señor de Tlacolula, which dates from the same era, are Indian interpretations in relief of the deaths of various saints—one with an ax in his head, a second boiled in oil. Another feature of this church is its antique tubular pipe organ.

There are several other archaeological zones in this area: *Dainzu* (stone carvings of ancient ball players), *Lambityeco* (beautiful carved friezes) and *Yagul* (breathtaking hilltop view and intriguing labyrinthine palace remains).

Before returning to Oaxaca stop in *Santa Maria del Tule* to see one of Oaxaca's natural wonders: the famous *Tule* tree, a giant *ahuehuete* (cypress) about 120 feet high and 144 feet around the trunk. Estimated to be more than 2,000 years old, the tree is like a forest unto itself.

To the south of the city is the *Zaachila*

Vestiges of pre-Columbian and Spanish cultures come into sharp contrast at Mitla

archaeological site, where two tombs decorated with beautifully preserved stucco sculpture are open to the public. For a typical Oaxacan meal stop at *La Capilla*, a pleasant restaurant with tables shaded by palapas.

Visits to all of these surrounding attractions, as well as city tours, can be arranged through *Turismo El Convento de Oaxaca*, with offices at the Camino Real (516-1806), Victoria, Mision de los Angeles and Holiday Inn hotels. They can also arrange a few days at the beach via regularly scheduled flights to Huatulco and Puerto Escondido.

Nature lovers interested in exploring Oaxaca's countryside should contact ecotourism outfit *Tierraventura*, Abasolo 217 (501-1363).

Oaxaca's traditional flavor makes it an inspiring place to study Spanish, and there are several good language schools.

The *Instituto de Comunicacion y Cultura,* or ICC, at Macedonio Alcala 307, offers college-credit courses, as well as workshops on regional cooking and weaving, tours and housing in Mexican homes. For more information, visit www.iccoax.com.

Dining

Oaxaca's bustling main plaza is lined with sidewalk cafes. Here you can breakfast on sweet rolls and hot chocolate, lunch on simple but tasty regional or continental dishes, and dine on *tamales Oaxaqueños*, Oaxacan-style tamales wrapped in banana leaves. Or simply enjoy the people-watching and quench your thirst.

Mornings or afternoons are a good time to try the gourmet coffee shops serving regionally grown blends. There's *Cafe La Antigua*, at Reforma 401, corner of Abasolo, which exclusively serves coffee brewed from Mexico's high-grade organically-grown Pluma beans; *Gecko*, a cafe-art gallery housed in an attractive restored home opposite Santo Domingo; and the *Coffee Bean*, which has a branch on Macedonio Alcala, about two blocks from the main plaza, and another on Cinco de Mayo, a block

north of the Camino Real Hotel.

Excellent restaurants in the downtown area include *La Asuncion* and *El Naranjo*, though neither faces or overlooks the main square. Following is a list of the leading restaurants around town.

El Asador Vasco
Portal de las Flores 10-A
Tel. 514-4755
Overlooking the central square. More popular for its ideal location than for its Basque fare. Try it in the evening, when typically Spanish entertainment is provided by an *estudiantina*, or group of young minstrels, and call ahead for a reservation; tables with a view of the square go fast.

El Naranjo
Valerio Trujano 203, downtown
Tel. 514-1878
Contemporary Oaxacan cuisine served in a lovely colonial home just a block and a half from the main square. Try the chicken or enchiladas served with one of seven types of Oaxacan *mole*, a complex sauce made of ground nuts and herbs; or the *chiles rellenos*, different peppers stuffed with a variety of fillings, from ancho chili with goat cheese and almonds to poblano chili with minced meat. Open 1 to 10 p.m.

El Refectorio
Camino Real Hotel
Tel. 501-6100
Located downtown, this spot features an authentic colonial setting and Oaxacan *mole*, a rich chocolate-and-chili-based sauce, as well as international specialties. Live music.

El Sagrario
Valdivieso 120, downtown
Tel. 514-0303
Housed in a colonial residence a few steps from the main square, this complex comprises a restaurant specializing in grilled steaks, with a lunch buffet from 1 to 5 p.m.; a pizzeria, a soda fountain, and a popular basement bar with live music nightly. Open 8 to 2 a.m.

El Tule
Victoria Hotel
Tel. 515-2633
This hilltop restaurant serves fine regional and international dishes, with a glorious panoramic view. Sunday buffet. Open 7 a.m. to 10:30 p.m.

Hosteria de Alcala
Macedonio Alcala 307, downtown
Tel. 516-2093
Housed in a restored colonial mansion, this spot offers an extensive international menu, indoor or patio dining, and live piano music nightly from 8 p.m. Open 8:30 a.m. to 11 p.m. Closed Sunday mornings.

La Asuncion
Hostal de la Noria Hotel
Tel. 514-7844
Located downtown, this spot serves beautifully prepared and presented contemporary Oaxacan and international dishes, both indoors or in a lovely umbrella-shaded patio. Prices are very reasonable, service is excellent. Open 7:30 a.m. to 11 p.m.

La Casa de la Abuela
Hidalgo 616 and Portal de las Flores, downtown
Tel. 516-3544
A good option overlooking the square and Alameda Park, it serves typical Oaxacan cuisine in a pleasant setting.

La Flor de Oaxaca
Armenta y Lopez 311, downtown
Tel. 516-5522
About three blocks south of the main square. A good place to sample Oaxacan dishes.

La Fonda de Santo Domingo
Cinco de Mayo 411, behind Santo Domingo
Tel. 514-8924
Gloriously Mexican, this cozy and colorful spot offers typical fare and an excellent house mezcal (that's also sold at its adjoining shop).

Los Cypresses
Hacienda Los Laureles Hotel
Tel. 501-5300
Located in the suburb of San Felipe del Agua, this European-style restaurant, with its garden and mountain views, is considered one of the city's finest. Try the Oaxacan, Mexican and international specialties, and don't miss their wonderful salads and homemade patés spread on fresh-baked black bread. Open 8 a.m. to 10 p.m.

Los Pacos
Constitucion 104-A, downtown
Tel. 516-1704
Next to Santo Domingo, this wonderful two-level restaurant-art gallery offers Oaxacan cuisine and a spectacular view from the top floor.

Nightlife

The Camino Real Hotel's lovely poolside bar, *Las Novicias*, is great for having drinks and listening to live music from 8 to 11 p.m.

The Victoria Hotel's *Terraza* terrace bar offers a panoramic view of the city and romantic trio music Tuesday to Sunday nights from 8 p.m. For reservations, call 515-2633.

There's live music at the *Candela* bar, corner of Murguia and Pino Suarez, and at the bars of the *El Sagrario* and *Catedral* restaurants.

There are a couple of good discos, including *Tequila Rock* next to the Mision de los Angeles Hotel, and *Sabina*. The Fortin Plaza and Mision de los Angeles hotels both have shows in the evenings.

You can also check MACO and *Teatro Alvaro Carrillo* for a schedule of plays, concerts, films and other cultural events.

Shopping

Oaxaca's crafts are admired all over Mexico and sold elsewhere for much more. On Saturday and Sunday evenings, you'll see Indians from surrounding villages display their handicrafts in front of the cathedral and around Alameda Park. This strong artistic tradition has found its modern expression in a thriving contemporary art scene best represented by famous Oaxacan-born artists Rufino Tamayo (1899-1991), Francisco Toledo, and Rodolfo Morales (1926-2001).

Many of the city's best shops and art galleries are located on streets around the main plaza and on Macedonio Alcala, the street leading to Santo Domingo. For handicrafts and folk art, don't miss these two spots: *Casa de las Artesanias de Oaxaca* and *MARO*.

Housed in a beautiful colonial building opposite Santo Domingo is a small shopping center called *Plaza Santo Domingo.* Inside you will find a variety of shops, including *Tapetes Mays* and *Arte Mexicano,* for rugs, prints, and a large selection of imaginative hand-painted animal figures.

Oaxacans observe the siesta tradition and most shops close between 2 and 4 p.m., but then remain open until 7 or 8 p.m.

Following are some recommended shops:

Amate Books
Macedonio Alcala 307-2
Tel. 516-7181
This bookstore offers an extensive selection of English-language books about Mexico, including its art, architecture, culture and cuisine. English spoken. Open 10:30 a.m. to 2:30 p.m. and 3:30 to 7:30 p.m.

Arte de Oaxaca
Murguia 105, half a block from Alcala
Tel. 514-0910

This attractive, centrally-located art gallery, housed in a restored colonial home, is run by personable and knowledgeable owners Nancy Mayagoitia and Dora Luz Martinez, who promote works by Oaxaca's established and up-and-coming artists, including Rodolfo Morales, Filemon Santiago, Virgilio Santaella and Rolando Rojas. Open 11 a.m. to 3 p.m. and 5 to 8 p.m.; to 3 p.m. Saturday.

Arte Mexicano de Antequera
Macedonio Alcala 407-16, downtown
Tel. 516-3255
In Plaza Santo Domingo. One of the major art galleries, with one exhibition room dedicated to paintings and sculptures by Oaxaca's leading young artists, including Ixrrael Montes, Crispin Vayadares and Carlomagno, and another featuring select pieces of Mexican folk art. Open 10 a.m. to 2 p.m. and 4 to 8 p.m.

Casa de las Artesanias de Oaxaca
Matamoros 105, downtown
Tel. 516-5062
Room after room dedicated to a different handicraft, from wool rugs and embroidered textiles to black pottery and silver jewelry. This marvelous shop features the works of 80 different communal organizations or family workshops from the state's seven regions.

Oaxaca's famed Tule tree, estimated to be more than 2,000 years old

Chris Luhnow

Cielito Lindo
Macedonio Alcala 407-2, downtown
Tel. 514-2913
Located opposite Santo Domingo, this string of three adjoining boutiques offers beautiful, ethnically inspired clothing by prestigious Mexican designers and design houses, including Girasol and Alejandro Julian. Also creative amber and silver jewelry. Open 10 a.m. to 8 p.m.

Galeria Quetzalli
Constitucion 104, next to Santo Domingo
Tel. 514-2606
A great selection of contemporary Mexican art, including works by Francisco Toledo, Luis Zarate, Jose Villalobos, Maximino Javier, Emy Winter and others. Also houses a wonderful restaurant-bar. Open 10 a.m. to 2 p.m. and 5 to 8 p.m.

La Mano Magica
Macedonio Alcala 203, downtown
Tel. 516-4275
Where collectors head for contemporary art, as well as fine folk art exemplified by the collection of hand-woven silk and wool tapestries created by master weaver Arnulfo Mendoza.

You can see the highly intricate tapestries being woven in the gallery's colonial patio. They pack and ship. Open 10:30 a.m. to 2:30 p.m. and 3:30 to 7 p.m.

Oro de Monte Alban
Macedonio Alcala 403, downtown
Tel. 514-3813
Located just a few steps from the Santo Domingo Church, this branch is the most spectacular, featuring exquisitely crafted reproductions of pre-Hispanic gold jewelry as well as wonderful creations in silver. You can visit the workshop at Adolfo C. Gurrion and see a fascinating demonstration of the lost wax process.

MARO
Cinco de Mayo 204, downtown
Tel. 516-0670
At MARO, which stands for the Regional Association of Craftswomen of Oaxaca, you'll find a superb variety of handicrafts from throughout the state as well as workshops where you can see the artisans at work on textiles, masks, sculptures and more. Items sold retail and wholesale.

Oaxaca Hotels

Camino Real
Cinco de Mayo 300
Tel. (951) 501-6100
www.caminoreal.com
The 16th-century former Convent of Santa Catalina, a historic landmark four blocks from the main plaza, was converted in 1994 into this charming deluxe hotel. The 84 rooms and seven junior suites surrounding flower-filled courtyards and secluded patios, are decorated with Spanish colonial art and Oaxacan handicrafts, and equipped with satellite TV, a/c, minibar, phone, safe. Swimming pool, restaurant, bar, meeting facilities. Valet parking. Rates FC.

Casa Bonita
Catalina 102, in San Felipe del Agua
Tel. (951) 520-0396
www.hotelcasabonita.com
Located a 10-minute drive from downtown Oaxaca, this stately converted home features 11 well-appointed guest rooms with cable TV and minibar, among other amenities, fine dining indoors or on a sunny patio, computer workstations, personalized service. Rates FC (includes breakfast).

Casa Cid de Leon
Morelos 602
Tel. (951) 514-1893
www.mexicoboutiquehotels.com
This lavish B&B two blocks from the main plaza has just four exclusive suites with terracotta floors, wood-beam ceilings, hand-embroidered linens, bronze chandeliers. Hotel-airport transfers. Member of Mexico Boutique Hotels. Rates FC (includes breakfast).

Casa de Sierra Azul
Hidalgo 1002
Tel. (951) 514-7171
A lovely B&B housed in a beautifully restored colonial-era mansion two blocks from the main plaza, with 15 guest rooms, some surrounding a central courtyard with fountain. Rooms have cable TV, phone, coffee maker. Rates MD.

Casa de Siete Balcones
Morelos and Macedonio Alcala
Tel. (951) 516-1856
www.casadesietebalcones.com
In the heart of the Historic Center, this 200-year-old home-turned B&B features seven charming, well-appointed guest rooms with balconies overlooking one of the most historic corners, and proximity to leading sights of interest. Attention to detail evident in the concierge service, fresh flowers in rooms, bath robes. Rates FC.

Casa Oaxaca
Garcia Vigil 407
Tel. (951) 514-4173
www.mexicoboutiquehotels.com
This exclusive inn, under German management, offers just seven simple yet tastefully decorated guest rooms in a renovated colonial home five blocks from the main plaza. Patio, pool, *temazcal*

(pre-Hispanic sweat lodge), fireplace, cocktail hour and breakfast service. Member of Mexico Boutique Hotels. Rates FC.

Hacienda Los Laureles

Hidalgo 21, in San Felipe del Agua
Tel. (951) 501-5300
www.mexicoboutiquehotels.com
Located a 10-minute drive north of downtown in a very exclusive but typical Mexican-style residential area, this attractive five-star hacienda hotel and spa with views of nearby mountains is ideal for weddings and small groups. The 23 rooms and suites surrounded by gardens have a safe, cable TV and minibar, among other amenities. Swimming pool with jacuzzi, gym, *temazcal* (sweat lodge), massage services, fine restaurant. Member of Mexico Boutique Hotels. Rates FC.

Hostal de la Noria

Hidalgo 918
Tel. (951) 514-7844
www.lanoria.com.mx
This beautifully restored three-level colonial home two blocks from the main plaza is decorated with large potted plants, hand-painted walls, and Oaxacan arts and crafts. The 52 rooms and suites, built around a central patio, have satellite TV. Small meeting rooms, valet parking. The restaurant is one of the best in town. Rates MD.

Mision de los Angeles

Porfirio Diaz 102
Tel. (951) 515-1500
A popular colonial-style hotel in the northeast of the city, with 145 rooms, including 18 air-conditioned suites, with satellite TV, built around lovely gardens. Swimming pool, tennis, restaurant, bar, disco, ample convention facilities. Rates MD.

Victoria

Lomas del Fortin 1
Tel. (951) 515-2633
www.hotelvictoriaoax.com.mx
On a hill overlooking the city, this is a lovely, well-run, family-operated hotel that has 150 rooms, junior suites and villas, all with satellite TV and air-conditioning. Gardens, heated swimming pool, tennis, excellent dining room, bar with live music, business center and meeting facilities. Close to everything despite its hilltop location. Free transportation to and from the downtown area from 8 a.m. to 10 p.m. Rates MD.

Pacific Coast Resorts

The Oaxaca coast is still remote enough to discourage hoards of tourists, but appealing enough to attract those who are looking for a tranquil and out-of-the-way spot with fine beaches and exceptionally good fishing and surfing.

The road from Oaxaca to Puerto Escondido by way of Puerto Angel is paved but mountainous. This route takes much more time than it would appear on a map, with slow-moving traffic and endless curves. The

coastal towns can also be reached via the highway from Acapulco. Flights connect Mexico City, Acapulco and Oaxaca with Puerto Escondido.

Puerto Escondido

Puerto Escondido is an ideal place to relax and enjoy the sunny days and starry nights, unless you have come to test its fame as Mexico's surfing capital.

The town centerpiece is a short, wide main street that has been closed to traffic and turned into a promenade lined with restaurants, souvenir shops and sporting goods stores. Unfortunately, you'll find little of the handicrafts for which the state of Oaxaca is known.

One of the best restaurants downtown is *La Perla Flamante*, serving great fresh fish at wonderful prices, accompanied by a good selection of tropical and reggae music. The *Santa Fe Hotel*, situated on Playa Zicatela, the surfing beach, is a charming colonial-style property with an excellent restaurant, where a romantic trio serenades diners in the evenings.

In the north end of town is the hilltop *Posada Real Hotel*, featuring a spectacular view of the beach below and a wonderful beach club. The rock formations on the beach here break the powerful waves, allowing some swimming and frolicking, as well as nature watching as

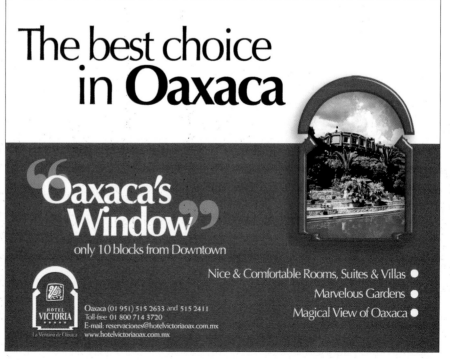

small fish and crabs take refuge among the rocks.

Budget hotels downtown include *Flor de Maria*, run by a Canadian-Italian couple, and *Rincon del Pacifico*.

If you're looking for an even more remote spot, try *Puerto Angelito,* a small bay accessible by cab from downtown Puerto Escondido, or by boat. You can reserve a colorful hammock on the beach, and not much else. The only building here is a palm-thatched seafood restaurant that serves good food and drinks.

An hour south of Puerto Escondido is the small town of *Puerto Angel*, a fishing village with only minimal accommodations and a population that brings to mind the flower children of the 60s. Its nearby beaches are favored by backpackers and other budget travelers who seek the economy and simplicity of a hammock, a bottle of beer, and an empty beach. *La Posada Cañon de Vata* (tel. 584-3048) has a good restaurant serving organically-grown vegetables and homemade breads.

From Puerto Escondido you can take day trips that combine visits to various sites of interest, including *Mazunte*, a sea turtle slaughterhouse-turned-sanctuary, *Zipolite*, a nudist beach, and *Huatulco,* Oaxaca's leading coastal resort.

The Isthmus

East of Oaxaca city, Mexico's land mass narrows to form the Isthmus of Tehuantepec, a strip of land that connects Mexico and Central America. Here the Gulf of Mexico and the Pacific are divided by only 140 miles of relatively flat terrain, tempting developers to think in terms of an alternative Panama Canal. So far, Mexico has shown no interest in such a plan, beyond devising rail transport between the gulf and Salina Cruz on the Pacific.

Tehuantepec is distaff color and grace. The tall, stately Tehuanas, reputed to be among the most beautiful women in the world, are famed for their lavish costumes (now only worn on special occasions). Their velvet blouses and skirts embroidered in gold and satin are crowned with huge lace bonnets fashioned, oddly enough, out of a little girl's dress. According to legend, the headdress originated hundreds of years ago when a box of lace baby dresses washed ashore from a shipwreck, and the only use the women could find for them was as a headpiece. Necklaces strung with gold coins accessorize the costumes, a vestige of the days when railroad workers laying tracks across the isthmus would woo their sweethearts with the medallions.

Native society in the area comes close to being matriarchal, with the women dominating home and economic life. They run the markets while the men work the fields. Sister town *Juchitan* has long carried on a rivalry with neighboring Tehuantepec over which of the two is most representative of Tehuantepec womanhood.

Puerto Escondido Hotels

Aldea de Bazaar
In Bacocho, north end of town

Tel. (954) 582-0508
This attractive Moorish-style property offers 47 rooms with two double beds and a sitting area with two single beds, making it ideal for families. Rooms have a/c, TV and hair dryer (baths with showers only). Restaurant, beautiful pool, spa with a *temazcal* (pre-Hispanic sweat lodge), nice beach area with sun umbrellas and lounge chairs. Rates MD.

Posada Real Puerto Escondido
Blvd. Benito Juarez, north end of town
Tel. (954) 582-0237
www.posadareal.com.mx
On a bluff at the ocean's edge, with a great view of the beach below, this attractive low-rise has 100 clean, simple rooms with satellite TV and a/c distributed in two buildings surrounded by well-kept grounds with a swimming pool and children's pool. A great beach club with a pool and restaurant (accessible via stairs leading down to the water) make this hotel a wonderful option. Travel agency and friendly management. A Best Western hotel. Rates MD.

Santa Fe
Playa Zicatela, south end of town
Tel. (954) 582-0170
www.hotelsantafe.com.mx
This delightful colonial-style hotel on the main surfing beach has 62 rooms and eight bungalows, each air conditioned and individually decorated, a swimming pool and an excellent restaurant with seafood and vegetarian specialties. Rates MD.

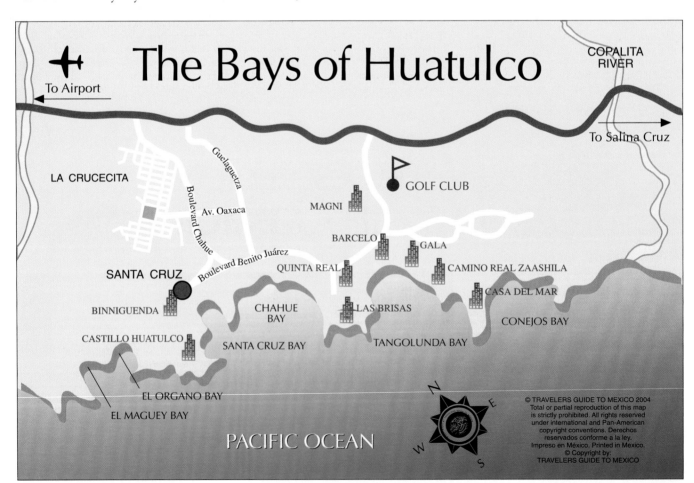

The Bays of Huatulco

COPALITA RIVER

To Airport

To Salina Cruz

LA CRUCECITA

Guelaguetza

Boulevard Chahue

Av. Oaxaca

GOLF CLUB

MAGNI

BARCELO

GALA

Boulevard Benito Juárez

SANTA CRUZ

QUINTA REAL

CAMINO REAL ZAASHILA

CASA DEL MAR

BINNIGUENDA

CHAHUE BAY

LAS BRISAS

CONEJOS BAY

CASTILLO HUATULCO

SANTA CRUZ BAY

TANGOLUNDA BAY

EL ORGANO BAY

EL MAGUEY BAY

PACIFIC OCEAN

Huatulco

Nine Bays to Explore

Verdant hills surround
Huatulco's secluded bays

Fonatur

Huatulco is one of Mexico's newer and more exclusive resort developments. Few people are familiar with its name and even fewer have visited its pristine shores, making the resort a kind of semiprivate playground for those who vacation there.

Located at the very southern tip of the country's Pacific coast, 180 miles south of Oaxaca city, Huatulco covers a 22 mile stretch of coastline carved into nine beautiful bays. The Sierra Madre Mountains provide a verdant backdrop to about 30 crescent-shaped beaches lapped by crystalline blue-green waters. Because of the hilly terrain, many of the beaches are accessible only by boat.

In 1983, a government tourism development agency, called Fonatur, picked this isolated wilderness to become Mexico's next Cancun or Ixtapa, both Fonatur creations. As part of a three-stage development plan, five-star and luxury hotels, and an 18-hole golf course were built on Tangolunda Bay, site of the hotel zone. Three and four star hotels, a marina for excursion boats, and locales for shops and restaurants were constructed on Santa Cruz Bay. A town designed to capture the flavor of a typical Mexican village was also built, becoming the urban center for local resi-

dents. La Crucecita's town square boasts an old-fashioned bandstand, creating an aura of timelessness.

An 8,850-foot jet airfield with palm-thatched terminals was built 12 miles north of the bay area. While the airfield caused some controversy when reports surfaced that the landing strip was built on an ancient Zapotec archaeological site, the palm-fringed *palapas* were approved all around for blending in nicely with the tropical surroundings. Two-thirds of the land has been set aside for conservation and building restrictions have kept the hotel zone looking somewhat harmonious with low-lying constructions painted in muted colors or earth tones.

About 60,000 national and international tourists visited Huatulco during its first year as a resort, in 1989. There are now slightly more than 2,000 hotel rooms in establishments ranging from luxurious properties on Tangolunda Bay to smaller, less expensive hotels in La Crucecita, Santa Cruz and Chahue. The goal is to build 16,000 rooms by the year 2018.

In anticipation of a steadily increasing number of tourists, the airport's national and international terminals were recently expanded and baggage carrousels installed. The expand-

able airstrips already accommodate 757s.

Due to the rising number of cruise ship arrivals, a new dock has opened in Santa Cruz Bay that can handle two 3,000-passenger cruise ships at a time. The dock is expected to give the slow-growing Pacific coast resort a shot in the arm, as shops, restaurants and other businesses open to cater to passengers. Other attractions under development include an "eco-archeological" park called Punta Celeste and the Museo del Mar.

The average year-round temperature is 85°F, with a wintertime low of 57 and a high of 100 during the summer months. Showers cool temperatures during the rainy season, from July to October.

If you seek pristine natural surroundings along with the comforts of world-class accommodations, then Huatulco is the place for you. Enjoy the exclusivity while you can. The infrastructure for Stage I, which encompasses Tangolunda, Chahue and Santa Cruz bays, is nearly complete. Stage II will open up a fourth bay, Conejos, to development.

What to See and Do

Huatulco's greatest attractions are the bays

Santa Cruz Marina

Fonatur

themselves—Conejos, Tangolunda, Chahue, Santa Cruz, El Organo, El Maguey, Cacaluta, Chachacual and San Agustin. Most harbor isolated beaches with soft sand and clear azure water thriving with marine life and unblemished by pollution. The air is fresh and scented with the sweet-spicy smell of tropical foliage.

Exploring the bays, each with its own unique natural beauty, is the favorite pastime.

Several bays are accessible only by sea. Independent entrepreneurs at the marina in Santa Cruz or on the beach in front of the hotels offer to take you there in *lanchas* (small, open boats), but it is safest to make arrange-

ments through a travel agency. You can book a boat for the day (captain included) and set your own itinerary, or join a group tour.

There are five- and seven-bay tours which include stopping for snorkeling, swimming and sunbathing at one or two of the bays, respectively. Your tour will invariably head out on one of three seagoing vessels: the deluxe *Tequila* and *Fiesta Huatulco*, both catamarans, or the *Zorro* speedboat. Ask for either of the first two if you prefer to take in the bays at a leisurely pace. The Zorro zips around at a fairly fast speed, hitting the waves of the open sea head on.

If you opt to visit the bays on your own, remember that snorkelers prefer the waters of *Playa la Entrega*, a protected marine park on Santa Cruz Bay. Opposite the beach, a 640-foot-long, 112-foot-wide coral reef creates a natural aquarium harboring more than 700 types of colorful fish and other sea life. Gear can be rented from a small concession stand.

The guided tours take passengers to beautiful *El Maguey* and *San Agustin*, as well as La Entrega, for snorkeling.

Favorite scuba diving spots are the reefs off Cacaluta and *La Montosa* islands, *Bufadero*, where there's a sunken ship, *Los Duendes* and *El Tigre*, areas typical of the Pacific, where the big fish swim among large rock formations.

Buceo Sotavento (581-0051) is a highly recommended scuba diving outfit for instruction and equipment. Reservations can also be made through in-house travel agencies at all major hotels.

Visitors can take in the bays and surround-

ing jungle by mountain biking, horseback riding, or driving the more popular all-terrain vehicles (ATVs). There are even guided walking tours through lush coffee plantations that dot the mountainside. English pirates are credited with first bringing coffee plants to the region, but it was the Germans who turned coffee into an industry in Mexico. The tours offer an opportunity to enjoy the scenery—coffee plants flourish under the shade of banana, lemon and avocado trees—learn about coffee production, and sample the quality.

Huatulco offers water sports fans a variety of activities, from deep-sea fishing to kayaking. Most hotels have water sports desks offering wave runners, banana boats and kayaks.

The Camino Real Zaashila and Quinta Real hotels have excellent tennis facilities. There's golf at the 18-hole public course inaugurated in Tangolunda in 1991, reputedly the most beautiful public course in the country.

Two rivers in the region, the Copalita and Zimatan, provide white-water rafting opportunities ranging from a Class I degree of difficulty to a Class V. Rafting company *Piraguas Aventuras* (587-1333) offers the gamut, including a leisurely trip down river that's fun for the whole family, from the six- to 60-year-olds.

A popular day trip from Huatulco is a visit to the turtle center at *Mazunte*. Derived from an Indian phrase meaning "I ask you to please

Deluxe hotels line Tangolunda Bay

lay eggs," Mazunte was the site of a sea turtle slaughterhouse near La Escobilla, Mexico's principal nesting beach for the endangered Olive Ridley. It was converted into a research and conservation center after laws were passed to protect the marine species. Escobilla is closed to the public, but visitors can see most of the world's variety of marine turtles at Mazunte's aquarium.

A trip to Mazunte can include a visit to a nearby cosmetics plant that serves as an example of an alternative, sustainable source of income for locals previously employed in the turtle trade. The small cooperative uses only natural ingredients, like avocado, beeswax and palm oil, to make its line of four basic products, called Mazunte, and they are available at a variety of shops in Mexico, including The

Body Shop.

Travelers can visit the state's other popular but more bohemian seaside resort, Puerto Escondido, or take a half-hour flight to the colonial city of Oaxaca aboard local carrier Aerotucan's 14-seater planes.

Dining

Popular spots in La Crucecita for Oaxacan fare include *Don Wilo* and *El Sabor de Oaxaca.* For sumptuous Italian cuisine try *Il Giardino del Papa,* owned by Mario Saggese, who has cooked for the Pope. *Oasis I* is known for its sushi, *Oasis II* for its grilled meats, and *Cactus* for its seafood specialties.

On the beach in Santa Cruz are several restaurants serving fresh seafood and two-pound lobsters, the favored local dish, accompanied by a *michelada,* the favored local drink, made of beer and lime juice on the rocks, served in a frosty salt-rimmed glass. Two of the most popular spots are *Doña Celia* and *Ve-el-Mar.*

Somewhat hidden from view, Celia's is a simple waterfront eatery that has garnered a loyal clientele with its fish and seafood specialties. Try the lobster *a la Doña,* served with beans and wrapped in flour tortillas, or the *Acapulqueña,* shrimp and octopus fried in olive oil, chopped green chilis and onions. Open for breakfast, lunch and dinner.

Leading restaurants in Tangolunda include Quinta Real's *Las Cupulas,* featuring fine international and regional specialties accompanied by a spectacular view of the bay (7 to 11 a.m. and 7 to 11 p.m.); Camino Real Zaashila's *Azul Profundo,* serving Mexican-Thai cuisine in elegant surroundings (6:30 to 11 p.m.); and Barcelo's *Don Quijote,* offering gourmet specialties, a cozy lounge and live piano music (7 to 11 p.m.).

The Barcelo also hosts dinner-shows with different themes, from a Broadway musical to a Fiesta Mexicana with mariachi and marimba music, folk dancing and games.

A good restaurant along the hotel strip in Tangolunda is *Don Porfirio,* which is especially popular for its bar scene. Around the corner, *Noches Oaxaqueñas,* or Oaxacan Nights, offers a mini version of the Guelaguetza, Oaxaca's famous festival of folk dancing, plus traditional Mexican cooking. For information or reservations call 581-0001, or consult your travel agent.

At the main kiosk in Santa Cruz, you can enjoy a cappuccino or espresso at *Café Huatulco,* which serves brew from beans grown regionally, as well as delicious pastries.

Nightlife

Until recently, the most action you were likely to see after sunset was the sand crabs skittering on the beach, but that has changed—a little. *La Crema* is the happening bar in town. If you're in the mood for dancing, there's *La Papaya* disco-bar on Chahue Beach.

The *Bitza* bar at the Camino Real Zaashila offers an attractive lounge and exotic tropical drinks (5 p.m. to midnight) while the Quinta Real's *Las Cupulas* terrace bar has live music Thursday to Saturday in a lovely setting with a wonderful bay view. For a taste of Mexico, try the Barcelo's El Jorongo bar, an old-style cantina featuring live entertainment and cocktails till 2 a.m.

Shopping

The *Museo de Artesania,* a block from La Crucecita's main square, on Flamboyan, is a museum of handicrafts, store and workshop, all in one. You can see artisans creating traditional Oaxacan arts and crafts, including woven rugs, *alebrijes,* or fantasy creatures carved out of wood, black pottery and other items.

There's a pleasant arts and crafts market in La Crucecita with a variety of *alebrijes,* as well as leather and woven goods. A more run of the mill market is located in Santa Cruz.

Several shops in *Plaza Oaxaca,* a string of stores lining the square in La Crucecita, carry good selections of handmade items, as well as books and magazines, and beach wear.

Major hotels usually have a boutique or two with a good selection of folk art, apparel or souvenirs.

Hotels

In addition to a wide range of hotels, an increasing number of bed-and-breakfasts, private villas and homes offer accommodations, including *Villa Azomalli* (co-owned and managed by Chicagoan Tony Palos (tel. (312) 226-7639) and *Villa Fa-Sol,* a nine-room retreat in a residential zone (tel. 581-0283).

Barcelo Beach Resort
On Tangolunda Bay
Tel. (958) 581-0055
www.barcelo.com
A great beach setting makes this six-story all-inclusive complex a popular resort. There are 344 comfortable oceanview rooms and suites with cable TV. Gardens, a la carte and buffet dining, cantina, lobby/piano bar, gym with steam room, sauna, massages, enormous swimming pools and children's pool, child care center, four tennis courts, 24-hour room service, convention facilities for up to 800 people. Rates FC (all inclusive).

Camino Real Zaashila
On Tangolunda Bay
Tel. (958) 581-0460
www.caminoreal.com
This beautiful beachfront resort on Playa Rincon Sabroso blends Santa Fe and Mediterranean-style architecture, with whitewashed walls, bright color accents, and wood beams shading private balconies. Guests enjoy access to a gorgeous expanse of secluded beach. There are 120 spacious rooms and suites (41 with private pools), award-winning cuisine, poolside snack bar, small meeting rooms, tennis court, and a beautiful 270-foot freeform swimming pool. Rates DX.

Casa del Mar
Balcones de Tangolunda 13
Tel. (958) 581-0102
Set on a bluff overlooking beautiful Tangolunda Bay, this attractive and intimate hotel features a spectacular panoramic view. Just 25 suites with spacious terraces and ocean views, large baths, cable TV, VCR. Lovely pool, restaurant, small meeting room. Free shuttle to beaches. Rates MD.

Flamboyant
Gardenia and Tamarindo
Tel. (958) 587-0113
www.flamboyant.com.mx
On the main square in La Crucecita. A congenial colonial-style hotel with 100 tastefully appointed rooms and four master suites with ac, color TV. Pool, delightful gardens, restaurant, beach club (with free transportation). Rates ECON.

Las Brisas
On Tangolunda Bay
Tel./Fax (958) 583-0200
www.brisas.com.mx
On a peninsula of its very own, with three beautiful private beaches, this former Club Med property is now under new management. Extensive remodelling features 338 newly-expanded rooms and suites with wonderful views of the ocean, three swimming pools, 12 tennis courts, spa, gym, conference facilities for 1,000, specialty restaurants, bar. Rates DX.

Marina
Tehuantepec 112
Tel. (958) 587-0963
www.hotelmarinaresort.com
On Santa Cruz Bay. A modest but tasteful Mediterranean-style hotel just steps from the marina, with 50 attractive guest rooms, each with a private balcony, some overlooking the bay, jacuzzi, kitchenette and satellite TV. Small pools, private beach club. Grill restaurant and snack bar. Rates MD.

Posada Chahue
Mixie and Mixteco
Tel. (958) 587-0945
This Best Western hotel a block from Chahue Beach offers a good budget option, with 21 clean and comfortable rooms with a/c, color TV, coffee service. Pool, delightful gardens, good restaurant, beach club just 300 meters away (with free transportation). Rates ECON.

Quinta Real
On Tangolunda Bay
Tel. (958) 581-0428
www.quintareal.com
This sophisticated tropical retreat features a great view of the bay and stunning moonlit evenings from its privileged hilltop location. There are 28 attractive suites with jacuzzi, including a two-bedroom presidential suite, overlooking the bay; some with private plunge pool and sun deck, some with telescope for stargazing. Excellent gourmet dining, breezy terrace bar. Beach club with two swimming pools, restaurant-bar. Tennis court. Palm-thatched palapa for hosting special events for up to 60 guests. Member of Mexico Boutique Hotels. Rates DX.

TRAVELERS GUIDE TO
Guadalajara

*The "Pearl of the West" is a modern city
that still retains much of her colonial charm.*

Guadalajara General

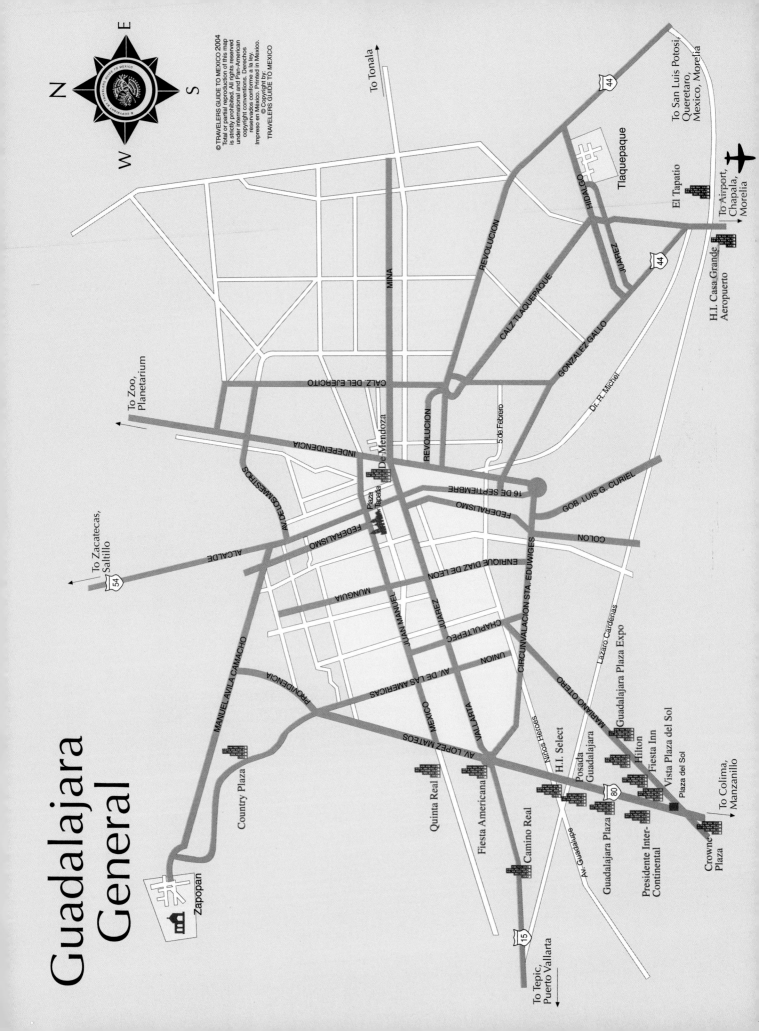

N E W S

To Tonala

To San Luis Potosi,
Queretaro,
Mexico, Morelia

44

Tlaquepaque

Hidalgo

El Tapatio

To Airport,
Chapala, Morelia

Juarez

44

H.I. Casa Grande
Aeropuerto

Revolucion

Calz Tlaquepaque

Gonzalez Gallo

Dr. R. Michel

To Zoo,
Planetarium

Mina

5 de Febrero

Calz. del Ejercito

Independencia

De Mendoza

Revolucion

Av. de los Maestros

Plaza
Tapatia

Federalismo

16 de Septiembre

Federalismo

Gob. Luis G. Curiel

To Zacatecas,
Saltillo

54

Alcalde

Colon

Enrique Diaz de Leon

Munguia

Circunvalacion Sta. Eduwiges

Juan Manuel

Juarez

Chapultepec

Lazaro Cardenas

Guadalajara Plaza Expo

Providencia

Manuel Avila Camacho

Union

Av. de las Americas

Mexico

Vallarta

Av. Lopez Mateos

Mariano Otero

Niños Heroes

H.I. Select

Posada
Guadalajara

Hilton

Fiesta Inn

Vista Plaza del Sol

Plaza del Sol

Country Plaza

Quinta Real

Fiesta Americana

Camino Real

Av. Guadalupe

80

Guadalajara Plaza

Presidente Inter-
Continental

To Colima,
Manzanillo

Crowne
Plaza

Zapopan

15

To Tepic,
Puerto Vallarta

What to See and Do

Parks, Churches, Markets, Murals and More

The capital of Jalisco state and Mexico's second largest city, Guadalajara is one of the most serenely beautiful and stately urban centers in North America. Blessed with an ideal climate and a location convenient to much of what Mexico has to offer, Guadalajara and its surroundings have attracted many American and Canadian expatriates.

"The Pearl of the West," as she's known, is a modern city of some five million people that still retains much of her colonial charm. Her rich heritage dates back to 1542 and is evident throughout the city. Amid skyscrapers, residential suburbs, golf and country clubs, are colonial mansions and lovely old churches.

Unlike Mexico City, where the Aztec civilization flourished, Guadalajara was wilderness when the Spanish arrived. Following the destruction of Moctezuma's Aztec empire, Hernan Cortes sent Nuño Beltran de Guzman in 1542 to conquer the lands to the west. Conquer he did, but only after a long and bloody campaign. It was not until 1551 that the Spaniards considered the area secure. Then the province of Nueva Galicia established Guadalajara, named after the Moorish city in Spain, as its capital.

For centuries Guadalajara languished in self-contentment. History, for the most part, passed her by, as evidenced by the lack of historical sites. Late in the 1920s, things began to change when the Southern Pacific Railroad extended its tracks southward from California to Jalisco. But what looked like a boom turned into a bust with the arrival of the Great Depression. The Southern Pacific never did as well as was hoped, and after 30 years sold its holdings to the Mexican government.

The sale of the railroad marked a major turning point for Guadalajara. The city decided to rebuild, without sacrificing its charm. It succeeded—today's metropolis, resembling modern U.S. cities, is the envy of much of the rest of Mexico.

Traditionally, Guadalajara has thrived on agriculture. It lies in Mexico's breadbasket, and grapes, melons, strawberries, bananas, coconuts, *jicama*, vegetables and grains grow abundantly.

The city is an industrial center as well, with first-class facilities for business travelers. The Expo Guadalajara exhibition center hosts many national and international trade fairs. The Guadalajara-Mexico City superhighway, which cut driving time to about four hours, linked the two major city's as never before.

Many U.S. and Canadian citizens have chosen to retire in Guadalajara and nearby Chapala, where there are English-language church services and clubs. The city also has two good medical schools and excellent hospitals with bilingual staff.

A weekly English language newspaper, *The Colony Reporter*, keeps residents and visitors up-to-date on happenings in Mexico and specifically Guadalajara, Chapala and the nearby resort of Puerto Vallarta.

Getting Around

Seven-block-long *Plaza Tapatia*—a stroller's paradise of colonial architecture, fountains, ancient and modern sculpture, and museums—dominates Guadalajara's Historic Center. At the west end of Plaza Tapatia is the "first block" of the city, which includes the very spot where the city was founded in the 16th century, the cathedral and four plazas juxtaposed to form a cross. Most of Guadalajara's great colonial buildings face these plazas.

In front of the cathedral is *Plaza Guadalajara.*

Teatro Degollado

Packed with laurel trees, for which it was previously named, it boasts a fountain with the Jalisco state seal, as Guadalajara is the state's capital.

The southern arm of the cross is *Plaza de Armas,* with its Victorian kiosk of lacy wrought iron, where locals gather for band concerts Thursday and Sunday evenings.

The eastern park behind the cathedral is *Plaza de la Liberacion,* dedicated to the heroes of Mexican independence. In the center of the plaza is a statue of Hidalgo, father of the independence movement. At both ends are beautiful fountains, and the entire plaza is bordered with flowers.

To the north is *Plaza de la Rotonda.* The center of this handsome square contains a circular group of columns set in a garden honoring illustrious Jaliscans. A series of life-size statues in bronze skirt the park.

All of these plazas are especially beautiful in April and May when the purple jacaranda trees shed their blue haze over the sidewalks and mingle with the flame-colored blooms of the poincianas.

The *Department of Tourism* is located in a beautiful 18th-century building at Morelos 102 (tel. 3613-0306). You can get maps and information about walking tours in English.

The Cathedral

Dominating the main plaza is the cathedral, Guadalajara's landmark. Begun in 1571 and completed nearly half a century later, the cathedral's half dozen architectural styles—including Gothic, Tuscan, Moorish and Corinthian—set it apart from other Mexican churches.

When its twin towers, 200 feet high, were toppled by an earthquake in the early 19th century, they were rebuilt in Byzantine style. Inside are 30 handsome columns leading to an altar designed in Italy. In all there are 11 altars, and in the sacristy hangs a masterpiece by the Spanish painter Murillo, the "Assumption of the Virgin." Many art treasures here were sent by a grateful King Ferdinand in appreciation for funds the city sent to Spain during the Napoleonic Wars.

Across the way is the *Government Palace,* office of the Governor of Jalisco. Dating from 1643, it is by far the most historic structure in Guadalajara. It was here in 1810 that the leader of Mexico's War of Independence, Father Miguel Hidalgo, decreed an end to slavery. And it was here in 1858, during the War of Reform, that Mexico's best-loved president, Benito Juarez, managed to escape assassination. The building is noted for its Jose Clemente Orozco murals depicting Hidalgo's heroic struggle.

Orozco

Orozco (1883-1949), who ranks as one of the greatest figures of modern Mexican art, along with Diego Rivera and David Alfaro Siqueiros, did much of his work in Guadalajara. He is perhaps the city's most famous son and a name you are likely to hear. His works hang in some of the world's finest museums, while his murals grace such places as Dartmouth College and the New School for Social Research in New York City.

In many ways, he owes his fame to an American woman, Alma Reed, who introduced him to U.S. art circles. It was really only after Orozco had been accepted in the United States that many Mexicans were willing to recognize his greatness.

At the *Casa Museo Jose Clemente Orozco,* the artist's former home, one can view his progression from a standard painter to a driving, powerful political force in art. The museum is located at Aurelio Aceves 27, and open Tuesday to Sunday, 10 a.m. to 2 p.m. Tel. 3616-8329.

Cabañas Cultural Center

The best known and most dramatic of Orozco's murals, including the world-famous "The Man of Fire," line the chapel of the former Hospicio Cabañas orphanage (between Republica and Miguel Allende streets), now converted into the *Instituto Cultural Cabañas.* Orozco's bold murals contrast vividly with the stark colonial architecture of the chapel; there's also a permanent exposition of his complete art works in originals and reproductions.

The orphanage itself is a remarkable structure consisting of 26 flower-filled patios linked by tile passages. Dating from the mid-1700s, it is a perfect example of neoclassical architecture and has witnessed much of Jalisco's history. The institute is open Tuesday to Saturday, 10:15 a.m. to 6 p.m.; Sunday to 3 p.m. Tel. 3614-4440.

The plaza outside the Cabañas Institute features wonderfully surreal bronze sculptures by Guadalajara native Alejandro Colunga, whose work also graces Puerto Vallarta's boardwalk. Resembling a living room set that Lewis Carroll would be proud of, Colunga's chairs, table and sofa have eyes, ears and feet, giving the impression they assembled there of their own accord and could at any time get up and walk away.

Museums

The *Regional Museum of Anthropology and History* at Liceo and Hidalgo streets, down the street from the Government Palace, is well worth a visit. You can spend hours browsing through the many rooms and admiring the religious art, pre-Columbian artifacts, colonial paintings (including some early works by Diego Rivera), colonial furniture, portraits of gov-

Trompo Magico children's museum

ernors, emperors, queens and notables, pottery, handicrafts, ethnography of the Huichol and Cora Indians, and more. In the last patios are the ornate carriage used by the ill-fated Emperor Maximilian and the more austere black carriage used by Benito Juarez. Open Tuesday to Saturday, 9 a.m. to 5:45 p.m.; to 5 p.m. Sunday. Tel. 3614-9957.

For an interesting glimpse into the lifestyle of one of Mexico's contemporary presidents (1976-1982), visit the *Casa Museo Lopez Portillo,* on Liceo just two blocks north of the cathedral. This mansion, once the former president's family home, houses an impressive collection of 18th- and 19th-century antiques, including a grand piano brought from Austria as a gift to Maximilian. Open Tuesday to Sunday, 10 a.m. to 6 p.m. Tel. 3613-2411.

The *Museum of the City of Guadalajara,* housed in a stately colonial building that once served as a Capuchin monastery, showcases Guadalajara's history, urban development, customs, art and traditions from pre-Hispanic times through the 20th century. The museum is located at Independencia 684, corner of Mariano Barcenas, and is open Wednesday to Saturday, 10 a.m. to 5:30 p.m.; to 2:30 p.m. Sunday. Tel. 3658-3706.

The *Museum of Folk Art,* at San Felipe and Pino Suarez, displays a small but interesting collection of handcrafted objects, ranging from embroidered saddles to pottery, in a lovely converted home. The tiny gift shop has some colorful items. Open Tuesday to Saturday, 10 a.m. to 8 p.m., Sunday to 4 p.m.

At Morelos 217, between Maestranza and Degollado, is Guadalajara's *Wax Museum.* Opened in 1994, it displays the figures of 120 prominent individuals, including Hernan Cortes, Emperor Cuauhtemoc, Cantinflas, Madonna and Bill Clinton.

In the nearby suburb of Zapopan, in a side room of the basilica, the tiny *Huichol Museum* is devoted exclusively to colorful and fanciful yarn "paintings," woven goods, embroidery, and intricate bead work by the Huichol and Cora Indians of Jalisco state. Open daily, 9:30 a.m. to 1:30 p.m. and 3 to 6 p.m. Tel. 3636-4430.

The *Zapopan Art Museum,* at 20 de Noviembre 166, features rotating exhibits of works by international artists and a room dedicated to the art of photography.

Also in Zapopan is *Trompo Magico,* a popular interactive science museum with fun touch-and-do exhibits on the universe, earth sciences, the human body, computing and more. Open 9 a.m. to 1 p.m. and 2 to 6 p.m.; weekends and holidays open 10 a.m. to 3 p.m. and 3:30 to 8:30 p.m.; closed Mondays. Tel. 3836-0555.

Degollado Theater

This theater on Plaza de la Liberacion is home to the Jalisco Philharmonic Orchestra and the center of the city's cultural activities. Operas and concerts are presented here, and visiting musicians perform throughout the year. More than two centuries old, the building is a perfect example of pure Grecian revival architecture.

The theater itself is an architectural masterpiece and has been compared to La Scala in Milan. The entrance is lighted by crystal chandeliers, and the center dome, also lighted by crystal chandeliers, is a mural of the fourth part of Dante's "Inferno." Its five tiers are trimmed in rich red and gold leaf.

Unless it's in the United States or Europe for a command performance, the *Ballet Folklorico* of the University of Guadalajara should be a "command attendance" for you. It's a colorful and thrilling presentation of the songs and dances of Mexico, Sundays at 10 a.m. at the Degollado. For reservations, call 3614-4773.

A Ballet Folklorico is also hosted by the Instituto Cultural Cabañas Wednesdays at 8:30 p.m. The Cabañas troupe has performed for international audiences in Tokyo, Havana and Guanajuato's Cervantino Festival. Tel. 3618-8135.

Parks

In this city of parks, the largest is *Parque Agua Azul* at Gonzalez Gallo and Independencia. It boasts an orchid house, aviary, butterfly sanctuary housing 160 varieties, acoustic shell seating 9,000, and the state-run *Casa de las Artesanias* (House of Handicrafts).

Alcalde Park, one block from Avenida Alcalde, between Los Maestros and Jesus Garcia streets, has a lake where local residents go boating.

Seven miles from the center of the city is *Oblatos Canyon*, where you can gaze for miles in any direction from its summit and see papayas, mangoes, *zapotes* and other tropical fruit at its lower elevations.

Huentitan Park has a fabulous zoo where sculptor Sergio Bustamante's fantastic animal figures mingle with live monkeys, elephants and giraffes. The real animals are protected by moats instead of bars and mini-trains take tourists around the grounds. The zoo is open Wednesday to Sunday, 10 a.m. to 6 p.m.

Libertad Market

This market at Calzada Independencia and Juarez is reputedly the biggest public market in the Western Hemisphere. In addition to aisles of scrubbed and artistically-arranged fruits and vegetables, fish and meat stands, and food and flower stalls, there's a great variety of shoes, toys, clothes for children, lamps, onyx, and acres of sombreros. It's a great place to buy leather goods, unpainted chairs, stools and big flower pots.

Plaza de los Mariachis at Calzada Independencia and Obregon, south of Libertad Market, is the place to relax in the afternoon and listen to the various bands taking requests. You can sit at tables and order refreshments.

Churches

Santa Monica Church, on the street of the same name between Reforma and San Felipe, in an authentic colonial neighborhood, is one of the finest examples of early 18th-century Mexican baroque, with a breathtaking facade of carved stone.

The church of the *Santuario*, on Avenida Alcalde, is dedicated to Mexico's Virgin of Guadalupe. Its interior is beautiful and worth seeing.

The *Gothic Expiatorio Church*, just behind the University of Guadalajara, on Tolsa and Madero streets, is fun at noon or at six in the evening when the clock in the steeple presents the 12 disciples marching forth.

Located at Corona and Prisciliano Sanchez streets, next to lovely San Francisco Park, *Templo de San Francisco de Asis* is a colonial

monument of great beauty. It dates from the first years of the conquest and was finished in 1684. The facade is plateresque with many ornamental details.

Across the street is the ancient church of *Our Lady of Aranzazu*, notable for the contrast between its churrigueresque altar and severe exterior.

A very small Gothic-style church located on Hospital Street, between Calzada Independencia and Alcalde, merits a visit. Take a close look at the carved figures on the facade—these celestial musicians are mariachis!

The *Basilica of the Virgin of Zapopan*, home of

Plaza Tapatia

Mexico Tourism Board

the "little virgin," is located in a large suburb in the northwest end of town. The church itself is imposing, with two towers elaborately adorned in the plateresque manner. The interior is decorated in the blue and white colors of Our Lady of Zapopan, who is the patroness of Guadalajara and offers protection against storms and plagues. The Virgin, which measures only 13 inches from head to toe, was donated to the local Indians by a Franciscan missionary in 1542 and now stands above the altar, the object of many pilgrimages.

Each year there is a great celebration when the "little one" returns home on October 12 from her yearly trek to all the churches in the diocese. Accompanying her, strolling, dancing or riding the nearly five miles from the cathedral to Zapopan, on Avenida Avila Camacho, are some 400,000 of her faithful adherents.

For a week after, Indian dancers perform twice daily in the courtyard of the basilica.

The renovated *Ex-Convento del Carmen*, at Juarez 638, is the site of continuous art and cultural exhibits, along with concerts, plays and poetry readings. You can buy tickets here for performances of the Jalisco Philharmonic Orchestra through Conciertos Guadalajara. Tel. 3613-2024.

Tlaquepaque

This suburb of Guadalajara, just five miles from the downtown area, is probably Mexico's largest and most important arts and crafts center, offering a wide variety of ceramics, blown glass, colonial-style furniture, and the uniquely Mexican leatherbound chairs, sofas and tables called *equipales*.

Once a town in its own right, Tlaquepaque still retains its unique character. It's a bit of Mexico of yore, of cobbled streets and quaint plazas with tiny outdoor cafes tucked under the arcades.

Today its number and variety of shops seem limitless, but it all started with glass factories. At Contreras Medellin 173, opposite El Refugio Cultural Center, is a small glass factory (3657-5775), one of the few left in the village where you can still marvel at the traditional art of glass blowing. They put on quite a show, with master craftsmen dipping 10-foot-long tubes into a roaring furnace to pick up a red hot glob that they puff into a bubble, then whirl and tease into a tumbler, coffee cup or vase. El Refugio, at Donato Guerra 160, hosts cultural events throughout the year.

There are also potters in Tlaquepaque, many originally from the nearby town of Tonala, who were attracted to Tlaquepaque by the success of the glass blowers. In turn, the success of these potters attracted a new, modern breed of artisans, some of whom are Americans. Their earthenware products are of handsome, contemporary design. If you visit the factories, you can watch these experts shape clay at their wheels, then glaze and fire it.

The town next produced a generation of artists—perhaps inspired by the atmosphere of creativity they grew up in—and many of them have achieved international acclaim. The highly original works of Sergio Bustamante, Alex Mata Taylor, Rodolfo Padilla and others have been widely imitated but never surpassed. Other artists, such as Agustin Parra, have launched entirely new ranges of products, including baroque-style furniture and accessories, employing traditional techniques and successfully rescuing long-forgotten secrets of the trade.

Along with the artistic generation came professional dealers, whose interest turned the town into a collection of fascinating specialty shops. Among the biggest-selling items are silver, leather goods and antiques. You can find everything from gold-leaf mirrors to wrought-iron furniture and old-fashioned brass scales.

The shopping mecca of Tlaquepaque has everything from fine original craftsmanship to inexpensive, mass-produced imitations, from genuine antiques to superb reproductions, from one-of-a-kind works of art to curios and souvenirs.

The heart of Tlaquepaque is *El Parian*, a popular place to relax, have a cold drink and enjoy the passing scene. Mariachis stroll about playing guitars among the lovely Mexican-tiled arches. Both Tlaquepaque and the town of Cocula, also in the state of Jalisco, claim to be the original home of mariachis—guitar, violin and trumpet bands outfitted like *charros* (Mexican cowboys). Legend has it that these groups first became popular during the brief reign of Emperor Maximilian. The Austrian archduke was a great promoter of things Mexican, and there is nothing more Mexican than these troubadours. The emperor, so the story goes, had the bands play at wedding banquets in Mexico City's Chapultepec Castle, hence the name, from the French *mariage*. Most scholars of Mexican custom, however, believe the word is derived from one of the local indigenous languages.

One block from El Parian is the beautiful main plaza, *Jardin Hidalgo*, with handsome fountains and a kiosk. Concerts, mariachis and folkloric events are often presented here on Sunday afternoons, in the shadow of the parish church of San Pedro.

Most of the major stores are located along four blocks of Calle Independencia, which is closed to traffic. Calle Juarez, one block south, takes second place in terms of the number and quality of stores.

At Independencia 237 is the *Regional Museum of Ceramics* with its impressive collection of pottery, spanning more than a century, from the entire state of Jalisco. It also has a collection of miniature art. Open Tuesday to Saturday, 10 a.m. to 5:30 p.m., Sundays to 3 p.m.

Tonala

Not far from Tlaquepaque, and a 30-minute drive from downtown Guadalajara, is the thriving crafts center of Tonala. Many of the better craftsmen have factory-stores here and showrooms in Tlaquepaque, such as *Ken Edwards*, whose beautiful stoneware is made at Morelos 184.

Tonala's bustling Thursday and Sunday street markets are famous, attracting buyers from around Mexico and abroad. As many as 2,500 to 3,000 stalls line the main square and central streets with handicrafts and everyday goods. Prepare yourself for the huge crowds and heavy traffic.

For a more select range of local handicrafts, visit *Casa de los Artesanos,* which showcases the work of established artisans in everything from blown glass to hand-carved wood. Open 9 a.m. to 7 p.m.; to 3 p.m. weekends, at Tonaltecas 140.

At Constitucion 104 is the former home of renowned local potter Jorge Wilmot, whose prize-winning pieces are displayed in museums around the world. Appropriately, the building now houses the *National Ceramics Museum*. The *Tonala Museum of Archaeology and Popular Culture*, at Ramon Corona 73, also features ceramics, from pre-Hispanic artifacts to modern pieces.

Tequila

You can tour the haciendas of leading tequila distillers *Casa Cuervo* and *Sauza* in the town of Tequila. The Panoramex travel agency offers tours to Sauza Mondays, Wednesdays and Fridays (3810-5057/5005). You can also go on your own; tours of Sauza's agave plantation, production plant and 18th-century hacienda are offered Monday through Saturday, 9 a.m. to 2 p.m.

Tequila Herradura, another leading distiller, is based in Valle de Amatitan, located between Guadalajara and Tequila. Their splendid hacienda, San Jose del Refugio, offers guided visits Monday through Thursday and Saturday, at 9, 10 and 11 a.m. and noon. For more information, call 3613-9585 in Guadalajara, or (374) 745-0531 in Amatitan.

On Saturdays, you can take the *Tequila Express* to the Herradura distillery. The train tour includes (a lot of) tequila tasting on board, mariachi music, folkloric dancing and a typical regional meal. Operated by the Guadalajara Chamber of Commerce, the train departs from the station, at Washington and Independencia, at 11 a.m. and returns at about 8 p.m. For tickets, call 3880-9099.

The tequila plantations and distilleries make great side trips, and some of the haciendas will even let you host events there.

Golf

They say scarcely a day passes that you can't play golf in Guadalajara, and the number of courses in and around the city seems to prove that. Many of the courses can be played for a green fee and a letter of introduction or proof of membership from your home club.

The 18-hole *Guadalajara Country Club* is the oldest and a traditional favorite. But it has stiff competition now. *El Palomar Country Club* serves an upscale planned community located high above the city (golf packages are available that include lodging at the deluxe Quinta Real hotel). *Atlas*, *Santa Anita* and *Las Cañadas* are also among the leading golf clubs.

Lake Chapala

The area around Lake Chapala, one of Mexico's largest natural lakes, is home to one of the largest retirement colonies in North America. Many foreigners, mostly Americans and Canadians, have chosen to retire here and enjoy the warm days and cool nights along the shores of this 55-mile-long body of water.

According to historians, the first American came to the area in 1885, but it wasn't until 1955 that the larger influx of foreigners began. Now it is estimated more than 10,000 expatriates live on the north shore.

While garden and bridge clubs, golf courses and yacht clubs have proliferated, you can still see burros trailed by a dusty farmer wending their way through the narrow streets, adding to the Mexican atmosphere and charm of the lake shore.

Chapala is the focal point of the north shore. The western shore is home to charming Ajijic—which has the largest concentration of expatriates—as well as San Antonio Tlayacapan, San Juan Cosala and Jocotepec. San Nicolas is to the east.

After the dry month of May, the rainy season is welcomed. It lasts from mid-June to October and brings rains most afternoons. The following morning is usually warm and sunny. Even during the rainy season, temperatures are mild, but because the lake is 5,200 feet above sea level, you may need a sweater for cooler evenings.

Though Lake Chapala is credited for the area's verdant landscape and mild temperatures, it has been sadly neglected. For years, water has been steadily drawn off to help supply growing Guadalajara's insatiable thirst. Constant extraction coupled with climatic fluctuations, such as rainfall and evaporation, have shrunk the lake and threaten its survival.

Chapala

Chapala was founded in 1538 by Father Miguel de Bolonio, who converted the area's Coca Indians to Christianity. One of their chiefs was named Chapa, giving the town its name. In those days, the Indian children of Chapala were sent once every two weeks to the island of Mezcala, one of several islands on the lake, for religious instruction.

Among the town's landmarks are the Church of San Francisco, built in 1528 and reconstructed in 1580; the villa where British author D.H. Lawrence wrote his widely read "Plumed Serpent," now a gorgeous small inn at Zaragoza 307; and a converted mansion on the lakefront which once belonged to the Braniff family of aviation fame and today houses a leading restaurant, *Cazadores*. Lunch and dinner are served on the veranda or in the picturesque dining room furnished in early 20th-century period decor.

It's interesting to stroll along Chapala's waterfront. Beautiful views, well-maintained gardens and handicraft stalls vie for your attention. Perhaps the best known landmark on the waterfront is the *Beer Garden*, the largest restaurant-bar along the lake. It celebrated its 70th birthday in 1999. On Sunday afternoons you can see colorful mariachis—guitar and trumpet musicians dressed like *charros* (Mexican cowboys)—taking requests.

Chapala is proud of its charming plaza, on Madero Street, with its graceful bandstand. Behind the plaza, the municipal market features scrubbed vegetables and fruits, fish, chicken, flowers, hats, shoes, flowerpots—a little bit of everything. You'll be captivated by the mixture of colors and aromas.

Chula Vista Country Club, five minutes west of Chapala, has a sporty nine-hole golf course set into the mountains, and two tennis courts. It's well worth driving around the Chula Vista development to see the beautiful flowers, trees and spectacular homes, many with a view of the lake.

Below Chula Vista is the sleepy little village of San Antonio Tlayacapan, right out of a storybook with its church, town square and cobblestone streets. It is here that Dane Chandos (actually the pen name of two British authors) wrote the charming book "Village in the Sun," which brought many people to the area.

A more modern work offering insight into this region of Mexico is Tony Burton's "Western Mexico—A Traveller's Treasury" (Editorial Agata, 1994). The book is available in both English and Spanish in Mexico, or through www.sombrerobooks.com.

Near the highway in San Antonio Tlayacapan is *Lakeside Little Theater*, where productions in English are presented throughout the tourist season, and *PAL Trailer Park*, one of the finest such facilities in Mexico.

On the lake shore is the lovely *Real de Chapala Hotel* which hosts a Mexican Fiesta Sundays in its beautiful garden overlooking the lake, with folk dances, mariachis and a Mexican buffet.

Next door to Real de Chapala is Ajijic's *Club Nautico*, perhaps the only yacht club in the world to lie about half a mile from the waterline; a tractor pulls the boats out to the steadily shrinking lake.

Ajijic

The charming town of Ajijic, with its delightful hiccuping sound (ah-hee-HEEK), was founded by Nahua Indians under their chief Xitomatl in the early 1400s. Its cobblestone streets were laid during the days of Spanish rule. The town's *San Andres Church*, as well as its little chapel dedicated to the Virgen de Santiago, date to the 1500s, though the church was rebuilt in 1749.

Tucked behind many of the crumbling walls are the upscale homes of interesting foreigners, but not even the "gringo" invasion has done much to alter the tempo of Ajijic. The Mexicans who live here have managed to maintain their customs and ways.

Many people's favorite place to dine out is *La Nueva Posada*, on the lake shore, at Donato Guerra 9. Indoors or out, both food and service at this hotel are always excellent.

The *Lake Chapala Society,* an organization with the largest membership of expatriates in Jalisco, is at 16 de Septiembre 116-A. Run by volunteers, the society has a beautiful garden and one of the most extensive English-language libraries in Mexico. Tel. 766-1140.

Addresses in downtown Ajijic are very confusing since most streets change name at the center of town. The main street, which runs from the highway to the pier, is Colon, which becomes Morelos nearer the lake.

At Independencia 9-A is *Coleccion Barbara*, easily the best antique shop for miles around. Owner Tom Thompson is an authority on Oriental rugs. All kinds of marvelous objects fill

A fountain adorns downtown Chapala

Barba Editores

this store, including century-old examples of Mexican folk art. Tel. 766-1824.

Mi Mexico, at Morelos 8, is an interesting boutique and art gallery in one of the village's oldest homes. It has hand-woven wool wall hangings, carpets, hand-printed fabrics, designer dresses, sweaters, jewelry, wood carvings and gifts from all over Mexico. Tel. 766-0133.

Across the street, at Morelos 15, is the charmingly decorated *Cugini's Boutique and Gallery*. It features the unique clothing lines of Girasol, Tachi Castillo, Manos Mexicano and Dunes, as well as a wide selection of designer and ethnic jewelry, including creations by Lozano, Luisa Conti, El Angel and Carin. The Mexican folk art is representative of Chiapas, Oaxaca, Jalisco, Michoacan and Guanajuato. This is a fun place to explore and find unusual gift items. Owner Lois Cugini is helpful and informative, having travelled Mexico for the past 20 years. Tel. 766-1790.

At the intersection of Morelos and 16 de Septiembre is the *El Mexicano* gift shop, specializing in silver jewelry and items incorporating precious and semiprecious stones. Rene Alvarez, the owner, is very friendly and a licensed tour guide.

At 16 de Septiembre 4 is *Centro Artesanal La Vieja Posada*, housed in part of a former tequila-making hacienda that dates back 146 years. You'll find selected arts and crafts from all over Mexico, as well as delicately hand-painted colonial-style furniture and cool cotton clothing, wholesale or retail.

A few steps away, *La Taberna* in *El Meson de Don Miguel*, a restaurant and handicraft shop, offers live music several nights a week, from 8 to 11 p.m. Further down the street, at 16 de Septiembre 7, is the studio of *Enrique Velasquez* (766-0162), whose excellent watercolors and local scenes make original gifts for the folks back home. Next door is a collective gallery showcasing the talents of several local artists and always worth a visit.

West of Morelos, at Ocampo 30, is *Galeria Daniel Palma*. Palma, who was born in Ajijic, is gaining international renown for his wonderfully powerful kinetic animal sculptures made by combining natural stone, wood and iron. Open 10 a.m. to 6 p.m., except Monday. Tel. 766-1688.

On the Ajijic-Chapala highway, in La Floresta, next door to the Lakeside Auditorium, is the state-run *Casa de Las Artesanias*, offering regional handicrafts at fixed prices.

San Juan Cosala and Jocotepec

Ten minutes west of Ajijic is the small village of San Juan Cosala and its spa, famous for its thermal baths and spouting geyser.

Jocotepec is the village at the extreme western end of the lake. Its history traces back to 1361, when the Nahua Indians settled there. In 1520 a Spanish expedition led by a cousin of Hernan Cortes conquered the Indians, and in 1529 Jocotepec was founded. In years past, Jocotepec was a rest stop on the fifth day of the stagecoach journey from Mexico City to Guadalajara.

Jocotepec has rustic charm and is widely known for its beautifully woven serapes with traditional flower motifs. There are good selections of serapes and other local handicrafts at *Artesanias Rodriguez* (Hidalgo Sur 66).

At Hidalgo Sur 71 is *La Carreta* restaurant, which serves Mexican home-style barbecues in the patio of an ancient colonial home.

Only limited accommodation is available in Jocotepec but professional artists Georg and Phyllis Rauch welcome discerning bed-and-breakfast travelers to their mountainside home and studio which overlooks the town and lake. *Los Dos B&B* offers two suites and a three-level cottage in addition to the hospitality and regional insights of the Rauch's, who have lived in Mexico for more than 20 years. Tel. 763-0657.

Dining and Nightlife

Fiesta Americana Hotel

Guadalajara has a wide variety of good restaurants around town and at the leading hotels. One of the region's major culinary contributions is *birria*, goat or mutton flavored with chilies, then cooked, shredded and served in a tomato and beef broth with a sprinkle of chopped raw onions and cilantro. Other local specialties include *torta ahogada*, a crusty roll filled with beef and "drowned" in a chili sauce, and *jericalla*, a rich custard-like dessert.

Mexicans usually have their main meal in the middle of the day. After 2 p.m. restaurants are often crowded with businessmen enjoying long, leisurely lunches. At night, if you arrive before 8, you may find yourself alone. Locals don't get serious about dinner until 9. Some restaurants close early or remain closed Sundays, so call first.

Alfredo di Roma
Presidente InterContinental Hotel
Tel. 3678-1234
The Guadalajara branch of the Italian restaurant famed for its fettuccini Alfredo, prepared tableside with rich cream, light semolina noodles, and fresh parmesan cheese, not to mention gold cutlery. The dishes are complemented by an extensive selection of fine French wines and attentive service. Open 1 to 11:30 p.m.; to 5 p.m. Sunday.

Angus
Hilton Hotel
Tel. 3678-0505

A popular steak house serving fine cuts of beef in a refined setting. Open 1 p.m. to midnight. Closed Sunday.

Aquellos Tiempos
Camino Real Hotel
Tel. 3134-2424
Celebrating 40 years in business, this award-winning restaurant features gourmet fare served in an elegant turn-of-the-century setting. The cuisine ranges from refined Mexican dishes to international favorites. Try the duck breast in brandy and black cherry sauce, or snails flambéed in mezcal with chipotle chili butter. Periodic gastronomic festivals feature the cuisines of different countries with theme menus and guest chefs. Winner of the AAA Four Diamond Award. Live piano and saxophone. Open 7 to 11 a.m., 2 to 5 p.m. and 7 p.m. to midnight, except Sunday.

Chez Pierre
España 2095
Tel. 3615-2212
Near the Niños Heroes monument and municipal art gallery in Plaza del Arte. In business for more than 30 years, this theme restaurant is all about France. The house specialty is prime rib. Live piano music. Open 1 p.m. to 1 a.m., except Sunday.

El Sacromonte
Pedro Moreno 1398
Tel. 3825-5447
This elegant courtyard restaurant serves meat and fish specialties in style. The star lanterns hanging from the ceiling and live mariachi music lend a romantic air. Open 2 p.m. to midnight. Closed Sunday. Reservations recommended.

Genghis Khan
Portal Expo Guadalajara
Tel. 3671-0130
From the owners of the popular Santo Coyote restaurant comes this oasis inside the city's exposition center, offering an interesting and original setting, and the house specialty, charcoal-broiled lobster.

Habana
La Paz 2199
Tel. 3616-0096
From the 1951 Plymouth parked out front to the 1930s architecture with tiled floors and arches, the ambience is pure old Havana. Try the *tostones,* crispy tortillas made of fried plantains heaped with different toppings; shrimp fricassee; and a minty *mojito,* a favorite island drink that resembles lemonade made with rum and crushed mint leaves. Cuban cigars, including Cohiba, available. Musicians at lunch and dinner. Open 1 p.m. to 1 a.m.

Hacienda La Mentirosa
Jose Maria Vigil and Ruben Dario
Tel. 3642-3253
Enjoy fine cuts of beef surrounded by portraits of movie stars from Mexico's golden age of cinema.

Jacarandas
Crowne Plaza Hotel
Tel. 3634-1034
Great French-influenced Mexican and continental cuisine, plus a terrific view of the city. Live piano music. Open 7 to 12:30 a.m. Closed Sunday.

Kamilos 333
J. Clemente Orozco 333
Tel. 3825-7869
For lots of local flavor, try this traditional establishment that has been going strong since 1975. Brick walls and rustic wood furniture provide a cozy, country atmosphere. The menu features *carne en su jugo,* a regional specialty of shredded beef simmered in its own juice, and such classic trimmings as beans, guacamole and fresh-made tortillas. Also Mexican-style breakfasts. Open 8 to 1 a.m.

Karne Garibaldi
Garibaldi 1306
Tel. 3826-1286
Listed in the Guinness Book of World Records for its speedy service, this spot serves tasty, traditional *carne en su jugo,* shredded beef simmered in its own juice, in record time. So popular, three other branches have opened around town, including at Plaza Galerias, Plaza del Sol and Lopez Cotilla 433.

La Fonda de San Miguel
Donato Guerra 25, downtown
Tel. 3613-0809
A restored 17th-century former convent of the Barefoot Carmelites houses this attractive restaurant. The menu features a variety of *moles* and other traditional Mexican dishes perfected in convents over the centuries; the "manchamanteles" is said to be a recipe of Mexican poet-nun Sor Juana Ines de la Cruz. Other popular dishes: *chiles rellenos* (stuffed poblano peppers), and chicken breast in *huitlacoche* (corn truffle). Live music. Open 8:30 a.m. to midnight; to 6 p.m. Sunday and Monday.

La Hacienda
Fiesta Americana Hotel
Tel. 3825-3434
Traditional Mexican atmosphere, superb Mexican cuisine, as well as some marvelous original creations, are the bill of fare at this outstanding hotel. Special Sunday buffet with mariachis. Open for lunch and dinner.

La Huerta
Camino Real Hotel
Tel. 3134-2424
A pleasant, airy spot for tasty snacks and meals. An extensive daily breakfast buffet is available till noon, and a not-to-be-missed Sunday brunch served under the shade of huge trees in the lovely gardens. Mexican and international cuisine. Mariachi music and entertainment for the kids at Sunday brunch. Open 7 a.m. to midnight.

La Rinconada
Morelos 86, Plaza Tapatia
Tel. 3613-9914
Next to the tourism office. An elegant island of tranquillity in the center of the city. Mexican and international cuisine and a popular bar in a lovely colonial-style house and patio. Open 8 a.m. to 9:30 p.m.; to 6 p.m. Sunday.

La Tequila
Mexico 2916

Tel. 3640-3440
This restaurant and tequila museum features stained-glass panels in the upstairs bar that pay homage to popular brands, and 230 different varieties. Menu offers Mexican specialties. Don't miss the fried cheese with salsa verde and tequila soufflé with a vanilla sauce. Open 1 p.m. to 12:30 a.m.; to 6 p.m. Sunday.

Ma Come No
Las Americas 302
Tel. 3615-4952
This lovely Italian restaurant features creatively prepared dishes accompanied by bread baked fresh on the premises, including focaccia to drizzle with flavored olive oils. Good salad buffet with homemade dressings of mango and grapefruit. Desserts feature chocolate-filled ravioli, tiramisu, vanilla mousse with raspberry liqueur. Open for lunch and dinner.

Nude
Lopez Cotilla 1589
Tel. 3616-5248
This spectacular sister restaurant to Santo Coyote offers an equally memorable dining experience in a setting with dramatically high ceilings, a glass wall facade and, in a nod to its name, modern paintings of nudes. Highlights from the eclectic international menu include skewered shrimp in fine herbs and duck in tamarind sauce.

Pierrot
Justo Sierra 2355, corner of Aurelio Gallardo
Tel. 3630-2087
This elegant spot in a residential zone features outstanding French and continental specialties. The very agreeable ambiance is orchestrated by the attentive Pierre himself, who provides top quality cuisine at fair prices. Menu includes lamb, duck and mahi-mahi. The three-pepper fillet is very popular. Piano music. Open 1:30 p.m. to 1 a.m., except Sunday.

Quinta Real
Quinta Real Hotel
Tel. 3669-0600
Refined Mexican and international dishes served in a beautiful setting, elegant atmosphere. Lives up to its motto of serving "sophisticated food for sophisticated people." Also has some of the best breakfasts in town. Great Sunday buffet. Excellent service. Live classical music during lunch and dinner. Open 7 a.m. to midnight.

Recco
Libertad 1981
Tel. 3825-0724
In a restored colonial mansion near the U.S. consulate, this restaurant is named after a famous Italian town. The Italian cuisine is among the best of its kind in Mexico. The menu offers a variety of pastas and such specialties as chicken cacciatore, and beautifully prepared meat and fish dishes. Both the shrimp Casamona and steak *au poivre* are superb, as is the chicken Kiev. A luscious tiramisu with amaretto and a delicious homemade Sicilian cassata compete with the crepes Suzette for the per-

fect dessert. Good wine selection. Owner Luigi Capurro is a gracious host. Open 1 to 11 p.m.

Santo Coyote
Lerdo de Tejada 2379
Tel. 3616-8472
A stunning lantern-lit garden, and chic southwestern-style architecture and decor provide the setting for Mexican, regional and international specialties; the garden is especially lovely at dusk as lanterns wink on and lawn sculptures seem to come alive. Menu highlights include beef carpaccio in balsamic vinegar, Dijon mustard and red wine; Mixteca soup with bone marrow and zucchini blossoms; grilled chicken in tamarind sauce; and charbroiled beef and rib specialties. Popular bar area. Open 2 p.m. to 2 a.m.

Nightlife

Aquellos Tiempos
Camino Real Hotel
Tel. 3134-2424
Get a taste of Mexico at this fine cantina. Tequila, mezcal and Mexican snacks, as well as imported scotch, brandy and more. Closed Sunday.

Bar Lafitte
España 2095, above Chez Pierre restaurant
Tel. 3615-6645
Named for the infamous pirate; the decor is nautical. Live shows feature musicians, singers, comics and more. Open 7:30 p.m. to 3 a.m., except Sunday.

Barzelona
Las Americas 1462
Tel. 3817-4410
This small, trendy hangout is where Guadalajara's young elite meet. Music ranges from Mexican pop to American rock and the walls are decorated with celestial scenes. Reservations recommended. Cover charge.

Boseé
Patria 1600
Tel. 3848-9395
All the rage among the young set. Techno music. Cover charge: 80 pesos.

Caballo Negro
Fiesta Americana Hotel
Tel. 3825-3434
An English-style pub with shows, good music (featuring salsa) and a dance floor. Open 9 p.m. to 1 a.m. Happy Hour 9 to 10 p.m. Closed Sunday.

Casa Bariachi
Vallarta 2221
Tel. 3615-2706
The house of mariachi music. There's also a folkloric ballet. Open from 1 p.m.; shows from 3:30 p.m. Another branch at Vallarta 2308.

Hard Rock Cafe/Hard Rock Live
Centro Magno
Tel. 3616-4560
Wall-to-wall rock memorabilia and rock mu-

sic. Rock 'n' roll bands play mostly cover songs in the evenings. Open till 2 a.m.

La Bodeguita del Medio
Vallarta 2320, opposite Centro Magno
Tel. 3630-1620
This replica of the celebrated 1940s Havana nightclub offers Cuban food, music and ambiance. The walls are decked with legends and photos of celebrities who visited the original hangout, including Ernest Hemingway. Try their *mojito*, served with white rum and mint leaves. Cuban trios play afternoons and evenings. Open from 2 p.m.

La Diligencia
Camino Real Hotel
Tel. 3134-2424
Lovely turn-of-the-century decor, international entertainers, and live music featured Thursday to Saturday. Open 6 p.m. to 2 a.m., except Sunday.

La Maestranza
Maestranza 179, downtown
Tel. 3613-5878
More than 3,000 pieces of bullfighting memorabilia deck the walls of this trendy cantina with a lot of ambiance. A great place to have drinks and enjoy the scene: a young crowd, loud pop music. Try their special *yerbabuena* (mint) house cocktail. Open 1 p.m. to 2 a.m.

La Rondalla
Hilton Hotel
Tel. 3678-0505
The hotel lobby bar features live music and a tequila gallery serving an extensive variety of the national drink. Open 1 p.m. to midnight.

Memories
El Tapatio Hotel
Tel. 3635-6050
A chic candlelit disco featuring music from the 50s and 60s. Highlighted is the great view of the city. Open 8 p.m. to 2 a.m.

Nude
Lopez Cotilla 1589
Tel. 3616-5248
A spectacular setting for drinks, with an inviting circular bar area. Elegant top-floor disco to open soon.

Peña Cuicacalli
Niños Heroes 1988, corner of Chapultepec
Tel. 3825-4690
Live folk music from Mexico, Latin America and Spain. Tasty snacks, from tacos and nachos to sandwiches and stuffed baked potatoes. Drinks and liqueur-flavored coffees. Don't be surprised if the audience joins in a sing-along. Open nightly from 8 p.m.; from 7 p.m. Sunday.

Quinta Real
Quinta Real Hotel
Tel. 3615-0000
A beautifully decorated bar—elegant, comfortable, romantic. Live classical music and jazz. Open noon to midnight.

Where to Shop

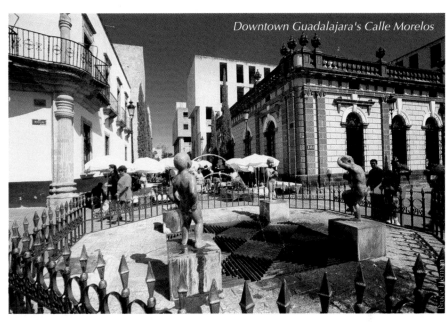

Downtown Guadalajara's Calle Morelos

For a real shopping treat, on Sundays only, visit the 200-year-old *Ex-Hacienda La Mora* in Zapopan. Its thick adobe walls and carved stone lintels provide the perfect backdrop for rustic handcrafted furniture, plus decorative ceramics, textiles, and more. A small restaurant on the premises serves authentic Mexican dishes under an ancient shade tree. Avenida Santa Margarita 606; we suggest you take a taxi. Open 9:30 a.m. to 6:30 p.m. Tel. 3633-7447.

Guadalajara's newest shopping center, *Centro Magno,* is a three-story complex built in neo-classical style. It features fine dining on the lower level, trendy shops on the second, a fast-food court and the city's largest movie complex (19 screens) on the last.

Other major shopping centers include *La Gran Plaza, Plaza del Sol, Plaza Galerias* and *Plaza Patria*. Guadalajara has two shopping centers dedicated entirely to footwear: *Shoe Forum* (Forum del Calzado) and *Shoe Gallery* (Galeria del Calzado), both located on Avenida Mexico.

Leave time to visit Tlaquepaque and Tonala, nearby towns where you'll find excellent selections of quality merchandise, right where it's made—blown glass, stoneware, hand-woven textiles, papier-mâché, furniture, antiques, and much more.

Most shops open from 10 a.m. to 8 p.m. daily, with an earlier closing, usually 4 p.m., on Sundays.

Guadalajara

Aplijsa
Fiesta Americana Hotel. Tel. 3615-6101

Plaza Universidad. Tel. 3610-1363
Airport (National Terminal). Tel. 3688-5669
For lovers of cultivated and natural pearls, diamonds, opals and other fine gems and jewelry, these are superb spots. They manufacture their products, and sell wholesale and retail. If jewelry is your business, be sure to stop here. The airport branch is ideal for last-minute buys. Branches in Mexico City and Monterrey.

Bazar Hecht
Garibaldi 1215
Tel. 3826-7923

Well-known in Tlaquepaque, Armando Hecht has this showroom of antiques, collectibles and furniture in Guadalajara. You never know what you might find and you certainly won't find better anywhere in the region. A pleasure for the browser and a delight for the connoisseur.

BordArte
Circunvalacion Agustin Yañez 2479
Tel. 3630-5406
In Arcos Vallarta. Intricately embroidered textiles in cross-stitch patterns. These designs on silk or linen add a touch of ethnic elegance to

any home. Cushions, tablecloths, bedspreads, wall hangings and other items.

Galeria Vertice
Lerdo de Tejada 2418
Tel. 3616-0078
Art collector Luis Garcia Jasso designed this gallery space where sculptures grace the spacious gardens and fine contemporary art decks the walls. Strong focus on Latin American artists, including Pablo Szmulewicz, Vladimir Cora, Francisco Toledo and Rafael Coronel.

Instituto de la Artesania Jalisciense
Calzada Gonzalez Gallo 20
Tel. 3619-1407
Around the corner from the entrance to Agua Azul Park. Where the state of Jalisco proudly displays its handicrafts, from ceramic plates and hand-blown glass to serapes, cotton clothing, leather, tin, brass, furniture and silver jewelry.

Juguetes Educativos y Tradicionales
Iturbide 562
Despite its pedantic name (Educational and Traditional Toys), this little shop carries charming, exclusively Mexican toys handmade out of such traditional materials as wood, cloth and ceramics. They make great gift items.

Omar Centeno
Vallarta 1075
Tel. 3827-1714
Unique art and accent pieces for the home, including textured three-dimensional paintings, paper weights in the shape of a hand, lion's heads, and more.

Sandi Bookstore
Tepeyac 718, Colonia Chapalita
Tel. 3121-0863
Canadian Sandi Day has put together the city's largest selection of English-language books and magazines. A special section includes hard-to-find volumes on Mexico. The bulletin board is a draw for foreigners searching for apartments, roommates, pets, etc. Open 9:30 a.m. to 2:30 p.m. and 3:30 to 7 p.m.; to 2 p.m. Saturday. Closed Sunday.

Takasami
La Gran Plaza
Tel. 3671-0446
An upscale boutique featuring clothing by talented designer Rosario Mendoza. Prewashed, unbleached cotton painstakingly handmade into elegant apparel adorned with appliqués, embroidery, crocheted lace and some beadwork detailing Mexican motifs like agave, corn, cactus and calla lilies. Styles flatter any age and shape. Long and short dresses, capes, caftans, accessories and more. Open 11 a.m. to 2 p.m. and 3:30 to 8 p.m.

Tane
Presidente InterContinental, Fiesta Americana and Camino Real hotels
This renowned store features beautiful sterling silver jewelry, as well as reproductions of an-

tique pieces and exclusive contemporary sculptures by outstanding Mexican and international artists. The jewelry items are often limited or one-of-a-kind pieces with lifetime warranties.

Tlaquepaque

Adobe Diseño
Independencia 195
Tel. 3657-2792
This large, wonderful shop features attractive, original furniture and decorative items by designer Martha Figueroa, as well as accent pieces from Indonesia. It also houses one of Tlaquepaque's best restaurants, Adobe. You can't miss it, just look for the Land-of-the-Giants-size *equipale* chairs out front.

Indigenous women sell beaded jewelry and other handmade items

Agustin Parra Diseño Barroco
Independencia 158
Tel. 3657-0316
The self-taught Parra has become a world-renowned creator of furniture, frames, altars, paintings and sculptures in the baroque tradition. Using extraordinary talent and techniques identical to those used in the 17th century, Parra crafts superb modern masterpieces. Absolutely unique. Open 10 a.m. to 2 p.m. and 3 to 7 p.m.; to 5 p.m. Sunday.

Ann Kary
Matamoros 28
Tel. 3659-7739
An extensive selection of pewter items, from plates and trays to decorative items. Open 9 a.m. to 6 p.m.

Antigua de Mexico
Independencia 255
Tel. 3635-3402
A beautiful 19th-century mansion provides a perfect setting for an outstanding collection of colonial furniture and objets d'art. You'll also find contemporary pieces, replicas of antiques,

decorative items and small gifts, as well as fine original paintings by some of Mexico's leading artists. If you like the best, you'll like this. Open 9 a.m. to 2 p.m. and 3 to 7 p.m. Closed Sunday.

Bazar Barrera
Independencia 205
Tel. 3635-1961
Filled to the rafters with items in brass, bronze, copper, clay, leather and wood. They feature an extensive collection of miniatures. Great for picking up gifts. Open 10 a.m. to 7 p.m.; to 2 p.m. Sunday.

Bazar Hecht
Juarez 162
Tel. 3659-0205
The eclectic tastes of Enrique Hecht featured in a split-level showroom: handicrafts, antiques, furniture (made in their own factory), religious icons, *estofado* art. Open 10 a.m. to 7 p.m.; to 2:30 p.m. Sunday.

Daniel Espinosa Jewelry
Independencia 186-D
Tel. 3587-5080
Bold, contemporary designs in silver by the talented Taxco-based jeweler, including many pieces with semiprecious stones. Espinosa's creativity and sense of fun is evident in his tie-style chokers made of silver cubes and red beads, hypnotic silver rings with black enamel swirls, and other unique jewelry.

El Palomar
Tlaquepaque 1905
A fascinating shop and production facility. Beautifully-executed stoneware takes shape before your very eyes. Many patterns in elegantly subtle colors, all certified lead free. The shop also displays jewelry, sculpture, woven goods and metalwork from all over Mexico, and a line of artistic furniture.

Esplendores de Tlaquepaque
Matamoros 33
Tel. 3657-6159
The place to find handmade icons, boxes, decorations and other items made in *repujado*, a method of molding and decorating aluminum. Open 10 a.m. to 3 p.m. and 4 to 7 p.m.

Galeria El Dorado
Independencia 145
This beautiful old house with a shady patio with a fountain, features an eclectic assortment of furniture and decorative items, from Huichol Indian beadwork to photographs by Ricardo Alarcon. Also an exciting selection of sculptures in ceramic, brass and copper signed by Mario Gonzalez. El Dorado manufactures and exports its wares. Open 10 a.m. to 6:30 p.m.; 11 a.m. to 6:30 p.m. Sunday.

Galeria Ken Edwards
Madero 70, just past the Jardin
Tel. 3635-2426
Don't miss this outstanding store; Edwards' name has become an institution in Tlaque-

paque. Displayed in an inviting old mansion are beautiful hand-painted, high temperature, lead-free stoneware vases, bowls, mugs, complete table services, and even some unusual items, such as an avocado cup. Also a few select antiques and some colorful folkloric costumes from Mexico's different regions. Open 10:30 a.m. to 7:30 p.m. The Ken Edwards factory in Tonala, at Morelos 184, is open to the public.

Galerias Preciado
Independencia and Gral. Garcia Barragan Blvd.
Tel. 3635-2822
Long-known in Tlaquepaque, the prestigious Preciado family has built a thriving furniture and home decorations business around their beautiful wrought-iron creations. You'll find their showrooms all over Tlaquepaque. This bazaarlike store carries everything from lamps and lanterns to carved wood items. Open 10 a.m. to 8 p.m.; 11 a.m. to 3 p.m. Sunday.

Jesus Guerrero Santos
Independencia 227-A, inside Casa Linda
Tel. 3659-7373
This artist shows extraordinary craftsmanship and imagination in combining hand-painted ceramic and alpaca to create highly original furniture pieces, decorative items, vases, mirrors, candle holders, chests and more.

La Casa Canela
Independencia 258
Tel. 3635-3717
One of Tlaquepaque's most beautiful shops is housed in an 18th-century mansion showcasing a very select collection of Mexican handicrafts, fine art and folk art. Each room represents a complete interior design concept and a different medium, including ceramic, glass, metal, textile and wood, with an emphasis on hand-carved and *estofado* furniture. Pieces can be made to order. Open 10 a.m. to 2 p.m. and 3 to 7 p.m.; to 6 p.m. Saturday; 11 a.m. to 3 p.m. Sunday.

La Ventana
Independencia 176-A
Tel. 3657-3800
Young architect Eduardo Navarro displays his talents in a great collection of wrought-iron furniture, Talavera ceramics, tin decorative items, candles and Mexican art. Open 10:30 a.m. to 7 p.m.; to 5:30 p.m. Sunday.

Las Tres
Independencia 286
Tel. 3631-5132
Featuring fashions by three local designers: More Martinez, Dunes and Ana R. Stylish casual clothing. Open 10:30 a.m. to 6:30 p.m. Closed Sunday.

Maria de Guadalajara
Independencia 270
Tel. 3639-1426
Selling soft, comfortable, casual clothing in wrinkled cotton designed by Maria Bennett. Mix-and-match one-size combinations, and jewelry.

Originales
Juarez 262
Tel. 3659-1337
Architect Ernesto Cruz displays his creative talents in highly contemporary wood furniture for the home and works of art in wax—his unique candles come in every shape and size, including four-foot-high columns, some etched with text.

Pineda de Tlaquepaque
Independencia 111
Silversmiths since 1945, they offer sterling silver jewelry in pre-Hispanic and modern designs. Open 10 a.m. to 7 p.m.; noon to 2 p.m. Sunday.

Plateria Tlaquepaque
Independencia 211
Tel. 3635-5089
This large store with a wishing well in the middle displays an extensive selection of sterling silver jewelry. Open 10 a.m. to 6:30 p.m.; to 3 p.m. Sunday.

Plaza de las Artesanias
Juarez 145
Tel. 3635-1194
This small bazaar houses several shops. Antiguo Tlaquepaque specializes in custom-designed hand-woven rugs, table linens and wall hangings. Sharing the same space is talented young designer Alex Mata Taylor's silver jewelry in pre-Hispanic designs, and native Huichol and Cora Indian art, including their much sought after yarn paintings and beadwork. Jimenez Hermanos manufactures fine leather items, from belts to golf bags. And Pascual Estudiante features original designs in mirror frames, lamps and oversized bird cages. Open 10 a.m. to 6:30 p.m.; 11 a.m. to 2 p.m. Sunday.

Rodo Padilla
Independencia 139
Tel. 3657-3712
This space features original ceramic sculptures by one of Tlaquepaque's most creative artists. Padilla's charming and amusing kinetic sports figures, angels and Mexican charros, reflecting the artist's sense of whimsy, have found a place in private collections worldwide. Some of his figures are interpreted into silver jewelry. Open 10 a.m. to 7 p.m.; 11 a.m. to 3 p.m. Sunday.

Segusino
Prisciliano Sanchez 36
Tel. 3639-3745
Two floors of fine Mexican colonial furniture, as well as textile, ceramic and wrought-iron accent pieces for the home.

Sergio Bustamante Gallery
Independencia 238
Tel. 3639-5519
Where the renowned Mexican artist displays his sculptures in papier-mâché, bronze and copper, as well as his line of silver and gold jewelry. An amazing talent on show in an exceptionally attractive gallery with a reflection pool and roaming peacocks. Also accent pieces for the home, works by other Mexican artists.

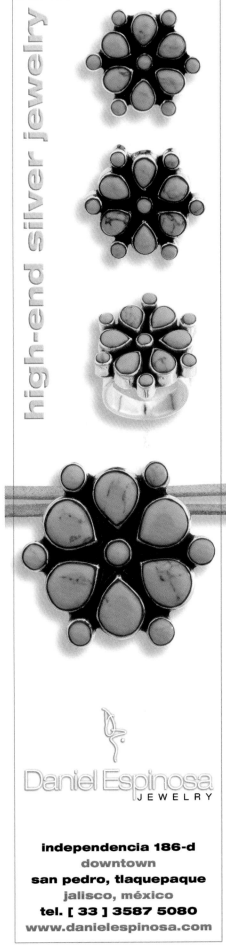

Where to Stay

Calinda Roma
Juarez 170, downtown
Tel. (33) 3614-8650
www.hotelescalinda.com.mx
On a main street, this old favorite is conveniently close to city attractions. It's one of the best of the economically-priced hotels, with rooftop garden, pool, restaurant-bar. There are 120 air-conditioned rooms, including non-smoking and executive women's sections, with satellite TV. Meeting facilities and business center. Rates ECON.

Camino Real
Vallarta 5005
Tel. (33) 3134-2424
www.caminoreal.com
Located in a residential area 15 minutes from downtown, this first-class hotel offers a pleasant country club setting and excellent service at moderate prices. Each of the 205 rooms has a balcony overlooking the landscaped gardens. Four swimming pools, lighted tennis court, well-equipped gym, putting green, and preferential green fee for guests at the Palomar Country Club. Gourmet Mexican restaurant, coffee shop, lobby bar and turn-of-the-century bar with live music. Business center and extensive convention facilities. Rates MD.

Crowne Plaza
Lopez Mateos Sur 2500
Tel. (33) 3634-1034
www.crownegdl.com
Across from Plaza del Sol shopping center. One of the nicest Crowne Plazas around, this modern colonial-style gem has 294 large rooms with all first-class amenities. Beautiful grounds, good restaurant, coffee shop, bar. Pool, gym, golf, playground. Convention and banquet facilities for up to 900 people, business center with computers. Very popular. Rates MD.

De Mendoza
Venustiano Carranza 16, downtown
Tel. (33) 3613-4646
www.demendoza.com.mx
A colonial-style hotel with lots of character, and 110 charming rooms with a/c, satellite TV, phone. Heated pool, good restaurant, business center, small meeting rooms, parking. Rates ECON.

El Tapatio
Blvd. Aeropuerto 4275
Tel. (33) 3837-2929
www.hotel-tapatio.com
About 20 minutes from town, near Tlaquepaque. A colonial-style resort and racquet club located on a hillside overlooking the city, with gardens and cobblestone paths. Each of the

117 large, comfortable rooms has satellite TV, minibar, balcony or terrace. Restaurant, disco. Pool, nine tennis courts, gym, sauna and steam room. Meeting rooms, business center. Rates MD (includes continental breakfast).

Fiesta Americana
Aurelio Aceves 225, at the Minerva Fountain
Tel. (33) 3825-3434
www.fiestamericana.com

This fabulous 25-story deluxe hotel is the tallest in Guadalajara. The twin towers have 351 rooms and 40 suites, a one-acre interior garden, four glass elevators and shopping arcade. Continental and Mexican restaurants, bars, nightclub. Tennis, gym, pool. Convention facilities. Rates FC.

Fiesta Inn
Mariano Otero 1550
Tel. (33) 3669-3200
www.fiestamericana.com
Between Expo Guadalajara and Plaza del Sol shopping center. A well-located 158-room hotel with heated pool, gym, lobby bar, cafeteria-restaurant, and meeting facilities. Rates MD.

HOTEL RATES	
LX: luxury, rates above 375 USD	
DX: deluxe, rates from 250-375 USD	
FC: first-class, rates from 150-250 USD	
MD: moderate, rates from 75-150 USD	
ECON: economical, rates under 75 USD	

Frances
Maestranza 35, downtown
Tel. (33) 3613-1190
www.hotelfrances.com
The city's oldest hotel, with a fascinating history dating from 1610, has been declared a national monument. Right on the main plaza, the colonial hotel's 60 rooms and suites are completely modern, with satellite TV; courtyard, restaurant, bar and nightclub with live music. Rates ECON.

Hilton
Av. de las Rosas 2933
Tel. (33) 3678-0505
www.guadalajara.hilton.com
This 22-story first-class hotel and recent winner of AAA's Four Diamond Award is in the World Trade Center and connected to Expo Guadalajara via a direct walkway. The property offers 402 rooms and 20 suites (including a presidential suite). Business center, meeting rooms, executive club, heliport. Restaurant, cafeteria, lobby bar. Rates FC.

Holiday Inn
Niños Heroes 3089, corner of Lopez Mateos
Tel. (33) 3122-2020
www.selectgdl.com.mx
A modern 15-story hotel catering to business travelers, with 220 rooms, each with a work station, coffee maker, 28-inch TV. Rooftop pool and sun deck, sauna, gym. Restaurant, lobby bar, meeting facilities for 600 people, business center with computers, Internet access. Rates MD.

Presidente InterContinental
Lopez Mateos Sur and Moctezuma
Tel. (33) 3678-1234
www.intercontinental.com
This modern glass pyramid with a 12-story atrium lobby is a flower-filled center for doing business and socializing, with two comfortable restaurants, lobby bar with live music, state-of-the-art meeting facilities for up to 2,000 people, fitness center and spa, outdoor swimming pool, and shops. The 409 recently renovated rooms and suites have a/c, full bath with hair dryer, satellite TV, minibar, direct dial phone, data port. Club floor offers personalized service and club lounge. Rates FC.

Quinta Real
Av. Mexico 2727
Tel. (33) 3669-0600
www.quintareal.com
Part of a fast growing Mexican chain, this lovely, elegant hacienda-style hotel has 76 luxurious and beautifully decorated suites, some with whirlpool bath. Personalized service, fine gourmet restaurant, bar with chamber music, pool, gardens, business center and meeting facilities for up to 200. Member of Mexico Boutique Hotels. Rates DX.

Villa Ganz
Lopez Cotilla 1739, Colonia Lafayette
Tel. (33) 3120-1416
www.mexicoboutiquehotels.com
Near the historical center and Expo Guadala-

jara. A colonial mansion-turned-B&B with just 10 spacious rooms and suites with French doors with beveled glass, plenty of natural lighting. Central salon/library with hot coffee in the morning, chilled Chardonnay in the afternoon. Garden and lounge with fireplace. Business center, meeting rooms, terrace bar. Rates DX.

Lake Chapala

Ajijic B&B
Hidalgo 22, Ajijic
Tel. (376) 766-2377
Conveniently located just a half block from the main plaza, this charming inn offers six attractive guest rooms, each with a king-size bed and satellite TV, surrounded by lovely gardens. Rates ECON (includes breakfast).

La Nueva Posada
Donato Guerra 9, Ajijic
Tel. (376) 766-1344
This Ajijic favorite is housed in a lovely colonial-style inn facing Lake Chapala, and five blocks from the main plaza. Its 23 guest rooms are spacious and charming, with double or king size beds, cable TV, phone. Also short-term garden villas available. The indoor and outdoor dining areas, with views of the lake and fine Mexican and continental cuisine, and the bar, which has live entertainment, are popular gathering places for American and Canadian expatriates and local residents. Swimming pool. Rates MD (includes breakfast).

Quinta Quetzalcoatl
Zaragoza 307, Chapala
Tel. (376) 765-3653
www.chapalaliving.com
This unique B&B, where author D.H. Lawrence wrote his novel "The Plumed Serpent," offers five individually decorated rooms and suites nestled among gardens behind 12-foot stone walls. Lovely tiled pool, jacuzzi, dining room, open-air bar area, game room with cable TV. Nearby golf (hosts Ricardo and Barbi Henderson keep clubs around for guests who like to travel light). Rates MD (includes breakfast, complimentary beers, soft drinks).

Tlaquepaque

Casa de Las Flores
Santos Degollado 175, near Matamoros Street
Tel. (33) 3659-3186
www.casadelasflores.com
Housed in a restored adobe home with a small patio and garden, this B&B offers six spacious guest rooms. Rates MD (includes continental breakfast).

La Villa del Ensueño
Florida 305, near Niños Heroes
Tel. (33) 3635-8792
www.mexonline.com/ensueno.html
An intimate Mexican B&B offering 14 guest rooms and four spacious suites, all colorfully decorated, half with a/c. Two pools, bar, lounge. Rates MD (includes breakfast).

Quinta Don Jose
Reforma 139
Tel. (33) 3635-7522
www.quintadonjose.com
A pleasant 10-room B&B with swimming pool, cozy bar, breakfast served on a sunny patio. Rates MD (includes continental breakfast).

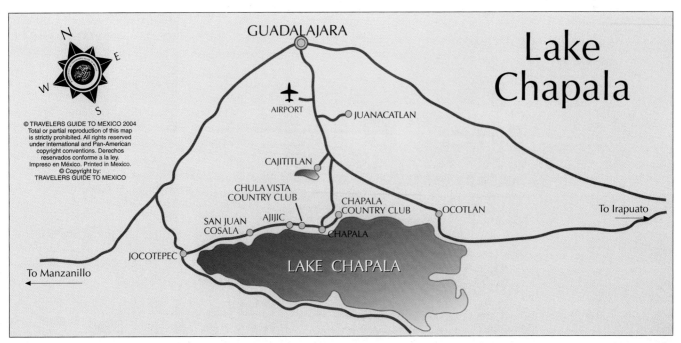

Lake Chapala

GUADALAJARA
AIRPORT
JUANACATLAN
CAJITITLAN
CHULA VISTA COUNTRY CLUB
CHAPALA COUNTRY CLUB
OCOTLAN
To Irapuato
SAN JUAN COSALA
AJIJIC
CHAPALA
JOCOTEPEC
To Manzanillo
LAKE CHAPALA

© TRAVELERS GUIDE TO MEXICO 2004
Total or partial reproduction of this map is strictly prohibited. All rights reserved under international and Pan-American copyright conventions. Derechos reservados conforme a la ley. Impreso en México. Printed in Mexico.
© Copyright by:
TRAVELERS GUIDE TO MEXICO

World's
Best Resorts
2003

ESCAPE THE URBAN JUNGLE AND COME TO OURS, FOR DINNER.

As you stroll through the streets of Puerto Vallarta, make your way to La Jolla de Mismaloya, where a whole new world of entertainment and dining experiences await you, including "John Huston's Restaurant" —featuring top quality seafood, caught fresh daily— and the world famous "The Sets of The Night of the Iguana Restaurant", the absolute best in Mexican and International cuisine, with live Mariachis!

For reservations 226-0660
www.lajollamexico.com

The Suites at
La Jolla de Mismaloya

Puerto Vallarta, Mexico

TRAVELERS GUIDE TO
Puerto Vallarta

Booming Vallarta offers visitors more than ever before.

Introduction

More Than Just a Beach Resort

By Jim Budd

Culture, cuisine and ecology are the big attractions in Puerto Vallarta these days. The quaintest town on the Mexican Pacific has become much more than just a beach. It is more than just a village, too, having grown to a point were it is something like half a dozen destinations rolled into one. You have Old Vallarta and New Vallarta, in between there's Marina Vallarta. You have the South-of-Town Hotel Zone and the North-of-Town Hotel Zone and, now, Punta Mita.

The town sits on Bahia de Banderas, the largest natural bay in Mexico, with 100 miles of coastline ringed by mountains. You find long stretches of beach to the north of town, and delightful coves to the south.

Few people come to Puerto Vallarta simply to relax. Basking on the beach is considered lazy when whale-watching expeditions beckon. Some 500 humpbacks honeymoon in the bay every winter, swimming down all the way from Alaska. Summer nights are spent waiting for sea turtles to lumber ashore and lay their eggs in the sand. Tourists join teams of biologists in rescuing these infant Ridleys, which might otherwise be gobbled by gulls. You can find everything from hikes into the jungle to horseback rides, excursions on mountain bikes and kayak outings.

Lounging around the pool is no longer enough. Nor is buying T-shirts and tacky souvenirs when it comes to shopping. Visitors to Puerto Vallarta scour the art galleries; there are more than a dozen selling fine paintings and sculpture. In high season, the third Wednesday of the month is when the new shows open and everyone goes gallery-hopping; it's the third Friday of the month for the marina area. Tours are also available to artists' studios.

The late Manuel Lepe, Mexico's premier primitive painter, gets credit for putting Puerto Vallarta on art maps. Lepe's trademark angels flying over the beaches delighted the Hollywood types who began flocking to the area in the 1960s.

Puerto Vallarta remained largely unknown until Mexicana Airlines saw profit-making potential in the sleepy village. At the time, rival Aeromexico had a monopoly on the route between Mexico City and Acapulco. Farseeing officials at Mexicana figured Puerto Vallarta could offer the same resort facilities to Guadalajara, the country's second largest city. And

the only way to get there was to fly. So they obtained a franchise in 1954 and began promoting the place.

However, it was the on-location filming of John Huston's "Night of the Iguana" in 1964 that really made people take notice of Vallarta. The film starred Richard Burton, and accompanying him was Elizabeth Taylor. Both were married at the time, but not to each other. The tabloids poured in and seldom did a day go by that some newspaper did not publish a report datelined Puerto Vallarta.

Hollywood in the 1940s made Acapulco famous. Puerto Vallarta's time had come. Soon Mexicana flights were booked weeks in advance by pilgrims who wanted to see where Dick and Liz had romanced—the two had purchased homes across the street from one another, and built a connecting bridge.

A third of a century has passed, but people talk about the filming as if it were only yesterday—a restaurant operates on the site of the original set.

Puerto Vallarta has evolved considerably since then.

Relatively isolated until 1969, when the first paved highway connected it to the rest of Mexico, it's now an easy four-hour drive from Guadalajara.

Cars jam Puerto Vallarta's narrow streets on weekends and holidays. Making the cobblestone streets one-way helped alleviate the congestion, as did building bridges across Cuale River, and the six-lane boulevard that connects the airport with the downtown area, Avenida de Las Palmas. Finding a parking space downtown still presents a challenge.

With the increase in tourism, a large hotel zone developed above town, a lesser one below town. Marina Vallarta is now home to a Marriott, Westin and half a dozen other luxury hotels.

Beaches to the south and especially the north are booming with new developments, so much so that increasingly the name "Vallarta" refers to not just the town but also the coast as far north as Punta Mita and beyond. On the northern edge of vast Banderas Bay, Punta Mita is home to Mexico's second Four Seasons Hotel and a Jack Nicklaus golf course. Many feel Vallarta has the potential to become Mexico's next big golf destination.

Perhaps the best newest development in Vallarta is the resurrection of the Playa los Muertos area, dubbed the "Zona Romantica." The downtown stretch of the *malecon*, or seafront, remains a rival, but appeals to a younger crowd. Streets leading down to Los Muertos, particularly Basilio Badillo and Olas Altas, have become the address of some of the best dining spots in Vallarta, once known for its mediocre cuisine.

Culture, cuisine and ecology—they've made Puerto Vallarta much more than just a beach resort.

Jim Budd is a travel writer living in Mexico.

Puerto Vallarta Convention & Visitors Bureau

What to See and Do

Discovering Hidden Treasures on Beautiful Banderas Bay

Playa los Muertos

YOU CAN BUY YOUR OWN COPY OF THIS BOOK. SEE THE LAST PAGE.

Vallarta Lifestyles

The heart of Puerto Vallarta, the downtown area, is easily explored on foot, even though it has grown to include two very distinct neighborhoods—*Old Town Vallarta* and *Zona Romantica*, otherwise known as the Playa los Muertos area.

In Old Town Vallarta, steep cobblestone streets climb their way uphill from the seafront. This is the traditional downtown area and home to Vallarta's single-most photographed feature, the crown atop Guadalupe Church. The graceful contour of the crown, a fiberglass replica of the original which caved in during a 1995 earthquake, has long been a symbol of Vallarta.

But there's no shortage of landmarks and photogenic runners-up to the church tower. *Vallartenses* have discovered that their elegantly simple seafront promenade, or *malecon*, provides an eloquent backdrop for numerous statues, monuments and works of art, including a lovely bronze statue of a sitting couple by renowned Mexican artist and Vallarta resident Ramiz Barquet, a boy astride a sea horse,

arches that are lit up at night like the entrance to an amusement park, Guadalajara-born artist Alejandro Colunga's intriguing congregation of bizarre creatures that locals refer to as "the fantasy figures," and Sergio Bustamante's ebullient "Three Figures with a Ladder."

On Sundays, around sunset, the malecon bustles with activity as residents gather with friends or family for a stroll beside the ocean, much like the inhabitants of a small town meet and mingle at the main square.

Wander southward and you'll pass Rio Cuale, the river that divides the downtown area in two. Across the river is where the Zona Romantica begins, a newer, more bohemian neighborhood that has sprung up around Playa los Muertos, Vallarta's most popular beach. Sidewalk eateries, fashionable boutiques, and the odd Internet cafe line the streets closest to the beach. The beachfront restaurants offer front-row seats to the activity on shore.

Between the two banks of Rio Cuale is a narrow island that is home to a few fine restaurants, a botanical garden, the Regional An-

thropology Museum and some handicrafts stalls.

Vallarta's more modest accommodations are located in the downtown area, including a couple of very charming hotels. Five-star and luxury properties are located in the hotel zone, Marina Vallarta, south Vallarta, and Nuevo Vallarta, a still-growing resort development just north of the airport.

Beaches

According to legend, Vallarta's preferred beach, *Playa los Muertos*, or Dead Men's Beach, was the site of a bloody clash between pirates and Indians. Over the years, there have been several failed attempts to give this lively beach a more cheerful name, including the sunnier Playa del Sol, but habit and history have prevailed.

For more secluded beach escapes, most visitors head south, where the shoreline is carved into inviting coves. When in 1963 director John Huston was scouting for a remote coastal jungle setting to film Tennessee Williams' "Night of the Iguana," he chose *Playa Mismaloya*. The beach, hidden in a cove sheltered by high cliffs, is located about six miles south of town via a scenic winding road. Today, Mismaloya is dominated by a major hotel, but you can still see the crumbling remnants of the film set where a restaurant named after the movie has been built.

Some of the more secluded beaches can only be reached by boat, including *Playa Las Animas, Quimixto, Majahuitas* and *Yelapa*. The village farthest south, Yelapa is a delightful spot straight out of Michener. After a couple of hours, the boat glides into a small, picturesque cove surrounded by green mountains. The Polynesian-style village sitting at the edge of the bay has a beautiful white sand beach, perfect for swimming, snorkeling, or relaxing with a drink in a hammock. You can eat lunch at one of several palm-thatched restaurants on the beach, and enjoy the freshest fish you've ever tasted.

The village, too, is worth a visit, with a handful of stores with interesting handicrafts and unique clothing. If you're adventurous, a 20-minute hike or 30-minute horseback ride up the mountain will bring you to a refreshing 150-foot waterfall, where you can take a dip in the cool waters at the base.

There is a small hotel on the beach and a bed-and-breakfast up the river for those who wish to stay the night. Nightlife centers around the Yelapa Yacht Club restaurant in the village. Locals and tourists mix on disco nights, Wednesday and Saturday. Bonfire beach parties are often held during a full moon.

Las Animas and Quimixto are much smaller than Yelapa, but do have restaurants, and horseback riding and hiking. Majahuitas is a small beach with a charming rustic hotel.

Boat Trips

Day or sunset cruises offer a great way to see the bay's attractions and admire the landscape from a different perspective. Most cruises hug the coastline, offering a good view of the inviting shore and *Los Arcos,* the giant boulders rising out of the water at the entrance to Mismaloya. Day cruises usually include snorkeling.

Boats leave every morning for Yelapa, Las Animas, Quimixto and Majahuitas to the south of the bay and for northerly mountain-rimmed beaches.

Princesa Bay Tours offers a variety of popular excursions, such as a day trip to Islas Marietas, a reserve off Punta Mita where Jacques Cousteau spent time exploring the abundant marine life, including sea turtles, dolphins and whales in winter. Tel. 224-4777.

For up close and personal encounters with marine life, contact *Open Air Expeditions*. Their 25-foot motorboats are equipped with hydrophone systems so you can see and listen to the song of the migratory whales that winter in the bay from December through March.

Modeled after Christopher Columbus' ship, the Santa Maria, the *Marigalante* offers trips to Islas Marietas and a sunset cruise. A below-deck museum displays relics recalling Columbus' voyage. Tel. 223-0309.

Superior Cruises, at Marina Los Peines, Dock No. 1, sails to secluded beaches north of Puerto Vallarta. The daily excursions accommodate a minimum of four and maximum of 12 people.

You can also rent a boat through a travel agency and design your own itinerary.

Sightseeing

A variety of tours highlight town sights and surrounding areas, from a three-hour city tour to a five-hour "see-all" city and tropical tour.

Casa Kimberley, a hilltop villa-turned-shrine to the most famous love affair of the 20th century, is open to the public. The love nest that once belonged to Richard Burton and Elizabeth Taylor has been preserved much as it was when the couple lived here. A pink bridge, built to join the his-and-hers homes facing each other, arches over the road. Movie posters, photo albums and mementos fill the different rooms. The villa, located just a couple of blocks behind the malecon, at Zaragoza 445, is easily accessible by foot. Daily tours are offered from 9 a.m. to 6 p.m. Tel. 222-1336.

The International Friendship Club offers twice weekly tours of beautiful Vallarta homes during the high season. These leave every Wednesday and Thursday at 11 a.m. from the Rio Cuale Hotel, and last about two and a half hours. Tickets cost 30 dollars and proceeds go to charity. Tel. 222-5466.

At *Terra Noble,* a hilltop retreat so unique it was featured in Architectural Digest (June 1996), visitors can take part in an Aztec-style sweat lodge ceremony, or have a variety of facial and body treatments, including massages. It's worth visiting this "spa and healing center" just to see its unique design and enjoy its panoramic view of Vallarta. Tel. 222-5400.

The movie "Predator" was filmed south of town at El Eden, where the Mismaloya River runs through a gorge deep enough at one point to create a swimming hole. A rope is suspended over the water for those who want to take a cooling dip by swinging in Tarzan style. There's a restaurant-bar on the bank. You can descend to the site on horseback.

Porfidio Distillery, a state-of-the-art tequila factory located just north of the airport, is open to the public for tours and tequila tasting, Monday to Friday from noon to 3 p.m. The Porfidio label has won top awards for its premium, triple distilled tequilas. Tel. 221-1236.

Bullfights are held Wednesdays at 5 p.m. at La Paloma bullfighting ring, located on the road to the airport.

Air tours provide a one-day jaunt to the colonial city of Guadalajara and the nearby handicrafts center of Tlaquepaque, and to the small mining town of San Sebastian in the Sierra Madre mountains. Packages usually include air fare, sightseeing, guide service and lunch.

Aerotaxis de la Bahia has daily scheduled flights to San Sebastian, as well as to Talpa and Mascota, two other quaint colonial towns only 15 minutes from Puerto Vallarta. Private charters are also available. Tel. 222-2049.

Water Sports

Good snorkeling and scuba diving sites offer an opportunity to see giant mantas, dolphins and sea turtles. The most popular destinations are Los Arcos, Quimixto and the Marieta Islands. Seasoned divers may want to ask about more remote locations, as well as night dives.

Chico's Dive Shop, at Diaz Ordaz 770-5, is Vallarta's premier snorkeling and diving outfit. In business since 1968, it is one of the most reliable centers in town for excursions, instruction and certification. Tel. 222-1895.

Though newer to the scene, tour operator and dive center *Vallarta Adventure*, at Marina Vallarta, is another leading outfit. It also offers jungle treks, whale-watching, and excursions into remote Huichol territory. Tel. 221-0658.

Ecotours

Humpback whales winter in Banderas Bay from about mid-December to mid-March, making whale-watching excursions one of the most popular outings during the high season. Tropical birds can be sighted year-round, including blue-footed boobies, terns, and frigate birds, but you need to know where to look.

Vallarta's leading ecotourism outfits offer these excursions and more, including visits to sea turtle breeding camps (from August to November), hiking through the Sierra Madre, and sea kayaking.

Expediciones Cielo Abierto, or Open Air Expeditions, located at Guerrero 339 (tel. 222-3310), was founded in 1994 by oceanologist Isabel Cardenas. *Ecotours de Mexico,* at Ignacio Vallarta 243 (tel. 222-6606), was established in 1991 by husband and wife team Astrid Frisch and Karel Beets. Both are staffed by responsible bilingual personnel, and are active members of the Mexican Association of Adventure Travel and Ecotourism (AMTAVE).

There are also biking tours of the surrounding countryside, with visits to waterfalls, ranches, hot springs and quaint towns. Call *Bike Mex* at 223-1680, or visit them at Guerrero 361. They also offer hiking and nature walks.

Horseback Riding

Horseback riding in the nearby jungle and countryside offer visits to mango orchards, cattle ranches and farms, small rural villages, a river you can swim in and, on Sundays, a typical Mexican rodeo.

Rancho el Ojo de Agua, the oldest establishment of its kind in Vallarta, has nearly 20 years of experience under its belt. The ranch provides quality horses, equipped with either English or Western saddles, experienced guides and personalized attention from the owners. Excursions include sunset rides and longer five-day trips on horseback to remote sites of interest, such as the old mining town of San Sebastian in the Sierra Madre. Tel. 224-8240.

A one-day trip to San Sebastian is also available, beginning with a 15-minute flight. Once there, a bilingual horseback tour takes you through the typical mountain town and its haciendas. You can return the same day or overnight. For more information, call *Rancho Charro*, 224-0114.

Golf and Tennis

The recent opening of the *Vista Vallarta Golf Club* and its two championship courses is destined to make Vallarta a major golf destination. The first course is designed by Jack Nicklaus and the second by Tom Weiskopf.

Also new is Nuevo Vallarta's *Paradise Village Golf and Country Club*, which features an 18-hole course designed by Robert von Hagge.

Marina Vallarta Golf Club, an 18-hole course designed by Joe Finger, opened in the summer of 1989. It is close to most major hotels and has excellent facilities. Though open to the public, guests at certain hotels enjoy preferential access. Tel. 221-0171.

About eight miles north of the airport is *Los Flamingos Golf Club*, with an 18-hole course. A handsome stone and stucco clubhouse and pro-shop overlook rolling hills that fade off into the distance toward the ocean. There's a pleasant lounge and good restaurant. Tel. 298-0280.

The Four Seasons resort at *Punta Mita* features a Jack Nicklaus designed 18-hole course overlooking the ocean.

The *Canto del Sol Plaza Vallarta Hotel* (tel. 224-0123) is a complete tennis complex with four indoor, four outdoor courts, night play, clinics and individual instruction, and tournaments.

Good tennis facilities are also found at Los Tules, Puesta del Sol Club de Tenis, and La Iguana Tennis Center.

Fishing

The waters of Puerto Vallarta rank with the best in the world for both deep-sea and small game fishing. November through May is the best season for sailfish. Throughout the year there are plenty of smaller fish, from red snapper and rooster fish to sea bass and tuna. Many fishing boats are available, most offering catch-and-release sport-fishing trips. An international deep-sea fishing tournament is held each year in November.

Nearby lakes offer the attraction of freshwater catches like black bass. Bass fishing tours to the *Cajon de Peña* reservoir, 70 miles south of Vallarta, are available.

Isla del Rio Cuale

A long and narrow five-acre island sits in the middle of Rio Cuale, the river that divides downtown Vallarta. The west end of the island is at the mouth of the river and looks out over the blue Pacific. The east end provides a vista of the canyons that border the river and the mountains in the background.

On the ocean side, a little museum displays a collection of archaeological artifacts from pre-Hispanic tombs in Jalisco, Colima and Nayarit states. Open Tuesday to Saturday from 10 a.m. to 7 p.m. and Wednesday from 10 a.m. to 4 p.m. In this same area, there is a small

Punta Mita golf course

botanical garden and the Casa de Cultura, or cultural center.

A few of Vallarta's leading restaurants, including *Le Bistro, The River Cafe* and *Oscar's*, are on the island, as well as several handicrafts stalls and a handful of small shops. There's also a statue of John Huston sitting in a director's chair, in homage to the man who helped put Vallarta on the map.

Studying Spanish

Mexico's most prestigious school of arts and language studies for English speakers, *Instituto Allende* in San Miguel de Allende, operates a Vallarta campus on Isla del Rio Cuale. Foreign students who wish to combine earning credits and degrees with travel abroad can study painting, ceramics, textile or jewelry making, and Spanish. Tel. 222-0076.

Under the slogan "learn Spanish in paradise," the *University of Guadalajara* offers Spanish language courses at its campus in downtown Vallarta. The semi-intensive and intensive programs are complemented by cultural activities and a tutorial service. Tel. 223-2082.

Getting Around

Taxis are plentiful and drivers charge predetermined fares set according to distance. The system appears to work wonderfully. Still, if you have any doubts about the fare you are being charged, just ask to see the driver's price chart—he should have one available—or check with your hotel regarding rates.

Bus routes are fairly extensive, going as far south as Mismaloya and as far north as Nuevo Vallarta. Shuttling from one end of town to the other is easy and inexpensive, costing only a few pesos. Pay attention to the destination marked on or over the front windshield.

North of Town

The northern curve of Banderas Bay has its own attractions, and the road there is currently being expanded into a four-lane highway that will bring them within easier reach.

Just eight miles north of town, crossing into the neighboring state of Nayarit, is *Nuevo Vallarta*, a 1,150-acre residential-resort development with nearly three miles of beachfront, a large

Puerto Vallarta

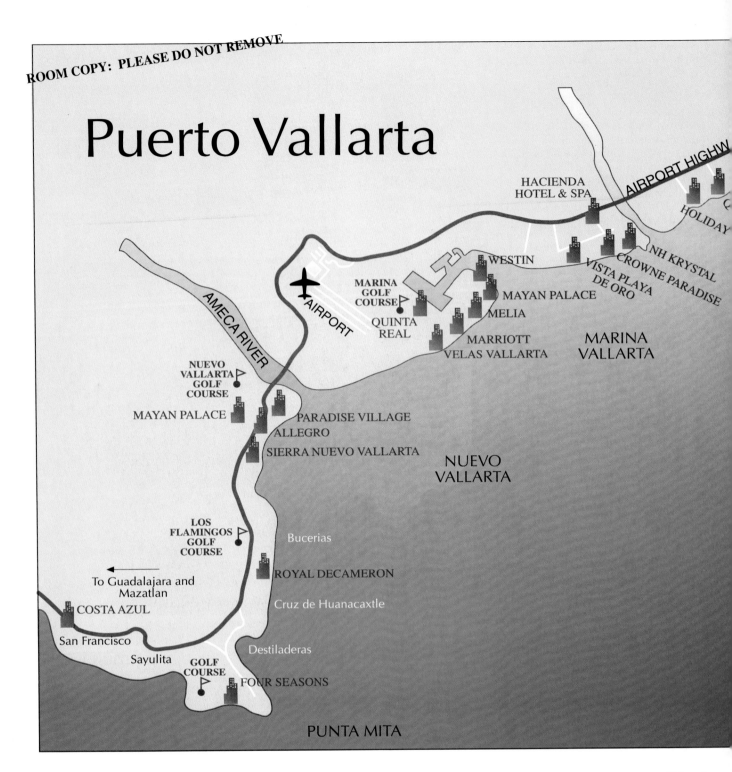

marina, several five-star hotels, mostly all-inclusives, three golf courses, an RV park, shopping center, and more than five miles of river and estuary frontage for home sites with private docks.

Dolphin Adventure, one of the few facilities of its kind in the world, has a colony of Pacific bottlenose dolphins in several, large ocean-water pens. A brief audio presentation prepares visitors who want to take the plunge with the gentle, curious creatures, and those who opt for the softer approach—submerging themselves waist deep in one of the pens for a petting session. Reservations must be made at least a day in advance. The facility closes Sundays. Tel. 221-0657.

Splash, the local water park, features Mexico's tallest (20 meters/60 feet) and most elaborate water slides. The park is open daily, 10 a.m. to 7 p.m. Tel. 297-0723.

African Queen, a replica of the steamboat that took Katharine Hepburn and Humphrey Bogart down the Congo in the 1951 film, takes up to 12 passengers on a two-hour tour of the area in search of crocodiles and tropical birds. The boat leaves every morning at 10:30 from the marina at the Paradise Village Hotel. Tel. 224-4880.

Quelele Lagoon, home to the crested caracara, or *quelele* in Spanish, comprises more than 100 hectares of tidal plain surrounded by white mangroves. The lagoon is the natural habitat

of the river crocodile, many varieties of fish and shrimp, and an amazing range of species of both resident and migratory birds. Considered one of the 100 most attractive sites in Mexico for bird watching, the lagoon is a protected natural area. For bird-watching tours of this and other prime birding areas, contact Open Air Expeditions, tel. 222-3310.

Seven miles farther north, on a beautiful beach, *Bucerias* is a popular spot for winter residents seeking a small-town atmosphere. Unique restaurants have opened up and jazz concerts have become a regular weekly event. From there you can follow the bend of the bay past several small, pristine beaches, such as *Cruz de Huanacaxtle*, *Destiladeras* and *Punta de Burro*.

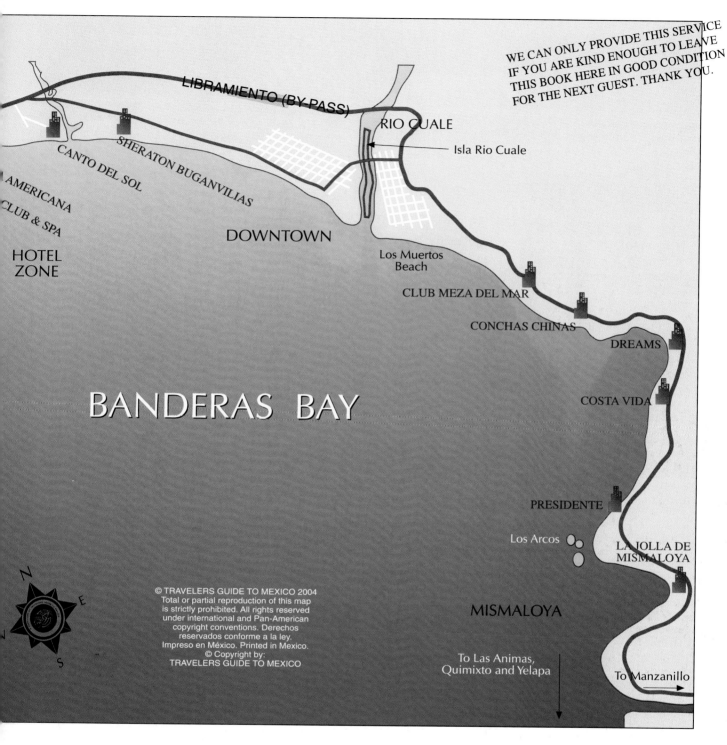

LIBRAMIENTO (BY-PASS)

RIO CUALE

Isla Rio Cuale

CANTO DEL SOL

SHERATON BUGANVILIAS

AMERICANA CLUB & SPA

HOTEL ZONE

DOWNTOWN

Los Muertos Beach

CLUB MEZA DEL MAR

CONCHAS CHINAS

DREAMS

COSTA VIDA

BANDERAS BAY

PRESIDENTE

Los Arcos

LA JOLLA DE MISMALOYA

© TRAVELERS GUIDE TO MEXICO 2004
Total or partial reproduction of this map
is strictly prohibited. All rights reserved
under international and Pan-American
copyright conventions. Derechos
reservados conforme a la ley.
Impreso en México. Printed in Mexico.
© Copyright by:
TRAVELERS GUIDE TO MEXICO

MISMALOYA

N E S W

To Las Animas,
Quimixto and Yelapa

To Manzanillo

The northern tip of the bay, called *Punta Mita*, is poised to become one of Mexico's most upscale resort communities. The 1,500-acre spear-shaped peninsula, surrounded by the Pacific on three sides, offers a varied coastline with miles of smooth, sandy beaches, rocky, shell-strewn stretches, and small coves. A shallow reef just off the coast offers ideal snorkeling and scuba diving. Currently there are a handful of exclusive resorts, including a Four Seasons Hotel and its oceanside signature Jack Nicklaus golf course. Playa Anclote is the popular beach for surfers and swimmers, and has several beachfront restaurants.

Heading farther north, following the highway marked "Tepic," is the small fishing village of *Sayulita*, thought to resemble Vallarta 40 years ago, with its secluded beaches and fishermen reeling in their nets.

Local artist Evelyne Boren resides in Sayulita and hosts an open-house workshop tour every Wednesday during the season.

One of the finest restaurants in the area, *Don Pedro's*, is right on the beach. Under a giant palapa with views of the ocean and jungle, chef Nicholas Parillo (formerly of Prego's in Beverly Hills and The Rex in L.A.) expertly prepares gourmet Mediterranean cuisine with a touch of the tropics—a combination of mesquite-grilled fresh fish and seafood, wood-burning oven thin-crust pizzas, and pastas.

Five minutes further up the highway is the small town of *San Francisco*, or "San Pancho" to regulars.

Turning right up a winding road, you arrive at a small gem of a hotel, *Costa Azul Adventure Resort*. Located at the end of a magnificent beach enclosed by two rocky points, this hotel has been a local pioneer in environmental awareness, sponsoring a sea turtle sanctuary and inviting hotel guests to participate in its operation. Visitors are welcome to come for the day and enjoy the water sports on the beach or take nature hikes and horseback rides in the jungle mountains behind the resort. On Fridays, the restaurant hosts one of the most charming Mexican Fiestas around, complete with a local singing star.

Marina Vallarta

Bruce Herman

One of Mexico's most attractive and well-planned marina developments, the 445-acre Marina Vallarta comprises slips for 355 boats, as well as one and a half miles of beach, an 18-hole golf course, water park, and two shopping centers.

Luxury hotels line the beachfront, while villas and a boutique hotel dot the course, and condominiums and timeshares surround the marina. A community park and the American School of Puerto Vallarta, which prepares young *Vallartenses* for a future in the local tourism industry, are located on the northern edge.

The well-protected marina is packed from November to May with leisure boats of every description. It's fun to stroll along the waterfront, or *malecon*, and see the beautiful sailboats and yachts, many with their owners living on board. Boats can be chartered here for day cruises and fishing trips.

The malecon is lined with sidewalk cafes, art galleries, craft shops and services. And one of the most spectacular views of the city is from atop the lighthouse-bar *El Faro*, which offers a 360-degree panorama of the entire area.

Each November, the *Fiestas del Mar* are celebrated in Marina Vallarta and other parts of Puerto Vallarta, culminating with a fishing competition, international gourmet festival and the Governor's Cup golf tournament.

Throughout the winter season, five top art galleries along the malecon host monthly events such as *Marina Art Night*, usually held on the third Friday of the month. The atmosphere is that of a block party with different musical groups entertaining gallery-goers as they walk from one exhibit opening to another.

Sailing regattas also take place throughout the winter months, many attracting international participants, such as the MEXORC and Banderas Bay regattas.

The marina was designed to be a self-con-

> *Sailing regattas, many attracting international participants, take place throughout the winter months.*

tained resort, which is convenient, since it's a good 15-minute drive from the downtown area. Still, it's easy enough to travel between the two districts. Taxis are plentiful and charge set fares: about four dollars from the marina to anywhere along the downtown malecon. Buses pass all the major hotels at the marina on their way downtown, and charge just a few pesos. On your return trip, make sure the bus' destination reads "Marina."

Heading toward town from Marina Vallarta is the Port of Puerto Vallarta, where deluxe cruise ships coming from California drop anchor, among them Princess Line's famous "Love Boat." In high season as many as 12 luxury liners per month make port for the day. Several bay cruisers and fishing boats also depart from this marina. Check the preceding chapter for details on specific activities in the area.

Restaurants

Argentina
Mayan Palace Hotel
Tel. 226-6000
An open-air terrace restaurant and bar specializing in Argentinian-style grilled meats. Open 7 to 11 p.m.

Bakal
Mayan Palace Hotel
Tel. 226-6000
This glass-enclosed cafe and restaurant with a view of the sea and open-air terrace seating offers international fare and a different dinner theme nightly, including a beachfront Mexican Fiesta Thursdays, 7 to 10 p.m., with folk dancing, mariachi music, fireworks and more. Open 7 a.m. to 11 p.m.

El Candil
Quinta Real Hotel
Tel. 226-6688
Award-winning cuisine served in an elegant glass-enclosed dining room overlooking the pool and golf course beyond. Specialties include honey-and-garlic duck and fillet of beef with mushroom sauce. Great Sunday brunch 9 a.m. to 3 p.m. Open for breakfast, lunch and dinner.

La Terraza di Roma
On the malecon, at Puesta del Sol Club de Tenis

Tel. 221-0560
Owned by popular men about town Esteban Gangoiti and Paolo Cavazzuti, this restaurant is a favorite spot for authentic Italian cuisine. Fresh-baked focaccia drizzled with olive oil gets the meal off to a delicious start. Follow with homemade pasta dishes or delicious brick-oven pizza. Air-conditioned dining room or lovely alfresco seating on a floating deck. Piano music. Open 8 a.m. to 11 p.m.

Mikado
CasaMagna Marriott Hotel
Tel. 226-0000
The price of dinner includes a show as expert chefs show off their teppanyaki cooking skills right at the table, effortlessly slicing, dicing, searing and sautéeing. Restful Japanese decor and outstanding attention to detail make this restaurant a great option. Open 6 to 11 p.m. Reservations recommended.

Morgan's Steak & Seafood Lounge
On the malecon, next to the lighthouse
Tel. 221-2576
At Puesta del Sol 20. Yachting enthusiasts and landlubbers alike will enjoy the nautical decor and tasty seafood dishes, including lobster and king crab, as well as crisp salads, steaks and the house specialty, BBQ ribs. Two air-conditioned bars and a covered terrace overlooking the marina. Open 11 to 1 a.m.

Nikki Beach
Westin Regina Hotel
Tel. 226-1150
Originating in Miami Beach, the Nikki Beach concept brings the jet set lifestyle to Vallarta (after first making a splash in Marbella, St. Tropez and St. Barth). Champagne and cocktails at noon, gourmet cuisine, and your very own private tent overlooking the beach, plus the latest music and fashions. The menu features chili-crusted beef tenderloin, satay chicken, crispy Atlantic salmon, and baked Florida snapper.

Porto Bello
On the malecon, at Marina Sol
Tel. 221-0003
This elegant Italian restaurant offers lunch or dinner in an art nouveau-style dining room or on a spacious patio overlooking the marina harbor. Homemade pastas and sauces are a tradition of Canadian owners Mario Nunes and Maurizio Pellegrini. Try the fusilli Porto Bello prepared from a traditional family recipe. Open noon to 11 p.m.

Tumtah
Mayan Palace Hotel
Tel. 226-6000
Fresh fish and seafood specialties in a setting evoking an Asian fish market, and overlooking the yacht harbor. Open 7 a.m. to 11 p.m.

Nightlife

Marina Vallarta is filled with activity in the evening hours, from musicians strolling along the malecon to sports bars. Most of the res-

taurants stay open late and provide a wonderful sidewalk cafe ambiance for enjoying after-dinner drinks and animated conversation. Several of the beachfront hotels also have entertainment in the evening, from open-air bars with live music to colorful Mexican Fiestas.

Champions
CasaMagna Marriott Hotel
Tel. 226-0000
Sports bar with snacks, comfortable seating and a pool table. Dance music nightly from 11 p.m. to 2 a.m.

Collage
Just south of Plaza Neptuno
Tel. 221-0505

This disco opens nightly at 10 and often doesn't close until dawn. Expect a dress code, which in Puerto Vallarta means no T-shirts, shorts or sandals.

El Faro
On the malecon, at Royal Pacific Yacht Club
Tel. 221-0541
Ride the elevator up to this circular bar perched atop the lighthouse and enjoy a tropical cocktail while taking in the stupendous view of the bay and city. Take a camera for that perfect sunset, and then make a night of it. Guitarist plays romantic tunes around 9 p.m.

La Cascada
Westin Regina Hotel
Tel. 221-1100
Enjoy cocktails in this beautiful and expansive open-air bar which overlooks the pool and gardens. The live guitar music nightly from 7 to 10 p.m. adds a romantic touch to the setting. Open noon to 1 a.m.

Shopping

On the malecon are several boutiques, galleries and convenience stores catering to visitors, residents and boat owners. Hours tend to run later in this area, with some places still open for business at 10 or 11 p.m. during high season.

Two shopping centers in the Marina Vallarta community are *Plaza Marina,* with a major supermarket, dry cleaners, fast-food spots, banks and shops, and *Plaza Neptuno,* at the main entrance, with over 20 specialty stores, decorator shops, a florist, medical center and trendy open-air deli. Lovely sculptures decorate the interior.

Andrea's Silver and Art
Plaza Neptuno
An attractive selection of sterling silver jewelry at reasonable prices. Also signed original pieces by gem cutter and metalsmith Juan Carlos Aguirre; his items are expensive but unique. Open 10 a.m. to 8 p.m. Closed Sunday.

Arte de Las Americas
On the malecon, at Marina Las Palmas II
Tel. 221-1985
Showcasing works by internationally celebrated artists and young emerging Mexican artists. A good spot to get orientation of the local art scene. Talk to Debora, the personable director of this gallery, which is associated with the long-established Galeria Uno. Late hours during high season.

Arte Primitivo
Plaza Neptuno
A vast collection of furniture and decorative items, much of it from the Orient.

Coleccion La Bohemia
Plaza Neptuno
Tel. 221-2160
Comfortable easy-care fashions with flair locally produced by designer Toody Walton in natural fabrics, from cottons to linens. Exclu-

Marina Vallarta

Vallarta Lifestyles

sive hand-painted "Artwear," collectible Mexican accessories and shoes built for comfort also featured. Special orders welcome. Open 10 a.m. to 8 p.m. Closed Sunday.

Galeria EM
On the malecon, at Marina Las Palmas II
Tel. 221-1728
Stained-glass decorative objects for the home designed by Estela Herrera and Mario Perez. At their workshop, located across from the Marina Vallarta entrance, you can watch craftsmen create these beautiful creations.

Maria de Guadalajara
On the malecon
Cool, comfortable resort wear in wrinkly, natural or dyed cotton designed by Maria Bennett. Mix-and-match one-size combinations.

Rodo Padilla
Plaza Neptuno
Tel. 221-2246
Original fine-quality ceramic sculptures by one of Tlaquepaque's most creative artists. Padilla's amusing figures, including his signature rollicking Mexican *charros* (cowboys), have found a place in private collections worldwide.

Vogue Vallarta
Plaza Marina
Tel. 221-0557
Original designs by Delia Cortez, who incorporates beautiful Mexican hand-crocheted lace into her mostly white and off-white creations. Her clothes have become classics in Vallarta.

Real Estate

By Silvia L. Elias

Important developments are taking place throughout Banderas Bay, where unique geological formations create a distinct variety of amazing landscapes, views and diverse real estate options along nearly 30 miles of drivable coastline, from Boca de Tomatlan, to the south, to Punta Mita, to the north.

South Shore

The bay's south shore enclave of world-class residences has set itself apart as the undisputed leader in luxury, selection, design, appreciation, and overall consistent return on investment. Nowhere else in the bay can you enjoy the same breathtaking panoramas.

The southside begins at the southernmost end of Los Muertos Beach (Zona Romantica) and gradually meanders, hugging the coast along the picturesque southern highway to the small fishing community of Boca de Tomatlan.

This area has always been considered the most popular and exclusive for purchasing or building a home or a condominium due to its impressive bay views, proximity to the downtown area, enchanting tropical ambience, and consistent appreciation of value.

Since there are few beachfront properties along the south shore, they demand the highest prices, but they also appreciate the fastest, which makes them wise investments and very desirable vacation homes.

As you head south from downtown Puerto Vallarta, the first hillside residential area is Alta Vista, followed by Amapas. Here we can find expansive hillside villas and high-end condominiums, many featuring one unit per floor and some exceeding 6,000 square feet. Amazingly, this area has tripled in growth over the past five years. Two reasons it has grown in popularity are its unparalleled views of the bay and city, and its proximity to downtown Puerto Vallarta.

Although few private homes and villas have been built in this privileged area, they offer a wide range of prices and styles, from 235,000 dollars for a smaller, freestanding home to 2.5 million dollars for a new contemporary villa with unsurpassed views.

Several new exclusive condominium projects, generally sold during the construction phase, have been developed in this area over the past five years, setting the standard for condominium living, including La Cima I, Selvamar, Brisa Lunar, Vista Amapas, Estrellita del Mar, and Vista Romantica, to name just a few. Resale prices range from 200,000 to 850,000 dollars for an exquisite two-story penthouse with a private pool (over 6,000 sq. ft. of con-

Marina Vallarta

Vallarta Lifestyles

struction). Other signature projects are planned for the very near future, such as the exclusive Villas La Teja and Horizon.

About a mile south of town lies prestigious Conchas Chinas Beach and mountainside. Its consistent rapid growth in high-end real estate is not surprising when you consider the views and infrastructure of this extraordinary location.

Conchas Chinas has historically been one of Puerto Vallarta's preeminent real estate markets, even jokingly referred to as Aspen South. The proximity of this area to downtown Puerto Vallarta, via either a scenic 20-minute walk or a five-minute drive, adds to its desirability. Originally, estates of grandiose proportions rose on sizeable oceanfront hillside lots along the west side of the highway, on chic Santa Barbara Street, otherwise known as Millionaires Row. These early residences afforded the luxury of great spaces where sparkling pools with cabanas and tennis courts were expected amenities. The astounding values placed on Santa Barbara's palatial residences range from 1.6 million to more than 7.5 million dollars.

Exclusive Conchas Chinas hillside villas vary in price from 700,000 dollars to 3.5 million dollars. Older homes fronting the beautiful sandy beaches of Amapas and Conchas Chinas, with their unique rock formations, were demolished and rebuilt or completely renovated to offer some of the most desirable villas in the entire bay. Many of these exclusive villas have been used as film locations and serve as vacation getaways for a select few. Even today, you'll find the homes of famous celebrities, such as Casa Septiembre. These marvelous villas can be purchased from 2.5 to 3.5 million dollars.

Traveling farther south along highway 200, we pass the former elegant Camino Real Hotel (today Dreams Resort). The site of this hotel sitting on its own beach in a natural cove is also shared by Los Venados and Las Estacas, where traditional villas in the romantic style of the South Pacific lie along the oceanfront, such as Casa Las Estacas, with its own tide pool and natural "geyser." This treasured cluster of beachfront homes, sitting on their own sheltered inlets, shares some of the bay's most exclusive addresses. Expect to pay more than 2 million dollars when one of these select homes becomes available.

Slightly further south is Punta Negra Beach, with several condominium buildings, such as the exclusive Punta Esmeralda (only one luxurious residence per level, starting at 820,000 dollars), Los Palmares, and the more affordable Punta Negra or Playa Esmeralda. Coto San Xoaquin is a recent addition to the select planned residential developments of the south shore.

Further along the southern coast, the coco palms seem to grow thicker as we reach Garza Blanca. Here, the atmosphere changes to one of a European coastal village. Prices range from 250,000 dollars to almost a million dollars for a contemporary or hacienda-style villa. Above it, the Sierra Vallarta development has opened for sale, offering 28 exclusive home sites from 27 dollars per sq. ft. to premier lots priced at 35 dollars per sq. ft.

Sierra del Mar, an upscale, gated residential community, is set in a manicured jungle setting directly above Playas Gemelas (Twin Beaches). This master-planned community offers extraordinary custom built villas from an affordable 850,000 dollars to more than 2 million dollars. Playas Gemelas offers a large selection of high-rise condominiums above the white sugarlike sands that made this area so famous. Inventory is scarce and prices range from 300,000 to 500,000 dollars for a more spacious unit.

On the south end of Playas Gemelas sits Paredon Colorado, a new gated community of only 10 luxurious custom built home sites. This prestigious development has been exclusively planned and designed by Elias & Elias Architects.

The bay's three natural arches, known as Los Arcos, provide a dramatic seascape for those fortunate enough to live in front. From the terraces at Villa Las Peñas, you can watch the seabirds soar over Los Arcos, listen to the waves crash below, and enjoy a spectacular panorama, which can be yours starting from 1.75 million dollars.

Mismaloya Bay is the site of La Jolla de Mismaloya Hotel, one of The Leading Hotels of the World, and many desirable villas and condominiums. Hillside residences, each overlooking the secluded emerald bay, range in price from 275,000 to more than 800,000 dollars. Oceanfront residences range in price from 1.2 to 3 million dollars, with condominiums priced at a more accessible 135,000 to 500,000 dollars.

Downtown

One of the few downtown areas anywhere with a nice sandy beach, *El Centro*, as it's called in Spanish, is a favorite of artists and romantics. The area is divided by the Cuale River, with its artsy island.

South of Rio Cuale is Colonia Emiliano Zapata, where some of the best-known condominium buildings are located along the main beach in town, Playa Los Muertos. This is the ideal location for those who like to be where the action is.

Prices of beachfront units in this area range from 150,000 dollars for a small one-bedroom unit to over 400,000 dollars for a two-bedroom. Units with partial views are slightly less expensive. Units that have undergone extensive renovations or penthouses go for quite more. These buildings are on average 10 or more years old. A newer project in this area is Playa del Sol, a combination of fractional ownership and fulltime units. Homes with a view can be purchased for around 375,000 dollars, large hacienda-style villas with interior gardens, for around 700,000 dollars.

Called El Cerro, or The Hill, the area located on the other side of the river and behind Guadalupe Church offers a spectacular view of the downtown area and is the location of numerous elegant homes and villas, many owned by foreign nationals. Locals call the neighborhood "Gringo Gulch" because the first foreign residents that owned homes in this area were from the U.S., among them celebrities such as Elizabeth Taylor, Richard Burton and John Huston.

Prices of homes along the riverside range from 275,000 to 650,000 dollars. Small fixer-uppers cost no less than 100,000 dollars. Just being constructed in this area are custom-built townhouses measuring approximately 3,000 sq. ft. and starting from 325,000 dollars.

Homes in the hillside are slightly more expensive than on the riverside, costing from 225,000 to 750,000 dollars; larger properties

sell for much more. The recently renovated Malecon II building offers 55 luxury condominiums, underground parking and a rooftop pool.

Colonial-style condominiums in this hillside garden setting, such as the acclaimed Puesta del Sol building, offer great variety. One-bedroom condominiums range in price from 68,000 to 145,000 dollars, and two-bedroom units, from 155,000 to 275,000 dollars.

The cost of recently sold view lots ranged from 50 to 80 dollars per sq. ft., depending on size and location.

Marina Vallarta

Puerto Vallarta boasts one of the country's finest marina developments. The Bay View Grand, with almost 500 condominium units, has been successful. A few affordable re-sales can be found in this exclusive project, including some corner penthouses for only 650,000 dollars. A couple of new mega-projects, Portofino and Shangri-La, are well on their way.

Condominiums in the marina area range from 85,000 dollars for a unit facing the avenue to over a million dollars for a villa in one of the waterfront complexes.

Private homes on the area's golf course fairways start at 285,000 dollars for a fully furnished two-bedroom duplex with a private pool, and go up to one million dollars for a home with a pool and top-of-the line materials.

North Shore

The Ameca River, one of the major rivers of Banderas Bay, divides the state of Jalisco from the state of Nayarit, where the north shore actually begins. Here, the master-planned development of Nuevo Vallarta and its excellent infrastructure of canal-front homes has gained the attention of a tourism market that previously overlooked Puerto Vallarta.

Nuevo Vallarta is designed to take full advantage of tropical seaside living. Seawater canals wind throughout, offering home sites with docks easy access to the bay. Grand hotels, luxurious beachfront estates and plush condominiums lie on the long stretches of beach. The area is home to the first fully enclosed shop-

ping mall in Vallarta as well as a first-rate marina. If golf is your passion, Nuevo Vallarta features three major courses with fairway homes already in full swing.

Home prices in Nuevo Vallarta range from 50,000 to more than 850,000 dollars. Since there are only 17 beachfront residential sites, beachfront home prices are generally in line with Puerto Vallarta prices, at more than 1.5 million dollars. Lots along the golf course are priced between 100,000 and 350,000 dollars. Waterfront canal lots are available and priced between 100,000 and 300,000 dollars. Along the northern Flamingos beachfront and golf course are several new condominium projects offering some of the most affordable units and townhouses on the north shore.

A visit to the small village of Bucerias makes you feel as if you have traveled back in time. Located north of Nuevo Vallarta, this hamlet has all the modern conveniences you need and the tropical beauty you expect; it only lacks tourists in the same numbers that flock to other beach destinations. This inviting beach community, home to many Canadians and Americans, has everything from beachfront homes and condominiums to hillside view properties. Prices range from 100,000 dollars for a condominium to more than 1.4 million dollars for a beachfront estate.

Further north is a cluster of homes on a small bay within the bay called Tizate. A series of individual beachfront homes line this hidden enclave of real estate gems. Prices range from 350,000 dollars for a beachfront lot to more than one million dollars for an oceanfront residence.

Taking advantage of superb views and ocean frontage is the master-planned community of Punta Esmeralda, a gated development with a private beach club where you can select from a condominium, some with private pools, to a freestanding home. Prices range from 250,000 to 700,000 dollars.

An easy walk north of Tizate, just before reaching La Cruz de Huanacaxtle, are three communities of Mediterranean-style homes called La Puntilla, Punta Pelicanos, and Vallarta Gardens. These oceanfront homes are priced from 350,000 to more than 750,000 dollars.

In the small fishing village of Huanacaxtle you'll find custom oceanfront homes, as well

as hillside view homes, with prices ranging from 350,000 dollars to over one million dollars for an oceanfront home.

Another master-planned development is Real del Mar, where view lots and waterfront living is set in an area of great natural beauty. The developers, taking advantage of the natural landscape, have located the community clubhouse on the beach, giving all owners the opportunity to share in the area's privileged cove. There are also tennis courts, a gym and spa. Home sites start from 360,000 dollars and villas, from 1.3 million dollars.

La Playa Estates is another pioneer beachfront gated community that has been developed on the north shore over the last five years.

Punta Tortugas, a charming small project, offers views of the bay and low-density development that is consistent with neighboring developments. All services, such as electricity, telephone and water, are available. Prices, depending on the view and access to the ocean, range from 250,000 to 600,000 dollars.

Paradise Coves truly describes this deluxe area of Costa Banderas, or Banderas Coast, offering only 12 home sites, all surrounded by an ecological reserve, priced from nearly 400,000 dollars. An exclusive beach club, walking trails and 24-hour security add to its allure.

Vast Pontoquito offers a mix of low-density (only 28) oceanfront and mountainside residential lots. Here, the lush tropical jungle surrounds you as you enjoy the views of the bay, and lots are attractively priced from 250,000 to 600,000 dollars.

Punta Caracol and Punta del Burro offer select clients a cluster of homes on one of the more desirable beaches. Punta Caracol, with only four homes planned, offers some of the bay's best buys in oceanfront living, with villas starting at 1.4 million dollars. Oceanfront homes in Punta del Burro have traditionally been sought by the discriminating buyer of oceanfront property; no other place in the Vallarta area reminds one of a sandy, palm laden Caribbean island like this spot does. Homes range from 650,000 dollars to more than 2 million dollars.

The masterpiece of planned development must be Punta Mita. With more than 1,600 acres of peninsula, all surrounded by white sandy beaches, this is the site of a Four Seasons and Rosewood resort. The infrastructure far exceeds expectations, with numerous amenities, such as a 19-hole championship golf course designed by Jack Nicklaus, for just 65 villa home sites. The price of a villa in this area can be expected to start at 1.8 million dollars and surpass 4.5 million dollars.

Clearly, the development of the north shore is attracting a clientele willing to exchange the charm of old Puerto Vallarta for the amenities and exclusivity of master-planned gated communities that meet the real estate demands of the sophisticated world traveler.

Among the most popular timeshare resorts in the Vallarta area are Paradise Village, Mayan Palace and Westin Regina. Prices vary greatly, ranging from 9,000 dollars for a week in low season to 40,000 dollars for a high-season week in December.

If you plan to vacation with your family or a group of friends, consider renting a villa or apartment. Exclusive properties available for rent include Villa Quinta del Sol, Brisas Altas, Cuatro Villas and the exceptional Villa Merissa, which comes with its own resident French chef. Prices vary from 400 to 1,200 dollars a night during low season to more than 1,500 dollars a day in high season. Condominiums rent for 80 to 200 dollars a night in low season, 150 to 300 dollars in high. Monthly rates are also available.

Long-term mortgages are now available through various U.S. financial institutions, allowing far more foreign investors to acquire property in Mexico.

Vallarta's real estate market continues to enjoy explosive growth; the major problem is a lack of inventory. Fortunately various new developments have started or are about to start, which may temporarily alleviate but not completely solve the inventory problem. Many private investors are purchasing older homes downtown or in the south shore area, remodeling and then reselling them.

We will definitely see more luxury condominium developments and private residences built on the south side due to the recent success of similar projects and increasing customer demand. The alternative to a south end or downtown property is to look northward, where there is still a fair amount of beachfront land available for development and hillsides with ocean views.

Owner and manager of her own realty firm since 1981, Silvia Elias has served as president and founding member of the Puerto Vallarta chapter of Mexico's Association of Real Estate Agents (AMPI) and is a Certified International Property Specialist (CIPS).

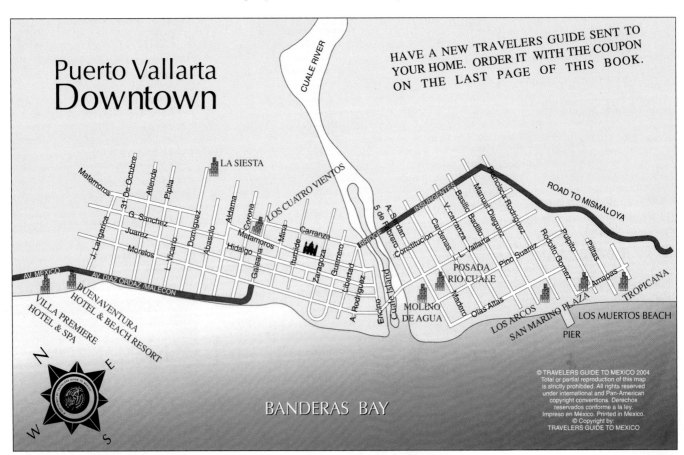

Puerto Vallarta
Downtown

HAVE A NEW TRAVELERS GUIDE SENT TO YOUR HOME. ORDER IT WITH THE COUPON ON THE LAST PAGE OF THIS BOOK.

BANDERAS BAY

Dining and Nightlife

For a serene little fishing village that used to roll up the sidewalks after sundown, Puerto Vallarta has come a long way.

At midday, visitors prefer to stay close to the beach. A local specialty is barbecued fish on a stick sold by beach boys who pluck them fresh from the ocean and cook them on the spot. It's delicious, especially accompanied by a cold drink.

Later in the day, it's customary to dress down and wander over to your favorite bar to watch the sunset—any place along the *malecon*, in the hills above it, or at Playa los Muertos offers a great vantage point.

Evenings are for sampling the better restaurants; in fact, many only open for dinner. The major hotels have excellent restaurants and dining at them is a good way to get to know some of the other properties. There are also many fine restaurants around town.

During peak tourist season, it's best to call ahead for reservations. Don't take much heed of taxi drivers' restaurant recommendations, since they may be pushing only those that give them a commission for bringing in customers.

Despite the variety of nighttime activity that Puerto Vallarta offers, dinner alone can make for a memorable evening. Of course, grilled fish and seafood dishes are big specialties here, but there's also a wide choice of Mexican and international restaurants.

The recommendations below have been grouped for your convenience according to geographic location. "Downtown" encompasses Old Town Vallarta, as well as the area south of Rio Cuale and along Playa Los Muertos, now called the Zona Romantica.

Velas Vallarta Hotel

Downtown

Abadía Café
Basilio Badillo 252
Tel. 222-6720
Enjoy Mexican and European specialties in a

Abadía
CAFÉ
BREAKFAST • LUNCH • DINNER

Mexican
&
European Specialties

Basilio Badillo 252
Reservations 222 6720

roberto_lavalle@hotmail.com
www.accessmexico.com/abadia

romantic indoor setting or on their pleasant terrace. A popular breakfast spot, featuring eggs Benedict, mimosas and classical music. Lunchtime offers three different pre-fixed lunch menus and two-for-one drinks, as well as tasty hamburgers and Mexican favorites. Early bird dinner available from 4 p.m. Open from 8 a.m.

Andale
Olas Altas 425
Tel. 222-1054
The bustling downstairs bar is a favorite with locals and tourists alike, and the covered sidewalk seating is perfect for people-watching. An upstairs dining area offers a tranquil setting for enjoying fine dining at a great value. The specialties of the house include osso bucco, juicy sirloin cheeseburgers with crispy cottage fries, and the catch-of-the-day cooked to order. All entrees accompanied by soup or salad. Open for breakfast, lunch and dinner; bar open after hours.

Archie's Wok
Francisca Rodriguez 130
Tel. 222-0411
A half block from the Playa los Muertos pier. Before opening Vallarta's legendary restaurant, Archie, the restaurant's namesake, was personal chef to movie director John Huston at his jungle villa, where he prepared daily feasts of tropical Asian cuisine based on Filipino, Thai and Chinese specialties. His wife Cindy successfully continues his legacy. Try their Thai garlic shrimp, spicy stirred vegetables, crisp egg rolls, or hoi-sin ribs, accompanied by zesty dipping sauces. And don't miss their Szechuan margarita! A classical duet plays Wednesday to Saturday evenings. Open 2 to 11 p.m. Closed Sunday.

Café des Artistes
Guadalupe Sanchez 740
Tel. 222-3229
Under the direction of chef-owner Thierry Blouet, who was admitted into the prestigious inner circle of the Maitre Cuisiniers de France in 2000, this leading restaurant features innovative French/Mexican cuisine served in attractive interiors or a multilevel garden setting, both decorated with contemporary art. Menu

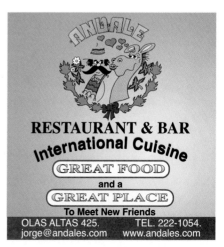

ANDALE

RESTAURANT & BAR
International Cuisine
GREAT FOOD
and a
GREAT PLACE
To Meet New Friends
OLAS ALTAS 425.   TEL. 222-1054.
jorge@andales.com   www.andales.com

favorites include fettuccini with stuffed mussels; chilled gazpacho with avocado cream; grilled tenderloin with camembert, chile chipotle and crusty pepper potatoes; and Moctezuma chocolate fondant. For an exclusive culinary treat, reserve a table at their top-floor Cocina de Autor dining room, where you get to rub elbows with the chef and his assistants. Reservations a must. There's a charming tapas bar with live music nightly. Open 6 to 11:30 p.m.; bar open till 2 a.m.

Coco Tropical
Basilio Badillo, on the beach
Tel. 222-5485
Fine dining on Olas Altas Beach in a tropical atmosphere with unforgettable sunsets. The

international cuisine with a Mediterranean influence includes fresh mushrooms, spinach and mozzarella in puff pastry; char-grilled tuna steak; coconut shrimp with banana-and-mango chutney; and delicious panna cotta brulée for dessert. Open 11 a.m. to midnight.

Daiquiri Dick's
Olas Altas 314, Playa los Muertos
Tel. 222-0566
This world class beachfront restaurant offers a wonderful unobstructed view of the ocean along with some of the best food and service to be found anywhere. Signature dishes include the unforgettable lobster tacos and the seafood Napoleon, part of a constantly changing menu of tempting specials. The restaurant's contemporary design (by Peter Bowman) exudes an understated elegance ideal for a quiet, relaxing breakfast, an alfresco lunch, or dinner under the stars. If you love the food, take a glance at the acclaimed "Sand in Your Shoes" cookbook authored by their ineffable chef and manager Rafael A. Nazario. Open 9 a.m. to 11 p.m. (closed Wednesdays from May through mid-October).

El Arrayan
Allende 344
Tel. 222-7195
The ideal spot for authentic Mexican fare, from the black bean soup garnished with pork rind to the traditional, sweetened *café de la olla*. Even the menu's typical design remains faithful to the style of neighborhood eateries. Don't miss the *pozole de camaron*, a hearty stew made with hominy corn and fresh shrimp. Owner-chef Carmen borrows from her great grandmother's own recipes and adds to it her Swiss culinary training. Open for lunch and dinner.

El Palomar de los Gonzalez
Aguacate 425, on a hill overlooking town
Tel. 222-0795
Excellent seafood and meat dishes in a romantic Mexican setting: tropical plants, waterfall, seating around a terrace pool. Spectacular view. Excellent service by the personable Juan Ramon Gonzalez, son of the owners. Open 6 to 11 p.m.

Fajita Republic
Pino Suarez and Basilio Badillo
Tel. 222-3131
A top spot in town for fajitas and Mexican food, all prepared with choice meats and fresh ingredients. Also try their BBQ ribs, steaks and seafood cooked to perfection on an open grill. Enjoy your meal under huge palm and mango trees in this casual and exotic setting, personally attended by the owner, Fernando, or try their walk-up seafood taco bar. Open 11 a.m. to midnight (taco bar open to 6 p.m.).

Kaiser Maximilian
Olas Altas 380-B
Tel. 223-0760
Longtime Vallarta hotelier turned restaurateur Andres Rupprechter offers fine European cuisine, including contemporary Austrian dishes, at his popular restaurant (named after a fellow

Austrian and onetime emperor of Mexico). Dine in a breezy sidewalk setting or in an air-conditioned, turn-of-the-century-style dining room. A favorite dish is *zwiebelrostbraten*, pounded beefsteak piled high with onion rings and sautéed potatoes. Top off your meal with chocolate mousse or *sachertorte and apfelstrudel*. Open 6 p.m. to midnight. Closed Sunday. The Espresso Bar features Austrian pastries, ice cream and more than 20 flavored coffees, plus full bar service, light breakfasts, lunches and dinners. Open 8 a.m. to midnight, except Sunday.

La Dolce Vita
Diaz Ordaz 674, on the malecon
Tel. 222-3852
This popular restaurant offers good Italian fare and a great view of the seafront promenade from its second-floor dining area. Enjoy freshly-prepared northern Italian specialties and 21 varieties of wood-burning brick oven pizza. On weekends the house band plays jazz. Open noon to 2 a.m., 6 p.m. to midnight Sunday.

La Hacienda
Aguacate 274
Tel. 222-0590
This hacienda-style restaurant is owned and operated by official town historian Carlos Munguia and his wife, Elena. Tables are set in a plant-filled patio and Mexican-style charcoal-broiled meats are the specialty. The Hacienda coffee doubles as dessert. Open 6 to 11:30 p.m. Closed Sunday.

La Nube
Matamoros 542
Tel. 223-0530
Occupying the top floor of a hilltop building, it offers a sweeping view and gourmet Italian cuisine. Owner Luigi's favorite menu items include sailfish carpaccio with arugula and leeks, grilled imported lamb marinated in rosemary, and sea bass in basil sauce. Don't miss the profiteroles with hot chocolate sauce. Open 6 to 11:30 p.m.

La Palapa
Pulpito 103, Playa los Muertos
Tel. 222-5225
A delicious blend of Mexican and Asian culinary traditions and an ideal setting by the ocean's edge have made La Palapa one of Vallarta's leading restaurants. Enjoy breakfast on the beach with original recipes and traditional favorites. Have a relaxing lunch at their new beach club, where you can sip a *cerveza* and watch the world go by. See the magic of sunset listening to live jazz and savoring the fresh flavors of the tropics in a torch-lit paradise. Try the pork won tons in pineapple relish, crab cakes with chipotle chili sauce, or pan-seared scallops with mango chutney. A memorable place. Open 8:30 a.m. to 11:30 p.m.

Las Cazuelas
Basilio Badillo 479
Tel. 222-1658
Since 1968, one of Vallarta's traditional fam-

ily-run restaurants, and well known for its gourmet Mexican cuisine and beautiful hacienda-style decor. Try the Aztec *mixiote*, a central Mexico delicacy of marinated meat slow-cooked in a maguey leaf. Indoor or terrace dining. Open 6 to 11 p.m. (closed part of the summer season). Reservations recommended.

Las Palomas
Diaz Ordaz 610, at Aldama, on the malecon
Tel. 222-3675
Especially popular for breakfast, this charming, casual spot has been serving good Mexican food and great drinks for 21 years. The atmosphere is comfortable with nightly sing-alongs. Open 8 a.m. to midnight or later.

Le Bistro
Isla Rio Cuale 16-A
Tel. 222-0283
Just off the southbound bridge. This leading restaurant has a unique garden setting beside the river and an attractive lounge bar featuring jazz tunes from the owners' ample collection. Increasingly popular with the foreign community, especially for its delicious crepes. The extensive menu includes fillet of red snapper baked in a crust of crunchy banana chips, and jumbo shrimp in toasted coconut and curry, plus Pacific spiny lobster cooked to order. Open 9 a.m. to midnight, except Sunday.

Los Arbolitos
Calle La Rivera 184, corner of Lazaro Cardenas
Tel. 223-1050
A family operation popular for its Mexican and seafood dishes, homemade flour or corn tortillas, reasonable prices and giant margaritas. Off the beaten track, but well known to locals. Open 11 a.m. to 11 p.m.

Los Xitomates
Morelos 570
Tel. 222-1694
A blend of traditional Mexican and European ingredients, the nouvelle Mexican cuisine has garnered write-ups in the L.A. Times and other publications. A tantalizing menu features coconut shrimp with spicy tamarind, ginger and lemon grass sauce, mushrooms stuffed with corn truffle, roasted tomato soup with goat cheese croutons, octopus sautéed with olive oil, garlic and three chilies, and other beef, chicken, seafood and vegetarian specialties.

Memo's Pancake House
Basilio Badillo 289
Tel. 222-6272
Run by Memo Barroso, writer of a popular guidebook to Mexico's Pacific coast. This bustling breakfast spot also attracts the crowds at night with its bar and grill specializing in "taco samplers." Breakfast 8 a.m. to 2 p.m., dinner 5 to 11 p.m.

Mezzaluna
Hidalgo 550
Tel. 222-0393
This intimate spot owned by three South Americans of Italian heritage offers a wonderful selection of homemade pastas. Menu high-

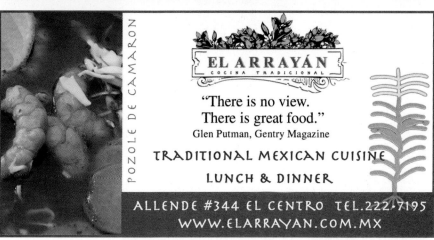

lights include goat cheese ravioli with sun-dried tomatoes, and fettuccini with smoked salmon and asparagus. Outdoor patio and small terrace. Open 6 p.m. to midnight. Closed Monday.

Oscar's
Isla Rio Cuale 1
Tel. 223-0789
Situated at the very tip of the island, this ideally-located spot offers alfresco dining with a wonderful view of the bay. The menu features classical international and seafood fare, including chateaubriand for two, grilled jumbo shrimp and lobster prepared to order. Live guitar music daily. Open 8 a.m. to 11 p.m.

Remembranzas
Pulpito 242, upstairs
Tel. 222-5342
One of Vallarta's most romantic spots for dining features two open-air terraces, a cozy colonial-style bar and a private dining room for small groups. Try the rack of lamb in fine herbs, chicken breast in peanut sauce, and a classic Mexican dessert with a twist, *flan de nuez*. Personal attention from owner Dora Macin. Open 6 p.m. to midnight.

Roberto's Puerto Nuevo
Basilio Badillo 283
Tel. 222-6210
A classic Vallarta-style restaurant offering indoor and terrace dining. Personable owner Roberto Castellon is always on hand to welcome his guests. Seafood is the specialty—try the smoked marlin, fish fillet mignon with mushrooms, or *mantarey* tacos.

Señor Mister Pepe's
Basilio Badillo 518
Tel. 222-0549
Charcoal-grilled Black Angus beef, lobster tail and jumbo shrimp, sizzling fajitas and excellent guacamole are some of the specialties. Personalized attention from owner Pepe and his family. The piano bar adds entertainment to the evening. Open October to May. Reservations needed.

Café Des Artistes Restaurant

The River Cafe
Isla Rio Cuale 4
Tel. 223-0788
An island of tranquillity featuring delicious international specialties, including deep-fried calamari with their special zesty house dressing, baked mahi-mahi in a garlic-and-fine herbs crust, and rack of lamb with rosemary and wild rice risotto. Popular jazz duo Beverly and Willow draw listeners in the evenings to this newly-remodeled setting of tropical palapas and gardens by the river's edge. Open 9 a.m. to 11:30 p.m. Reservations recommended.

The Shrimp Factory
Ignacio Vallarta 237
Tel. 222-2365
A branch of the popular Mazatlan establishment that serves peel and eat shrimp fresh from Mexican waters, never frozen. Open 11 a.m. to 11 p.m.

Trio
Guerrero 264
Tel. 222-2196
This casually elegant eatery in an old townhouse with a rooftop bar is run by two European chefs who combine their experience and passion for the culinary arts. Their classic Mediterranean menu features beef carpaccio with aged balsamic vinegar and shaved Parmesan cheese, Tuscany roasted garlic and rosemary soup, pan-roasted sea bass with white pepper sauce, and warm chocolate cake soufflé with vanilla ice cream. Open 6 p.m. to midnight. Reservations recommended.

Hotel Zone

Avanzare
Holiday Inn Hotel
Tel. 226-1700
An intimate setting with art nouveau touches and Mediterranean specialties, including breast of chicken stuffed with goat cheese and red peppers, and, for dessert, iced Grand Marnier soufflé with vanilla sauce. Open 6 p.m. to midnight. Closed Sunday.

Bogart's
NH Krystal Hotel
Tel. 224-0202
Upscale Moroccan decor and an elaborate menu. The white dining room with reflecting pools and fountains is staffed by waiters in white turbans. The international cuisine features flambéed specialties and a noteworthy rack of lamb. Live dance music Thursday to Saturday from 7 to 10 p.m. Open from 6 p.m. to midnight.

Los Murales
Villa Premiere Hotel
Tel. 226-7001
Gourmet Mexican cuisine served in an attractive, intimate contemporary Mexican setting surrounded by art. The menu changes with the seasons. Personalized service. Reservations required. Open 6 to 11 p.m. Closed Wednesday.

Kamakura
NH Krystal Hotel
Tel. 224-0202
Craving authentic Japanese cuisine? This is the place. Charming Oriental ambiance, dishes prepared tableside. Popular and fun. Open 5 p.m. to midnight; closed Monday.

La Petite France
Fiesta Americana Hotel
Tel. 293-0900
Toulouse Lautrec posters deck the walls of this casual bistro and wine bar. Try a variety of wines by the glass and typical French favorites like homemade paté, coq au vin, canard a l'orange or entrecote a la bordelaise. Live piano music or recorded French artists. Open for breakfast, lunch and dinner.

Las Gaviotas
Sheraton Buganvilias Hotel
Tel. 226-0404
This elegant restaurant with a tropical setting, excellent international cuisine and attentive service hosts a lively Fiesta Mexicana Thursdays from 7 to 10 p.m., featuring Mexican music, folk dancing, an extensive buffet and drinks. Open for dinner, 5 p.m. to midnight, with live piano music. Sunday Champagne brunch with mariachi music, from 9 a.m. to 2 p.m.

Outback Steak House
On Francisco Medina Ascencio
Tel. 225-4906
In front of NH Krystal Hotel. The Vallarta branch of the famous Aussie steak house offers the same favorites, including Bloomin' onion, deep fried and served with horseradish-cheese dip, shrimp on the barbie, and beef imported from Outback's own U.S. ranch. Wines from Down Under. Open 4 to 11 p.m.

Tarantino's
Francisco Medina Ascencio 1952
Tel. 224-3939
Opposite Villas Vallarta mall. A five-time winner of Mexico's Eagle award for quality and presentation, Tarantino's serves 18 varieties of pizza and other Italian favorites. Free home and hotel delivery. Open noon to 11:30 p.m., except Monday.

South of Town

Chico's Paradise
Km. 20 on the highway to Manzanillo
Tel. 222-0747
This large, rustic, palm-thatched restaurant sits where river waters flowing down the mountainside gather in a large natural pool; you can have a swim and work up an appetite. The restaurant's specialties include *ceviche* Mismaloya, a lemon-and-coconut marinated fish cocktail, jumbo shrimp cooked to order, and coconut pie. Live music. Open for breakfast, lunch and dinner.

Da Antonio
Presidente InterContinental Hotel
Tel. 228-0507
Gourmet Italian cuisine served by candlelight with views of the bay. Attentive service. Open for dinner only.

John Huston's Restaurant
La Jolla de Mismaloya Hotel
Tel. 226-0660
Named in honor of the film director who helped put Vallarta on the map, this casual hilltop restaurant features fresh fish and seafood specialties accompanied by a sweeping view of the ocean and Los Arcos. Try a traditional *raicilla* aperitif made with mezcal and served with zesty orange slices. Open 11 a.m. to 11 p.m.

The Sets of the Night of the Iguana
La Jolla de Mismaloya Hotel
Tel. 226-0660
This elegant hilltop restaurant-bar, built on the

film site of the famed Hollywood movie, offers international and seafood specialties, including charcoal-grilled steaks, shrimp or whole fish, beef fillet stuffed with shrimp, and crab-filled pear. You can have a relaxing brunch with a view, or romantic dinner by candlelight. Indoor and outdoor seating. Mariachi music in the evenings (in high season). Open 11 a.m. to 11 p.m.

Special

Don Pedro's
Sayulita
Tel. (329) 291-3090
On the beach in the small fishing village of Sayulita, north of the bay. Housed under a giant palapa with views of the ocean and jungle, this spot features Chef Nicholas Parillo's (formerly of Prego's in Beverly Hills and The Rex in L.A.) gourmet Mediterranean cuisine with a touch of the tropics. Mesquite-grilled fresh fish and seafood, wood-burning oven thin-crust pizzas, and pastas. Open 11 a.m. to 11 p.m.

Tino's
Pitillal
Tel. 224-5584
Avenida 333, corner of Revolucion, in Pitillal, a small town on the outskirts of Vallarta. A 10 to 15-minute drive from the hotel zone or marina, this colonial-style restaurant-bar is famed for serving some of the best seafood in the area. Specialties include *pescado sarandeado*, whole red snapper barbecued in a rich sauce, and shrimp *diablo*, grilled and served with a spicy tomato dip. Trio music from 3 to 6 p.m. Open noon to 11 p.m. Their sister restaurant in Nuevo Vallarta, Laguna Tino's, offers lagoonside dining.

Nightlife

A few short years ago, painting the town would have taken only minutes to do. Now you can sip a drink and listen to jazz at a swanky bar, sway to tropical rhythms, or swoon to the sounds of a romantic trio. You can even dance the night away to pulsating music at laser-lit

discotheques or seafront restaurants that turn into dance clubs as the night wears on.

Many nightclubs and a few of the resort's leading restaurants feature live music. In the downtown area, *La Bodeguita del Medio,* a replica of Havana's famed 1940s nightclub, brings the tropical rhythms of that Caribbean nation to Vallarta, with a Cuban band that plays salsa and merengue. At *Zapata,* you can hear pre-Hispanic and Latin American folk music; at the *Hard Rock Cafe,* there's live rock 'n' roll; at the *Kit Kat Lounge,* you can reminisce to classic hits; and there's jazz at *Mogambo*.

Many top restaurants have pleasant bars, including *Café des Artistes* and *De Santos,* where lights are dimmed for after-dinner dancing from midnight to 4 a.m.

After dark, the *malecon* is aptly called the "wild malecon," a reference to the dancing, often on table tops, that takes place at several restaurant-cum-nightclubs lining the seafront promenade.

Probably the best-known area for nightlife is the Zona Romantica, along Ignacio Vallarta Street. Within a few blocks are numerous bars and nightclubs with live music and entertainment that continues into the wee hours. It's a great place for bar hopping.

For a change of pace, English-language musical theater is staged at the Santa Barbara restaurant on Olas Altas; check the local listings for schedules.

Andale Bar
Olas Altas 125
Tel. 222-1054
This watering hole is very popular with locals and tourists, and is open at all hours.

Carlos O'Brian's
Diaz Ordaz 786, on the malecon
Tel. 222-1444
A restaurant-bar especially popular with the young set. What it lacks in elegance, it makes

up for in atmosphere created by the blasting music, impromptu stage shows, and eye-popping color scheme. Wild, leaning towards scandalous. Open to 2 a.m.

Christine
NH Krystal Hotel
Tel. 224-6990
This disco ranks among Mexico's more sophisticated and attractive. Always crowded and lots of fun. Open from 10 p.m.

Club Paco Paco
Ignacio Vallarta 278
Tel. 222-1899
Vallarta's gay disco. Rooftop bar and grill, pool table and video bar. Open 3 p.m. to 6 a.m.

Club Roxy
Ignacio Vallarta 219
Tel. 223-2404
Live R&B, pop rock and dance tunes from 10 p.m. Happy Hour, from 6 to 9 p.m., features fruit-of-the-season margaritas. Open 6 p.m. to 1 a.m., except Sunday.

Costantini
Guadalupe Sanchez 740
Tel. 222-3229
An ultra-chic tapas bar and lounge with live music nightly. Open until 2 a.m.

De Santos
Morelos 771
Tel. 223-3052
This sleek, upscale restaurant-bar features eclectic music, from salsa to swing. After dinner the lights are turned down and the music turned up. Open until 4 a.m.

Hard Rock Cafe
Diaz Ordaz 652, at Abasolo, on the malecon
Tel. 222-5532
Live rock 'n' roll every night, except Wednes-

day, from 10 p.m. to closing.

Kit Kat Lounge & Café
Pulpito 120
Tel. 223-0093
A retro cocktail lounge that brings back the drinks, tunes and look of yesteryear. Martinis, Manhattans and a wide range of exotic mixed drinks, Frank Sinatra and Nat King Cole hits, and leopard-skin decorative touches. Open 6 p.m. to 2 a.m.

La Bodeguita del Medio
Diaz Ordaz 858, on the malecon
Tel. 223-1585
This replica of the celebrated 1940s club in Havana offers Cuban food, music and ambiance, as well as a spectacular view of the malecon from its second-floor, open-air dining area. Try their *mojito,* a popular Cuban drink that resembles lemonade served with white rum and crushed mint leaves. A Cuban band entertains in the afternoons and evenings; dancing in the aisles.

Mariachi Loco
Lazaro Cardenas, corner of Ignacio Vallarta
Tel. 223-2205
This lively cantina presents mariachis in concert 7:30 p.m. to 4 a.m.

Señor Frog's
Venustiano Carranza and Ignacio Vallarta
Tel. 222-5171
A restaurant-bar especially popular with the young set. Cavernous warehouse setting with sawdust-strewn floors. Quiet by day, frat party atmosphere at night. Open noon to 4 a.m.

Zapata
Diaz Ordaz 522, on the malecon
Tel. 222-4748
This second-floor Mexican restaurant features live pre-Hispanic and Latin American folk music. Open from noon.

Mexican Fiestas

The Fong family are the genial hosts of Vallarta's longest-running Mexican Fiesta, started more than 30 years ago and still going strong. Their Mexican dinner-show includes folk dancers, lasso-spinning *charros* (Mexican cowboys), ranchero singers, a "harmless" cockfight, piñatas, and more. Shows are held at *La Iguana,* downtown at Lazaro Cardenas 311, Thursdays and Sundays. For reservations, call 222-0105, or consult your hotel travel desk.

Many major hotels, including the NH Krystal, Mayan Palace, Sheraton, and Buenaventura, stage weekly Mexican Fiestas with a Mexican buffet and open bar, mariachis, marimbas or other types of regional music, and folk dancing from different parts of the country.

Where to Shop

Shops on Isla Río Cuale offer colorful handicrafts and souvenirs.

Puerto Vallarta is uniquely positioned to offer visitors a wide range of high quality arts and crafts since it is part of Jalisco state, home to Mexico's handicraft centers of Tlaquepaque and Tonala.

Vallarta is also a major center of contemporary art, as its number of long-standing art galleries can attest. Since the early 70s, artists have been moving to this tropical paradise, enticed by the spectacular scenery and beautiful light. Many have attained international status. Several galleries organize a joint exhibition night during the high season known as the Art Walk, and tours of artists' studios. Remember, art brought into the United States is duty free.

Huichol Indians, who live in the remote regions of the Sierra Madre mountains in the states of Jalisco and Nayarit, are a large presence in Vallarta (and easily recognized by their colorfully embroidered native garb). One of the most reclusive and thus pure pre-Columbian peoples in the Americas, the Huichol come to the resort exclusively to sell their unique yarn "paintings," woven goods, beaded masks, beaded wrist cuffs and other ornaments.

A truly local product in Vallarta is resort wear—clothing designed with the tropics in mind. Beginning in the 60s several small shops began to sell dresses and shirts made from beautiful woven fabrics hand-embroidered by local women. A casual, loose-fitting style emerged that is now interpreted by several local designers, such as Delia Cortez, Laura Lopez Labra and Toody Walton. Beautiful hand-painted cotton clothing is also offered by several textile artists in town. Durable Mexican-style leather sandals, called *huaraches,* are another good buy and can be made to order.

Most shops and galleries are located along Old Town Vallarta's main shopping strips, Juarez and Morelos, and the streets that intersect them. Interesting shops and boutiques can also be found in downtown's Zona Romantica, the neighborhood located south of Rio Cuale, especially along Basilio Badillo Street. Vallarta's top shopping centers are *Plaza Neptuno,* at the entrance to Marina Vallarta, and Nuevo Vallarta's *Paradise Plaza*. The *Mercado Municipal,* a typical market located downtown between the two bridges, offers Mexican curios.

As in most beach resorts, stores often close during the hottest time of the day, from 2 to 4 p.m. Most open at 10 a.m. and remain open until 8 or 9 p.m. Several shops in the restaurant zones can be found open until 10 or 11 p.m. Better shops tend to close on Sunday, although some galleries will open by appointment.

Jewelry

Astrid
Dreams Puerto Vallarta Hotel, NH Krystal Hotel, La Jolla de Mismaloya Hotel - Pto. Vallarta. Paradise Village Shopping Center - Nvo. Vallarta.
Exclusive designs in 18k and 14k gold jewelry, many featuring precious or semiprecious gems backed by a certificate of authenticity. Also a select range of silver jewelry from Taxco and great gift items.

Cerroblanco
Leona Vicario 226
Tel. 223-3546
Pepe Cerroblanco, third generation jeweler of the famous San Miguel de Allende family, and his American-born wife Kate offer his export line of contemporary silver and gold creations with semiprecious stones. Many of his designs have been in Sak's Christmas catalogue. Stays open late as it is just below Café des Artistes.

Daniel Espinosa Jewelry
Morelos 600
Tel. 223-0863
Bold, contemporary designs in silver by the talented Taxco-based jeweler, including many pieces with semiprecious stones. Espinosa's creativity and sense of fun is evident in his tie-style chokers made of silver cubes and red beads, silver and leather combinations, hypnotic silver rings with black enamel swirls, and other unique jewelry.

Sergio Bustamante Gallery
Juarez 275
Celebrated Mexican artist Sergio Bustamante, known for his whimsical sculptures and decorative items, has created a distinctive line of 22k gold, gold-plated sterling silver, and sterling silver jewelry featuring his signature faces, hands, blazing suns and moons. Two other locations downtown.

Viva
Basilio Badillo 274

Tel. 222-4078
An inviting emporium of eclectic jewelry representing the work of more than 70 designers from around the world. Pieces range from tribal-style ornaments made with shells and bone to strings of pearls or semiprecious stones mounted in gold, prices range from 3 dollars to 3,000 dollars. Open 10 a.m. to 10 p.m. daily.

Clothing and Accessories

Coleccion La Bohemia
Basilio Badillo and Constitucion
Tel. 222-3164
Featuring comfortable easy-care fashions with flair locally produced in natural fabrics by designer Toody Walton. Exclusive hand-painted "Artwear," collectible Mexican accessories, and shoes built for comfort can all be found in this shop, a favorite with visitors and residents for more than 15 years. Call to find out where their weekly fashion shows are being staged. Open 10 a.m. to 9 p.m.

Mar de Sueños
Leona Vicario 230-C
Tel. 222-2662
Luxurious swim wear and fine lingerie from La Perla.

Mosaïqe
Basilio Badillo 277. Tel. 223-3146
Juarez 279. Tel. 223-3183
Attractive original designs in clothing and accessories, including exotic silver jewelry, some of it with semiprecious stones, beaded bags, beach wraps and mix-and-match combinations made of rich hand-dyed and handmade fabrics.

Handicrafts and Folk Art

Alfareria Tlaquepaque
Mexico 1100
Tel. 223-2350
Operated since 1953 by the Fregoso family, this outlet has featured many of the lovely hand-crafted items you've admired as decor in restaurants and hotels, especially painted pottery and earthenware. Good selection and very reasonable prices. Stays open Sunday.

Artes Mexicanos
Honduras and Colombia
Tel. 222-0525
Fine, handmade violins and acoustic guitars produced in Paracho, Michoacan, and personally selected by the owners. Large assortment of wonderfully colorful baskets as well.

Galeria de Ollas
Morelos 101
Tel. 223-1045
Famed pottery from Mata Ortiz, a small town in Chihuahua that has revived the sophisticated ceramics making of Mexico's ancient Paquimé civilization. The intricately designed pieces are made using the same technique (without the use of a potter's wheel or kiln). Prices range from less than a 100 to more than 1,000 dollars, depending on size and intricacy of design.

Hecho a Mano
Zaragoza 160
Tel. 223-2819
Inspired decorations by well-known Jalisco designer David Luna, using typical handicrafts.

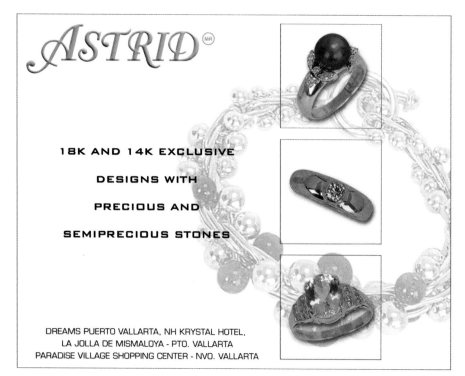

Also teak furniture and decorative items from Bali. Open 10 a.m. to 10 p.m.

Indigo
Basilio Badillo 241
Tel. 223-0107
Hand-loomed textiles from Guatemala made into fabulous decorative items and accessories: pillows of all sizes, table linens, hammocks and bedroom coordinates. Woven bags and shawls are some of the wearable items. Open 10 a.m. to 10 p.m. Closed Sunday.

Olinala Gallery
Lazaro Cardenas 274
Tel. 222-4995
This museumlike gallery specializes in fine Mexican folk art, especially authentic ceremonial masks. Also beaded Huichol art, lapidary work and rare, one-of-a-kind pieces. Free crating and airport delivery.

Patti Gallardo's Eclectic Art
Basilio Badillo 250
Tel. 222-5712
Unique hand-painted clothing and accessories, and decorative items. Everything from the whimsical rugs and cushions to duvet covers, figurines and hand-carved furniture reflect Gallardo's creative style.

Querubines
Juarez 501, corner of Galeana
Tel. 222-2988
A charming, labyrinthine emporium of high quality Mexican arts and crafts. Lose yourself among stacks of intricately embroidered cotton dresses, bolero jackets, Panama-style hats, and more.

Talavera, Etc.
Ignacio Vallarta 266
Tel. 222-4100
Three blocks south of Rio Cuale. Exclusive distributors of leading Talavera maker Uriarte.

Art Galleries
Galeria Arte Latinoamericano

Josefa Ortiz Dominguez 155
Tel. 222-4406
A showcase for local talents, most notably painter Martha Gilbert, who puts on two shows a year, in November and February. A great place for posters also.

Galeria Dante
Basilio Badillo 269
Tel. 222-2477
Vallarta's only gallery dedicated exclusively to sculpture. Classical to contemporary pieces from Mexico and Italy, including works by Agustin Alfaro, Gabriel Colunga and Octavio Gonzalez, author of the whale sculpture at Marina Vallarta.

Galeria Pacifico
Aldama 174
Tel. 222-1982
Wide selection of sculptures and paintings in various media by midrange masters to rising stars, including Ramiz Barquet, author of "Nostalgia," the bronze couple sitting on the *malecon*; Evelyne Boren and Rogelio Diaz. Affable owner Gary Thompson has 20 years of experience in Latin American art, has curated exhibits in the U.S., works as easily with new art enthusiasts as with experienced collectors.

Galeria Uno
Morelos 561
Tel. 222-0908
Representing a wide variety of well-known artists, including Esau and Raymundo Andrade, Lee Chapman and Oscar Zamarripa.

Galerie des Artistes
Leona Vicario 248
Tel. 223-0006
Opening an art gallery was a natural step for Thierry Blouet and his wife Adriana, whose restaurant, Café des Artistes, has long lived up to its name by serving as a venue for art exhibits. Paintings and sculptures by major Mexican artists, such as Rivera, Orozco, Bejar, as well as antiques and unique sculpted glass art. Open noon to midnight. Closed Tuesday.

Kathy Von Rohr Studio
Manuel M. Dieguez 321
Tel. 222-5875
For many years the artist lived an idyllic life in a beach house by John Huston's former residence, developing her skills using nature as her inspiration. Her studio features sculptures, lithographs, watercolors, oils.

Manuel Lepe
Juarez 533
Tel. 222-5515
This museum/gallery displays a handful of original works by the late Manuel Lepe, Mexico's pioneer painter of primitive art, and a few of his personal items. Lepe's paintings of Vallarta, known for their trademark angels in the sky, have found their way into the art collections of John Huston, Peter O'Toole, John Travolta and England's Queen Elizabeth.

Where to Stay

Vallarta Lifestyles

Andale
Olas Altas 425, downtown
Tel. (322) 222-1054
www.andales.com
Vallarta regulars will recognize the name of the casual and popular restaurant-bar that now offers 13 standard rooms and two penthouse suites with ocean view. Rates ECON.

Buenaventura Hotel & Beach Club
Av. Mexico 1301
Tel. (322) 226-7000
www.buenaventuraonline.com.mx
On the beach, near the downtown area. A popular five-story hotel with a tropical look and 236 comfortable air-conditioned rooms and suites with color TV; four with private jacuzzi. Palapa restaurant, bar, large swimming pool, jacuzzi. All-inclusive option available. Rates MD.

Dreams Puerto Vallarta
Playa las Estacas, south of town
Tel. (322) 226-5000
Recently acquired by AMResorts, operators of top-of-the-line all-inclusives, this property (formerly Camino Real) is on a secluded cove. There are about 330 spacious rooms and suites distributed in two towers, some with terrace jacuzzi, all with spectacular views. Pool, fitness center, tennis. Meeting facilities for 1,200 people. Rates DX (all inclusive).

Fiesta Americana
Francisco Medina Ascencio Blvd., Km. 2.5

Tel. (322) 224-2010
www.fiestaamericana.com
In the hotel zone. This attractive nine-story beachfront property has 291 rooms, including 35 suites, with satellite TV, hair drier, safe; a spectacular open-air palapa lobby, pool area with jacuzzi, fountains, three restaurants, pool and beach bars, children's activities, and courtesy Marina Golf Club membership. Meeting facilities for 600. Rates FC.

Hacienda Hotel & Spa
Francisco Medina Ascencio Blvd. 2699
Tel. (322) 226-6667
www.haciendaonline.com.mx
In the hotel zone, a block from the beach. A pretty Mexican colonial-style hotel and spa with good service and a relaxed atmosphere. Most of the 155 air-conditioned rooms have a balcony and overlook beautiful gardens and a large pool; satellite TV. *Temazcal* (pre-Hispanic sweat lodge). Small well-equipped meeting room, restaurant, bar. Rates MD.

Hacienda San Angel
Miramar 336, downtown

> ## HOTEL RATES
> **LX**: luxury, rates above 375 USD
> **DX**: deluxe, rates from 250-375 USD
> **FC**: first-class, rates from 150-250 USD
> **MD**: moderate, rates from 75-150 USD
> **ECON**: economical, rates under 75 USD

Tel. (322) 222-2692
www.haciendasanangel.com
Housed in Richard Burton's former home in the hills overlooking the town and bay below, this boutique hotel offers a unique resort experience: nine suites exquisitely decorated with antiques, all modern amenities, in-room spa services. Large heated pool with panoramic view, rooftop sun deck with jacuzzi, fine dining, and more. Not suitable for children. Rates FC (includes continental breakfast).

Holiday Inn
Francisco Medina Ascencio Blvd., Km. 3.5
Tel. (322) 226-1700
www.holidayinnpvr.com
In the hotel zone. A nine-story building with 231 comfortable rooms with private balconies facing the Pacific, and an 18-story tower with 144 junior suites. Restaurant, lobby bar with live music, tennis courts, pool, jacuzzis, gym with steam room. Meeting facilities for up to 700 people. Rates MD.

La Jolla de Mismaloya
Twelve minutes south of town
Tel. (322) 2 26-0660
www.lajollamexico.com
This all-suite resort on Mismaloya Bay offers 303 one- and two-bedroom suites with ocean-view terrace. The Spanish-colonial-style grounds feature four large pools, fitness center, jacuzzis, lighted tennis courts, bars, restaurants, kids club, convention center. All-inclusive option available. Rates FC.

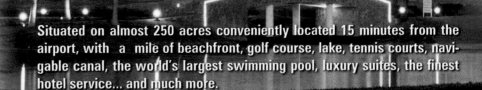

Los Cuatro Vientos
Matamoros 520, downtown
Tel. (322) 222-0161
A small budget hotel located high above town. The 14 simple but comfortable rooms have domed ceilings and colorful flowers stenciled on the walls. Good restaurant, rooftop bar with panoramic view. Rates ECON.

Majahuitas
On Playa Majahuitas, south of town
Tel. (322) 221-5808
www.mexicoboutiquehotels.com
20 minutes by boat from Boca de Tomatlan. This secluded, solar-powered, environmentally-friendly beach resort offers eight one- to four-person *casitas* built around a lush cove. Good dining, private beach. Member of Mexico Boutique Hotels. Rates FC (AP).

Molino de Agua
Ignacio Vallarta 130
Tel. (322) 222-1907
www.molinodeagua.com
This downtown hotel features 60 units scattered around nicely-landscaped gardens, including oceanview and oceanfront rooms, all with a/c, terrace. Two pools, jacuzzi, beachfront and patio dining. Rates MD.

NH Krystal
Av. de las Garzas, on the beach
Tel. (322) 224-0202
www.nh-hotels.com
Built on 12 hectares of land in the hotel zone, this attractive resort has been designed to resemble a typical Mexican village with 128 colonial-style rooms and 8 suite villas with private pool. New fully-equipped beach club, lovely swimming pools, hot tub, massage area. Specialty restaurants, disco. Well-staged Mexican Fiesta with delicious buffet. Banquet and convention facilities, kids club year-round. Rates MD.

Playa Conchas Chinas
Barra de Navidad Hwy., Km. 2.5
Tel. (322) 221-5230
www.conchaschinas.com
South of town, on Playa Conchas Chinas. This Mexican-style property built on a hillside offers 19 rooms, four junior suites with jacuzzi, and a three-bedroom master suite with a private pool, all with terraces overlooking the ocean (known for its great sunset views). Rooms have a/c, satellite TV. Swimming pool, restaurant. Rates MD.

Presidente InterContinental
Barra de Navidad Hwy., Km. 8.5
Tel. (322) 228-0507
www.intercontinental.com
12 minutes south of town. Remodelled and operating under a new, no longer all-inclusive concept, this hotel is nestled on a lovely private cove with a mountain backdrop. The 120 suite-size rooms, including 19 with whirlpool tubs, have ocean views, private balconies, sitting areas, a/c, TV, minibar. International restaurants, lobby bar, wet bar. Swimming pool, lighted tennis court, fitness center facing the ocean, supervised kids program. Meeting rooms for up to 150 people. Rates DX.

Sheraton Buganvilias Resort & Towers
Francisco Medina Ascencio Blvd. 999
Tel. (322) 226-0404
www.sheratonvallarta.com
In the hotel zone. Newly remodeled and better than ever, this deluxe beachfront offers 501 rooms and 150 suites with cushy Sweet Sleeper Beds, ocean views; 72 exclusive Towers section units have added amenities. Two expansive swimming pools, four tennis courts, gym, jacuzzi, vacation-time kids program, restaurants, bars, one with entertainment, meeting facilities for up to 1,200. Rates FC.

Villa Premiere Hotel & Spa
San Salvador 117, on the beach
Tel. (322) 226-7046
www.villapremierehotelspa.com
Located on the edge of the downtown area, this deluxe oceanfront hotel and spa offers 83 well-appointed rooms and suites with private balcony with ocean views and whirlpool tubs. Lovely swimming pool area, gym and spa. Restaurants, bar, 24-hour room service. All-inclusive option available. Rates FC.

Marina Vallarta

CasaMagna Marriott Resort
Paseo de la Marina 5
Tel. (322) 226-0000
www.casamagnapuertovallarta.com
An impressive oceanfront property with 433 rooms and suites with deluxe amenities, private balconies. Health club, jacuzzi, sauna, swimming pool, lighted tennis courts, formal and casual restaurants, bars. Business center, extensive meeting facilities and resident meeting planner. Rates DX.

Mayan Palace
Paseo de la Marina Sur 220
Tel. (322) 226-6000
www.mayanpalace.com
This modern Mexican-style hotel and timeshare offers a beachfront location and expansive grounds with a large freeform swimming pool, navigable canal for canoeing, and watersports marina. The 292 spacious rooms and luxury suites, some with kitchenette, are distributed in three towers. An aquapark makes a terrific playground for kids. Three swimming pools, gym, spa and tennis courts. Steak and seafood restaurants, lobby bar. Rates DX.

Melia
Paseo de la Marina Sur 7
Tel. (322) 221-0200
www.solmelia.com
This attractive property features a huge pool in the shape of Pablo Picasso's "Dove of Peace" and nicely landscaped grounds. A leading all-inclusive with 360 attractive rooms, meeting facilities. Rates FC (all inclusive).

Quinta Real
Pelicanos 311

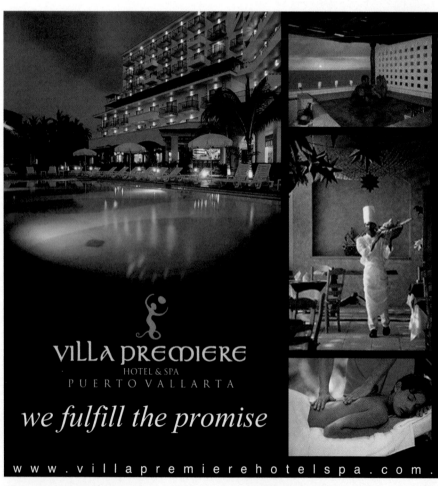

Tel. (322) 226-6688
www.quintareal.com
This lovely colonial-style mansion is set on the edge of the golf course (reduced green fees for guests), with 42 lavish suites and 25 villas, most with jacuzzi or individual plunge pool. Private beach club, spa, excellent gourmet restaurant, lovely tiled swimming pools, lighted tennis courts, gym, meeting room. Member of Small Luxury Hotels of the World and Mexico Boutique Hotels. Rates DX.

The Westin Regina Resort
Paseo de la Marina Sur 205
Tel. (322) 226-1100
www.westinpv.com.mx
Situated on a lovely 21-acre beachfront with 266 attractive rooms and 14 suites with Mexican decor, private balconies with ocean views, and deluxe amenities. Fitness center with spa services and three tennis courts, four clover-shaped pools, restaurants, bars, kids club. Meeting and convention facilities for 900 people, secretarial/business services. Rates FC.

Velas Vallarta
Paseo de la Marina Norte 585
Tel. (322) 221-0091
www.velasvallarta.com
On the beach, in front of the golf club, this modern-colonial-style resort has 339 one- to three-bedroom suites with a/c and ceiling fans, cable TV, and other amenities. Three swimming pools, four tennis courts, fitness center, restaurants, bar, and meeting facilities. Golf packages available. Rates FC.

Nuevo Vallarta

Mayan Palace
Tel. (329) 226-4000
www.mayanpalace.com
Situated along a mile of beachfront, this 250-acre hotel and timeshare resort features a huge freeform swimming pool with fountain, a navigable canal for canoeing, golf course, tennis courts, and marina with water-sports facilities, plus 449 spacious rooms and luxury suites with all amenities. Rates FC.

Paradise Village
Paseo de los Cocoteros 001
Tel. (329) 226-6770
www.paradisemexico.com
A Mayan-style resort and spa on the beach with 509 spacious units with ocean, marina or mountain views and terrace. Spa, pools, jacuzzi, restaurants, lobby bar, meeting facilities, lighted tennis courts. Rates DX (all inclusive).

Sierra
Paseo de los Cocoteros 19
Tel. (329) 297-1300
www.misvacaciones.com.mx
An all-inclusive resort with 366 rooms with oceanview balcony, marble bath. Health club, tennis, disco, bar. Rates DX (all inclusive).

Costa Vallarta

Editor's Note: Costa Vallarta, the stretch of coast that lies north of Puerto Vallarta, is developing fast, with new hotels opening regularly. Since Puerto Vallarta's international airport serves as the main point of departure for resorts along this coast, the destinations in this section are listed in geographical order, starting with those closest to the airport.

Bucerias

Royal Decameron Costa Flamingos
Lazaro Cardenas 150
Tel. (329) 298-0424
www.decameron.com
This attractive beachfront hotel has 227 rooms with satellite TV, restaurant-bar, pool, tennis, kids activities. All-inclusive option. Rates MD.

Punta Mita

Casa Las Brisas
Playa Careyero, Punta Mita
Tel. (322) 306-2122
www.mexicoboutiquehotels.com
10 minutes from Four Seasons Hotel and golf course. Guests at this six-room beachfront villa enjoy rooms with private oceanview balconies around a pool with submerged sunning chairs and a small fountain. White stucco walls, tile floors and patios, thatch roofs and guayaba wood balcony detailing reflect Vallarta-style architecture and design. Gourmet restaurant. Gym, recreation room, health and beauty services. Rates DX.

Four Seasons
Ramal Carretera Federal 200, Km. 19
Tel. (329) 291-6000
www.fourseasons.com/puntamita
About a 30-minute drive north of Vallarta airport, this luxury beachfront resort boasts a nearby coral reef ideal for snorkeling, an oceanside championship Jack Nicklaus-designed golf course, large freeform pool with whirlpool, kids club and separate children's pool and play area, and fitness center with full spa services. There are 140 oceanview rooms; including 26 suites, most with private plunge pool. Ample indoor/outdoor convention and banquet facilities. Rates LX.

San Francisco

Costa Azul
Located 20 miles north of the airport
Tel. (311) 258-4120
www.costaazul.com
This ecotourism and adventure resort is ideal for nature lovers, with myriad outdoor activities, including horseback riding through the surrounding jungle or on the beach, and snorkeling excursions around the bay. Accommodations include 34 rooms, 24 suites and 10 villas. Nice beachfront pool. Rates MD.

Rincon de Guayabitos

Decameron Los Cocos
Retorno las Palmas
Tel. (327) 274-0190

www.decameron.com
Attractive beachfront hotel with 240 rooms, suites and bungalows, restaurant, bar, pools, tennis court, meeting rooms. All-inclusive option. Rates ECON.

San Blas

Garza Canela
Paredes 106 Sur
Tel. (323) 285-0112
www.garzacanela.com
This attractive family-run hotel with 51 air-conditioned rooms and suites with satellite TV, is set on nicely-landscaped grounds about a 10-minute walk from the beach. Good restaurant, bar, pool. Rates MD.

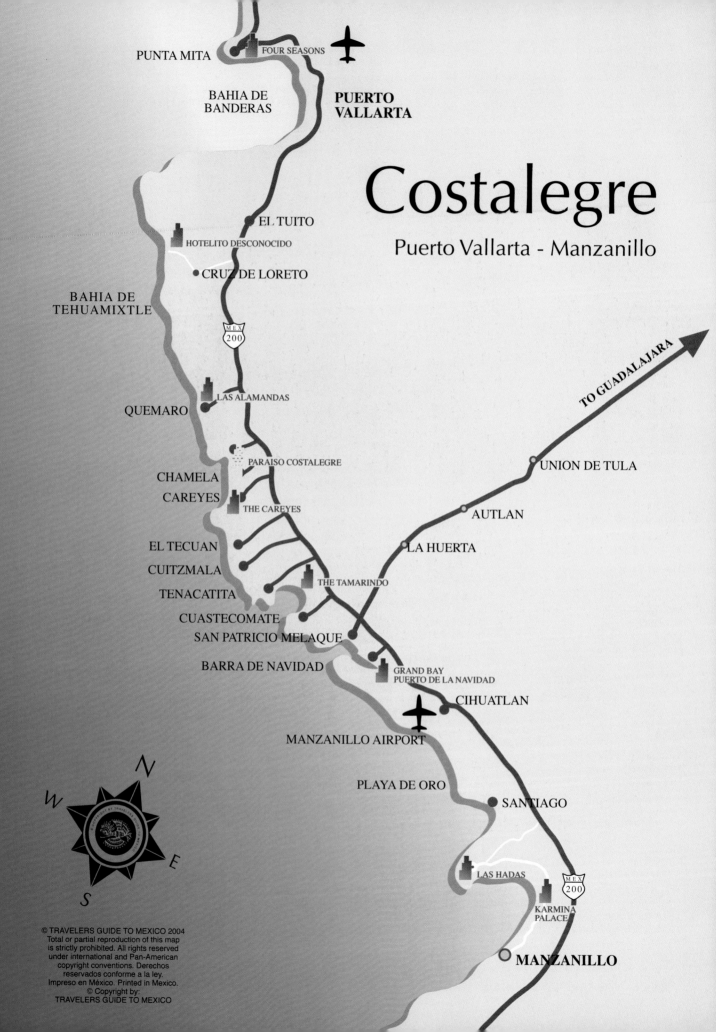

Costalegre
Puerto Vallarta - Manzanillo

PUNTA MITA

FOUR SEASONS

BAHIA DE
BANDERAS

**PUERTO
VALLARTA**

EL TUITO

HOTELITO DESCONOCIDO

CRUZ DE LORETO

BAHIA DE
TEHUAMIXTLE

MEX 200

TO GUADALAJARA

LAS ALAMANDAS

QUEMARO

PARAISO COSTALEGRE

UNION DE TULA

CHAMELA

CAREYES

THE CAREYES

AUTLAN

EL TECUAN

LA HUERTA

CUITZMALA

TENACATITA

THE TAMARINDO

CUASTECOMATE

SAN PATRICIO MELAQUE

BARRA DE NAVIDAD

GRAND BAY
PUERTO DE LA NAVIDAD

CIHUATLAN

MANZANILLO AIRPORT

PLAYA DE ORO

SANTIAGO

N
W   E
S

LAS HADAS

MEX 200

KARMINA
PALACE

MANZANILLO

© TRAVELERS GUIDE TO MEXICO 2004
Total or partial reproduction of this map
is strictly prohibited. All rights reserved
under international and Pan-American
copyright conventions. Derechos
reservados conforme a la ley.
Impreso en México. Printed in Mexico.
© Copyright by:
TRAVELERS GUIDE TO MEXICO

Costalegre

Pristine Beaches From Manzanillo to Puerto Vallarta

Poolside view of the Mexican Pacific

An important seaport since before the Spanish Conquest, Manzanillo is a popular though low-key international tourist destination, as well as home to the Mexican navy.

The resort is stretched out along twin bays divided by a small finger of land called Peninsula de Santiago. The old, provincial port, which has seen its share of colorful, historical episodes involving pirates and hidden treasures, is situated on the southern end of Manzanillo Bay, on a narrow isthmus separating the Pacific from a large lagoon called Cuyutlan. The better resort hotels are located on or near the peninsula.

Manzanillo is not your typical resort town. As you approach the harbor, the scene changes into one of a marine beehive. You might even encounter the Japanese fleet in town. The docks are downtown, and the railroad tracks to the wharves cut across the main street. Although the harbor is fenced off and heavily patrolled, it is possible to observe some fishing boat activity from harbor-front restaurants. This area has seen major renovation work re-

cently, including the installation of a gargantuan statue of a sailfish by Mexican artist Sebastian.

Today Manzanillo ranks as one of Mexico's most important west coast ports, largely because of its rail connections to the interior. It

Vast coconut plantations stretch out in every direction ...

is a shipping center for coconuts, bananas, limes, avocados, mangoes and sugarcane from local plantations. It is also Mexico's main door to the increasingly important Pacific Rim.

Coming in from the airport, vast coconut plantations stretch out in every direction. The fruit is harvested for its oil, which the state exports, and its juice is the thirst quencher of choice among locals. Restaurants serve the subtly-flavored drink on ice and most convenience stores carry it bottled.

Cortes arrived here early in his conquest.

In 1531, he named the town after the beautiful chamomile, or *manzanilla*, plants he found in abundance. The place where Cortes met with the Indians is still called Audiencia, meaning "audience," and is one of the finest beaches in the area. Cortes founded the first shipyard in Latin America at the mouth of this area's Santiago River. He also spent part of his retirement at this west coast port, a straight line across Mexico from Veracruz, where he first arrived!

In 1564 Captain Basque Lopez de Legazpi led a fleet of galleons across the Pacific to conquer the Philippines in the name of the Spanish Crown. His ships were built by Indians and Spaniards on the beaches of Salahua, not far from the site of the Las Hadas Hotel.

Other explorers sailed from here to discover La Paz, Ensenada, Santa Barbara and San Diego. Such an important shipping center also attracted a few notorious pirates, among them Drake, Cavendish and Speijelbergen. Consequently, the area is rumored to be a veritable cemetery of buried treasures, some of which have allegedly been found. In 1862 a steamer caught fire near here and sank with a cargo of a million and a half dollars in gold and silver. In 1900 a U.S. expedition recovered some half million dollars' worth of the booty, but the rest may still be there.

Before the Spanish came, Manzanillo was an important fishing village said to have hosted junks from the Orient. Today the resort is known as the Sailfish Capital of the World and hosts an international competition in November, as part of the annual *Colima Fair*, and a national tournament in February. Red snapper, marlin and giant tuna also abound in the warm waters.

Manzanillo's *May Festivals* are an important annual coastal event celebrating the anniversary of the port. The festivals include water sports competitions, as well as cultural events and handicrafts exhibits.

Aero California, Mexicana and *Aeromar* make the nearly one-hour flight from Mexico City to Manzanillo, and *Alaskan Airlines* flies from Los Angeles.

Beaches

In the area known as Salahua is *Playa el Tesoro*, a beach popular with locals for its fine surf. Between the town and Santiago Peninsula is *Playa las Brisas*, a broad white beach facing west.

Playa Azul starts at La Posada Hotel, a Hemingwayesque inn, and curves northwest towards Las Hadas. The sea is relatively calm along this beach from December through May. On this stretch lie most of the moderately priced hotels, motels and suites. There are also a few attractive condominiums here, including *Roca del Mar*, *Pacifico Azul* and *Palomar*.

Playa Santiago, one of the best beaches in the area, starts at the Playa de Santiago Hotel and continues around Santiago Bay to the Club Santiago development. Waves on the open bay can be rough, but the inlet in front of the hotel is shallow, with small waves and no undertow.

Several residential developments, mostly condominiums, are located along the highway between Playa Las Brisas and Santiago Bay. Part of the highway itself has been expanded to four lanes to accommodate the increase in tourism.

On the west side of Santiago Peninsula is *Playa la Audiencia*, a favorite with visitors and locals alike. The Gran Bahia Real Resort & Spa (formerly Sierra Manzanillo) is here.

Playa Miramar is a wide expanse of beautiful curving beach, with excellent swimming surf, on the western extreme of Santiago Bay. There are hookups and great facilities here for recreational vehicles. The all-inclusive Club Maeva resort is located across the road.

Nearby is *Club Santiago*, a residential development, including a beach club, a nine-hole golf course and tennis courts. High above the ocean, the view is spectacular.

This area of Manzanillo is slated for growth, and dredging has begun for the 600-slip marina of Port Juluapan. When completed, the development will feature condominiums, hotels, a yacht club and private homes with their own slips.

Playa de Oro, about 20 miles north of Manzanillo, near the airport, is a secluded and very attractive beach. You can rent a car for this trip; *National* maintains offices at the Manzanillo airport, as well as at the Las Hadas Hotel, and they deliver.

Because of the area's volcanic nature, the waters around Manzanillo feature underwater fissures, cracks and crevices, archways, tunnels and sea mounds with visible lava flows. Among the best dive sites are La Ahogada, La Audiencia, El Arrecife, El Carizal and Los Frailes (for experienced divers only), Las Hadas (for beginners), and Elephant Rock. The sand's high mineral content gives it a beautiful black-and-gold two-tone look in places.

Sites and Side Trips

Don't miss the *University Museum of Archaeology*, at Glorieta de San Pedrito, which has a small but wonderful collection of pre-Hispanic artifacts. The museum is open Monday to Friday. Tel. 332-2256.

Bahias Gemelas travel agency (representatives of American Express, tel. 333-1000) and *Viajes Lujo*, located at Av. Mexico 143-2, are reliable agencies that can arrange sightseeing, fishing, horseback riding and other activities.

For a complete change of pace, they can arrange a visit to the state capital, *Colima*, a charming provincial city just an hour away via a four-lane highway. The city has several interesting museums, including the *Museum of Western Cultures* (Museo de las Culturas de Occidente), which displays a fine collection of "Colima dog" figurines, and the fabulous *University Museum of Folk Art* (Museo Universitario de Artes Populares), which features an amazing array of arts and crafts.

A highlight of the trip is sighting the twin volcanoes that rise above Volcan de Colima National Park, about 25 miles north. One of the volcanoes has been emitting sulfurous fumes since its eruption in 1941.

Just minutes away from Colima, *Comala* is a great place to experience small-town Mexico. Families and friends gather under the arcades at the main square to enjoy live traditional music and a midday meal at one of the plaza's popular cantinas, which serve cold beer and tequila accompanied by a nonstop flow of typical snacks at no extra charge.

The local cottage industry is *ponche*, homemade liqueurs flavored with fruits and nuts like pistachio, coffee and, of course, coconut. You'll see them sold all over town.

While in Comala, visit the *Alejandro Rangel Hidalgo Museum*, where the charming works of the late celebrated local artist, as well as his impressive collection of pre-Hispanic artifacts, are on display in a beautiful former hacienda.

Operated by Amanresorts, Comala's *Mahakua-Hacienda de San Antonio* offers luxurious privacy and pampering in a beautiful countryside setting at the foot of two volcanoes. The property features 26 spacious guest rooms with a fireplace, a plant-filled courtyard, richly appointed living and dining rooms, rooftop terrace and gourmet dining. Tel. (312) 313-4411.

Dining

Manzanillo restaurants feature the bounty of the sea, with lots of fish and shrimp dishes, and its coconut plantations, with everything you can think of made from the tropical fruit, from soup to ice cream.

Agua de coco, coconut juice on ice, is served here the way ice water is elsewhere. Other favorites are *tuba*, a mild, fermented beer-like drink made from palm sap, and *agua de granada*, a beverage made from local pomegranates. Colima is also renowned for its coconut brandy, a comforting end to a leisurely meal.

L'Recife, on a cliff overlooking the ocean at the Vida del Mar condominium complex, features excellent food and service, and a talented saxophone/clarinet player, in a stunning alfresco setting. Take your swimsuit for a dip in the clifftop pool. Open noon to midnight during high season only. Tel. 335-0900.

Feeling homesick? Drop by *Juanito's*. Expat John Corey's hamburger joint is where locals and visitors gather to watch ESPN on a giant screen, check their e-mails and enjoy the classic American staple.

Chef Jean Francois Laroche, owner of the long famous and then suddenly washed away Willy's, serves European-style fare at *La Toscana*. Tel. 333-2515.

Las Hadas offers several fine restaurants, including the elegant *Legazpi*, which serves continental cuisine in a Moroccan setting with a great view of Manzanillo across the bay (open Thursday to Saturday); and a great open-air palapa restaurant above the beach. This was the setting for the Bo Derek-Dudley Moore romantic dinner in the movie "10."

The Vista Playa de Oro hotel's *La Margarita* beach club has an open-air restaurant-bar built on a terrace that juts out over the beach, with a wonderful view and cool breezes. Try their big goblets of fresh coconut juice on ice.

Other favorites include *Los Delfines,* for seafood, and *Chantilly,* for traditional Mexican dishes.

Nightlife

One of the liveliest spots is Club Maeva's *Boom-Boom* disco, which is usually jammed to the rafters on weekends. It has good sound and light systems, is popular with the young at heart, and closes at about dawn.

Another favorite night spot is *Solaris* disco at Vista Playa de Oro hotel, just north of Playa Miramar. The best light and sound show is at *Vog* disco, at Km. 9.2 on the Costero. For reservations call 333-1875 or 333-1992.

At Las Hadas nightlife centers around the piano lounge in the lobby.

During the winter season, Las Hadas and Club Maeva feature weekly Fiestas Mexicanas with traditional dancing, music and food.

Shopping

Shopping is not one of the resort's major draws, but a few establishments stand out.

At Las Hadas, a small, circular plaza called *Plaza Doña Albina* has a beauty salon, tobacco shop and clothing boutique.

In the Santiago area, *Las Primaveras* carries quality crafts, including blown glass, papiermâché and leather. Other shops displaying native crafts are *La Cordoñiz,* at Camino Real 399, outside Los Candiles Hotel, and the *DIF* shop, downtown at Andador Constitucion and Zaragoza. *Plaza Manzanillo* and *Plaza Pacifico* are the town's leading shopping centers.

Hotels in Manzanillo

Gran Bahia Real
On a cove overlooking La Audiencia Bay
Tel. (314) 333-2000
www.realresorts.com.mx
A beach resort (formerly Sierra Manzanillo) with 317 rooms and suites (suites have whirlpools). Restaurants, disco-bar with entertainment. Swimming pool, tennis courts, fitness center, meeting rooms. Rates MD (all inclusive with room-only option).

Karmina Palace
Av. Vista Hermosa 13
Tel. (314) 334-1313
www.karminapalace.com
A five-star all-inclusive beach resort designed to evoke the majestic temples and palaces of Mexico's Mayan civilization; its grand, central staircase is flanked by serpents. There are 324 spacious junior and master suites with 27- and 20-inch TVs; some with private pool or jacuzzi. European-style spa, gym, 10 tennis courts, access to adjoining golf course, eight interconnecting pools with cascades, private beach cove, excellent dining, day-care center, open-air theater, 24-hour room service, business center, extensive meeting facilities for up to 1,200 people. Rates FC (all inclusive).

Las Hadas
Peninsula de Santiago
Tel. (314) 331-0101
www.brisas.com.mx
In a class by itself, the resort evocative of a "Thousand and One Nights" is the dream come true of multimillionaire Antenor Patiño, also known as the "Bolivian Tin King." An elegant setting with Moorish minarets and cupolas, a wonderful private beach, golf course, and modern marina. The 234 rooms and suites are distributed among beautifully landscaped palm-studded grounds; there are 10 types of accommodations, including units with private terrace plunge pool. Fine restaurants, piano lounge. Large freeform swimming pool, excellent beach, water sports, 70-slip marina, 10 tennis courts, 18-hole golf course. Meeting and banquet facilities. One of The Leading Hotels of the World. Rates FC.

Pepe's Hideaway
Tel. (314) 333-0616
www.pepeshideaway.com
This unusual all-inclusive option offers 7 palm-thatched huts on stilts in a jungle setting, each with king-size bed and a sunken tub (as well as electricity and running water). Swimming pool, spa, palapa restaurant. Rates MD (all inclusive).

Costalegre

A relatively remote and still largely untouched coastline lies between Manzanillo and Puerto Vallarta, though long-term plans are to turn this area into a prime tourism destination.

Popularly known as Costalegre (Happy Coast), this region was opened by highway for the first time in 1973, making it possible to drive north from Manzanillo (or south from Puerto Vallarta) along a 175-mile stretch of still secluded and unspoiled hills, mountains, beaches, lush tropical jungles, bays, inlets and islands.

This coastal stretch is home to three idyllic bays—Tenacatita, Chamela and Navidad—and destinations like Cruz de Loreto, Quemaro, San Patricio Melaque and Barra de Navidad. Accommodations ranging from ultra luxurious to low budget dot the coastline.

Barra de Navidad

About 37 miles north of Manzanillo, the fishing village of Barra de Navidad is built on a sand bar adjacent to a large lagoon. *Isla Navidad,* the area's top development, includes the luxurious *Grand Bay* resort, a 500,000-hectare property with 200 spacious guest rooms, convention facilities, fine restaurants and a deluxe full-service spa. Its spectacular 27-hole golf course allows all levels of players to enjoy the game. Combining colorful plants and trees, sand traps, rolling fairways and lagoons, the landscaping is more typical of a classic European garden than a golf course.

About seven miles past Barra de Navidad, *San Patricio Melaque* is a bay with a host of small, clean beaches nestled at the foot of the hills. The Melaque area is relatively well developed with about 24 economy and moderately-priced hotels. Popular with boaters is *Los Pelicanos,* a seafood restaurant.

Costa Careyes

Due north, on still another bay, is Costa Careyes (Sea Turtle Coast), an area featuring eight miles of beautiful coastline, small beach inlets and coves, palm-strewn foothills, and lagoons surrounded by tropical vegetation. *El Tamarindo,* an exclusive resort in this area, features an attractive oceanside 18-hole golf course, tennis courts and yacht club.

Tenacatita

Traveling north along the coast is Tenacatita, a quiet, secluded area where the all-inclusive *Blue Bay Village Los Angeles Locos* and *Punta Serena* holistic retreat are located. A river flows into the sea here, making the best swimming beach for miles in either direction. Nine miles away is *El Tecuan,* a budget beachfront hotel with a pool, restaurant and its own lagoon.

Chamela

One of three bays on the Costalegre, picturesque Chamela is well liked for bird watching at nearby Isla de los Pajaros (Isle of Birds), reachable by boat from the beach; Isla Cocinas, an island known for its Caribbean-style white sand; and succulent lobsters at very reasonable prices. Chamela is also home to the *Paraiso Costalegre,* a small resort that recalls the islands of Fiji or Tahiti with its Polynesian-style villas surrounded by abundant palms. There are small villas for two as well as family-size villas that can accommodate up to 15 people.

Quemaro

Following in the footsteps of her celebrated grandfather, Antenor Patiño, Isabel Goldsmith has created an exclusive hideaway resort near the town of Quemaro. *Las Alamandas* offers very

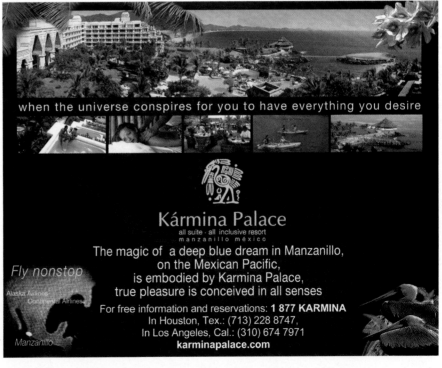

private and exquisitely decorated villas that can be yours for roughly 400 to 2,800 dollars a night, depending on whether or not you splurge for an entire villa.

Cruz de Loreto

The leading exclusive resort here is *Hotelito Desconocido* (The Little Unknown Hotel). Created by a prominent Italian fashion designer, this unique hideaway features Polynesian-style palm-thatched cottages on piles rising above a freshwater estuary.

Hotels in Costalegre

Cabo Blanco

Paraiso Costalegre
en Villa Polinesia
CHAMELA JALISCO MÉXICO.

a true encounter
with nature...

Located in the center of astounding Chamela Bay, Paraiso Costalegre is a small resort just 17 Km. from Careyes that consists of Villas equipped with all services and with an extraordinary view of the ocean, where you can experience a close encounter with nature.

Enjoy visiting the nearby island, the beaches, the mountain, as well as scuba diving, surfing, fishing, sailing or watching the beautiful wildlife of the Pacific Coast.

Paraiso Costalegre
Tel. 01 (315) 333 97 77
Fax: 01 (315) 333 97 79

Info and Reservations
Tel. 01 (33) 3625 0906
Fax: 01 (33) 3616 2872
www.paraisocostalegre.com

Armada and Bahia de la Navidad
Tel. (315) 355-6495
At the Pueblo Nuevo tourism complex. A pretty colonial-style property five minutes from Playa Barra de Navidad, with 100 rooms with satellite TV, a/c. Floating marina, beach club, tennis, large pool, wading pool. Restaurant, bar, game room. Rates MD (all inclusive).

Casas de Careyes
Careyes
Tel. (315) 351-0240
www.mexicoboutiquehotels.com
Puerto Vallarta-Barra de Navidad Hwy., Km. 53.5. Luxurious one- to seven-bedroom *casitas* and villas offer 35 guest rooms in a splendid beachfront setting near Tamarindo and Isla Navidad golf courses. Rates DX.

El Careyes
Careyes
Tel. (315) 351-0000
www.mexicoboutiquehotels.com
Puerto Vallarta-Barra de Navidad Hwy., Km. 53.5. This upscale resort is situated on its own private bay, 60 miles north of Manzanillo airport and two and a half hours south of Puerto Vallarta. There are 48 beautifully decorated rooms and suites, most with panoramic views of the ocean, some with private balconies with plunge pools. Health club, freeform pool with jacuzzi, tennis and paddle tennis. Lounge, game room. Restaurant, bar, gourmet deli. Small meeting rooms for 60. Polo and horseback riding November to April. Member of Mexico Boutique Hotels. Rates DX.

El Tamarindo
Cihuatlan
Tel. (315) 351-5032
www.mexicoboutiquehotels.com
Situated 40 minutes north of Manzanillo airport (Melaque-Puerto Vallarta Hwy., Km. 7.5), this exclusive resort lies on a spectacular coastline with three private beaches surrounded by palm groves. 30 palm-thatched bungalows equipped with luxurious amenities (each has its own plunge pool and jacuzzi) create a setting of tropical sophistication. Restaurant, bar, room service. Freeform pool, two clay tennis courts, 18-hole golf course, health club. Member of Mexico Boutique Hotels. Rates DX.

Grand Bay
Barra de Navidad
Tel. (315) 355-5050
www.islaresort.com.mx
Situated on the 1,200-acre Isla Navidad residential resort, 35 minutes from Manzanillo airport, three and a half hours by car from Guadalajara, minutes by boat from Barra de Navidad. This exclusive resort features deluxe beachfront accommodations and recreational facilities in a private setting that blends Mexican colonial and Mediterranean architecture. There are 199 spacious, attractively decorated guest rooms with all deluxe amenities, restaurants, bars, kids club, convention facilities, a signature Robert von Hagge 27-hole golf course, 187-slip marina, small beach, three swimming pools, including kids pool, two

jacuzzis, three tennis courts, gym. Full-service spa with facial and body treatments. Rates LX.

Hotelito Desconocido
Cruz de Loreto
Tel. (322) 281-4010
www.hotelito.com
The creation of a prominent Italian fashion designer, this unique seaside hotel 2 hours south of Puerto Vallarta resembles an idyllic fishing village, lit after dark by candles and torches (no electricity; solar-power heats water, drives ceiling fans). The 32 guest rooms are housed in Polynesian-style palm-thatched cottages on piles rising above a freshwater estuary; guests get about by row boat and scattered foot bridges. Restaurants, bar/game room with billiards, saltwater pool, mini-spa with gym, whirlpool, herbal sauna. Room service. Phone in lobby. Rates LX (AP).

Las Alamandas
Quemaro
Tel. (322) 285-5500
www.alamandas.com
This luxurious beachfront resort is located on a 1,500-acre tropical reserve about halfway between Puerto Vallarta and Manzanillo. Like staying at an elegant private estate with six villas (14 suites) sumptuously decorated with Mexican art and handicrafts; villas can be rented in their entirety. Restaurant, beach club, bar with large screen satellite TV, in-room TV and VCR. Swimming pool, flood-lit tennis court, gym, horseback riding, boat excursions on nearby river. Private airstrip; charter plane rentals arranged. Rates LX.

Meson Doña Paz
Rinconada del Capitan, Isla Navidad
Tel. (315) 355-6441
www.mexicoboutiquehotels.com
An exclusive refuge of peace and tranquility, this grand mansion houses 14 rooms and suites with crystal doors that open onto a marvelous pool and bay view, and a breathtaking lobby overlooking a man-made saltwater cove/swimming pool. Gourmet restaurant. Beach, jacuzzi, tennis, gym, guests enjoy preferential rates at Grand Bay Hotel's spa. All-inclusive option. Rates DX.

Paraiso Costalegre
Chamela Bay, 17 Km. north of Careyes
Tel. (333) 122-3943
www.paraisocostalegre.com.mx
This charming resort features Polynesian-style villas for two on a palm-studded beach; each villa has a view of the ocean and all amenities. There are also family-size villas that can accommodate up to 15. Good dining, water sports, friendly management. Rates MD.

HOTEL RATES

LX: luxury, rates above 375 USD
DX: deluxe, rates from 250-375 USD
FC: first-class, rates from 150-250 USD
MD: moderate, rates from 75-150 USD
ECON: economical, rates under 75 USD

GRAND BAY HOTEL
ISLA NAVIDAD RESORT

WYNDHAM
LUXURY RESORTS

475 YEARS IN THE MAKING.
NOW READY FOR YOUR CLIENTS TO EXPLORE.

Seeking new worlds, Hernan Cortés found a hidden Eden on Mexico's Pacific Gold Coast. Centuries later, history is made. Travel professionals seeking the new and extraordinary are discovering a resort hotel of unprecedented grandeur, at the heart of the exclusive 1200-acre Isla Navidad residential community. Robert Von Hagge's 27-hole championship golf course, Golf

Magazine's Gold Medal Award Winner 1998, a 187-slip marina, and 199 exquisite guest accommodations reflect the passion for perfection that defines the name Grand Bay. For your most discerning clients, now you can expand the boundaries of pleasure. Located near Manzanillo in Colima, Mexico. Call for brochures, rates, and more details.

U.S. Reservations Office **1-800-WYNDHAM.**
In Mexico
Toll free **01-800-849-2373** or **(315) 355-5050**

www.islaresort.com.mx

WYNDHAM
LUXURY RESORTS

Mazatlan

A Different Kind of West Coast Resort

Mazatlan, aglow with thousands of shining lights

Mazatlan Tourism Council

Mazatlan is both a thriving fishing port and a successful tourist resort, which gives it an appealing air of self-assurance. Since it doesn't depend solely on tourism dollars to survive, unlike other major resorts, its welcome of visitors is that much more sincere. And while less glamorous than its closest west coast rival, Puerto Vallarta, it is also less commercial and often less crowded.

Most locals earn their livelihood from the abundance of shrimp, swordfish, marlin and tuna in the surrounding waters. But miles of sand-strewn coastline—Mazatlan boasts the longest stretch of uninterrupted beach in Mexico—have sprouted a sizeable though secondary tourism industry.

The largest West Coast port facility between Los Angeles and the Panama Canal, Mazatlan is built on a peninsula that separates Mexico's largest shrimp fleet from more than 15 miles of wide beaches that extend northward. Because its sheltered harbor is where the Pacific Ocean and the Sea of Cortez meet, creating the greatest natural fish trap in the hemisphere, sport fishing is the resort's premiere pastime.

Behind the lowlands surrounding the resort rises the beautiful Sierra Madre. The most memorable feature of the town—home to about 300,000 friendly inhabitants—is the *malecon*, the seafront promenade that borders the downtown area and bay as it stretches north towards the hotel zone, putting about five miles of ocean beaches at your feet. Ringed by a brightly lit, modern four-lane boulevard, the bay becomes a brilliant necklace at night with the *Puerto Viejo* (old port) its pendant.

The resort is growing, as a fledgling development to the north, called *Nuevo* (or New) *Mazatlan*, can attest. Initial plans for that area call for residential resorts, hotels and a golf course. A highway from the airport is planned that will bypass the old resort and head directly to the new.

Situated just a few miles below the Tropic of Cancer (same latitude as Honolulu), Mazatlan marks the beginning of the Mexican tropics and offers an absolutely superb winter season climate with mild to warm temperatures and virtually no rain from the end of October to June. Its beautiful beaches merge with waters that rarely get colder than 68°F or warmer than 75°F.

Each year since 1898, Mazatlan has hosted a pre-Lenten carnival, a Mardi Gras-style five-day bash that usually falls in late February or early March (just before Ash Wednesday). As one of the country's most spectacular carnivals, with parades, floats and fireworks, it is well attended, with hotel reservations usually made six months in advance. A more sober month-long cultural festival in November features opera, ballet and symphony concerts with international performers.

Mazatlan's monthly bilingual newspaper, *Pacific Pearl*, is a handy guide to community events and activities of interest to visitors. Hotels distribute them free, or you can pick up an issue at the tourism booth opposite the Playa Mazatlan Hotel. Tel. 916-5160.

Aero California, Alaskan Airlines, Mexicana and *Continental* connect Mazatlan with major U.S. and Mexican cities. International Pan-American Highway 15 connects Mazatlan with Nogales, Arizona, 720 miles north; Guadalajara, 315 miles south; and Mexico City, 683 miles southeast. There is daily bus service from Nogales and a ferry makes daily runs across the Sea of Cortez to La Paz. The city is also a port of call for several U.S. cruise ships, some on round-the-world itineraries.

History

Indians first settled Mazatlan, which means "land of deer" in Nahuatl—large herds once migrated along this beautiful coast. While there still is an abundance of game in the surrounding countryside, tourism and the fishing trade changed the pattern of migration considerably.

Mazatlan became an important city in the early 17th century because of gold and silver mines in nearby Rosario, Copala and Panuco. The pirate ships of Drake and Cavendish preyed on the treasure-laden Spanish galleons that traded with the Philippines. What is now known as *Icebox Hill* was a sentinel post for the Spanish garrison 15 miles away at Villa Union.

The town was not incorporated until 1806 and lacked a municipal government until 1837. A group of immigrant German businessmen, who wanted to import agricultural equipment to work their ranches, was actually responsible for developing the port.

Two decades later, during the French intervention, Mazatlan was the stronghold of Mexican independence troops. They seized large quantities of gold from the nearby mines—a coup that helped contribute to the defeat of Emperor Maximilian.

By the end of the 19th century, Mazatlan was the center of a large fishing industry and a thriving port involved in international trade with countries as far away as China and Japan.

Nearly 40 million pounds of shrimp are processed each year in Mazatlan, home of Mexico's largest shrimp fleet. Tons of shrimp are frozen daily, at nine different plants, and shipped off to the United States, Mexico's biggest customer. Mazatlan also has one of the largest tuna canning factories on the Pacific coast and a fleet of tuna boats that fish as far south as Panama.

What to See and Do

The main square is the centerpiece of a 20-

Heading out for a day of deep-sea fishing

block historic district undergoing a resurgence, with renovated colonial-era mansions housing restaurants and shops. An interesting cathedral built of a melange of styles dominates the square, site of band concerts every Friday. *Plazuela Machado,* a small plaza with charming sidewalk cafes, is where you'll find *Museo Casa Machado*. Built in 1846, the preserved former home illustrates upper class life in the late 19th century. Nearby is Mazatlan's most prized architectural jewel, the *Angela Peralta Theater,* built

in the 1860s; and *El Tunel*, a traditional eatery dating from 1945. The *Museo Arqueologico*, with a small but good collection of pre-Columbian artifacts, is downtown also, at Sixto Osuna 76.

Located at Av. de los Deportes 111 is *Acuario Mazatlan,* featuring about 200 marine species from all over the world, a fun sea lion show, and a small museum. Open daily from 9:30 a.m. to 6:30 p.m.

The port area is located at the very southern end of town, before the malecon begins.

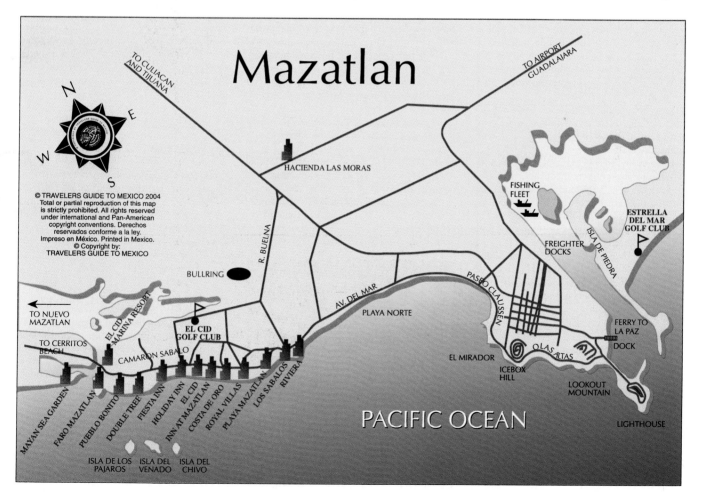

Mazatlan

TO CULIACAN AND TIJUANA

TO AIRPORT GUADALAJARA

HACIENDA LAS MORAS

© TRAVELERS GUIDE TO MEXICO 2004
Total or partial reproduction of this map is strictly prohibited. All rights reserved under international and Pan-American copyright conventions. Derechos reservados conforme a la ley. Impreso en México. Printed in Mexico.
© Copyright by:
TRAVELERS GUIDE TO MEXICO

FISHING FLEET

ESTRELLA DEL MAR GOLF CLUB

FREIGHTER DOCKS

ISLA DE PIEDRA

R. BUELNA

BULLRING

TO NUEVO MAZATLAN

EL CID MARINA RESORT

EL CID GOLF CLUB

PASEO CLAUSSEN

AV. DEL MAR

PLAYA NORTE

FERRY TO LA PAZ

DOCK

TO CERRITOS BEACH

CAMARON SABALO

EL CID

COSTA DE ORO

ROYAL VILLAS

PLAYA MAZATLAN

LOS SABALOS

RIVIERA

EL MIRADOR

OLAS ALTAS

ICEBOX HILL

LOOKOUT MOUNTAIN

LIGHTHOUSE

MAYAN SEA GARDEN

FARO MAZATLAN

PUEBLO BONITO

DOUBLE TREE

FIESTA INN

HOLIDAY INN

INN AT MAZATLAN

ISLA DE LOS PAJAROS

ISLA DEL VENADO

ISLA DEL CHIVO

PACIFIC OCEAN

Mazatlan has two major 18-hole golf courses

Mazatlan Tourism Council

Here you can see the large ferries that ply the waters of the Sea of Cortez each night to La Paz, 235 miles northwest. The bow of the ferry opens to take on cars, trailers, motorcycles and trucks. Once closed, the vessel is more like an ocean liner, complete with staterooms, restaurants, and a bar with live music. The trip takes 18 hours and sleeping cabins are available.

Heading toward town along the water, you'll come to the fishing fleets and yacht club, where a thin strip of land connecting the hilltop lighthouse with the mainland provides an unforgettable landscape. For the fit, a visit to *El Faro* lighthouse is a pleasant 25-minute hike up a meandering path. The lighthouse is 505 feet above sea level, ranking as the second-highest natural lighthouse in the world, after Gibraltar.

Strolling along the malecon at sunset is a must. This lovely palm-lined coastal road changes names as it runs its course from south to north—Paseo Centenario, Olas Altas, Paseo Claussen, Avenida del Mar and finally Avenida Camaron Sabalo. Where the malecon becomes Paseo Claussen is *El Mirador*, a tower of rock jutting out into the ocean where local boys make daring dives into the rocky crevice. The tide must be in and the timing just right for a successful dive.

For good views of the city and surrounding countryside visit the Spanish fort (*Casa del Marino*), Icebox Hill (*Cerro de la Nevera*), especially at night, and Lookout Mountain (*El Cañon del Cerro del Vigia*).

During the winter season, you can see bullfights or rodeos. *Caliente*, at Avenida del Mar 48, in the Cima Hotel, features horse and greyhound races, and major sporting events. There's also a restaurant and bar.

City tours by bus with English-speaking guides depart daily at 10 a.m. and again at 3 p.m. *Olé Tours*, at Camaron Sabalo 7000-5, offers private tours of the city and surrounding attractions, and can also make special arrangements to accommodate the disabled. Tel. 916-6288.

Taxis are plentiful and charge fixed rates.

A more popular, though not necessarily cheaper, form of transportation is the "*pulmonia*," an open-air taxi that looks like a golf cart. Unique to Mazatlan, this vehicle is called pneumonia because that's what you'll get if you are caught in one during a heavy rainstorm.

Beaches

Olas Altas, the beach where the seafront promenade begins, lives up to its name: High Waves. It is the first swimming beach on the peninsula, but not the best, being somewhat rocky and sometimes a little rough. It is, however, a popular spot for surfing, strolling, shopping, having a beer, or just relaxing. After sunset, it serves as a popular gathering place. The older hotels in town are on this small stretch, as are some restaurants.

The beaches get better the farther north you go. *Playa Norte* (North Beach), popular with local residents, is a slender strip of white sand extending for six miles beyond the coastal road, and has lockers, showers, umbrellas and beach chairs for rent, as well as several small restaurants, most with mariachis. Be careful when swimming. There are few lifeguards, except during major holidays. The last beach to

the north is *Playa Brujas,* popular among young surfers, as is *Playa los Pinos,* otherwise known as "The Cannon."

Beach activities also include sailing, scuba diving, parachute gliding, water-skiing, jet-skiing and banana boat rides. Bicycles and horses are also for rent.

Boat Rides

The most popular excursions are to the three islands that dot Mazatlan's horizon, *Isla de los Pajaros* (Bird Island), great for bird watching, *Isla del Venado* (Deer Island) and *Isla del Chivo* (Goat Island), both favorite water-sports sites with tranquil and undisturbed beaches.

From the beach next to the El Cid Hotel, you can take an interesting ride on the amphibious *Super Pato* to Deer Island for swimming, snorkeling and scuba diving. It leaves every two hours from 10 a.m. on. Motor launches and catamarans head to Goat Island and *Isla de Piedra*, which also has pristine beaches that are usually less crowded than those on the mainland.

Not technically an island, Isla de Piedra (Rock Island) forms part of the peninsula. Its mangrove-lined waterways are home to many exotic birds, including herons, pelicans and sea hawks. Its coconut, mango, lemon, and avocado plantations give way to secluded beaches ideal for horseback riding, water sports and sunbathing. You can take a guided horseback tour of the village and plantations by the beach, or sightsee aboard a horse-drawn carriage.

Randi's Happy Horses offers excellent one- to two-hour horseback or horse cart tours of the area, including an old cemetery, two lagoons and an extensive plantation. The return journey is along 15 miles of undeveloped beach. There are morning and sunset tours led by bilingual guides. Tel. 985-2740.

You can get to Isla de Piedra on your own—just cab over to Embarcadero Isla Piedra, where launches make the trip regularly—or join a group tour. A good outfit offering excursions is *Sunny Island Cruise*, whose 33-foot catamaran, *Renegado*, takes up to 60 passengers on a six-hour sightseeing excursion. Tel. 914-2477.

Harbor cruises depart daily from the south side of the peninsula, near the fishing boats. *Fiesta Mazatlan* yacht sails Tuesday through Sunday at 11 a.m. from the lighthouse dock on a three-hour cruise. Tel. 985-2237.

Fishing and Hunting

Undoubtedly Mazatlan's biggest single attraction is its superb fishing—eight fleets of charter boats stand ready all year long. About 12,000 billfish are caught and released annually; Mazatlan promotes and adheres to a catch-and-release policy. The record to break is a 988-pound, 12-foot, black marlin caught February 14, 1980. Swordfish, tuna and shark are in abundance year-round, and light-tackle fishing in the lagoons, which teem with rainbow runners, snook and barracuda, is also very popular.

Three-time world record breaker Bill

Heimpel is an area expert at *Star Fleet,* a sport-fishing outfit with sleek yachts and excellent crews. They organize fishing trips daily from 6 a.m. to 3 p.m. Tel. 982-2665. Another leading sport-fishing outfit is *Aries Fleet.* Tel. 916-3468.

Since Mazatlan is situated on what's known as the Pacific Flyway, meaning it is on a major southward migratory route for ducks and doves, hunting is also popular. A long narrow island separates the lagoon from the sea and provides some of the best wildfowl hunting. Many species of duck (from pintail to blue-wing) as well as dove, quail and pheasant are found here. The surrounding hills are home to deer, wild boar, rabbit and coyote. *Angler's Inn,* run by Billy Chapman, can arrange hunting and lake fishing excursions. Tel. 916-6013.

Golf and Tennis

Mazatlan's star golf course is *Estrella del Mar,* an 18-hole oceanside course designed by Robert Trent Jones II on Isla de Piedra. Located some 45 minutes from the hotel zone, the course is the centerpiece of a development project that comprises private villas, condominiums, a deluxe hotel and tennis club. The owners' prior developments include Colorado's Telluride Ski Resort and Arizona's Biltmore Golf Resort. Estrella's high-season rate, including transportation from your hotel and golf cart, is about 100 dollars (about 70 dollars in low season). Tel. 982-3300.

In the hotel zone, *El Cid* offers an 18-hole course complemented by the addition of nine holes at its sister resort on the marina. The Marina Nine, as the course is called, was designed by Lee Treviño using water on seven of the nine holes. Golf Today rated the course "an absolute winner." Tel. 913-3333.

Most of the major hotels have tennis courts.

Side Trips

Just 20 minutes from the hotel zone is an upscale country inn, *Hacienda Las Moras,* where you can spend the day enjoying its beautiful grounds, fine food and attentive service, and swimming pool, horseback riding, tennis and nature walks. Taxis charge about 20 dollars to make the trip. Tel. 916-5045.

Day tours are available to the nearby colonial villages of *Concordia* and *Copala,* as well as the surrounding villages of *Rosario, Panuco, Villa Union del Presidio, Malpica, Teacapan* and *Agua-caliente,* and the jungle-covered *San Blas* area. Some of these are abandoned mining towns dating back to the Spanish Conquest, others are colorful coastal villages.

The most popular trip is to Concordia, a small town an hour and a half drive from Mazatlan with an interesting square and church, and Copala, a quaint colonial mining town deep in the hills. Copala has attracted government officials, writers and others in search of a secluded hideaway. This is a furniture-making area and your tour will probably include a visit to a workshop.

The San Blas jungle tour takes you into the tropical forests of Nayarit. First you take a dug-out up a river for lunch and a swim, and later visit the old *Father Kino Mission* and the colorful town of San Blas, approximately four hours from Mazatlan via the winding road to Tepic (the turnoff for San Blas is at Km. 36). Take insect repellent.

Dining

As a major exporter of fish and seafood, Mazatlan restaurants feature abundant fresh shrimp as well as smoked marlin. You'll also find a wide variety of restaurants specializing in Mexican cuisine, grilled meats and U.S.-style fast food. Try Mazatlan's *Pacifico* beer, a local brew now being exported.

Angelo's
Pueblo Bonito Hotel
Tel. 914-3700
Fine Italian and international cuisine served in a refined intimate setting; singer and piano player add to the romantic ambiance. Specialties include osso bucco, *gamberoni alla Luciana,* and *cioppino.* Extensive selection of domestic and imported wines. The setting calls for formal resort attire. Attentive service. Open 6 p.m. to midnight.

Casa Loma
Las Gaviotas 104
Tel. 913-5398
In business since 1976, this spot offers tasty international cuisine and fine service in a casual open-air patio or a more formal dining room decorated in dark wood and red velvet. The house salad, made with shrimp, pineapple, bacon and a secret dressing, is a favorite menu item. Owner Ramon greets you personally and never forgets a name! Open 1:30 to 11:30 p.m. Reservations recommended.

Cilantro's
Pueblo Bonito Hotel
Tel. 914-3700
A wonderfully rustic and airy beachfront, palm-thatched restaurant with tropical decor. Lunch features seafood specialties and excellent grilled sandwiches, dinner offers seafood delights and prime cuts of beef. Favorites include shrimp cocktail, chicken sandwich, petals of fish, shrimp in chipotle chili-tamarind sauce, and the New York cut and seafood combo plate. Open 9 a.m. to 10:30 p.m.

Cowboy
Opposite Los Sabalos Hotel
Tel. 983-5333
This steak house and saloon features a country atmosphere accented by log beam ceilings, and steak and seafood specialties. Open for lunch and dinner.

El Palomar
Paseo Claussen and Virgilio Uribe
Near Playa Norte. In business for more than 30 years, this beachside restaurant and bar specializes in grilled meats and seafood dishes. Favorites here include *carne asada* and *quesos fundidos,* Mexican-style cheese fondues. Open 7 a.m. to midnight.

El Shrimp Bucket
Olas Altas 11-126, downtown
Tel. 981-6350
The original Anderson restaurant and a longtime favorite. Good breakfasts, box lunches, great seafood, with a nice view of the sea. Marimba music makes for a fun evening. Open 6 a.m. to 11 p.m.

El Tunel
Calle Carvajal, downtown
Opposite Angela Peralta Theater. A Mexican-style diner that has been serving authentic regional dishes since 1945. Try their *pozole* stew and other traditional favorites served in a friendly, family-oriented setting. Entrance is through a long, narrow hallway, thus the name. Open noon to midnight.

Faro Mazatlan
Playa Real Hotel
Tel. 913-1111

Mazatlan Tourism Council

A romantic open-air thatched-roof restaurant and bar overlooking the ocean. Known for its wonderful grilled fish and excellent service. Open 9 a.m. to 11 p.m.

Gringo Lingo
Rodolfo T. Loaiza 315
Tel. 913-7737
Opposite Playa Mazatlan Hotel. Great for people watching, this is a popular place to hang out and grab a bite before hitting the discos. Indoor and outdoor seating.

Hacienda Las Moras
On road to La Noria, 20 min. from hotel zone
Tel. 916-5045
This picturesque hacienda hotel located in Mazatlan's lush countryside offers excellent dining in a unique colonial-era setting. Favorites of the country-style cuisine with a cosmopolitan flair are crisp shrimp salad in a zesty dressing, and shrimp fajitas with beans, guacamole and freshly-made flour tortillas. You can spend the whole day and enjoy the swimming pool, horseback riding, tennis, green surroundings and attentive service. Taxi fare is about 20 dollars.

La Cabaña
Pueblo Bonito Hotel
Tel. 914-3700
This palm-thatched hut by the pool is ideal for a light snack or quick bite. The menu features sandwiches on homemade breads, and salads. The juice bar creates exotic fruit cocktails and fresh fruit juice combinations. Some outdoor seating. Open 9 a.m. to 5 p.m.

La Casa Country
Av. Camaron Sabalo
Tel. 916-5300
Opposite Holiday Inn Hotel. A fun country-and-western-style restaurant with a Tex-Mex menu featuring grilled meats. Specialties include *arrachera*, rib eye, and "Adelita," a Mexican combo plate. Waiters dance to the country music. Open noon to 2 a.m.

La Costa Marinera
Privada del Camaron and La Florida
Tel. 914-1928
On the beach, next to Oceano Palace Hotel, with indoor and outdoor seating. This is one of the premier seafood restaurants in Mazatlan. Great for lunch or dinner.

La Hacienda de la Flor
Royal Villas Resort Hotel
Tel. 916-6161
Traditional Mexican ingredients prepared with culinary flair and served in an attractive hacienda-style setting. Try the cream of poblano chili soup, chateaubriand topped with marinated onions and a zesty 10-chili sauce, and cheese-filled battered jumbo shrimp in a sweet-and-sour tamarind sauce. Live romantic music at breakfast and dinner. Open 7 a.m. to 11 p.m.

Las Palomas
Pueblo Bonito Hotel

Tel. 914-3700
Traditional Mexican dishes served in informal interiors featuring hand-painted tile murals, or out on a breezy terrace. Extensive breakfast buffet and outstanding Sunday brunch. Open 7 a.m. to midnight.

Mariscos La Puntilla
Near the ferry dock
Tel. 982-8877
Locals flock to this popular seafood restaurant for its fresh fish and shrimp specialties served in an airy outdoor setting overlooking the water and a busy pier; local tours take off from here. Try their *pescado zarandeado*, whole fish marinated in spices. Live norteño music adds to the ambiance. Open 11 a.m. to 7 p.m.

Mister Ace
Av. Camaron Sabalo and Gabriel Ruiz 3
Tel. 914-4948
A favorite spot for its supper club atmosphere and classic dishes at reasonable prices. Try the cream of lobster soup, broiled shrimp stuffed with cheese and wrapped in bacon, or your catch of the day prepared as you like it. A variety of after-dinner coffees prepared at your table. Indoor or outdoor dining. Great breakfasts. Live piano music from 6 p.m. to midnight. Open 8 to 2 a.m.

Papagayo
The Inn at Mazatlan
Tel. 913-5500
Fine international and Mexican cuisine served in a delightful and romantic seaside setting, with tables on an open-air terrace overlooking the ocean or in air-conditioned comfort. The menu features creative fish and seafood dishes like the Coco Loco, jumbo shrimp flambéed in tequila, orange liqueur, coconut milk and pineapple, and served over rice in a coconut shell. A la carte and buffet breakfasts daily. Live music 6 to 9 p.m. Open 7 a.m. to 11 p.m.

Señor Frog's
Av. del Mar 225
Tel. 985-1110
This sister restaurant to El Shrimp Bucket features good food, friendly service and a lively ambiance. Try the BBQ ribs or oysters Madrazo. Don't pay any attention to the prominent sign advertising "Lousy food and warm beer." Open noon to 2 a.m.

Sr. Pepper
Av. Camaron Sabalo, opposite Playa Real Hotel
Tel. 914-0101
Mazatlan's premier steak house offers understated elegance with candlelit tables, ceiling fans and abundant plants. The specialties include filet mignon, mesquite-grilled steak, lobster and shrimp. There's a dance floor and live music, plus an attractive bar. Dinner 5 to 11 p.m.; open until 2 a.m. No reservations.

Sombrero Bay
Opposite Los Sabalos Hotel
Tel. 983-6330
This beautiful Mexican restaurant offers a delightful, open-air setting with umbrella-shaded

tables and colorful handicrafts. Contemporary Mexican cuisine, wide range of tequilas, live marimba music. Open 11 a.m. to midnight.

Terraza Playa
Playa Mazatlan Hotel
Tel. 913-4444
The traditional favorite for relaxed dining by the beach. Good food and friendly service in a terrace restaurant overlooking the ocean. Salad bar. Live music for dancing from 7 p.m. Fireworks show Sundays at 8 p.m. Open 7 a.m. to 11 p.m.

Vittore
Rodolfo T. Loaiza 100
Tel. 986-2424
Opposite Los Sabalos Hotel. This chic Italian grill serves tasty fare in attractive interiors or in a pleasant sidewalk terrace. Pastas, and grilled fish and seafood are the specialties. A selection of wines to accompany meals. Open for lunch and dinner.

Nightlife

Most of the major hotels feature live music in the evenings, whether at the bar or beachside, including the Riviera Beach Resort and Playa Mazatlan. Dominating the seaside promenade, at the beginning of the hotel zone, is *Fiesta Land*, a Moorish-style complex that houses several eateries and nightclubs, the most popular being *Bora-Bora*.

Bora-Bora
Fiesta Land
Tel. 986-4949
This outdoor venue features a palm-thatched bar and disco on the beach. Extremely popular with the young crowd. Open from 9 p.m.

El Cenote
Royal Villas Resort Hotel
Tel. 916-6161
Enjoy your favorite drinks in a romantic tropical garden setting near cooling ocean breezes and the sound of the waves. Soft music for dancing Tuesday to Sunday from 7 p.m. Popular with a more mature crowd. Happy Hour 5 to 6 p.m. and 8 to 9 p.m.

El Shrimp Bucket
Olas Altas 11, downtown
Tel. 982-8019
The marimba music, in an outdoor patio, under the stars, with a nice view of the sea, makes for a fun evening. Open until 11 p.m.

Joe's Oyster Bar & Grill
Los Sabalos Hotel
Tel. 983-5333
There's dancing at night to U.S. pop hits at this friendly beachfront spot. Open until 2 a.m.

Mexican Fiestas

Mexican Fiestas are an important part of nightlife throughout Mexican resorts and Mazatlan is no exception. The *Playa Mazatlan Ho-*

tel features a complete folkloric dinner-show three times a week, and a fireworks show every Sunday. Tel. 913-5320.

The *Royal Villas Resort* hosts a Mexican Fiesta with a folkloric ballet every Sunday (tel. 916-6161), as does *The Inn at Mazatlan* (tel. 913-5500). *El Cid Mega Resort* hosts a Carnival Fiesta every Wednesday at 7 p.m. Tel. 913-3333.

A new venue for Mexican theme shows, including dinner and drinks, is *Spectaculare*. The open-air theater features two shows weekly: Mexico Through the Centuries, showcasing the music and dances of different regions, and Millennium of Mexico, which takes the audience through 100 years of Mexican music. Tel. 914-0040.

Shopping

Mazatlan's largest shopping center, *La Gran Plaza*, is near the hotel zone at Reforma and Apolo. The air-conditioned complex has more than 200 stores selling everything from swimsuits to rustic Mexican furniture, as well as beauty parlors, a travel agency, bookshops and fast-food restaurants. In the hotel zone stores line the major avenue, Camaron Sabalo, as well as Rodolfo T. Loaiza. You'll find lots of Mexican vanilla, both clear and dark, in powder or liquid form, plus leather goods, handicrafts, and gold and silver jewelry.

Designers Bazaar
Rodolfo T. Loaiza 217; Playa Mazatlan Hotel
Exotic and unusual clothing, mostly for women, in both dressy and casual styles. Superb hand-painted and batik fabrics in brilliant colors. Large selection on two floors. Also a good collection of jewelry and folk art.

Dr. Jorge Morelos Chong
Av. Camaron Sabalo 204-30
Tel. 913-6068
For dental care and emergencies. Dr. Morelos specializes in porcelain crowns (*coronas de porcelana*) and fillings, as well as root canals (*endodoncias*). English spoken. Hours: 9 a.m. to 1 p.m. and 4 to 6:30 p.m. For regular checkups, making an appointment is recommended.

El Delfin
Balboa Towers
Tel. 914-3209
This highly reputable jeweler offers a unique collection of gold and sterling silver items creatively displayed. Handmade 14k and 18k gold pieces, most set with precious or semiprecious gems, are their specialty. They also offer a wide selection of loose precious and semiprecious stones, including diamonds, in different shapes and cuts. Custom-made designs, jewelry repairs. Open 9 a.m. to 7 p.m.

Michael Gallery
Av. Camaron Sabalo 19
Tel. 916-7816
A great place to browse and admire Mexican creativity, this store features a wonderful selection of Mexican handicrafts, including items made of blown glass, carved wood, wrought iron, and more, plus an excellent collection of silver jewelry. Open 9 a.m. to 10 p.m., except Sunday.

Miguel's Jewelry
Av. Camaron Sabalo 1448, opposite Pueblo Bonito Hotel
Tel. 916-5792
A carefully-selected range of fine Mexican sterling silver jewelry, as well as handicrafts. Open 9 a.m. to 7 p.m., except Sunday.

Mundo Tropical
Rodolfo T. Loaiza 204-43
This tiny shop carries Mexican vanilla and ready-made spice mixes for making such typical Mexican dishes as *enchiladas* and *huevos rancheros*.

Rubio Jewelers
Costa de Oro Hotel; Av. Camaron Sabalo 5108
Tel. 914-3167
Offering high quality and reliability, with attractive displays of gold and silver jewelry set with precious and semiprecious stones chosen by owner Jose Rubio Lizarraga, a graduate of the Gemological Institute of America. Costa de Oro branch is also the exclusive distributor of Mexican artist Sergio Bustamante's distinctive line of jewelry and art work. Open 9 a.m. to 6:30 p.m.; 10 a.m. to 2 p.m. Sunday.

Sea Shell City
Rodolfo T. Loaiza, near Playa Mazatlan Hotel
A supermarket of sea shells with aisles of common to rare shells in all sizes, shapes, colors. Mobiles, curtains, jewelry, accessories. Some fine items, many kitschy souvenirs.

Hotels

Costa de Oro
Av. Camaron Sabalo

Tel. (669) 913-2005
www.costaoro.com
A popular beachfront hotel and timeshare resort with 290 rooms and one-bedroom suites with kitchenette and cable TV. Restaurant, sports bar. Large, nicely landscaped swimming pool right on the beach, three tennis courts, meeting facilities, gym. Rates MD.

El Cid Mega Resort
Av. Camaron Sabalo
Tel. (669) 913-3333
www.elcid.com
A sprawling resort with 1,320 rooms and suites distributed in two beachfront towers and a low-rise country club complex. Championship golf course, 17 tennis courts, gym and health spa, eight swimming pools. Access to Marina El Cid for water sports and sailing instruction. Kids club. Myriad on-site activities and tours. Restaurants, bar, disco. Business center and extensive convention facilities for more than 4,000 people. All-inclusive option available. Rates MD.

Faro Mazatlan
Punta del Sabalo
Tel. (669) 913-1111
www.faromazatlan.com.mx
Located on a rocky point overlooking a fine beach, this attractive all-inclusive (formerly the Camino Real) has 165 nicely decorated rooms and suites with all first-class amenities. Beach club with seafood restaurant and live tropical marimba music, tennis courts, beautiful swimming pools, meeting and banquet facilities, kids club, excellent service. Rates FC (all inclusive).

Fiesta Inn
Camaron Sabalo 1927
Tel. (669) 989-0100
www.fiestainn.com
This friendly, modern hotel with a business bent has 117 simple yet attractive rooms with satellite TV; beachfront restaurant, pool, well-equipped gym. Rates MD.

Hacienda Las Moras
On the road to La Noria
Tel. (669) 916-5045
www.lasmoras.com
20 minutes from the hotel zone. Nestled in the countryside, this upscale retreat housed in a former mezcal-producing hacienda dating from 1835 offers six villas and five individual casitas, excellent dining, swimming pool, tennis courts, horseback riding, attentive service. Rates DX.

Holiday Inn SunSpree
Camaron Sabalo 696
Tel. (669) 913-2222
www.holiday-inn.com
A modern hotel with 183 large rooms with satellite TV, a/c, phone, minibar. Nice beach club, kids club, great pool area, poolside restaurant, tennis court, business center, meeting facilities

for 600. Rates MD.

Los Sabalos
Rodolfo T. Loaiza 100
Tel. (669) 983-5333
www.lossabalos.com
A newly renovated gleaming white-stucco hotel on the beach with 200 attractive rooms and suites, each with satellite TV, air-conditioning. Four restaurants and the popular beachfront Joe's Oyster Bar. Swimming pool, health club with sauna, steam room, jacuzzi and masseuse, beach club, and child care. Convention facilities for 300 people. Rates MD.

Marina El Cid
Av. Camaron Sabalo
Tel. (669) 913-3333
www.elcid.com
This first-class hotel and yacht club offers 210 Mediterranean-style suites overlooking the marina entrance, beach and Sea of Cortez beyond. Two lagoonlike freshwater pools surrounded by tropical gardens, nine-hole golf course; restaurant, lobby bar with live music, exclusive yacht club with 90 slips, meeting rooms. Rates MD.

Mayan Sea Garden
On Sabalo Cerritos, north of the hotel zone
Tel. (669) 988-0032
www.seagarden.com.mx
On six acres of gardens, this popular beachfront hotel and timeshare resort has 300 one-bedroom suites with kitchenette and cable TV, some with balconies overlooking the ocean or mountains. Large swimming pool with cascading waterfalls, three lit tennis courts, gym. Restaurant, bar, disco. Rates MD.

Playa Mazatlan
Rodolfo T. Loaiza 202, on Playa las Gaviotas
Tel. (669) 913-1120

www.hotelplayamazatlan.com
This horizontal low-rise on the beach is an ultra-popular hotel offering lots of activity or relaxation. There are 427 comfortable air-conditioned rooms with oceanview balconies, satellite TV, phones. Large swimming pools, indoor and outdoor jacuzzis, gym, and terrace restaurant-bars facing the ocean and featuring live music. Rates MD.

Pueblo Bonito
Camaron Sabalo 2121
Tel. (669) 914-3700
www.pueblobonito.com
A beautiful colonial-style beachfront property with gardens and 247 attractively-decorated suites with kitchenette, cable TV and ocean view. Excellent restaurants (Italian and seafood specialties), spectacular pool area, gym, spa, small meeting room, children's activities, and several nice shops. Rates FC.

Pueblo Bonito at Emerald Bay
Ernesto Coppel Campaña 201, Camino al Delfin, in Nuevo Mazatlan
Tel. (669) 989-0525
www.pueblobonito.com
Located on a pristine bay, this neo-classical-style all-suite beachfront hotel and timeshare resort features 78 attractive units (258 when completed) ranging from junior to penthouse suites. Lovely pool area with jacuzzi, extensive banquet facilities, tennis, fitness center, specialties restaurant, bar, gourmet deli. Rates FC.

Riviera Beach Resort
Camaron Sabalo 51
Tel. (669) 983-4822
www.riviera.com.mx
A tastefully remodelled older hotel on the beach with 118 rooms and 57 suites with balconies, air-conditioning, TV; lovely pool area, beachfront restaurant, separate bar with live music. Rates MD.

Royal Villas Resort
Camaron Sabalo 500
Tel. (669) 916-6161
www.royalvillas.com.mx
This modern Mexican-style property on the beach offers 125 one-, two- and three-bedroom suites with oceanview balcony, satellite TV, including two penthouses with jacuzzi. Pool, gym, game room, meeting facilities for 150, business center, children's activities, excellent restaurant and lobby bar with live music. Rates MD.

The Inn at Mazatlan
Camaron Sabalo 6291
Tel. (669) 913-5500
www.innatmazatlan.com.mx
The original small inn has grown into an impressive 223-suite oceanfront property with upscale accommodations ranging from studios to penthouse suites, all with oceanview balconies and cable TV, some with kitchenette, living room. Popular restaurant-bar, oceanfront swimming pool, tennis (with 2 complimentary hours of play daily), children's activities. Meeting facilities for up to 200 people. Rates FC.

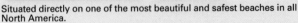

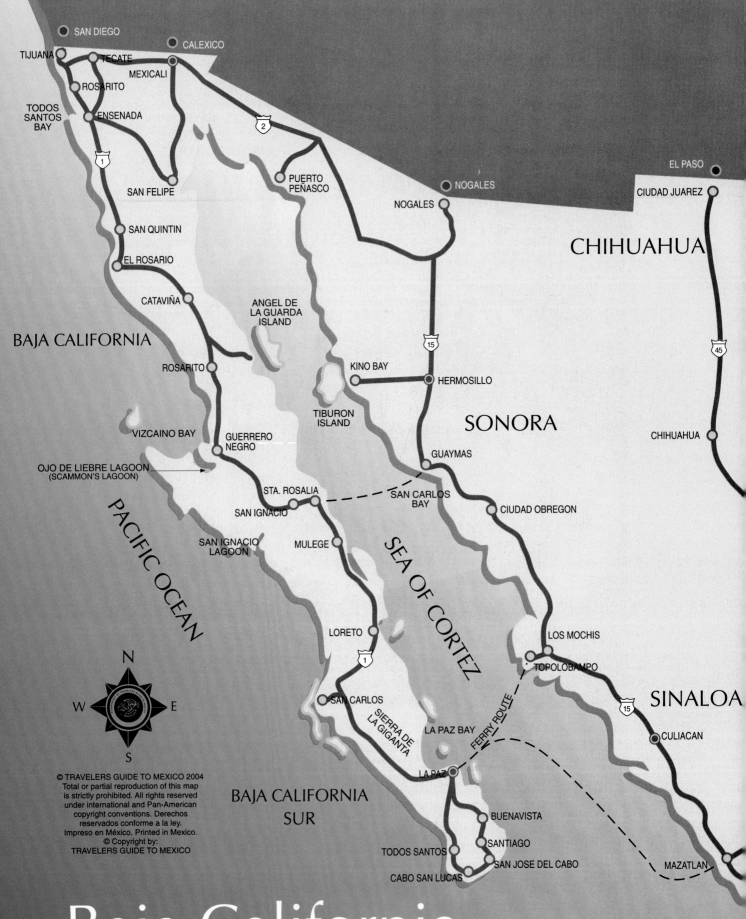

Baja California

TRAVELERS GUIDE TO
Baja California

Ministry of Tourism

The peninsula features landscapes
full of stunning contrasts.

Tijuana to Land's End

Mexico's Last Vacation Frontier

North Baja is home to Mexico's leading wineries

Exotic and exciting, Baja California is Mexico's last vacation frontier. While it was nearly as remote as the moon a few years ago, it's now well-established as a holiday haven.

Baja means "lower." The Spaniards called what is now the U.S. state *Alta,* or Upper, California. They paid little attention to either, and almost none at all to Baja. Only in the past two decades has Mexico awakened to its potential.

Longer than Italy's boot, the peninsula is divided into two states: Baja California, with Mexicali as its capital, and Baja California Sur, with La Paz as its capital. Dotted by the remnants of Catholic missions and exotic cactus, its topography consists of desertlike barren hills with an occasional green strip of irrigated farmland or vineyard, and a vast stretch in the northern middle of the peninsula that resembles a surrealistic lunarscape. Mostly, however, it's an 800-mile-long desert poking into the boundless sea.

The peninsula's midriff is flanked by headlands and islands, and features the 25-mile-long Bahia de Concepcion, reputedly the world's largest bay, and certainly one of the most beautiful. From Mulege down the coast to Loreto/Puerto Escondido's safe harbor, clear waters teeming with fish are juxtaposed against barren landscapes, making a picturesque backdrop for boaters.

Transpeninsular Highway 1, from Tijuana down to Los Cabos, is in good condition for the most part, but gas stations, few and far between, are known to run out of unleaded gas, called Magna Sin or Premium, so fill up whenever possible. It's advisable to travel the highway only during daylight hours to avoid being stranded all night with a breakdown.

Baja weather tends to be hot and dry in summer and a bit cooler in winter. Spring presents a fabulous sight with myriad cactus in bloom.

The beaches between Rosarito and Ensenada are popular surfing areas, and Baja abounds in sporting events year-round. Bicycle races are held between Ensenada and Tecate, and auto racing includes the famous Baja 1000 in November and the Baja 500 in June, as well as various off-road races.

Mexico's national tourism development agency, Fonatur, is building a nautical route along the Baja peninsula and Sea of Cortez to lure more seafaring tourists from the U.S. southwest. The project calls for upgrading existing ports and building new ones along the coasts of both north and south Baja Californias, as well as Sonora and Sinaloa.

Tijuana

Tijuana's transformation from seedy border town to cosmopolitan urban center appears to have picked up speed as its burgeoning population of 2 million residents demands a higher standard of living. The city in Mexico with the lowest unemployment rate now offers more cultural activities and a wider range of fine restaurants than ever before.

In the process of shedding its old skin, the city has closed some of its traditional attractions. If you used to go for the horse races and jai alai games, then you're in for a major disappointment. They have both closed. The gargantuan jai alai palace, an architectural marvel dating from the mid-1900s, is being remodeled to serve as a concert venue.

Still, there's plenty of kitsch to be had at the *Wax Museum*, where Tia Juana's likeness resides, and at *Avenida Revolucion*, the famed shopping strip flanked by stores and stalls selling piles of T-shirts and leather goods. To be fair, there's more to this celebrated boulevard: here you can also buy a key with your name carved on it, get a prescription filled at any of numerous pharmacies (though prices are double what they are in other parts of the city), and see "girls, girls, girls!"

But Avenida Revolucion represents the old face of Tijuana. The town's future lies in Zona Rio, a 20-block-long area that stretches along the banks of the Tijuana River and modern Paseo de Los Heroes Boulevard. This district is home to the architecturally unique Tijuana Cultural Center, leading restaurants, the attractive Camino Real Hotel, and a modest shopping center.

In September of 2002, Newsweek stunned everyone by naming Tijuana one of the world's top seven cultural centers. "*La Bola,*" or "The

Ball," as the city's spherical cultural center is affectionately called, is probably the reason why. The center hosts world-class exhibits, concerts, seminars, workshops and film festivals, and screens movies at its IMAX theater. The center also houses the *Museum of the Californias*, which relates the history of the Baja California Peninsula from pre-Hispanic times to the present, including the Prohibition-era surge in tourism.

Located just a few miles south of San Diego, Tijuana grew into a center of cabarets and nightclubs in the early 1900s, when U.S. Prohibition laws drove Americans in search of nightlife across the border. Nearly a century later, it's still struggling to shed its "sin city" image. It is plagued by police corruption and attempts to clean things up have been less than successful. But change is slowly taking place. A small but significant sign of increased government regulation is the new fleet of reliable orange-and-white taxis that charge passengers according to the meter.

New Baja Cuisine

As the city where Italian restaurateur Alex Cardini tossed the very first Caesar salad, where the clamato was first mixed, and the revered national cocktail, the margarita, was invented, Tijuana takes special pride in its gastronomy.

One of the newest restaurants in Zona Rio and one you shouldn't miss is *Palmazul*, which aims to showcase everything about Baja California, including its regional architecture, wildlife, art, crafts and cuisine. In keeping with this idea, the stone-paved entrance leads to an inviting lounge bar decked with representations of Baja's prehistoric cave paintings. Behind the wavy bar, a desert landscape dotted with cactus provides a beautiful, and cleverly parched, backdrop. At the entrance to the dining room is an Ensenada-style seafood cocktail bar brimming with fruits of the sea on ice. Fresh ingredients and grill-top cooking characterizes the "new peninsular cuisine." A few highlights from the menu include oven-baked duck burrito, grilled swordfish with pineapple sauce, oysters au gratin, shellfish fantasy, and roasted quail. Tel. 622-9775.

Also forming part of Zona Rio's growing restaurant row are *Villa Saverios*, for Mediterranean-style cuisine prepared with locally grown ingredients and served in a pleasant Romanesque setting, and *La Diferencia*, for Mexican specialties surrounded by traditional folk art.

Less than 30 minutes south of Tijuana, at the golf resort of Real del Mar, chef Martin San Roman's culinary skills have turned him into somewhat of a local celebrity. Featured at his *Rincon San Roman* restaurant are such creations as tuna tartare flavored with a blend of sesame oil, balsamic vinegar, honey and thyme; oyster soup in a Pernod spiked tomato broth; Baja-style coquille San Jacques; and layered crepe cake with white chocolate. It's no wonder the talent behind Tijuana's once famed Tour de France restaurant is considered Baja's No. 1 chef. Tel. 632-2241.

Wine Fest

Naturally, with all this good food, fine wine can't be far behind. Baja winery *L.A. Cetto* has a downtown bottling plant and wine cellar that lets visitors see part of the production process. Visitors can tour the facility, participate in a wine tasting of their award-winning wines, and browse their gift shop. Tel. 685-1644.

Each year around August, regional wineries host a Wine Harvesting Festival, or *Vendimia*, at their vineyards about two and a half hours south of Tijuana. Celebrations typically begin with a traditional mass followed by the blessing of the first grape press, a grape stomping competition, wine tasting, late-afternoon picnic-style lunch, pop music concert, bullfight, *taquiza* (tacos) and fireworks. Go prepared for some jostling and many hours spent outdoors in sunny weather; take plenty of water and sunscreen, a hat, and a sweater for nighttime.

Thanks to new local microbrewery Cerveceria Tijuana TJ, beer is also making a splash in these parts. The company's downtown headquarters, featuring *La Taberna TJ* restaurant and bar, a beautiful wood-paneled tavern, is the perfect place to try their five delicious brews, with names like Morena (Brunette) and Dorada (Golden). Made with imported European know-how and equipment, their top-quality beer has no additives or preservatives of any kind. Tel. 684-2406.

Popular nightspots in town include *Tia Juana Tilly's*, *Hard Rock Cafe* and *Señor Frog's*.

Where to Stay

Tijuana's leading hotels, the *Camino Real* and the *Grand Hotel*, bespeak a demanding business clientele.

Located just outside Zona Rio, on the edge of the Agua Caliente Golf Course, the traditional two-tower Grand Hotel really knows how to pamper its guests with friendly and attentive service, and serves excellent coffee to boot. Tel. 681-7000.

Conveniently located in the heart of Zona Rio, the Camino Real Hotel offers chic, modern surroundings and proximity to major sights of interest. Tel. 633-4000.

Aeromexico operates as many as 13 daily flights to Tijuana, reflecting the city's importance to the business sector, not just as a gateway to the United States, but also for its role in commerce here in Mexico.

Rosarito

About a 20 minute drive from Tijuana, the town of Rosarito is best known for its attractive long beach and famed *Rosarito Beach Hotel*, a classic built a half century ago and once a getaway for Hollywood celebrities. Lana Turner, Orson Welles, Gregory Peck and Debbie Reynolds were among its frequent guests. Opened during the Prohibition era, the hotel's tile-and-mirror decor is a perfect blend of Hollywood and Mexico.

In those days, Rosarito was a playground for the stars. Today it serves more as a stage for the stars. "Titanic," the biggest box office hit of all time, was filmed here at the six-acre, seaside Fox Studios Baja. Film productions continue at the facility (Pearl Harbor was partially shot here), especially those that call for a 17 million-gallon tank of seawater (built for Titanic).

For a fun behind-the-scenes look at moviemaking, visit the studio's movie theme park, Foxploration. Here you can learn, and demonstrate, how miniature model ships can be used to depict doomed oversized ocean liners, and other cinematic sleights of hand. Tel. (866) 369-2252.

Nearby *Puerto Nuevo* is famed for its numerous restaurants serving grilled lobster accompanied by refried beans, rice and flour tortillas. In fact, Puerto Nuevo-style lobster is increasingly served throughout the Baja peninsula. Among the best places to try this local delicacy are the Rosarito Beach Hotel and *Ortega's* in Puerto Nuevo, where you get excellent seafood and a view to boot.

Tecate/Mexicali/San Felipe

Tecate, one of Baja's three border towns, is located 34 miles east of Tijuana. The town is famed for its beer (visitors can tour the brewery), wine, and health resort, *Rancho La Puerta*. Established more than 40 years ago, La Puerta is in the same league as the *Green Door* and *Maine Chance*.

An interesting spectacle staged each year in Tecate is the running of the bulls, a local version of the event made famous by the city of Pamplona, in Spain. The attractive *Hacienda Santa Veronica* offers all resort amenities, plus a "bloodless bullfight."

Mexicali, due south of the California-Arizona border, is 65 miles east of Tijuana. Capital of Baja California, Mexicali is a unique border town in that tourism is unimportant to its economy. The city of 800,000 inhabitants is the center of a rich farming region. Lack of tourism is one reason many people enjoy visiting Mexicali. Unlike Tijuana, it is a typical Mexican town. Its one unusual trait is that it is home to more than 50 Chinese restaurants.

On the eastern side of the peninsula, 125 miles south of Mexicali, is San Felipe, fast growing into northern Baja's newest resort. The reason is the fishing—the village is on the shores of the Sea of Cortez, the greatest fish trap in the Western Hemisphere.

Sites of interest here include the *Valley of the Giants*, populated by huge 50-foot-tall cardon cactus; seaside hot springs; and *San Pedro Martir National Park*, a 151,000-acre park that's home to Baja's tallest summit, the 10,126-foot double-crested Picacho del Diablo, or Devil's Peak.

Ensenada

Charming and picturesque Ensenada, located 70 miles south of the U.S.-Mexico border and a 90-minute drive from San Diego, is Baja California's third largest city and most important resort. More than half a million people visit each year.

According to local lore, the Spanish priests who discovered the area's bay were so impressed by its size that they felt the name of a single saint was insufficient and called the harbor *Bahia de Todos los Santos,* or Bay of All Saints. It's one of Mexico's principal ports of call for cruise ships and pleasure boats.

A new seafront promenade, or *male-con,* and a remodeled shopping and dining corridor, Paseo Calle Primera, have made the town more attractive. Water sports, from snorkeling to kayaking, are popular in the waters north and south of town. Yellowtail season is May through October and anglers have their choice of taking a party boat or chartering a vessel. On land, visitors can golf, play tennis, hike and horseback ride.

Camino Real Hotel, Loreto

Sites of interest include the oldest winery in the Baja peninsula, *Bodegas de Santo Tomas,* which offers wine tastings; *La Bufadora* ("The Blowhole"), where wave action through a passage in the cliffs produces a spectacular geyser that spouts sea water high into the air; and *Punta Banda,* a delightfully secluded beach about 19 miles south of Bufadora that is frequented by sea lions.

Among the best restaurants in town is the award-winning *El Rey Sol,* a family-owned operation that has been serving classic French cuisine since 1947, as well as original seafood recipes and European-style pastries. It's located at Paseo Calle Primera 1000 and is open daily for breakfast, lunch and dinner. Tel. 178-1733.

There's plenty of action after dark, especially at the landmark *Hussong's Cantina,* a wild and woolly sailors' hangout renowned for being the oldest bar in the Californias. Established as a stagecoach stop in 1892 by German-born Johan Hussong, the cantina has hosted its share of celebrities, including Marilyn Monroe, Steve McQueen and Bing Crosby. Mariachi musicians and caricature artists liven up the atmosphere of this informal watering hole with sawdust strewn floors. It's located at Avenida Ruiz 113, and is open from 10 a.m. until past midnight.

Wine enthusiasts, and anyone who wants to learn more about Mexico's leading wineries, will enjoy a visit to *SeDe Vino,* a stylish wine bar that features national wines and varieties from around the world, both by the glass and by the

bottle. Av. Ruiz 138, downtown. Tel. 178-3433.

Galeria de Perez-Meillon, at Plaza Hussong's, has one-of-a-kind ceramics and *Mario's,* with four locations on Paseo Calle Primera, carries large selections of sterling silver jewelry, as well as leather goods, and arts and crafts.

Recommended hotels include *Hacienda Bajamar,* part of an oceanfront golf resort 30 minutes north of town (tel. (646) 155-0151), and *Posada El Rey Sol,* located in the downtown area (tel. (646) 178-1601).

Guerrero Negro

Numerous charming sites lie southward, on the Pacific side of the peninsula, including *Valle de San Quintin,* where La Pinta Hotel has a broad private beach and a wide range of recreational facilities, and *Cataviña,* home to another La Pinta, this one on the site of an old Spanish mission. Weird *cirio* "elephant" trees, nearby cave paintings and colonial-era missions make this area especially interesting for photographers.

Located 29 miles south of San Quintin and 80 miles north of Cataviña is *El Rosario,* a fishing and agricultural village that as recently as 1974 was the last outpost of civilization before the adventurous plunged into the desolate central and southern tracts of Baja. The paved road ended at *Mama Espinoza's,* a general store and restaurant with a few rustic rooms available for the drivers of the annual *Baja 1000* auto race. Doña Anita, the articulate and spry octogenar-

ian owner, still makes delectable lobster tacos for her guests, with a menu featuring *Parnelli Jones, Mickey Thompson* and *Steve McQueen* tacos, named after past participants in the big race that traditionally ends at her place.

On the border between north and south Baja is Guerrero Negro, a Pacific coast town renowned as the site of *Laguna Ojo de Liebre,* also known as *Scammon's Lagoon,* a body of water that gray whales consider their own lovers' lane. The whales swim down from the Arctic Ocean to mate and bear their young off the beaches of Baja California between December and March. Declared Gray Whale National Park, the lagoon is one of the best places to see them frolic.

Guerrero Negro is also the site of the world's largest sea salt extraction mine. The facility, run by a Japanese-Mexican conglomerate, is the biggest of its kind in the world. Ocean water is evaporated in great ponds and the salt that is left behind is quarried for shipment abroad. This area has been the focus of much conflict since environmentalists believe the salt industry poses a threat to the whales.

At the entrance to town is *Malarrimo,* a restaurant featuring excellent seafood, especially abalone. Enrique Achoy, who can be found here, runs excellent natural history tours during the winter. In the spring and fall he takes people to visit the famous prehistoric cave paintings of *El Vizcaino,* which have been named a World Heritage Site by UNESCO.

Below Guerrero Negro, the highway cuts southeast across the peninsula, passing through the delightful oasis of *San Ignacio*. Its old Jesuit mission is one of the most beautiful to be found along the peninsula.

Santa Rosalia

On the Sea of Cortez is Santa Rosalia, with its ferry terminal offering regular car service to Guaymas on the mainland. Santa Rosalia began its existence as a French-occupied manganese mining town in the 1870s, and the Gallic influence remains. The prevailing architectural style is French Provençal throughout this picturesque seaport, which was one of the last ports in the world to be served by the age of sailing. Its protected man-made harbor boasts a recently constructed marina.

The town claims to have some of the best bakeries in all Mexico (probably thanks to the French), *El Boleo* being a favorite. It definitely has an unusual local church—a prefabricated, 19th-century iron structure built in Paris and shipped halfway around the world. The designer was long believed to have been none other than Gustav Eiffel, but researchers now believe it was built by a fellow student of Eiffel's who studied at the same academy.

Mulege

Located 38 miles south of Santa Rosalia, at the mouth of beautiful *Bahia de Concepcion*, is Mulege. This tropical seaside oasis is built beside the peninsula's only navigable river, lined with date palms and olive groves, and graced by a lovely old mission.

Here fishermen can combine freshwater angling with sea adventures. Pleasant boat trips can be arranged both up river and to rock islands offshore, where sea lions make their home. Among Mulege's attractions is its former prison-without-bars, which allowed inmates to work daily in town. No longer in operation, the hacienda-style building overlooks the charming town. Prehistoric cave paintings preserved in the surrounding hills are accessible by jeep.

Recommended hotels include *Posada de las Flores*, a pretty hacienda-style property on Santa Ines Bay, and *Serenidad*, a popular gathering place, especially for its Saturday night pig roast and fiesta with mariachis.

Loreto

Little-known Loreto is a charming town 85 miles south of Mulege, on the Sea of Cortez. As the first capital of the Californias, it boasts famous missions built by Jesuits in the 17th century. In fact, "300 Years Old and Still Undiscovered" is the town motto.

Blissfully tranquil, its big draws are deep-sea fishing and scuba diving. Tuna, sailfish, marlin and mahi-mahi are available during the summer, and yellowtail and red snapper in the fall and winter.

Loreto has a quaint downtown area with shaded plazas and an attractive *malecon* (seaside promenade) that draws locals and tourists alike for strolls along the waterfront. The resort also comprises an area 17 miles south

of town called *Puerto Escondido* that sits on the edge of a gorgeous mountain-ringed bay, *Bahia Nopolo*. Puerto Escondido has long been known as the home of the *Tripui Trailer Park*, considered the best and most complete RV park in all of Baja California Sur.

Don't miss the opportunity to visit several stunningly pristine islands nearby, such as *Isla Coronado*, where you can snorkel in the crystalline waters and sun bathe on the fine white sand beach. You can hire a private boat or contact *Las Parras Tours*, which offers island excursions, as well as kayaking, mountain biking, mule riding and whale watching. Tel. 135-1010.

Loreto won't remain undiscovered much longer. While today it is home to just a handful of hotels, a small marina, an 18-hole seaside golf course and a John McEnroe Tennis Center, a major development project plans to turn this secluded spot into a leading residential resort, mainly for the U.S. and Canadian markets.

Loreto Bay—a project launched by Mexico's tourism development agency Fonatur (creator of Cancun, Los Cabos and Ixtapa) in partnership with U.S. and Canadian investors—aims to establish a master-planned seaside community on 3,000 acres along three miles of coastline to the south of town.

When completed in about 10 to 15 years, the Villages at Loreto Bay will comprise 5,000 homes, hotels, businesses, and cultural and recreational facilities. Touted as a showcase of sustainable development practices, the Villages are being designed to "harvest" more potable water than they consume, through re-use and desalinzation, and create more energy than they use, through solar power. Developers have already broken ground and sold the first batch of homes.

Good beachfront hotels include the *Camino Real* and *The Whales Inn*.

Located on its own sandy, secluded cove adjacent to an 18-hole golf course, the deluxe Camino Real features (at less than deluxe prices) 156 modern Mexican rooms and suites with air-conditioning, fan, satellite TV, safe and other amenities, as well as an alfresco specialties restaurant, wet bar, lobby bar and 24-hour room service. Tel. (613) 133-0010. www.LoretoBaja.com.

The Whales Inn, the gloriously remodelled former Eden Resort, is an all-inclusive beach and golf resort with 250 guest rooms and lots of recreational activities, including archery. Tel. (613) 133-0700. www.whalesinn.com.

An excellent option in the heart of town, right on the main plaza, is *Posada de las Flores*. This charming little hotel features 14 guest rooms, each individually decorated and named after a different flower, and an outdoor pool. Posada's *The Roof Garden*, for Mexican fare, and *Vecchia Roma*, for Italian favorites, are excellent dining options. Tel. (613) 135-1162. www.posadadelasflores.com.

You can fly direct to Loreto from Los Angeles on *Aero California* and from San Diego, on *Aeromexico*. You can also fly to La Paz or Los Cabos, rent a car and make the scenic three and a half hour drive north.

La Paz

The tranquil capital of Baja California Sur is aptly named (*paz* means "peace"), but it was not always this peaceful. Its past includes a host of pirates, cruel soldiers and missionaries.

The city once thrived on a brisk trade in pearls, as its nearby oyster beds produced the coveted black pearl until an epidemic brought an end to production in 1940. It later began to attract sport fishermen from the United States, and rapidly grew into an important resort served by ferries, a jet airport and the Transpeninsular Highway.

Home to more than 250,000 inhabitants, La Paz boasts one of the highest per capita incomes in Mexico. Its flourishing economy is reflected in clean, well-kept streets, homes and businesses. The whole atmosphere is quietly cosmopolitan and romantic in an adventurous sort of way.

Tourists come primarily to fish, a sport that costs less here as boat rentals aren't quite as expensive as in other parts of Mexico. If you're not keen on fishing, there are lots of water sports to enjoy, as well as tours of various local attractions. The *Reina Calafia* glass-bottom boat offers excursions to nearby islands with a seal colony and spectacular rock arch.

La Paz is a duty-free port, so you will find imported goods from around the world, as well as Mexican arts and crafts. The town's major department store, *La Perla,* carries imported items from the United States, Europe and the Orient.

Recommended hotels include the *Crowne Plaza, La Concha Beach Resort* and *La Posada de Engelbert* (as in Humperdinck).

La Paz is served by *Aeromexico* from Los Angeles, El Paso, Tucson, Phoenix, Mexico City, Tijuana, Culiacan, Guadalajara, Manzanillo and Guaymas; and by *Aero California* from Los Angeles, Loreto, Mazatlan, Mexico City and Tijuana.

Baja Ferries recently launched new passenger and vehicle ferry service between La Paz and Topolobampo, Sinaloa. Ideal for travelers combining a tour of the Copper Canyon with Baja California, the Italian-built vessel is equipped with private cabins for up to four people, regular seating, restaurant-bar, coffeeshop and shops. The six-hour trip costs about 60 dollars per person (about double that for a cabin); vehicles pay about 160 dollars. For more information, call (612) 125-7593. Ferry service is already available between La Paz and Mazatlan.

East Cape

Located 45 minutes north of Los Cabos' international airport, about halfway between Cabo San Lucas and La Paz, the East Cape is home to the towns of *Buena Vista* and *Santiago*, and is known for its sport fishing. The few two- to four-star hotels in the area together maintain a fleet of 150 fishing boats, including some two dozen fly-bridge cruisers. Since 1952, this has been where the pros hang out. Spring and summer are the high season.

Los Cabos

Sightseeing Among Lunar Landscapes, Beautiful Beaches

Accommodations along The Corridor overlook the Sea of Cortez

Winding its way down from the border, and covering nearly a thousand miles before it reaches the tip of the peninsula, is perhaps Mexico's most fascinating route, Transpeninsular Highway 1. The southern section, from La Paz to Cabo San Lucas, was inaugurated in 1974, opening up a desert wilderness with secluded beaches and waters teeming with fish.

Los Cabos, the area at the very tip of the Baja California Peninsula ("*cabo*" means "cape"), has become a major resort destination thanks largely to its climate: dry year-round, with an average temperature of 75° F and about 300 days of sunshine annually.

The isolated fishing camps that once catered to a handful of visitors who came in their own private planes or yachts, are now among luxury hotels that dot the coast around two towns—San Jose del Cabo and Cabo San Lucas—and the 20-mile stretch of coastline that lies between them, known as "The Corridor."

San Jose seems to play Yin to Cabo's Yang. In the spirit of Taoist philosophy, each complements the other. San Jose is quaint, charming and serene. Cabo is brash, animated, lively.

The heart of San Jose is a broad, tree-lined boulevard with canopied outdoor cafes and plant-filled patio restaurants. Cabo's center of activity is a modern marina that bustles with yacht and fishing boat traffic by day, and teems with revelers at night. There's the laid-back village and the definitive party town.

Los Cabos, whose total population has reached 100,000, was first visited by European missionaries in the 1500s. At that time the

> *Whales can be sighted not far from coast, spouting, breaching, lobbing and occasionally spyhopping.*

native Indians, a nomadic tribe called the Pericu that is thought to have migrated from the South Pacific, were the only inhabitants. Early records left by the missionaries describe the Pericu as dark-skinned and sturdy with a kind nature, as long as they were allowed to practice their polygamous ways.

In the 1800s, whaling came to the cape. Laguna Ojo de Liebre, one of Baja's three leading whale sanctuaries, is also known as Scammon's Lagoon, after American whaling captain Charles Scammon, who followed the migrating whales and discovered their wintertime refuge.

Along with the whalers came a few pirates, and more than a few of Los Cabos' best families proudly trace their roots back to the captains of these pirate ships. Fishing continued to dominate the economy of the region, and at the beginning of the 1900s a tuna cannery was built in Cabo, drawing fishing boats from around the world. The cannery was shut down in the 1960s and since then tourism has thrived.

Major airlines, as well as small feeder lines, serve the Los Cabos airport, located seven miles north of San Jose, which is 20 miles north of Cabo. In 1999 a second international airport terminal opened south of the original, serving as a base for special charter flights and *Alaska Airlines*, which flies to major U.S. cities.

Mexicana provides daily service to Los Angeles. Direct flights from Houston via *Continental*, from Dallas/Ft. Worth, Los Angeles, and

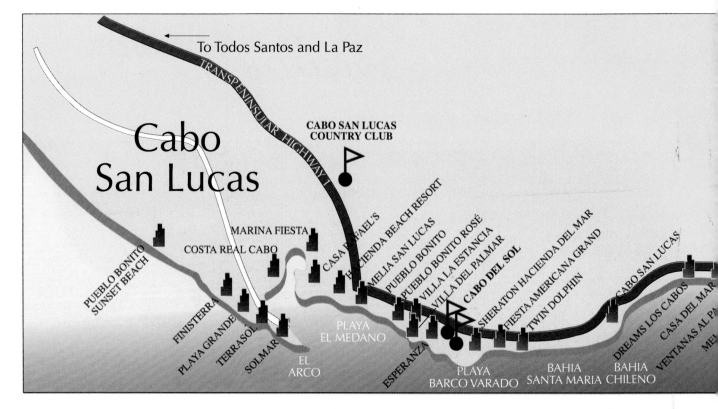

To Todos Santos and La Paz

TRANSPENINSULAR HIGHWAY 1

Cabo San Lucas

CABO SAN LUCAS COUNTRY CLUB

MARINA FIESTA
COSTA REAL CABO

PUEBLO BONITO SUNSET BEACH

FINISTERRA
PLAYA GRANDE
TERRASOL
SOLMAR

EL ARCO

PLAYA EL MEDANO

CASA RAFAEL'S
HACIENDA BEACH RESORT
MELIA SAN LUCAS
PUEBLO BONITO
PUEBLO BONITO ROSÉ
VILLA LA ESTANCIA
VILLA DEL PALMAR
CABO DEL SOL
SHERATON HACIENDA DEL MAR
FIESTA AMERICANA GRAND
TWIN DOLPHIN
DREAMS LOS CABOS
CABO SAN LUCAS
CASA DEL MAR
VENTANAS AL PA
MEI

ESPERANZA
PLAYA BARCO VARADO
BAHIA SANTA MARIA
BAHIA CHILENO

Chicago via *American Airlines*, from San Diego via *Aeromexico*, and from Phoenix via *America West*, make this destination even more accessible. *Delta* has begun to service the area out of Atlanta, while Continental is adding a weekly flight out of Newark.

Ocean liners that cruise the Mexican Riviera make regular stops at Los Cabos year-round.

Boat Rides

Boat outings are a great way to view this coast and its attractions.

Caborey, a catamaran measuring 134 feet, is a newly launched, family oriented floating cabaret offering three decks of live entertainment, including a nightly tango show, and gourmet dining, as well as shopping and daytime snorkeling tours. Tel. 143-8260.

Cabo Expeditions, at the Costa Real Cabo Hotel, has a popular three-hour snorkeling excursion to three different sites, as well as whale-watching tours, aboard convenient Zodiac rafts. Tel. 143-2700.

The *Oceanus* double-deck catamaran cruiser offers a four-hour sightseeing excursion along the coast, from Cabo to San Jose and back, so you can get a good look at the various beaches in between. Tel. 143-3929.

You can sightsee in style aboard *Kaleidoscope's* deluxe 100-foot-long power catamaran. Tel. 148-7318.

To enjoy the underwater sights without diving take a ride aboard the *Nautilus*, a boat with a below-surface viewing area.

More low key and economical, glass-bottom boats offer a pleasant way to see both the landmarks and the underwater life.

For Nature Lovers

Several nature tours highlight the area's flora and fauna, and take in a few nearby towns.

A Pacific-side tour takes you to a secluded beach that's home to sea lions and puddles of exotic marine creatures, and the town of *Todos Santos*. An eastward-bound tour features a fossil field, rock paintings, a visit to the leather-manufacturing town of *Miraflores*, and the town of *Santiago*, noted for its colonial mission dating from 1723. For more information, call *Rancho Tours*. Tel. 143-5464.

The Trailer Park in San Jose rents bicycles by the day or hour, and various bike tours lead to the eastern area known as *Punta Gorda* (Fat Point) or Santiago, where hot springs lie a short hike away. At Cabo's Playa el Medano you can rent mountain bikes for tackling nearby desert trails and sand dunes.

Nature lovers should not miss *Desert Park Natural Reserve*. A guided tour on state-of-the-art Honda ATVs (all-terrain vehicles) takes you into the desert and 2,000 feet up into the mountains, through pristine canyons and sand arroyos, to natural springs surrounded by unique flora and fauna. Reservations must be made in advance; custom tours are available. Tel. 144-0127, 144-0121.

Each winter gray whales migrate thousands of miles from as far north as the Bering Strait to the warmer, protected waters of Baja's Pacific bays and lagoons, where the females give birth to their calves. Like their human counterparts, baby whales are especially curious creatures and make for interesting encounters.

From January through March whales can be sighted not far from coast, spouting, leaping out of the water (called breaching), splashing water with their tales (lobbing), and occasionally poking their heads and one eye above the surface and appearing to survey the surroundings (spyhopping). The best places to catch sight of these gentle giants are Ojo de Liebre Lagoon, near Guerrero Negro, San Ignacio

Key Facts About Baja Gray Whales

Order: cetacean (includes whale, dolphin, porpoise)
Size: 1.5 tons and about 15 feet long at birth; average adult weighs approximately 30 tons and measures 30 to 45 feet in length
Habitat: feeds in waters above Arctic Circle, around Alaska, mates and breeds off Baja coast
Diet: amphipods (small crustaceans living on the ocean bottom)
Annual Migration: 6,000 miles from Bering Strait to the Baja coast, the longest of any mammal on the planet
Velocity: 2 to 5 mph during migration, up to 18 mph when breaching or fleeing
Status: population currently numbers 21,000 after having neared the brink of extinction and been placed on the endangered species list
Predators: killer whale (orca), white shark, man

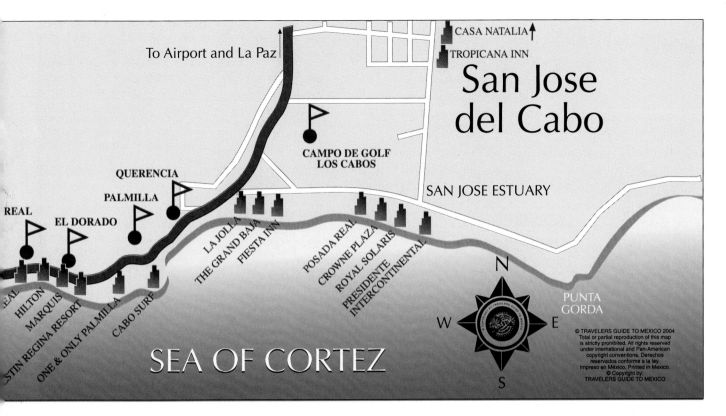

To Airport and La Paz

CASA NATALIA
TROPICANA INN

San Jose del Cabo

CAMPO DE GOLF LOS CABOS

SAN JOSE ESTUARY

QUERENCIA

PALMILLA

REAL

EL DORADO

LA JOLLA
THE GRAND BAJA
FIESTA INN
POSADA REAL
CROWNE PLAZA
ROYAL SOLARIS
PRESIDENTE INTERCONTINENTAL

HILTON
MARQUIS
STIN REGINA RESORT
ONE & ONLY PALMILLA
CABO SURF
REAL

N
W E
S

PUNTA GORDA

SEA OF CORTEZ

Lagoon and Bahia Magdalena.

Local two-hour whale-watching excursions are available from the marina. However, it's worth making the trip to the more distant sites mentioned above, where sightings are better. *Aereo Calafia* (tel. 143-4302), since 1994 Los Cabos' premier air tour operator, offers whale-watching excursions to Magdalena Bay aboard a panoramic high-wing Cessna. Professional and friendly, with certified bilingual guides, this tour operator works with local people and designs outings to make the most of the natural environment. Their full-service tours handle all transportation, from boat to mule, in addition to scenic flights over spectacular shorelines, accommodations, gear, meals, snacks and beverages. For more information on whale watching, turn to the chapter titled "The Great Outdoors."

The earliest inhabitants of Baja California left their mark with primitive cave paintings that have been declared World Heritage Sites by UNESCO. Organized tours take visitors to two sites, Sierra San Francisco and Sierra Guadalupe, where they can compare these fascinating prehistoric remnants.

Increasingly, travelers to Baja are taking the opportunity to visit the most famous natural attraction in northern Mexico, the Copper Canyon. Just across the Sea of Cortez, the Copper Canyon Express train departs from Los Mochis on its journey across the canyons.

Water Sports

Scuba diving and snorkeling rival golfing and sport fishing as major attractions.

Diving, primarily in the Sea of Cortez, is good year-round, although the very best time to dive is during the warmer months, from May through September, when visibility can reach 120 feet.

Scuba divers flock to the area facing the Fiesta Americana Grand Hotel for a 65-foot dive along the remains of an old Japanese shipwreck, amidst schools of dorado, amber jack and tropical fish.

For more experienced divers, *Cabo Pulmo*, the only living coral reef on the west coast of North America, offers a concentration of tropical and game fish, and stunning coral formations. Thirty miles northeast of San Jose, by an inlet frequented by colonies of barking seals, is *Bahia los Frailes.* These are the only areas in the Sea of Cortez where you can dive amid living coral reef.

Other favored places are the lovely and secluded 20- to 40-foot-deep *Bahia de Santa Maria*, located between the two towns, and the 35- to 70-foot-deep *Bahia Chileno*, next to the Cabo San Lucas Hotel, recommended for beginners, with its large rocky reef and some coral trees.

A must for divers is a visit to the *Sand Falls*, a natural underwater phenomenon first discovered by Jacques Cousteau. A five-minute boat ride will take you to the 30- to 100-foot-deep site where a "sand fall" is created when the current drags fine sand (tons of it per second) over an undersea crag and into the deeper waters.

Several well-equipped dive shops with guide, boat and tank refill services are in Cabo. *Amigos del Mar* has certified instructors, dive masters, guides (all bilingual) and a good dive boat. It also refills tanks and has all types of diving gear available for rent, including wet suits.

Another reliable shop is *Cabo Acuadeportes.* One of the newest dive shops is *Underwater Divers*, located at the Costa Real Cabo Hotel's shopping arcade, where there's also a decompression chamber manned by professional physicians, and an experienced diving rescue team.

Snorkeling, reputedly best in Baja, is extremely popular at *Del Amor, Santa Maria, Palmilla* and *Chileno* beaches. Several snorkel rental stalls are located at *El Medano Beach* and other locations.

Los Cabos is legendary among surfers the world over. Some of the best waves can be found along the stretch of coastline between Cabo San Lucas and Todos Santos, on the Pacific coast, and between San Jose del Cabo and Cabo Pulmo.

The most popular beaches for the novice surfer are *Playa Costa Azul* (Blue Coast), *Barco Varado* (Shipwreck), and *Acapulquito* (Little Acapulco). Seasoned surfers seeking a challenge favor *Punta Gorda.*

Other outdoor activities include windsurfing, jet-skiing, water-skiing, kayaking, horseback riding, rock climbing, mountain biking, mountain hiking, and hunting.

For horseback riding, note that Los Cabos has two equestrian centers: *Cuadra San Francisco*, located on The Corridor, and *Rancho Collins*, in Cabo.

During the dove and deer-hunting season, standard local hunting tours are available; guide service, license, transportation, and gear are included.

Sport Fishing

By Tracy Ehrenberg

Cabo San Lucas is known as the "Marlin Capital of the World" and deservedly so, as there are more marlin caught here than any other place on earth. Unlike other well known fishing destinations, where days and many dollars can be spent in pursuit of this most prized

A fishing party sails past Los Arcos

Bruce Herman

sport fish, it is not unusual to capture one or even more on your very first trip, whether you are a beginner or an expert.

Once reserved for the wealthy, fishing in Cabo is now within reach of almost all visitors and an encounter not to be missed. Not only will you experience the thrill of battling a creature of incredible beauty and size, or landing smaller species and eating them, but your fishing excursion will give you an opportunity to view the cape and its landmarks from a unique perspective, and often allow you to get a close up look at whales, dolphins and seals.

If possible decide ahead of time when you plan to fish, as advance reservations assure you will get the type of boat you want on the days you want. Most major fleets have stateside booking agents with 800 numbers, or you can call the fleet office in Mexico. Most of the year chartering a fishing boat with a day or two's notice at various fleet offices around town or through your hotel is not a problem.

The best way to decide on a fleet is through recommendations from friends or by talking with different fleet operators to see what each has to offer. If conservation is important to you, make sure you check out the fleet's policy regarding catch and release.

Most day charters (8 hours) include tax, fishing licenses, tackle, crew and ice. Some fleets will include beer and soda, and the cleaning and freezing of your catch. Live bait is normally available year-round and at least 10 should be purchased for your trip. The booking agent will advise what time (normally 7 a.m.) and where to meet your boat.

If you have a tendency towards seasickness, Dramamine is sold at various pharmacies in town. It is non prescription and an inexpensive insurance policy for feeling good on the ocean. For maximum effect, take one pill at least one hour before boarding. Sunscreen, hat and sunglasses are a must, as is a light jacket for the early morning. It is wise to bring along a towel or two, as you can sometimes get quite

wet when the boat is backing down on a fish. Your camera should not be left behind, as the fish are normally quite willing to put on amazing acrobatic performances that can be captured on film even if you release your catch.

At the dock in the morning you will see an array of booths lining the wharf, each announcing a different fleet name. The dispatcher will greet you, walk you down to your boat, and introduce you to the captain and mate. Most crews speak some English and will be happy to coach complete novices in the techniques of big game fishing.

Once underway the deckhand will bring out rods and reels from inside the cabin and set them in rod holders. The captain decides in which direction to head depending on where fish are likely to be biting. He may head straight for the fishing grounds without lines in the water or start trolling lures soon after leaving the harbor.

All charter boats have a selection of artificial lures on board. These look like bait to the fish, and normally have fairly heavy resin heads, metallic in color, with large eyes and a plastic skirt (fringe) representing the body, which can be any color combination. Upon reaching the fishing grounds the deckhand will attach lures to the lines of the rods and position the lures at various distances behind the boat as it slows to trolling speed. The captain will then systematically cover an area of the ocean where he believes the fish are. The type and size of the lure does not necessarily dictate what kind of fish will be caught as most smaller game fish will be attracted to lures intended for marlin. Although it is not always perceptible, the crew are on a constant lookout for fish, spotting birds, bubbles or fins that are indicators of activity in the area.

Getting a hook into a fish's mouth and getting it to stay there is known as "setting the hook." If you are an experienced angler, you should let the crew know in advance that you prefer to handle your own rod completely. If

you are not totally sure, unfamiliar with the species you will be targeting, or not used to the different tackle, it is probably best to let the deckhand set the hook on the first fish while you observe. If you are a complete novice don't worry, the crew will help you through every step of the fight; by day's end you'll be feeling like a seasoned professional.

Depending on the season and hunger of the fish, you can spend minutes or several hours trolling and looking for fish. Occasionally you will not catch anything—that is why this sport is called fishing and not catching—but by fishing the waters of Los Cabos your chances of success are improved.

The artificial bait or lures pulled behind the boat attract fish that, when hungry, will attack. Your crew will nearly always be aware when fish are about to bite on lures and will accelerate the boat, catching most first time anglers by surprise as frenzied activity begins.

When a fish strikes, the reel announces it with a loud zinging noise as the fish takes line, thrilling even the uninitiated with the excitement this causes. Once the deckhand is sure that the hook is well set, he will ask you to sit in the fighting chair, placing the rod in the holder attached to the seat. A crew member will stay at your side until the battle is finished, teaching you to pull up on the rod, crank the reel handle rapidly as you lower the rod tip, and rest and wait patiently when the fish takes more line.

Depending on the size and strength of the fish and your determination, the fight can last from a few minutes to an hour or more before you have your prize alongside the boat. If your catch is a marlin and you plan to release it, the deckhand assisted by the captain will gently wiggle the hook free before letting the fish go. On the way back to the docks, the crew will bring out the flags corresponding to your catch, announcing to the world the success of your day.

There are several options available as to what to do with your catch. Most people will want to have their photo taken with their fish if of notable size. If your fish needs to be cleaned it will be taken to the filleting tables at the dock, skinned and cut into manageable-size fillets. The fleet operator can also freeze the fish for you to collect at a later date. Smoking your fish is another option and can be arranged by your dispatcher.

To take your catch home you will need a cooler. Passing your cooler through as luggage at customs is not a problem at either end of your journey and once home your catch will provide you with plenty of tasty meals as memories of your fishing adventure.

Tracy Ehrenberg, owner and manager of Pisces Fishing Fleet, also supplies fishing information to the Los Angeles Times and is regularly featured on radio sports shows.

Golfing Mecca

Fast becoming North America's leading golf destination, Los Cabos features courses by some of the top names in golf design, such as Tom Fazio, Jack Nicklaus, Robert Trent Jones II, The Dye Corporation and Tom Weiskopf, as well as a truly diverse landscape incorporating mountains, desert and ocean.

Seven championship courses and a fine municipal course are currently open for play, each offering golfers a distinct and memorable golf experience.

A Must Golf Destination

Golf World predicted not long ago that Los Cabos would "become a 'must' golf destination." Three of the championship layouts—Cabo del Sol, Cabo Real and Palmilla—have played host to the prestigious PGA Senior Slam and its most renowned players: Lee Treviño, Dave Stockton, Raymond Floyd, Hale Irwin and Jack Nicklaus.

Shell's Wonderful World of Golf Series has selected Los Cabos on two occasions. In 1995 the series featured Treviño and Nicklaus on the Ocean Course at Cabo del Sol, and in 2001 it featured two of the PGA Tour's top players, Phil Mickelson and Sergio Garcia, at the private golf club *Querencia*.

The immaculate fairways of Querencia make it unmistakably a Tom Fazio design. You may not even notice the spectacular scenery just beyond the course, which represents his first golf course outside the United States in decades. Querencia's design draws on the natural rolling terrain and breathtaking coastline views, which give plenty of visual drama and challenges to this world-class 18-hole course, the only private golf experience in Los Cabos. Tel. 145-6600.

A Top Course

The Nicklaus-designed *Cabo del Sol* course remains on Golf Magazine's list of "Top 100 Courses" and has been touted as Mexico's answer to Pebble Beach. It includes one and a half miles of oceanfront play, with the Sheraton Hacienda del Mar and Fiesta Americana Grand hotels nestled among the ocean holes. You will be rewarded for your good shots on this 18-hole course, but to maximize your enjoyment, be selective when choosing the set of tees you play.

Another terrific playing field, Tom Weiskopf's recently opened Desert Course, is now part of the ambitious Cabo del Sol development.

Cabo del Sol's peak-season (December-April) green fee is around 230 dollars, with low-season (June-October) fees of about 150 dollars. Rates also vary according to the weekday/weekend schedule played, as well as any fees charged by your booking company or travel agency. Green fees at the Desert Course are slightly lower (about 10%) and do not vary on weekends. Tel. 145-8200.

Breathtaking Scenery

The *Palmilla* resort's 27-hole golf course was the first Nicklaus signature course in all of Latin America. You will be faced with breathtaking scenery when on this property—the ocean, desert and mountains come into stark contrast when you look towards Bahia de San Jose. The arroyo/mountain combination of 18 holes presents many interesting challenges, including lakes and arroyos. The ocean nine offers a good balance of holes, and it not only places you at the ocean's edge, but it also offers many directional changes. To many the Palmilla resort and residential development has long epitomized luxury and state-of-the-art architectural design in Los Cabos. Green fees range from about 100 dollars to 200 dollars, depending on the season. Tel. 144-5250.

A Good Challenge

With its two lakes and challenging holes, the 18-hole Trent Jones signature *Cabo Real* course offers golfers an opportunity to hone their skills. The front nine feature some unparalleled elevated vistas of the Sea of Cortez, and as you move through the back nine you'll play along the shores of the sea. A truly enjoyable course to play, it offers all levels of golfers a good challenge. This course also forms part of a mega-development that includes the Melia Cabo Real, Casa del Mar, and luxurious Ventanas al Paraiso resort overlooking the striking 14th hole. The master plan calls for other deluxe properties and extensive, high-tech sports facilities. High-season green fee, about 200 dollars, low-season, 150 dollars. Tel. 144-0040.

A Challenging Layout

The championship course at the *Cabo San Lucas Country Club* offers stunning fairway views of Land's End, San Lucas Bay and the Sea of Cortez. Designed by the talented Dye family, the course flows gently through groves of magnificent *palo blanco* trees and stately cardon cactus, and is accented by lush expanses of broad fairways and eight sparkling lakes. All areas of your game need to be on to score a low number on this challenging layout. Length off the tee will certainly give you an advantage. Golf aficionados can stay right on the course at Spanish colonial villas located at the 8th and 16th tees overlooking both the Sea of Cortez and the Pacific. High-season green fee, about 150 dollars, low-season, 120 dollars. Tel. 143-4653.

El Dorado, also a Nicklaus signature course, is in a class by itself. With six holes that hug the ocean, you'll be inspired by the views and the highly accomplished design. The inland holes are as dramatic as being beach side, with the natural rugged beauty of the mountains and desert. The course is very well balanced with generous fairways, which will ensure your enjoyment of the game. The course sits on both sides of the main highway, between the Westin, Hilton, and Melia Cabo Real hotels. High-season green fee, about 250 dollars, low-season, about 170. Tel. 144-5451.

For Beginners

Ideal for beginners or families, the *Los Cabos Golf Club* is a pleasant surprise. You need all your clubs on this full-length nine-hole course. Expect to find a good mix of holes and affordable green fees. Tel. 142-0905.

If you are going to be in Los Cabos during peak tourist season, it's best to book your tee times before your arrival. You can call the courses directly or Los Cabos tourism information at (888) 828-4448, or ask your hotel to make your reservations. Golf vacation packages can also be arranged through several agencies. For more information, visit www.golfin mexico.com.

El Dorado golf course

Real Estate

Five Unique Sites to Choose From

A clifftop mansion in Pedregal, Cabo San Lucas

Bruce Herman

By John Glaab, CIPS, and Mike Schaible

Cabo San Lucas: Bustling Cabo continues to be the center for nightlife and shopping, as well as fishing. The town is home to several sport-fishing fleets and hosts international tournaments. Puerto Paraiso, a major shopping and recreational center that opened on the marina in 2001, has several major new tenants. It houses three hotels (one five-star), a cineplex, bowling alley, and branch of Ruth's Chris U.S. steak house. Its boutiques and restaurants regularly attract passengers from cruise ships sailing the Mexican Riviera.

Pedregal is Cabo's original gated community. Situated on a hill overlooking the harbor, one side faces the emerald Sea of Cortez and the other the blue Pacific. Building lots at Pedregal are available starting from 85,000 dollars. A 12,000-square-foot resale villa recently sold for more than 3 million dollars.

Villa La Estancia, a luxurious condominium project, has gone up alongside *Villa del Palmar,* an oceanfront hotel and timeshare development. Together they form a mini community complete with a full-service grocery store and many other amenities.

Rancho Paraiso Estates, located just outside of town on 40 acres of gently sloping land, provides panoramic views of the famous arch at "Land's End." The 90 building lots range from 8,500 to 22,000 square feet. Prices start at 69,000 dollars and financing is available.

Todos Santos: Originally the home of a sugar cane mill, this charming village on the Pacific side of the peninsula has been likened to Carmel, Calif. Its remote location has attracted artists, writers and others looking for a place to get away from it all, while the long stretch of coast that lies between Cabo San Lucas and Todos Santos, with its lagoons, sandy beaches and pounding surf, has lured surfers and sports enthusiasts. The village is being spruced up, with buildings painted pastel colors and restored to house galleries, boutiques and restaurants. Oceanview lots in the 30,000-dollar range and a few oceanfront lots priced slightly above 70,000 dollars are still available.

Much of the land in the Todos Santos area, as throughout Mexico, is *ejido* land, or state-owned property that is worked communally. The government only recently adopted measures that allow an ejido's transformation into private property. As in all cases when buying real estate, in Mexico as elsewhere, it is imperative to check title. (In Mexico, three stamps are required on a registered deed: that of the public registry, the property tax office and the notary public, which has the ultimate

Investor confidence continues to spur growth in Los Cabos, as the construction of new golf courses, hotels, condominiums, commercial centers and residences shows.

While Los Cabos is home to some of the world's best fishing grounds, golf is bringing people by the plane loads. Today, the resort boasts eight of the most beautiful and challenging courses anywhere—surrounded, of course, by premium real estate.

Those considering making a long-term commitment to Los Cabos have five geographically unique sites to choose from. If golf is your passion, you may lean toward The Corridor, a 20-mile stretch of coastline between Cabo San Lucas and San Jose del Cabo that is home to

all of the major golf courses, many of the leading hotels, and numerous residential and condominium developments.

If your reason for choosing Los Cabos is mainly sport fishing, you will probably want to be in or close to Cabo San Lucas, proximity to the marina and boat launching facilities being a major factor. Marina San Lucas is considered by many to be one of Mexico's finest marinas and home to one of the highest rated sport-fishing fleets in North America.

If you seek peace and quiet, San Jose del Cabo's serenity may be ideal. The town has seen significant development in recent years, with old or abandoned buildings converted into boutique hotels or restaurants and shops.

responsibility for the accuracy of the deed.)

The Corridor: Locals call the 20-mile stretch of four-lane highway between Cabo and San Jose "The Corridor." Running alongside the Sea of Cortez, this length of coast is home to megaresorts Cabo del Sol, Cabo Real and Palmilla, a range of hotels and golf courses.

La Sierra at Cabo, a new residential resort financed by Fortune 500 company Textron, is taking shape not far from Cabo. The development comprises 160 lots over 74 acres, with 19 acres on the highway designated for commercial use. Building lots at the full-service gated community range from 70,000 to 160,000 dollars.

Cabo del Sol is a 1,800-acre development with five-star hotels, residences, condominiums and two golf courses. The full-ownership condominium *Puerta del Sol* offers 140 one-, two- and three-bedroom units starting from 339,000 dollars and reaching 1.6 million dollars. Laced with pools and waterfalls, it overlooks the 7th and 8th fairways, the beach and Sea of Cortez. *Las Brisas,* a 20-lot planned community, is situated above the second hole of the Jack Nicklaus signature "ocean" golf course. A few lots with excellent views are still available. Ranging from 11,000 to 14,000 square feet, they sell for between 115,000 and 155,000 dollars. Seven hacienda-style homes have been completed, priced from 600,000 dollars.

One of The Corridor's most picturesque beaches extends for a mile along the *Cabo Real* megaresort, which comprises a Robert Trent Jones II course and the Nicklaus-designed El Dorado course. The following hotels are part of the development: Dreams Los Cabos, Melia Cabo Real, Casa del Mar boutique hotel, an integral part of the Casa del Mar condominium complex, and Las Ventanas al Paraiso, member of the upscale, Dallas-based Rosewood Hotels and Resorts. A room here can cost as much as 1,500 dollars a night. Adjacent to the hotel is *Residences at Paraiso,* with prices starting from 725,000 dollars. A penthouse condominium at Las Ventanas recently sold for 4 million dollars. Across the highway, *Fairway Villas at Gardenias* offers one-bedroom condominiums for 169,000 dollars and two-bedroom condominiums for 259,000 dollars.

Closer to San Jose, another fractional ownership project is being offered. Called *Club Perla Rosa,* it is located at the El Zalate condominium project, next to World Mark's luxurious Coral Baja resort, Mañanitas. Lots of up to eight and a half acres will be available.

The luxury resort community of *Palmilla* is anchored by the historic and legendary Palmilla Hotel, which recently changed ownership and is now called the One & Only Palmilla. Just two years after a major 13 million-dollar renovation, the new owners made further refurbishments and added a convention center. Since it was built in 1956, this unique hideaway has attracted such visitors as Bing Crosby, John Wayne and, more recently, Lee Iacoca. The hotel's Mexican architecture inspired the design of the fairway homes, villas and condominiums. Above the highway, adjacent to the first golf course in Latin America designed by Nicklaus, lots start at 115,000 dollars. A lot on the Sea of Cortez is available for 1.4 million dollars. Beachfront villas at *Villas del Mar* are priced at a little more than 1.8 million dollars.

San Jose del Cabo: San Jose prides itself on its peaceful parklike setting, with a newly renovated town plaza graced by benches, a gazebo, and a 200-year-old cathedral. The downtown area has enjoyed significant development—older, sometimes derelict buildings have been transformed into small hotels, restaurants, shops and art galleries.

Real estate surrounding the municipal golf course consists of single-family homes and condominiums. Prices start at 79,000 dollars for a one-bedroom condominium and 179,000 dollars for a home.

Along the palm-lined main boulevard dramatic changes are taking place, including *Las Mañanitas*, a charming Mediterranean-style condominium complex. Attention to detail is evident in the construction of its one- to three-bedroom units, and oceanfront villas. Its developer boasts it will have the most lavish landscaping in Los Cabos. Having sold all of the original 52 units, construction is now underway on phase two: 26 large condominium-style units and 26 two- and three-bedroom villas, with prices starting at 415,000 dollars.

East Cape: Some of the most remarkable beachfront property, with a multitude of coves and unspoiled beaches, is located right outside San Jose, just east of the sleepy fishing village of La Playita. Prime real estate is still available at reasonable prices, with beachfront lots ranging from 69,000 to 300,000 dollars. Luxurious self-contained beachfront homes are available from 450,000 dollars.

Timeshare: Timeshare units are available at a wide range of prices. Options include the *Pueblo Bonito Rosé* and *Melia San Lucas*, on the beach in Cabo, neighbor *Club Cascadas*, a luxurious, private, membership resort, and the larger *Villa del Palmar*. Along The Corridor, *Sheraton Hacienda del Mar* and *The Westin Regina* are very popular. And three miles from downtown San Jose is *Coral Baja*.

Realtors in Los Cabos: While Mexico does not have licensing for realtors, it does have the Mexican Association of Real Estate Professionals (AMPI), which is the Mexican counterpart of the National Association of Realtors in the United States and CREA in Canada. AMPI is recognized by the Mexican government and affiliated with similar associations worldwide. Founded in 1956, it now has chapters in more than 40 cities. The site www.icrea.org can help you locate a professional agent in Mexico.

John Glaab, CIPS (Certified International Property Specialist), is vice president of international marketing for title and land use specialists The Settlement Company, and a founding member of the Mexican Association of Real Estate Professionals (AMPI) in Los Cabos. Before coming to Mexico from Canada in 1991, he worked as a marketing consultant for multinational corporations. Mike Schaible is the owner/broker of Baja Properties, as well as past president of AMPI Los Cabos, member of the Los Cabos Developers Association, and past president of the Los Cabos Multiple Listing Service Association. Mike came to Los Cabos from Vail, Colorado, in 1986.

Cabo San Lucas

The town of Cabo San Lucas is only about 30 years old. Originally a fishing village with a population of a few hundred, the town is now growing by leaps and bounds—with new first-class hotels, restaurants and shops opening regularly—and has outgrown its primitive paradise label.

The *San Lucas Harbor,* home of a world-renowned fishing fleet, has facilities for 250 fishing boats. The docking area, with an open-air public market, is the scene of much activity, especially early in the morning as the fishing parties cast off, and after midday when the boats start returning with their bounty.

At the far end of the harbor is a modern marina with slips for 350 boats. Surrounding the marina are two hotels, the Costa Real Cabo (formerly Plaza Las Glorias) and Marina Fiesta; a condominium complex; and the city's leading shopping center, the newly opened *Puerto Paraiso,* a huge mall with gourmet and informal dining, nightclubs, shops, cinemas, a bowling alley and other services.

Cabos' greatest attraction, after golfing, fishing and diving, is its natural setting. Here the warm Sea of Cortez (called Mar de Cortes or Golfo de California in Mexico) meets the much cooler Pacific Ocean, at times creating a spectacular rainbow of colors.

A must for visitors to Cabo is a boat excursion to the landmark *El Arco* (The Arch), a dramatic rock formation right at the tip of the peninsula, where seals, sea lions and pelicans bask in the sun. Formed by the erosive action over millions of years of the ocean pounding into the rocks, the arch marks a marine refuge for hundreds of species of fish and an under-ground canyon believed to be as deep as the Grand Canyon. Every few years, the water level drops, exposing the sandy bottom directly below El Arco and giving visitors a chance to walk under its stony arch. You can take a glass-bottom boat, departing frequently from the marina, that circles around El Arco and drops you off at its *Playa del Amor* (Lovers Beach), where you can picnic.

The Pacific side of the beach offers a wonderful sight, but is too dangerous for swimming. Swimmers can enjoy the calmer, clear, snorkeler's-dream water of the Sea of Cortez. During the winter, you can take a boat ride to see the now famous migrating whales leaping and cavorting while engaged in their mating rituals. Just as famous as El Arco are the world-famous underwater sand cascades discovered and explored by Jacques Cousteau.

Beaches

Despite appearances, finding the beach is easy. All entrances to roads leading to swimming, snorkeling and surfing beaches are marked by signs that give the name of the beach, whether they are in town or along the Cabo San Lucas-San Jose del Cabo highway known as "The Corridor."

If you aren't driving, you can reach most of the distant beaches by taxi, or on one of the buses or *colectivos* (minibuses) that shuttle between Cabo and San Jose.

Try these favorite beaches:

Playa el Medano is the most popular sunning, swimming and people-watching beach in town. According to locals, it is also world renowned for its annual Easter holiday bikini contest, which involves a big jackpot.

The Villa del Palmar, Villa La Estancia, Melia San Lucas, Pueblo Bonito, Pueblo Bonito Rosé, Marina Fiesta and Hacienda hotels, as well as the Club Cascadas timeshare, have access to Medano Beach.

You can also take a water taxi from the marina, or simply walk the length of the marina (and get a good look at the sleek yachts) until you get to the beach.

Here you'll find jet-skis, Hobbie Cats and plenty of other beach "toys" for rent by the day or hour. There are giant, seagoing tricycles, colorful kayaks, and lounge chairs. Swimming conditions are good even for small children nearly year-round, and there are plenty of restaurants for a snack or fancy lunch. Take mosquito repellent.

Playa del Amor is the tiny, charming beach at El Arco that connects the Sea of Cortez with the Pacific Ocean. Enjoy swimming on the sea side, but do not swim on the Pacific side. Take a water taxi or glass-bottom boat (they will return to pick you up if you arrange for it).

Playa Barco Varado, or Shipwreck Beach, is at Km. 10 of The Corridor. The sparkling clear tide pools along the shore and the rock formations to hike along make this a favorite spot for family outings. Overnight camping is no longer permitted, but you can set up for the day. A deluxe resort complex that includes the Sheraton Hacienda del Mar Hotel and Pitahayas restaurant is near the beach, but there are no water sports rentals, so bring your own gear and explore the wreck of an old Japanese vessel.

Bahia de Santa Maria, or Santa Maria Bay, located at Km. 18, next to the Twin Dolphin Hotel, has a beach well worth visiting and water that's ideal for swimming. You can get there on your own or take a scenic tour, with snorkeling gear and meals included. Take a hat or beach umbrella, and sunscreen; the brilliant white, powdered coral reef sand is extremely reflective.

Playa el Chileno, right before reaching the Cabo San Lucas Hotel on The Corridor, is great for snorkeling, and all sorts of water sports equipment is available for rent. Swimming here is best right near the hotel.

El Bledito and *Buenos Aires* beaches (in Cabo Real) have strikingly white sand and open ocean swimming in deep-blue waters. Bledito is better for swimming.

Playa Palmilla, on The Corridor, next to the One & Only Palmilla Hotel, is excellent for swimming and snorkeling; equipment rental is available.

Playa Costa Azul (in San Jose del Cabo) is highly popular among surfers, especially during the summer, when the surf is tops!

Other Attractions

A popular excursion is a visit to *El Faro Viejo*, a turn-of-the-century lighthouse on the dunes at the extreme southern tip of the peninsula. The building is currently undergoing renovation and may soon house a sea-related museum, but the location's real attraction is a view of a Pacific sunset that is unforgettable. Much of the film "Troy," starring Brad Pitt, was shot here.

The lighthouse was built at *Cabo Falso* (False Cape) in 1905 of fired adobe brick. In 1967 a red-and-white striped lighthouse, built of cement, was erected nearby, as the old one suffered from the ravages of the sea. The original French-manufactured Fresnel lens from the first structure was adapted for motorized use and installed in the second lighthouse. Occasionally the lighthouse keeper will permit visitors to see the inner workings of the newer lighthouse. Photographers find the contrast of the two lighthouses within sight of each other irresistible.

Half the fun of a visit to the lighthouse is getting there on an ATV (all-terrain vehicle) or on horseback. Organized ATV tours are the most common way to visit and the best tours are organized by *Tio Sports Adventure & Nature*. This experienced outfit offers a wide range of outdoor activities, including snorkeling and scuba diving. Tel. 143-3399.

For horseback riding tours to the lighthouse contact *Rancho Collins Horse Rentals* at the Melia San Lucas Hotel.

If you embark on an unguided tour of this site, be sure to carry extra water for yourself and extra fuel for your vehicle. Cabo Falso is a windswept and remote area, and more than a few cars get stuck in the soft sand, so use caution.

Guided ATV tours, perhaps the area's best, are also offered at *Desert Park*, a protected nature reserve in Cabo Real. There you can go on a low-key two-hour botanical and panoramic tour or a four-hour safari that includes lunch. Tel. 144-0121.

The *Los Cabos Museum of Natural History*, on the main square, houses many interesting exhibits relating to area history, including artifacts from notable shipwrecks and ancient fossils. Admission is free.

Near the village of *Santiago*, 20 minutes from San Jose del Cabo, is a desert dotted with marine fossils, indicating that this entire area was underwater centuries ago. You can see remnants of giant clams, reptiles, fish and snails. *Baja Outback Tours* offers an excellent guided tour of the area on a comfortable bus.

Todos Santos, a sleepy town that has in recent years become home to a growing community of artists, is located some 40 miles, or about an hour's drive, north of Cabo, on the Pacific coast. A good number of art galleries feature works by local artists, including N.E. Hayles, Catherine Wall, and Eli Alexander. Since 1998, the town has hosted an annual art festival the first week of February, featuring art exhibts, folk dancing, cultural events and more.

If you go, don't miss the opportunity to dine at the renowned *Café Santa Fe* (closed Tuesdays), where lunch or dinner alone can make the trip worthwhile. Another must is a visit to *La Poza*, a charming European-owned boutique hotel featuring fine food, an art gallery, and a delightful oceanfront setting with gardens and meandering paths.

Back in Cabo, the *Pedregal Tennis Club*, located on top of a hill a few blocks from the marina, in the residential zone of Pedregal, offers well-kept courts, good lighting for evening matches, private instruction and weekly membership rates. Most of the major hotels have their own courts.

Many of Pedregal's Beverly Hills-style homes belong to Mexico's or the U.S.'s rich and famous who summer in the area. The contrast between the old-fashioned and ultramodern homes presents a good photo opportunity.

Dining

Casa Rafael's
Casa Rafael Hotel
Tel. 143-0739
This offbeat inn houses a piano bar (with equally offbeat entertainment), cigar lounge, and restaurant featuring classic international fare, including Black Angus beef, lobster, and smoked fish paté, served by white-gloved waiters. Wine selection. Live music. Open 6 to 10 p.m.; to 11 p.m. Friday and Saturday.

Cilantro's
Pueblo Bonito Hotel
Tel. 142-9797
A casual oceanfront terrace restaurant-bar specializing in seafood and international dishes, including scallop and salmon custard, mahi-mahi fillet with a polenta tart, and Jamaican-style lamb chops with plantains. Open noon to 11 p.m.

Baja waters are ideal for scuba and snorkeling

Edith's
Playa el Medano
Tel. 143-0801
A popular open-air restaurant on the beach offering a romantic setting with views of the lighted yachts and sailboats. Outdoor mesquite grill turns out a wide array of seafood specialties. Attentive service, nice attention to detail, including homemade tortillas and salsas. Wine selection. Open 5 p.m. to midnight.

El Michoacano
Leona Vicario and Alvaro Obregon
This modest family-run establishment specializes in one of Mexican cooking's favorite country dishes, *carnitas*, pork slow cooked in its own

Visitors take an ATV tour of the lighthouse

juices until tender inside, crusty outside—delicious with fresh, warm tortillas. The Graciano family has been perfecting their recipe since 1899. Branch also in San Jose del Cabo's Colonia El Zacatal.

El Shrimp Bucket
Marina Fiesta Hotel
Tel. 143-2598
Facing the marina, with a great view of the boats and luxury yachts. Shrimp by the bucket and a frat house atmosphere typical of Anderson restaurants. Early breakfasts and box lunches prepared for seafarers. Dine indoors in air-conditioned comfort or outdoors on a terrace. Open 6 a.m. to 10:30 p.m.

El Squid Roe
On Marina Blvd.
Tel. 143-0655
A Quonset hut across from Plaza Bonita. Tasty BBQ ribs and seafood, but more popular as a nightspot with live DJ. The split-level interior features colorful posters and unusual mobiles. Rambunctious waiters add to the lively, irreverent ambiance. Part of the Anderson chain. Open from noon.

Felix'
Hidalgo and Zapata
Tel. 143-4290
Creative Mexican cuisine from chef and proprietor Spencer Moore, known as "The Salsa King." His "world's biggest salsa bar" offers everything from roasted corn to mango chutney and habanero. Specialties include hearty *pozole* stew, stuffed chilies, and *panuchos.* Patio dining. Open 2:30 to 10 p.m.

La Dolce
Hidalgo and Zapata
Tel. 143-4122
Fans of Italian food flock to this popular trattoria and pizzeria offering traditional favorites in a colorful setting with indoor or sidewalk seating. Branch in San Jose. Open 6 p.m. to midnight.

La Golondrina
Paseo del Pescador
Tel. 143-0542
Opposite the Pemex gas station. This former trading post, nicknamed "The Swallow" after a trader who, like the birds, returned year after year, is extremely popular for its generous seafood specialties and luscious desserts served in a nicely-lit garden, under ancient trees. The blackboard menu offers everything from oysters on the half shell to grilled lobster, and all of the entrées include soup, salad, garlic bread, and steamed rice or mashed potatoes. Full bar. Open 5 to 10:30 p.m. Closed Monday.

La Nao
Pueblo Bonito Sunset Beach Hotel
Tel. 142-9999
This fine restaurant is housed in a glass and marble pavilion overlooking the Pacific Ocean. Open for breakfast, lunch and dinner.

La Palapa
Melia San Lucas Hotel
Tel. 143-4444
This poolside restaurant with a spectacular view of the Sea of Cortez serves fine international and Mexican cuisine, especially barbecued lobster, shrimp, fish and beef accompanied by a lavish salad bar. Different dinner theme nightly. Open noon to 10:30 p.m.

La Republica
Morelos and 20 de Noviembre
Tel. 143-3400
A beautiful garden setting for enjoying gourmet Mexican cuisine. Menu highlights include grilled red snapper in fine herbs, Yucatan-style sea bass, and charbroiled rack of lamb in chipotle chili sauce. Open 6 to 11 p.m.

La Roca
Solmar Suites Hotel
Tel. 143-3535
Famous for its catch-of-the-day dishes, great margaritas and strolling guitarists. Mexican Fiesta Saturday nights with mariachis, folk

dancing and piñatas. Open for breakfast, lunch and dinner.

Las Palmas
Playa el Medano
Tel. 143-0447
This palapa and adjoining sun deck offers a spectacular view of El Arco, and good fish and seafood dishes. Shrimp cocktail fans will love their version, with beautifully arranged jumbo shrimp. Home of the local bikini contest. Sports bar, live guitar music. Happy Hour 3 to 6 p.m. Open 8 a.m. to 11 p.m.

Las Palomas
Pueblo Bonito Hotel
Tel. 142-9797
A pleasant poolside restaurant with indoor or outdoor dining on a plant-filled terrace. Mexican Fiesta dinner-show Tuesdays, Tex-Mex fare Thursdays, and grilled specialties Saturdays, with piano music. Open 7 a.m. to 11 p.m.

L'Orangerie
Pueblo Bonito Rosé Hotel
Tel. 142-9898
French-influenced international cuisine from award-winning chef Jean Pierre Le Boursicalt, accompanied by a marvelous ocean view. Live piano music. Open 6 to 11 p.m. Closed Monday.

Lorenzillo's
On Marina Blvd.
Tel. 105-0212
This rooftop restaurant with a spectacular view of the marina features fresh, live lobsters, as well as great steak and seafood dishes. Open noon to midnight.

Mama Roma
Marina Fiesta Hotel
Tel. 143-5142
Italian food with an attitude, brought to you by Grupo Anderson, a restaurant chain known for its tasty fare and late-night frat party atmosphere. Enjoy hearty pasta dishes and sizzling pizzas in a pleasant setting facing the marina—ideal for people-watching. Open for lunch and dinner.

Mama's Royal Cafe
On Hidalgo, between Zapata and Madero
Tel. 143-4290
This cozy, colorful restaurant is one of the town's most popular breakfast spots. Favorites include French toast stuffed with cream cheese and topped with fruits and nuts, eggs Benedict, tropical fruit-filled crepes, mimosas and bloody marys. Open 7:30 a.m. to 1 p.m., except Tuesday.

Mare Nostrum
Pueblo Bonito Rosé Hotel
Tel. 142-9898
An open-air restaurant overlooking the sea and serving Mexican, French and California cuisine, especially fish and seafood specialties. Excellent Sunday brunch. Live piano music—and the pianist is great. Open 7 a.m. to 11 p.m.

Mi Casa
Av. Cabo San Lucas, on the square
Tel. 143-1933
This charming Mexican restaurant, set in a delightful tree-shaded courtyard, serves traditional Mexican fare, including delicious *barbacoa*, pit-roasted goat, and *cochinita pibil*, a Yucatecan dish of shredded pork marinated in a zesty sauce. Tortillas freshly made on the premises. Romantic trios serenade diners in the evening. Open noon to 3 p.m. (except Sunday) and 5 to 10 p.m.

Mi Casa del Mar
Av. del Pescador
Tel. 143-6898
Deliciously prepared seafood dishes by the famous chef-owner of the popular Mi Casa and Peacocks restaurants. Try the *mariscada real*, a delectable seafood platter. Open 1 to 10:30 p.m.

Mocambo
Leona Vicario and 20 de Noviembre
Tel. 143-6070
One of the best seafood restaurants in Los Cabos, offering the freshest dishes at reasonable prices under a huge palapa. A favorite among locals, now being discovered by tourists. Open 11 a.m. to 11 p.m.

Pancho's
Hidalgo and Zapata
Tel. 143-0973
This colorful, casual, popular restaurant offers traditional Mexican dishes and seafood. Specialties include *pozole,* a hearty stew made with pork and hominy kernels, and grilled red snapper with garlic butter. Fixed-price breakfast, lunch and dinner menus at very reasonable prices. Guitarist plays nightly. Bar carries more than 200 types of tequila and mezcal. Open 6 a.m. to 11 p.m.

Peacocks
Next to the Melia San Lucas Hotel
Tel. 143-1858
Innovative international fare served in a luxuriously large palm-thatched palapa. Menu highlights include blackened salmon fillet, saffron mussels casserole, jumbo shrimp with four different sauces. Patio bar. Open 6 to 10 p.m. Reservations recommended.

Ruth's Chris Steak House
Puerto Paraiso
Tel. 144-3234
Excellent choice cuts of beef served in a well-appointed setting with a spectacular view of the marina. Well-crafted menu, from the onion soup au gratin to the custom-aged Midwestern beef broiled in a special high-temperature oven to lock in the flavor. Also lamb, veal, lob-

ster, fish. For dessert, try the fresh baked pecan pie or chocolate espresso cake. Open 1 to 11:30 p.m.

Sancho Panza
Costa Real Cabo Hotel
Tel. 143-3212
This wine bar and bistro near the marina is a local favorite for its "Mediterranean food with a Latin flair," selection of fine wines, and live jazz and blues nightly. Open 4 p.m. to midnight.

The Giggling Marlin
On Marina Blvd.
Tel. 143-0606
A popular watering hole opposite the marina serving fresh seafood and international dishes at very reasonable prices. "Must Wear Shorts" is the dress code, probably because you can take home a souvenir snapshot of yourself posing upside down like a hooked marlin. Open 6 to 1 a.m.

The Office
Playa el Medano
Tel. 143-3464
Combines all the necessary ingredients for a fine meal at the beach: sand under your feet, a view of the water, and good food. The mostly Mexican menu features flour tortilla quesadillas stuffed with cheese and mushrooms, topped with guacamole, and broiled fish fillet bathed in spinach and cheese sauce. Mexican Fiesta Thursdays and Sundays at 6:30 p.m. Happy Hour 3 to 5 p.m. Open 7 a.m. to 10 p.m.

The Shrimp Factory
Marina Blvd. and Guerrero
Tel. 143-5066
A branch of the popular Mazatlan establishment that serves shrimp by the kilo, prepared

any way you like it. Open noon to 11 p.m.

Dining in The Corridor

Arrecifes
The Westin Regina Resort
Tel. 142-9000
Fine Mexican cuisine, and seafood and steak specialties served in attractive Mediterranean-style surroundings. Menu highlights include marinated scallop salad with a hazelnut dressing, and grilled tuna in sweet-and-sour basil sauce. Live music. Open 6 to 11 p.m. Closed Tuesday.

Casa del Mar
Casa del Mar Hotel
Tel. 144-0030
This luxurious hacienda-style hotel features a lovely dining room overlooking the beautifully-landscaped grounds and sea beyond, with seating indoors or on a breezy terrace. Highlights from the menu of fine Mexican and seafood dishes include cream of cilantro soup, flaky sea bass in basil sauce, and grilled shrimp marinated in fine herbs. Open 7 a.m. to 11 p.m.

Canto del Mar
Marquis Los Cabos Hotel
Tel. 144-0906
This specialties restaurant features a different chef's tasting menu every night. Reservations required.

Charlie Trotter's Sea Restaurant
One & Only Palmilla Hotel
Tel. 144-5000
Chicago's famed Charlie Trotter brings his unique, organic Mediterranean and European-style dishes to a beautiful and refined setting in Los Cabos. Serving breakfast, lunch and dinner. Dinner reservations required.

lar ocean view. Attractive Mediterranean setting, excellent service.

Twin Dolphin
Twin Dolphin Hotel
Tel. 145-8190
Serving classic "Sonoran Desert Cuisine" and other savory dishes prepared with organic vegetables and herbs grown in the hotel's own gardens; they even have a few goats for making their homemade cheese. Try the *olla de arroz con pollo*, chicken, rice, chilies, tomatoes and onions cooked in an earthenware casserole; Baja cassoulet, preserved duck, marinated lamb, pork and chorizo simmered in an *olla* with beans; and vegetarian tamales, a medley of vegetables served over sweet red pepper tamales, and drizzled with epazote cream sauce.

Da Giorgio
The Corridor, Km. 25, near San Jose
Tel. 144-5304
Misiones del Cabo, near Cabo
Tel. 145-8160
Both hilltop restaurants feature panoramic views; the Cabo branch caters especially to sunset lovers with a multilevel, cliffside bar with a view of El Arco. Live music during the season. San Jose branch open noon to 11 p.m., Cabo branch open 9 a.m. (with a limited breakfast menu) to 11 p.m.

El Restaurante
Esperanza Hotel
Tel. 145-6454
Fresh, seasonal gourmet fare served in a spectacular palapa overlooking the sea, with balconies cascading toward the oceanfront. Open 7 a.m. to 10 p.m. Reservations required for non-guests.

El Restaurante
Las Ventanas al Paraiso Hotel
Tel. 144-0258
Expertly prepared Mediterranean cuisine with a Mexican touch and French flair (courtesy of chef Casiano Reyes), as well as specialties from the seaside grill. Extensive wine selection and cellar that converts into a private dining room. Open 7 to 11:30 a.m., noon to 4 p.m. and 6 to 10 p.m. Reservations a must.

Fenicia
Hilton Hotel
Tel. 145-6500
Dine indoors or under the stars on a terrace overlooking the sea. The gourmet Mediterranean specialties are created by master chef Mario Maggi, founder of Bice restaurants. The dishes combine the best of Italian, French, Spanish and Greek cuisines. Open for dinner only.

French Riviera
On The Corridor
Tel. 104-3125
Owned and operated by two French chefs, this spot offers fine dining in a spectacular setting facing the sea. Patrons have a choice of two fixed-price menus, both wonderful. Open for lunch and dinner.

Pitahayas
The Corridor, Km. 10
Tel. 145-8010
At Sheraton Hacienda del Mar Hotel in Cabo del Sol. This leading restaurant is housed under a large, breezy palapa overlooking the beach. The open kitchen, supervised by executive chef Volker Romeike, features Pacific Rim cuisine, combining fresh seafood or fine cuts of beef with exotic spices and sauces such as mango, curry, black bean, tangerine-plum, and more. Favorites include the Oriental steamer basket of stuffed dumplings, curried swordfish salad, blackened fish with mango chutney, and coconut shrimp. Mesquite grill and wok cooking give the dishes their special flavor. Extensive wine cellar. The setting calls for formal resort attire. Open 7 to 11 p.m. Reservations recommended.

Puerta Vieja
The Corridor, Km. 6
Tel. 104-3252
Villa Serena owners' new venture, this restaurant has a nice ocean view and specializes in lobster, steak, and seafood dishes. Full bar. Open noon to 11 p.m.

Rosato
Fiesta Americana Grand Hotel
Tel. 145-6200
Delicious Northern Italian cuisine, with seafood specialties, accompanied by a spectacu-

Villa Serena
The Corridor, Km. 7.5
Tel. 145-8244
This hilltop restaurant-bar features a panoramic view of the sea, and Mexican and seafood specialties, including delicious lobster tail, served under a giant palm-thatched hut. Take your swimsuit for a dip in the pool. Open 7 a.m. to 11 p.m.

Vista Ballena
Marquis Los Cabos Hotel
Tel. 144-0906
Excellent cuisine served in a setting with a spectacular view of the hotel pool area and the Sea of Cortez. Open for breakfast, lunch and dinner.

Zippers
The Corridor, Km. 28.5
On Playa Costa Azul, a popular surfing beach. Watch surfers tackle the waves from this beachfront bar and grill. Mesquite-grilled steaks and hamburgers, beer-battered shrimp, fish 'n' chips. Live music Friday and Saturday. Open 11 a.m. to 10 p.m.

Special

Café Santa Fe
In Todos Santos
About an hour's drive from Cabo. Considered "a culinary oasis," this attractively-converted Santa Fe-style home offers gourmet international cuisine in a pleasant flower-filled patio setting. Everything is excellent, from the tender beef grilled to your exact order to the courteous, attentive service. The menu features Italian and seafood specialties, and fine wines. Worth making the trip. Open for lunch and dinner, except Tuesday.

Nightlife

Cabo a Go Go
Plaza Bonita
Tel. 105-1573
Cabo's newest dance club features baby boomer music, as well as salsa, rock 'n' soul, and Romantic Nights.

Caborey Dinner Cruise
Tel. 143-8260
For a different experience, board the new deluxe Caborey cruiser for cabaret-style entertainment and fine dining.

Cabo Wabo Cantina
Guerrero, downtown
Tel. 143-1188
Originally opened by Sammy Hagar and Eddie van Halen, this bar and dance hall features a DJ, loud rock music, and the occasional band. Open noon to sunrise.

Caliente Casino Real
Plaza Nautica
Tel. 143-1934
All major sporting events, plus dancing, casino, pool tables. The restaurant serves seafood and continental cuisine. Open 7 a.m. to 11 p.m.; to midnight weekends.

El Squid Roe
On Marina Blvd.
Tel. 143-0655
A mandatory stop on the Los Cabos nightlife circuit, this lively restaurant-bar turns into an impromptu disco after dark. DJ plays the best dance tunes. Very popular.

Hard Rock Cafe
Plaza Bonita
Tel. 143-3779
Wall-to-wall rock memorabilia and live rock bands six nights a week. A very popular hangout. Open noon to sunrise.

The Giggling Marlin
On Marina Blvd.
Tel. 143-1182
Among the most popular bars with tourists and locals alike. Resident mambo and salsa pro Gabriel invites guests to a dancing lesson and video tapes the results for later viewing.

The Nowhere Bar
Plaza Bonita, overlooking the marina
Tel. 143-4492
This favorite meeting place among young locals is also called "The House of Shots." Need we say more? Well, there is one more thing: it's the best spot in Cabo for people-watching.

Nightlife in The Corridor

Havana Supper Club
Opposite Costa Azul Beach
Great live tropical music and jazz until the wee hours of the morning. Dinner menu of fish and seafood dishes.

La Cantina/Cigar Bar

The Westin Regina Resort
Tel. 142-9000
A selection of the world's finest cigars and a great setting to enjoy them in. Open 1 p.m. to 1 a.m. (from 5 p.m. in low season).

Mexican Fiestas

Many area hotels feature lively Mexican Fiestas with a Mexican buffet, tequila, mariachis, folk dancing and fireworks. We recommend you consult your concierge for information.

Shopping

In addition to stores around town, you may want to visit the gift shops of some of the better hotels, which often carry quality resort wear, jewelry and art.

Those who want to purchase an original gift should consider a bottle of *damiana* liqueur, made from an infusion of the herb of the same name. It is touted as an aphrodisiac, and most commonly served on the rocks, straight or mixed with carbonated water. Throughout Baja California, bartenders put a dash into margaritas.

Puerto Paraiso, a huge new shopping and entertainment complex with sweeping views of the marina, houses more than 200 specialty shops and exclusive boutiques. There are smaller shopping centers around town, including Plaza Bonita, also on the marina.

Store hours vary, and some close during the lunch/siesta hours, but most remain open well into the evening (especially during the high season). On Sundays, many stores open half a day.

Puerto Paraiso

Animale
Attractive selection of clothes for women by French designer Jacques Ruc.

Astrid
In business for 20 years, this firm, with branches at several Mexican resorts, carries its own exclusive designs in 14 karat and 18 karat gold, some incorporating precious or semiprecious stones backed by a certificate of authenticity.

Kaki Bassi
A tasteful display of works by the popular local artist.

Mormaii
Brazilian wetsuits and surfing gear.

IX Mandamiento
Asian and exotic items.

Ruta de las Indias
A delightful adventure for those who love sailing the Seven Seas.

Tanya Moss Designer Jewelry
Original gold and sterling silver jewelry, and wearable art by designer Tanya Moss, whose innovative and sophisticated designs reflect their Mexican heritage. Individually handcrafted by skilled artisans, many of her cre-

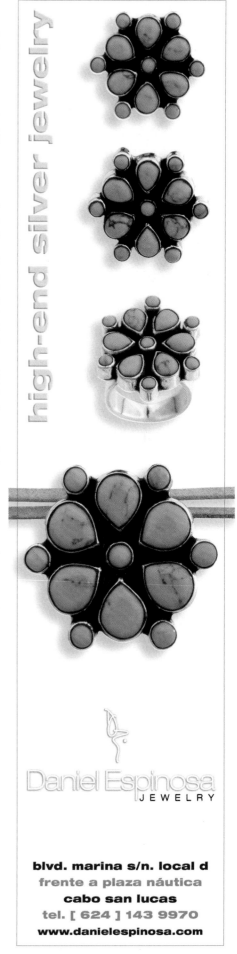

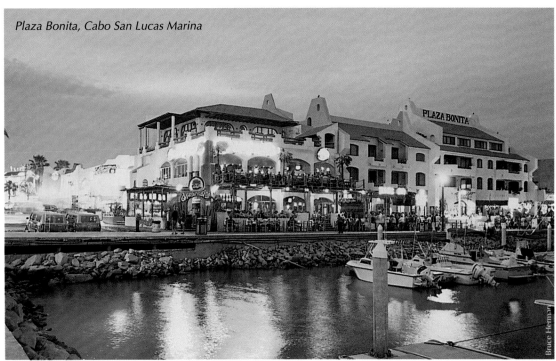

Plaza Bonita, Cabo San Lucas Marina

ations incorporate freshwater pearls, amber, precious or semiprecious stones. Her new collection features the intensity of 18k gold, and silver combined with strands of multicolored semiprecious stones and pearls.

Plaza Bonita

Cartes
Quality Mexican colonial-style furniture, as well as unique rugs, Talavera plates and pottery, and accent pieces for the home, all attractively displayed.

Dos Lunas
Attractive resort wear for both men and women, including light cotton tops, sarongs and bathing suits, plus hats, bags and other accessories. Stays open Sunday.

Sergio Bustamante Gallery
Fantastic whimsical sculptures by one of Mexico's most celebrated artists, plus his stunning line of gold and silver jewelry, including his signature blazing suns and half moons.

Other Locations

Alternarte
Posadas Building 7
This art gallery, shop and cultural center located opposite the Pemex gas station is dedicated to all types of art. You'll also find books, CDs, courses and more.

Artesanos
At the entrance to town
A huge emporium of quality Mexican furniture, handicrafts, and all sorts of home decorative items.

Books Books
Plaza de la Danza

Cabo's best selection of English-language newspapers, paperbacks and magazines. Plus a good selection of postcards, maps and souvenirs.

Daniel Espinosa Jewelry
On Marina Blvd., facing Plaza Nautica
Tel. 143-9970
Bold, contemporary designs in silver by the talented Taxco-based jeweler, including many pieces with semiprecious stones. Espinosa's creativity and sense of fun is evident in his tie-style chokers made of silver cubes and red beads, hypnotic silver rings with black enamel swirls, and other unique jewelry.

El Callejon
Vicente Guerrero and Lazaro Cardenas
A wonderful place to browse for home furnishings and decorative items, from hand-painted tables and chairs to rugs hand woven from hemplike rope. Custom designs made to order.

El Faro Viejo
On Mijares
Between Abasolo and Matamoros, in a trailer park. The souvenir shop carries an interesting selection of ceremonial masks from different parts of Mexico, and handicrafts and books on Baja. Open from 5 p.m. Closed Wednesday.

Feinstein Custom Designed Jewelry
Pedregal Park, Local 4
Hidden away, this gem of a store features owner and designer Ed Feinstein's custom-designed jewelry and imported gift items from around the world, including his line of "magic motion clocks," a must-see. Enjoy a glass of wine or cold drink while you browse. Also full line of English-language greeting cards. Open 9 a.m. to 6 p.m., except Sunday.

Galerias Gattamelata
On road to the Hacienda Hotel

An attractive store featuring colonial-style furniture, antiques, gifts and home decorating items. Quality merchandise on consignment from collectors.

Glass Factory
On road to Todos Santos
Watch original pieces of blown-glass being created by local artisans, 8 a.m. to 2 p.m. Factory store open until 5 p.m.

Golden Cactus Gallery
Guerrero and Madero, second floor
One of the town's leading galleries is owned by fellow artists Chris MacClure and Marilyn Hurst, and features contemporary artwork by leading Cabo artists, including MacClure, Dave Pinto, Fernando Tamez.

J&J Habanos
On Madero, half a block from Marina Blvd.
This leading tobacco shop has been recognized for its knowledge, selection and care of cigars. Also carries rare tequilas, and its own exclusive line of accessories and casual wear for the cigar aficionado.

Magic of the Moon
Hidalgo and Zapata
Original designs by designer Pepita, known for her romantic off-the-shoulder dresses and sexy beaded bustiers. Sizes XS to 4X. Custom-made apparel ready in three days.

Mexico Lindo
Plaza del Sol
An attractive selection of sterling silver, and 14k and 18k gold jewelry. Designs made to order. Six branches in all, including a factory-store at Madero and Guerrero where you can see craftsmen fashioning pieces out of precious metals and semiprecious stones.

Necri
On Marina Blvd.
Across from Plaza Nautica. A boutique of Mexican handicrafts, especially Talavera items, and pewter picture frames and candle holders.

Sunset Weddings
Posadas Building 7, opposite Pemex gas station
Tel. 143-5016
Los Cabos' wedding planners, with the experience and knowhow to organize the perfect special event on the beach or at other picturesque sites around the cape. Leave the planning and coordination to the professionals and enjoy the uniquely romantic setting of Baja's spectacular coast.

San Jose del Cabo

Fountains Add Color to Downtown San Jose del Cabo

Bruce Herman

San Jose del Cabo has a flavor all its own—that of a small Baja California settlement steeped in tradition. This nearly 300-year-old semitropical town is not as sleepy as it appears. It is an important commercial center, and an agricultural and cattle-raising community. Mango, avocado and orange trees grow abundantly in the region. A communal organic farm in the nearby town of San Jose Viejo exports fine herbs and produce to the United States and Canada.

The main boulevard, Paseo Mijares, is a wonderful place to stroll, with its ancient, ornate stone arches and quaint white and pastel-colored cottages decorated with profusions of colorful flowers.

Sightseeing in San Jose can include the *Parroquia de San Jose* (San Jose Parish Church), founded in 1730 by Jesuit Padre Nicolas Tamaral. A mosaic on its main facade depicts Tamaral suffering at the hands of the rebellious Pericu Indians. The church sits facing the town's main square, surrounded by colonial-era buildings among which the Palacio Municipal (city hall) stands out handsomely.

Don't miss *Cacti Mundo-Los Cabos Botanical Garden*, home to approximately 500 species of cacti from all over the Western Hemisphere, including many rare or endangered varieties. This botanical garden is affiliated with the prestigious Le Jardin Botanique (Montreal), Le Jardin Exotique de Monaco and the British Cactus and Succulent Society. Open daily, 9 a.m. to 5 p.m. Admission: 6 dollars. Facilities include a snack bar, a gift shop that features fine talavera and glass souvenirs with cactus motifs, and parking space.

Bird lovers will enjoy the estuary, a natural lagoon that's home to about 200 species of birds. Visitors can rent kayaks to explore its many fingers and enjoy the beautiful environment. The estuary is located next to the Presidente InterContinental Hotel.

Downtown San Jose's Alvaro Obregon Street is lined with charming art galleries. During the winter season, a weekly Thursday afternoon (5 p.m.) Art Walk lets you gallery hop and mingle with the artists.

A city ordinance for the preservation of old buildings is faithfully adhered to and a Historical San Jose tour is now available. Many of the more interesting buildings are located in the downtown area, on Doblado, Hidalgo, Morelos, Obregon and Zaragoza streets, as well as on Paseo Mijares, the main boulevard. The old *Casa de la Cultura* (or cultural center), on Mijares, served as a refuge for U.S. citizens during the 1847 U.S.-Mexican War.

The tourist zone includes a handful of major hotels, a good number of condominiums, several small shopping centers and the *San Jose Golf Club,* a challenging nine-hole par-35 course, with deep traps and a lake located on a beautiful 26-acre tract. The course is well maintained and the view of the ocean from the clubhouse terrace is inspiring.

Among the sites that can be reached easily from San Jose are the towns of *Santiago* and *Miraflores*, both about 40 minutes away. The former boasts an old mission built in 1723 by Jesuit padres, and is also home to a dilapidated zoo. Miraflores is noted for its rustic leather works, especially *huaraches* (sandals) and saddles.

Another interesting place to visit is the *Buenavista-Los Barriles* area (about 45 minutes from San Jose), where international windsurfing championships are held every year. Fishing here is excellent, and snorkeling, diving and kayaking in nearby Los Frailes and Cabo Pulmo, home to the only live coral reef on the North American west coast, are sensational.

Tio Sports Adventure & Nature operates ATV (all-terrain vehicle) tours around San Jose and the East Cape, and also offers a snorkeling tour to Cabo Pulmo and other excursions. Drop by their offices in front of the Presidente InterContinental Hotel or call 142-4599.

You can also horseback ride through surrounding farmland and fruit orchards or take a day trip to the state capital, La Paz, that includes a museum visit, shopping and lunch.

Puerto Los Cabos, a resort development in the neighboring town of La Playita, will soon offer exceptional oceanfront properties along three miles of pristine coast, a marina, and a Greg Norman championship golf course.

Dining

Baan Thai
On Morelos
Tel. 142-3344
Pan-Asian cuisine in a pleasant setting. Open noon to 10 p.m. Closed Sunday.

Café Flora
On Plaza Garufi, next to the Fiesta Inn Hotel
This small outdoor cafe serves light fare prepared with organic ingredients and also sells fresh organic produce. Cooking classes offered. Open for lunch and dinner.

Da Antonio
Presidente InterContinental Hotel
Tel. 142-1001

Excellent Italian cuisine by chef Alessandro Brandi served in a beautiful setting overlooking an estuary. Open for dinner only.

Damiana
Mijares 8
Tel. 142-0499
This colorful and romantic restaurant-bar is housed in a lovely 150-year-old colonial home decorated with Mexican folk art. There's a cozy bar with a high wood-beam ceiling and just a handful of tables under a big shade tree in a bougainvillea-filled patio, where the romantic sound of guitar strumming fills the air. The menu has been featured in Bon Appetit magazine, and with good reason. Try the garlic-and-guajillo chili mushrooms Diablo or the cream

AUTENTICO ITALIANO

cheese-filled fried jalapeños to start with, followed by the shrimp steak or charbroiled lobster (from the day's catch) in achiote sauce. Savor the region's damiana liqueur compliments of the house. Open 10:30 a.m. to 10:30 p.m. Reservations recommended.

El Chilar
Benito Juarez and Morelos
Tel. 142-2544
Exquisite Mexican nouvelle cuisine by former Las Ventanas chef Armando served in a charming Mexican setting. The creative menu changes monthly. Try the *tlayudas,* a popular dish from Oaxaca. Open for lunch and dinner. Reservations suggested.

El Patio de San Jose
Mijares 1357
Tel. 142-5508
Between Doblado and Coronado, near the Palacio Municipal. Run by former Westin Regina chef Ayub, this outdoor patio restaurant offers a casual setting for well-prepared continental fare, and great margaritas. Try the Caesar salad with grilled shrimp, coconut shrimp with chipotle chili sauce, and grilled lobster in orange butter and chives. A lighter lunch menu offers grilled beef and fish burgers. Open 11:30 a.m. to 10 p.m.

Fandango
Alvaro Obregon and Morelos
Tel. 142-2226
Housed in one of San Jose's colonial homes, this cozy, rustic restaurant offers excellent food, outstanding fish and salads. Open for lunch and dinner, except Monday.

French Riviera Coffee Shop
On Doblado
Tel. 142-3350
A delightful bakery and coffee shop owned and operated by two French chefs who make the best baguettes in town. Don't miss their chipotle chili bread. Nice selection of pastries, homemade chocolates, fruit tarts, and cakes. Breakfast and lunch only.

La Dolce
On Hidalgo, facing the main square
A converted old home offering patio or indoor dining and excellent Italian favorites like pizza, pasta and focaccia at reasonable prices. Open for dinner only.

La Panga
Plaza Bahia las Palmas, hotel zone
Tel. 142-4041
Wonderful seafood in an attractive setting with an ocean view. Delicious dishes prepared in innovative ways. Open for lunch and dinner.

Local Eight
Mijares and Finisterra
Global cuisine featuring an extensive menu, including a five-course chef's tasting menu. Open for dinner only. Closed Sunday.

Mi Cocina
Casa Natalia Hotel

Tel. 142-5100
This beautiful restaurant is on a terrace surrounded by palm trees. Everything is delicious, from the homemade bread to the desserts. Try the fried Camembert with grapes, and beef medallion in Roquefort cheese and chipotle chili sauce. Owners Natalia and Loic personally supervise the establishment. Open for breakfast, lunch and dinner.

Morgan's Encore
On Alvaro Obregon
Tel. 146-9733
Canadian interior designer-turned-restaurateur Morgan MacLeod's newest venue offers great food in an elegant atmosphere featuring multi-level terraces, three fireplaces and a baby grand. The original spot at Doblado and Hidalgo, Morgan's Restaurant & Cellar, continues to serve international fare and seafood specialties in a traditional Mexican setting with murals and fountains (closed August and September). Open 6 to 10:30 p.m.

Pescaderia el Mercado del Mar
Mauricio Castro 1110, on road to the airport
Tel. 142-3266
Extremely popular, especially at lunch, for its delicious fish and seafood. Try their famed *toritos,* jalapeños stuffed with shrimp or smoked marlin. There's a fish market and smokehouse right on the premises (which explains the name) and personalized attention from owner Carlos Ceceña. Open noon to 10 p.m. Closed Tuesday.

Posada Terranova
On Degollado, between Doblado and Zaragoza
Tel. 142-0534
A cozy Mexican-style inn offering air-conditioned interior or terrace dining. Good Mexican home cooking, especially at breakfast with *huevos con machaca,* eggs with shredded beef, and *chilaquiles,* strips of chicken and fried tortillas smothered in salsa verde and sour cream. Sports bar. Open 7:30 a.m. to 10 p.m.

Rusty Putter
Hotel zone
Spacious palapa (thatched-roof) restaurant and sports bar serving burgers and sushi accompanied by an ocean view. Adjacent miniature golf.

Tacos Rossy
On the Transpeninsular Hwy.
A real favorite among locals and tourists alike, this spot serves delicious seafood tacos. Open for breakfast and lunch only.

Tequila
On Doblado, between Mijares and Hidalgo
Tel. 142-1155
A charming patio restaurant featuring innovative Mediterranean cuisine, with an emphasis on fish and seafood dishes, served in a romantic setting. Open 5:30 to 10:30 p.m.

Tropicana
Tropicana Inn Hotel, Mijares 30
Tel. 142-1580
Recently renovated, some of the original splen-

dor of this converted mansion is still evident in the lovely patio and fountain. Tasty seafood and Mexican dishes served on a beautiful thatched-roof terrace. Try the outstanding fajitas, served with wheat tortillas, and frozen margaritas mixed with a dash of regional damiana liqueur. A popular local watering hole with a sports bar. Live music nightly during the winter season. Open 8 a.m. to 11 p.m.

Nightlife

Damiana
Mijares 8
Tel. 142-0499
This colorful and romantic restaurant, housed in a lovely 150-year-old colonial home decorated with Mexican folk art, has a cozy bar. Strolling guitarists add to the romantic atmosphere. Open till 10:30 p.m.

Tropicana
Tropicana Inn Hotel, Mijares 30
Tel. 142-1580
The bar at this lovely small hotel is famed for its frozen margaritas.

Shopping

In addition to the stores listed here, don't overlook gift shops at the better hotels, which often carry one-of-a-kind jewelry, resort wear, or art by Mexican and local artists.

Adobe
Plaza San Jose
Home furnishings by famous Guadalajara designer David Luna, who has one of the leading stores in the handicrafts center of Tlaquepaque.

Arte, Diseño y Decoracion
Zaragoza and Hidalgo, across from the church
ADD carries rustic Mexican home decorating items made of wood, pewter and Talavera, as well as modern jewelry.

Cabo Wabo Cantina
On Mijares, near the main square
Good assortment of tequilas, plus souvenirs with the Cabo Wabo logo.

Casa Paulina
Zaragoza, across from Bancomer
Rustic Mexican-style furniture, decorative items and handicrafts.

Copal
Mijares 10
Handicrafts from around the nation, from silver jewelry to paintings on *amate* (tree bark paper). Prices can be steep.

Galeria Sol Dorado
Mijares 27
Lovely shop in an old home featuring handicrafts, art, fine home furnishings.

La Mina
On Mijares
A small shop carrying an attractive selection of silver jewelry.

Los Cabos Tourism Board

Mercado Municipal
On Mauricio Castro
Sample local life at this traditional market selling flowers, fresh fish, produce and handicrafts.

National Arts & Crafts Center
On The Corridor, close to Cabo Real
This hacienda-style complex features a wide variety of handicrafts from around the country and holds alternating exhibitions in basket weaving, lacquerwork, pottery making, and other Mexican arts and crafts. The pleasant courtyard restaurant serves Mexican cuisine at lunchtime. Open 8 a.m. to 5:30 p.m. Closed Sunday.

Opalos de Mexico
Mijares 5
A large jewelry factory specializing in Mexican fire opals. Also all sorts of gold and silver jewelry. Other branches on Hidalgo and two shops off the main square.

Pacific Jewelry
On Mijares, off the main square
This huge jewelry shop features gold, silver, and precious stones.

Veryka
Mijares 6, next to Casa Natalia Hotel
Tel. 142-0575
This wonderful shop carries the finest Mexican handicrafts from around the country, including rare pieces you won't find anywhere else, plus traditional clothing made of hand-loomed fabrics. With branches in San Miguel de Allende and Oaxaca, they can truly offer a great selection.

Villa Valentina
Transpeninsular Hwy., Km. 31
Tel. 142-6612
Impressive and unique home furnishings, rustic, antique and custom-made furniture, large selection of decorative pieces for every home. Weekly Saturday bazaar features special exhibits and a patio luncheon by reservation only.

Art Galleries

El Encanto
On Alvaro Obregon, next to El Encanto Inn
Good collection of interesting art.

Kaki Bassi
On Hidalgo
Talent and personality have made Kaki a leading local artist. Stop by for a chat—she loves it!

Pez Gordo
Alvaro Obregon 19
Tel. 142-5788
This unusual gallery is well worth a visit.

Wentworth Porter Gallery
Alvaro Obregon 20
Tel. 142-3141
One of Los Cabos' foremost contemporary artists, impressionist painter Dennis Wentworth Porter displays his fine work in this gallery. Visits to the artist's studio are available by prior arrangement. (Closed from mid-August to mid-October.)

Where to Stay

Bruce Herman

Royal Surf Hotel

Cabo San Lucas

Cabo Villas Resort
Playa el Medano
Tel. (624) 143-9199
www.cabovillasresort.com
42 luxury suites with ocean views. Gourmet dining, sports bar and grill with spectacular view of The Arch. Two swimming pools, rooftop jacuzzi, gym, spa. Rates FC.

Costa Real Cabo Resort & Spa
On the marina
Tel. (624) 143-1220
www.realresorts.com.mx
This sprawling hotel (formerly Plaza Las Glorias) dominates the marina with 206 rooms with satellite TV, some with jacuzzi. Restaurant, bar. Pool, gym, beach club. Meeting facilities for 1,000. Rates FC.

Finisterra
On Marina Blvd.
Tel. (624) 143-3333
www.finisterra.com

Named "land's end," this hotel at the tip of the peninsula, on a hill with a view of the Pacific and Sea of Cortez, has 286 guest rooms with deluxe amenities, including Palapa Beach Club suites with private balconies, living/dining areas. Four pools, lighted tennis courts, gym. Famed Whale Watcher bar, good dining. Rooftop meeting room for 100. Rates MD.

Hacienda Beach Resort
Playa el Medano
Tel. (624) 143-0663
www.haciendacabo.com
A colorful Spanish-mission-style hotel on 27 tropically landscaped acres with 115 oceanview rooms, including charming little *cabañas* right

HOTEL RATES
LX: luxury, rates above 375 USD
DX: deluxe, rates from 250-375 USD
FC: first-class, rates from 150-250 USD
MD: moderate, rates from 75-150 USD
ECON: economical, rates under 75 USD

on the beach. Good restaurant, open-air bar, oyster bar-game room, secluded beach, pool. Rates MD.

Marina Fiesta
On the marina
Tel. (624) 143-2689
www.marinafiestaresort.com
A popular hotel-timeshare in a pueblo-style building with 155 attractively furnished one- and two-bedroom suites with balcony overlooking the pool or marina, satellite TV, a/c, fully equipped kitchenette. Nice swimming pool, wet bar, sun deck with jacuzzi, kids playground. Rates FC.

Melia San Lucas
Playa el Medano
Tel. (624) 143-4444
www.solmelia.com
This lovely colonial-style resort offers 150 rooms with private balconies, most with ocean views. Two beautiful swimming pools. Restaurant, bar, 24-hour room service, two tennis courts, small meeting room. Rates DX.

Playa Grande Resort
Playa Solmar
Tel. (624) 143-6647
www.playa-grande.com
Built along 1,000 feet of Pacific beachfront, this hotel-timeshare resort offers 130 elegant units (260 when complete) in a hacienda-style low-rise, each with a spacious living/dining room, oceanview balcony, fully-equipped kitchen and world-class amenities. Two pools, restaurant-bar, gym, tennis court.

Pueblo Bonito Los Cabos Resort
Playa el Medano
Tel. (624) 142-9797
www.pueblobonito.com
An attractive Mediterranean-style all-suite hotel on the beach with 148 units with private oceanview balcony, kitchenette, a/c, and satellite TV. Poolside and oceanfront restaurants, bar, health club, freeform swimming pool set amid lovely gardens. Small meeting rooms. Rates FC.

Pueblo Bonito Rosé
Playa el Medano
Tel. (624) 142-9898
www.pueblobonito.com
Adjoining its sister resort, this pink Mediterranean-style all-suite property has Romanesque decorative accents. The 260 super spacious suites have private oceanview balcony, kitchenette, ceiling fan, a/c and satellite TV. Gourmet restaurant. State-of-the-art health spa/fitness center with sauna, massage. Pool, lighted tennis court, scuba instruction. Rates DX.

Pueblo Bonito Sunset Beach
Tel. (624) 142-9999
www.pueblobonito.com
Located on a spectacular stretch of beach on the Pacific Ocean, the chain's newest and most luxurious property is a hotel-timeshare resort featuring 118 suites (519 when complete), a lovely pool with jacuzzi and wet bar with sweeping views of the ocean, 24-hour room service, international restaurant, deli, in-room massages and free transportation hourly to its sister property on El Medano Beach. Rates DX.

Solmar Suites
Av. Solmar 1
Tel. (624) 143-3535
www.solmar.com
Built against the cliffs, this attractive all-suite beachfront hotel incorporates its natural stone backdrop in some rooms. The 84 junior to deluxe suites have private balconies or ground-floor patios overlooking the Pacific and beautiful Solmar Beach. In-room amenities include satellite TV, minibar, phone, safe. Heated pools, giant jacuzzi, tennis court, good restaurant-bar. Complete fishing fleet. Rates FC.

Terrasol
Av. Solmar
Tel. (624) 143-1803
An attractive low-rise condo-hotel resort and spa on the beach facing the Pacific Ocean. Complete hotel service, with 67 studio or one- to three-bedroom units with ocean or mountain views, full kitchen and fireplace. Pool, restaurant, tennis, health spa, gym, jacuzzi. Electric car service within complex. Rates FC.

Villa del Palmar Beach Resort & Spa
Playa el Medano
Tel. (624) 143-2694
www.villadelpalmarloscabos.com
A modern beach resort and spa with 457 units ranging from studios to three-bedroom suites with oceanview balcony, full kitchen, satellite TV. Tiered pools, two lighted tennis courts, water-sports rentals, restaurants, deli, meeting room for 200. Full-service spa and fitness center with gym, jacuzzi, sauna, steam room, massages. Fine swimming beach. Rates DX.

Villa La Estancia
Playa el Medano
Tel. (624) 143-8121
www.villalaestancia.com
Behind hacienda-style wrought-iron gates, this new luxury hotel-timeshare resort features two- and three-bedroom villas on El Medano Beach (next to Villa del Palmar). The 58 guest rooms (160 when complete) have oceanview balconies, maple finishings, full kitchens. Restaurants, bar, infinity pool, tennis courts. Guests have access to Villa del Palmar spa facilities and other services. Rates LX.

The Corridor

Cabo Surf Hotel
The Corridor, Km. 28
Tel. (624) 142-2666
www.cabosurfhotel.com
Located on Palmilla Bay's Acapulquito Beach, this beachfront boutique hotel faces one of the best longboard surf spots in Baja. An intimate property with just 16 suites attractively furnished in old California style. A restaurant-bar with open-air terrace serves fresh seafood and Mexican favorites, plus great margaritas and piña coladas. The gated grounds include pool, heated spa, gardens. Just steps from two of the resort's top golf courses. Rates FC.

Casa del Mar
The Corridor, Km. 19.5
Tel. (624) 145-7700
www.casadelmarmexico.com
A lovely hacienda-style hotel and spa on the beach offering deluxe accommodations and proximity to two championship golf courses: Cabo Real and El Dorado (special discounts available to guests). There are 56 attractive rooms, and suites with kitchenette, seven blue-tiled pools, four tennis courts, gym, beachfront massage palapas, restaurant and bar. Small meeting rooms. Rates DX.

Dreams Los Cabos
The Corridor, Km. 18.5
Tel. (624) 144-0202
www.solmelia.com
Recently acquired by AMResorts, operators of top-of-the-line all-inclusives, this all-suite oceanfront spa and golf resort (formerly Melia Los Cabos) has 160 spacious units with private oceanview balcony, kitchenette, satellite TV, and more in a hacienda-style setting. Excellent European-style spa and fitness center, infinity pool, tennis, meeting facilities, 24-hour room service, lobby bar. Rates FC (all inclusive).

Esperanza
The Corridor, Km. 7
Tel. (624) 145-6400
www.esperanzaresort.com
In Punta Ballena, just four miles from Cabo. This new, exclusive Auberge resort features 50 guest rooms and six suites distributed in palm-thatched *casitas* on a hill gently sloping toward two secluded crescent-shaped coves with sandy beaches. Rooms feature ocean views, expansive terraces, original art and luxurious amenities. Indoor or alfresco dining in a beautiful palapa overlooking the sea, with terraces cascading down to the oceanfront, coffee bar, bar with entertainment. Full-service spa, infinity pool, outdoor plunge pools. Rates LX.

Fiesta Americana Grand
In Cabo del Sol
Tel. (624) 145-6200
www.fiestaamericana.com
This modern Mexican-style property, elegantly decorated with Mexican furnishings, features 290 rooms and suites with a view of the sea distributed in 13 four-story buildings along the beach. Spa and fitness center, freeform swimming pools, tennis courts, kids club. Beautiful and extensive convention facility with 20,000 square feet of meeting space, business center. Casual and formal dining, bars. One of The Leading Hotels of the World. Rates FC.

Hilton Beach & Golf Resort
In Cabo Real
Tel. (624) 145-6500
www.hiltonloscabos.com
Located on a spectacular swimming beach, this hacienda-style resort and spa features an open-air courtyard entrance with fountain. The 375 deluxe oceanview rooms, including 66 suites, have private balcony, cable TV, safe, 3 phones, high-speed Internet access, iron and ironing board, and more. Casual and specialties restaurants, 24-hour room service, wet bars, cozy piano bar. More than 11,000 square feet of meeting space, business center. Two swimming pools, two lighted tennis courts, spa, fitness center, kids club and pool. All-day shuttle service to both towns (cost: 10 dollars).

Las Ventanas al Paraiso
In Cabo Real
Tel. (624) 144-0258
www.lasventanas.com
The ultimate in luxury, this exclusive property has been beautifully designed to blend in with its surroundings. Each of the spacious 61 suites features a fireplace, telescope for stargazing, original Mexican crafts, and panoramic sea and desert views. Amenities include a spa and fitness center, swimming pool, fine restaurant, two 90-foot yachts for fishing and overnight expeditions, meeting facilities and conference center, and a 2,400-bottle wine cellar that's ideal for hosting special events. Preferential access to championship golf course. Rates LX.

Marquis Los Cabos
In Cabo Real
Tel. (624) 144-2000
www.marquisloscabos.com
This second Marquis property (Mexico City's is one of The Leading Hotels of the World and a member of Small Luxury Hotels of the World) is a beach, golf and spa resort with 240 rooms, including 30 casitas, five master suites and a presidential suite, each with its own private pool. All suites are oceanfront with a private balcony and hydro-massage bathtub. Oceanfront pools, two gourmet restaurants and wine cellar, ballroom and meeting facilities, state-of-the-art spa and gym. Continental breakfasts delivered every morning via a "butler box." Rates DX (includes continental breakfast).

Melia Cabo Real
In Cabo Real
Tel. (624) 144-0000
www.solmelia.com
Combining European service and Mexican flavor, this all-inclusive beachfront convention center and golf resort offers 302 deluxe rooms and suites with satellite TV with Internet access, minibar, private balcony, 24-hour room service; most with ocean views. Two semiprivate swimming beaches, complimentary shuttle service to Cabo, PADI water-sports center, attractive pool area, open-air restaurants, bars with entertainment, lighted tennis courts, fitness center, state-of-the art business center. Winner of 2003 Gold Key Award. Rates DX (all inclusive).

One & Only Palmilla
The Corridor, Km. 7.5
Tel. (624) 146-7000
www.palmillaresort.com
About four kilometers from San Jose. Re-opened in early 2004 under new management, and still sparkling from a recent multimillion-dollar renovation, this premier golf resort and spa offers deluxe accommodations and service in a beautiful hacienda-style setting on the beach. The beachfront and oceanview suites, and standard rooms (172 in all) have terraces and are beautifully appointed in Mexican colonial style. Personal valet, star-gazing telescope, aromatherapy menu, and 24-hour room service are some of the wonderful in-room amenities offered. The hotel features a signature 72-hole Jack Nicklaus golf course and rambling gardens. Three restaurants, two bars, spa, fitness center, two pools, tennis courts, meeting facilities. Rates DX (AP).

Sheraton Hacienda del Mar
In Cabo del Sol
Tel. (624) 145-8000
www.sheratonhaciendadelmar.com
This gorgeous hacienda-style property on a secluded beach offers 186 deluxe rooms and suites with satellite TV, a/c, jacuzzi and cushy Sweet Sleeper Beds. There's a beautiful freeform pool, spa and fitness center with sauna and steam room, and excellent dining. Named No. 1 golf hotel in Los Cabos by Conde Nast Traveler. Rates DX.

The Westin Regina Resort
The Corridor, Km. 22.5
Tel. (624) 142-9000
www.westin.com
Near San Jose del Cabo. This striking, recently renovated 243-room luxury resort, winner of several architecture awards for its modern Mexican design, is located on a scenic coastline. All guest rooms offer a view of the Sea of Cortez from a private balcony, and deluxe amenities. The resort also features seven pools, jacuzzi, tennis courts, nine-hole synthetic putting green, spa and fitness center, kids club, restaurants, bars, business center, extensive meeting facilities. Rates DX.

Twin Dolphin
On The Corridor
Tel. (624) 145-8190
www.twindolphin.com
On a bluff overlooking a lovely secluded beach, six minutes north of Cabo San Lucas. An exclusive 165-acre property that beautifully showcases the region's dramatic cactus-strewn landscape. Stunning architecture, lovely pool, 50 charming guest rooms with spectacular ocean views, tile floors. Fine restaurant, bar, lounge with TV/VCR, tennis, massage, jogging trail. No in-room phones or TVs. Rates DX.

San Jose del Cabo

Casa Natalia
Mijares 4, downtown
Tel. (624) 142-5100
www.casanatalia.com
A beautifully-designed boutique hotel in Mexican contemporary style, with 14 deluxe rooms and two jacuzzi suites, all tastefully decorated with fine Mexican handicrafts; in-room spa services, his and hers bathrobes, safe. Room service, concierge service. Heated pool, outdoor palm-thatched bar, excellent restaurant. Arrangements made for use of the Casa del Mar Hotel beach club. Member of Small Luxury Hotels of the World. Rates FC.

Crowne Plaza Los Cabos
Hotel zone
Tel. (624) 142-9292
www.farodelcabo.com.mx
An all-inclusive property featuring a 186-foot lighthouse, at the top of which is a restaurant with a spectacular view. The 333 spacious rooms and suites offer top-notch amenities, balconies with ocean views, 24-hour room service. All suites are oceanfront with jacuzzi. Two swimming pools, including saltwater infinity pool, four restaurants, oceanfront dining, live entertainment, gym, tennis, convention center, kids club and juniors club. Rates FC (all inclusive).

Posada Real Los Cabos
Hotel zone
Tel. (624) 142-0155
www.posadareal.com.mx
On the beach, across from the golf course. Looking better than ever after a major 2.5 million-dollar renovation, this moderately-priced low-rise offers 148 rooms and suites with satellite TV, a/c, minibar, phone. Restaurant, bars with live music, cactus garden, pool, jacuzzis, tennis and water-sports rental. A Best Western hotel. Rates MD.

Presidente InterContinental
On Mijares Blvd.
Tel. (624) 142-0211
www.intercontinental.com
On a secluded stretch of beach (beautiful but rough for swimming) adjacent to a freshwater lagoon that's home to many birds. This service-oriented all-inclusive resort (there's 24-hour room service) is built around an attractively landscaped garden and appeals to outdoor enthusiasts with three swimming pools, three lighted tennis courts, putting green and driving range, fitness facility, kids club and pool, desert excursions and more. The 400 rooms and suites, available in four categories, have private balconies with ocean, lagoon or garden views, TV, minibar, a/c, direct dial phone. A la carte or buffet dining, two bars, wet bar. Rates LX (all inclusive).

The Grand Baja
Hotel zone
Tel. (624) 142-4393
www.thegrandbajaloscabos.com
This upscale all-inclusive beachfront features 252 lavishly decorated units, from 322-square-foot studios to a spectacular 7,534-square-foot penthouse suite. Indoor/outdoor dining, nightly live entertainment, lovely pool, two jacuzzis, fitness center, naturalistic organic spa, meeting and banquet facilities. Rates FC (all-inclusive).

Tropicana Inn
Mijares 30, downtown
Tel. (624) 142-1580
This former residence serves as a traditional Mexican-style inn with 40 guest rooms overlooking a cobblestone courtyard. Each of the colonial-style rooms is equipped with a direct dial phone, coffee maker, a/c and satellite TV. Pool with swim up palapa bar, good restaurant, popular sports bar, parking. Rates MD (includes continental breakfast).

Todos Santos

Alegria Inn
Tel. (612) 145-0700
www.alegriainn.net
A charming inn north of town, near the beach. Rates MD (includes breakfast).

Posada La Poza
Tel. (612) 145-0400
www.lapoza.com
This elegant boutique hotel, restaurant and art gallery offers the town's only beachfront accommodations.

The Todos Santos Inn
Tel. (612) 145-0400
www.mexonline.com/todossantosinn
This beautifully restored 19th-century mansion in the heart of town houses exquisite guest rooms and a popular wine bar. Rates MD.

*A trip through Copper Canyon
rewards visitors with memorable vistas.*

Bruce Herman

Chihuahua

The Romance of the North

At once ancient and modern, Chihuahua is home to both ruins of bygone civilizations and monuments of a thriving industrialized society. Prosperous U.S.-style suburbs flourish on its flat desert plains while mysterious cave dwellings built thousands of years ago nestle in mountain crevices, awaiting exploration. Add to this the fact that it is also home to one of the country's most famous natural attractions, the Copper Canyon, and you have the makings of a fascinating destination.

Mexico's largest state, covering 150,000 square miles, is the country's leading producer of apples, walnuts, oats, cotton and jalapeño chilies. But its strategic location along the U.S. border has made assembly plants, called *maquiladoras* in Spanish, the mainstay of the economy. As many as 400 plants assemble mostly electronic and automotive goods for export. Lumber production and cattle ranching are the next biggest revenue earners.

Chihuahua City

Chihuahua city is modern, with outlying industrial parks and some historic attractions, including the home-turned-museum of revolutionary Pancho Villa.

The large main patio of the state capitol is decorated with impressive murals depicting the state's history, from the arrival of the Spanish to the Mexican revolution. The Apache tribe that roamed the northern plains played an important role in Chihuahua in the late 1800s, plundering the vast ranches with some regularity.

The capitol was built in 1892 on the very site where a priest named Miguel Hidalgo, a key figure in Mexico's War of Independence, was executed before a firing squad in 1811. Di-

rectly across the courtyard, there is a haunting portrayal of Hidalgo at his execution. The dungeon where he was incarcerated is beneath the main post office and is open to the public.

The home of Pancho Villa, leader of the northern rebellion during the Mexican Revolution of 1910, has been turned into the *Museum of the Revolution*. On display is the 1919 Dodge touring car in which he was shot dead by political enemies. Upstairs, visitors can see Villa's death mask, showing the bullet hole in his skull.

The many rooms are filled with revolutionary memorabilia and period photos of Villa and his army. Villa was a teetotaler who had all liquor destroyed upon capturing a town, and one 1913 photograph taken in Ciudad Juarez shows his men standing among smashed barrels of local brew. A "Wanted" poster issued in 1916 by the chief of police of Columbus, New Mexico, offers a 5,000 dollar reward for Villa's capture after he and his men stormed the city, the only time a foreign army has invaded the United States.

Villa's widow Doña Luz Corral, one of his 23 wives, lived in this house until her death in 1981. Today the army operates the museum, open 9 a.m. to 1 p.m. and 3 to 7 p.m., except Monday.

Another interesting home-turned-museum is *Quinta Gameros,* a lavish French-style mansion built in 1910 for a local mining magnate who never got the chance to enjoy it. The start of the revolution forced Manuel Gameros to flee to El Paso, Texas, just as construction was completed. The mansion was intended to impress the daughter of Luis Terrazas, one of the world's richest men before the revolution who was known to brag that the state of Chihuahua was "on my ranch." His son-in-law, Enrique

Creel, for whom the town of Creel, in Copper Canyon, is named, served as governor of the state, ambassador to the United States, and secretary of state.

The mansion houses a stunning collection of art nouveau furniture, as well as a second-floor exhibition space, and a basement-level gallery displaying paintings by accomplished local artists. Open 11 a.m. to 2 p.m. and 4 to 7 p.m.

Other interesting sites are the *cathedral*, which was built between 1726 and 1825, and its underground *Museum of Sacred Art*; and the *Center of Contemporary Art*, with works by Rivera, Siqueiros and others.

The government-run *Casa de las Artesanias*, at Avenida Juarez 705, behind the main post office, has a large selection of regional handicrafts, most of it made by Tarahumara Indians who live in the Copper Canyon.

Chihuahua produces a regional brand of firewater that, like the tequila of Jalisco and mezcal of Oaxaca, is made from a variety of agave. Called sereque, the agave native to this area's harsh desert is processed much the same way as the blue agave used to make tequila, including being aged in oak barrels for a minimum of six months, and is bottled as *sotol.*

Dining and Nightlife

Bolivar Avenue, where Quinta Gameros is located, is home to a few fashionable restaurant-cafes that open in the late afternoons and feature live entertainment, including rock or pop bands, on weekend evenings. One such place is *Del Paseo Café*, which serves regional fare and features live Latin American music from 8 p.m. (open from 4 p.m.).

El Calicanto, at Aldama and Ocampo, is a charming bohemian-style eatery with regional dishes, outdoor tables, and live music in the evenings. *La Galera*, on Reforma, is a popular restaurant-bar that's also a cafe and art gallery.

Excellent restaurants are located within a few blocks along Avenida Juarez, including *Tony's*, a longtime favorite for fine international cuisine in an elegant setting (Juarez and 39th, tel. 410-2988).

For good food in a fun, friendly setting, try *Applebee's*, at Periferico de la Juventud 5708. For a special treat, especially at sunset and in the evening, have a light meal at *Mandala*, an informal restaurant-cafe high on a hill at Mirador de la 11. The tables are set on a terrace with a sweeping view of the city; in winter each guest gets a poncho to ward off the chilly night air. On Friday nights, from 9 p.m., live music is provided by a romantic trio or Latin Ameri-

can ensemble. Mandala is open 5 p.m. to midnight, except Mondays.

The Westin Soberano Hotel offers fine dining with a view and live piano music at its specialties restaurant, *Los Candiles*.

Chihuahua has several lively night spots, including *Juventus Bowl*, an entertainment complex with a restaurant, disco, pool hall, and bowling alley; *Old Town*, a nighttime rodeo show; and *La Taberna Cerveceria*, a converted brewery featuring Mexico's Cuauhtemoc brand beers.

Side Trips

Chunks of desert in the state of Chihuahua have been transformed into fertile fields thanks to a small but significant Mennonite colony that settled here in the early 1920s.

Near the city of *Cuauhtemoc*, located a two-hour bus ride west of Chihuahua city, fruit farming (mainly apples and peaches) is the major economic activity of the Mennonite community. And if you have ever bought Chihuahua cheese then you are already familiar with the community's most famous product.

Mennonites originated in northern Germany and arrived in Mexico via Canada and the United States. Known for their strict adherence to the Bible, they have largely preserved their 16th-century way of life, including their language, a dialect of Old Low German. While the community retains many of its orthodox customs, such modern conveniences as pickup trucks and station wagons have replaced the horse and buggy.

A tour to the area generally includes a visit to a cheese processing plant and a schoolhouse, where children up to the age of 12 are taught exclusively from the Bible, and where recess sees girls in bonnets and flowery frocks, and boys in cowboy hats and boots play outdoors, evoking scenes from America's pioneer days.

About 150 miles northwest of Chihuahua city or about 120 miles southwest of Ciudad Juarez, near the town of Nuevo Casas Grandes, lies the most important archaeological zone in north Mexico—the ruins of *Paquimé*.

Designated by the United Nations Educational, Scientific and Cultural Organization (UNESCO) as a World Heritage Site, Paquimé comprises the remnants of a 1,000-year-old city with multi-story dwellings and an advanced water distribution and drainage system that supplied homes with fresh running water. Of special interest is the House of the Guacamayas, a string of mud cages that researchers believe were used to breed tropical birds, probably for their valuable plumage.

Many aspects of Paquimé culture, which reached its zenith during the 11th century, are similar to those of Amerindian groups of the American southwest.

The on-site *Museum of Northern Cultures*, inaugurated in 1997, illustrates the day-to-day life of Paquimé, which was suddenly abandoned in 1400 A.D. after what appears to have been a devastating fire. The museum also displays ancient samples of the now famous pottery that was made here. A museum shop offers an extensive selection of Paquimé-style

pottery, some illustrated books on the region, and souvenirs.

You can see Paquimé-style pottery being made in *Mata Ortiz,* a small town located 34 miles, or an hour's drive (mostly on dirt road), south of Nuevo Casas Grandes.

The residents of Mata Ortiz have revived the sophisticated ceramics making of Paquimé, producing works using the same technique (without the use of a potter's wheel or kiln), and incorporating highly intricate designs. The artisan responsible for reviving this art form, Juan Quezada, has a gallery exhibiting his work and that of other artisans in town. Pieces can range in price from less than a 100 to more than 1,000 dollars, depending on size and intricacy of design.

The best place to stay in Nuevo Casas Grandes is at the *Hacienda,* a pleasant motel with clean, spacious rooms surrounding a grassy courtyard and swimming pool. *Bandido,* the best restaurant in town, serves Mexican fare and fine cuts of grilled beef in a picturesque Western-style setting. There's live music in the evenings, and a dance floor that is packed on weekends. From May to September, you can catch a weekend rodeo show at *Pistolero.*

Vestiges of northern Indian culture are also found directly south of Paquimé, near the town of Ciudad Madera, where the archaeological site of *Cuarenta Casas* features remnants of adobe dwellings built into mountain caves and niches.

South of Chihuahua city, the towns of *Ciudad Delicias, Ciudad Camargo* and *Parral* are worth visiting. Delicias, famed for its walnut tree orchards, is also known for good bass fishing and duck hunting, and its Museum of Paleontology. Camargo is known for its good fishing and hot springs. The former silver mining town of Parral, where Pancho Villa was assassinated, has several attractions, including its Catedral de San Jose and Museo del General Francisco Villa.

Chihuahua city is a departure point for road or train trips to Copper Canyon. Daily flights connect Chihuahua with Mexico's major cities, as well as El Paso, Dallas, Phoenix, Los Angeles, Houston and Atlanta.

Hotels in Chihuahua

Fiesta Inn. Ortiz Mena 2801. Designed with the business traveler in mind, this hotel offers 152 rooms and suites with cable TV. Pool, gym, restaurant-coffee shop, lobby bar, business center, meeting rooms, parking, car rental. Rates MD. Tel. (614) 429-0100.

Holiday Inn Hotel & Suites. Escudero 702. Ideal for longer stays, this modern colonial-style property resembles a small suburban community with 74 guest rooms distributed in clusters. Amenities include cable TV, equipped kitchenette, living room. Guests-only club with restaurant-bar, game room, gym, indoor pool, sauna; also outdoor pool. Parking. Rates MD (includes breakfast). Tel. (614) 439-0000.

San Francisco Park Place. Victoria 409, right behind the cathedral. A classic hotel ideally located for sightseeing. There are 132 spa-

cious, air-conditioned rooms and two suites, all with satellite TV. Beautiful banquet room (Salon Ingles) with panoramic view, parking, restaurant, coffee shop, and a helpful staff. Rates MD. Tel. (614) 439-9000. www.hotel sanfrancisco.com.mx.

Westin Soberano. Barranca del Cobre 3211, on a hill overlooking an industrial park. This deluxe property offers 204 guest rooms, executive floor, business center, extensive meeting facilities, outdoor pool with sun deck, gym, tennis/racquetball courts, steam room. Restaurant with panoramic view, lobby bar. Rates FC. Tel. (614) 429-2929.

Copper Canyon

One of Mexico's most spectacular natural attractions is where the Sierra Madre mountain range forms one of the longest and deepest canyon systems in the world, covering 25,000 square miles of rugged land. Three of the canyons—Urique (6,200 feet), Sinforosa (6,039 feet) and Batopilas (5,940 feet)—are not only deeper than Arizona's famous Grand Canyon (4,702 feet), but are also considered to be the world's eighth, ninth and tenth deepest, respectively.

Known in Spanish as Las Barrancas del Cobre, or Copper Canyon, this natural marvel boasts beautiful scenery and an unforgettable train ride, and is home to Mexico's Tarahumara Indians.

The Tarahumara—who call themselves Raramuri, or the "light footed ones," in ref-

Victoria 409 Centro
Chihuahua, Chih., México
Tel. (614) 439.9000 Fax (614) 415.3538
Toll free from USA 1 800 847 2546
www.hotelsanfrancisco.com.mx

erence to their running skills—are often described as reclusive, but weren't always that way. When the Spanish arrived, the Tarahumara inhabited Chihuahua's central plains. In trying to escape forced labor in Spanish-owned mines or haciendas, they slowly retreated into the canyons. Now they exclusively inhabit the Sierra Tarahumara, though the women, colorfully dressed in multilayered skirts and frilly tops, are often seen on the streets of Chihuahua city hawking their wares.

It was back in 1872 that Albert Owen, a U.S. engineer, dreamed of a railroad that would provide coastal access to logging, ranching and mining interests. With delays caused by engineering difficulties, the 1910 Mexican Revolution and World War II, the project wasn't completed until 1961.

Today, the Copper Canyon railroad stretches for 300 miles across the mountains, taking passengers over 35 bridges (the highest about 300 feet above Rio Chinipas) and through 86 tunnels (the longest measuring more than a mile).

Facilities on the *Copper Canyon Express* train, also called "Chepe" for the Spanish initials of the route (Chihuahua al Pacifico), have greatly improved since the national railroad company was privatized not long ago. Money has been invested in upgrading both the trains and stations. Passenger, dining and lounge cars have been remodeled, with roomy, newly-upholstered reclining seats, and large windows that let you appreciate the passing scenery.

Upscale train tours are also available through various companies, including *Finlay Fun-Time Tours* based in North Hollywood, Calif., which hooks its private sleeping, dining and observation cars onto the regular train.

Five days is the minimum amount of time recommended for a tour of the canyon, whether starting off from Chihuahua or Los Mochis, and a seven-day tour is pretty ideal. If you don't plan to overnight at one of the stops along the rail route, it is best to make the 12-hour trip eastward from Los Mochis, to be assured of hitting the most impressive sights during daylight hours.

The first stop, about 50 miles east of Los Mochis, is the charming town of *El Fuerte.* Built in 1564, the town has seen a lot of history, but is now a sleepy village with cobblestone or dirt streets. Most of the activity centers around the *Posada del Hidalgo Hotel,* a delightful remodeled mansion with a pool and good restaurant.

During the four-hour ride to the next stop, *Bahuichivo,* the flat farmland around Los Mochis gives way to rolling hills and mountain ranges that plunge into river beds hundreds of feet below. Here, you can choose to overnight in the town of Cerocahui, located a 45-minute drive away. The town's charming *Mision Hotel* offers the best accommodations and dining; wine aficionados will be pleasantly surprised by their red or white made from grapes grown right at their own on-site vineyard.

Cerocahui is a departure point for horse-back-riding or hiking tours through lush landscapes to a nearby cascade, as well as excursions to the rim of Urique Canyon or down to its valley. To include the seven-hour tour to the canyon bottom, it's best to spend two nights here.

Back on the train, after about two hours you arrive at *Barrancas/Divisadero,* twin stations about five minutes apart. At both stops, hotels built on the very edge of the canyon offer stunning vistas, as well as visits to surrounding lookouts and Tarahumara cave homes.

About an hour and a half east is *Creel,* considered the gateway to the Copper Canyon for those coming from Chihuahua. Like a bustling trading post, this western-style town is filled with stores selling Tarahumara-made handicrafts to visitors, such as woven baskets and wood utensils, and fabrics, hardware and other items to the Tarahumara.

Creel serves as a base for numerous day trips combining visits to nearby sites of interest, including beautiful *Arareko Lake,* the Valley of the Mushrooms, a Jesuit mission decked with indigenous wall paintings, Tarahumara dwellings, and waterfalls, such as *Cusarare* or *Basaseachi,* which at 811 feet is Mexico's highest. If you can spend an extra night in Creel, you can squeeze in a trip to the picturesque town of *Batopilas,* situated by a river at the bottom of a canyon. Batopilas was a bustling silver mining town in the late 1800s and the remnants of the once-grand hacienda of the town's major mining magnate, American Alexander Shepherd, grace the banks of the river.

From Creel, the train ride to Chihuahua city takes about five hours through an enormous agricultural valley with extensive apple orchards, north Mexico's Mennonite country (in fact, the train first stops in the Mennonite town of Cuauhtemoc). Creel is also accessible by road from Chihuahua city. This is the first tract of a planned highway that roughly follows the rail route and is designed to offer cars access to the canyon. The next towns to be linked via highway will be Divisadero, Bahuichivo and Los Mochis. The highway, a planned hotel zone along the canyon's edge, and recreational facilities are all part of a long-range government project to boost tourism to the region.

During the rainy season in late summer and early fall, canyon vistas are particularly lush and the cloud formations spectacular. In mid-December and at Easter, Tarahumara communities hold elaborate religious celebrations and festivals.

If you plan on hiking or camping in the canyons, keep in mind that nighttime temperatures at the higher altitudes can be freezing in winter while the lower altitudes remain tropical, with bamboo, oranges and orchids in abundance. In fact, many Tarahumaras "go south" for the winter simply by relocating from the top of the canyon to the base.

A good Chihuahua-based outfit specializing in tours of the canyon is *Turismo al Mar,* Calle

Tarahumara women sell handicrafts at the Divisadero train station

Berna 2202 (410-9232). In business for 20 years, they also offer city tours and excursions to Mennonite country and other nearby sites.

Travel light, as getting on and off the train with heavy luggage can be difficult, pack warm clothing in case of rain or cool temperatures, and take lots of change—there are no banks in the remoter parts of the canyon.

Recommended hotels in the Copper Canyon include the *Mirador* (near the Posada Barrancas train station; Los Mochis tel. (668) 818-7046), *Divisadero-Barrancas* (at the Divisadero train station; Chihuahua tel. (614) 415-1199), *Mision* (in Cerocahui; Los Mochis tel. (668) 818-7046), *Cascada Inn* (in Creel; tel. (635) 456-0253), and *The Lodge at Creel* (tel. (635) 456-0071).

Northwest Mexico

North Mexico is a vast expanse of arid land between two bodies of water, the Gulf of Mexico to the east and the Sea of Cortez to the west.

The hard terrain gives nothing up voluntarily and the *norteños* who inhabit the region pride themselves on what they have been able to achieve—Mexico's highest standard of living. Around the major metropolises, stretches of dry desert framed by jagged mountain ranges give way to rambling cattle ranches and fruit orchards. The cities boast affluent U.S.-style suburbs lined with neat rows of houses and manicured lawns.

Northwest Mexico is made up largely of plains, mountains and deserts, often harsh but always fascinating in their contrasts of scenery, from mineral rich mountains to coastal resorts and broad extensions of productive grain fields.

The coastal states of Sinaloa and Sonora, along the Sea of Cortez, have several resort areas. Sinaloa keeps the United States supplied with fresh tomatoes during the winter months,

while Sonora is the cotton and wheat growing capital of Mexico. In addition to having rich farmland, the coastal strip has marshes that are popular for duck hunting.

Increasingly, cruise companies that ply the waters of the Sea of Cortez also offer pre- or post-cruise tours to Copper Canyon, so travelers can visit all of the region's major attractions.

Los Mochis

Los Mochis is a transplanted California town near the Sinaloa coast. It was settled by U.S. immigrants spurred on by two men whose names are still prominent here, Albert Owen and Benjamin Johnston. Visitors can see interesting displays of relics and photos depicting the area's history at the *Los Mochis Museum,* downtown.

The town's major attraction is its location near the Sea of Cortez, where there's good hunting and fishing. There are also good seafood restaurants and comfortable hotels. Most tourists, however, go to Los Mochis to embark on the train ride through Copper Canyon, terminating in Chihuahua, 300 miles away.

A few miles from Los Mochis, on the Sea of Cortez, is the port of *Topolobampo,* where the 850-foot-deep natural harbor ranks as the third deepest in the world, after Sydney and San Francisco.

The town itself is struggling to bring its hodgepodge development under control and become one of Mexico's leading ports. From here, ferries take passengers and cars across to La Paz, in Baja California Sur. The trip takes about 12 hours.

San Carlos Nuevo Guaymas

Above Sinaloa is the state of Sonora, which is much like Arizona, but with a Mexican accent and a coastline. Travelers not fascinated by deserts usually head for the fishing port of

Guaymas in San Carlos Bay, or Kino Bay to the north. Both areas are popular seaside getaways for people living in the parched U.S. southwest. The *San Carlos Country Club* is one of the most ambitious residential/tourist developments in northwest Mexico.

Puerto Peñasco

Better known in the United States as "Rocky Point," Puerto Peñasco is a flourishing seaside resort on the Sea of Cortez. Because of its proximity to the Arizona border, it is a popular vacation spot for residents of Tucson and Phoenix. A major development project for the area will eventually include a Jack Nicklaus signature golf course and five-star hotels.

In the southernmost part of the state is *Alamos*, one of the earliest Spanish settlements in this part of Mexico, and once a prosperous mining town. Alamos is the most colonial of Sonora's cities and has been declared a national monument.

Hacienda de los Santos, a member of Small Luxury Hotels of the World, offers exclusive accommodations in a beautifully renovated 17th-century hacienda originally built for a local silver baron. Tel. (647) 428-0222.

Kino Bay

Lovely Kino Bay is a resort of the future. Right now it's big with the trailer and camper set, but insiders say major hotel developers will be arriving soon. All of Sonora may be getting ready for a boom in travel. After all, a big potential market lies just across the border.

About two and a half miles out to sea are several islands. The largest, *Isla del Tiburon* (Shark Island), covers 3.7 square miles. It is inhabited by nomadic groups of Seri Indians, who are noted for their sleek carvings of birds and fish from *palo de fierro* (ironwood), a tree that grows on the island. Isla del Tiburon is a biosphere reserve and the few animal species that inhabit the island, including the desert turtle, mule deer and *cimarron* (wild mountain goat), are almost extinct.

Durango

To the south, the state of Durango is known for its superb outdoor life, as well as logging and mining industries. When the Spanish arrived here in the 16th century, they discovered a wealth of natural resources, including lumber, gold, silver, lead, copper and iron.

Centuries later, filmmakers discovered its consistently sunny skies and rugged scenery made it an ideal location for shooting westerns. From the 1950s to the 1970s, during the western's heyday, John Wayne, Robert Wagner, Burt Lancaster, Paul Newman and Emilio "El Indio" Fernandez were among the Hollywood and Mexican actors who made movies here. The trend slowed in the 80s with the decline of the western genre.

Pantera Excursions (tel. 825-0682) offers tours of Durango city, the picturesque countryside/movie sets, the Sierra Madre mountains, nearby archaeological ruins, the Zone of Silence and other sites of interest, and bird watching, hiking and mountain biking tours.

Durango is known as the land of scorpions and while practically extinct, the arachnid still features prominently in local crafts, appearing in key chains, ash trays and other souvenirs.

Northeast Mexico

Composed of the three border states of Coahuila, Nuevo Leon and Tamaulipas, plus the inland states of San Luis Potosi and Zacatecas, northeast Mexico represents about one-quarter of Mexican territory and is almost as large as Texas, which sits just north. Because of their pronounced colonial character, San Luis Potosi and Zacatecas are grouped with the colonial cities of Central Mexico described earlier in the book.

In the northeast you'll find extreme differences in terrain, culture and people. There are colonial plazas and cathedrals, modern cities and suburbs, Gulf of Mexico beaches and deserts, mountains and caves. A leisurely trip might include visiting the largest cities: Monterrey, Saltillo, San Luis Potosi, Tampico and Zacatecas.

Nuevo Leon

This industrial power, one of the main pillars of the economy, has many attractive tourist destinations: besides the capital, Monterrey, and its environs (described in the following chapter), there are the towns of Sabinas, Linares, Galeana, Bustamante, Montemorelos and Aramberri, full of peaceful and lovely panoramas of life in Mexico today.

Coahuila

Saltillo, Coahuila state's capital, is a popular weekend getaway for residents of Monterrey thanks to its proximity (less than an hour away) and cooler temperatures. Settlers were originally attracted to this corner of the Chihuahua Desert by a small spring, a little *salto de agua* or *saltillo*.

Today, one of the city's main attractions is the stunning *Museo del Desierto*, where visitors learn that the desert is not nearly as lifeless as it looks. *Museo de las Aves de Mexico* exhibits a collection of more than 700 different species of birds (about 2,400 specimens), from a tiny hummingbird to a magnificent eagle in flight.

For a memorable meal try *El Tapanco*, housed in a converted 250-year-old mansion at Allende Sur 225. There, you'll also find fine Mexican folk art at *Fonart*. While downtown, take the time to visit *El Serape de Saltillo*, where they make famed Saltillo serapes from fine hand-spun and dyed wool. A tourist trolley offers two-hour tours of the city's major sights Friday, Saturday and Sunday at 10 a.m. and 3 p.m. The city's leading hotels are the *Quinta Real* and the *Camino Real*.

About an hour west of Saltillo is the *Museo Paleontologico de Rincon Colorado*, where scientists found the remains of a duckbilled dinosaur, and where thousands of fossils underfoot indicate the area was once covered by ocean.

The town of *Parras*, a little more than an hour's drive west, is where the oldest winery in the Western Hemisphere was founded in 1597 and still exists today as *Casa Madero*. The town hosts a wine harvesting festival in August. For more information, call (842) 422-0111.

Mexico's only ski resort is located in Arteaga, between Saltillo and Matehuala. Situated on 700 hectares of pine forest high in the Sierra Madre, *Monterreal* boasts two artificial slopes made of Dendix, skiing's answer to AstroTurf. There's also a golf course (at more than 3,000 meters above sea level, golf balls fly farther), swimming pool, tennis court, hiking trails and chalets. Equipment rental and instruction are available.

Across the border from Eagle Pass, Texas, *Piedras Negras* is where Ignacio "Nacho" Anaya, a maitre d' at a local restaurant, served the very first plate of nachos in 1943. The appetizer of tortilla chips topped with melted cheese and jalapeños, originally known as "Nacho's specialty," hence nachos, went on to become a classic of Tex-Mex cooking. The town hosts an annual nacho competition the second weekend of October (Anaya's son serves as a judge).

Tamaulipas

A popular hunting and fishing destination, Tamaulipas is home to numerous rivers, lakes and beaches, and has some 270 miles of coast on the Gulf of Mexico. Its well-known border cities—Nuevo Laredo, Reynosa and Matamoros—attract millions of visitors annually.

Reynosa is the port of entry for most of the white-winged dove hunters who flock to the state's hunting and fishing camps. Matamoros is an industrial city where many U.S. businessmen work, mostly as managers at assembly plants.

Tampico, where the Panuco River meets the Gulf of Mexico, is one of Mexico's leading ports and oil-refinery centers, and the site of a growing petrochemical industry. Since the expropriation of the oil companies more than 50 years ago, the city has lost its international flavor. Today, its only real attraction is the wonderful crab native to its waters, and the good fishing in the gulf and nearby freshwater lagoons, *Laguna de Chairel* and *Laguna del Carpintero*, where there are several fishing camps. Northeast of the city is *Playa Miramar*, a long stretch of relatively undeveloped beach.

Nogales

The states of Sonora and Chihuahua border Arizona, New Mexico and southwest Texas. Directly opposite each other in Arizona and Sonora are the twin cities of Nogales. This is the starting point for the highway that goes directly south to Hermosillo, Ciudad Obregon and Guaymas.

Nogales, Mexico, has limited tourist attractions and facilities and is one of several border cities in which the Mexican in-bond industry has extensive assembly operations for U.S. firms, especially in electronics and textiles. Here also, the two nations share the huge Sonora-Arizona desert, with its spectacular scenery and remarkable animal and plant species.

Monterrey

Mexico's Industrial Powerhouse

El Faro de Comercio, Monterrey's tribute to business and industry, dominates the downtown area

Monterrey Convention & Visitors Bureau

Better known for its high-tech convention center, Cintermex, than for its mountain-top retreat, Chipinque, the city of Monterrey is often overlooked as a tourist destination.

As the legions of suit-clad, briefcase-carting passengers aboard Monterrey-bound flights attest, northern Mexico's industrial capital is a place for doing business.

But there's another side to this modern fast-paced metropolis that warrants packing some jeans and suntan lotion, toting a camera, and inviting the family along.

The city offers a wide range of attractions, enough to entice any visitor into extending a business trip a day or two, or more, to get a firsthand look at how residents enjoy their time off at world-class museums, a burgeoning nightlife district, and the surrounding mountains.

Those are just a few of the most popular places where *regiomontanos*, as they call themselves, let down their hair or, more to the point, lay down their briefcase.

History

Founded in 1596 by Don Diego de Montemayor, the city was named in honor of the Viceroy of New Spain. In 1612 disastrous floods wiped out much of the original city, but the imprint of the Spanish colonial era can still be seen in the Barrio Antiguo, or Old Quarter, located behind the cathedral.

Regiomontanos (think of it as Monterrey spelled backwards) exude a palpable confidence, perhaps derived from the knowledge that their town is a vital engine of Mexico's economy.

Unlike the more languid ambiance characteristic of Mexico's southern cities, life here is energetic and fast paced. In contrast to the quaint, tree-shaded plaza so typical of colonial towns, the plaza here is new, more functional than decorative, and crisscrossed by pedestrians bent on arriving punctually at their next destination.

Monterrey's strategic location near the U.S. border, combined with a diligent, skilled and well-educated work force, and access to key natural resources, have helped make it what it is today—headquarters of the country's largest corporations, including beer maker Cerveceria Cuauhtemoc, cement giant Cemex, and leading glass manufacturer Vitro.

The city is also the most important in the northeastern region for its institutions of higher learning (there are four major universities and five small colleges), medical facilities and cultural activities. The *Monterrey Institute of Technology* (TEC) is considered the best university in Latin America in computer sciences and engineering.

This thriving metropolis is the country's third-largest city, with about three million inhabitants living in the metropolitan area, which includes six municipalities. The one called San Pedro Garza Garcia, located southwest of the downtown area, is home to the most affluent residential and commercial district. A low mountain ridge divides these two Monterrey hubs—the downtown area and Garza Garcia—but the city has bored a hole through it.

The Loma Larga Tunnel has cut the former 30-minute drive from one neighborhood to the other to 10 minutes.

Nestled at the foot of the Sierra Madre mountains, in a 1,800-foot-high valley, the city is dominated by a uniquely shaped 5,700-foot peak called *Cerro de la Silla*, or Saddle Hill. Temperatures above 80°F are common from April through October. During the winter, nights can get very crisp and chilly, and a thick sweater or jacket is necessary. It generally rains in August and September.

What to See and Do

Like their Texan neighbors, regiomontanos are inclined to think BIG. Downtown's main square, which is actually more of a rectangle, stretches the length of six city blocks. Covering almost 100 acres, this plaza is among the world's largest, along with Moscow's Red Square and Mexico City's Zocalo. It is aptly called the *Gran Plaza* or *Macroplaza*. And with an efficiency that befits an industrious city, almost every single important building has been made to occupy it, from city hall at one end to the post office at the other, and everything in between, including the cathedral, Government Palace, central tourism office, two of the top museums, the 1,500-seat municipal theater, and the legislature. This means that a casual stroll along the plaza can easily lead to an impromptu city tour, and a fairly organized one at that.

The vast plaza is home to many monuments and sculptures. The *Explanada de los Heroes*, a chunk of more than 19,000 square meters, features statues of Mexican heroes Hidalgo, Morelos, Juarez and Escobedo. The gigantic multitiered *Neptune Fountain*, which serves as a wading pool for kids on hot summer days, has bronze sculptures of Neptune and other figures of the water kingdom designed by Spanish artist Luis Sanguinio.

On the southeast side of the plaza is a 250-foot-tall tribute to the forces that built Monterrey—the *Faro del Comercio*, or Beacon of Commerce. Designed by the "Father of contemporary Mexican architecture," Luis Barragan, the red tower emits a blue-green laser beam at night in the direction of various city landmarks, including Saddle Hill.

In front of the light tower is the *Catedral de Monterrey*, begun in 1603 and finished 150 years later. Its beautiful three-tiered bell tower was installed in 1851. The cathedral contains murals and sculptures by some of the country's finest artists, and is home to one of the country's great art treasures, an image of the Purisima Virgen.

The *Barrio Antiguo*, or Old Quarter, is an

Cola de Caballo waterfall

Monterrey Convention & Visitors Bureau

island of colonial-era charm and tranquility amid the bustling city. Buildings dating from the 18th and 19th century, with wrought-iron grillwork on the windows and pastel-colored facades, line the cobblestone streets. This is what Monterrey looked like before its industrial revolution.

Many of the structures are undergoing renovation, but already residing in the colonial enclave are a few corner cafés and antique shops, and enough bars and nightclubs to satisfy even the most avid bar-hopper. The barrio encompasses a three by five block area bordered by Dr. Coss to the west, Padre Mier to the north, Av. Constitucion to the south and Felix Gomez to the east.

Culture Makes Its Marco

Not long ago, Monterrey was derided for being long on cash but short on culture. Not anymore. Art, history and science are venerated at three excellent museums.

Monterrey's *Museum of Contemporary Art* (Marco) is not only home to major works of modern art, it *is* a major work of modern art. Designed by renowned Mexican architect Ricardo Legorreta, famed for his modern-day interpretations of traditional Mexican architectural themes, the building evokes a classic Mexican *casona*, or mansion, with a ground floor interior courtyard surrounded by geometric arches. Open 11 a.m. to 7 p.m. (stays open till 9 Wednesdays and Sundays); closed

Mondays. Tel. 8342-4820.

The impressive *Museum of Mexican History*, located at Dr. Coss 445 Sur, offers a fascinating audio-visual journey through pre-Hispanic Mexico, the colonial era, war of independence, revolution and up to modern times. The many interactive displays let you delve further into the topics that interest you most. Open Tuesday to Friday 11 a.m. to 7 p.m.; Saturday and Sunday till 8 p.m. Tel. 8345-9898. The Zaragoza station of the city's No. 2 subway line leaves you near the museum.

The history museum is located alongside picturesque *Paseo Santa Lucia*, a miniature riverwalk that seems to have taken its inspiration from San Antonio's. Here you can rent pedal-powered launches, or while away the time at one of several riverside eateries.

Most science museums would be content to fill you with a sense of wonderment once they got you inside. Not *Planetario Alfa*. Monterrey's sophisticated touch-and-do science museum is awe-inspiring from a distance. It is housed in a giant silver cylinder that rises out of the earth at an angle defying the laws of gravity. Inside, each level is dedicated to a different aspect of science and technology, with games and interactive displays.

Alfa also features an ImaxDome theater where movies are projected on a hemispheric screen, making viewers feel as if they are part of the action, an outdoor aviary with exotic bird species, and a science garden. Open Tuesday to Friday 3 to 9 p.m. and Saturday and Sunday from noon. Tel. 8303-0002.

Though not one of the big three, the wonderful *Glassworks Museum*, located at Zaragoza and Magallanes, inside the city's old glassworks, is definitely worth a visit. A tour of the quaint 19th-century building begins with a ground-floor exhibit of the early days of glass manufacturing and ends with a top-floor exhibit of contemporary works of art in glass. Both the antique and avant-garde displays are memorable. Open Friday to Wednesday 9 a.m. to 6 p.m. Tel. 8329-1000, ext. 1222.

An old-fashioned trolley makes the rounds of the downtown area Tuesday through Sunday from 10 a.m. to 5 p.m. Its route takes passengers past the main square, Marco, the history museum, cathedral, and the shopping district of Plaza Morelos. Look for signs marking boarding stops; tickets can be purchased on board.

Taxis are plentiful and inexpensive, with rates fixed according to the zone you're going to.

Infotur (the tourist information center) maintains offices near the plaza. Tel. 8345-6745.

Located a brisk walk west of the downtown area, at Purisima Plaza (famous for its *troles*, or crushed ice flavored with natural fruit syrups), is the ultramodern *La Purisima Church* designed by Enrique de la Mora. Built after World War II, it was the first to reflect modern ecclesiastical architecture in Latin America, and attracts architectural aficionados from all over the world.

An interesting place to visit is *El Obispado* (Bishop's Palace), located high on a hill overlooking the city, providing an excellent view. Built in 1787 to employ farmers whose crops had been destroyed by an unusually cold winter, it became the seat of the Catholic diocese during the remainder of the colonial period. Surrounded by cannons, it served as headquarters for U.S. General Taylor during the 1847 U.S. invasion of Mexico, and for revolutionary general Pancho Villa. Declared a national monument in 1932, it has housed a museum of regional history since 1956. Its magnificent exterior lighting makes it resemble a jewel in the evenings.

A good place to put your finger on the pulse of Monterrey is *Cintermex* (Centro Internacional de Negocios), the city's renowned convention facility. This is where Monterrey's top corporations are showcased, with about 150 businesses maintaining permanent offices here.

A visit to *Cerveceria Cuauhtemoc* should be on every beer lover's list. The business that started it all was established in 1890 by two local brothers and today is the largest brewery in Mexico. Maker of popular brands Tecate, Carta Blanca and Bohemia, the brewery also produces a special edition Christmas-time beer called Nochebuena.

Visitors can tour the plant or simply enjoy a complimentary freshly-brewed beer in their beer garden Monday through Saturday 11 a.m. to 3:30 p.m. Groups larger than 15 should make prior arrangements. Tel. 8328-5000.

Located on the grounds of the beer factory is the small *Museo de Monterrey*, integrated into a 19th-century building that once held the fermenting vats. Giant copper cauldrons still form part of the museum, which exhibits works by contemporary Mexican artists.

Next door is the *Baseball Hall of Fame*, which records great moments in Mexican baseball, and boasts a new interactive area where visitors can test their game skills.

Monterrey has several excellent options for the entire family, among them *Plaza Sesamo*, an amusement park incorporating the Sesame Street theme and characters. The park features 17 giant water slides, a Space Shot that launches passengers at 45 miles per hour, and other rides and games. Tel. 8354-5400.

Bioparque Estrella is a safari-style park where more than 700 animals representing 50 different species roam free. Located an hour outside the city, the park also has a number of rides and recreational facilities. Tel. 8190-3100.

Bullfights are held November to March at *Plaza Monumental* on Av. Universidad.

Side Trips

Just a 15-minute drive up the mountains from Monterrey's prosperous U.S.-style, two-car garage suburbs is *Chipinque National Park*, a popular weekend getaway, especially on hot summer days. Temperatures in this densely wooded area located 5,000 feet above sea level are on average 10 degrees cooler than they are in town. Residents aren't the only ones taking refuge here—you can spot blue jays, crested flycatchers living up to their name, and squirrels by the dozens feasting on the abundant nuggets that fall from the trees.

On Sundays, locals in jogging gear tackle the park's mountainside trails, earning the right to indulge in the hearty country-style breakfast buffet offered by the site's *Chipinque Hotel*. Named for the last Indian patriarch who lived on the plateau until driven out by the Spanish,

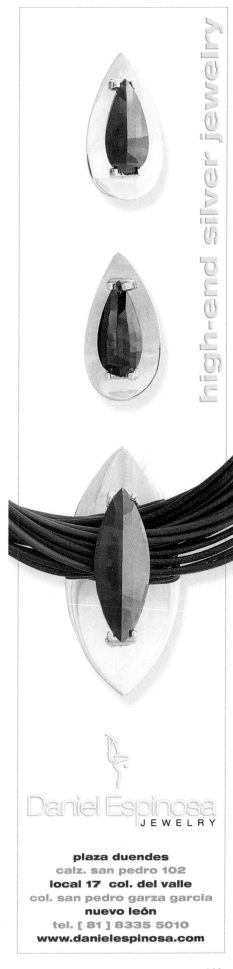

the park is also popular for its horseback riding, playgrounds and picnicking.

A 45-minute drive southwest of downtown Monterrey, off Route 6, are the *Garcia Caves*, a mile and a half of passageways and chambers. Cable cars go up *Friar's Mountain* to the cave entrance 2,500 feet above ground level. Daily 90-minute tours take you through well-lit winding passageways that snake through the 16 chambers within the mountain. On weekends, estimate an hour-and-a-half wait to get on a cable car.

Another natural attraction, *Cascada Cola de Caballo* (or Horse Tail Falls), is located 25 miles south, off Route 15. Horses are available for exploring the countryside around the spectacular 80-foot falls, including the charming, colonial village of *Santiago*, a lovely town with a central plaza and restored colonial buildings.

Hacienda Cola de Caballo now stands where the pecan-growing Hacienda Vista Hermosa prospered 50 years ago, and visitors can stop here for the night or a meal with a panoramic view. Tel. 8369-6644.

Nearby is *Presa La Boca* (Rodrigo Gomez Dam), where accommodations are available at the private aquatic club *Bahia Escondida*, a hideaway nestled among lush foothills sloping gently toward the reservoir. A beautiful, placid lake, formed by the dam, is a favorite swimming, water-skiing and boating site. Picnic grounds amid lovely greenery frame the lake.

Huasteca Canyon, a spectacular natural monument, is six miles south of Monterrey at

Cumbres de Monterrey National Park. The 1,000-foot canyon is a giant maze of rock formations and strangely-shaped mountain ridges where prehistoric people left pictographs on rock faces thousands of years ago.

The terrain around Monterrey is ideal for outdoor sports such as mountain climbing, biking and trekking. For information about these excursions, call *Aventur* at 8335-6119.

Dining

Monterrey is carnivore country and the two most popular local dishes are *cabrito*, roast kid, and *machaca*, shredded dried beef.

Machaca is popular breakfast fare, most commonly mixed with scrambled eggs. You may also find *carne seca* on the menu, sheets of dried beef similar in taste to beef jerky.

Cabrito is both expensive and somewhat heavy, making it more of a dish to be served and savored at special occasions, like Sunday family gatherings. To make cabrito, a young goat, about 40 days old, is roasted for three to four hours over a mesquite fire.

Following are some of the leading restaurants:

Barandales
Radisson Gran Ancira Hotel, downtown
Tel. 8345-7575
The Ancira's elegant turn-of-the-century restaurant, located in the majestic lobby, features exquisite buffets and a Sunday champagne brunch. Live music.

El Granero Grill
Calz. del Valle 333 Ote.
Tel. 8378-4408
In Garza Garcia. One of the city's leading restaurants offers a wide ranging menu, from Mexican specialties to sushi, served in an attractive mountain lodge-style setting. Specialties include prime rib, shrimp-stuffed mushrooms, stuffed peppers in a pastry shell, cabrito *estofado* (stew), and orange duck. Open 12:30 p.m. to 12:30 a.m.; to 11:30 p.m. Sunday.

El Paraiso
Gomez Morin 305 Sur

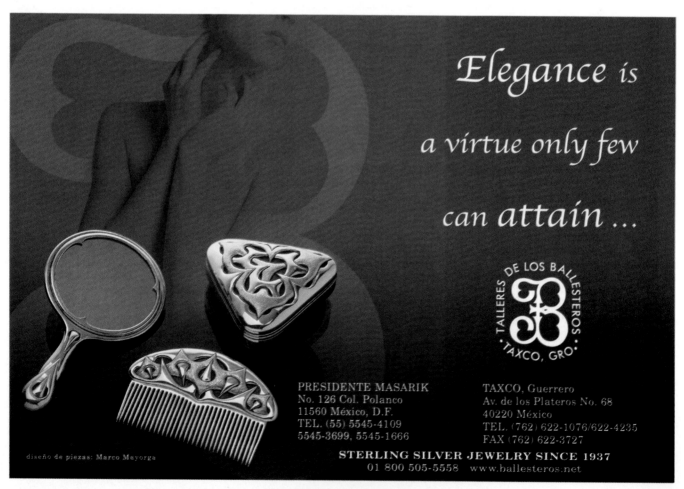

Tel. 8356-6690
In Del Valle Campestre. A grand setting for gourmet international cuisine. Try the duck in black cherry sauce. Open noon to 1 a.m.; to 6 p.m. Sunday.

El Tio
Hidalgo 1746 Pte., downtown
Tel. 8346-0291
A thriving family-run business since 1931 thanks to the excellent food, service and personalized management (today *tio's* nephew manages the restaurant). Lunch is served in a spacious dining room decorated with bullfighting memorabilia, and dinner is enjoyed in a romantic, candle-lit garden patio. Regional dishes such as *cabrito* and *carne seca* are the specialty, but great care goes into everything, including the fresh seafood, soups, salads and homemade desserts, all served in generous portions. Ample wine list. Open 12:30 p.m. to 12:30 a.m.

Il Capriccio
Enrique C. Livas 315
Tel. 8348-4374
In Colonia Vista Hermosa. Authentic Italian fare served in a cozy setting. Menu features homemade pastas and mesquite-burning brick-oven pizzas. Branch also in Villa de Santiago (tel. 2285-3045).

La Casa de Sandor
Crowne Plaza Hotel, downtown
Tel. 8319-6010
A restaurant-bar popular with residents as well as visitors. Open 1 to 11 p.m.; from 6 p.m. Saturday; closed Sunday.

La Catarina
Morones Prieto 2525
Tel. 8345-3357
The place to go for a memorable Mexican meal. Open 1 p.m. to 2 a.m.; to 6 p.m. Sunday.

Los Continentes
Presidente InterContinental Hotel
Tel. 8368-6000
In Garza Garcia. International cuisine served in an attractive setting.

Los Vitrales
Sheraton Ambassador Hotel, downtown
Tel. 8380-7000
This handsome restaurant, located in the lobby, under a lovely stained-glass ceiling, offers excellent international and regional cuisine. Wonderful breakfast buffets, great service. Open 24 hours a day.

Luisiana
Hidalgo 530 Ote., downtown
Tel. 8343-1561
Centrally located near the leading hotels. A favorite of Monterrey's movers and shakers, and for good reason. This elegant but casual restaurant serves fine continental cuisine and luscious desserts. Outstanding service. Open daily, noon to midnight.

Pangea
Bosque del Valle 110-20
Tel. 8114-6601
In Garza Garcia. Pangea's fine international fare and handsome setting has attracted a loyal clientele. Menu highlights include the tomato tower stacked with avocado and goat cheese in a basil vinaigrette, smoked salmon pizzeta with sour cream and capers, and glazed salmon fillet with a hint of ginger and soy sauce. Open 1 p.m. to midnight. Closed Sunday.

Quinta Real
Quinta Real Hotel
Tel. 8368-1000
In Garza Garcia. A truly elegant setting for enjoying refined international and regional dishes. Piano and violin duet at dinner. Open 6 a.m. to midnight.

Wall Street
Presidente InterContinental Hotel
Tel. 8368-6000
In Garza Garcia. An American-style steak house featuring prime cuts of beef prepared to your exact order. Open Monday to Saturday for breakfast and dinner, Sundays all day.

Nightlife
Nightlife in Monterrey thrives at the major hotels and, increasingly, in the Barrio Antiguo.

In fact, the Barrio joints have been drawing so many revelers that some of the streets are now closed to traffic in the evenings.

One of the most popular venues in the Barrio is *La Fonda de San Miguel*, at Morelos 924. This lively bar features rock bands playing to an invariably packed and receptive house—as the night progresses, so do the spontaneous sing-alongs. Tel. 8342-6659.

For a truly *norteño* night out, try the *Far West Rodeo*, located at Av. Los Angeles 309 (tel. 8351-3030). This rodeo-disco features a huge dance hall, country-and-western music, rodeo show, and lots of dancing cowboys and cowgirls.

Carlos n' Charlie's is a favorite nighttime watering hole for the young set, especially on Thursdays. *Havana*, San Pedro 202 in Del Valle (tel. 8401-2020), is the current rage. El Tio restaurant has a separate, inviting bar area, *El Campanario*.

Among popular hotel nightspots is the Sheraton's *Le Pavillon* bar, for listening to soft jazz and Bohemian music (open 6:30 p.m. to 2 a.m., except Monday). Quinta Real's posh, elegantly-appointed bar, *Los Murales*, features alternating sets with a guitarist or romantic trio from 7 p.m. to midnight, except Sundays. The Presidente InterContinental's *Fifth Avenue Bar* also features live music.

Shopping

Monterrey's premier shopping centers are *Galerias Monterrey*, at Gonzalitos and Insurgentes, *Plaza San Agustin*, at Real de San Agustin 222, in Garza Garcia, and the newly-opened *Valle Oriente*, at Lazaro Cardenas 1000. Downtown, five blocks of Calle Morelos were paved with brick, closed to traffic and turned into a shopping promenade called *Plaza Morelos*. Nearby is the two-story *Patio Santa Rosa* mall.

Antique lovers should visit *Villa Amadeus*, a Romanesque-style villa displaying works of art and antiques from around the world. Collected by antique dealer Horacio Saenz, the antiques are lovingly distributed throughout the rambling mansion located on Calzada del Valle 109 Ote., in Garza Garcia. Tel. 8378-2874.

Daniel Espinosa Jewelry, at Plaza Duendes (8335-5010), features bold, contemporary designs in silver, including many pieces with semiprecious stones. Espinosa's creativity and sense of fun is evident in his tie-style chokers made of silver, hypnotic silver rings with black enamel swirls, and other unique items.

Talleres de los Ballesteros features sterling silver jewelry, silverware, table settings and decorative accents for the home, all crafted by the famed Taxco-based Ballesteros family of silversmiths. For pearls and gems, visit *Aplijsa* at the Presidente InterContinental Hotel (8363-3533).

Monterrey has several fine galleries. *Galeria Ramis Barquet*, at Real de San Agustin 302, in Garza Garcia (8363-2802), deals in contemporary international art. Famed Mexican sculptor *Sergio Bustamante* maintains a gallery at Plaza San Agustin (8368-4832), featuring his fantastic animal sculptures and jewelry.

An interesting selection of Mexican handicrafts and folk art can be found at *Carapan*, opposite the Sheraton Ambassador Hotel. The different rooms display a little of everything, from Talavera pottery to silver jewelry. Tel. 8345-4422.

A traditional stop on guided tours of the city is *Cesar's Mexican Arts & Crafts*, at Isaac Garza Ote. 900. Tel. 8374-1854.

At *Tequilarte*, a restaurant-bar at Padre Mier and Dr. Coss (8340-4003), you can find premium tequilas as well as books on Mexico's national drink.

Hotels

Chipinque
Meseta de Chipinque 1000
Tel. (81) 8378-1100
20 minutes from the downtown area, in a national park. A mountain-top hotel with a friendly atmosphere and a great view of the city. There are 60 cozy rooms with satellite TV, phone, fireplace and heating distributed in rustic stone cabins. Restaurant with panoramic view, bar, swimming pool and jacuzzi, tennis, gym, steam room and sauna, meeting facilities for 300. Rates MD.

Crowne Plaza
Constitucion 300 Ote., downtown
Tel. (81) 8319-6000
A popular and bustling lobby bar lends this hotel a party atmosphere almost round the clock. The modern, atrium-style, 18-story tower has 403 rooms with cable TV and double doors that keep out noise. Restaurants, nightclubs, pool, tennis, gym, sauna, business center, banquet and meeting facilities for 1,200 people. Rates FC.

DoubleTree Rio
Padre Mier 194 Pte., downtown
Tel. (81) 8344-9040
On the main plaza. This modern high-rise offers 394 rooms with cable TV, coffee maker, iron, ironing board. Heated pool, tennis court, gym, indoor parking, restaurant, lobby bar, meeting room and business center. Rates MD.

Fiesta Americana Centro
Corregidora 519 Ote., downtown
Tel. (81) 8319-0900
This hotel has 207 rooms with cable TV, minibar, sofa bed, dataport. Business center, banquet facilities, restaurant-cafe, lobby bar, small indoor pool and gym. (Also Fiesta Inn Centro and Fiesta Inn Valle). Rates MD.

Hilton Garden Inn
Antonio L. Rodriguez 1880 Pte.
Tel. (81) 8122-8000
www.hiltongardeninn.com/monterrey
A modern hotel for the business traveler with 150 comfortable rooms with work stations, cable TV; meeting facilities for small groups, restaurant and lounge. Indoor pool and whirlpool, gym. Parking. Rates MD.

Holiday Inn Parque Fundidora
Privada Parque Fundidora 100

Tel. (81) 8369-6000
Adjoining the Cintermex convention center via a covered walkway. There are 250 rooms, restaurant, lobby bar, pool, sun deck, tennis, gym, banquet and meeting rooms, and business center. (Also Holiday Inn Express Tecnologico and Holiday Inn Monterrey Norte.) Rates MD.

Presidente InterContinental
Vasconcelos 300 Ote., in Garza Garcia
Tel. (81) 8368-6000
www.intercontinental.com
A modern hotel with 305 well appointed rooms with high speed Internet access, two-line phones, and coffee maker, among other amenities. Club floors and business rooms offer personalized service. Business center and fine convention hall. Two restaurants, popular Sunday buffet, lobby bar with music nightly. Fitness center with indoor pool and jacuzzi, spa services, tennis. Rates DX.

Quinta Real
Diego Rivera 500, in Garza Garcia
Tel. (81) 8368-1000
www.quintareal.com
Opposite Plaza San Agustin shopping center. This stunning colonial-style property brings luxurious accommodations to Monterrey. In fact, its lovely garden courtyard is the setting of choice for elegant local weddings. There are 165 exquisitely appointed suites in all, 40 in a new wing designed to cater to the top-level executive. Fine restaurant, stately bar, gym, spa, business center, and meeting and banquet facilities for up to 320 people. Rates FC.

Radisson Plaza Gran Ancira
Hidalgo and Escobedo, downtown
Tel. (81) 8150-7000
Near the main plaza. Graceful Belle Epoque architecture gives character to this grand hotel; legend has it that Pancho Villa hitched his horse in the cavernous lobby. There are 246 spacious rooms and suites with cable TV, popular cantina, pool, gym, business center, and meeting rooms for 750 people. Rates MD.

Santa Rosa Suites
Escobedo 930 Sur, downtown
Tel. (81) 8342-4200
www.mexicoboutiquehotels.com
More like an English-style townhouse with rooms to let than a hotel, this small property offers 29 junior and master suites. Courtesy valet service. Small meeting room, porterhouse steak restaurant-bar. Member of Mexico Boutique Hotels. Rates FC.

Sheraton Ambassador
Hidalgo 310 Ote., downtown
Tel. (81) 8380-7000
Near the main plaza. A downtown favorite with low-key Belle Epoque decor that reflects a sense of tradition and comfort that extends to the 239 spacious rooms and suites equipped with work stations. Business center, banquet and meeting facilities for more than 1,000. Superb restaurants, lobby bar. Fitness center, swimming pool, jacuzzi, jogging track, tennis court. Rates FC.

Maya World

Millenniums ago, the Maya created a civilization now considered one of the most important ever to exist in the ancient world. In an extraordinary burst of creativity which lasted around 600 years, they built immense cities, temples and pyramids, created a huge trade network and made breakthroughs in the arts and sciences that placed them leagues ahead of their contemporaries. Then, for reasons unknown, their culture went into decline and their cities were abandoned.

To appreciate and understand a little more about the ancient Maya and their civilization, travelers can visit the remnants of their cities and ceremonial centers. The areas they reigned—collectively known as the Mundo Maya, or Maya World—include the five Mexican states of Chiapas, Tabasco, Yucatan, Campeche and Quintana Roo, as well as the Central American countries of Guatemala, Belize, Honduras and El Salvador.

Chiapas

Though it is one of the country's more impoverished regions, the southernmost state of Chiapas is rich in ways that cannot be measured in monetary terms. It is rich in cultural and ethnic diversity, and wildlife.

The state capital, *Tuxtla Gutierrez*, is the center of a thriving coffee-growing region and home of Mexico's famed marimba music. Accessible by air service from Mexico City, Tuxtla offers a good base for exploring picturesque villages where pre-Hispanic customs have survived.

To see the state's variety of wildlife there is no better place than the *Miguel Alvarez del Toro Zoo*. It is acclaimed for exhibiting only animals native to the region and for faithfully preserving their natural habitat. A number of the animals are extremely rare, including the beautiful quetzal bird, with its long train of tail feathers.

Also worth visiting is *Sumidero Canyon*. The Alquimia Group, operator of such major parks in Mexico as Xcaret, Xel-Ha and El Garrafon,

Temple of the Inscriptions, Palenque

Mexico Tourism Board

all in the Riviera Maya, is now operating the Sumidero Canyon Ecological Park. You can take two-hour river cruises along the 26-mile-long Grijalva River, which is flanked by towering canyon walls, some as high as 6,000 feet. There's also kayaking, mountain biking and hiking.

The nearby town of *Chiapa de Corzo* serves as a departure point for the boats, and has a few attractions of its own, including an impressive Moorish fountain and the former Convent of Santo Domingo, which now houses the *Museum of Enamel*. At *El Campanario*, a restaurant on the main plaza, you can try some of the regional specialties, including *cochito*, a delicious pork dish, and *chipilin*, a hearty soup made with corn dumplings.

Tuxtla's leading hotel, *Camino Real*, offers two great restaurants; *Montebello*, specializing in fine cuts of beef and lobster (closed Sunday), and *Azulejos*, specializing in regional dishes. At night bands entertain in the lobby bar.

San Cristobal de las Casas

San Cristobal de las Casas is a characteristically indigenous Chiapaneca town nestled in the heart of the state's jungle highlands, at a 7,200-foot elevation. It's a short flight from Tuxtla Gutierrez, or a scenic two-hour drive away. The winding, ascending road offers a pleasant way to arrive at this mountain top town. En route, the tropical heat and plant life prevalent in Tuxtla gradually give way to the nippy mountain air and pine forests that surround San Cristobal, where days are sunny and warm, and nights chilly, or even cold when it rains.

Shortly after arriving in San Cristobal, the town's singular 17th-century *cathedral* comes into view, standing adjacent to the main plaza. Breathtakingly unconventional, it is a festive mixture of Spanish baroque architecture and naïf indigenous art. The combination appears to be a compromise between a Spanish colonial aesthetic and an Indian one, with the native influence having clearly gained the upper hand.

By contrast, the stately 17th-century *Church and Convent of Santo Domingo*, near the municipal market, is a gorgeous example of unadulterated classic European baroque architecture, with its highly ornate carved facade and gold leaf covered interiors. Both of these unique temples are dazzling in their own way. It is the cathedral, however, that best symbolizes San Cristobal, where unlike many other parts of the country the indigenous presence is overwhelming.

As a market town, San Cristobal draws Indians from surrounding areas who come to sell their hand-woven goods and earthenware. The most prominent group are the Chamulas, members of the Tzotzil and Tzeltal Mayan tribes. On most days, the grounds around Santo Domingo are turned into an outdoor market where Chamula women, wearing their distinctive blue tops, and black woolen skirts and serapes, display stacks of fine hand-loomed fabrics, from richly embroidered cotton tablecloths and pillowcases to thick woolen sweaters.

San Juan Chamula and *Zinacantan* are interesting nearby towns and guided tours (some on horseback) are readily available. Chamula is located just eight miles north of San Cristobal. A small collection of stands near the town square has interesting samples of coarse woolen jackets and cotton tops. But the town's main attraction is its church, ordinary enough on the outside, but highly unusual inside, where the Chamula practice an intriguing blend of Christianity and ancient Indian religious beliefs.

Another of Chiapas' well-known indigenous groups are the Lacandon Indians. Living deep in the Chiapas rain forest, the Lacandon have resisted the changes of the 20th century more successfully than probably any other indigenous group in North America.

Today there are only about 600 Lacandon left and they maintain a symbolic presence in San Cristobal through *Na Bolom*, the museum, library, research center and guest house which was once the home of the late scholar-photographer Gertrude Duby Blom, widow of famed

Agua Azul cascades

Mexico Tourism Board

archaeologist Franz Blom. Duby Blom won international acclaim for her efforts to preserve the isolated Lacandon Maya and their way of life. "Na Bolom," a playful corruption of the couple's surname, means "House of the Tiger"

in Tzotzil. Located at Av. Vicente Guerrero 33, Na Bolom is open Tuesday through Sunday. English-language tours of the grounds are given at 4:30 p.m. Here you can also inquire about guided tours to other sites of interest. Tel. 678-1418.

Amber, the translucent stone derived from fossilized coniferous resin, is plentiful in the region, and attractive shops in town display creative jewelry fashioned out of silver and the ancient rock. To find out more, visit the *Amber Museum*, at Ex-Convento La Merced, where displays illustrate, among other things, the different types of amber found around the world, and its mining and extraction. Tel. 678-9716.

Recommended hotels include *Casa Mexicana, Casavieja* and *Flamboyant Español*. Leading restaurants include the Swiss-owned *Plaza Real,* and *El Faisan*, featuring regional (Tzotzil-style) dishes in a pleasant refurbished building.

Calle Real de Guadalupe is to San Cristobal what Fifth Avenue is to New York—the length of this major street is flanked with shops, many selling amber jewelry.

Horseback excursions can be arranged over winding mountain trails. By car, a favorite destination is the *Lakes of Montebello,* located practically on the border with Guatemala. This is one of Mexico's loveliest areas, with a chain of lakes in myriad colors.

Drop by the State Tourism Office at Miguel Hidalgo 2, about half a block from the main plaza. They have a stock of travel brochures on San Cristobal. Tel. 678-6570.

The Ruins

The Mayan ruins of *Bonampak* and *Yaxchilan,* in the west of the state, near the border with Guatemala, are reachable from San Cristobal and Palenque by road or charter flights.

Bonampak, Mayan for "Painted Walls," is known for its striking murals depicting bloody scenes of preparation for warfare and actual battles. If you do not have the chance to visit the real thing, reproductions of the murals are on display at Mexico City's Museum of Anthropology, at Chetumal's Museum of Mayan Culture, and in Villahermosa.

From Bonampak, a 45-minute boat ride on the Usumacinta River separating Mexico from Guatemala brings you to Yaxchilan, set amid jungle in the heart of Classic Mayan territory. Known as the home of the "decapitated god," a Buddhalike stone sculpture whose severed head lies close by, it appears to have reached its apogee around 750 A.D. under the rule of Bird Jaguar and been abandoned in the 10th century.

Closer to Palenque, about 120 kilometers or 75 miles south, are the less well known but equally impressive ruins of *Tonina,* which means "the stone house" in the Mayan Tzeltal tongue, and its on-site museum. Home to fascinating high reliefs in stone and stucco depicting monsters of the underworld, Tonina's tall acropolis also offers a spectacular panoramic view of the surrounding fertile fields.

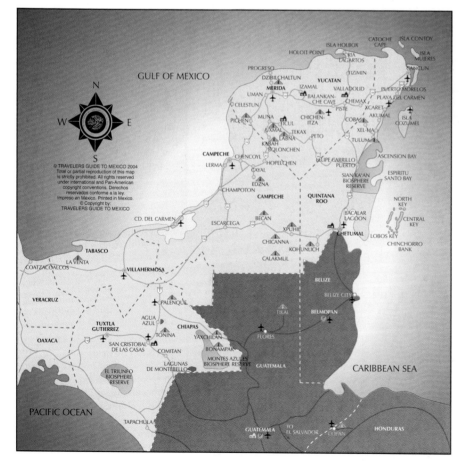

Tabasco

Today this region bears little evidence of its historical significance as the New World's cradle of civilization. It does, however, claim some of the most beautiful unspoiled landscapes in Mexico, marked by tall palms, limpid lagoons, and snowy egrets. With an abundance of rivers, streams and waterfalls—more than half the state's territory is covered by water—Tabasco is probably similar to South Florida before it was settled.

In a marshy delta across the state line, in neighboring Veracruz, is *La Venta*, one of three major Olmec sites and the most accessible. But even here there is little to see; the principal pieces are on display at La Venta Archaeological Park and Museum in Tabasco's capital, Villahermosa.

Other nearby Olmec sites are *San Lorenzo* and *Tres Zapotes*. About 88 kilometers/55 miles north is the westernmost Mayan site, *Comalcalco*, where kiln-fired bricks were used for construction in an area lacking stone.

Tabasco, which begins at the Tonala River, just east of Coatzacoalcos, can be reached from Oaxaca via the Trans-Isthmus Highway, or from Tuxtla Gutierrez, Chiapas, or, as most tourists prefer, via the approach from Veracruz. There is also air service connecting Mexico City with Villahermosa.

Villahermosa

This region's petroleum industry spurred the growth of the state capital, Villahermosa, into a bustling tropical metropolis. The city takes advantage of the *Grijalva River* for much of its trade, especially with the interior of the state, and a broad boulevard follows the western bank. The river is usually busy with river boats carrying people and produce to and from the interior or the gulf port city of Frontera, 73 kilometers/46 miles north. Each May an international speedboat marathon is held on the Grijalva.

Villahermosa's most famous site is *La Venta Archaeological Park and Museum,* located between Paseo Grijalva and Laguna de las Ilusiones Park. This unique outdoor museum features the massive sculptures, particularly the giant Olmec stone heads, found in La Venta jungle. Here numerous ancient stone carvings are on display in a natural jungle setting similar to where they were found, with bushy-tailed animals scampering about and a variety of birds residing in the trees. The colossal 18-ton heads, altars and mosaic jaguar masks are outstanding. There is a small indoor exhibit area with maps worth looking at and a gift shop halfway through the park trail with a nice selection of handicrafts. It takes about two hours to comfortably see everything. The museum-park is open daily from 8 a.m. to 4 p.m.

The immense *Research Center for Olmec and Mayan Cultures* (CICOM) includes a museum of native costumes, library, classrooms, the state theater, restaurants and the *Carlos Pellicer Camara Regional Museum.* The museum has a fairly impressive collection of archaeological artifacts representing the state's important gulf coast cultures, and is open daily from 10 a.m. to 1 p.m. and 5 to 8 p.m.

The *Museum of Popular Culture* displays items relating to music and dance in Tabasco—costumes, instruments, masks—and household utensils, as well as rotating temporary exhibits. There is also a *Casita Chontal,* a reproduction of a typical home and furnishings used by the Chontal Indians. The museum is open weekdays from 9 a.m. to 8 p.m.

An interesting outing on the Grijalva River is offered by the floating restaurant *Capitan Beulo*, named after a Tabascan who was captain of the boat when it served originally as a floating clinic. The Beulo offers three excursions a day, at about midday, late afternoon and evening, from Tuesday through Sunday, featuring excellent regional cuisine.

Construction began on the Villahermosa *cathedral* in March of 1963, and still continues. Of Corinthian design, its 230-foot steeples are reportedly the tallest in Mexico.

The downtown *Zona Luz* (Zone of Lights), with tiled roads open only to pedestrians, is a good place for a beguiling walk through streets lined with shops and dotted with caged parrots.

Tabasco 2000 is an urban complex with a zoo, planetarium and shopping center. Good handicrafts—particularly woven palm and wood carvings—can be found at *El Baul.* A spectacular sight at dusk is the flight of millions of birds returning to roost in the city's trees.

Villahermosa has two excellent hotels: the *Hyatt Regency,* a nine-story deluxe hotel across from La Venta Park, and the *Camino Real,* an attractive 11-story property adjoining the Tabasco 2000 shopping center. Other good hotels are the *Calinda Viva* and the *Cencali.*

When eating out, you're bound to find *pejelagarto* on the menu. Called gar in English, this ugly but delicious mutation between a fish and an alligator is considered a delicacy and prepared in many different ways. Markets sell the fish usually already grilled.

Restaurants featuring Tabascan cuisine and seafood include the renowned *Los Tulipanes*, in the cultural center, and *Meson del Duende.* The Camino Real's *Azulejos* offers lavish breakfast and dinner buffets featuring local and international dishes, and *Bougainvillea,* at the Hyatt, serves delicious regional and international cuisine in a refined setting.

Night spots include the Hyatt's *Flamboyan* lobby bar, featuring live music, and *La Plataforma*, a video bar resembling an oil refinery.

Cacao, the bean chocolate is derived from, flourishes in this tropical climate, and you can visit a nearby plantation and see how it's processed and packaged for making hot chocolate. Indians used the prized cacao bean as currency, even after the arrival of the Spanish, and a gold peso could be exchanged for about 1,500 beans.

Set on 250 spectacular acres of jungle, savanna and lagoon, just minutes from the Villahermosa airport, is *Yumka'* (in the Chontal culture, Yumka' is the dwarf that protects flora and fauna). It is a nature study center-cum-wildlife park in which the wild animals roam free on land resembling their natural habitat, while the humans are confined to special safarilike vehicles.

Palenque

Located in Chiapas, but more easily reached via an excellent highway from Villahermosa, 144 kilometers/90 miles to the northwest, is one of the most significant and beautiful

Giant Olmec head, Villahermosa

Bruce Herman

archaeological sites anywhere. Its pyramid structures feature intricately carved bas-reliefs depicting historical and mythical events relating to the reign of a Mayan ruler, Lord Pacal, and his descendants.

Though today Palenque is shrouded in the mists of a tropical jungle, from 500 to 800 A.D. it was a major power in the Mayan world. Dominating the site is the *Temple of the Inscriptions*, so named because of the wall of hieroglyphics at its summit. In 1952 Mexican archaeologist Alberto Ruz Lhuillier investigated some holes in a slab of the temple floor and discovered a stairway, then filled with rubble, leading to the tomb of a ruler since identified as Lord Pacal (615-683 A.D.). The lid of his sarcophagus is a work of art and is on view in the tomb.

The next building is the *Palace,* with multi-level chambers, hallways and patios decorated with now-crumbling stucco figures. Acid rain and dust from a volcanic eruption a few years ago have destroyed much of the delicate artwork. On a wall near the main staircase is an oval tablet depicting Pacal's accession to power, a royal headdress being presented to him by his mother, Lady Zac-Kuk. In one corner of the Palace is a reconstructed square tower affording a view of the entire area, but currently closed to visitors.

On a nearby hill is a complex built by Chan-Bahlum, son of Pacal. It is believed his tomb is beneath one of the buildings. Some of the area's most outstanding art is at the Anthropology Museum in Mexico City, but an on-site museum houses many fine pieces, including beautiful hieroglyphics.

Recently uncovered, and still not open to the public, are several tombs dating back about 1,200 years. The most spectacular of the tombs includes a mortuary chamber with an underground staircase leading to one of the main temples.

At the entrance to Palenque, Lacandon and Chamula Indians in native dress sell bows and arrows, and colorful hand-woven belts and bags. Other souvenirs here are reproductions of Palenque art hand carved on small stone slabs or burned into a feltlike fabric. You can see them being made at *La Cañada,* a small bungalow hotel-restaurant owned by the Morales family. The food is good, and the family has catered to countless archaeologists, so they have lots of stories. Art historian Dr. Merle Greene Robertson's research center is across the street.

On the road to the site is a lovely hotel, *Chan-Kah Resort Village,* with rustic-chic Mayan-style bungalows, a good restaurant and an attractively landscaped pool. Another lovely hotel is the *Ciudad Real Palenque,* located about 10 kilometers/6 miles from the site.

In town, next to the main plaza, is a sister hotel to the Chan-Kah called *Chan-Kah Centro.* A bit removed from the center of town is *Mision Palenque,* an attractive hotel with a pool, restaurant and bar. Just outside of town, on the road to Ocosingo, is *Calinda Nututun Palenque,* a pleasant hotel with a natural river-made swimming area.

A good restaurant near the ruins is *La Selva,* serving both regional and international cuisine in an attractive tropical setting. *Mero-Lec,* a small, popular restaurant-bar on La Cañada street, in town, offers a charming, candle-lit setting in the evenings for dinner or drinks.

Other good restaurants include *Innominado,* on Cinco de Mayo, and *Tulija,* Km. 27, Palenque Highway. Good regional specialties are served at *Maya,* Independencia 5.

About an hour's drive south of Palenque are the beautiful *Agua Azul Cascades,* a great place to go after a visit to the ruins for a refreshing swim, a picnic, or just to admire the unusual blue of the cascades. Rock formations break up the flow of water into a series of calm pools that are wonderful for wading. The water is freezing, but the weather is hot, and the combination terrific.

Visitors can follow a trail up the hill to the source of the cascade. Set aside about two hours for the hike and a swim.

(Continued from page 307)
And Yucatecos prefer their elaborate regional dishes to the foreigner's hamburgers.

Their loose, cotton clothing is ideal in this warm, humid climate. Men wear pleated white or pastel shirts called *guayaberas,* often embroidered in the color of the fabric, and women use the traditional white, richly embroidered *huipil* and underlying slip, or *justan.*

The flat countryside is covered with scrub brush and henequen, the spiky plant used to make rope, hammocks and baskets. Beginning in the 1950s, plastic supplanted henequen for many of these products, severely affecting the Yucatecan economy. Poor soil and lack of rain make farming difficult; corn is and always has been the main staple.

Campeche

Long a favorite spot for hunters and fishermen, Campeche is beginning to attract tourists with its culture and history. Today travelers come to discover its charming colonial capital and Mayan archaeological treasures, including *Edzna, Chicanna, Xpuhil, Calakmul* and *Becan.*

A town of about 50,000 people, the capital, also called Campeche, was neglected for years, its colonial-era homes crumbling and dilapidated. Now pretty pastel-colored facades with white trim and delicate wrought-iron balconies line the cobblestone streets of the renovated downtown area. UNESCO recently declared the city a World Heritage Site. Old-fashioned street cars offer one-hour tours of the city center, departing from the main plaza at 6 and 8 p.m.

Located on the Gulf of Mexico, the city was the principal seaport on the Yucatan Peninsula from the 16th to the 18th centuries, and subsequently a major target of pirates such as Lorenzillo, Diego "The Mulatto" and William Parker.

To protect the port from attacks, the Spanish Crown ordered the fortification of the city. Remnants of the original fortress that surrounded the entire town still stand, including ramparts and gates, giving the city a decidedly romantic, swashbuckling air. The ramparts now house museums and the Land Gate is the site of a dramatic light and sound show that relives the pirate era.

Campeche is famed for its seafood and one of the most traditional restaurants in town is *La Pigua,* where the specialty is delicious coconut-battered jumbo shrimp. The city is also famous for its fiestas, the largest being the pre-Lenten carnival celebrations. *Fiesta de San Roman* in September and *Fiesta de San Francisco* in October are also popular.

Improved infrastructure, including better roads and hotels, have made it easier to visit the state's as yet little-known but remarkable archaeological sites. Tours to Edzna, the closest major ruin to Campeche, located just 55 kilometers/34 miles away, depart daily from Baluarte Santiago (Santiago Rampart) at 9 a.m. and 2 p.m.

Ciudad del Carmen, southwest of Campeche, is a charming, small fishing village of 15,000 with palm-shaded plazas, fishnets set out to dry, beautiful beaches and excellent seafood restaurants. The city is Mexico's chief gulf shrimp fishing center, and is popular with anglers for tarpon fishing.

Quintana Roo

Quintana Roo became a state in 1975. The jungle territory on the Caribbean side of the Yucatan Peninsula is sparsely populated, with endless miles of sandy beaches and numerous Mayan ruins. Between 2,000 and 2,500 archaeological sites have been identified throughout the Yucatan Peninsula—most of them have yet to be explored.

Cancun, Cozumel, Isla Mujeres are the state's best known destinations. The state capital, *Chetumal,* is located on the border with Belize. A small waterfront city with wide boulevards and two-story homes painted in pastel shades, Chetumal's biggest attraction is its impressive *Museo de la Cultura Maya.* The museum depicts the everyday life and spiritual practices of the Maya through engaging interactive multimedia exhibits.

Recommended hotels include *Los Cocos* and *Holiday Inn Puerta Maya.*

The city is well situated as a base for exploring the nearby archaeological zone of *Kohunlich,* as well as *Chicanna, Xpuhil, Calakmul* and *Becan,* in neighboring Campeche. A different lodging option for visitors to these sites is offered by *Chicanna Ecovillage,* an environmentally-friendly hotel in the jungle.

Chetumal's beaches and lagoons (including *Bacalar,* known as "The Lake of the Seven Colors") are ideal for water sports. Nearby is a beautiful freshwater sinkhole, *Cenote Azul,* with intense blue waters. Its exact depth has not yet been determined. Just a few miles off the coast is one of the world's top dive sites, 26-mile-long, 10-mile-wide *Chinchorro Reef.*

The Yucatan Peninsula

The Yucatan Peninsula is the land of the Maya—another Mexico, a country within a country. Its ancient cities, now in ruins, stand as monuments to one of history's greatest civilizations. Not that the Maya belong in the dustbin of history. Theirs is a living race; most *Yucatecos* still speak the clipped Mayan language, and their distinctive facial features attest to their ancestral heritage.

A giant land mass jutting out between the Gulf of Mexico and the Caribbean Sea, the Yucatan Peninsula includes the states of Yucatan, Campeche and Quintana Roo. The peninsula is actually a limestone shelf, honeycombed with underground rivers, caverns and sinkholes which form giant freshwater wells, called *cenotes* in Spanish.

Far from Pacific coast and Sierra Madre earthquake faults, the peninsula's only problem with Mother Nature is a rare Caribbean hurricane. The area is comprised of vast expanses of green jungle, pristine beaches, villages peppered with typical Mayan thatched huts, colonial cities such as Merida and Valladolid, modern resorts such as Cancun and Cozumel, and magnificent archaeological sites, many still unexplored.

For centuries this region was isolated from the rest of Mexico by dense jungles, rivers, lagoons and immense swamps. Only in the latter half of the 20th century have some of the area's treasures been brought to the world's attention.

History

The Mayan chronicle began more than 3,000 years ago along the coast of present-day Belize, where nomadic ancestors of the Maya came to settle. By the time of Christ they were building cities and ceremonial centers bigger than any in Europe. By the 10th century A.D. their civilization had largely vanished. No one knows exactly why.

During the Classic period, 600-900 A.D., the Maya built towering monuments to their gods, engaged in far-reaching trade, conducted warfare, and studied the stars and planets, using astronomy to guide their spiritual lives and establish agricultural cycles. Many scholars have said the Maya were obsessed with time.

The Maya understood the concept of zero, which eluded the Greeks and Romans.

For years scholars have puzzled over Mayan hieroglyphic writing. In addition to stone and wood carvings, the Maya produced numerous codices and books written on bark paper, recording astrological and other information. The conquering Spaniards were quick to denounce these writings as "works of the devil." Diego de Landa, a zealous Franciscan friar and later Bishop of Yucatan, publicly burned the

Kohunlich, a unique Mayan site near Chetumal

codices in the town square of Mani, south of Merida, in July of 1562. The Maya were forced to convert to Catholicism and abandon traditional rituals central to their culture.

Only three Mayan codices are known to have survived, and all of them are in foreign museums. The codices remained largely mute until only very recently, when several scholars of Mayan civilization succeeded in decoding portions.

Around 1000 A.D., the Toltecs, a warring tribe from Central Mexico, conquered a Mayan civilization in decline. Their carvings of warriors and war scenes are superimposed over the original Mayan ones.

One hundred years before the Spanish arrived, the Maya-Toltecs abandoned the main religious centers and returned to subsistence living. The causes of the Maya-Toltec decline are still hotly debated. But experts agree it may have been a combination of factors, including a lack of sufficient arable land and water to support a growing population, increasing hostilities against other cities, class conflicts, disease and outside agitation.

Despite their decline, the descendants of the Maya proved difficult for the Spanish to conquer. Francisco Cordoba met strong resistance when he and his Spanish expedition landed at Cozumel in 1517, and again at Campeche. Scores died on both sides, but the Spanish survivors returned to Cuba carrying significant relics, including gold, that would inspire their countrymen to return in force.

It wasn't until 1528 that the Spanish seriously undertook to conquer the Yucatan. Don Francisco de Montejo, sponsored by Spain's King Carlos V, began a campaign that his son concluded in 1542 with the defeat of the Maya.

The Spanish built the cities of Merida and Campeche (on top of existing Mayan cities), began cattle and sheep raising, and made virtual serfs of the Indians.

Yucatecos got a chance to break away from three centuries of misery following the 1821 War of Independence, which freed Mexico from Spain. Independent-minded Yucatan separated from Mexico a few times in the following decades and as late as 1907 tried to join the United States.

But even after the Spanish left, the wealthy *ladino* landholders did not. Huge haciendas were constructed to support the henequen (sisal) industry, fueled by virtual slave labor. Stately mansions were built in Merida, mainly on Paseo de Montejo, and frequent trips to Europe—especially France—by the wealthy resulted in the marked French architectural influence that is still noticeable in Merida.

Discontent among the Maya finally exploded in 1847 in the long and bloody War of the Castes. Yucatan would not see peace until 1901, when the last dissident outpost of a particularly fierce Mayan group was captured by the Mexican army.

Following the Mexican Revolution early in this century, land reforms enabled the natives to work land for themselves and this stability gradually integrated Yucatan with the rest of the country.

Yucatan

Yucatan's descendants of the Maya and the Spanish have a strong respect for custom and tradition. Many Maya still practice nature worship, although it remains veiled in Catholicism.

(Continued on page 306)

Merida

La Ermita Church

larly in the cuisine offered at many restaurants.

Quite unusual for Mexico is Merida's system of naming streets *(calles)*. Except for a few major avenues, most streets are numbered rather than named, with even ones running north-south, odd ones east-west. You'll often see addresses written as follows: Calle 57 No. 485 x 58 y 56, which means "485 57th street, between 58th and 56th streets."

Merida's weather is hot and steamy in the summer until predictable afternoon rains lead to comfortable evenings. It is cooler in the winter, with occasional nighttime winds making it chilly enough for a sweater.

What to See and Do

Begin your tour of the city at *Plaza de Arma*, the elevated main square shaded by Indian laurels. An oasis of greenery that is especially pleasant toward evening, it invites you to sit on a *confidente,* one of its S-shaped, love seat-style benches, enjoy an ice cream, have your shoes shined, read the newspaper, and watch other people do the same.

The *cathedral*, completed in 1598, is the largest in Yucatan. The *Government Palace*, on the north side, is the seat of the state government, and the *Municipal Palace*, on the west side, is the city hall. On the south side is the *Casa de Montejo*, built by the Spanish family that founded the city in 1542. Of particular interest is the stone carvings above the entrance, depicting armorclad conquistadors standing with each foot firmly planted on the head of a Mayan Indian. The mansion now serves as the main branch of Banamex, a Mexican bank.

On Sunday, the main square explodes with activity. Streets are closed to automobile traffic, folk dancers twirl, marimba bands play, and Indian women sell handicrafts.

One block from the main plaza is *Parque Cepeda*, also known as *Parque Hidalgo*, where horse-drawn carriages called *calesas* offer leisurely rides through town. Two blocks north of the main square is the *University of Yucatan*, founded by Jesuits in 1618.

Within easy walking distance of the main plaza is Merida's wonderful *Municipal Market*. A vast complex of tiny stalls, shops and booths, this is where Mayan farmers, craftsmen and suppliers bring their goods. You'll find rare fruits and honey and, in a special handicrafts section, elaborately-embroidered huipils (the regional dress for women), matrimonial-size hammocks (big enough for two), and Panama-style hats.

At the corner of Paseo de Montejo and 43rd, in the stately mansion that formerly served as the governor's residence, is the *Museum of Anthropology and History*. In an area of such archaeological significance one expects the local museum to be good, and it is. It is a good idea to visit the museum both before and after seeing the ruins in order to put it all in perspective.

The *National Museum of Popular Art*, on Calle 59 between 50th and 48th, features fine examples of folk art from around the country, including some antiques. Other cultural attractions include the small *City Museum*, at 61st and

Built more than 450 years ago on the site of the ancient Mayan city of T'ho, Merida is the social and economic center, as well as the capital, of the state of Yucatan.

"The White City," as it is often called, probably derives its nickname from the whitewashed facades of colonial-era buildings. Though the name could have easily derived from the traditional garb of locals—the pleated *guayabera* shirt worn by men and lacy *huipil* dress worn by women.

Merida's downtown area features a large, tree-shaded central square. The city's main boulevard, Paseo Montejo, is home to impressive European-style mansions whose pastel shades and elaborate trim are reminiscent of lavishly iced wedding cakes.

Though a bustling city of about 700,000, Merida retains its colonial charm and has a laid-back tempo that delights visitors. It makes a good base from which to explore the Mayan archaeological sites of Chichen-Itza and Uxmal. Pink flamingo sanctuaries and swimmable crystal-clear *cenotes* (sinkholes) are some of the natural attractions of the Yucatan Peninsula that are easily accessible from Merida. Some of the cenotes are found in caves with centuries-old stalactite formations.

Founded in 1542 by Francisco de Montejo, Merida and all of the Yucatan remained virtually isolated until the middle of this century. Trade and commerce, based on the profitable henequen (or sisal) industry, were long directed toward the United States, Cuba and Europe. Wealthy *Yucatecos* were far more likely to visit Havana, or even Paris, than Mexico City.

Rope products are still produced here from the fiber of the ubiquitous henequen plant, but the advent of petroleum-derived nylon effec-tively wiped out the industry. Sisal, a tiny gulf coast village, gave its name to the fiber used to make everything from floor mats and hammocks to industrial cording and sacks.

Yucatan is dotted with plantation-style haciendas built in henequen's heyday. The 17th-century *Hacienda Yaxcopoil*, on the road to Uxmal, has been conserved and converted into a museum. One of the most interesting exhibits is the building itself, a reconstructed relic from another era, with a Moorish double arch at the entrance. Several former haciendas have been converted into deluxe hotels or restaurants.

It wasn't until 1951 that a railroad was completed linking Merida with Mexico City, and the highway was not opened until 1956. Previously, on the rare occasions when Yucatecos needed to visit the capital, they had to go by ship to Veracruz and continue from there on land.

All this contributed to Merida's independent attitude. It wasn't uncommon for wealthy landowners during the height of the late 19th-century henequen boom to import clothing, materials, food, wine, books and even brides from Europe, especially France. They built palatial homes along Paseo de Montejo, a tree-lined boulevard modeled on the Champs Elysees.

The Spaniards erected a wall around the city to protect it from frequent pirate attacks. It had only eight entrances, through large Spanish arches. Three of these are still standing. As customary, the city is built around a central plaza where the cathedral stands. Early in this century Merida attracted a large number of Syrian and Lebanese settlers, whose influence is seen in the architecture and particu-

58th streets, the *Museum of Natural History*, at 59th and 84th streets, and the *Museum of Instruments*, where musical instruments from pre-Hispanic times to the present are on display. The museum is located on the corner of 36th and 21st.

Santa Lucia Park, on the corner of 60th and 55th, is a center of activity on Sunday. From here south on Calle 60 to the plaza, the street closes for a flea market between 9 a.m. and 10 p.m. It is one of the town's most popular events, with concerts in the Municipal Palace, art exhibits and other attractions.

One of the most enjoyable treats is a stroll or horse-and-buggy ride down tree-lined *Paseo de Montejo*, where impressive French-colonial mansions with curved driveways and colonnaded facades stand witness to the wealth of yesteryear's henequen barons.

Farther up the boulevard is the *Monumento a la Patria*, a large semicircle of rose-colored stone depicting the colonial history of Mexico on one side and that of pre-Hispanic Mexico on the other.

South of the main plaza, beyond *San Juan Arch* (one of eight original entrances to the city), is the small but impressive *La Ermita Church*. The tiny chapel has an exquisite statue of the Virgin over the main altar, but the real attractions are the Mayan and Toltec sculptures in the garden.

Not far from here is the municipal cemetery, uniquely attractive because of its hundreds of colorful mausoleums.

City tours aboard open-air trolleys are available every morning (9 a.m.) and evening (6 p.m.) from Tuesday to Sunday, departing from the main plaza in front of the cathedral. There's a 60-peso charge.

Check with *Merida's English Library* about house and garden tours. The library is at Calle 52 No. 544, between 49th and 51st. Tel. 923-0083.

The bilingual monthly magazine *Yucatan Today*, distributed free at hotels, restaurants, shops and travel agencies, includes maps and information on events of interest to tourists.

For ecotours and adventure travel in the region, including cave exploration and scuba diving, contact *Balam-Beh*, run by the bilingual Carlos Sosa Estrada. Tel. 924-1871.

Dining

Yucatecan cuisine differs vastly from the regional cuisines in the rest of the country, relying heavily on marinated meats, especially pork. Turkey meat is another dietary staple, as is Yucatan's delicious twist on the humble tortilla, the *panucho*, a small fried corn tortilla stuffed with refried beans. Panuchos are traditionally served with shredded turkey, but you can ask for pork, chicken or beef toppings.

Another famous Yucatecan dish is *cochinita pibil*, marinated suckling pig baked in banana leaves. Its variation, *pollo pibil*, substitutes pork with chicken. All pibil dishes are first mari-

nated in *achiote*, a piquant sauce made from orange juice and annatto seeds. Two popular Yucatecan beers are *Leon* and *Montejo*.

Yucatecan dishes tend to incorporate less chili than other Mexican regional fare, preferring instead to serve it on the side, which is fortunate, because the area's chili of choice is the deadly *habanero*, a small bright green or yellow chili found only in the Yucatan Peninsula. It was purportedly imported centuries ago from Java.

Following are Merida's leading restaurants:

Casa del Paseo
Paseo de Montejo 465
Tel. 920-0528
A block from the Fiesta Americana Hotel. A lovely setting for international dishes and Yucatecan specialties. Open 1 p.m. to 1 a.m.

El Mural
Fiesta Americana Hotel

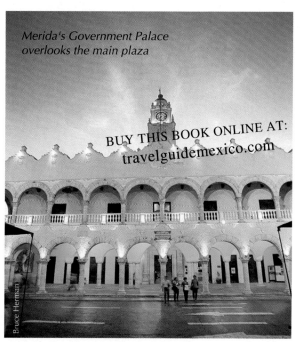
Merida's Government Palace overlooks the main plaza

Bruce Herman

BUY THIS BOOK ONLINE AT: travelguidemexico.com

Tel. 942-1111
An elegant restaurant offering refined Mexican cooking and Yucatecan specialties. Open noon to midnight. Closed Monday.

Hacienda Teya
Km. 12.5, Merida-Chichen-Itza Hwy.
Tel. 928-1885
About 10 minutes from the city. Dine on traditional Yucatecan dishes in a restored hacienda dating from the 17th century. The menu features strictly regional fare. Try the superb custardlike *flan* and *manjar blanco con leche de coco*, which tastes like a creamy coconut-flavored rice pudding. Open noon to 6 p.m.

Hacienda Xcanatun
Km. 12, Merida-Progreso Hwy.
Tel. 941-0273
About 20 minutes from the downtown area. This beautifully refurbished hacienda houses an excellent restaurant offering gourmet interna-

tional and regional fare, including grilled salmon and skewered marinated shrimp. Delicious desserts, selection of wines. Live music Thursday to Saturday evenings. Open 1:30 to 11 p.m.; to 7 p.m. Sunday. Closed Monday.

La Casona
Calle 60 No. 434
Tel. 923-8348
A block north of Los Aluxes Hotel. One of Merida's most attractive restaurants is housed in a beautifully restored mansion with period furnishings, a verandah and garden. The specialty is Italian cuisine. Restaurant open 1 p.m. to midnight; bar to 2 a.m. (except Sunday).

La Habichuela
Calle 21, corner of Calle 8
Tel. 926-3626
A Cancun favorite since 1977, this award-winning restaurant has brought its special blend of international and regional fare to Merida. The house specialty is Cocobichuela, chunks of lobster and shrimp bathed in a curry sauce and served in a coconut shell. After dinner, try their Mayan coffee, aflame with Kahlua and regional Xtabentun liqueur. Dine in their handsome dining room or open-air patio. Open noon to midnight. Reservations recommended.

Los Almendros
Calle 50 No. 493, between 57th and 59th
Tel. 923-8135
A tradition in the Yucatan, this family-style restaurant serves delicious, typical Yucatecan dishes. The cochinita pibil is outstanding, as are the panuchos with a variety of toppings. The margaritas are good, too. Second branch at Parque Mejorada (tel. 928-5459). Open 11 a.m. to 11:30 p.m.

Muelle 8
Calle 21 No. 142
Tel. 944-5343
In the north of the city. Popular with residents for its excellent seafood, wharf warehouse decor and good service in a relaxed setting. Open noon to 6 p.m.

Peregrina Bistro
Hyatt Regency Hotel
Tel. 942-0202
A charming hacienda-style setting for delicious regional and international specialties, including blackened New York steak, red snapper pibil, turkey in black *mole*. Breakfast buffet or a la carte service. Open 7 a.m. to 11 p.m.

Portico del Peregrino
Calle 57 No. 501, between 60th and 62nd
Tel. 928-6163
Sample regional cuisine and international favorites in the colonial-style dining room or lush garden patio. Open noon to 11 p.m.

Spasso
Hyatt Regency Hotel

Tel. 942-0202
This trattoria offers delicious Italian specialties, and transforms into a night spot in the evenings, with live music Wednesday to Saturday nights. Open-air terrace dining. Open 5 p.m. to 2 a.m.

Tratto
Prolongacion Paseo Montejo 479
Tel. 927-0434
The gourmet international cuisine with Italian and Asian influences and oversized open-air bar have made this a popular spot with both locals and visitors. Open 7 p.m. to 2 a.m.

Villa Italia
Calle 21 No. 69
Tel. 927-5867
Traditional home-cooked Italian fare served in a pleasant alfresco setting. Open 1 p.m. to 2 a.m.

Nightlife

Every Wednesday at 9 p.m. in the Jose Peon Contreras theater, on the corner of 60th and 57th streets, the *Folkloric Ballet of the University of Yucatan* presents a lively program of music and dance called "Yucatan and its Roots." The same group performs regional songs and dances Fridays at 8 p.m. in the central patio of the university for a smaller admission charge.

La Trova, the popular bar of the Merida Mision Hotel, features live music, including traditional Yucatecan melodies, Monday through Saturday till 2 a.m. Traditional music is also played Thursdays at 9 p.m. at Santa Lucia Park. *La Trova del Bohemia*, at 55th street, opposite Santa Lucia park, is one of the city's older establishments, featuring Latin American folk music and mariachis in the evenings.

Shopping

The best buys in Merida are guayaberas, the handsome tailored shirt of the tropics; hammocks; Panama-style hats, here called *"jipis"*; huipils, embroidered white cotton dresses worn by traditional Yucatecan women; and *xtabentun*, the sweet, licorice-flavored regional liqueur made of anise and honey.

The municipal market has a section dedicated entirely to handicrafts, and their selections are admirably first rate. Across the street from the market, at Calle 56 No. 561, you'll find more choices from a cooperative of artisans from nearby Tixkokob.

Casa de las Artesanias, on Calle 63 between 64th and 66th, is a state-run shop carrying fine arts and crafts, including handmade leather sandals, and straw baskets and handbags. It's open from 8 a.m. to 8 p.m. Tel. 928-6676.

An outdoor handicraft market is set up Sundays at Santa Lucia Park and the central square. Shops usually close between 2 and 4 p.m.

Casa de Cera
Calle 74 No. 430, between 41st and 43rd
Tel. 920-0219
Unique Mexican sculpture made of beeswax, including Mayan pyramids and other objects inspired by pre-Hispanic art and culture.

Guayaberas Finas Evan
Calle 62 No. 508, between 59th and 61st
A fine assortment of cotton-blend, all-cotton or linen guayaberas.

Guayaberas Genuina Yucateca
Calle 58 No. 520, second floor
Great source for guayaberas, including pleated and embroidered varieties.

Guayaberas Jack
Calle 59 No. 507, downtown
Tel. 928-6002
The city's oldest manufacturer and retailer of guayaberas, in business for 38 years.

Hecho A Mano
Calle 31 No. 308
Tel. 954-0344
Facing Cinco de Mayo Park. A fine selection of folk art from around the country, from lacquerwork to glazed pottery. Catalogue available.

La Poblana
Calle 65, between 58th and 60th
A highly reputable hammock shop that exports all over the world.

Maya Chuy
Calle 60 No. 430, corner of 47th
Beautiful hand-embroidered traditional clothing and accessories, as well as contemporary apparel and items for the home decorated by hand. Funded in part by the U.N. and Canada, this small store is part of a project to train and promote local women artisans. No credit cards accepted.

Mexicanisimo by Masud
Calle 60 No. 496, between 59th and 61st
Tel. 928-2891
Facing Parque de la Madre. Elegant dresses for women in natural undyed cotton, and leisure wear for men in the same fabric.

Hotels

Casa del Balam
Calle 60 No. 988
Tel. (999) 924-2150
Two blocks from the main plaza, this picturesque neo-colonial hotel has 52 spacious rooms, small pool, plant-filled courtyard entry, good dining room, bar. Rates MD.

Casa Mexilio
Calle 68 No. 495
Tel./Fax (999) 928-2505
This charming and historic bed-and-breakfast located four blocks from the main plaza offers 10 rooms in a tastefully converted 19th-century neo-classical townhouse. Small pool, sun deck, dining room, and tavern bar serving casual fare. Rates ECON (includes full breakfast).

El Castellano
Calle 57 No. 513, between 62 and 64
Tel. (999) 930-0100
Complete remodelling has allowed this traditional hotel to take its place among the city's better five-star properties. Swimming pool, specialty restaurant, cafeteria, piano bar, business center. Rates MD.

Fiesta Americana
Av. Colon 451, corner of Paseo Montejo
Tel. (999) 942-1111
Resembling the stately European-style buildings of Merida's colonial epoch, this attractive hotel offers deluxe services and facilities at less than deluxe prices. The 350 well-appointed rooms and suites have 24-hour room service. Banquet and meeting facilities for 800, business center. Fitness center, swimming pool, tennis. Good restaurants, lobby bar, shopping arcade. Rates FC.

Hacienda Katanchel
Merida-Cancun Hwy., Km. 26
Tel. (999) 923-4020
Located 30 minutes from Merida, this lovingly restored 17th-century hacienda is on nearly 700 tree-shaded acres. The 40 deluxe guest rooms and suites, called "pavilions," are scattered about the vast grounds, offering wonderful privacy, and have an outdoor plunge pool and terrace with hammock. Pool, tennis court. Restaurant-bar with outdoor terrace; game room, TV lounge. Member of Small Luxury Hotels of the World. Rates DX (includes breakfast, airport transport).

Hacienda Temozon
In Abala
Tel. (999) 949-5001
A 30-minute drive from Merida's airport. This marvelously restored 17th-century hacienda features 29 beautifully-decorated ample suites, spectacular pool, excellent dining, bar. There's an underground *cenote* on the premises for exploring. Rates LX.

Hacienda Xcanatun
Merida-Progreso Hwy., Km. 12
Tel. (999) 941-0213
www.mexicoboutiquehotels.com
Offering the special ambiance of a hacienda just 20 minutes from downtown Merida, with 18 attractive suites with private terraces, excellent restaurant, two swimming pools, gardens. Enjoy holistic treatments in the jade-toned spa or in-suite, and access to a nearby country club with golf and tennis. Member of Mexico Boutique Hotels. Rates DX (continental breakfast and airport transfers included).

Holiday Inn
Av. Colon 498, near Paseo Montejo
Tel. (999) 925-6877
This 213-room hotel has been remodeled to reflect the colors and architecture of the region's famous haciendas. Restaurant, lobby bar with entertainment, swimming pool, tennis, gym, business center, convention facilities. Rates MD.

Hyatt Regency
Calle 60 No. 344 and Av. Colon

Tel. (999) 942-0202
Steps from Paseo Montejo. This modern high-rise offers deluxe accommodations at less than deluxe prices. There are 300 rooms with first-class amenities. Restaurants, nightlife, swimming pool, lighted tennis courts, outdoor jacuzzi, health club, business center, banquet and convention facilities for 650 people. Rates FC.

La Mision de Fray Diego
Calle 64 No. 524
Tel. (999) 924-1111
Near the main plaza. This renovated colonial-era mansion offers 26 rooms and suites around a courtyard with fountain or a swimming pool. Restaurant-bar. Rates MD.

Villa Mercedes
Av. Colon 500, near Paseo Montejo
Tel. (999) 942-9000
A newly built hotel resembling a turn-of-the-century mansion, with 84 rooms and suites with all modern amenities, some with jacuzzi. Pool, restaurant, bar, meeting facilities, 24-hour room service. Rates MD.

Side Trips

A little more than an hour from Merida is the village of *Becal*, where local women weave *jipi* (pronounced hippie) hats and other items in underground caves. The moisture in the caves keeps the leaves of the jipi palm that they use pliable, preventing it from breaking when knotted or twisted. Most houses in the small village boast a cave in the backyard, dug out of the soft limestone. You can see weavers at work at the *Bel-Ha* workshop, then visit nearby *Artesanias Jipi y Palma*, where the hats are pressed into shape.

Just an hour-and-a-half drive (57 miles) west of Merida is the gulf coast fishing village of *Celestun*, site of a wildlife preserve where colonies of pink flamingos spend the winter months feeding in the nutrient-rich waters of the area's estuary. Local fishermen offer boat rides to see the flamingos and the great number of other flora and fauna that thrives here.

Though the birds are the big draw, this stretch of coast also has beautiful, soft, white beaches strewn with seashells and lapped by clear blue water. If you can spend more than a day here, deluxe accommodations are available at *Eco Paraiso Xixim*, a splendid, rigorously ecological resort featuring spacious palm-thatched beachfront cabins, fine dining, and expert knowledge of the area's natural treasures. Tel. (988) 916-2100.

The road from Merida to Celestun is good, but avoid driving at night as there are numerous bicycles on the road, the locals' main means of transport. You can call *Ecoturismo Yucatan* (tel. 925-2187), an established travel agency geared to ecotourism and adventure travel, to arrange a day trip.

Half an hour north of Merida is the gulf coast town of *Progreso*, a shipping port with the world's longest pier (two and a half miles) and a retreat for summer-weary residents of Merida. The beaches along this coast are good, but

windswept in the winter months; sailing is a popular sport. The beachfront restaurants, including *El Capitan Marisco* and *Sol y Mar*, serve good seafood. *Sian-Ka'an,* a small inn in nearby Yucalpeten, offers pleasant accommodations and a beach club.

All along the coast east of Progreso, a resort area known as *Nuevo Yucatan* (New Yucatan) is slowly taking shape, but there is little there as yet. An all-inclusive Reef Club spa and beach resort attracts North American tourists, especially Canadians, to this area.

Canadian company Scotia Prince Cruises has launched ferry service between Tampa and Progreso aboard its luxury M/S Scotia Prince. The 1,100-passenger *Yucatan Express* shuttles between the two ports from November to May, offering passage (crossings take 36 hours), as well as gambling and duty-free shopping (the same ship is used from May to October to provide ferry service between Maine and Nova Scotia). For more information, visit www.yucatanexpress.com or call (866) 461-5812.

An hour's drive east of Merida is *Izamal*, a colonial town nicknamed "The Yellow City" —bright mustard-yellow paint covers its impressive Franciscan convent and most every other building in town. The Convento de San Antonio, built atop the base of a destroyed Mayan temple, boasts the largest enclosed atrium in Mexico, and a lovely stained-glass image of the Virgin.

The Yucatan state tourism office offers Sunday train tours to Izamal that depart from the train station at 8:15 a.m. and arrive at 9:50 for five hours of sightseeing, including lunch and a presentation of a folkloric ballet. For more information, call 924-9495, or consult your hotel concierge.

Maya Express (Expreso Maya) offers visitors a new way to see this region's archaeological gems—by train. The rail journey begins in Merida, or Villahermosa, and takes in the Mayan ruins of Chichen-Itza, Uxmal and Palenque, as well as the colonial city of Campeche, as it winds its way through Mexico's Mundo Maya. The five-day train tour, aboard restored 1940's

vintage cars, is offered by The Train Collection.

Chichen-Itza

Just 80 miles east of Merida, on a highway that cuts almost straight through dry scrub forest towards Valladolid and Cancun, Chichen-Itza suddenly looms above the treetops. It's an impressive sight.

Early information about the six-square-mile site and its hundreds of structures is sketchy. Chichen-Itza was built late in relation to more southerly Mayan areas. Major buildings weren't begun until possibly 600 A.D. Late in the 10th century the Toltecs arrived from central Mexico, following their god/ruler Quetzalcoatl in 987 A.D. This god, the Plumed Serpent, is known here as Kukulcan.

At about the same time a new group arrived from the southern part of the peninsula. Considered "tricksters and rascals" by the natives, the newly-arrived Itza proceeded to take charge. Eventually they moved on to northern Guatemala, where they established an equally poor reputation.

The architectural and artistic differences between the older pure Mayan constructions and the newer Toltec-inspired sections is pronounced. When the Spaniards arrived in the 16th century, the city had been reclaimed by the jungle.

In 1885 the U.S. consul in Yucatan, Edward H. Thompson, purchased the abandoned site. In 1904 he dredged the *Cenote Sagrado,* or Sacred Well, and verified the legends of sacrificial humans and valuables being cast into the sinkhole as offerings to the Mayan gods. Offerings to Chaac, the crooked-nosed rain god, were particularly significant in this lakeless, riverless region where water was precious. In the 80-foot well, Thompson found the remains of human bones and 240 artifacts of jade, copper and gold. The Carnegie Institute continued to explore the area from 1923 to 1943.

The dominant structure at Chichen-Itza is *El Castillo* (also known as the Pyramid of Kukulcan), 75 feet tall and capped with a square

Kukulcan Pyramid, Chichen-Itza

Bruce Herman

Uxmal

Mexico Tourism Board

temple. You climb 91 steps to the top. The total number of stairs is 365 (there is one top step), a figure which attests to the Maya's knowledge of the heavens.

Twice a year, during the spring and autumnal equinoxes, thousands gather around the Kukulcan Pyramid for a spectacular show. Mayan architects designed the pyramid so that the afternoon sun at these times of the year produces the shadow of a snake (representing the Plumed Serpent deity) descending the staircase, its giant head resting at the base.

Kukulcan is built over a series of previous constructions. An interior staircase leads to the *Throne of the Red Jaguar*, a chamber containing a reclining Chac-Mool and a stunning, popeyed jaguar. Access to the chamber is from 11:30 a.m. to 3 p.m. and 4 to 5 p.m.

To the west of Kukulcan is the great 272-foot-long *Ball Court*, where the Maya played a ball game popular in many parts of Mesoamerica. Friezes show the game had religious significance and was played with deadly seriousness: the captain of one team is shown being decapitated. What is intriguing is that experts cannot say with any certainty whether he represents the winning or losing team. Sacrifice was not only accepted, but considered an honor in serving the gods. Chichen-Itza has 22 ball courts, more than have been found at any other Mesoamerican site.

Aesthetically beautiful and unique in Mesoamerica is the *Observatory*, a circular dome built atop a massive terraced temple in the old, Mayan section. A circular interior stairway leads to a chamber at the top that served as an observatory for astronomers. Small slits in the wall provide fixes on celestial bodies, and the readings were used to calculate agricultural timetables.

Nearby is another complex, the *Nunnery* and *Church*. A massive structure 300 feet long and 55 feet high, it is full of connecting rooms the Catholic Spaniards interpreted to be a nunnery. The gaping hole in one side was made by an early French explorer who dynamited the

building to see what was inside.

Good accommodations are available near the ruins, including *Mayaland*, a colonial-style hotel set in lush tropical gardens with a panoramic view of the ruins, *Villa Arqueologica*, an attractive Mediterranean-style hostelry operated by Club Med, *Hacienda Chichen*, a perennial favorite with a rich history, and, in the village of Piste, the modern *Mision Chichen-Itza Park Inn*. Another option is to stay in nearby Valladolid.

Near Chichen-Itza is *Balankanche Cave*, with an altar room of ceramic and carved stone offerings left by the Maya at least 800 years ago. Until 1959 it was believed the cave was nothing more than a large entry room containing a few watery passages of more interest for their fish species than for their archaeological value. Then Humberto Gomez, a local tour guide long familiar with the cave, discovered some loose rocks in the back wall and slowly made his way into the altar room—becoming the first person to enter since the Maya had sealed it.

Another interesting archaeological site is *Dzibilchaltun*, 22 kilometers north of Merida. Dating from around 500 B.C., the 30-square-mile site features the *Temple of the Seven Dolls*, which registers the autumnal and vernal equinoxes, and a beautiful cenote, called *Xlakah*, whose limpid waters invite visitors to take a refreshing dip.

Uxmal, Kabah and Labna

On the road to Campeche, 58 miles south of Merida, is *Uxmal*. While it is smaller than Chichen-Itza, its architecture is considered to be among the most magnificent in the ancient world.

Founded around 600 A.D., Uxmal, which means "Thrice Built," was developed in stages, with beautifully carved facades, corbelled arches and majestic terraces and columns facing broad plazas. Dominating the site is the 100-foot-tall *Pyramid of the Magician* consisting

of five superimposed temples. A steep 118-step climb to the top rewards you with a panoramic view of the half-square-mile city.

Not to be missed is the *Nuns' Quadrangle*, a vast plaza flanked on four sides by numerous rooms. Note the beautiful carvings over the doorways of the typical thatched-roof mud and wattle homes still used today by the Maya.

"The most spectacular single building in all pre-Columbian America," is what noted early archaeologist Sylanus G. Morley said of the *Governor's Palace*, a long, rectangular building on a series of three terraces encompassing a five-acre area. Its facade is composed of more than 20,000 intricately-carved stones, giving the appearance of delicate latticework.

There is a Spanish-language light and sound show at Uxmal; individual headsets are available offering narration in English, French and German.

Just in front of the entrance to Uxmal is the charming colonial inn *Hacienda Uxmal*, with tropical gardens, tiled corridors and spacious rooms. The hilltop *Mision Uxmal* has attractive balcony rooms overlooking the ruins. Club Med has a *Villa Arqueologica* directly across from the site entrance.

Twelve miles south of Uxmal, the archaeological zone *Kabah* has an impressive 160-foot-long palace building called the *Kodz-Poop*, its facade covered by 250 Chaac masks. It is believed Kabah was connected to Uxmal by an ancient roadway, or *sacbe*. A short way beyond is *Sayil*, with its magnificent palace, and *Labna*, known for its beautifully-decorated arch.

Past Labna are the expansive *Loltun Caverns*, with seemingly endless passageways and huge rooms, some opening to the sky. In places the lighting is poor and the rocks slippery. Be prepared for a cave much as nature created it, with few paved walkways or handrails.

Along the way you'll see vignettes of rural Yucatecan life and numerous brush-covered Mayan ruins by the roadside. Throughout this region are typical, oval, thatched mud-and-wattle-homes, like those depicted at Uxmal.

Hacienda Ochil, a tastefully converted hacienda located at Km. 175 of the Merida-Uxmal Hwy., offers a wonderful place to lunch on delicious regional fare, a small henequen museum and shop, and an underground cenote. Reservations are necessary. Tel. 944-3637.

Valladolid

Travel between Merida and Cancun, which lies just two and a half hours away via an excellent highway, has brought the lovely colonial city of Valladolid into the spotlight.

Lying just a short distance east of the ruins, Valladolid offers a wonderfully picturesque place to lunch if visiting the ruins, or to overnight on longer road trips. *El Meson del Marques*, facing the main square, is a 16th-century colonial home converted into a charming hotel with a courtyard restaurant. Tel. 856-3042.

The town's Franciscan *Convent of San Bernardino*, built to double as a fortress should the Indians rebel against the Spanish, is worth visiting, as is the main square, where local women sell beautifully embroidered huipils.

TRAVELERS GUIDE TO
Cancun

Mexico Boutique Hotels

*The top resort serves as the gateway to the Riviera Maya
and its unique sites of interest, such as Tulum.*

Gateway to Mundo Maya

Fonatur

No more than 30 years ago Cancun was merely a peculiar geological formation—called a sand bar—clinging to Mexico's Caribbean coast. Until keen-eyed developers in the 1970s saw the appeal of the area's shimmering turquoise waters and sparkling white sand, it had remained largely untouched since the mysterious decline of the Mayan empire around the 13th century. Today Cancun is a favorite Caribbean playground and gateway to the Mundo Maya, or Maya World, hosting more than 3 million visitors a year.

In the beginning, travelers were drawn only to its crystal-clear waters and talcum-soft sand. But soon its proximity to breathtaking Mayan ruins, exotic wildlife, and colonial gems became added attractions.

Cancun serves as an ideal coastal base from which to explore numerous remnants of the extraordinary Mayan civilization that flourished in the Yucatan Peninsula more than a thousand years ago. Nearby are the ruins of Chichen-Itza, Tulum and Coba. Archaeology buffs will want to visit the more distant sites of Uxmal, Labna, Sayil and Kabah—all part of Western Yucatan's Puuc Route—located outside Merida. Colonial towns such as Valladolid, Izamal and Merida are also worth visiting.

There are seven species of heron and four of egret that fly Cancun's skies. You can also spot magnificent frigate birds, cormorants, wood storks and white ibis. Iguanas are regularly seen sunning themselves by the side of the road, and in the evenings you can spot crocodiles gliding across the surface of the lagoon. The mangroves lining the lagoon are home to gray squirrels, collared anteaters, weasels, gray foxes and raccoons.

Magnificent beaches combined with unique historical sites, some of the best snorkeling and diving in the world, and tropical flora and fauna, give Cancun an added dimension.

What Is Cancun?

Technically, Cancun's L-shaped Hotel Zone is an island unto itself. It is separated from the mainland at each end by channels less than 100 yards across that connect the beautiful 18-square-mile Nichupte Lagoon with the sparkling Caribbean Sea. Each channel is crossed by a low bridge.

The island is a coral-based sand bar more than 13 miles long and one-quarter of a mile wide. The sand isn't just soft and brilliantly white, but composed of age-old porous limestone that is comfortable to lie on and never gets too hot. The aerated fossil grains are cool to the touch even at high noon, but so fine that they can easily cling to the skin (talcum powder helps rub them off). There are some intimate coves around the island, spectacular limestone rock formations, and sand dunes up to 35 feet high.

In September of 1988, Cancun was struck by Hurricane Gilbert, a powerful storm un-precedented in this century and the first to hit the area in 50 years. While there were no fatalities and most hotels were closed only a matter of days, the storm rearranged several of Cancun's gorgeous beaches. Most have regained their precious grains of sand through the efforts of either Mother Nature or man (some hotels trucked in huge quantities). However, beaches here continue to fluctuate in size, their sand deposits waxing and waning with the tide.

One good way to see how the resort is laid out is from the top of Cancun's rotating scenic tower at El Embarcadero Plaza, where ferries shuttle between the Hotel Zone and Isla Mujeres. Resembling a flying saucer caught on a pole, the tower offers a 360-degree bird's-eye-view of Cancun from about 300 feet (100 meters). Look for the towers in Cozumel, Isla Mujeres and Xcaret also.

Climate

The average daytime temperature in Cancun is 80º F, with only about a five degree variation year-round. Unlike the rest of Mexico, the rainy season here is during the late fall and winter months. It can sometimes even get chilly at night; lightweight sweaters, jackets or shawls are recommended for cool winter evenings. The summer months are generally hot and humid with frequent but brief showers.

Cancun has an average of more than 200 sunny days a year and has less annual rainfall than the Virgin Islands or the Bahamas. While it is not directly within the Caribbean hurricane belt, the old Mexican adage "hurricanes have no helm" sometimes applies. You may run into some rain, overcast weather and days with bothersome wind gusts. Usually a light breeze blows across the island, keeping things cool.

Red or yellow flag warnings are common on the open-sea side of the island, and swimming there is not recommended. Black flag warnings are posted at especially treacherous spots.

What to wear? Strictly casual resort wear, especially during the day. Jackets and ties are never needed, but it is customary to dress up for the discos, and most nice restaurants and bars require men to wear shirts and slacks (some allow Bermudas). Most frown on sandals. Women are allowed more leeway, but would likely feel under-dressed in tank tops and flip-flops.

Downtown Cancun is where most of the resort's 750,000 residents live. Patterned more after a U.S. suburb than a typical Mexican town, the area is sprawling and easier to negotiate by car than on foot. You can stroll down Avenida Tulum, where many sidewalk stands sell Mexican souvenirs and handicrafts, and visit the neighborhood park, Palapas.

Taxis are plentiful, with reasonable predetermined fares; taxis stationed outside hotels may apply higher rates. Every few minutes, 24 hours a day, white buses barrel up and down Kukulcan Boulevard on their way to and from downtown Cancun, passing all the major shopping centers and hotels along the way. The fare is nominal.

Aqua Bus, a water taxi service, takes passengers from one end of the Hotel Zone to the other via Nichupte Lagoon, stopping at eight different docks along the way, including La Isla and El Zocalo. The 60-minute ride costs three dollars (daily and weekly passes are available), and departs from the Royal Yacht Club (southern terminal) or the Jardin del Arte (northern terminal).

A Planned Resort

Cancun is the product of a long-range government plan to turn tourism into a major industry. The strategy calls for identifying coastal locations with resort potential and then orchestrating their development, as opposed to letting them happen naturally. A special government agency called Fonatur was set up and given the responsibility of scouting for sites, drawing the master plans, soliciting private and foreign investment, supervising development, and promoting the outcome.

As Fonatur's initial project, Cancun may well be the world's first completely fabricated vacation resort, from the basic infrastructure (roads, potable water, phone lines, electricity) to the superstructures (hotels, shopping centers, golf courses, convention facility). So what you see now is not the result of haphazard growth, though it appears that way in parts, but the completion of phases one and two of a three-phase development plan.

Unfortunately, all the pre-planning didn't guarantee uniformity or controlled growth. Garish signs, outlandish constructions and overbuilding blight parts of the landscape while well-tended promenades and green areas lined with slender palms and cascading bougainvillea characterize others.

Phase three will see the completion of Puerto Cancun, a megaproject comprised of a 400-slip marina, golf course, and 2,000 additional hotel rooms. The project spans the northern Hotel Zone and stretches all the way to Punta Sam. The resort expects to soon be hosting more than 3.5 million visitors a year, and the airport has already been expanded to handle increased air traffic.

The coastline stretching from Cancun to Tulum, called the Riviera Maya, is now booming. The area is home to the beach town of Playa del Carmen, the Sian Ka'an nature reserve, and tropical parks Tres Rios, Xcaret and Xel-Ha. New hotels, from sprawling all-inclusives to intimate inns, open regularly and

Dining tables overlook the lagoon

a four-lane highway is nearing completion.

The state of Quintana Roo hopes to replicate the success of the Riviera Maya with a southern counterpart called Costa Maya. As part of this effort to lure tourists to the state's lesser traveled southern half, officials are developing the coastline below the Sian Ka'an nature reserve, and paving the way for tourism by building airports and roads, and making other infrastructure improvements.

Kukulcan Boulevard, the resort's main strip, stretches the length of the hotel zone

BAHIA DE MUJERES

PUNTA CANCUN

DOWNTOWN CANCUN

KUKULCAN BLVD.

AV. TULUM

BULLRING

BLUE BAY
BLUE BAY
CARROUSEL
AQUAMARINA
OASIS BEACH
CLUB INTERNACIONAL
CASA MAYA
RIO CARIBE
VILLAS TACUL
AVALON BAY
DOS PLAYAS

Plaza Nautilus
CLUB LAS VELAS

CANCUN MARINA CLUB

PRESIDENTE INTERCONTINENTAL
OASIS VIVA
FIESTA AMERICANA

Plaza Caracol
Convention Center
FIESTA AMERICANA
GRAND CORAL BEACH

DREAMS

HYATT REGENCY

NH KRYSTAL

Forum by the Sea

POK-TA-POK

H.I. EXPRESS

BOJOR-QUEZ LAGOON

ARISTOS
MIRAMAR MISION
SUNSET
SIERRA CANCUN
HYATT CANCUN CARIBE

GRAN CARIBE REAL

Flamingo Plaza

FLAMINGO
AVALON
BEACH PALACE
MELIA TURQUESA
SHERATON

La Isla

CARIBBEAN VILLAGE

Kukulcan Plaza

TUCANCUN
CASA TURQUESA
THE ROYAL SANDS
THE RITZ CARLTON
JACK TAR VILLAGE
LE MERIDIEN
CANCUN PALACE
JW MARRIOTT
MARRIOTT CASA MAGNA
GRAN MELIA CANCUN

FIESTA AMERICANA CONDESA

OASIS
OMNI

THE ROYAL MAYAN
THE ROYAL CARIBBEAN
THE ROYAL ISLANDER
HILTON BEACH & GOLF RESORT
EL PUEBLITO
CROWN PARADISE CLUB
OASIS PLAYA

KUKULCAN BLVD

NICHUPTE LAGOON

WE CAN ONLY PROVIDE THIS SERVICE
IF YOU ARE KIND ENOUGH TO LEAVE
THIS BOOK HERE IN GOOD CONDITION
FOR THE NEXT GUEST. THANK YOU.

HILTON GOLF COURSE

EL REY RUINS

CARIBBEAN SEA

To Tulum, Playa del Carmen

SOLYMAR
ROYAL SOLARIS

SUN PALACE

INGLES LAGOON

WESTIN REGINA
CLUB MED

Cancun

PUNTA NIZUC

N
E
W
S

KUKULCAN BLVD.

Airport

What to See and Do

From Scuba Diving the Blue Waters to Golfing the Green Fairways

Cancun's greatest attractions are its stunning beaches, and swimmers have a variety to choose from. Most hotel beaches are excellent, so try several, particularly on the other end of the Hotel Zone from where you are staying. Beaches in Mexico are government property and therefore open to the public.

The beaches facing the open Caribbean Sea (on the long part of the L-shaped island, from the Dreams Cancun Resort & Spa toward the airport) are usually wide and beautiful, but the strong undertow, abrupt drop-off, and pounding surf make it a challenge to swim. One nice public beach in this area is *Playa Delfines*. There is a lookout and several stone benches for sitting and contemplating the sea, showers, and no hotel (as yet).

The beaches facing Bahia de Mujeres (on the short end of the L-shaped island, toward town) are smaller, shallow for some distance out, and have little surf, making them great for swimming, snorkeling and other water sports. These beaches, including *Playa Tortuga* and *Playa Caracol*, tend to be more crowded, as locals favor them as well. Another drawback here is that the blue of the Caribbean is sometimes marred by dark seabeds of algae and other flora.

Schools of small fish can often be spotted swimming in knee-deep waters a few feet from shore. Still, if you have never been scuba diving or snorkeling, muster up some courage and try it here. More than 500 types of tropical fish

inhabit the reefs around Cancun and visibility is excellent. A few of the reefs are shallow enough for easy snorkeling, including in the area off Punta Nizuc, on the south end of the island. Tour operators always have life vests available and even the best swimmers often opt to wear them for added security.

The real fun is scuba diving or snorkeling around the four reefs between Cancun and Isla

---

Schools of small fish can be spotted in knee-deep waters a few feet from shore.

Mujeres, where you can see to depths of 40 feet. The rainbow color of marine life is something you will never forget. In fact, many snorkeling/diving excursions out of Cancun take in Isla Mujeres' famed Garrafon National Park and its shallow coral reef.

Two new underwater activities available at Xel-Ha and Garrafon parks are the *sea trek* and *snuba*. Sea trek involves getting fitted with a funny-looking helmet that has air pumped into it from the surface so you can walk around on the sea floor and look at the pretty fish. More

than a snorkel, but less than a scuba, snuba lets you breathe underwater while your oxygen tank floats above you.

AquaWorld is one of the resort's largest and most long-standing tour operators, offering everything from scuba diving to deep-sea fishing. Its full-service marina is easy to locate; just look for the twin rockets (which offer reverse bungee jumping) rising above the Hotel Zone. Tel. 848-8300.

Dives and snorkeling excursions are also offered by *EcoColors*, a Cancun-based ecotourism outfit and member of the Mexican Association of Ecological and Adventure Tourism (AMTAVE). Tel. 884-9580.

You don't have to get wet to enjoy the Caribbean's colorful underwater life, just board boats with below-surface viewing areas, such as AquaWorld's *Sub See Explorer* or *Nautibus* (883-2119).

Over in Cozumel, *Atlantis Submarines* takes passengers aboard a high-tech sub to depths of more than 100 feet as a multilingual guide points out the more unique fish and plant life that goes by. Tel. 872-5671.

You can get acquainted with a wide variety of marine life at La Isla's *Interactive Aquarium*, home to the flat flounder, whose bulbous eyes reside on the same side of his face, and other extraordinary creatures. The aquarium's petting tanks let you feel the unique textures of stingrays, nurse sharks, starfish and urchins. And for an "up close and personal" encoun-

Boats wait at a lagoonside dock

ners take you through the dense mangrove-lined canals of Nichupte Lagoon, where you can get a close look at tropical birds, plants and marine life. The tours are usually combined with snorkeling. You can also hire a boat and a guide to show you around the canals.

Another activity you may want to try is parachute gliding, individually or with a friend (offered by AquaWorld).

Parque Nizuc, on the south end of Cancun, is home to the *Wet'n Wild* water park, which has a beach club and marina, wave pool, lazy river ride, twister and kamikaze water slides, and restaurants and shops. Nizuc also offers swimming with dolphins at *Atlantida* (reservations recommended), snorkeling in a protected 65,000-square-foot area of ocean water alongside stingrays and nurse sharks at *Baxalha*, and bungee jumping for three intrepid souls at a time. The park is open from 10 a.m. to 6 p.m. Tel. 881-3030.

Dolphin Discovery also offers encounters and swimming with dolphins at its facility on Isla Mujeres, just a half-hour boat ride away. For reservations, call 849-4748.

ter with the most fearsome inhabitants of the sea, you can dive into a tank and feed the resident sharks. Reserve in advance for feeding the sharks (883-1773) or swimming with dolphins (883-0413).

Water Sports

Deep-sea fishing is a bonanza in this remote part of the Caribbean. The waters abound in bluefin tuna, white marlin, sailfish, mackerel and grouper. There are daily deep-sea fishing

excursions or charters of from four to eight hours.

You can try your hand at bonefishing, also called "fishing the flats," in Nichupte Lagoon or at Boca Paila in the Sian Ka'an reserve. Arrange a trip through your hotel travel desk, or call AquaWorld or *Mundo Marino* (849-7258).

Windsurfing is popular here and the colorful sails against the blue-green water are visible everywhere. You can have windsurfing lessons at the *Royal Yacht Club*. Tel. 885-0391.

Jungle tours aboard two-seater wave run-

Cenotes

The Yucatan Peninsula is riddled with some 2,000 *cenotes*, freshwater wells (or sinkholes) that were created where cavern roofs collapsed, forming a natural pool that was then filled by rain and underground rivers. The most famous cenote is Chichen-Itza's giant Sacred Well. Many Mayan ceremonial centers were built near cenotes, the only source of freshwater in this riverless region.

Surrounded by jungle or found inside caves, cenotes can be small or vast oases of limpid water and marine life that invite swimmers, intrepid and experienced divers who come to explore their underground passages, or simply sightseers who come to enjoy the scenery.

Several cenotes are located within an hour or two of Cancun, near the archaeological site of Tulum and the beach town of Playa del Carmen, including Aktun Chen, Dos Ojos, Cristal, Escondido and Grande.

Run by marine biologist Kenneth Johnson, the EcoColors ecotourism company offers tours of cenotes and other natural wonders of the region. A typical tour includes hotel pickup and transport to Puerto Morelos for snorkeling around the offshore reef, then visits to the cenotes of Kantun Chi and Tankah for snorkeling and exploring.

EcoColors also offers tours to Holbox Island and the Yum Balam Reserve, a sanctuary for hundreds of birds, including pink flamingos, and home to the Yalahua Lagoon, where you can occasionally encounter dolphins. For more information, call 884-9580.

Sports

Pok-Ta-Pok, meaning "ball game" in Mayan, is a magnificent 18-hole golf course designed by Robert Trent Jones II, and features gently rolling fairways bordered by palms, two greens at the edge of the Caribbean, and even a small ruin by the third hole. There's on-course beverage service, a driving range, pro-shop and restaurant-bar. Tel. 883-0871.

The *Hilton Beach & Golf Resort* added another great course to the island landscape. The 18-hole championship course, designed by Japan's Aoki Corporation, incorporates some of the Mayan archaeological site Ruinas del Rey. Tel. 881-8000.

The *Mini Golf Palace* at the Cancun Palace Hotel offers two 18-hole putt-putt courses featuring waterfalls and replicas of Mayan ruins. Open 11 a.m. to 11 p.m. Tel. 885-0533.

Most hotels have one or two tennis courts and there are also courts at Pok-Ta-Pok. The Fiesta Americana Grand has three fabulous indoor installations. The courts at the Hyatt Hotel are also popular.

Bicycling is a good way to see much of the island and lagoon. A six-mile pink-brick bicycle path and promenade, bordered with flowering shrubbery and lofty palms, runs all the way to downtown Cancun from the Hotel Zone.

The Cancun bullfighting ring, located downtown on Av. Bonampak, is the only venue of its kind to host bullfights year-round. Every Wednesday at 3 p.m. you can see some of the country's fine matadors in action, as well as folk dancing and *charreria*, or Mexican-style rodeo riding. Tickets are available at the gate, or at travel agencies and major shopping centers, where they can also arrange for transportation.

Folk Art

El Embarcadero is home to Cancun's new *Museum of Mexican Folk Art,* which has quickly taken its place among the resort's must-see sites. The museum features a stunning array of handicrafts from throughout the country, with each room showcasing a different media or art form. One of the museum highlights is an authentic reproduction of a typical kitchen from Puebla, a state renowned not only for its cuisine, but also its Talavera tile and pottery, examples of which are used to accessorize the display.

Archaeological Sites

A trip to Cancun should include a visit to one of the famous nearby archaeological sites. A miniature sample of these sites is right on Cancun island. The *Ruinas del Rey*, or King's Ruins, which border the lagoon on the south end of the island, date back to the Late Pre-Classic period (300 B.C.-100 A.D.). The site's original Mayan name is unknown; it derived its current name from the discovery of a stone figure whose headdress and ear plugs were believed to depict a person of high ranking.

Though minor compared to other sites, Del Rey did reveal something of the way its inhabi-

tants lived, subsisting primarily from fishing and mollusk gathering. They also developed a far-reaching trade system that bartered seafood, and conch and snail shells used to make utensils and ornaments, for imported items such as grinding stones and flint knives. The stone figure and other artifacts, including conch and jadeite ornaments, have been removed, but visitors can still see remnants of a mural painting, glyphs, and human figures painted in red, black, yellow and blue.

Artifacts from this and other sites in the state reside in the small *Museum of Cancun* at the Convention Center. The museum is open 9 a.m. to 7 p.m. daily.

Only two and a half hours from Cancun, toward Merida, is one of the most impressive of all Mayan ruins, *Chichen-Itza.* The site dates to the Classic period, around 600 to 900 A.D., but most of the structures for which Chichen-Itza is renowned date from the Toltec-Maya, or Post-Classic period (900 to 1200 A.D.).

Near Chichen-Itza are the *Balankanche Caves,* the major portion of which remained sealed until the middle of this century, protecting the secrets Mayan priests left inside.

There are light and sound shows at both Chichen-Itza and Balankanche. Fifty miles south of Merida are several smaller Mayan sites, among them *Uxmal, Kabah, Sayil* and *Labna.* For more information, refer to the Merida chapter.

A little beyond is *Loltun Cave,* a huge cavern left much as nature created it, with little commercialism, other than guided tours, and minimal footpaths.

The Mayan civilization extended through Central America, so more archaeological treasures lie across Mexico's southern border, in neighboring Guatemala and Belize, and in Honduras and El Salvador. One- and two-day tours are available from Cancun to *Tikal* in Guatemala, and two-day tours to *Copan* in Honduras.

Once a bustling city of 55,000, the Late Pre-Classic site of Tikal is famed for its set of twin pyramids that face each other across vast plazas. The area's wildlife nearly rivals the ruins as an attraction; in fact, Tikal is located within a national park.

Copan features a unique, magnificently carved staircase, dedicated in 755 A.D., that records the history of 17 rulers of the royal dynasty. The site is believed to have flourished for more than a thousand years and served as a center of learning.

At Avenida Coba 5, downtown, you'll find the offices of *Aviateca,* the Guatemalan airline, and *Lacsa,* the Costa Rican airline, which handle these tours. Tel. 884-3938.

Aerocaribe, Mexicana's regional carrier, also offers one-day tours to Tikal. Tel. 884-2000.

Side Trips

Many interesting sites and locations near Cancun are reachable by boat, and these trips often combine sightseeing with snorkeling. One of the most popular day trips for nature lovers is to *Isla Contoy*, a protected breeding colony for nearly 100 species of seabirds, among them double-crested cormorants, ro-

Jungle tours zip through the lagoon's mangrove-lined canals

BUY THIS BOOK ONLINE AT:
travelguidemexico.com

Mexico Tourism Board

seate spoonbills and frigate birds. On the island, located about an hour and a half by boat from Cancun, visitors can take a guided walking tour, explore the beaches, snorkel, and visit the open-air museum on the area's wildlife.

Isla Mujeres is a great day trip or overnight jaunt. You can ferry over from either Puerto Juarez or Punta Sam for a nominal fee—both ports are about 10 minutes north of downtown Cancun (the car ferry runs from Punta Sam, which is about 5 minutes farther along on the same road after you pass Puerto Juarez).

Cozumel is a 15-minute flight from the Cancun International Airport, or a five-minute flight from Playa del Carmen's airport. Or you can ferry over from Playa (most people do); the trip takes 45 minutes.

Playa del Carmen is a burgeoning beach town about an hour and a half by bus from downtown Cancun, or a 40-minute drive from Cancun's International Airport. It is growing by leaps and bounds, and is no longer the off-the-beaten-track destination it once was. But Playa's marked European influence, fine eateries, and bustling nightlife make it an interesting spot.

About 30 minutes south of Cancun is *Puerto Morelos*, a small laid-back fishing village that is gradually attracting tourists. It's a favorite snorkeling site since this is where the region's barrier reef comes closest to the coast. See the "Riviera Maya" for more information on these and other sites, including the ruins of Tulum

and Coba, Xcaret and Xel-Ha, Tres Rios, Puerto Aventuras and Akumal, and the Sian Ka'an nature reserve.

Merida, the marvelous colonial capital of the state of Yucatan, is about three hours (320 kilometers/200 miles) west of Cancun on an excellent four-lane highway. The city is a showcase of Yucatecan culture, and especially nice to visit on Sunday, when streets close to traffic and the main square turns into a huge handicrafts market. Other charming colonial towns worth visiting are *Valladolid*, located just before reaching the ruins of Chichen-Itza, and *Izamal*, about 30 minutes away from the ruins. Both can be combined with tours of the archaeological site.

If you don't like organized tours, you can rent a car. Leading car rental agency Avis has offices in the area.

Isla Mujeres

Just six miles from Cancun, Isla Mujeres offers excellent snorkeling and diving—so much so that an island visit is included in most seafaring tours out of Cancun. Most of these day trips include *Garrafon,* a spectacular national park that features a shallow coral reef just offshore that's ideal for swimming and snorkeling. There are dozens of recreational activities in addition to the varieties of brightly colored fish, and cannons and anchors from sunken Spanish galleons that have been placed on the sea bottom to add to the scenery. Tel. 849-4950.

The island's best beach, an expansive stretch of sand at the northernmost lee side, is *Playa Norte.* The water is shallow, and as calm and clear as a swimming pool, and the soft porous limestone sand never gets hot (though it is blinding white; sunglasses are advisable). Here, jet-skis, windsurf boards, aqua-tricycles, banana boats and other water gadgets are available from *Tarzan's Water Sports* (ask for Tarzan, of course).

About one kilometer off the southern tip of the island, *Los Manchones* (so called because from the surface there appear to be large dark stains or *manchones*) is a series of beautiful coral reefs only 30 to 50 feet deep. Scuba divers find this one of the area's main attractions.

Fascinating for experienced scuba divers is the *Cave of the Sleeping Sharks,* 60 feet deep in the open Caribbean northeast of the island. This bizarre phenomenon of immobile sharks (ordinarily, they must be in constant motion

in order to breathe) was discovered by a local diver-fisherman who chanced upon the cave.

South of Macax Lagoon is a marine biology station and turtle farm called *Tortugranja.* Turtles have been nesting on this strip of beach for centuries, but they are now under strict protection, with their nests monitored and hatchlings placed in tanks for a few months to mature before being turned loose. About 40,000 baby turtles are set free annually, and resident marine biologists offer interesting talks on the endangered species in several languages (small admission fee). Tel. 877-0595.

You can swim with dolphins, or simply have an up-close and personal encounter with them, at *Dolphin Discovery*. Reservations are recommended as sessions are limited. Tel. 877-0207.

Varied theories explain the origin of the Island's provocative name, "Isle of Women." The most common claims Spaniards found idols depicting the Mayan goddess of fertility. Another holds that when Spaniards arrived, all they saw were women, because the men and boys were out fishing at sea. And by the time they returned home with their catch, the name had already been logged in by the now disappointed captain and crew.

For dining, *Casa Rolandi* is popular for its delicious Italian specialties cooked in a traditional brick oven (Villa Rolandi Hotel offers free transportation to its property south of town: 877-0500). In town, *Rolandi's Pizzeria* serves equally delicious but more casual Italian fare. *Zazil-Ha,* the restaurant at the Na-Balam Hotel, serves great food in a setting of beachside simplicity. Garrafon Park's palm-thatched *Tamarindo* restaurant is another good choice (open 11 a.m. to 5 p.m. only).

Ferries shuttle between Isla Mujeres and Cancun's Hotel Zone from El Embarcadero Plaza. Ferries also make the trip from Puerto Juarez, just north of downtown Cancun.

Aerobanana, a fleet of *one* bright-yellow six-passenger Cessna which can take visitors from the island's small airstrip to Chichen-Itza and other points of interest, is operated by Cozumel-based Juan Rachat. For reservations, call 872-5040.

Hotels in Isla Mujeres

La Casa de los Sueños
On the road to El Garrafon
Tel. (998) 877-0651
www.lossuenos.com
This lovely hilltop B&B features striking modern Mexican architecture, with an open-air lounge overlooking the bay, an infinity pool and sun deck. Each of the nine guest rooms has its own oceanview balcony or terrace, plus marble bathroom, satellite TV, a/c. Bar service, pre-breakfast eye-opener. Small private dock offers access to the sea; snorkel, kayak gear available. Nonsmoking, no children allowed. Rates FC (includes breakfast, water sports, bicycles).

Na-Balam
Zazil-Ha 118, east end of Playa Norte
Tel. (998) 877-0279
www.nabalam.com

A two-story hotel with extra large rooms, each with a small private patio on the ground floor, or balcony on the second, with sea views. Private beach with lounge chairs and hammocks. Palapa restaurant-bar. Attractive units across the road cater to yoga buffs, with separate pool and kitchen/dining area. Rates MD.

Secreto
Punta Norte
Tel. (998) 877-1039
www.hotelsecreto.com
Luxuriously simple, this chic new hotel offers nine air-conditioned suits with private veranda overlooking the swimming pool and Caribbean beyond, CD player, minibar, other amenities. Rates MD (includes breakfast).

Villa Rolandi Gourmet & Beach Club
Fraccionamiento Laguna Mar
Tel. (998) 877-0700
www.rolandi.com
Sandro Muller, who comes from a long line of Swiss hoteliers and is widely known for his string of fine Rolandi restaurants, now offers this attractive beachfront hotel with 20 suites with terrace jacuzzi, swimming pool, gym, ex-

Isla Mujeres

Bruce Herman

cellent dining, 24-hour room service. Private catamaran transports guests from Cancun. No children under 13. Rates DX (MAP).

Villa Vera Puerto Isla Mujeres
Puerto de Abrigo, Macax Lagoon
Tel. (998) 877-0330

www.mexicoboutiquehotels.com
A deluxe retreat with a marina and 24 Mediterranean-style suites and villas with whirlpool and many other amenities (four have kitchenette). Pool, beach club, saltwater pool, jacuzzis; hammocks, spa treatments, restaurants. Member of Mexico Boutique Hotels. Rates FC.

Dining and Nightlife

Enjoying the Caribbean's Fresh Fare

Where to dine in Cancun is often a question of setting, since seafood specialties, traditional Mexican fare, Italian cuisine and other international favorites are readily available whether you are in the Hotel Zone or the downtown area.

If you want to enjoy a panoramic view of the Caribbean Sea and feel its cooling breeze, or dine in a waterfront setting beside vast Nichupte Lagoon, then the Hotel Zone is the place to be. If you want to experience the more Mexican side of Cancun, then the smaller downtown restaurants are ideal. Avenida Yaxchilan is restaurant row, with mostly Mexican restaurants lining both sides of the street.

For a quick bite or take out, there are fast-food restaurants in all the major shopping centers. A variety of dinner cruises with pirate or carnival themes are another option for dining out in the evenings. Following are descriptions of Cancun's leading restaurants:

Arrecifes
Westin Regina Hotel
Tel. 848-7400
A romantic dinner spot, this attractive, softly-lit, award-winning restaurant features seafood and Italian specialties served on a terrace overlooking the Caribbean. Live piano music. Open 6 to 11 p.m. Closed Sunday.

Blue Bayou
Hyatt Cancun Caribe Hotel
Tel. 883-0044

Fans of Louisiana cooking and music will love this multilevel restaurant overlooking a beautiful waterfall and lush bayou setting. Menu features Cajun-Creole specialties like blackened fish, gumbo and jambalaya. Live jazz. Winner of the Dirona (Distinguished Restaurants of North America) award. Open 6:30 to 11 p.m.

Bogart's
NH Krystal Hotel
Tel. 848-9800
Pays tribute to "Casablanca" with its name and exotic Moroccan decor. The gourmet international cuisine includes crepes filled with cheese, sour cream and caviar; roast duck a l'orange with figs and dates; and flaming bananas with Kahlua. There's an intimate bar with live piano music. Smoking and nonsmoking sections. Open 6:30 p.m. to midnight. Reservations recommended.

Caribeño
Presidente InterContinental Hotel
Tel. 848-8700
An attractive Caribbean-style restaurant serving international and Mexican dishes. Open 7 a.m. to midnight.

Carlos 'n Charlie's
Forum by the Sea
Tel. 849-4057
Part of the famed Anderson chain, this restaurant is also a popular night spot. Well-liked for its barbecued ribs and frat party atmosphere.

Open noon to 2 a.m.

Casa Rolandi
Plaza Caracol
Tel. 883-2557
Delicious Swiss-Italian dishes and fresh breads baked in a wood-burning brick oven that seals in the flavor. Try the charcoal-grilled Caribbean lobster, brick oven-baked lamb chops with thyme, and famous Swiss chocolate cake made from a traditional family recipe. Open 1 to 11:30 p.m.

Celebrity
Casa Turquesa Hotel
Tel. 885-2924
A palm-thatched dining room decked with plants, and serving seafood specialties, Angus steaks and pasta, plus flambés prepared tableside. Live music. Open 5 p.m. to midnight.

Cenacolo
Kukulcan Plaza
Tel. 885-3603
A longtime favorite for its traditional Italian fare, attractive setting and convenient location. The tantalizing menu features clams sautéed in white wine, cheese and spinach ravioli in tomato and basil sauce, broiled swordfish, beef rolls stuffed with bacon, garlic and parmesan, and chocolate mousse.

El Cejas
Mercado 28, locales 90-100

Yaxchilan 31, downtown. Tel. 887-1080
Where locals go for fresh fish and seafood. Have a tangy *ceviche* (marinated seafood cocktail), whole grilled fish (ask for it *"doradito,"* crispy outside, flaky inside), and an ice cold *chelada*, beer with lime juice on the rocks served in a salt-rimmed glass.

El Mitachi
Hilton Hotel
Tel. 881-8000
Fresh fish and seafood, plus select Japanese specialties served in an attractive airy setting with terrace tables overlooking the Caribbean. Menu highlights include the fresh seafood medley on ice, grilled salmon or jumbo shrimp, crab-and-avocado California sushi roll, tempura ice cream with caramel coulis, and hot chocolate cake with vanilla ice cream. Dining by candlelight makes for a romantic evening. Open noon to 11 p.m.

El Pescador (The Fisherman)
Tulipanes 28, downtown
Tel. 884-2673
This simple establishment has been going strong since 1980 thanks to its delicious fish and seafood specialties, as well as tasty Mexican side dishes. There's interior or sidewalk seating that's great for people-watching. Open 11 a.m. to 11 p.m.

El Shrimp Bucket
Kukulcan Blvd., Km. 5.5
Tel. 849-7339
This lagoon-side restaurant-bar offers the same tasty dishes and frat party atmosphere that characterize Anderson establishments. Open noon to midnight.

Fantino
The Ritz-Carlton Hotel
Tel. 885-0165
Italian specialties served in an elegant setting with a view of the Caribbean. Menu highlights include grilled vegetable salad with aged balsamic vinegar, Tuscan white bean soup with chunks of lobster, and sautéed swordfish. Live piano music. Open 7 to 11 p.m. Closed Sunday. Reservations recommended.

Hacienda El Mortero
NH Krystal Hotel
Tel. 848-9800
A replica of an 18th-century Mexican hacienda, complete with painted tile floors, graceful arches and strolling musicians. Regional specialties from all over the country; the *arrachera* tacos are especially tasty. Great margaritas. Live mariachi music. Open from 6 p.m.

Il Piacere
Labna and Tulum
Tel. 868-3044
A romantic spot to dine by candlelight, enjoying flavorfull traditional Italian fare accompanied by a good wine. You'll want to order everything on the menu, from the fish carpaccio with caviar to the beef fillet cooked in brandy, Madagascar green pepper and cream, as well as the rich panna cotta dessert. Also a

wide variety of vegetarian pasta dishes, and homemade pizza. Open from 2 p.m.

La Casa de las Margaritas
La Isla Shopping Village
Tel. 883-3222
This colorful theme restaurant offers Mexican home cooking with a twist, like baked chicken marinated in tequila, brown sugar and chipotle chili, or beef fillet stuffed with goat cheese and spinach in green tomato sauce. The friendly staff dresses in regional costumes. Musical groups provide entertainment in the evenings. Open noon to 1 a.m.; to 5 p.m. Sunday.

La Cascada
Gran Melia Cancun Hotel
Tel. 881-1100
Mexican cuisine served in a colorful, casual setting with a view of the beach. Try the house specialty, Mushrooms Monte Alban, sautéed with marrow and mezcal; lobster enchiladas, grilled shrimp flambéed with tequila, and marinated lamb cooked in maguey leaves. Open 7

to 11 p.m.; Sunday brunch 1 to 4 p.m.

La Destileria
Kukulcan Blvd., Km. 12.65
Tel. 885-1087
Opposite Kukulcan Plaza. Enjoy Mexican cuisine in a setting reminiscent of an old tequila processing hacienda. Menu highlights include tropical seafood and mango salad, crunchy fried cheese in green salsa, and ancho chilies stuffed with lobster. Indoor or outdoor seating overlooking the lagoon. Mariachi music on weekends. Open 1 p.m. to midnight; to 6:30 p.m. Sunday.

La Dolce Vita
Kukulcan Blvd., opposite the Marriott Hotel
Tel. 885-0150
A favorite spot with locals and visitors for its excellent Italian cuisine served indoors or on a terrace overlooking the lagoon. Menu features grilled seafood platter cooked with fine herbs, charcoal-broiled jumbo shrimp, and chocolate truffle cake. Trumpet player provides

soft jazz. Open noon to 11:30 p.m. Reservations suggested.

La Habichuela
Margaritas 25, downtown, off the park
Tel. 884-3158
A favorite for 25 years, this award-winning restaurant serves excellent international and regional fare. The house specialty is Cocobichuela, chunks of lobster and shrimp bathed in a curry sauce and served in a coconut shell. After dinner, try their Mayan coffee, aflame with Kahlua and regional xtabentun liqueur. There are two different dining areas to choose from, including a beautifully-lit plant-filled garden, so let your mood decide. Open noon to midnight. Reservations recommended. Tel. 884-3158.

La Joya
Fiesta Americana Grand Hotel
Tel. 881-3200
A massive stained-glass window dominates the attractive interiors of this AAA Five Diamond Award-winning restaurant. Gourmet Mexican cuisine and international specialties served in a relaxed setting with live piano and mariachi music. Open from 6:30 p.m. Closed Monday.

La Madonna
La Isla Shopping Village
Tel. 883-4837
Dramatically lit and decorated, with floor-to-ceiling statues, this theatrical setting sets the stage for fine Italian cuisine. Creative pasta dishes and a good variety of wines. Also an upstairs martini bar, open from 6 p.m. Open for lunch and dinner.

Laguna Grill
Kukulcan Blvd., Km. 15.6, at Marina del Rey
Tel. 885-0320
This beautiful restaurant overlooking the lagoon, with an interior waterfall and running river, features outstanding "New World Cuisine," international and seafood specialties that combine Asian and Mexican flavors. Try the sesame and spice pan-seared tuna with wasabe and soy vinaigrette, lobster confit slow cooked in butter and olive oil with lemon and parsley, barbecued salmon, or honey roasted chicken. Open 2 p.m. to midnight.

Lorenzillo's
Kukulcan Blvd., Km. 10.5
Tel. 883-1254
This attractive palm-thatched restaurant built over the lagoon features excellent fish and seafood dishes, as well as prime cuts of beef, named after famous seafarers and seafaring vessels. Try The Bounty, breaded soft shell crab; El Capitan, seafood lasagna; or Jean Lafitte, grilled fillet mignon. Live lobsters and softshell crabs brought in daily. Open noon to midnight.

Los Almendros
Tulum 1 and 2, downtown
Tel. 887-1332
A tradition in Cancun, this spot features delicious Yucatecan fare served in a spacious, un-adorned cafeteria-like setting. Try the *poc-chuc* (Los Almendros' original recipe for pork), *pollo pibil* or *cochinita pibil* (chicken or pork baked in banana leaves and a zesty sauce). A trio serenades diners in the evenings. Only American Express accepted. Open 11 a.m. to 11 p.m.

Los Soles
Presidente InterContinental Hotel
Tel. 848-8700
Mexican specialties served in an attractive setting. Open 6 p.m. to midnight. Closed Sunday.

Mango Tango
Kukulcan Blvd., Km. 14.2
Tel. 885-0303
Overlooking the lagoon, this open-air restaurant features a tropical Caribbean show and menu, including shrimp in lime and coconut sauce, and beef and shrimp shish kebab with pineapple, papaya and plantain served over rice. The shows, at 7 and 9:30 p.m., reggae music and atmosphere are what keep people coming back. No cover. Open noon to 2 a.m.

Mikado
Marriott CasaMagna Hotel
Tel. 881-2000
This spot offers Thai cuisine in addition to such Japanese favorites as sushi and teppanyaki prepared tableside. Excellent food and service make for a memorable evening. Open 5 to 11 p.m. Reservations suggested.

100% Natural
Sunyaxchen 6, downtown. Tel. 884-3617
Plaza Terramar. Tel. 883-1180
Kukulcan Plaza. Tel. 885-2903
Fresh fruit and vegetable platters, delicious chunky hot or cold sandwiches, and great fruit shakes. A nice change of pace, especially for breakfast. Terramar branch open 24 hours.

Outback Steak House
Flamingo Plaza
Tel. 883-3350
An informal "Aussie"-style steak house specializing in imported prime rib and steaks seared in 17 spices. Famed for its Bloomin' Onion, deep-fried and served with dip. Open 4 p.m. to midnight; from 2 p.m. Saturday and Sunday.

Palm
Presidente InterContinental Hotel
Tel. 848-8747
This branch of the celebrated New York eatery features the same winning dishes, including thick cuts of U.S. prime beef, and jumbo lobsters from Nova Scotia broiled to perfection. Outstanding setting and service. Open 5 to 11:30 p.m.

Rolandi's Pizzeria
Coba 12
Tel. 884-4047
Popular for its wood-burning brick-oven pizzas and calzones. Try the special calzone Rolandi stuffed with Caribbean lobster and cheese in a tomato, olive oil and oregano sauce. Indoor or outdoor seating. Open 11 to 12:30 a.m.

Ruth's Chris Steak House
Kukulcan Plaza
Tel. 885-0500
Deliciously prepared sizzling steaks cooked to your exact order. Extensive range of side dishes to choose from. Attractive indoor dining room or outdoor terrace seating facing the main boulevard. Open 1 to 11:30 p.m.

The Club Grill
The Ritz-Carlton Hotel
Tel. 885-0165
An elegant setting for creative dishes that combine regional ingredients with European cooking techniques and Asian spices. The place to enjoy an after-dinner Cuban cigar accompanied by a fine cognac. Dance floor and live jazz. Open 7 to 11 p.m. Closed Monday. Reservations recommended.

The Plantation House
Kukulcan Blvd., Km. 10.5
Tel. 883-1433
Hand-cut crystal and sterling silver table settings set the tone for elegant dining at this posh open-air restaurant overlooking the lagoon. The menu features Caribbean-style seafood, with dishes named after the different isles, such as Jamaica, lobster sautéed with pineapple and coconut au gratin; and Puerto Rico, grilled yellowfin tuna with a mild and creamy chipotle chili sauce. Nonsmoking sections. Piano bar and live music 8:30 to 11:30 p.m. Open 5 p.m. to midnight.

The Royal Bandstand
The Royal Sands Resort
Tel. 848-8220
Dining and dancing to live music in an elegant hacienda setting. Golden oldies, romantic classics and the latest hits. Open 5 to 11 p.m.; bar to 1 a.m.

Yamamoto
Uxmal 31
Tel. 887-3366
An extensive selection of authentic Japanese cuisine, with a menu that features more than 100 traditional dishes that you can accompany with Japanese beer, sake or green tea. Try the fried tofu, mixed teppanyaki, and shrimp-and-

avocado sushi. Take-out and delivery service. Open 1:30 to 11 p.m.; to 8 p.m. Sunday.

Yan-Kin Grill
Sheraton Hotel
Tel. 891-4400
Fine beef and seafood dishes grilled on a terrace with a breathtaking view of the Caribbean. Also pastas. Open noon to 11 p.m.

U'Mediterraneo
Forum by the Sea
Tel. 883-4848
Enjoy Neapolitan cuisine in air-conditioned comfort or on an open-air terrace overlooking the Caribbean. The dishes, named after famous Italians, include calamari Dolce & Gabbana (fried squid), scallopine alla Leonardo da Vinci (veal scallops with mozzarella), and Versace baked clams in white wine. Disco/bar. Open 11 a.m. to midnight.

Nightlife

Bulldog
Next to NH Krystal Hotel
Tel. 883-1793
The Cancun branch of a popular Mexico City nightclub that bills itself as "the home of rock & roll."

Carlos 'n Charlie's
Forum by the Sea
Tel. 849-4057
Part of the famed Anderson chain, this restaurant is also a popular night spot. Well-liked for its barbecued ribs and frat party atmosphere. Open noon to 2 a.m.

Champions
Marriott CasaMagna Hotel
Tel. 881-2000, ext. 6341
This sports bar offers both sports and dancing: 40 monitors and a giant screen for watching sporting events, live DJ and dance floor. Also pool tables. Open noon to 2 a.m.

Coco Bongo
Forum by the Sea
Tel. 883-0592
Dance music and occasional stage shows in an intimate disco. Also an upstairs tequila bar, open from noon, and an open-air terrace bar, open from 6 p.m. Disco open from 9 p.m.

El Shrimp Bucket
Kukulcan Blvd., Km. 5.5
Tel. 849-7339
This lagoon-side restaurant-bar offers the same frat party atmosphere that characterize Anderson establishments, plus live salsa, merengue, Latin jazz and other rhythms.

Glazz
La Isla Shopping Village
This new and popular night spot features jazz and martinis in a sleek modern setting.

Hard Rock Cafe
Forum by the Sea
Tel. 881-8120

Wall-to-wall rock memorabilia, huge bar, big dance floor. Rock bands play from 11 p.m. every night but Wednesday. Popular and usually crowded in the evenings. Open 11 to 2 a.m.

Jazz Lounge & Sports Bar
Hyatt Cancun Caribe Hotel
Tel. 848-7800
The lobby bar features live jazz nightly, 6 p.m. to 1 a.m.

La Madonna
La Isla Shopping Village
Tel. 883-4837
Dramatically lit and decorated, with floor-to-ceiling statues, this restaurant features a second-floor martini bar. Open from 6 p.m.

Lorenzillo's Sunset Pier
Kukulcan Blvd., Km. 10.5
Tel. 883-1254
Choose from their wide variety of tropical cocktails and watch the sun set over the lagoon from the spacious open-air deck. Jazz band and singer entertain Wednesday to Saturday with three sets starting from 8:45 p.m. Happy Hour 6 to 8 p.m. Open 4 p.m. to midnight.

Pat O'Brien's
Flamingo Plaza
Tel. 883-0418
Unofficial headquarters of spring breakers, this lively New Orleans-style bar offers a lagoonside setting and famed "Hurricane" cocktails. Live music from 7 p.m. Open until 2 a.m.

Perico's
Yaxchilan 71, downtown
Tel. 884-3152
"Forever fiesta" is the ambitious motto of this lively Mexican restaurant featuring nightly conga lines that often spill out into the street. Live mariachi and marimba music from 7:30 p.m. Open 1 p.m. to 1 a.m.

Planet Hollywood
Flamingo Plaza
Tel. 885-3044
A restaurant-bar and boutique with a glamorous yet casual Hollywood atmosphere. New Studio Planet Hollywood for disco dancing. Open 11 to 1 a.m.

Rincon Latino
Casa Turquesa Hotel
Tel. 885-2924
A palm-thatched bar featuring a Cuban band. Open from 7 p.m. Closed Monday.

Roots
Tulipanes 26, downtown
Tel. 884-2437
This popular bohemian-style restaurant-bar features a Latin jazz band in the evenings from 9 p.m. No cover charge. Open until 1 a.m. Closed Sunday.

Señor Frog's
Opposite Playa Chac Mool
Tel. 883-1092
This popular restaurant is part of a successful chain known for its tasty food and frat party atmosphere. Late night dancing and reggae bands. Open noon to 3 a.m.

The City
Next to Forum by the Sea
Look for this high concept nightclub, beach bar, lounge and Porterhouse Grill to open soon.

Tragara Club
Kukulcan Blvd., Km. 15.6, at Marina del Rey
Tel. 885-0320
This beauiful lagoonside bar and lounge offers a relaxing spot for drinks. Open from 8 p.m.

Where to Shop

La Isla Shopping Village

Cancun offers excellent shopping and most stores are conveniently concentrated in several ultramodern and attractive shopping centers located in the Hotel Zone.

La Isla Shopping Village opened in late 1999 and quickly became one of the resort's leading commercial centers. Exclusive boutiques and attractive restaurants flank the center's brick-lined streets. A man-made river, fountains and benches, as well as an outdoor setting beside the lagoon, make it a pleasant place to stroll and browse. The center is also home to Cancun's *Interactive Aquarium*, featuring close encounters with sharks, and *Dilema*, a children's play center.

Forum by the Sea is another unique shopping complex, this one boasting a beachfront location. The atrium-style center has three floors of popular restaurant-bars, a disco, and a variety of shops. Fine jewelry, in particular, is featured here at such stores as Berger and H. Stern. A fast-food court on the upper level is open till 5 a.m., offering everything from pizza to health food with a view of the comings and goings on the main strip. Their beach club offers a great place for a family outing, with snacks and meals provided by Johnny Rockets and the Hard Rock Cafe.

Kukulcan Plaza, the resort's largest shopping center, is undergoing a complete renovation. In addition to green areas, giant cupolas, and other new architectural touches, the center will feature Luxury Avenue, a passageway lined by such upscale shops as Fendi, Cartier, Dior and Versace. It currently houses numerous shops and boutiques, a bowling alley, fast-food court, beauty salon, several fine restaurants, espresso bars, and a video arcade and games to keep kids entertained. Part of the space is dedicated to local artists whose works can be seen on display.

Located near the convention center, *Plaza Caracol* was designed by an internationally-re-

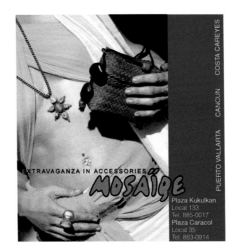

nowned architect (creator of Galerias in Houston and Dallas, among others). Its mazelike passageways are lined with fine jewelry shops, clothing boutiques, shoe stores, and cosmetics outlets. Both Kukulcan and Caracol have ATMs for making cash withdrawals, and money exchange houses.

The finest international and Mexican retailers maintain branches at the centers mentioned above.

Imported goods, such as perfumes, and gold and silver jewelry, are among Cancun's best buys thanks to low import taxes and a sales tax exemption, which lead to prices that can be 15 to 40 percent lower than in the United States.

Those looking for scenes of the Caribbean to take back home can find them at *Jardin del Arte*, an open-air art exhibit at El Embarcadero, the docking facility located at the downtown bridge. Paintings, sculptures and other works of art are sold by the artists themselves Monday to Saturday from 1 to 9 p.m.

El Zocalo, in front of the convention center, is an outdoor bazaar with stands displaying Mexican handicrafts and silver jewelry. It's a good place to find *huaraches*, attractive, durable handmade leather sandals for men and women. The bazaar hosts a Mexican Fiesta nightly from 6:30 p.m.

Most shops in downtown Cancun are located along Avenida Tulum and on the side streets that run between Tulum and Kukulcan Boulevard at the southern end, and between Tulum and Uxmal avenues at the northern end.

Catering mostly to locals, *Plaza Las Americas* is a recently-opened shopping center in the downtown area, with a branch of leading Mexican department store chain Liverpool, a Sears, and a multiplex cinema with VIP food and beverage service.

Shops generally open at 9 or 10 a.m. and stay open until 9 or 10 p.m. A few close during the lunch hour, from 2 to 4 p.m., and on Sundays. Following are just some of Cancun's more noteworthy shops.

La Isla Shopping Village

Blue Dream
Beautiful home decorative items and wearable art made of patterned Italian glass.

Casa Bonita
An emporium of Mexican handicrafts from around the country, including items made of pewter, silver and glass. Also hand-painted tiles and oil paintings by the store's artist-owner.

L.A. Cano
Tel. 883-5632
Striking pre-Hispanic-style jewelry based on actual archaeological finds from Mexico and Colombia. Most items made of 24 karat gold-plated brass, some incorporating semiprecious gems or polished stones.

La Casa del Habano
Tel. 880-5368
A wide selection of fine Cuban cigars perfectly preserved in a walk-in humidor, with each box bearing its seal of authenticity. Also stylish accessories for the cigar aficionado.

Los Castillo
Creations by the well-known Taxco family of silversmiths, including their trademark sterling silver trays and tableware inlaid with mother-of-pearl. Worth a visit just to see the wide assortment of jewelry and decorative objects.

Paul & Shark
Tel. 883-5601
Rugged sportswear inspired by the yachting life. Slickers, sweaters, khakis, and more.

Paulsen
Contemporary jewelry in yellow and white gold, many pieces incorporating pearls or semiprecious stones.

Sergio Bustamante
Striking 22 karat gold, gold-plated sterling silver, and silver jewelry designed by the celebrated Mexican sculptor, featuring his trademark blazing suns and half moons.

Kukulcan Plaza

Amazon
Clothing and accessories from Central and South America. Here you'll find genuine

Panama hats imported from Ecuador—they're woven from straw, yet famed for their supple, silky texture.

Dali
The town's best collection of books on Mexico at the best prices, including the chronicles of Stephens and Lawrence's travels through the Yucatan, maps, guide books, magazines and novels.

Fendi
The world-famous brand of leather goods and accessories, including handbags and luggage, ties, scarves, perfume and watches.

Gaitan
Handmade leather boots, jackets, bags, and more, at good prices.

Harley-Davidson
Mexico's first outlet of Harley-Davidson attire carries leather pants, jackets and accessories—all, interestingly enough, with one-year warranties. Also at Forum by the Sea.

Mama Sabina
A nice selection of traditional Mexican handmade and embroidered cotton dresses and tops from Oaxaca and Chiapas.

Mordo
Boots, jackets and Western-style accessories made of leather. Excellent quality. Also at Plaza Caracol.

Mosaïqe
Tel. 885-0017
Original designs in clothing and accessories, including exotic silver jewelry, some of it with semiprecious stones, beaded bags, beach wraps and mix-and-match combinations made of lush hand-dyed and handmade fabrics. Also at Plaza Caracol.

Ronay
Fine gold and sterling silver jewelry and unique silver-plated art work in limited editions. Also at Plaza Caracol and Forum by the Sea.

Silver Factory
A mind-boggling selection of silver jewelry and accessories, from rings to belt buckles. Pick up one of the little wicker baskets by the door and drop in whatever catches your eye.

Xaman-Ek, The Bird Sanctuary
Colorful tropical birds made of leather, ceramic and papier-mâché, as well as the unique art work and gold and silver jewelry of famed Guadalajara-born sculptor Sergio Bustamante. Also at Plaza Caracol.

Plaza Caracol

Delmar
Shells, shells, shells. More than 200 varieties from around the world. Everything from Yellow Helmets to sea urchins, some mounted as jewelry, others just finely polished to bring out their natural lustre. Also at Kukulcan Plaza.

Galerias Colonial
Ceramics, black Oaxacan pottery, papier-mâché fantasy figures, wood carvings, tapestries, onyx sculpture, and replicas of pre-Columbian artifacts.

Mosaïqe
Tel. 883-0914
Original designs in clothing and accessories, including exotic sterling silver jewelry, some of it featuring semiprecious stones. Also beaded bags, beach wraps and mix-and-match combinations made of lush hand-dyed and handmade fabrics. Also at Kukulcan Plaza.

Opals
A tiny shop with an excellent selection of Mexican handicrafts, including wooden masks from Guerrero and devil pottery from Michoacan. Branch at Playa del Carmen.

Sybelle
One of the resort's finest stores for clothing and accessories for both men and women, including fine costume jewelry, shoes and sandals. Also at Kukulcan Plaza.

Ultra Femme
A large selection of imported perfumes, colognes, cosmetics and accessories. Also at the airport, Kukulcan Plaza, La Isla, and downtown on Tulum Avenue.

Flamingo Plaza

Marti
Sporting goods, from golf balls to camping equipment. Everything you need for the great outdoors.

Tikal
Contemporary clothing and accessories fashioned from authentic Guatemalan fabrics.

Other Locations

Foto Omega
Tulum 103; and Uxmal 45, downtown
Tel. 885-2198
The best-stocked photo supply shops in the area. Film, developing, convenient single-use recyclable cameras for daytime, nighttime and underwater photography. Also at La Isla, Kukulkan Plaza, Forum by the Sea, Plaza Caracol and Flamingo Plaza.

La Fiesta
Kukulcan Blvd., opposite convention center
A supermarket of Mexican handicrafts.

Morgan's
Coba 47, downtown
Tel. 884-4433
A first-class tobacco shop with a good selection of fine cigars, including top-of-the-line Cuban brands.

Tierra Mia
El Embarcadero Plaza
Handmade clothing from Chiapas, Oaxaca and Guerrero.

Where to Stay

Casa Turquesa
Kukulcan Blvd., Km. 13.5
Tel. (998) 885-2924
www.casaturquesa.com
An elegant Mediterranean-style mansion on a dazzlingly white beach with 33 spacious suites with all amenities (including CD player, VCR), and private balconies with jacuzzi. Restaurant and bar with live music. Personalized service, private setting. Rates LX.

Club Med
Punta Nizuc
Tel. (998) 881-8200
On a wide expanse of beach on the south end of the island. The 410 rooms are set in three-story bungalows facing the sea or lagoon. Three excellent restaurants, water sports, complete schedule of daytime and nighttime activities and entertainment. No children under 12 admitted. Rates DX (all inclusive).

Dreams Cancun Resort & Spa
On Punta Cancun
Tel. (998) 848-7000
Recently acquired by AMResorts, operators of top-of-the-line all-inclusives, this property (formerly Camino Real) lies on one of Can-cun's most privileged slices of coast, offering a spectacular setting and attractive accommodations. There are 381 deluxe rooms and suites with private lanais and ocean views; Club Tower offers rooms with a stunning view and added amenities. Lovely private beach safe for swimming, large swimming pools, man-made lagoon. Well-equipped gym with steam room, jacuzzi, three tennis courts; instructor available. Meeting facilities, business center. Rates DX (all inclusive).

El Pueblito
Kukulcan Blvd., Km. 17.5 on Playa Delfines
Tel. (998) 881-8800
An attractive and popular all-inclusive resembling a colorful Mexican village. The 350 rooms with cable TV, a/c, balcony are distrib-uted in 29 beachfront low-rises. Pools, tobog-gan, tennis, a la carte dining, theme nights, lobby bar. Rates MD (all inclusive).

Fiesta Americana
Kukulcan Blvd., Km. 9.5
Tel. (998) 881-1400
www.fiestaamericana.com
A Mediterranean-style village surrounding a palm-filled plaza with a lovely freeform pool; 266 deluxe rooms and 15 suites with balco-nies. Beautiful beach, water sports, in-house movies, outdoor dining. Rates DX.

Fiesta Americana Condesa
Kukulcan Blvd., Km. 16.5
Tel. (998) 881-4232
www.fiestaamericana.com
Three Mediterranean-style buildings on the beach with 476 rooms and 26 suites, many with jacuzzi. Restaurants, bars, spa with sauna and jacuzzi, two-level freeform pool with wa-terfall, three indoor tennis courts, extensive convention facilities. One of The Leading Ho-tels of the World. Rates FC.

Fiesta Americana Grand Coral Beach
Kukulcan Blvd., Km. 9.5

HOTEL RATES
LX: luxury, rates above 375 USD
DX: deluxe, rates from 250-375 USD
FC: first-class, rates from 150-250 USD
MD: moderate, rates from 75-150 USD
ECON: economical, rates under 75 USD

Tel. (998) 881-3200
www.fiestamericana.com
AAA Five Diamond Award-winning beachfront hotel with 602 suites with all deluxe amenities, including 80 super spacious master suites. Fine restaurants, bars, gorgeous meandering pool, air-conditioned indoor tennis, gym, spa, year-round kids club. Extensive meeting facilities for up to 2,000 people, convention management, business center. One of The Leading Hotels of the World. Rates DX.

Gran Caribe Real
Kukulcan Blvd., Km. 11.5
Tel. (998) 881-5600
www.realresorts.com.mx
An attractive 638-room property on the beach (formerly Continental Villas Plaza) with some Mediterranean-style villas with terrace. Restaurant, cafeteria. Banquet facilities for 900. Three swimming pools, two lighted tennis courts, two squash courts, gym. Rates FC (all-inclusive with room-only option).

Gran Melia
Kukulcan Blvd., Km. 16.5
Tel. (998) 881-1100
www.solmelia.com
Located along 1,500 feet of white sandy beach, pyramid-shaped glass towers house 680 rooms with sea or lagoon views. "Follow the sun" pool, restaurants, bars, 24-hour room service, outdoor massage *cabañas* famed for their moonlight massages, fitness center, tennis courts, nine-hole golf course. Extensive convention and banquet facilities, business centers. Rates FC.

Hilton Cancun Beach & Golf Resort
Retorno Lacandones, Km. 17
Tel. (998) 881-8000
www.hiltoncancun.com
A modern pyramid construction with Romanesque architectural touches. The 426 fully redecorated spacious rooms and suites, distributed in a main tower and Beach Club villas, have sea or lagoon views. Fine restaurants, 7 heated pools, jacuzzis, lighted tennis courts, gym, 18-hole golf course, regulation soccer field. Spa to open soon. Experts at handling groups and conventions. Rates FC.

Holiday Inn Express
Av. Pok-Ta-Pok 21
Tel. (998) 883-2200
www.hiexpress.com
This pleasant low-key hotel next to the golf course has colonial touches and 119 rooms built around a garden and swimming pool. Rooms have a/c, satellite TV, bathtubs; second-floor units have balconies. Pool bar, deli. Free shuttle to beach club. Rates MD (includes continental breakfast buffet).

Hyatt Cancun Caribe
Kukulcan Blvd., Km. 10.5
Tel. (998) 848-7800
www.cancun.hyatt.com
On a wide expanse of secluded beach are 10 acres of gardens and 226 spacious rooms with ocean views, cable TV, a/c. Beachfront Regency Club villas have private balcony or terrace,

open-air private pool and jacuzzi. Beautiful pool, water-sports marina, tennis courts, running track, poolside massages. Restaurants, jazz bar, banquet facilities. Rates DX.

Hyatt Regency Cancun
Kukulcan Blvd., Km. 8.5, on Punta Cancun
Tel. (998) 883-1234
www.cancun.hyatt.com
This tower has 300 well-appointed rooms with balconies, most facing the Caribbean. Split-level pool, sand-covered sun deck with palapas, pier leading to the water, fitness center. Restaurants, bars. Convention facilities. Newly opened MCM World Spa. Free shuttle service to its sister hotel. Rates MD.

JW Marriott
Kukulcan Blvd., Km. 14.5
Tel. (998) 848-9600
www.marriotthotels.com
This luxury hotel features 450 rooms and suites with a spacious, private balcony, 24-hour room service. A three-level 30,000-square-foot spa offers the latest treatments; freeform pool facing the ocean, adults-only pool with wet bar, lighted tennis courts. Extensive meeting and banquet facilities, business center. Fine restaurants, lobby bar, kids club. Rates DX.

Le Meridien
Kukulcan Blvd., Km. 14
Tel. (998) 881-2200
www.meridiencancun.com.mx
A beachfront hotel-spa with a European flavor: 213 rooms and suites with Caribbean or lagoon views, or both, and all amenities. Pool area gets sun all day, excellent restaurants with fresh breads baked daily, kids club and playground, meeting facilities, artificial grass tennis courts, health spa with jacuzzi. One of The Leading Hotels of the World. Rates DX.

Marriott CasaMagna
Kukulcan Blvd., Km. 14.5
Tel. (998) 881-2000
www.marriotthotels.com
On a beautiful stretch of beach, this property offers 450 rooms and suites with private balconies, 24-hour room service. Health club, swimming pool, lighted tennis courts, kids club. Banquet and meeting facilities. International restaurants, lobby bar. Rates FC.

Melia Turquesa
Kukulcan Blvd., Km. 12
Tel. (998) 881-2500
www.solmelia.com
A pyramid-shaped all-inclusive beachfront complex with 450 spacious rooms and suites with balconies overlooking the sea; satellite TV, minibar, safe, 24-hour room service. Restaurant, lobby bar, pool, lighted tennis courts, meeting and banquet facility for up to 400. Rates DX (all inclusive).

Miramar Mision
Kukulcan Blvd., Km. 9.5
Tel. (998) 883-1755
www.hotelesmision.com
On a fine beach with 266 rooms and suites with a/c, satellite TV, minibar, safe, private balcony. Swimming pool with children's wading pool, large seventh-floor jacuzzi with panoramic view, game room. Restaurant, cafeteria. Meeting facilities for 350. All-inclusive option. Rates MD.

NH Krystal Cancun
Kukulcan Blvd., Km. 9, at Punta Cancun
Tel. (998) 848-9800
www.nh-hotels.com
Well-run and popular, this deluxe property on a great beach has 325 rooms with satellite TV, half with sea views. Fine restaurants. Large

pool, jacuzzi, sauna, gym, lighted tennis court, racquet court. Convention and banquet facilities. All-inclusive option. Rates DX.

Presidente InterContinental
Kukulcan Blvd., Km. 7.5
Tel. (998) 848-8700
www.intercontinental.com
On a superb swimming beach with minimum surf, this 300-room resort offers lots of recreational facilities, including two swimming pools, five jacuzzis, lighted tennis court, Ping-Pong tables, health club, wet bar, water sports. Oversized rooms available in three categories, with a/c, TV, direct-dial phones. Meeting facilities for up to 650 people. Winner of AAA's Four Diamond Award. Rates FC.

Radisson Hacienda
Nader 1, downtown
Tel. (998) 887-4455
www.radissoncancun.com
Hacienda-style architecture and lots of greenery make this a pleasant hotel (formerly Holiday Inn) with 248 rooms with cable TV, safe, iron, hair dryer, coffee maker. Swimming pool with wet bar, wading pool, tennis court, gym (nominal daily fee). Free beach transfers 4 times a day. Restaurant, lobby bar. Small meeting rooms. Rates MD.

Sheraton Resort and Towers
Kukulcan Blvd., Km. 12.5
Tel. (998) 891-4400
www.sheraton.com

On a wonderful half-mile stretch of beach, this hotel offers 471 rooms and suites in a pyramid with sea, lagoon or garden views, or a tower with terraces overlooking the Caribbean. Pools with wading pools, sun decks with hammocks, fitness center, lighted tennis courts, playground, miniature golf, 24-hour room service. Convention facilities. Guests enjoy access to Westin property via shuttle bus. Rates FC.

The Ritz-Carlton
Retorno del Rey 36
Tel. (998) 885-0808
www.ritzcarlton.com
Resembling a manor house, this stately hotel has 365 elegantly furnished rooms and suites with private balconies overlooking the Caribbean. Large swimming pools, three lighted tennis courts, fitness center. Supervised kids camp and kids menus. Fine restaurants. Business center, executive floors, extensive convention and banquet facilities. Five Diamond Award winner for service, cuisine. Rates DX.

The Westin Regina Resort
Kukulcan Blvd., Km. 20.5, on Punta Nizuc
Tel. (998) 848-7400
www.westin.com
Occupying a gorgeous stretch of beach, this beautiful property is decorated with refined Mexican touches. The 293 spacious rooms and suites are simply yet elegantly decorated and have all amenities. Five pools, three tennis courts, health and fitness center, *temazcal* (sweat lodge), restaurants and meeting facilities. Kids club. Guests enjoy access to Sheraton property via shuttle bus. Rates FC.

Villas Tacul
Kukulcan Blvd., Km. 5.5
Tel. (998) 883-0000
www.mexicoboutiquehotels.com
Originally a presidential retreat for visiting dignitaries, this hideaway is nestled on a sparkling, sandy beach cove with calm waters superb for swimming. The 80 guest rooms are distributed in 23 one- to five-bedroom Mexican-style villas, nine right on the beach (36 standard rooms with garden view and 27 Superior rooms with ocean view). Palm-thatched restaurants, bars, lovely pool with floating "islands," tennis courts, water-sports marina, playground. Member of Mexico Boutique Hotels. Rates FC.

Isla Holbox

Villas Delfines
Tel. (984) 875-2196
For those who want to get away from it all, this environmentally-friendly hotel on a beautiful beach offers spacious palm-thatched bungalows, each with a private terrace with a hammock. Restaurant-bar.

Xaloc Resort
On Playa Norte
Tel. (984) 875-2160
www.holbox-xalocresort.com
Eighteen tropical palm-thatched bungalows on the beach. Charming, rustic rooms with king-size beds. Restaurant, game room, two pools.

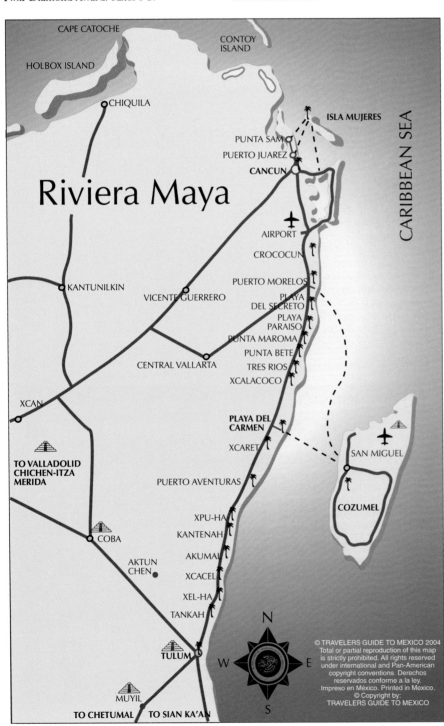

Playa del Carmen

Attractions Along the Riviera Maya

Quintana Roo's 100 miles of Caribbean coastline from Cancun to the archaeological site of Tulum is the state's fastest growing region. Tropical parks, snorkeling havens, and rustic to luxurious hotels dot this corridor called the Riviera Maya.

A nearly completed four-lane highway connects Cancun to Tulum, and buses regularly shuttle back and forth between downtown Cancun and the corridor's favorite resort town, Playa del Carmen, making stops along the way to leave or pick up sightseers at various points of interest.

Perfect for snorkeling, scuba diving, fishing or simply enjoying the Caribbean scenery, the area is peppered with nature parks and hotels, most of which are set on the beach about a half mile from the road, and hidden behind dense tropical vegetation. You can choose from facilities that range from a hammock strung between two palms to a luxurious beachside villa.

The first attraction you see after leaving Cancun is the *Palancar Aquarium,* with 17 displays of area marine life. Next door is *Crococun,* a crocodile farm and regional zoo.

Playa del Carmen

Bruce Herman

Puerto Morelos

About 30 kilometers/18 miles from Cancun is the small but burgeoning coastal fishing village of *Puerto Morelos.* Its attractive beaches and bohemian village life are drawing comparisons to Playa del Carmen's early days as a haven for tourist-weary visitors to the Mexican Caribbean. At Puerto Morelos the region's barrier reef comes closest to the coast, making it an ideal spot for snorkeling.

The opening of the *Ceiba del Mar,* an upscale boutique hotel and spa, has taken accommodations in the quaint fishing village to a new level. More typical is the pleasant budget beachfront hotel *Casita del Mar,* on Calle Heriberto Frias. Tel. 871-0301.

Near the main square, on Rafael Melgar, is *Johnny Cairo's,* a popular beach bar and grill. It's open Monday to Friday from 6 p.m., and Saturday and Sunday from 1 p.m. Tel. 871-0015.

A short distance beyond Puerto Morelos is the *Dr. Alfredo Barrera Marin Botanical Garden,* which features a replica of a typical Mayan home, a nature trail and native plant species like *cacao* and *chicle* trees, from which we get chocolate and chewing gum, respectively.

Playa del Carmen

Located 45 minutes south of Cancun's airport is the beach town of Playa del Carmen, the fastest growing destination in the state of Quintana Roo. Just a few years ago, this former fishing hamlet served merely as a springboard for visitors taking the ferry to Cozumel. But as more and more ferry-bound travelers lingered to enjoy its Caribbean beaches and rustic charms, the town came into its own as a resort destination.

Luxury cruise ships which regularly dock offshore add to the ever greater number of travelers who visit each year from the United States and Canada, as well as Europe, especially Germany, Great Britain and Italy.

"Playa," as it is called by locals, is growing by leaps and bounds, but still preserves a certain small-town charm and bohemian following.

> *"Playa" is growing by leaps and bounds, but still retains a certain small-town charm and bohemian following.*

Hotels in Playa tend to be small, chic yet rustic establishments with palm-thatched roofs. Three of the leading beachfront hotels are *Las Palapas* and *Shangri-La,* both on the north edge of town, and the downtown *El Faro.* Leading hotels in town include *Deseo* and *Mosquito Blue.*

The larger hotels are located in Playacar, the residential-resort development south of the ferry dock. These include one of the Mexican Caribbean's most exclusive all-inclusive resorts, *Royal Hideaway.*

Playacar is home to the *Playacar Golf Club,* with an 18-hole course designed by Robert von Hagge that is open to the public, and *Xaman-Ha,* a lovely refuge for guacamayas, parrots, pelicans, toucans and pink flamingos; the birds are not caged and roam about the park freely.

Almost everything in Playa is within walking distance, including the bird sanctuary; a 10-minute walk south on Avenida 10, starting from Avenida Juarez.

Playa del Carmen's main strip, Quinta Avenida (or Fifth Avenue), is flanked by numerous sidewalk restaurants interspersed with stores carrying handicrafts, myriad brands of tequila, amber and silver jewelry, and other items made in Mexico. *Daniel Espinosa Jewelry,* at Plaza Paseo del Carmen, features bold, contemporary designs in silver, including many pieces with semiprecious stones. Espinosa's creativity and sense of fun is evident in his tie-style chokers made of silver, hypnotic silver rings with black enamel swirls, and other unique items.

You can also find a variety of handmade goods from neighboring Guatemala, as well as casual resort clothes, and even fine cigars. *Morgan's Tobacco Shop,* with branches at Quinta Avenida and Calle 6, and at the Mosquito Blue Hotel, carries top-of-the-line domestic and imported brands, as well as pipes and other accessories. If property is what you are looking to buy, *Playa Real Estate,* on Quinta Avenida, specializes in the booming Riviera Maya.

The European influence in Playa has led to a crop of Italian trattorias serving up fresh pasta and brick-oven pizzas, including *Rolandi,* at the

Xcaret

Riviera Maya

dance floor/stage that is usually hopping at night with a young crowd. At *Deseo,* a chic new minimalist-style hotel, oversized beds, a live DJ and martini cocktails beckon visitors to the poolside lounge area.

Coffee mavens have a few places to choose from. One of the nicest is *The Coffee Press,* a modest little sidewalk cafe on Calle 2 with a small library of paperbacks, a sliver of a view of the Caribbean, freshly baked cakes, fruit juice cocktails and, of course, great coffee.

The beaches are Playa's main attraction, especially the more isolated stretches north and south of town. If you decide to explore them, leave anything of value in your hotel; sunbathers have been known to have their belongings pilfered from their beach towels.

A Playa-based ecotourism outfit, *Altournative,* offers expeditions to surrounding attractions, including rappeling or diving in nearby cenotes, and visits to local Mayan communities. Tel. 873-2036.

Travelers can fly direct to Cancun, and then make the short drive to Playa del Carmen, located about 66 kilometers/40 miles to the south. Airport taxis charge 50 dollars for the trip (returning from Playa, regular taxis charge 30 dollars).

Buses shuttle between Cancun and Playa at a very nominal fare, but expect this option to

Paseo del Carmen shopping center (tel. 803-4121) and *Da Gabi.* A popular French spot is *Byblos. Media Luna* is a small, low-key sidewalk restaurant offering an eclectic menu culled from different world cuisines; try their delicious grilled vegetable plate.

For Mexican fare, try *La Parrilla,* which serves good food and great drinks, with live mariachi music nightly, or *Pancho's,* a branch of Merida's famed restaurant and bar. Delicious Yucatecan specialties are available at

Yaxche, a restaurant with sidewalk tables at Calle 8, just off Quinta Avenida. Their *cochinita pibil* is outstanding.

Some restaurants close during the low season.

After dinner, try *Ted's Mescaleros,* a huge palm-thatched bar and dance hall on the beach that often features reggae bands and rock groups. Another popular night spot with live bands is the beach bar at the *Blue Parrot.*

Señor Frog's, a restaurant-bar overlooking the beach just past the dock, features a small

add about 40 minutes to the trip as the bus station is located in the downtown area, at the opposite end of Cancun from the airport.

Turboprop charter planes also make the 10-minute flight to Playa, which has a landing strip capable of handling light aircraft.

Tres Rios

The Riviera Maya's most pristine natural attraction, Tres Rios is a tropical reserve featuring three crystalline rivers that give the site its name. Because little was done to alter the natural environment while still providing all the necessary facilities, Tres Rios looks and feels like virgin jungle territory.

Visitors can float, swim or canoe down the jungle-flanked rivers towards the Caribbean, kayak or horseback ride on the beach, swim and snorkel in the cenotes, see an ostrich ranch, or simply enjoy the beautiful scenery. You can join group excursions through the park or design your own itinerary.

Bicycles are the preferred mode of transportation here, but you can also ride comfortably in a bike-pulled two-seater cart. There's a palm-thatched restaurant on the beach, as well as lockers, showers and a shop.

A nominal entrance fee covers most activities at the reserve, but an all-inclusive option is also available that includes a snorkeling tour to nearby reefs. Located about 30 minutes from Cancun, the reserve is open daily from 9 a.m. to 6 p.m. Tel. 887-4977.

Xcaret

Xcaret, a beautifully landscaped tropical theme park and pioneer in the region, is situated just 5 kilometers/3 miles farther south. Covered in lush vegetation and home to a few small Mayan ruins, Xcaret bills itself as an "eco-archaeological park," though "seaside playground" would probably be more descriptive.

In high season, the park draws more than 1,500 people a day who come to swim and snorkel the length of underground rivers, swim among schools of tropical fish in crystal-clear inlets and lagoons, see exotic animals, and enjoy folkloric and Mayan theme shows.

Apart from being a colorful place to snorkel and frolic in the sun, Xcaret has some scattered ruins, a wonderful aquarium featuring exotic sea creatures and a sea turtle hatchery, a butterfly pavilion and hatchery, an aviary, and excellent Mexican and seafood restaurants, some right on the beach.

One of the park's stellar attractions are its dolphins, which you can swim with for an added fee. This is a very popular activity and you must arrive at the park early to sign up for it.

The park has added nighttime shows to its roster of offerings (at no extra charge), including a fascinating reenactment of the Mayan ball game that pits two teams against each other, concerts of pre-Hispanic music and rituals, and excellent folkloric dancing and singing.

Xcaret's entrance fee is around 40 dollars. The park has its own comfortable air-conditioned fleet of colorful converted school buses that leave from the Xcaret terminal, across from Plaza Caracol, at 9, 10 and 11 a.m. for the scenic one-hour ride to the park. If you want to visit both Tulum and Xcaret, the bus leaves at 8:15 a.m. No reservations are necessary. Snacks and souvenirs are available at the terminal. For more information, call 883-3143.

Puerto Aventuras

Puerto Aventuras is a tranquil resort community about 45 miles south of Cancun. There are private homes, villas and condominiums, hotels, small-scale shopping centers with restaurants and stores, including a branch of one of Mexico's leading silversmiths, *Talleres de los Ballesteros*, a dive center, CEDAM nautical museum, marina and 18-hole golf course.

The community's main feature is its 240-slip deep-water marina capable of handling large luxury yachts. This is the first full-service marina in this part of Mexico and includes light maintenance facilities and a 24-hour marine radio station.

At Puerto Aventuras, you can swim with dolphins or simply pet them at *Dolphin Discovery*, which operates three such facilities in the Mexican Caribbean, including in Cozumel and Isla Mujeres. Making reservations in advance is recommended as sessions with dolphins are limited. Tel. 883-0779.

Xpu-Ha

Located about an hour's drive south of Cancun, Xpu-Ha is a new tropical water park that operates under an all-inclusive concept.

The all-inclusive entry price of 59 dollars, which covers transportation, all meals, drinks, and almost all activities, allows visitors to snorkel in natural inlets, scuba dive, or head out to sea in catamaran boat rides.

Visitors can see tropical fish at its aquarium, tropical birds at its aviary, and other animals, including deer, tapirs and turtles, that are native to the jungle.

Meals and drinks at the park are provided at two snack stations and a gigantic palapa-style restaurant that serves a buffet lunch.

Xpu-Ha, open daily from 9 a.m. to 5 p.m., has its own shuttle service from Cancun and Playa del Carmen with departures at 9, 10 and 11 a.m. Tel. 884-2411.

Akumal

Some 65 miles south of Cancun, or 14 miles north of Tulum, lies the hidden beach resort of Akumal, a beautiful, crescent-shaped palm-fringed bay at the edge of dense brush land.

Developed by Mexican industrialist and scuba diving enthusiast Pablo Bush, Akumal is famous for excellent snorkeling and diving. Expert instruction and equipment are available, and there are several good hotels in the area.

Aktun Chen

The caverns of Aktun Chen feature thousands of stalactite and stalagmite formations, as well as a clear 40-foot-deep cenote. Lighting and a foot path have made it easy to explore the inside of the largest of the three caves, which is 600 yards long. Around the site, visitors can hike through jungle trails or join a jungle tour aboard four-wheel all-terrain vehicles (ATVs).

Tulum and Xel-Ha

Most tours out of Cancun combine an early morning visit to the archaeological site of Tulum with an afternoon of snorkeling at Xel-Ha.

Located about 80 miles south of Cancun, Tulum is the only walled city the Maya built and the only one by the edge of the Caribbean. When the Spanish first came upon the site in 1518, they recorded that it was as large as Seville. Tulum's delicate small-scale buildings date from 1200 to 1400 A.D. and show a decline in construction techniques as compared with sites like Chichen-Itza and Uxmal.

The major construction is the *Castle*, a handsome pyramid perched on the edge of a cliff high above the pearl-white beaches below. Its serpent columns show Toltec influence. From here one can see most of the ancient city, only partially restored, as well as a magnificent

view of the coastline.

An expanded parking lot has made it easier to visit the site, and consequently people do, by the bus load. Try to visit in the early morning hours if you want to avoid the crush.

On the way back you can visit fascinating Xel-Ha, a park and natural aquarium with four interlocking lagoons where swimming and snorkeling are superb. There are also jungle trails, a shell-strewn beach (not for swimming, but great for exploring), and dolphin pen where you can swim with the unique creatures (at an additional cost).

The park encompasses a small archaeological zone with constructions dating from the Post-Classic period; Xel-Ha is believed to have been a major port for the Mayan merchant marine, which had a thriving trade that reached from the Gulf of Mexico to Honduras.

The newest feature at the park is the *Aquatic Institute*, which offers snorkeling instruction with an emphasis on the identification and responsible handling of underwater flora and fauna. The park is open from 8:30 a.m. For more information, call 884-9422 in Cancun or the park directly at (984) 875-6000.

Coba

Archaeology buffs, bird watchers (more than 200 species of birds migrate here annually) and nature lovers will want to visit Coba, about 30 miles northwest of Tulum. A Classic-era site that peaked around 500-800 A.D., Coba could be the largest Mayan city yet discovered—and only a portion of the site has been uncovered.

Coba is decidedly unique among Yucatecan archaeological sites: it is the largest (nine square miles), it has the tallest pyramid (Nohuch Mul, 122 feet), and it has four lakes and numerous stele—none of which have been found at any other site in the peninsula.

The turnoff for Coba along Highway 307 (Carretera Corredor) is just about parallel to the Tulum turnoff: for Tulum you turn east, for Coba you turn west. The road to Coba goes inland, eventually ending at Highway 180, which leads out of Cancun to Chichen-Itza and Merida.

Club Med operates a *Villa Arqueologica* right next to the site where you can stop for a meal or spend the night.

The small farming community of *Punta Laguna*, located on the highway between Coba and Nuevo Xcan, shares its forest enclave with the endangered spider monkey. Visitors can follow a jungle trail, spot the monkeys swinging from tree tops overhead, swim in the lagoon, and even see traditional farming methods and plots.

Sian Ka'an

About two and a half hours south of Cancun is the *Sian Ka'an* nature reserve, Mexico's largest protected area and a UNESCO-designated World Heritage Site. Here visitors can appreciate the region's varied wildlife while boating or even floating in clear winding canals.

Covering more than one million acres, the reserve is composed equally of semi-evergreen tropical forest, wetland, savanna and marine habitats. Not surprisingly, the varied landscape is home to an abundance of birds and animals.

More than 340 species of birds thrive here, including the rare jabiru stork and more than a million wintering migratory song birds from the United States and Canada, which make wintertime tours ideal for bird watching aficionados.

All of the endangered cat species of southern Mexico are also found here, including the jaguar, puma and ocelot, though their nocturnal habits make sightings rare.

What's more, the remnants of some 27 Mayan sites, including one building which may have served as a customs check point for traders transporting goods via the canals, have been found on the reserve.

For guided day trips of the reserve call *Amigos de Sian Ka'an* (887-3080), a respected local conservation group that also offers authentic ecological tours to other parts of Mexico's Caribbean coast, including visits to Coba and Contoy Island, a protected breeding colony for sea birds.

Another site worth visiting is *Ria Lagartos,* located about 160 miles northwest of Cancun. It is a federally-protected area with nesting flamingos and lots of interesting flora and fauna. The area has good fresh seafood, but accommodations are minimal.

For more information on these and other sites, refer to the chapter titled "The Great

Outdoors" found at the beginning of the book.

Where to Stay

Editor's Note: The Riviera Maya, a 100-mile stretch of coast that lies south of Cancun, is developing fast, with new hotels opening regularly. Because Cancun serves as the main point of departure for resorts along this coast, the destinations in this section are listed in geographical order, starting with those closest to Cancun's airport.

Puerto Morelos

Ceiba del Mar
Costera Norte, Lote 1
Tel. (998) 872-8060
ww.ceibadelmar.com
This attractive beachfront hotel and spa features 126 rooms and suites with oceanview terraces distributed in eight thatched-roofed buildings with sunroof, jacuzzi, bar and concierge. "Butler box" for discreet 24-hour room service. Spa, spa cuisine, *temazcal* (sweat lodge). Two swimming pools, oceanfront whirlpool, tennis court and jogging path. Meeting facilities for up to 120. Rates LX (MAP).

Paradisus Riviera Cancun
Just north of Puerto Morelos
Tel. (998) 872-8383
www.solmelia.com
Thatched rooftops and swaying palms give a tropical look to this all-inclusive beach and spa resort with 500 spacious rooms with terrace, including 96 ocean-view junior suites with private jacuzzi. A la carte and buffet dining, 24-hour room service, nightly shows. Shuttle to Cancun 4 times a day, unlimited scuba diving, tennis, Tai Chi, two swimming pools. Rates FC (all inclusive).

Paraiso de la Bonita
Carretera Cancun-Chetumal, Km. 3.28
Tel. (998) 872-9500
www.paraisodelabonitaresort.com
Located just 13.5 km./8 mi. south of Cancun's airport, and 16 km./10 mi. north of Puerto Morelos, this intimate and elegant luxury hotel and spa resort blends design elements from around the world, including Africa, India, Asia, the Mediterranean, Caribbean and Orient. There are 90 oceanview suites: first-floor units with private swimming pools, upper-level units with terraces, hammocks and umbrellas, all with spacious living rooms, Internet access, 24-hour room service. Offshore coral reef for exploring, three swimming pools, two tennis courts, 6,000-square-foot thalassotherapy spa (using heated, mineral-rich sea water). Fine restaurant and grill. Rates LX.

Punta Maroma

Maroma
Punta Maroma, Hwy. 307, Km. 51
Tel. (998) 872-8200
www.orient-express.com

Xel-Ha

Riviera Maya

About 20 miles south of Cancun airport. A romantic hideaway offering privacy and personalized service along a mile of Caribbean beachfront. The 58 rooms and suites are distributed in palm-thatched stucco villas surrounded by gardens and have a canopied king size bed, terrace with hammock, sunken tub, CD player, a/c, phone. Lounge with satellite TV. Indoor-outdoor gourmet dining, piano bar. Three swimming pools, beachfront jacuzzi, body and facial treatments, *temazcal* (sweat lodge). Rates DX (includes breakfast, airport transfers).

Playa del Carmen

Allegro Resort
Playacar hotel zone
Tel. (984) 873-0340
An attractive all-inclusive property on the beach. The 300 rooms distributed among two-story palm-thatched villas have balconies, cable TV, ceiling fans and a/c. Two pools, four tennis courts, kids club, restaurants, piano bar, disco, nightly entertainment. Banquet and convention facilities. Access to other Allegro resorts (two in Cancun, one in Cozumel, another at Playacar). Rates FC (all inclusive).

Caribbean Village
Playacar hotel zone
Tel. (984) 873-0506
Surrounded by a professional 18-hole golf course, this all-inclusive resort offers 296 rooms with satellite TV distributed in 22 two-story villas. Restaurants, disco, three pools, three tennis courts, kids club, beach club, daytime activities and nightly entertainment. Access to other Allegro resorts (two in Cancun, one in Cozumel, another at Playacar). Rates MD (all inclusive).

Continental Plaza
Playacar hotel zone
Tel. (984) 873-0100
www.hotel.sidek.com.mx
A beachfront hotel and timeshare complex of modern colonial design right next to the dock, with 185 rooms and suites with a/c, satellite TV, phone. Pool, tennis, water sports. Restaurants, bar. Meeting facilities for 200. All-inclusive option. Rates MD.

Deseo
Quinta Avenida and Calle 12, in town
Tel. (984) 879-3620
www.hoteldeseo.com
A place to be experienced not just stayed at, this stunning minimalist-style property bills itself as a "hotel + lounge." The 15 rooms and suites, some with terraces, are equipped with a beach and party kit, wireless phone, hammocks and other amenities. Pool deck/lounge area with oversized beds, live DJ in the evenings, jacuzzi, self-service kitchen, library.

El Faro
Calle 10 Norte, in town
Tel. (984) 873-0970
This charming beachfront hotel, built around a privately-owned functioning lighthouse, offers casual elegance with 28 tastefully decorated guest rooms, lovely swimming pool with a "floating" island of palms, good restaurant and bar. Rates MD.

Gala
Playacar hotel zone
Tel. (984) 877-4040
www.galaresorts.com.mx
This all-inclusive resort on a white sand beach offers 460 spacious rooms and suites with full or partial sea views, cable TV, a/c, phone and minibar. Specialty restaurants, bars, disco. Swimming pools, including an adults-only pool with jacuzzi, spa/gym with steam room and modern exercise equipment, meeting and banquet facilities for 500. Rates FC (all inclusive).

Ikal del Mar
Playa Xcalacoco
www.slh.com
This luxurious resort and spa along eight miles of Caribbean beach 10 km/7 miles north of Playa del Carmen features 30 villas built of native wood and stone, health and beauty treatments, gourmet Mediterranean and Yucatecan cuisine, 24-hour room service. Member of Small Luxury Hotels of the World. Rates LX.

Las Palapas
Two kilometers north of Playa
Tel. (984) 873-0616
www.laspalapas.com.mx
This attractive beachfront property offers 75 tastefully designed palm-thatched *cabañas* in a jungle setting, including seven right on the beach. All guest rooms have private balcony with hammock, ceiling fans, safe; no phone or TV. Pool, good restaurant, beach bar, clubhouse/game room. Largely European clientele. Rates FC (MAP, includes breakfast, dinner,

RESORT & THALASSO

Paraiso de la Bonita
RIVIERA MAYA·QUINTANA-ROO

| Paraiso de la Bonita: fountain of eternal youth |

Discover the curative powers of the sea at Paraiso de la Bonita, the first resort with a Thalasso Center in the Americas. On the shores of the Caribbean Sea, you can enjoy the most innovative spa treatments, which take full advantage of the curative properties of the sea and its algae to revitalize your mind, body and spirit. Our Thalasso Center has over 22,000 square feet of extraordinary facilities where you can enjoy a massage (reflexology, shiatsu, and lymphatic drainage) and our Fitness Center (yoga, tai-chi, aqua-gym, jacuzzi and sauna) as well as hydrotherapy, physiotherapy and algae treatments conducted by trained therapists. Paraiso de la Bonita is a new and exclusive boutique hotel with just 90 suites , designed in harmony with its environment and natural surroundings. The resort is situated near the most remarkable Mayan archaeological sites and has direct access from its private beach to one of the most beautiful coral gardens in the world. A visit to Paraiso de la Bonita is an encounter with beauty and health in an utterly exclusive ambiance.

PRESIDENTE
INTERCONTINENTAL.
HOTELS & RESORTS

The first Boutique-Hotel with a Thalasso Center in the Americas operated by Presidente InterContinental Hotels & Resorts

For reservations call: 1 (800) 327 0200 - E-mail: resa@paraisodelabonitaresort.com

A member of
The LeadingSmall Hotels of the World

www.paraisodelabonitaresort.com

taxes, tips).

Mosquito Blue
Quinta Avenida, between 12th and 14th streets
Tel. (984) 873-1245
In the north end of Playa, about two blocks from the beach. This two-story Italian-owned property offers understated elegance with 45 simple yet tastefully-appointed guest rooms, some with private balconies, overlooking lovely courtyards. The English colonial-style rooms feature Indonesian teak wood furnishings, and have cable TV, a/c, minibar, phone, safe. Small pool, large palapa lounge/game room with pool table, restaurant with gourmet fare, 24-hour room service. Rates MD.

Riu Palace
Playacar hotel zone
Tel. (984) 877-4200
Formal elegance characterizes this extensive all-inclusive beach resort operated by a Spanish hotel chain. Rates FC (all inclusive).

Royal Hideaway
Playacar hotel zone
Tel. (984) 873-4500
One of Mexico's most upscale all-inclusive resorts, with the personalized service of a small luxury hotel. The beautifully landscaped grounds feature 200 well appointed rooms and suites distributed in Caribbean-style villas, each with its own concierge. Rooms have balconies with hammocks overlooking the sea or gardens, whirlpool and all deluxe amenities. Lovely swimming pools, excellent beach, spa and fitness center, lighted tennis courts. A la carte gourmet dining, nightclub with excellent shows, sports bar with pool table, cigar lounge. Meeting and convention facilities. Weddings a specialty. Access to other Allegro resorts (two in Cancun, one in Cozumel, two others at

Playacar). Rates DX (all inclusive).

Shangri-La Caribe
Two kilometers north of Playa
Tel. (984) 873-0611
For the modern Robinson Crusoe, the 50 palm-thatched stucco cottages right on the beach house 107 rooms with private bath, attractive furnishings, hammock. Pool, bar/clubhouse, water sports. Represented by Turquoise Reef Group. Rates FC (MAP, includes breakfast, dinner, taxes).

Puerto Aventuras

Oasis
Tel. (984) 873-5050
www.oasishotels.com
This hotel boasts 500 meters of beautiful beach and a small saltwater lagoon. There are 296 air-conditioned rooms with a view of the sea, satellite TV, terrace, safe. Restaurants, bars. Gym, tennis, large pool, golf tours and clinics. Kids club. All-inclusive option. Rates MD.

Omni
Carr. Chetumal-Puerto Juarez, Km. 269.5
Tel. (984) 873-5101
www.omnihotels.com
An attractive beachfront property with 30 spacious rooms with marble floor, Mexican decor, terrace jaccuzi overlooking the Caribbean, hammock, "butler box" for unintrusive room service, and more. Oceanview dining, gym and massages, two adjoining pools and jacuzzi, dive shop. All-inclusive option available. Rates FC (includes continental breakfast).

Coba

Villa Arqueologica
Just a 10-minute walk from the ruins

Tel. (984) 874-2087
One of Club Med's attractive archaeological site hotels with 40 simple air-conditioned Mediterranean-style rooms, a good restaurant, bar, library-video room, nice pool, tennis court, pool table, beautiful gardens. Rates MD.

Akumal

Akumal Cancun
On the road to Tulum
Tel. (984) 875-9026
On a snow-white beach among coconut palms. Lovely and peaceful, and perfect for getting away from it all. There are 92 rooms and 10 suites, all with Caribbean views, restaurants, beach bar and disco. Dive shop, fishing, horseback riding, diving in *cenotes*, tennis. Rates MD.

Club Akumal Caribe Villas Maya
Tulum-Puerto Juarez Hwy., Km. 104
Tel. (984) 875-9012
A small hotel with 62 air-conditioned guest rooms distributed in bungalows with garden views and a three-story low-rise with sea views. Facilities include pool, palapa restaurant and snack bar, diving and water-sports center. Rates MD.

Oasis
Carr. Chetumal-Puerto Juarez, Km. 251
Tel. (984) 875-7300
www.oasishotels.com
Set on a beautiful beach, the 182 rooms are divided among three buildings. Tennis, four pools, outdoor jacuzzis, gym, PADI dive center, children's activities. Restaurants, bar. Rates MD (all inclusive)

Tulum

Cabañas Ana y Jose
Carretera Ruinas-Boca Paila, Km. 7
Tel. (984) 887-5470
www.tulumresorts.com
In the Sian Ka'an nature reserve, 90 minutes south of Cancun, near the ruins. A rustic romantic hideaway offering 15 rooms in white-stucco palm-thatched cottages on the beach, swimming pool, a good restaurant-bar, lots of serenity and a range of activities, including scuba diving, snorkeling. For those who really want to get away from it all, though in-house car rental makes it easy to get around. Rates MD.

Villa Las Ranitas
Carretera Ruinas-Boca Paila, Km. 9
Tel. (984) 845-8647
This charming, environmentally-friendly beachfront resort offers 16 rooms with balconies beautifully furnished with colorful native crafts. Solar-heated swimming pool.

A boat tour of Sian Ka'an

Susan Kaye

Bruce Herman

Mexico's original Caribbean playground was named Cuzamil, meaning "Land of the Swallows," by its first inhabitants, the Maya. However, it was Ixchel, the goddess of fertility, that they worshiped here and the remains of centuries old Mayan temples and ceremonial centers still dot the island.

This is where Europeans first stepped on Mexican soil, and a plaque on the beach marks the spot Catholic mass was first celebrated in Mexico. But the Spanish explorers didn't stay. Fresh water was in short supply and the mainland natives were hostile, so the conquerors pushed on in their search for El Dorado. Cozumel was largely forgotten, except by pirates such as Jean Lafitte, who frequented the island. Popular legend notwithstanding, no buried treasures have been found to date.

During World War II, the U.S. built an air base on Cozumel for planes hunting U-boats in the mid-Atlantic. Drawn by the clear waters, frogmen came to train and returned home with stories of magnificent underwater vistas. After a visit to the island in 1962, oceanographer Jacques Cousteau proclaimed Cozumel to be one of the world's finest diving destinations.

The island, approximately 30 miles long and 10 miles wide, is home to the world's second-largest coral reef and is ringed by some 30 dive sites, most of them concentrated along the west coast. The abundance of reefs coupled with the transparency of the Caribbean, which allows visibility of up to 200 feet, and the water's year-round warm temperature, which ranges from 77 to 82 Fahrenheit, have helped make Cozumel a major diving destination.

Recent developments include the opening of the *Cozumel Country Club*, which features an 18-hole Nicklaus Group signature golf course; the beachside wildlife park *Punta Sur*, which offers snorkeling and a marine turtle observation center; and *Punta Langosta*, a major shopping center.

Cozumel lies 11 miles east of the northern coast of the Yucatan Peninsula, and rapid ferry service is available from Playa del Carmen, about 45 minutes south of Cancun. The schedule for these passenger-only ferries changes seasonally, with hourly service generally running from 4 or 5 a.m. to 11 p.m.; the trip takes 40 minutes and a ticket costs about nine dollars. Check at the pier for a given day's schedule or call 872-1588.

A couple of vehicle ferries shuttle between the island and the mainland several times a day, charging about 50 dollars. The trip to Puerto Morelos, south of Cancun, takes upwards of three hours; the trip to Calica, south of Playa del Carmen, takes upwards of an hour.

Continental connects the island with Houston and New York, *U.S. Air* with Charlotte, N.C., and *Aeromexico* with Miami. *Aerocaribe* (Mexicana's

regional airline) operates a rather irregular shuttle service from Cancun with one or two daily departures.

Island Life

Life on the island is relaxed, somewhat akin to a ski resort, only the climate is tropical and the sport is scuba diving. Cutoffs and tank-tops seem to be as dressy as anyone ever gets, except at the nicer restaurants, where a higher level of casual is expected.

Only the mainland side of the island is settled, with a small hotel zone to the north and a larger one to the south. The island village, *San Miguel*, lies between the two, and is where most of the budget hotels are. The portion of San Miguel of interest to the visitor spans little more than 10 blocks along the waterfront, called Avenida Rafael Melgar, and five blocks inland, though the town itself has grown much beyond that.

The streets radiating away from the bustling central plaza are lined with restaurants, souvenir stalls, scuba diving outfits and sporting goods stores. Shops along the waterfront sell mainly diamonds and gems, catering to cruise ship passengers. More cruise ships dock in Cozumel than in any other destination in the Mexican Caribbean. During high season, all three piers are full to capacity every day with up to three ships each. Some days even, ships are anchored offshore and the passengers tendered into town.

The *Museo de la Isla de Cozumel*, the island's regional museum, is located on the waterfront, near the pier. The various halls relate island history as well as ecology with displays of mysterious Mayan artifacts, fascinating relics from the early days of deep-sea diving, and beautiful underwater fossils. There's a casual and popular terrace cafe on the top floor with one of the best views around. The gift shop offers one-of-a-kind T-shirts and a variety of souvenirs. Check at the entrance for notices of films and other cultural events. English-speaking guides are available. Open daily 9 a.m. to 5 p.m. There's a small admission charge.

The east coast of the island is home to miles of beautiful white sand beaches that are nevertheless empty because of the powerful open-sea surf. Here you'll find a handful of beach clubs, usually situated along the more tranquil stretches of the shoreline.

What to See and Do

Take a drive around the island, especially if it's your first visit. The 35-mile excursion along the road that hugs the coastline of this flat, largely jungle-covered island can be done aboard a rented moped, buggy,

Jeep or taxi. You can also join a group tour; some take passengers to the eastern side of the island aboard four-wheel all terrain vehicles, or ATVs.

Mopeds are fun for leisurely exploring on your own. However, riding one on the narrow two-lane blacktop (now undergoing badly-needed expansion) can be dangerous because of occasional speeding taxis, trucks and cars. Practice a bit before you hit the road, wear a helmet, and be super cautious. If that sounds too risky, opt for a Jeep or small car. Cozumel has two gas stations now, on the corner of Juarez and 30th, and Juarez and 75th. They're open 7 a.m. to midnight.

As you begin your tour by heading south of town, you'll see the road hugs the beach off and on. What seems like an impenetrable wall of jungle to your left conceals several horseback riding outfits, including the *San Miguel Ranch*, and farther down the road, the *Palma Ranch*.

Chankanaab Park

Cozumel's most famous site, Chankanaab Park, is about six miles south of the village. Here, a lagoon teeming with tropical fish is like a gigantic natural aquarium with water so clear the fish can be seen and admired from the water's edge. Connected to the sea by underground channels (that are off-limits to the public), the lagoon has a lovely reef just offshore, where scuba divers and snorkelers can view the coral, sunken cannon and anchors. There's also a fine beach for swimming and sunning.

Cozumel's clear waters are ideal for snorkeling and scuba diving

Bruce Herman

At the park, *Dolphin Discovery* lets visitors swim with the curious creatures. Four 30-minute swims, preceded by a 30-minute educational program, are scheduled daily. Reservations should be made in advance by calling 872-6605.

Another major attraction at Chankanaab is the botanical garden, home to over 200 species of tropical and sub-tropical plants brought from all over the world, and some native iguanas. The garden includes a life-size display of a typical Mayan home.

On-site dive shops rent equipment, and offer guides and instruction. Thatched-roof restaurants serve good food and Mexican specialties in a casual setting, with excellent drinks and marimba music.

Not far from Chankanaab Park are several popular public beaches, most with palm-thatched restaurant-bars and/or beach clubs offering fresh seafood dishes and cold drinks, and water-sports rentals. Much of the coast along this stretch is iron shore and the following spots are generally where the few sandy beaches are located: Playa San Francisco, Playa Sol, Sr. Sancho's Nachi Cocom, and Playa Palancar.

Next is the agricultural village of *El Cedral*, known for hosting a lively festival each year from April 30 to May 3.

The southern tip of the island, Punta Celarain, is home to a lighthouse offering a great view, if you can tackle the more than 100 steps to the top, and a Mayan temple. Once past this point, you'll be heading north again, up the eastern shore towards *El Mirador*, a rock structure that makes a great lookout, which is what the name means in Spanish.

As you go north up the coast, the best beaches are: Playa Bonita, Chen Rio, Punta Morena, and Punta Este, some with beach clubs. Remember that swimming off the eastern shore can be dangerous; currents are

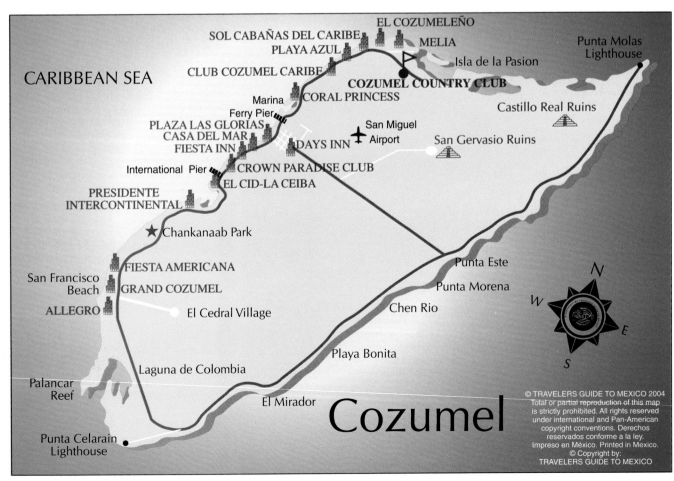

CARIBBEAN SEA

EL COZUMELEÑO
SOL CABAÑAS DEL CARIBE
PLAYA AZUL
MELIA
Punta Molas Lighthouse
CLUB COZUMEL CARIBE
Isla de la Pasion
COZUMEL COUNTRY CLUB
Marina
Ferry Pier
CORAL PRINCESS
Castillo Real Ruins
PLAZA LAS GLORIAS
CASA DEL MAR
FIESTA INN
San Miguel Airport
San Gervasio Ruins
DAYS INN
International Pier
CROWN PARADISE CLUB
EL CID-LA CEIBA
PRESIDENTE INTERCONTINENTAL
★ Chankanaab Park
FIESTA AMERICANA
Punta Este
San Francisco Beach
GRAND COZUMEL
Punta Morena
ALLEGRO
El Cedral Village
Chen Rio
Playa Bonita
Laguna de Colombia
Palancar Reef
El Mirador
Cozumel
Punta Celarain Lighthouse

strong and the sea can be rough.

At Punta Este you turn left and head back to town on the cross-island road that connects the eastern and western coasts. *Mezcalitos*, a small but very popular restaurant-bar sits on the beach here. Next to Mezcalitos is the access to the dirt road leading to the northern tip of Cozumel, Punta Molas, and a second lighthouse. A huge sign warns drivers against making the journey, which should be attempted only by jeep. Heed this sign.

There are several small archaeological sites on the island, some difficult to reach. The most interesting and easily accessible, via the cross-island road, is *San Gervasio*, which is also excellent for bird watching.

Avoid the cross-island road at night (the one connecting the western and eastern sides of the island). It's poorly lit and you run the risk of hitting one of the many islanders that walk it at dusk and after dark. Some are on tricycles (carrying cargo).

Underwater Adventure

About half the people who visit Cozumel come to dive, and those who do say there's no place quite like it. Swimming among the coral and tropical fish in the clear turquoise waters of the Mexican Caribbean is the next best thing to visiting another planet. Check with experts before venturing out; some areas off the island are recommended only for experienced divers.

Palancar Reef is internationally famous among the fin-and-mask fraternity. Just about every spot offers a picture-perfect chance for underwater photography. A great photo opportunity is a 12-foot bronze statue of Christ standing at a depth of 35 feet, located offshore in Chankanaab. Another picturesque dive site is the Santa Rosa Wall, a 70-foot drop-off with a strong current but a spectacular view of over-hanging coral and schools of colorful fish.

There are good spots for shore diving to depths of 10 to 15 feet at Chankanaab Lagoon's Beachcomber Cavern, and at the Sunken Airplane in front of the El Cid-La Ceiba Hotel.

There are more than 60 scuba diving out-fits operating in Cozumel; listed below are a few of the leading ones:

Scuba Du, at the Presidente InterContinental Hotel, is reliable and experienced. Tel. 872-0322, ext. 6845.

Del Mar Aquatics, at the El Cid-La Ceiba Hotel, is a small, professional outfit. Tel. 872-1900.

Dive Palancar, at the Grand Cozumel and Allegro hotels (872-9730), and *AquaWorld*, near El Cid-La Ceiba Hotel (872-1210), are also among the island's leading agencies.

Those who don't want to snorkel or scuba dive can still come face-to-face with the inhabitants of the deep thanks to *Atlantis Submarines*. The exhilarating ride aboard a high-tech submarine submerged to depths of more than 100 feet takes passengers on a journey to the bottom of the sea. A multilingual guide points out the more unique fish and plant life that goes by. Atlantis, which operates in only 11 locations in the Caribbean and Hawaii, offers five

trips a day, Tuesday through Saturday. Taking pictures will be easiest with 400 ASA or more sensitive film. For reservations, call 872-5671.

Another way to stay dry and view the fish is from the hold of a glass-bottom boat like the *Nautilus*. Tel. 872-1044.

Other Activities

Boat trips, some of which offer a picnic on one of the island's more remote beaches, are a favorite pastime. The outing lasts a full day and by the time it's over, strangers have become fast friends. Consult your concierge or a local travel agent about outings aboard *Gilligan's* catamaran.

The annual springtime Billfish Tournament attracts sportsmen from all over, but just about any month is good for going after white marlin, bluefin tuna or sailfish. Mackerel and grouper can be caught in abundance.

Club Nautico de Cozumel is a reliable sport-fishing outfit (872-0118). Well organized, well equipped and punctual, they arrange deep-sea and flats fishing.

Dining

There are some excellent restaurants on the island, offering everything from authentic Yucatecan specialties to flavorful Italian fare. And, of course, fresh grilled fish and seafood are on every menu.

Many of the smaller establishments in town don't accept credit cards, and none of the beach clubs do, so go prepared.

Acuario
Rafael Melgar 779, at Calle 11
Tel. 872-1097
This attractive restaurant on the waterfront offers a classic menu, with lobster and prime rib specialties. An enormous aquarium of exotic fish serves as a centerpiece. Soft guitar music adds to the ambiance. Open 4 p.m. to midnight.

Alfredo di Roma
Presidente InterContinental Hotel
Tel. 872-9500
The Cozumel branch of the Italian restaurant famed for its fettuccini Alfredo prepared tableside with rich cream, light semolina noodles, and fresh parmesan cheese, not to mention gold cutlery. The dishes are complemented by an extensive selection of fine French wines and attentive service.

Caribeño
Presidente InterContinental Hotel
Tel. 872-9500
A casual setting under a giant palapa with a wonderful view of the sea and great international and Mexican fare. The best breakfast buffet on the island. Live marimba and trio music at lunch and dinner. Open 7 a.m. to 10 p.m.

Carlos 'n Charlie's
Punta Langosta mall (Rafael Melgar 551)
Tel. 869-1646

One of Carlos Anderson's wacky establishments—as raucous as a college frat party. The menu offers wit and nutty house rules as well as a wide variety of fresh seafood, Mexican cuisine and their famed BBQ ribs. Have an ice-cold beer or tropical drink in a souvenir *yarda* (yard-long glass). Winner of the government's "H" award for good hygiene in food management. Open for lunch and dinner; from 5 p.m. Sunday.

Casa Denis
Calle 1 Sur 132, between Av. 5 and Av. 10
Tel. 872-0067
This family-run business, the island's first restaurant, has been around for more than 30 years and has the memorabilia to prove it.

Menu features tasty Yucatecan specialties. No credit cards accepted. Open 7 a.m. to 11 p.m., except Sunday.

Coffee Bean
Calle 3, steps from the waterfront
Tel. 872-4918
A New York-style coffee bar featuring gargantuan slices of luscious homemade cakes, pies, muffins. No credit cards accepted. Open 8 a.m. to 11 p.m.

Del Museo
Museo de la Isla de Cozumel
Tel. 872-0838
A second-floor terrace cafe offering a casual spot for breakfast or a snack accompanied by a great view of the waterfront. Good American and Mexican-style breakfasts. No credit cards accepted. Open 7 a.m. to 2 p.m.

Ernesto's Fajitas
South of town, next to Casa del Mar Hotel
Tels. 872-1154
Ernesto Diaz is credited with popularizing this Tex-Mex dish south of the border. Also serves good breakfast fare from 7 a.m. to 1 p.m. Open until 11 p.m.

Guido's
Rafael Melgar 23, on the waterfront
Tel. 872-0946
For 25 years this family-run restaurant has been perfecting the art of dining out, fine tuning everything from the courteous service to the flavorful dishes. Hosts Yvonne and Adolfo preside over this comfortable, breezy setting with a plant-filled patio and background music. Wood-fired oven pizzas and classic pastas are the backbone of the menu, but the Swiss-Italian cuisine also allows for great combinations with regional ingredients such as tuna, wahoo, and tropical fruits like mango. After dinner, enjoy the homemade *gelatis*, espresso and liqueurs. The wine selection, carefully stored in a climate-controlled cellar, offers a good variety in a range of prices. American Express card accepted only. Open 11 a.m. to 11 p.m.

La Cabaña del Pescador
North of town, opposite Playa Azul Hotel
Tel. 872-0795

The Fisherman's Cabin, as it's called, is a bit out of the way, but well worth it if you like lobster, the only featured dish. Lobster tails of your choice are sold here by the pound. No credit cards accepted. Open 6 to 11:30 p.m.

La Choza
Rosado Salas 190, at Av. 10
Tel. 872-0958
A longtime favorite, this traditional Mexican restaurant serves delicious and authentic home cooking in a cozy, rustic setting under a giant palapa. Delicately flavored soups included with each dish. Menu features several Yucatecan specialties. Prices very reasonable. Open for breakfast, lunch and dinner.

La Cocay
Calle 17, at Av. 25
Tel. 872-5533
Off the tourist track, but well worth it, this attractive Mediterranean restaurant features the innovative culinary creations of its talented French Canadian chef. Menu highlights include grilled rosemary skewered shrimp wrapped in prosciutto, and pan seared filet mignon with roasted garlic mashed potatoes. Good selection of wines. No credit cards accepted. Open 6:30 to 11:30 p.m., except Monday and Sunday.

La Veranda
Calle 4 Norte 140, between Av. 5 and Av. 10
Tel. 872-4132
This restaurant quickly garnered a reputation for serving delicious Caribbean cuisine in a lovely tropical garden or air-conditioned dining room. Open 6 p.m. to 1 a.m.

Pancho's Backyard
Rafael Melgar 27, in Cinco Soles
Tel. 872-2141
A lovely open-air patio featuring wonderful Mexican decor and tasty traditional Mexican fare. Famed for its "awesome" margaritas. Marimba music at lunch and dinner. Open 9 a.m. to 10:30 p.m.; from 5 p.m. Sunday.

Nightlife

A favorite island nightclub is *Joe's Lobster Pub*, now located where the main plaza meets the waterfront. The talented house band plays reggae and tropical music from 10:30 p.m.

Everyone seems to end up here, drawn by the friendly informal ambiance and excellent live music. There's a small and often packed dance floor, and Mexican and seafood dishes.

For a fun frat party atmosphere and pop music try *Carlos 'n Charlie's* at Punta Langosta mall. The local *Hard Rock Cafe*, on the waterfront, is reputedly the world's smallest, but features the same great American classics—burgers, fries, and rock 'n' roll bands (playing from 10 p.m.).

Viva Mexico, above the handicrafts emporium of the same name on Rafael Melgar, has a lively top-floor snack bar with a great view of the waterfront and live dance music from 10 p.m. until the wee hours of the morning. Tel. 872-0234.

Evenings begin earlier and end earlier in Cozumel than in much of the rest of Mexico. By 8 p.m., restaurants are doing a thriving business. Crowds at nightclubs begin to thin out soon after midnight. This may be due to divers getting hungry and sleepy sooner than the rest.

Shopping

Cozumel's first major shopping center recently opened at the Punta Langosta cruise terminal, just outside of downtown San Miguel. The open-air complex has been designed to house about 100 bars, restaurants and boutiques, such as DKNY, Versace, Nike, Sony, and TGI Friday's.

The town, particularly the waterfront, brims with shops selling handmade Mexican arts and crafts, especially articles for the home, and sterling silver jewelry, as well as imported brand-name perfumes, gold jewelry, gems, watches, crystal and porcelain.

Prices for imported goods in Cozumel are higher than on duty-free Caribbean islands, but usually lower than in much of the rest of Mexico, because of low import taxes and a sales tax exemption.

Several handicraft markets are located on the main square, including *Plaza del Sol* and *Confetti*.

Bugambilias
Av. 10, between Rosado Salas and Calle 1
This small shop carries fine handmade Mexican table linens, pillow cases, doilies, and more.

Cinco Soles
Rafael Melgar 27 and Calle 8, on the waterfront
Great for browsing, this colonial-style emporium of quality, handmade Mexican goods houses various interconnecting rooms, each dedicated to a different item. There are decorations and furnishings for the home, designer cotton clothing, sterling silver jewelry, and many souvenir items. There's also a fine Mexican restaurant on the premises.

Mi Casa
Rafael Melgar, between Calle 1 and Calle 3, on the waterfront
A beautiful shop carrying quality Mexican-made items for the home, including dishwash-

er-safe non-leaded ceramic tableware.

Pro Dive
Rosado Salas, between Av. 5 and Av. 10
A complete sporting goods store with everything for the beach and ocean, including single-use cameras for daytime, nighttime and underwater photography.

Roberto's Black Coral Studio
Av. 5 Sur 199, at Rosado Salas
Tel. 872-5383
A studio and gallery where you can watch the artist at work, sculpting delicate black coral into sea creatures or jewelry. The sculptures and distinctive accessories made here are shipped around the world. The craftsmanship is excellent and the selection varied. Open 9 a.m. to 2 p.m. and 4 to 9 p.m., closed Saturday and Sunday.

Tanya Moss Designer Jewelry
Punta Langosta mall (Rafael Melgar 551)
Tel. 869-1612
Original gold and sterling silver jewelry, and wearable art by designer Tanya Moss, whose innovative and sophisticated designs reflect their Mexican heritage. Individually handcrafted by skilled artisans, many of her creations incorporate freshwater pearls, amber, precious or semiprecious stones. Her more recent collections feature the intensity of 18k gold and silver combined with strands of multicolored semiprecious stones and pearls. Also in Mexico City and Los Cabos.

Viva Mexico
Rafael Melgar 27, on the waterfront
Tel. 872-5466
A huge emporium of Mexican handicrafts, tequila, silver jewelry, and other items. Open daily until 10 p.m.

Hotels

Days Inn
Calle 11 Sur 460, at Av. 20
Tel. (987) 872-1600
Five blocks from the waterfront and 10 from the main plaza. A colorful modern hotel with 45 rooms with cable TV, a/c, coffee maker; some with kitchenette. Swimming pool. Rates ECON.

El Cid-La Ceiba
Road to Chankanaab, Km. 4
Tel. (987) 872-0844
Recently acquired and renovated by El Cid resorts, this hotel is popular with divers for its location in front of a sunken airplane; Del Mar Aquatics dive center is headquartered here. There are 70 rooms with private oceanview balcony, a/c, ceiling fan, satellite TV. Swimming pool, jacuzzi, good restaurant overlooking the water. All-inclusive option available. Rates MD.

Fiesta Americana
Road to Chankanaab, Km. 7.5
Tel. (987) 872-9600
www.fiestamexico.com
Overlooking the Caribbean on the south side of the island, this first-class hotel offers 172 well appointed rooms in a horizontal low-rise and 54 Tropical Casita Suites with private terraces and hammocks set amid the jungle. Private beach club and pier, pool, fishing and other water sports, tennis, gym, restaurants, bar, meeting room. Rates FC.

Bruce Herman

Grand Cozumel by Occidental
Carretera Costera Sur, Km. 17.5
Tel. (987) 872-9730
www.grandcozumel.com
An attractive all-inclusive resort on Playa San Francisco, with 255 rooms and suites distributed among colonial-style buildings. Great beach, pier for diving and water sports, three pools, restaurants, bars, kids club, entertainment, spa services. Guests enjoy access to other Allegro resorts. Rates FC (all inclusive).

Melia Cozumel
Playa Santa Pilar
Tel. (987) 872-0411
www.solmelia.com
On the beach in the north end of the island. This first-class all-inclusive resort (formerly Paradisus Cozumel) features 147 units, including honeymoon suites with jacuzzi, overlooking the sea or garden, and unlimited golf privileges at the new adjacent course. Formal and

casual restaurants, 24-hour room service, cocktail lounge with live music, nice pool area, tennis, horseback riding, dive shop. Rates FC (all inclusive).

Playa Azul
Carretera a San Juan, Km. 4
Tel. (987) 872-0199
www.playa-azul.com
On the north end of the island. This charming owner-managed hotel nestled on a small but lovely beach has been expanded to offer 50 renovated, spacious air-conditioned rooms and suites with balconies facing the beach or garden; oceanfront suites have jacuzzi. Unlimited golf, private pier for scuba excursions, beachfront swimming pool, good Mexican and seafood restaurant, bar, pool table, lounge/library with TV and VCR. Rates MD.

Plaza Las Glorias
Rafael Melgar, Km. 1.5
Tel. (987) 872-2000
An attractive Mediterranean-style dive resort on the waterfront, about a 10-minute walk from the downtown area. The 174 rooms, 162 suites and 12 duplexes have private oceanview terrace, cable TV, minibar, hair dryer. Restaurant, popular lobby bar, scuba school, swimming pool, jacuzzi. Rates MD.

Presidente InterContinental
Road to Chankanaab, Km. 6.5
Tel. (987) 872-9500
www.intercontinental.com
Situated on a privileged stretch of coastline, this award-winning and beautifully-landscaped property offers guests the best this island has to offer without their ever needing to leave the hotel: ideal snorkeling and scuba diving locations (and instruction with an on-site PADI dive center), a beautiful little beach and tranquil cove perfect for swimming, and wonderful indoor and outdoor restaurants. Plus a gym with a view of the beach and sea, 253 spacious rooms and suites available in four categories, with private oceanview balconies, including beachfront rooms with direct access to the beach, 24-hour room service, swimming pool with jacuzzi, lighted tennis courts, Ping-Pong tables, meeting facilities for up to 350 people, children's activities. Full-service spa opening soon. AAA Four Diamond Award winner. Rates DX.

Sol Cabañas del Caribe
Carretera Costera Norte, Km. 5.8
Tel. (987) 872-0411
www.solmelia.com
This attractive low-rise on lovely Playa San Juan offers 48 rooms with oceanview balconies or patios with hammocks, including nine private *cabañas* near the water's edge. Well known for its attentive service, casual atmosphere and oceanfront palapa restaurant with live trio music in the evenings; nice bar. Swimming pool, kids pool, water-sports center. Rates MD.